NOV 18 2014

 LIBRARY

D0045463

NO LONGER PROPERTY OF
SEATTLE PUBLIC LIBRARY

BY SYLVIA JUKES MORRIS

Edith Kermit Roosevelt: Portrait of a First Lady

Rage for Fame: The Ascent of Clare Boothe Luce

Price of Fame: The Honorable Clare Boothe Luce

PRICE OF FAME

Ambassador Clare Boothe Luce

Oil portrait by René Bouché

PRICE OF FAME

THE HONORABLE CLARE BOOTHE LUCE

Sylvia Jukes Morris

RANDOM HOUSE   NEW YORK

Copyright © 2014 by Sylvia Jukes Morris

All rights reserved.

Published in the United States by Random House,
an imprint and division of Random House LLC,
a Penguin Random House Company, New York.

RANDOM HOUSE and the HOUSE colophon are registered
trademarks of Random House LLC.

Permission credits can be found on page 611.

LIBRARY OF CONGRESS CATALOGING-IN-PUBLICATION DATA
Morris, Sylvia Jukes.
Price of fame : the honorable Clare Boothe Luce / Sylvia Jukes Morris.
pages cm
Includes bibliographical references and index.
ISBN 978-0-679-45711-4
eBook ISBN 978-0-8041-7969-0
1. Luce, Clare Boothe, 1903–1987. 2. Ambassadors—United States—Biography.
3. Legislators—United States—Biography. 4. Dramatists, American—20th century—
Biography. 5. Journalists—United States—Biography. I. Title.
E748.L894M668 2014
996.9'3041092—dc23 2013046243
[B]

Printed in the United States of America on acid-free paper

www.atrandom.com

2 4 6 8 9 7 5 3 1

First Edition

For Edmund

Quod Ero Spero. I Will Be What I Hope to Be.

—Boothe family motto

CONTENTS

CONTENTS

CONTENTS

PRICE OF FAME

1

DELAYED ENTRANCE

He who would accomplish anything must learn to limit himself.

—Johann Wolfgang von Goethe

Two dozen red roses and a contingent of Washington correspondents and photographers awaited the new Republican Congresswoman from Fairfield County, Connecticut, at Union Station on Monday, January 4, 1943. Clare Boothe Luce was by far the smartest, most famous, and most glamorous member of the House of Representatives—the last quality not much evident elsewhere in the wartime capital.

When the cars of her express emptied onto the windy platform, twenty-two minutes late, a United Press man noted perplexedly, "Mrs. Luce wasn't on it." Had Clare been coming only from New York, she might have chosen to take the next commuter special. But she was booked on the last leg of a journey from Los Angeles, where she had just finished a screenplay for 20th Century-Fox.[1]

Aware that the thirty-nine-year-old Congresswoman had written four Broadway comedies—three of them hits and made into movies—the UP reporter suspected she might have pulled off an old theatrical trick, the incognito step from the wings, melting into the crowd in nondescript clothing. Also, as the wife of the publisher of *Time*, *Life*, and *Fortune*, Clare was media-savvy enough to know that the best way to attract press attention was to elude it. On a hunch, he called the swank

3

Wardman Park Hotel, and asked to speak to Mrs. Henry Luce. A secretary answered, and professed not to know where her employer was.

Sure now that Clare had concealed her arrival, he complained that he and his colleagues were being given the brush-off. There followed a click as the secretary hung up.[2]

Next morning, the elusive Representative called a press conference in her new quarters, suite 1631 on the sixth floor of the new House Office Building. Attendees were baffled as to how a freshman member of Congress had acquired such a coveted space, with its two entrances, ample reception hall, large office with private bathroom, and second office for three or more assistants, with enclosed "lavabo."[3]

Freshman or not, Clare knew how to operate on Capitol Hill. She was the stepdaughter of the late Representative Dr. Albert Elmer Austin, and had just won back the seat he had lost in 1940. She had often visited him in his cramped quarters in the old Cannon Building, and realized that they would not satisfy her fastidious standards. Throughout her life she had aimed for the best of everything, and usually gotten it. Hearing shortly after her election that a few suites were available, she had sent an aide to stand in line for this one, and beaten out seventy or so other applicants.[4]

She arrived ten minutes late—another coup de théâtre—and faced a battery of flashbulbs and newsreel klieg lights. Her appearance touched off pandemonium. Photographers stood on tables and unpacked storage boxes, yelling for her attention: "Just one more shot, please."[5]

Female reporters seemed more irritated by Clare's tardiness than their male colleagues, as well as envious of her stylish beauty. Cool, slender, and immaculately groomed for her "debut," she wore a red wool-crepe dress with deep pockets, and daisy-patterned gold-and-diamond earrings. Black velvet bows nestled in her blonde hair, upswept and softly waved above the brow. Her extraordinary translucent skin and blue eyes, shimmering with intelligence, invariably captivated men, as did her outsize personality and charm. Much of her seductiveness—and success as a playwright—came from her wit. "The difference between an optimist and a pessimist," she would drawl, in cultivated tones harking back to private school, "is that the pessimist is usually better informed."[6]

She began by apologizing for having sneaked away from Union Station the day before. Claiming to have been four days without a change

Congresswoman Clare Boothe Luce, 1943

of clothes, she said that she had exited the last car and rushed to her hotel to freshen up for an evening appointment. In any case, she had assumed reporters on the platform were waiting for some labor officials on the same train.[7]

Even the most hardened Washington pressmen were beguiled. One was overheard saying that there was "no labor leader living who would interest him if Mrs. Luce were around."[8] A barrage of questions followed. What were her views on taxation, women's rights, the war, and the GOP's election chances next year?

"I hope to do what I can," Clare said. "It might be little, or nothing, or much." Not wanting to sound flip, she added that voters in her district were "interested in precisely the same things as other people—gasoline rationing among them." Some issues she was not yet "up on." But she had been an advocate of women's rights for some twenty-five years now, and vowed to continue fighting for them. As for her party, the GOP, its priorities must be to defeat President Franklin Roosevelt in 1944, and to win the war.[9]

Never one for false modesty, Clare stated that since she had spent many months of the past three years reporting from both the East and West battlefronts, she felt qualified for a spot on the Foreign Affairs Committee.

"Places on that committee are supposed to go to seasoned Congressmen," a reporter reminded her. Clare realized she had let her ambition show, and said lamely that she would of course abide by House rules.[10]

"When are you going to make your maiden speech?" a voice shouted.

"When I have something to say."[11]

At this point a lobbyist for a dried-milk company, who had managed to infiltrate the room, asked if she would vote in favor of his product. She replied with a straight face that as yet, she had taken no position on the desiccation of anything.[12]

The bedlam increased. Newsmen scrambled over wires. Somebody kicked an electric socket, causing a loud explosion. The room grew increasingly airless, but with her customary sangfroid, Clare began talking about her three weeks in Hollywood. She said she had worked on a script about the birth of modern China, called *The 400 Million*. The Red scare in that overpopulated country had been on her mind when she visited a state-of-the-art steel mill, set not in a town but amid the orange groves of Fontana, California.

"Why can't there be more of this kind of thing?" she asked. "If we can move the factories to the farms and give our people some land to live on, most of their troubles will disappear. . . . Communism does not thrive when people are satisfied and happy." With a prod at the current administration, she asserted that "little people" deserved a better incentive to succeed in life "than they are likely to get from the New Deal."

Only capitalism was capable of satisfying the world's material, spiritual, and cultural aspirations.[13]

Thus, on her first full day in Washington, Representative Luce touched on vital themes that would preoccupy her for the next four years: equal rights, foreign affairs, and democracy versus authoritarianism. With only ten minutes left before the Republican caucus was due to begin, she edged toward the door.

"Are you going to hold regular press conferences?" a woman called out.

"I think not. In fact I know not. The answer is No. Period."[14]

▽

Clare rose early on Wednesday. Before leaving for the Hill, she went to the Wardman Park beauty shop. In the manner of one used to giving orders, she asked the proprietor to telephone her maid or chauffeur and tell them to bring her some reading material. After several calls, and irritated promptings from the Congresswoman, a package was delivered. Other customers looked on intrigued as Clare ordered coffee and a rye crisp. When told that the café served only toast, she said she would take that. But when it appeared, she waved it away and demanded a proper breakfast from room service. Soon a waiter appeared with a loaded table. Evidently she could be, in the words of one of her profilers, "a lady with a whim of iron."[15]

The scene, duly reported in a Washington gossip column, could have come from *The Women*, Clare's greatest Broadway success. Her script for that play, with its lacerating portraits of spoiled New York socialites in beauty and exercise salons, had given her a reputation for astringency. Few in the shop had ever seen such a fuss over food. Yet after the perfumed whirlwind had gone, they felt bereft, such was the force of her persona.[16]

▽

At noon, the 78th Congress of the United States convened. Clare again made a delayed entrance, this time from behind Speaker Sam Rayburn's platform, and slipped into her assigned seventh-row seat, fifth from the right aisle. The six other women on the floor—five of them Republicans—were already in place, dressed uniformly in black, corsages being their only splash of color. Clare thought them all frumps, except for Margaret Chase Smith of Maine, an unassuming, effective politician whom she admired. The others were Edith Nourse Rogers of

7

Clare at a congressional hearing

Massachusetts, an advocate of programs for veterans; Frances P. Bolton, a fluffy-haired two-termer from Ohio; and Jessie Sumner of Illinois, a prim isolationist. From New York came a slim lawyer, Winifred Stanley, six years younger than Clare but prematurely gray. The sole Democrat, senior to all of them, was New Jersey's Mary T. Norton. Her party held a working majority of 222, compared with 209 Republicans, 3 Progressives, and 1 Labor member.[17]

In contrast with her soberly clad peers, Clare dazzled in a custom-made, formfitting purple dress. Her black-and-blue-striped ascot matched her hair bows, clipped atop two golden coronet braids. Flat-heeled black shoes supported her regal five-foot-five frame.[18] To observers in the visitors' gallery, she looked like a leading lady, with her lustrous complexion, straight thick brows, discreetly remodeled nose, and pearly, slightly crooked teeth. Most enchanting of all were her ready smile and infectious laugh.

Other freshmen might have been awed by the presence of the President's wife in the visitors' gallery, but Clare was not. Some years earlier, Mrs. Roosevelt had seen her satire *Kiss the Boys Goodbye*, and publicly predicted that "Miss Boothe" would become a first-class playwright someday, "when the bitterness of the experiences which she has evidently had are completely out of her system." She had invited Clare to visit the White House for a talk. "I think it would be pleasant for both of us."[19] Later, at the war's onset, Clare had accompanied her husband to a private dinner with both Roosevelts. FDR had welcomed them as anti-isolationists and proponents of his Lend-Lease program, which made old American ships available to the embattled Royal Navy. He shared the anti-Nazi views that Time Inc. magazines had propounded many months before Pearl Harbor.[20]

Few Congressmen looked happy that afternoon at having yet another woman invade their domain. On either side of the aisle, it was the most conservative House since the days of Herbert Hoover. However, the man to Clare's right shook hands with her, and the one on her left engaged her in a lengthy conversation.

Not wanting to miss anything of the opening ceremony, she took out a white handerkerchief and polished a pair of horn-rimmed spectacles. She seemed nervous, removing and chewing the glasses, folding and refolding a pamphlet in her lap. From time to time, she rested a cheek on one hand. Her reply of "Present" to the roll call was scarcely audible.[21]

▽

Though much of Clare's adult life could be seen as preparation for elective office, her origins were not auspicious.[22] She had been born illegitimate in 1903, in an insalubrious part of New York City's Upper West Side, to William Franklin Boothe, a gifted violinist and former piano executive, who had come down in the world, and was reluctantly working as a patent-medicine salesman. Women found the handsome, clever, and athletic "Billy" irresistible. Son of a Baptist clergyman, he had forsaken his moralistic upbringing and drifted into multiple liaisons and marriages. While still wedded to his second wife, he had met Anna Clara Schneider, a violet-eyed beauty less than half his age. The poor daughter of Bavarian Lutheran immigrants, she was no stranger to Manhattan saloons. In two successive years, 1902 and 1903, she had given her lover his only children, David Franklin and Ann Clare Boothe.

Clare had always found it hard to acknowledge, or even look into, the more obscure facts of her parents' relationship. But apparently they never married. In 1907, William Boothe had taken his family first to Memphis and then to Nashville and Chicago, where he became a member of the Lyric Opera orchestra. But his musician's salary had not satisfied the luxury-loving Anna, and in 1913 she had left him and returned

East with her son and daughter. Clare had seen her father only once after that. He was to die estranged from his children in 1928, eking out a living as a violin teacher in Los Angeles.

As the self-restyled "Ann Snyder Boothe," Clare's mother had prospered in New York City from the largesse of lovers. The most generous of her gentleman callers was Joel Jacobs, a Jewish industrialist. He helped finance city apartments for her, as well as a summer house in Sound Beach, Connecticut, and paid the private school fees of both children. At age ten, in early evidence of theatrical talent, Clare had contributed to the family income by understudying Mary Pickford on Broadway, and two years later acted in an Edison silent movie, *The Heart of a Waif.*[23]

In 1922, at age forty, Ann had married a Connecticut physician, Albert Elmer Austin—the future Congressman whose seat Clare now occupied. Dr. Austin was not wealthy, to his stepdaughter's chagrin ("Mother always told me to marry for money, but she didn't do it herself").[24] But Jacobs had become part of the Austin ménage, lavishing jewelry on Ann, escorting her to the racetracks, and playing pinochle with the doctor.

Clare, removed early from her father's academic and cultural influences, had acquired much of Ann's money mania, vampishness, and free attitude to sex. Some teenage trips to Europe had helped mitigate this dominance and nurture Clare's intellectual curiosity. Chatting to traveling diplomats confirmed the precocious penchant for politics she had shown in debates at the Castle School in Tarrytown, New York. Flirting with a White Russian spy interested her in the Bolshevik Revolution, and sparked a lifelong passion for espionage. Collecting mementos of World War I on the battlefields of northern France helped her understand the importance of military preparedness. She experienced at first hand the devaluation of the currency in Weimar Germany, which taught her the importance of national solvency. Her aptitude for the theater was fed by avant-garde performances of Wedekind plays in Berlin. On one homebound crossing, she had impressed the Austrian producer Max Reinhardt, who seriously considered casting her in his extravaganza *The Miracle.* The role went to Rosamond Pinchot, but her friendship with Reinhardt endured.

Another shipboard encounter, with the millionaire activist Alva Belmont, had led Clare to a suffragette stint in Washington, D.C. On the cusp of turning twenty, she had walked the marble halls of Congress, lobbying for equal rights with Alice Paul and other members of the

National Woman's Party. But after only ten days, she had seen enough of her "dowdy dumpy" fellow crusaders—particularly those "who get a crush on girls."[25] She had returned to New York, and five months later married George Tuttle Brokaw, a hard-drinking millionaire of forty-four.

On August 22, 1924, she had given birth to her only child, Ann Clare. Six years of George's alcoholism, and living in his dreary, moated Fifth Avenue mansion, had propelled Clare to Reno in 1929. Divorced with ample alimony, she had settled with little Ann into a spacious apartment on Manhattan's East Side.

As Clare Boothe Brokaw, she could have continued life as a social-ite, summering in Newport and wintering in Palm Beach. But mother-hood did not fulfill her, and her brilliant mind and restless spirit needed more than upper-class diversions. So when she met the magazine owner Condé Nast at a dinner party, she had asked him for a job. Soon she was writing captions and essays at *Vogue*, and in two years had become man-aging editor of Nast's showcase publication, *Vanity Fair*. She had also published a critically praised book entitled *Stuffed Shirts*, consisting of linked tales that exposed the vanity, stupidity, hypocrisy, and decadence of the so-called elite.[26] By her thirtieth year, Clare had matured into a professional and social sensation, as well as one of the most desirable women in Manhattan.

In 1935, Henry Robinson Luce, admitting to a "coup de foudre," had left his wife, Lila, and two young sons to marry Clare—just in time to see her first play, *Abide With Me*, flop on Broadway. A grim melo-drama based on her Brokaw nightmare, it gave little foretaste of the acid wit that made *The Women*, her next play and most enduring accom-plishment, one of the hits of the 1936–1937 season. Produced by Max Gordon, with Robert B. Sinclair directing an all-female cast of forty, and Jo Mielziner designing lavish sets, the play was a stinging satire of naive, vacuous, and malicious Park Avenue gossips. It broke Broadway attendance records for a nonmusical, and went on to become a peren-nial staple in theaters around the world. *The Women* also reached the screen as a lavish MGM movie, adapted by Anita Loos and directed by George Cukor. Starring Norma Shearer, Joan Crawford, Rosalind Rus-sell, and Joan Fontaine, it featured 237 outfits by the designer Adrian, and was second only to *Gone With the Wind* in 1939 box office receipts.[27]

Well before that, Harry Luce had planned to make use of his wife's editorial skills on his new, hugely successful picture magazine, *Life*, for which she had given him many seminal ideas. But editors at Time Inc. had rejected having another Luce on the masthead, not to mention

Clare's domineering feminine presence in the office. Unbowed by this disappointment, and by the death of her mother in a particularly gruesome automobile accident, Clare had followed *The Women* with two more Broadway successes, both made into movies: *Kiss the Boys Goodbye* and the anti-Nazi *Margin for Error*.[28]

Hitler's subsequent invasion of Poland had revived Clare's military interests. In early 1940, she spent several weeks in France and England collecting material for a nonfiction book, *Europe in the Spring*. It became a bestseller, but the author was so self-referential in her accounts of meetings with refugees and generals that Dorothy Parker sardonically entitled her review "All Clare on the Western Front."[29]

Inured after *Abide With Me* to adverse criticism or sarcasm, Clare had next turned her reporting skills to the Sino-Japanese War. She had toured the Far East on military planes, documenting the blitz on Chungking for *Life*, befriending a beleaguered Chiang Kai-shek, and undertaking to raise American funds for him. In the Philippines, while researching a profile of General Douglas MacArthur, she had begun an affair with the Supreme Commander's mysterious intelligence chief, General Charles Willoughby—"the one man that I could have run away with."[30] In his dark, handsome Germanic persona, Willoughby combined her favorite preoccupations: spying, warfare, and romance.

Upon returning stateside, Clare had pulled off one of the biggest scoops in contemporary journalism when her *Life* cover story on MacArthur appeared on December 7, 1941, the day of Pearl Harbor.

▽

Thirteen months after that lethal attack, Representative Luce knew that she was uniquely qualified to help influence the course of the war. In 1942 alone, she had flown seventy-five thousand miles reporting on the various fronts.[31] What other member of Congress had dodged bullets in France, and bombs in Belgium and Indochina? Who else on Capitol Hill had reported on desert battles against Field Marshal Erwin Rommel in North Africa, stood in trenches in Burma on assignment to interview General Joseph Stilwell, or struck up a friendship with Jawaharlal Nehru in India? The widely read articles resulting from these experiences had been a major factor in her election to Congress.

Clare supported American armed entry into both Eastern and Western theaters, but, like President Roosevelt, she was not interested in saving the British Empire. On the contrary, she hoped to see all colonies disbanded after the war. But first she wanted German and Italian

Fascism destroyed, Japanese expansionism brought to an end, and international Communism's threat to democracy curbed. Her impatient nature notwithstanding, she was determined to do all she could to have such injustices redressed during her time in Congress. To these ends, it was imperative that she obtain a seat, if not on the House Foreign Affairs Committee, then on the almost equally prestigious Committee on Military Affairs.

2

GLOBALONEY

*Anyone who has never made a mistake has
never tried anything new.*

—ALBERT EINSTEIN

W hile waiting for a committee assignment, Clare was not shy of
crossing party lines. She let it be known that she approved of
the President's recent State of the Union speech, in which he had aggressively declared, "The period of our defensive attrition in the Pacific
is drawing to a close. . . . This year we intend to advance." In Europe,
too, "we are going to strike, and strike hard. . . . The Nazis and Fascists
have asked for it—and—they—are—going—to—get—it," FDR added
with trademark forcefulness. Clare called these words "heartening," and
praised his modesty in not taking more credit for last November's successful North Africa landings.[1]

Roosevelt was amused by a poem in the newspaper *PM* that mocked
her for having once accused him of fighting a "soft war."

O Lovely Luce—O Comely Clare!
Do you remember—way back there—
Holding your lacquered nails aloft,
"The war we fight," you said, "is soft."

And while the vote hung in the balance
You turned the trick with all your talents.
You were the keystone brave and buoyant.
By Lucifer, were you clarevoyant![2]

The President sent the verses to John W. McCormack, the House majority leader, with a note asking, "Can't you find a freshman Congressman on our side who will wait his chance until the first time Clare talks and then quote this poem?"[3]

Clare bided her time before voicing any opinions in Congress, but continued to speak her mind to reporters. When Eleanor Roosevelt suggested that the voting age for servicemen be lowered to eighteen, so that those willing to die for their country should have a say in governing it, Clare disagreed. "If boys in uniform are allowed to vote, boys out of uniform . . . must be allowed to vote. So must girls of eighteen."[4]

On Tuesday, January 12, she spoke at a sold-out Women's National Press Club dinner for new Congresswomen. Supersvelte in a black silk suit and flowered scarf, she challenged the view of some of her colleagues that after the war there would be greater economic opportunities for the six million American women who now held jobs. Female factory workers in her constituency had told her that given a choice, they would prefer to return to homemaking. The reason for this preference was "biological," she said. Women had an innate need to procreate and be nurturers.[5]

Evidently, Clare Boothe Luce was not a strict feminist. She had succeeded in a man's world, and believed that women were entitled to careers if they wanted them. But she was also an accomplished seductress, having married once, if not twice, for money, social position, and power.

In the question period that followed, someone asked Clare if she intended to write any more plays. She jokingly said that it reminded her of the boy who put twelve eggs under a hen, explaining to his father, "I just wanted to see the old fool spread herself."

Clare's saving grace was her talent to amuse, sweetening her frequent flights of pomposity and startling frankness. Another reporter had to admit he had lost his earlier prejudice toward her. "From the serious to the humorous, with a most refreshing vocabulary which had us in stitches . . . it was evident that she had made good and knew it. She has a warm smile . . . the effect is irresistible."[6]

The following day, Clare learned that she would not be appointed to the House Foreign Affairs Committee. This was hardly a surprise, because two senior Republican women—Rogers of Massachusetts and Bolton of Ohio—were already on it. She focused her hopes on the all-male Committee on Military Affairs. Since her teens, she had been fascinated with things military, naval, and aeronautical.

On Thursday, January 14, Clare was told that she was indeed being considered for the military panel. This was exciting news to share with her husband, who took the midnight train to Washington to spend his first weekend with her since the election.

▽

Henry ("Harry") Luce at age forty-four was an imposing presence in his custom-tailored suit and gray Chesterfield overcoat with velvet collar. But he wore his fine clothes awkwardly, as if Clare had coaxed him into them. This was often the case. Among his peers, he appeared engaged, informed, and charming, a perfect escort for his wife in the political circles in which she now moved.[7]

Henry and Clare Luce, 1943

16

He left behind him in New York a number of gossipy, protective senior employees who had long watched Clare's progress with skeptical interest, and were wondering if they could be unbiased in covering her in public office. Chief among these "Time Incers" was John Billings, who had been managing editor of *Life* since its inception in the mid-1930s. A wellborn Southerner, Billings was quiet and deferential to Harry, but he was a shrewd observer and an indefatigable, acerbic diarist. He noted that Clare was getting a lot of attention in Washington, not all of it favorable. "I'm glad for I really don't like her."[8]

For more than seven years, Harry had faced the question of how extensively his wife's activities should be reported in his magazines, aside from how much space they should give to her writings. He felt that it was appropriate to review her plays, even unfavorably, if warranted, and that her war articles should receive the same ruthless editing as anybody else's. During her recent election campaign, he had made sure that she was not covered more extensively than other contestants. In fact, Clare could, and did, argue that she got less newsprint than she deserved, considering how celebrated she had become on Broadway. Now, with *Time* selling more than a million copies a week, and *Life* more than three million, Harry faced a delicate challenge in doing justice to Representative Luce while avoiding accusations of neglect or nepotism.

Although always proud of Clare's successes, he believed that her canny political instincts and oratorical skills, combined with beauty and a mind able to penetrate to the core of the most complex issues, would now take her to greater heights. He had been astounded by her stamina on Fairfield County's grueling campaign trail. It had included early-morning visits to humid, smelly hat factories in Danbury, shouted conversations in deafening munition plants in Bridgeport, and trudges through the muddy barnyards of Trumbull farmers. She had even gone to a Norfolk tire mill at three o'clock one morning to discuss labor problems with carbon-dusty rubber puddlers, and was probably the only Connecticut candidate to slide down a firehouse pole to solicit votes.[9]

Harry had earlier marveled at his wife's physical bravery in war zones, and relished her fearlessness in attacking not only populist Democrats, but the Old Guard snobs of the GOP. Speaking at a dinner in her honor given by bejeweled supporters, she said, "One of the troubles with the Republican party is that it contains too many prehistoric millionaires who wear too many orchids."[10]

Henry Luce aspired to politics himself, but lacked one essential quality: a penchant for pressing the flesh. A shy, sometime stutterer, he was so in awe of Clare's ease in talking with all kinds of people, from the most brilliant scientist to the humblest manual worker, that he admitted wanting to "bow inwardly with admiration."[11] He hoped that by having Clare in Congress, he could go beyond his influence as a media tycoon, and directly affect legislation advancing his own ideological goals. The most passionate of these—a cause deriving directly from his missionary childhood in the Far East—was that the United States should support Chiang Kai-shek in freeing China, first from its Japanese conquerers, and then from Mao Tse-tung's Communist insurgency.

Phenomenally successful though Harry was in his own right, his awe of Clare had damaged their once rapturous marital relationship. She frequently absented herself from him in the hope that apartness might revive his libido. For years it had been flagging, at least vis-à-vis her. His frankly admitted problem was that having put her on a pedestal, he felt it was sacrilegious—at least according to his Presbyterian scruples—to have sex with someone so sanctified. Bewildered by this, Clare had spent months in Europe in 1940, researching a book on the Phony War, hoping for a cable of sexual yearning from her husband. But she had waited fruitlessly, right up to the eve of the German army's arrival in Paris. Her dedication to *Europe in the Spring* read, "To HRL, who understood why I wanted to go."[12]

The problem went far back. After a mere two years of marriage, both Luces had "wandered off the reservation," as a character in *The Women* put it. Clare hankered for the intensity of her teenage romance with Julian Simpson, an English army officer, and was nostalgic about her later affair with Bernard Baruch, the famous Wall Street speculator and supporter of FDR. She had enjoyed a few European assignations with Joseph P. Kennedy (whose son John occasionally dated her daughter), and was in the second year—mainly epistolary now—of her romance with General Charles Willoughby.

Harry's infrequent extramarital exploits tended to be more fraught. As a churchgoer, he felt equal guilt about one-night or long-term liaisons. Although tall and attractive to many women, he had begun in his forty-fifth year to show the effects of heavy smoking, steady drinking, and indifference to food and exercise. His skin sagged in places, and his hair was receding.

▽

Confirmation of Clare's election to the Committee on Military Affairs came on Monday, January 18. She told her home newspaper, *Greenwich*

General Charles Willoughby on duty in the Pacific, c. 1943

Time, that she was "well satisfied" to be the only woman among its thirty members.[13]

But that feeling dwindled as the reality of the committee's typical agenda began to dawn on her. Its discussions tended to be about infrastructure, inefficiency, and profligate spending, rather than far-flung battles. She found herself having to deal with such dry subjects as irregularities in the construction of airfields by U.S. Army engineers, delays in expanding a Florida hospital, wasteful operations in a General Electric supercharger plant, and a report of fifty-five cases of gonorrhea in a Missouri barracks.[14]

The Committee on Military Affairs could, at least, divert itself in late January by monitoring President Roosevelt's two-week trip to Casablanca for a conference with Winston Churchill. The main purpose of this meeting (prompted by Josef Stalin's urgent request for the opening of a second Western Front to relieve pressure on his defenses in the East) was to plot when, where, and how Allied forces might cross the English Channel and invade the European mainland. Although that day was obviously far off, FDR and Churchill also wanted to discuss post-invasion strategy. The President had a dramatic proposal: that the Axis must submit to no less than "unconditional surrender." Churchill was likely to agree, but the danger was that if this policy became known, plotters within the Reich would see no ultimate advantage in over-throwing Hitler, thus prolonging the war.[15]

▽

Clare's office was already receiving some 150 letters a day, a record for a House newcomer. She told her assistants to answer mail from service-men and constituents first. About a third of the letters came from women, and most were friendly, asking for autographs, photographs, or endorsements. Others offered legislative suggestions. Lecture invita-tions came from groups hoping to enjoy her much-publicized candor and humor.

Her impact on everyday Washington life was evident all over town. Hairdressers advertised styles called "the Clarette" or "the Lucian" or "the Clare Bo." One correspondent reported that visitors to the nation's capital wanted to see three things: "The Washington Monument, The Lincoln Memorial, and Clare Boothe Luce."[16]

Social mavens predicted that "Mrs. Henry R. Luce" would buy or rent a large house in a fashionable neighborhood, in order to entertain lavishly. But Clare already had a Georgian-style mansion on fifty-nine acres in Greenwich, Connecticut, and a spacious suite at the Waldorf Towers on Park Avenue in New York City. Determined to focus on work while she was in Washington, she chose to remain in her five-room, $750-a-month, air-conditioned apartment in the residential annex of the Wardman Park Hotel on Woodley Road, N.W.

She quickly established a daily routine. Assisted by a maid—her only domestic luxury, due to the city's lack of manpower—she took a foamy bath, sprayed herself with pine scent bought during her Califor-nia trip, checked her nail polish for chips, and pinned a rose to her lapel, its stem in a tiny vial of water. After breakfast, she was chauf-feured to Capitol Hill, until she decided to forgo that convenience, in the interests of economy and gas rationing, and took a taxi instead. She was generally at her office by nine.

On arriving, she reviewed mail with Isabel Hill, her superefficient, Wellesley-educated secretary for the past eight years.[17] Then, after dis-cussing important calls with her staff, she would retreat to her private sanctum with its two couches, one armchair, electric kettle, and small, carved figure of a Chinese god whose stomach she scratched every morning for luck. Maps of Atlantic and Pacific war theaters hung along-side pictures of George Washington and Douglas MacArthur, as well as a plaque of Abraham Lincoln, her most admired President. On her desk were photographs of her mother and daughter, orderly stacks of letters, carefully clipped newspapers, press releases, and an upturned, ceramic Uncle Sam hat holding sharpened pencils. Shelves housed books on topics ranging from government and economics to sociology and war. A side table with a large globe and surmounted silver airplane symbolized her interest in aviation.

After dealing with urgent matters, Clare usually attended committee meetings or met with other Representatives on legislative affairs. At noon, she crossed over to the House and lunched there, sometimes with constituents. When not on the floor for votes and debates, she spent the rest of the day in her office, usually working past 9:00 P.M. Though she suffered from persistent neuralgia and anemia, the pace she set exhausted her employees, who often looked paler than she did. She most often dined in the Wardman Park restaurant, either alone or with friends or business acquaintances.[18] Afterward, she sat in her sitting room with its historic prints of Connecticut and the District of Columbia, reading office documents or a book. Her personal library included Arnold Toynbee's six-volume *A Study of History*, as well as *How to Reach the Top in the Business World* and *How Never to Be Tired*.[19]

▽

Having a low boring point, Clare likely could not have endured the tedium of much of her congressional work without Albert P. Morano, her executive assistant. A tireless, astute Italian Catholic of thirty-five, he had performed the same job for her stepfather. It was he who had persuaded her to run for the seat Dr. Austin narrowly lost in 1940, saying, "You can't miss."[20] After her election, she had given him a watch inscribed with those optimistic words.

Morano proved to be worth every cent of his $5,000-a-year salary. A Washington radio station rated him the best House aide, in recognition of his meticulous scouring of forty newspapers a day, while keeping track of the status of numerous bills. Clare owed her coveted suite to his willingness to stand in line for it in last December's cold. He managed her other staff, monitored her schedule, and never forgot a name—an essential attribute for one who hoped to run for public office himself someday. (His middle initial, he liked to joke, stood for "Politician.") With his swarthy build and thick dark hair, Morano reminded Clare so much of her brother, David, that she told him to call her "Sis."

Though married, he was obviously a little in love with his employer.

He said her mind "worked better than a man's," and that by using her wily instincts and uncanny ability to predict the future, she "might even get to be President."[21]

▽

Less than a month after settling in Washington, Clare wrote a letter to Alice Basim, a young nurse who had married Dr. Austin shortly before his death. Depressed by a four-day blizzard, she admitted to being disillusioned with her new job. "It's hard and dreary and thankless and I only half guessed . . . what the life of a 'public servant' was. They do shove you about, whittle away at you. . . . A creeping paralysis of the brain seems to set in."[22]

Clare considered herself a loner, but loneliness did not suit her, particularly now that she was living less stylishly than she was used to, with fewer sophisticated friends to see. Being thespian by nature, she needed to perform for appreciative audiences. Yet even in congenial company, she could switch in a flash from enchanting extrovert to gloomy introvert. Her attacks of what she called "the dismals" were frequent, and she admitted to uncontrollable mood changes.[23] Even in New York, soul mates who shared her myriad interests were few. In Washington they were practically nonexistent, given that most of the people she encountered were politicians or journalists.

She had the gift—or curse—of instant intimacy, tending to unburden herself indiscriminately on strangers, regaling them with hilarious or tragic stories from her life, so that they soon came to feel they had known her always. But then they were puzzled when the solid relationship they thought they had established with her evaporated. This happened the moment anybody presumed a closeness she did not reciprocate. Even old friends fell victim to her quixotic temperament, and were desolate after she withdrew from them, either temporarily or, in some cases, permanently.

Clare's husband and daughter suffered most of all. In her absence, they missed her common sense, decisiveness, organizational skills, and love of fun, not to mention her creative and athletic abilities. It seemed to them that she could do everything except sing and cook. In turn, she regretted not having Harry as a sounding board during her solitary evenings at the Wardman Park, and with Ann now in college on the West Coast, she also felt the lack of someone young to impress and instruct.

As an antidote to her current gloom, she looked forward to showing off the gift for oratory she had discovered in herself at a Wendell Willkie rally in Madison Square Garden in 1940.[24] At some point soon, she would have to deliver her first congressional speech.

▽

The initial prompting for Clare's headline-capturing debut on the House floor came from Sam Pryor, chief assistant to the president of Pan American Airways. He alerted her to a new magazine article by Henry Wallace, in which the socialist-minded Vice President suggested that after the war there should be an international "Freedom of the Air," similar to the prewar policy of "Freedom of the Seas."

Pryor's boss, Juan Trippe, had been a contemporary of Henry Luce at Yale. The two CEOs often dined together in the Chrysler Building's Cloud Club, where they talked about their separate careers. As self-made men, they shared Clare's dislike of the kind of governmental utopianism espoused by idealists like Wallace, particularly the notion of unrestricted civil aviation. Trippe in particular was afraid that the United States, which had never ratified the prewar Convention Relating to the Regulation of Aerial Navigation, would allow its territory to be crisscrossed at will by foreign carriers, even those flying to neighboring countries such as Mexico or Canada. Clare knew she was being lobbied, but asked Speaker Rayburn to allot her time to address the issue.[25]

Late in the afternoon of Tuesday, February 9, at the close of legislative business, Clare rose in the House and was recognized. Customarily at that hour, a Congresswoman making her maiden speech would have spoken to an almost deserted chamber, with only the presiding officer and a representative of each major party there to forestall any unplanned parliamentary move. But about a third of the Representatives were curious about her, and stayed to listen. They had no idea what subject she wanted to address, although some Democrats anticipated a plea for aid to China.[26]

"Mr. Speaker," she said, "may I take this occasion to thank the people of Fairfield County in Connecticut who elected me to this body?"[27]

Since beginning her public career, she had learned it was more effective not to scold, clench a fist, or wag a finger when addressing a crowd, but rather to be witty and smiling. She had worked to keep high frequencies out of her voice, knowing that female orators could be hard on the eardrums. One of the greatest assets a woman could have, she believed, was to speak in mellow, low-pitched tones. "The drone of the bee is easier to bear than the whine of the mosquito."[28]

There was a resolution before the House, Clare reminded her colleagues, "to form a permanent standing committee on civil and commercial aviation, domestic and overseas." She admitted that she knew little about how such a group would organize and operate, but stressed what she did know: that the airplane was "the most dynamic instrument" of the war, and surely would be of the peace. If the United States did not address itself to the question of its present and future place in the civilian air world, it might lose that peace.

In January 1939, she recalled, President Roosevelt had declared that "an economically and technically sound air transportation system" was the backbone of national defense. But now, four years later, she felt that his administration had become shortsighted in favoring "the total militarization of our airlines." Meanwhile, Great Britain continued to operate its civil and military air networks as separate entities. At war's end, Churchill's ministers would be ready "to put muscles and flesh on their international airways system."

Waxing rhetorical, Clare continued.

> Make no mistake. Our far-sighted British cousins have already clearly seen the vision of the air world of tomorrow. They have seen that the masters of the air will be the masters of the planet, for as aviation dominates all military effort today, so will it dominate and influence all peacetime effort. . . . Perhaps the Russians have seen this too, although we have no way of knowing. Certainly the Chinese know, because I have discussed it with many of them, that when peace comes it will then be too late to plan America's future role in the air.
>
> The shape of all postwar air policy is being beaten out now on the anvil of war.

Clare pointed out that the policy of "sovereignty of the skies," sanctioned at the Versailles Treaty of 1919, had allowed the United States to protect itself strategically by denying free access to its air lanes and airports. Yet it had also profited from the exchange of reciprocal landing agreements and become the foremost commercial airpower, in terms of mileage routes and total passengers. Now she saw that American preeminence was being challenged by the advocates of "Freedom of the Air." Unleashing skills honed in her Broadway scripts, she identified the main culprit.

I call your attention to a recent article written by the Vice President of the United States, Mr. Henry Wallace, which has just appeared in the *American* magazine. . . . It is called "What We Will Get Out of the War." Now, in passing, I would like to say that I am a great admirer of some of Mr. Wallace's ideas. He has a wholly disarming way of being intermittently inspiring and spasmodically sound. . . . However, one usually finds that the higher the plane he puts his economic arguments upon, the lower, it turns out, American living standards will fall.

Mr. Wallace's article . . . is on a very high plane indeed. In it he does a great deal of global thinking. But much of what Mr. Wallace calls his global thinking is, no matter how you slice it, still globaloney.

Clare's coinage of the flippant last word shocked her audience and delighted reporters in the press gallery.[29] Unfortunately, its zing deflected attention from her reasoned follow-up. She quoted Wallace's words, "Freedom of the Air means to the world of the future what Freedom of the Seas meant to the world of the past," and said that neither principle guaranteed peace, much less fairness in international trade.

Freedom of the seas, Clare declared, had nearly killed American merchant shipping after World War I, due to competition from "all the cheap-labor, low-operating cost, government-subsidy countries of the world." She speculated that freedom of the air would have the same effect. Giving full rein to fantasy, she imagined herself standing one day in some great Midwestern terminal, watching the arrivals of "the airliner *Queen Elizabeth* . . . the Stalin *Iron Cruiser,* the Wilhelmina *Flying Dutchman,* the *Flying De Gaulle,* the airships of all the nations on earth—perhaps even those of the German and Jap," while looking in vain "for an American Clipper against the clouds."

She conceded that she might be going too far in pressing an analogy between the freedoms of air and sea. But she drew it only because "Mr. Wallace himself had seen fit publicly to slice another piece of globaloney off the apparently inexhaustible ration he keeps in his mental larder."

Clare ended her forty-minute address with a paraphrase of Winston Churchill. Members of the House of Representatives, she said, were not elected "to preside over the liquidation of America's best interests, either at home or abroad."[30]

Although a Senate committee reiterated Clare's misgivings about freedom of the skies the following day, press reports of her speech focused
disapprovingly on the gibe of "globaloney." Even *Fortune*, Harry's most
sedate magazine, dubbed it "an ill-mannered crack." *Time* gave space to
her detractors, including Henry Wallace, who huffed, "I am sure the
vast bulk of Republicans do not want to stir up animosity against either
our Russian or English allies." Eleanor Roosevelt weighed in with,
"Well, are we going to have a peaceful world or aren't we? All nations
should have free access to the world's travel lanes."[31] The writer Dawn
Powell, who had depicted Clare as a ruthless self-promoter in her 1942
novel, *A Time to Be Born*, remarked in her diary that Mrs. Luce, in attacking the Vice President, had "made such evil use of her new Congressional power."[32]

Of 183 nationwide press clippings about the speech gathered by
Clare's staff, only 70 were favorable.[33] A friendly columnist lamented

Congresswoman Luce makes good "copy."

that "it had to be left to a pretty woman to make the most-needed he-man speech on foreign policy that has been heard from either floor of the House since the war began." Mrs. Luce, he wrote, was so well-known "for pulchritude, chic, wit and wisecracking that these got the headlines instead of the sound doctrines expounded and the grave warnings sounded."[34]

Forty-seven periodicals criticized her for creating disunity, or for being an imperialist as well as an isolationist. Perhaps the most damning reaction was that of the *Saturday Review*. Under the headline LUCE THINKING, it declared that the word *globaloney* was worse than a lapse of taste. It was "an unforgivable insult to Americans who happen to be fighting and dying in a global war."[35]

Clare's own reaction was that she had "rocked a lot of people back on their heels." Criticism notwithstanding, "What I said . . . did a whale of a lot of good to the cause of postwar aviation."[36] She would have to wait for proof of that claim.

President Roosevelt made no comment about Clare's oratorical debut, but neither did he publicly support Wallace's air plans. The administration, however, appointed one of its top defenders in the House, Representative J. William Fulbright of Arkansas, to refute the new member from Fairfield County. He began by saying that Mrs. Luce had "inferred" that the Vice President's proposal would endanger America's security. She had also "inferred" that planners were working secretly on a new air policy.

In her response, Clare gave the Rhodes scholar and former university president a grammar lesson. "The gentleman said that I had inferred this or that. I inferred nothing. I implied, and the gentleman from Arkansas did the inferring."[37]

Fulbright's face turned red. Far from being amused at his discomfiture, most of Clare's male colleagues agreed that she had "a tongue like a dragon's."[38]

3

TURNING FORTY

The intellect of man is forced to choose
Perfection of the life, or of the work.

—WILLIAM BUTLER YEATS

On February 12, 1943, three days after her controversial address, Congresswoman Luce had lunch at the Louis XIV restaurant in New York with John Billings and two other Time Incers. *Life*'s dyspeptic editor recoiled from Clare's "overpowering perfume." He noted that she ate only scrambled eggs, and looked "thinner and bonier than ever." The purpose of the meeting soon became plain. She boasted about the success of her maiden speech, then offered him an article on "modernizing Congress." He silently wondered how after just five weeks in such an "ancient and honorable institution," she could criticize it without jeopardizing her political career. But Clare insisted that American lawmakers should be as efficient and up-to-date as captains of commerce, industry, and communications. She said she would propose that automatic voting machines be installed in the Capitol, to speed up legislation, and that the standard of debate in the House would be improved if it was wired for broadcasting. Billings felt such ideas showed her to be "pretty ignorant of Congressional history," and did not commit to an article.[1]

Unfazed, Clare treated the newsmen to her views on the next presidential election. Many Republicans, she said, thought that even a

"Chinaman" could beat FDR in 1944. But she was not so sure. The only potential candidates worthy of the GOP nomination, in her view, were Herbert Hoover and General Douglas MacArthur, and both would be "politically impossible."

Once in full monologue mode, Clare brooked no interruption. She was, Billings concluded, "theatrical in essence—and talks more like an actress than a politician."[2]

▽

In Washington on February 15, Congresswoman Edith Rogers of Massachusetts spoke at a ceremony marking the birthday of Susan B. Anthony. "With women in every phase of war work," she said, "from the WAACs and WAVES to welders, it is only justice that they should have equal rights with men."[3]

To do her part in the celebration, Clare put before the House a list of Anthony's feminist precepts. Among them were the pioneer's last publicly spoken words, "Failure is impossible." She did not add that Anthony privately, just before her death, had sounded disenchanted with the results of her sixty-year struggle for justice: "Young women who are benefitting from the changes haven't the least idea of how they came about."[4]

This could not be said of the young Clare Boothe. Exactly twenty years earlier, she had come to Washington to lobby Congress alongside Alice Paul and Alva Belmont for an Equal Rights Amendment to the Constitution.[5] She had even scattered leaflets from an airplane over New York State. After her divorce in 1929, with ample means to settle for the life of a socialite, she had chosen to capitalize on her own abilities in the workplace, and had done so ever since. She had seen opposition to the Equal Rights Amendment—first offered in the Senate by a man in 1923—grow. Ironically, female trade union organizations had balked at it, insisting that women in industry needed special protections that would vanish with equality. Joining them was the League of Women Voters, which held that the business of curbing discriminatory laws should be left to the states. The amendment's chief promoter remained the National Woman's Party, or NWP.[6]

By 1943, only half of the women in Congress were willing to join Clare in supporting another submission. Representative Louis Ludlow of Indiana reintroduced the amendment on January 6, 1943. Not one of his forty-two co-sponsors was female. This might have been avoided had an invitation from the Connecticut State Committee of the NWP, asking Clare to be co-sponsor, been answered promptly when she first arrived in Washington. But it had lain neglected in her mound of mail, and the group had assumed she was indifferent.[7]

The *Bridgeport Herald* facetiously reported that the failure of "Blondilocks" to introduce the ERA bill had disappointed NWP supporters in her home state.[8] To make amends, Clare announced her full backing for passage of the bill. But she did not think the feminist issue as important as winning the war, and keeping the nation secure and solvent.[9]

▽

Custom required the President to invite freshmen members of Congress to an informal reception at the White House. Franklin Roosevelt saw it as an opportunity, under the guise of a casual exchange of views, to probe each new arrival for collaborative potential—or the reverse. Clare, for her part, seized on it as an opportunity for a serious discussion with the Chief Executive. To let FDR know what was on her mind in advance, she accepted his invitation in a letter, releasing a copy to the press.[10] It brazenly questioned his handling of the war and criticized his attempts to increase the powers of the executive branch.

She wrote that she and her Republican colleagues were worried that food shortages might arise in the United States because of the dual demands of the military and farm programs. Meanwhile, the inability of the War Manpower Commission to figure out how many workers were needed for specific programs, and how to get them, "may lead to a calamitous cramping of war industry." Not mincing her words, she informed Roosevelt that Congress was feeling "the people's long-delayed fury against the swollen and wasteful Washington bureaucracies that have burgeoned through the years." Finally, she said that the GOP hoped to win power soon, because it had confidence in "the political validity and human worth of historical Republicanism."[11]

This was hardly the best way to ingratiate herself with FDR, and a prompt reprimand came from his press secretary, Steve Early. The publication of her letter, Early wrote, had created a "widespread" misapprehension that the upcoming reception would be substantive. To spare her "any possible disappointment," he stressed that she should not expect a purely social evening to "hold promise of political discussions."[12]

Clare arrived at the White House on Wednesday, March 10, ten minutes late. This time her tardy entrance violated executive protocol. Consequently, she did not feel welcome. In the State Dining Room, she found small tables laden with mostly masculine fare: beer, cheese, crackers, cigars, and cigarettes. There was no opportunity for an extended conversation with the wheelchair-bound President, since leaders of the House and Senate were introducing their 117 new members to him party by party, in groups of 20 or 30. Roosevelt did most of the talking, telling anecdotes of his Casablanca trip, and apologizing for not being routinely available to congressional visitors now that he was so busy with war reports and conferences. He was especially effusive with Winifred Stanley, holding her hand as he chatted, and addressing only a cool "Good evening" to Clare. When she left, he patronizingly called out, "How's Henry?"[13]

The President's peremptory treatment added to Clare's distaste for political life. She shared her malaise with General Willoughby, who was some ten thousand miles away in Australia, planning MacArthur's return to the Philippines.

> I hate Washington, I don't like being in Congress . . . and the bleak way it circumscribes my life. After only two short months of it I know that power and office are two things I don't want . . . yet I'll go through it cheerfully for the next two years, if only I could feel anything could be accomplished on the plus side for either the war, or the peace. . . . Frankly my health is wretched. I am abominably tired, and feel like chucking it all and going off to a sandy beach somewhere.[14]

Years of listening to Bernard Baruch notwithstanding, economic policy was not Clare's strongpoint. She found herself confused by the reaction of Congress and business to the President's 1943 budget proposals. With war costs approaching $7 billion a month, and the national debt near $150 billion, it did not surprise her that Roosevelt called for $16 billion in extra taxes and/or savings. Her puzzlement grew when, of all people, the treasurer of Macy's, Beardsley Ruml, proposed that the government reduce the deficit by forgiving all or part of individual taxes for 1942. This was presumably in the hope that Americans would use their gains to invest in industry and the war effort. Roosevelt said he could not simultaneously agree to cuts that would benefit mostly the rich, and ask for an increase "in taxes and savings from the mass of our people."[15]

After pondering both policies, Clare offered an amendment to what became known as the Ruml-Carlson bill, limiting tax relief to the first $25,000 of income. She said that wealthy citizens, herself included, did not need a windfall from the Treasury. In fact, she advocated "taxing the rich almost to the point of constitutional confiscation." These were not exactly sound Republican sentiments, and her amendment was defeated in the House on March 30 with a roar of, "No!"[16]

▽

On April 9, Clare appeared in Greenwich for the first time since her election, to address a war bond rally. The following afternoon, after attending a lunch in her honor co-hosted by her former campaign manager, William Brennan, and the Fairfield County Republican Committee, she went to New York to celebrate what was nominally her fortieth birthday. Actually, that anniversary had been on March 10, but she had long since changed the date because she preferred being an Aries to a Pisces.[17]

Rather than dine in some intimate setting with her husband, Clare went to see the movie version of her play *Margin for Error*, directed by and starring Otto Preminger, which had just opened in New York. Afterward, she went to a party at the apartment of an old friend, Margaret ("Maggie") Case, society editor of *Vogue*. Other guests included the movie producer Sir Alexander Korda and his wife, Merle Oberon, the journalist and travel writer John Gunther, Marcia Davenport, author of the novel *The Valley of Decision*, the actor Raymond Massey, and John Foster, a British barrister whom Clare had met and flirted with on trips to London. As wine and liquor flowed, Foster joked about the congressional corpse that had gone unnoticed for four days because people were so used to legislators "lying in the House."[18]

Although Clare may not have accepted it at the time, this party marked the onset of her middle age. She had grown used to the preferential treatment afforded her as a smart, wealthy, and humorous woman, able to impress all in her orbit. But the traditional end of youth brought with it the likelihood of more loneliness.

4

THE MOST
TALKED-ABOUT MEMBER

▽

In this world there are only two tragedies. One is not getting what one wants, and the other is getting it.

— OSCAR WILDE

Before a broadcast speech to fifteen hundred Republicans in Bridgeport on April 17, Clare was introduced by a state leader as "the daughter of a Yankee fiddler who knew poverty in her youth." She did not dispute this description, and launched into a mini-sermon on the need for tax reform. Then, taking advantage of the traditional privilege of office to speak at length on multiple subjects, she shifted topics to military matters: the "bloody" battles American servicemen were fighting, the shortage of submarines, escort vessels, and blimps to confront the Axis U-boat menace, and the Pentagon's incompetent handling of manpower recruitment, which might soon lead to the forcible drafting of not only men, but women, boys, and girls. She criticized Washington politicians for having "one eye on the war and the other one on the next elections," and complained about "jurisdictional jealousies that swirl about the head of every legislator, and the red tape which tangles his feet." Although President Roosevelt was a patient and cheerful man, she said, he lacked "administrative ability." As for Congress, it was dilatory in leaving its most significant work to be done by committees.[1]

The Boston Globe reported this litany of complaints, adding that

Mrs. Luce had "already told her friends that two years on Capitol Hill will be plenty." After returning to the House, Clare found herself ostracized by fellow members, who left the seats on either side of her empty.[2]

Displaying a combination of ingenuousness and conceit, Clare admitted to a *New York Mirror* columnist that she had been curious enough to find out what her colleagues thought of her. Most, she discovered, were "secretly proud" to be associated with a celebrity. One had stated that when he asked constituents what he could do for them, they said they wanted to meet Representative Luce. She did not hesitate to quote his bemused, "If I only knew her well enough to take them all over to her office, I wouldn't have to worry about the next election."[3]

Clare also managed to dismay and alienate some major figures in the other branches of government. In mid-May, she attended an exclusive dinner in honor of the Under Secretary of Foreign Affairs, Richard Law, and found herself talking to Felix Frankfurter, the recently appointed Supreme Court Justice and Roosevelt confidant. The opportunity to match wits with one of the best minds in the country was one she would normally welcome. But Frankfurter seemed neither to warm to her as a woman nor to care to engage her in serious dialogue.

She might have been further discomfited had she known that at least three other guests, including Mrs. Frankfurter, thought she was dull and humorless. "She is undoubtedly what Dick Law calls 'decorative,' i.e. has all the style that money can buy and a slim figure can carry off," the Justice wrote later in his diary, "but no real charm, no beauty except big and attractive eyes (doll's eyes that close and open), no give and take of spirit or mind. She behaves like a schoolteacher . . . makes little speeches and has unmitigated self-assurance. . . . I wholly distrust her motives."[4]

On May 17, three days after her encounter with Frankfurter, Clare had lunch with another Roosevelt intimate, Secretary of the Interior Harold Ickes. She wanted to find out, on behalf of her constituents, how much oil would be available for driving and home heating in the coming winter. Ickes could have told her over the phone that the outlook was not encouraging. But he was curious to meet the new Congresswoman who, Hill gossip had it, had once been the mistress of Bernard Baruch. In his diary, Ickes described her as the most talked-about member of the House. "She has not attempted to hide her light under a bushel and on two or three occasions she has made herself look foolish." He conceded that Clare was good-looking, if "brittle," but said her vaunted sex appeal escaped him.[5]

The condescension of jurists and cabinet officers did not gall Clare as much as the continuing false gallantry of her male colleagues in the House. In a letter to Pearl S. Buck, the Nobel Prize–winning novelist, she complained of the "myriad little snubs and discriminations" inflicted on her and other Congresswomen. They were treated "with the traditional solicitude strangers are wont to show old ladies crossing Fifth Avenue, or with the teasing deference uncles and older brothers show to girls on the day they graduate from High School." Behind the mask of courtesy was "an unwillingness to assign 'the girls' . . . to good committee jobs, or to permit us to speak on important and newsworthy legislation."[6]

This was not entirely fair, since she had a seat on a prestigious committee and had been allowed, in her maiden speech, to address one of the most crucial issues facing the postwar world. Her male colleagues in Military Affairs had to listen when Clare slammed such patronizing legislation as the "Wayward Wives Bill," whose aim was to cut off benefits from any woman who was unfaithful while her husband fought abroad. She proposed an amendment "that if the *serviceman* is unfaithful overseas, the wife's allowance be doubled."[7]

Chairman Andrew J. May agreed with her that this would be an extremely hard bill to implement, so it was not recommended for passage.[8] But duller members continued to be intolerant of Clare's combination of logic and wit.

Weary of the pettiness and superficiality of much of her four months in Washington, Clare welcomed an opportunity to write a weekly column called "Here the Gavel Fell" for *CBI* [China-Burma-India] *Roundup*, an official magazine for servicemen in the Far East. Her first piece appeared on May 13, 1943, and caused an immediate stir.

"Young people of the United States," she wrote, "are raised in a decade of the rubber stamp Congresses." This implied that her own was one of them, and suggested that her colleagues of both parties were too much in awe of President Roosevelt. In follow-up essays, she accused FDR of being too busy with military maneuvers to help stabilize the economy, and recommended that "guerilla sorties" be made to reduce New Deal bureaucracies. After twelve such columns, an exasperated War Department banned them, saying that Congresswoman Luce's views on controversial political questions had "no place in an Army publication."[9]

Clare felt the cancellation was probably due to her having "been in the hair of those who are not anxious to have our men overseas know how many people feel about the home front."[10] One GI in the CBI theater protested her ouster in verse:

Come brothers, let us mourn forsooth:
They nipped the nib of fair Clare Boothe.
Hushed in her journalistic prime
No sinner she: the printed word
Was all in which the lady erred
Her dreadful controversial ink
Induced poor Army lads to think!
(A heinous habit which a man
Must strive to conquer if he can.)[11]

▽

During the mid-June brouhaha over Clare's *CBI Roundup* columns, General Willoughby arrived in Washington. The boom to nominate his chief, Douglas MacArthur, for the presidency in 1944 was gathering strength, and Clare was all for it, especially if it meant she would see more of Charles. "In two years, people grow away from one another. . . . Even a month, a week together from time to time would bridge the gap." He too was unhappy over their enforced two-year separation. At times, he confessed, she scared him off with her feelings of "habit, belonging, obligation" vis-à-vis Harry.[12]

Although Willoughby was officially in town for meetings at the Pentagon, he needed to find out, as discreetly as only an intelligence officer could, just how much support there was among Republican leaders for MacArthur's candidacy.[13] He dined with Senator Arthur Vandenberg of Michigan, whom Clare had already lobbied to the same end. Willoughby's effusive praise of his chief convinced the Senator to organize a MacArthur-for-President Committee, and publish an article in *Collier's* magazine, "Why I Am for MacArthur," saying that the general was the only man capable of defeating Roosevelt during wartime.[14]

Willoughby stayed at the Wardman Park Hotel, conveniently near Clare's apartment. Given her high profile, and the extreme delicacy of his mission—an army officer trying to whip up political opposition to his Commander in Chief—they were careful not to be seen too much together, enjoying private moments instead.

▽

Clare made her second controversial House speech on June 24, 1943, this time to a full chamber. It was entitled "What Is America's Foreign Policy?" and argued that the country had none. As presently governed, the United States had only nationalistic ideals, and idealism, however noble, did not necessarily win the respect of other powers. "There is a world of difference between sentiment and policy," she pointed out, defining the latter as "procedure . . . based on self-interest [that] may be at total variance with the accepted principles, or spiritual concepts of a nation."

If the United States had had a firm, unsentimental foreign policy during the 1930s, she said, the "isolationist" President Roosevelt would not have sent a message of congratulation to Chamberlain after Munich, and Japan would not have been allowed to buy American steel in order "to beat our only potential ally in the Far East [China] to her knees." It was only after Pearl Harbor that FDR had hastily and unimaginatively adopted the worldview of Winston Churchill.[15]

Helen Essary of the *Washington Times-Herald* described the address as "one of the most daring ever heard in Congress." As Clare, looking innocent and ultrafeminine in a black-and-white-flowered silk dress, spoke of programs being "midwifed by secret diplomacy," and the administration plunging the American people into "an abyss of moral confusion," she drew the ire of some of the ablest Democratic scrappers in Congress.[16] But Republicans cheered, and one on the Foreign Affairs Committee passed her a note, saying the speech was the best he had heard on the subject.[17]

Essary divined that if Clare was to succeed over time, she "must prove that in addition to brains, beauty, and audacity she also has stamina. There is a chance that so dazzling a butterfly may be bored—too soon." The reporter ended her article by suggesting Congresswoman Luce for Vice President on the Republican ticket in 1944, to put "zip, drama, and light into the campaign."[18]

▽

On Sunday, June 27, Clare appeared in Appleton, Wisconsin, to give the keynote speech at the state Republican convention. It was rare for a freshman Representative to be offered such a high-profile role. She began with criticism of her own party. Business-friendly "Old Deal" policies in earlier GOP administrations, she said, had failed to do justice to farm and other laborers, and led to Roosevelt's New Deal. Corrective Democratic programs had also been useless, in her view, discouraging individual enterprise. Should FDR run for a fourth term, she predicted that he would have to campaign on his foreign policy record—for what it was worth—and his management of the war, rather than his ineffectual domestic record. She criticized the President's "windy" political rhetoric as "dazzle dust terms thrown in people's eyes in order to be able to complain that [they] do not see."[19]

Her speech was widely reported, with left-wing newspapers and magazines being incensed by its dismissal of the welfare state. *The New Republic* remarked that she had made a "classic fool of herself." But *Time* called her address a model of partisan politics. An editorial in Oregon's *Salem Capital-Journal*, a newspaper of small circulation but considerable political influence, remarked that in Clare Boothe Luce the Republicans had found "their ablest campaign orator, next to Wendell Willkie. In fact, she excelled him as "a better master of satire [and] invective . . . using the rapier rather than the broadsword."[20]

Nine days later, she spoke in New York at a Columbia University gathering of the Institute of Arts and Sciences. Showing her versatility, she broached the vexed question of immigration, calling for the repeal of the Chinese Exclusion Act of 1882, and noting that it had been proved unjust even in its own time. Now in place for sixty-one years, the law seemed to condone "the whole Hitler doctrine of race theology." It was time to guarantee Chinese aliens a part in "the long-established quota system." Issuing a hundred or so work permits a year hardly posed a threat to American labor, or "even our so-called white civilization."[21]

Such challenging rhetoric, coupled with Clare's ever-stylish appearance, assured her of continued media coverge, and compounded the already considerable jealousy of less noticed legislators.

▽

As part of his job, Henry Luce regularly visited different parts of the country, lecturing and looking for article and pictorial subjects for his magazines. On a trip to meet with the Governor of Georgia, he had spent a night at Redcliffe, the estate of John Billings in South Carolina. It reminded him sadly of Mepkin, his own nearby plantation on the Cooper River—closed for the war's duration. He had bought the crumbling property for Clare early in their marriage, and restored it extensively.

As he and Billings sauntered through Redcliffe's gardens, the managing editor, a large, shy man, was pleased to feel no social strain with his boss. Somewhat solitary now that his wife lived mostly in Washington, Harry seemed to have a need to talk.[22] China was a big subject for him, going back to his birth and schooling there. He raised money for the Nationalists and gave frequent coverage to their leader. Rather self-importantly, he told Billings that after a recent China Relief rally at Madison Square Garden, he had spent three hours with Madame Chiang Kai-shek. She had told him confidentially that "after the war, China's capital would be moved to Peking."[23]

▽

In the final House debate before the two-month summer recess began on July 8, Representative John W. Flannagan, Democrat from Virginia, launched into a diatribe against members who were "wrangling and fussing" on partisan issues instead of supporting their Commander in Chief. Without mentioning Clare by name, he made an overwrought attack on the "slim blonde creature of symmetrical lines and a face of beauty," who had emerged as such a maverick during the current session. She, "whose graceful form was richly gowned, whose long swan-like arms and tapering fingers were encased in jewels," had distracted the attention of the House from serious military matters. Clearly struggling with an erotic fixation, Flannagan even invoked her "left breast . . . bedecked with a rose crimson as the precious blood that oozed out of the ghastly wounds suffered by our boys as they fought from the foxholes of Bataan." These feminine attributes had not stopped the gentlewoman from Connecticut from giving "vent to spleen that I would never associate with a form so fair." In his view, her voice lacked "the ring of American motherhood."[24]

Another colleague tried to flatter Clare by suggesting she had "a masculine mind." She declined the compliment. "Thought has no sex. One either thinks, or one does not think."[25]

As the last day of her first six months in Congress came to an end, she stopped at her office to sign a batch of mail. Though she was obviously tired, reporters peppered her with questions. Would she be interested in running for the seat of Connecticut's retiring Republican Senator, John A. Danaher? Clare said no. She thought that a Democrat would win it. She intended to seek reelection to the House, "if the party wants me to run." What about the vice presidency? Clare laughed, saying the time for an American woman in such an exalted position was "a long way off."[26]

This did not quell rumors of her ambition. A few days later, the *Philadelphia Inquirer* ran a picture of her taking leave of Speaker Rayburn. "Home to Henry goes Clare Luce," the accompanying article read. "And if Henry isn't careful he's likely to find himself the hubby of a Senator. That Clare is just loaded down with ideas!"[27]

5

SUMMER INTERLUDE

It is better to be rare jade and broken,
than to be common tile and whole.

— CHINESE PROVERB

During the recess, Al Morano and two or three other staffers handled business from Clare's old campaign headquarters in downtown Greenwich.[1] She stayed mostly at home in the thirty-room country house on King Street that Harry had bought before the war. There she caught up on sleep, swam, played tennis, and wrote—usually in bed and sometimes at a circular desk facing it in her aquamarine boudoir.[2] As a member of the Committee on Military Affairs, she felt obliged to venture out occasionally to inspect war plants in Bridgeport, Norwalk, Stamford, and Danbury. Harry, meanwhile, commuted to his New York office.

Clare's solitude was soon interrupted by the appearance of David Boothe—"that wicked and wonderful brother of mine," as she ambivalently described him. He was attracted, as always, by the prospect of free accommodation, plentiful liquor, and the company of his adored sister.[3]

The siblings could not have been more different. David, one year older, was as dark and swarthy as Clare was fair and ethereal. In manner, too, they were opposites. He was coarse and brusque, she was smooth and deliberate. Three attributes they shared in abundance were physical courage, charm, and sex appeal. David had been no older than thirteen when he seduced his first girl, and Clare had begun to attract adult men in her mid-teens.[4] They also had mutual memories of maternal domination that had damaged them both—David perhaps more seriously. His early alienation from conventional mores had been sparked by his mother's tendency to identify him with his nomadic, untamable father, not to mention her repeated predictions that he would be a failure.[5]

Divorced since January from Nora Dawes, his Canadian wife of three and a half years, David, as always, needed money. He was currently a staff sergeant in the army. But having qualified as a pilot (thanks to a $10,000 training course paid for by Harry), he aspired to a commissioned rank with better pay in the overseas Army Air Corps. At forty-one, and suffering from high blood pressure, he was unfit for aerial combat, so Clare had used her influence to get him assigned as a liaison or service pilot. She hoped a career in military aviation might give her brother's life the structure it lacked. He was now set to leave for the Far East, where he expected to fly reconnaissance and transport planes in the Pacific theater.

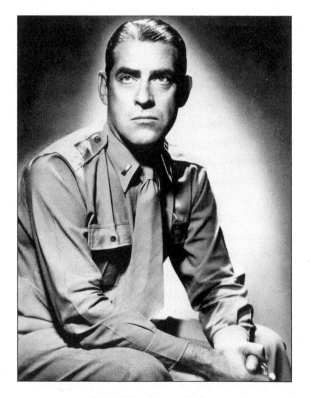

David Boothe, c. 1943

Although always in arrears on income taxes, David habitually shopped at Brooks Brothers or Abercrombie & Fitch, and had his bills sent to the Luces. Even Nora, the daughter of a wealthy Montreal brewer, seemed to think her in-laws should take care of any purchases at Bonwit Teller over and above the $300 monthly stipend they already allowed. This Harry refused to do, although he felt compassionate toward Nora, who had undergone a hysterectomy after David infected her with gonorrhea.[6]

In advance of her brother's arrival, Clare had written him an angry letter itemizing $190,000 in loans or cash gifts that she and Harry had given him since 1936.[7] "I doubt if there is any man in the world who has had as much help so constantly and has fallen down so often as you have," she wrote, telling him he should get "once and for all off my husband's shoulders." Now that he had a respectable job, he must not expect either of them to finance him again.

> I have no doubt that it will always be possible for us to keep track of your whereabouts as you borrow money from whatever friends of ours you can manage to lay your hands on. But I would just as soon not keep track of you. I know this is hard and harsh, but after twenty-five years of having been pretty much of a softie about you, I don't feel it's so bad.[8]

Unfortunately, she would always be "a softie" for David, as for nobody else. And he would forever find in his sister the only anchor he had or wanted. Time and again, he sailed back into her secure harbor, hauling his myriad physical, psychological, and financial problems with him.

Clare saw an opportunity that July to unite the three people she currently most cared about. General Willoughby was still in the United States, on temporary duty in San Francisco. Ann was at Stanford, taking extra classes in order to graduate a year early, in the spring of 1944. David, en route to the Far East, could use his considerable powers of persuasion to ingratiate himself with Willoughby, and travel there in more comfort with him.

On July 17, Clare and David flew to San Francisco. Ann Brokaw, eager to meet the high-ranking officer she had heard so much about, went north from Palo Alto in advance of their arrival, and dined with

Willoughby and a Colonel and Mrs. Davis at the Hotel Mark Hopkins. They talked until midnight, and then all four spent the night in the Davises' quarters at Fort Mason.[9]

The combination of a general's star, battle ribbons, and tall, dark good looks worked its inevitable spell on the eighteen-year-old. "General Willoughby is the most romantic, one of the handsomest, and most intriguing men I have ever met," she wrote in her diary. "If he were twenty years younger (he's 51) I should be madly in love with him! I can understand why mother is so fond of him."[10]

The following morning, Ann reunited with Clare and David at the Saint Francis Hotel. Her mother, she thought, looked "beautiful and lovely as ever." But the change in her uncle's appearance shocked her. David, formerly well built and copiously thatched, seemed "so thin and small and different in his Sargent's [sic] uniform and new haircut."[11]

At dinner that night, Ann again met Willoughby. Her infatuation with him deepened: "Oh the General is divine!"[12] Next morning, she attended Sunday services with Clare and "Charles." David, typically, had something else to do. After lunch, they went to Clare's suite, where she and Willoughby entertained Ann by reading aloud all three acts of Jacinto Benavente's *Princess Bebé*. That night, the three of them dined in the hotel restaurant. By now Ann was in love. "Oh gawd why isn't the general 20 years younger!"[13]

▽

At her best, when not combating teenage angst, Ann was a lighthearted and uncontentious young person. She brought a breath of warm air into the chilly atmosphere between David and Clare. Her relationship with her mother, however, was not uncomplicated. Though she loved her deeply, she was in awe of her beauty, and found her more intellectually challenging than anybody except Buckminster Fuller, whom Ann had judgment enough to realize had a greater mind.[14] Equally important, for a girl about to turn nineteen, was Clare's wisdom. She seemed to have an answer to all the pesky questions of life, such as "how people get in trouble by having affairs before they're married."[15]

Mother and daughter understood each other's mercurial temperaments. Both could switch from happy to sad in a flash.[16] Otherwise, they had little in common except melodious speaking voices. Ann lacked Clare's wit, multicreativity, lightning perceptions, luminosity, and seductive charm. In addition, she had a plain Brokaw face, with a long nose and crooked teeth. At almost five feet eight, she felt too tall for most men, and lamented her bony feet and large-knuckled fingers. "I've always wanted long artistic hands like Mummy's."[17]

She was not without social graces, although the mother of the violinist Yehudi Menuhin found her "spoiled, headstrong, self-centered."[18] Educated at the prestigious Foxcroft School in Virginia, with good grades in English literature, American history, and French, she had poise and was at ease in society. Her most striking physical assets were her slender figure, dark blue eyes, fair, slightly freckled skin, and long, chestnut hair.

At Foxcroft, Ann had shown a talent for playing the piano and violin, inherited no doubt from her maternal grandfather, William Boothe, a prodigiously gifted musician.[19] She sang well, too, and even tone-deaf Clare thought Ann had "a voice as pretty as a bird's."[20] Not surprisingly, she loved opera and could lip-synch arias from *Madame Butterfly* and other vocal works.

Having no illusions about a professional music career, and prevented by the war from going to the Sorbonne, her first university choice, Ann had opted to major in political science at Stanford, in the hope of eventually becoming a diplomat.[21] She joined the esteemed sorority Kappa Kappa Gamma, and was due that fall to be treasurer of the Stanford chapter of Pi Delta Phi, the national French honorary society. To her serious mind, proms, dates, and small talk felt like a waste of time. Her professors and peers, no matter how cosmopolitan or well-read, could not compete with Clare's stimulating presence, not to mention the endless stream of elevated conversation at Henry Luce's dinner table.[22]

Well aware of the superiority of her parents, Ann compared herself unflatteringly with Clare. "I have none of Mother's versatility or brains. I'm so mediocre it hurts and I get dumber (and less hair I might add) all the time."[23]

Stanford being even more remote geographically from the Luces' world than Foxcroft had been, Ann pined for her mother to write, telephone, or visit. But Clare always had excuses. In the past, she had been forever traveling somewhere, or "working on a new play."[24] Now she was in Congress, and often too preoccupied to keep in touch. Ann pleaded for the slightest snippet of news. "Do call me again when the budget permits. You've no idea how good it is for my morale!" And, "Mother dear what have you been doing? I haven't heard from or about you in ages!"[25]

More recently, she had begun to blame herself: "Forgive all my stupid little letters in which I normally ask you to write me! Somehow I always forget how very busy you are—and all the good you are doing—until I get a batch of clippings! Then it's always a wonder to me how you even manage to survive the work you have to do."[26]

Introspective and often lonely, Ann kept a diary at her mother's suggestion. Writing it, she said, made her think more clearly, and took the place of friends.[27] During her freshman and sophomore years, she had emerged from her shell, and carried on a flirtation with Walton Wickett, a tall, fair, twenty-nine-year-old engineer at Pan American Airways. She thought him "brilliant," and said that he was the first boyfriend with whom she "felt the fun of thrust and parry with words." He also played the piano "beautifully." But she found his parents lackluster and his bourgeois world too remote from her own, complaining that he was too much like her in being moody, introspective, and selfish.[28]

Walton was a devoted beau, but bothered by the fact that he had less money than Ann. She was, after all, a Brokaw heiress, with an income of more than $30,000 a year, and the stepdaughter of a press tycoon who gave her gifts of Time Inc. stock.[29]

Since he frequently irritated her, Ann was puzzled by the endurance of their friendship. She fantasized about what might have developed romantically had Walton "been truly handsome." Reading *Ethan Frome*, *Anna Karenina*, *Madame Bovary*, and other novels of passion made her long for a "feverish inner life and a lover."[30] When Walton querulously asked, "If I were famous, Ann, would you marry me?" she said she didn't know.[31] She continued to feel ambivalent about him, possibly because of a streak of violence in his normally sedate behavior. She recorded him slapping her face in a fit of jealousy, with "the strangest glint in his eye."[32]

Clare had met Walton briefly on her last trip to California, and quite liked him.[33] But when the young man tried to confide in her, writing that her daughter was "the most stimulating person" he had ever known, Clare had written back frankly, saying that she did not object to him as a son-in-law. But with a playwright's perspicacity, she dissected their situation:

> You see Ann is plainly greatly impressed by her family, fascinated
> by the lives we lead (and totally unaware that great chunks of
> them are very boring and shallow and sterile really). At any rate
> Ann is determined either to go on living that life *with* us, as our
> "unmarried and much sought after daughter," or if she marries,

make a similar life for herself. As she doesn't have (at 18 anyway) the intellectual equipment or talent, forthwith and overnight to recreate the atmosphere of the Luce household, she knows she will need help, lots of help in doing so! In short, she *is* looking for "another Henry Luce." The unhappy part of it—and which she will not face, is that she wouldn't *know* another Henry Luce at the age of 22 to 28 say, if she met him face to face tomorrow. (He stuttered slightly, was already a baldish fellow in his middle twenties, covered with cigarette ashes, endlessly opinionated—was always broke—had no artistic friends, and few journalistic ones.) He would decidedly *not* have impressed Ann *at that time*, as being either handsome, charming or "fascinating." But it is quite useless to tell Ann all this; she doesn't believe it. Neither does she quite believe (although she has seen with her own eyes to the contrary) that my "success" is largely the result of infinite patience, and hard work, and, in earlier days, considerable sacrifice of many of the things which she believes now, I have always enjoyed. In short, Ann, having no true perspective on the lives of the Luces—in spite of my constant efforts to give her one—can have, but does not have, a true perspective on her own life, since (*quod erat*) she wants hers to be exactly like ours.

Now to return to the question which interests you most— yourself vis-à-vis Ann. Well, you don't fit in, as a husband, in the heroic, or rather outsize, Luce mold; you don't fit into this false picture she has of her world—and ours. Nor, I predict, can you be *made* to fit, unless you become a national military hero overnight, write a great opera or novel, become managing editor of *Time*, run for Congress, be appointed ambassador to Spain, or inherit five millions. . . .

My advice is this: ignore Ann completely for the next six months—or better for a year. Go away, don't write her, if possible find another girl to go out with. Behave exactly as you would if you had grown tired of her.

And truly Ann *is* very young. I find myself fundamentally angry with you for importuning her in such a serious matter when she is still so far from graduating. I think it shows a lack of adult comprehension on your part too, my lad.

For the rest, you are quite right to love her, for she is a darling and lovely girl, with enormous possibilities. And she is quite right not to love you: you are far too demanding and insistent, in

the circumstances. So, alter your tactics, and you may succeed. I
do wish you well.[34]

As it happened, Ann had other suitors, who were no more successful
than Walton in proposing to her. There was Geza Korvin, a thirty-four-
year-old Hungarian actor with a chiseled face, thick dark hair, and copious Continental charm.[35] "If *only* he were younger and better off!!!!"[36]
And there was Captain James Rea, a short, good-looking test pilot who
drove an expensive car and took her on trips to Yosemite.[37] He believed
that her too-small breasts could be improved by regular massage.[38]

In rejecting him, Ann wrote a letter that unwittingly confirmed
Clare's analysis of her.

> I live for the day when I graduate—when I can begin to lead a re-
> ally interesting life, when because of the fortunate—or maybe
> unfortunate—accident that I happen to be the daughter of a very
> brilliant, famous & powerful woman & stepdaughter of a bril-
> liant, famous & powerful (for he is that) man . . . when I can be
> around the leaders of, or at least the people who influence the
> lives of millions, whether politically, artistically, intellectually or
> spiritually. And not just be around either—but learn & absorb
> from them as much as possible. . . .
>
> The price is that I know no field well & many superfi-
> cially. . . . A still greater price is loneliness—you must have
> guessed how lonely I am though one shouldn't admit it. [39]

Ann continued to toy with Walton—"something keeps drawing my
thoughts to him."[40] She told him she hoped to marry soon and have
several children.[41] But her ideal man was still her stepfather. Harry
loomed in her mind as a sort of god whose passions made the whole
house rumble. "Until the thunder has quieted down," she wrote, "an
atmosphere of intensity—electrical discharge and excitement pervades
our lives."[42]

After Ann, David, and Willoughby had gone their separate ways, Clare
arrived back East in a low frame of mind. Alone again in her big country
house, she dwelt on the often tedious first months in Congress, her deteriorated marriage, and the irresolution of her affair with Willoughby.

She had hoped in San Francisco to make sense of her complex feelings for the general, and whether after the war she could make a life with him. Willoughby seemed a more substantial figure now than the officer she had met in Manila, if only because of his greatly increased responsibilities as intelligence chief for the whole Pacific theater.

What Clare had not anticipated was that Charles would be so taken with her daughter. Ann had apparently already heard from him that he had enjoyed dancing with her at the Saint Francis Hotel. She rapturously quoted his words: "I have found you most charming, and good looking and, of course, I liked you being tall."[43]

Emboldened by this, Ann felt free to write reprovingly to her mother:

> The General is a far better correspondent than you. I had a letter
> from him the other day from Hawaii. He and Uncle David had a
> quiet trip that far together and the General says he intends to
> keep an eye on him for our sakes. I still think the General is the
> most romantic guy I ever met—don't you?
>
> P.P.P.S. I'm mad as an old wet hen that you went off with the
> General's stars. Now you hang on to them for me won't you?[44]

The allusion was to combat medals that Charles had won in the Philippines, and had casually given to Ann as souvenirs. Clare had sneakily taken them back to Connecticut.[45]

David could hardly believe his luck in having been taken under Willoughby's wing. A letter telling Clare of his safe arrival in Brisbane in late July was written on notepaper from the Supreme Commander's headquarters. "Thru the courtesy of Gen'l Sir Charles, from his office, a line . . . I'm delighted to be here and have an opportunity of serving in this particular section of the world. The men are mature, in direct contrast with my USA companions . . . The Gen'l is a great and good guy."[46]

Mindful of her brother's short attention span, his lack of self-esteem, and his weakness for women and drink, Clare was not sanguine about his long-term commitment once he reached the steamy, sparsely populated Pacific Islands.

When intimates retreated from her into their own lives, Clare had a narcissistic tendency to feel abandoned. Even Harry's commutes seemed like desertions. As her depression worsened, she tried to work through it by committing her thoughts to paper. They tumbled out in a bilious ten-page letter to Helen Lawrenson, a *Vanity Fair* colleague from the early 1930s.

Sounding a little unhinged, Clare wrote that Washington was a cancerous place, and compared men there to cockroaches and ants. Her own "bird-dropping liberalism" revolted her. It signified nothing in a meaningless world. All human effort for social change was a wasted attempt to resuscitate "an already dead body." Her work on the Military Affairs Committee convinced her that Allied soldiers did not know what they were being asked to die for. The letter degenerated into gruesome images of corpses caked with blood, and eyeless beggars oozing pus. Finally, she advised Lawrenson to warn her own daughter—a child of four—that life was nothing but "struggle, struggle, struggle."[47]

Lawrenson saw this "weird paean of disgust" as proof of inner hopelessness and "something akin to loathing" for mankind. A left-wing, even radical, thinker herself, she was not convinced that Clare had a social conscience.[48] She wrote back as tactfully as possible, disagreeing that humanism was a dead cause, and praising Congresswoman Luce's efforts in that direction. "You've voted correctly, and you've spoken out with courage and spoken the truth. Your speech about Roosevelt's lack of foreign policy was brilliant and true. He *has* no foreign policy . . . and therefore he has adopted the British one."[49]

▽

Eight years before her current midsummer doldrums, a more optimistic Clare had written an article suggesting that there was nothing "untoward or illogical, or subversive of masculine supremacy" in the idea of a female President of the United States.[50] When the women's division of the Republican National Committee announced in August that she would make a four-week speaking tour of twenty states that fall, speculation grew that it would inevitably whip up a "Luce for Vice President" boom—perhaps for a ticket headed by General MacArthur.[51] But Clare postponed the tour until the new year, giving as her reason that important bills were up for consideration in the next session of Congress.

This did not stop talk of her political potential. If anything, it intensified after a foreign policy address she wrote for the August 9 gathering of the India League of America at New York's Town Hall. The speech was read for her, because she claimed to be ill.

It began with an attack on Roosevelt and Churchill for regarding freedom as "the white man's monopoly," and went on to demand the release of Jawaharlal Nehru and Mahatma Gandhi, who were in prison for their efforts to end the British Raj. Clare called for all colonies to be given independence after the war, and urged Americans not to "lift a finger to help the British defeat the Indians in their fight for freedom."[52]

Her sympathy for subjected peoples was largely the result of meeting Nehru while covering the Far East for *Life* at the start of the war. She had been "utterly captivated" by him, as she confided at the time:

> It wasn't the dusky sweep of his eyelashes nor his poetic face; nor yet the fact that he smoked rose-petal cigarettes, nor even that he gave me a golden sari. It's just that I thought him one of the most brilliant and certainly "the goodest" man I have ever met, in a lifetime spent meeting great and, I regret to say, not very good men.[53]

She saw the Harrow- and Cambridge-educated Nehru as a liberated India's best prospect in the postwar world.[54] In a grateful letter to her, he predicted the ultimate defeat of the Axis powers, but not until "their empires are ended." The same applied to the Allies. He said that Stafford Cripps, the leader of the British House of Commons, talked to Indians as if it were still the nineteenth century. "Burma and Malaya show up the rottenness of the British Empire."[55]

Clare had suggested that Nehru travel to America to discuss "the Indian question" with President Roosevelt.[56] But before he could act on her proposal, he had been arrested. Among the few papers he managed to take with him was a letter from her, which he read repeatedly during his captivity in Ahmednagar Fort. It ensured that he would never forget her.[57]

Neither would Charles Willoughby, who wrote awkwardly of their recent trysts: "Remember how quickly we defeat time and absence and separation. Remember the few days that were natural, because we were free, how wonderful they were; how much of a forecast, and an accurate blue print of living."[58]

6

LUMINOUS LADY

*If we only wanted to be happy it would be easy. But we want to
be happier than other people, which is almost always difficult,
since we think them happier than they are.*

—Charles de Montesquieu

After Ann Brokaw finished her summer classes at Stanford, she traveled East for a short stay with Clare in Washington before the fall semester began. Congress had reconvened by the time she arrived in mid-September. She was able to watch Representative Luce participate in a "Wake Up America" forum, hear her on the radio show *Information Please*, and even accompany her to the famous Stage Door Canteen.

This facility for servicemen in Lafayette Square was one of the few spots where socialites and politicians could carouse in the war-dreary capital.[1] Clare as usual captured most of the attention. Besieged by servicemen from all sides of the dance floor, she twirled nonstop for the best part of an hour. Ann was photographed behind the counter, ladling food.[2]

She was accustomed by now to fielding questions about her famous mother's beauty and activities. But a young man she met took her aback when he asked why *Time* magazine was forever taking cracks at Congresswoman Luce.

"What should I have answered?" Ann said on returning to the Wardman Park apartment.

Clare was tempted to reply acidly, "Well, the truth I suppose."[3]

Ann Brokaw at the Stage Door Canteen, September 1943

Harry's editors still tended to belittle her political doings, as if they feared being accused of favoring the boss's wife. The remark passed on by Ann stayed with her overnight, and by the next evening, October 3, Clare was so upset that she typed a long plaint to Harry. It began philosophically, but soon became an almost masochistic mea culpa, indicating that her recent depression had not altogether lifted:

> Please do not be unhappy or disturbed at the irritation I some-times show with *Time*, or its text. Knowing that *Time* is objective, that its opinions are reached by a magnificently informed group of men . . . doesn't exactly set me up, however, when they take (over a period of so many years) such a consistently dim view of me. . . .
>
> That is as much a matter of pain to me, as it is embarrass-ment to you. All the more so, as I know *they* are right: I'm not a particularly admirable person, fundamentally. . . . I am a kind of pretty phenomenon. . . . I have failed perhaps in everything—in being a good daughter, a good mother, a good wife, a good artist. To the list of long failures I now add that I have not been a good, or constructive public servant, and I know I never shall be. . . .
>
> But all that is neither here nor there: the salient fact, the in-disputable evidence is that you are, unhappily, married to a woman your own editors simply cannot like (because they should

not). And that is a great hardship for you, and a constant cause for pain and uneasiness. What is indicated is not that you should change either your policy or your editors, but that you should change your wife, or that she should change her ways, her convictions, or her character. . . . I can, of course, get out of politics, and will, when the time comes. I could not . . . get far in them anyway, married to you, because too many people down here think of me first as your wife (and blame me for everything they don't like that *Time* says about them) or, when they find out that I really have no "power," which they do find out after a while, the wise ones—check me off the list. . . .

Anyway, the net of it is that I have to stand and do stand pretty much on my own feet, without any support in the public prints. . . . There ISN'T anything you can or should do about it. God's designs for a man's working and living can often be at variance with his own designs for loving. I have contributed nothing to the scope or purpose of your work, little to the comfort of your living, and only spasmodically and that a long time ago, to your joy of loving. The fault is largely mine, I am bitterly aware of it. I curse myself these days, every time I hang up the phone after having talked to you. I never seem able even conversationally to contribute anything of comfort or inspiration or interest. . . . What should I say that would please you? That I miss you? I do of course, but I never expect you to come back to me anyway, there is some dark, immutable barrier between us that I am quite powerless to conquer, and talking about it does nothing but make you miserable or angry.[4]

Clare ended by wishing Harry joy in something or somebody, if not her. After her political career was over, she wrote, she would be gone from any scene that might cause him difficulty. "Okay darling?"[5]

Harry did not reply at once. Clare sensed that he was angered by having to come up with an editorial policy that would be fair to both her and himself. She shared her malaise with Ann and, after the girl left, tried to distract herself with work.

Her priorities for this session of Congress, she informed *The Washington Post*, were a tax bill to help pay for the war, a bipartisan resolution to cooperate in the immediate postwar period, and another to straighten the critical "manpower tangle." She proposed the creation of an Army-Navy Maintenance Corps to enlist men physically disqualified from fighting for jobs in essential industries. She said this would postpone the dreaded further drafting of fathers.[6] Encouragingly, there was movement on another of her causes: President Roosevelt had agreed to back repeal of the Chinese Exclusion Act.[7]

Harry remained silent. "I expect, in a little while, I'll call up and apologize," Clare wrote Ann.[8] Whether it was he or she who eventually telephoned, a truce of sorts was worked out between them by October 22. On that day, John Billings bemusedly noted in his diary, "Luce orders that the name of Clare Boothe Luce be not mentioned in any of the magazines until further notice. O.K.—but why? Because Luce thinks his wife is regularly misinterpreted and put in a bad light in *Time*."

It was a Pyrrhic victory for Clare, who now found herself honor-bound to kill a flattering profile of her written by Noel Busch for *Life*. She did so in a call to Billings, her voice sounding to him like "icy poison."[9] The editor presumed that Harry would moderate the ban as soon as his writers showed a willingness to treat Clare fairly.

"Dad is in a better than average mood," Clare told Ann at the end of the month. "Like a *lamb* he bought me the big Segonzac painting from Frank Crowninshield's art sale. $7,500 wheeeeee. It was a 'peace offering' for certain, and so I am being peaceful too."[10]

Adding to her own improved mood was news from New York that Moss Hart might direct a revival of her 1942 comedy, *Love Is a Verb*, with Myrna Loy set to star.[11]

▽

Infinitely larger theaters—the European and Pacific wars—absorbed Clare when she returned to her seat on the House Military Affairs Committee. The spring and early summer of 1943 had brought significant Allied victories in Europe, North Africa, and the Soviet Union. American and British divisions had forced Field Marshal Rommel's once invincible desert corps to surrender in Tunisia while he was on leave, freeing the Mediterranean for Allied shipping and an invasion of Sicily. There, Generals Patton and Montgomery, attacking from different points on the island, had routed the Axis in thirty-eight days. Mussolini had fallen at the end of July, Naples was taken by the Fifth Army, and Roosevelt's demand for "unconditional surrender" had been yielded to by the Italians on September 8. Even more dramatically on the Eastern Front, the Red Army had defeated the Germans at Stalingrad and at Kursk, and pushed them into retreat mode across the Dnieper River.[12]

Fewer victories were reported, as yet, from the other side of the world. But the Japanese were now driven from Guadalcanal and Tarawa, and more islands would soon fall to the Americans. Clare was particularly well briefed on what General Willoughby called "the War of Distances," because he used his connections to get uncensored mail to her.[13] He reported that U.S. troops were already halfway along the north coast of New Guinea, where David Boothe was flying transport planes. Others were set to attack New Britain, a springboard for the recapture of the Philippines.[14]

The campaign that MacArthur's army and Admiral William Halsey's navy were now embarked on covered an area equal in size to that between England and Iran. Island-hopping, meticulously planned by the Supreme Commander, would require eighty-seven amphibious landings on malarial terrain where temperatures sometimes rose to over 115 degrees in the shade, and rain fell at the rate of up to sixteen inches a day. Snakes, crocodiles, and head-hunting cannibals hardly made the campaign easier, but Willoughby proudly reported that his fellow soldiers had already immobilized a quarter of a million Japanese in jungle fighting, and had done it with fewer deaths than even the U.S. Marines had incurred in capturing Saipan.[15]

More personally that October, Charles wrote that he had just seen an old *Time* magazine photograph of Clare that to him had "the luminous quality of Sargent."[16] She was shown getting into a car in a small toque hat, giving a queenlike glance at the camera, and her stylish loose coat suggested "the subtle outline of a beautiful and ravishing body." The apparition undid him.

> I was seized with the most frantic longing . . . like a fever, that shook me and devoured me . . . a savage, savage fire that consumed me . . . a sudden knowledge of the menace of slow years; a fierce jealousy of your time and milieu; and yet . . . a sense of belonging; and the hope of the hour between us that will set everything right again; and the feel of your lips that will vanish all these months as if they were not. . . . Love me, my dearest, my wife, my own.[17]

He added that he appreciated the intimate notes she wrote him in the small hours, saying how much she loved and longed for him. He

Clare "in bed" with General Willoughby

desired her, too, "maddeningly so at times, as if some fire were dormant and suddenly, with a gust of wind, roars into a fierce blaze. Then my imagination runs riot—but it is wholly delightful."

Apparently, Willoughby saw his long-term future in the Far East, because he talked of Clare joining him there. But could she bear the dislocation and the material sacrifice? "You have been unconsciously accustomed to a certain scale of living: it would jar you to change it."[18]

▽

Clare was again a little down when she wrote Ann on Sunday, November 7, but tried to sound cheerful. "Annie my pudding-cake, my peach pie, and all assorted delicacies." She enclosed a flattering newspaper reference to Ann by a reporter who had met her in Washington. Every word of the piece was true, Clare said, and showed that "perliteness pays—to the press, anyway!" Her daughter certainly had "enchanting" manners, "except of course sometimes about one o'clock in the morning, when you don't have to get up and I do the next day, and you insist . . . on a pow-pow with mom-ma."[19]

Aware that Ann might be concerned about the strain between her and Harry, Clare reported that he was due in Washington that afternoon. They had to perform the kind of formalities expected of a power couple: pay a hospital visit to the ailing President of the Philippines,

Manuel Quezón, then attend a party at the Soviet Embassy to dutifully "celebrate" the Bolshevik Revolution.

The news from Mepkin was not good. Two years of neglect had taken a toll. "Dat ole debil jungle," she wrote, had crept over the cottages, infusing their furnishings with mold. In contrast, winter had come to the Potomac. "The lawn outside is covered with a tattered carpet of brown and yellow leaves, the tennis courts are shut, a few roses still bloom. . . . I am lonely and depressed, and wish you were here." Instead she had only her dog, Speaker, who looked at her with tragic eyes and drooled so much as she ate that she ended up giving him her dinner.

Closing on a hopeful note about the war, Clare predicted that it would end in Europe in 1944 and in the Pacific a year later.

> And then whoops it's off we go, you and I, to assay the damage
> the whole thing did, around the world. Better get yourself ready
> by then with typing and shorthand, because *together* we will get a
> lovely book out of it. Notes by CBL, footnotes by her shrewd lit-
> tle *tochter*.
>
> Kiss, hugs, moist smacks, and all other embraces such as slaps
> on derrières, and pinches on the cheek, which show that a fond
> mamma wishes to convey the impression that she idolizes her
> only offspring.[20]

That fall, Clare spoke out increasingly against imperialism. In a speech at the University of Rochester on November 18, she accused Great Britain of holding on to India for economic rather than altruistic reasons. If 390 million Indians wanted to be free and self-sufficient, she declared, they should be. Britain's commercial losses could be made up by the United States, which might then assume responsibility for the security of all Asia. She repeated what she had prophetically written Harry after Pearl Harbor, that if the Allies won a "multiple-front war" against the Germans and Japanese, freed subject nations might then ally themselves with their "former master's enemies." Hence America was fated "to police the world."[21]

A few nights later, she attended a dinner in New York for the famous British explorer Freya Stark. Perhaps the last of the empire-trotting travelers in the tradition of Sir Richard Burton, Stark was fifty years old and at the crest of an enviable literary career. She was in

America to lecture on the Middle East, with the approval of the British Foreign Office, which hoped she would persuade audiences that Palestinian Arabs deserved their own homeland along with the Jews. This mission met with disapproval in Zionist circles, but Stark was charming, well-informed, and not easily thwarted.

Clare seized the occasion to pontificate about the fate of colonies, and Britain's obligation to free India. Stark said before that happened, the conflicting ambitions of Hindus and Muslims had to be reconciled, or independence would bring civil war and bloodshed.[22]

"Let there be massacres," Clare shot back. "Why should the white races have a monopoly on murder?"

Stark, smiling, said that if the Congresswoman wanted to give poor countries immediate independence, she might coin a slogan, "Freedom for Fratricide."

Clare countered with an icy stare.

In a report to London, Stark dismissed her as "an enemy on sight, with lovely eyes firmly fixed on the middle distance."[23]

▽

November also saw the publication of *Au Clare de Luce: Portrait of a Luminous Lady*, a biography that did not enhance Clare's reputation.

The author was Faye Henle, a business reporter who had monitored her election campaign, and the controversy surrounding the "Globaloney" speech, and concluded that she was a dangerous symbol "of press agentry."[24] Henle had since been in pursuit of the real woman (as she thought), talking to Clare, observing her in Congress, and interviewing friends such as the novelist Laura Z. Hobson. Having no access to private documents, she relied on morgue articles (in particular a 1941 *New Yorker* profile by Margaret Case Harriman) for information about her subject's early life.[25] She thus recycled misconceptions, many of them propagated by Clare herself. Had Henle taken more time with her 205-page book, completed in three months, she might have avoided such checkable errors as the date of Clare's birth, the fact that "Joyce Fair" was not young Miss Boothe's stage name, but that of another actress, and that *Europe in the Spring* had been dedicated to Harry, not David. Nevertheless, the book was occasionally perceptive, as in a metaphorical description of Congresswoman Luce's effect on the House. "The new member was politely attentive to the goings-on, but those who continued to observe her began to realize that this radiance, this aura or spotlighted circle that seemed to surround her invisibly, was not merely the cool of magic moonlight; there was insulation in it, too—something of the thin chill that protects dry ice from careless handling."[26]

Henle harped throughout on Clare's presumed coldness, and also questioned her intentions.

> Practically all the desirable accomplishments are credited to her except warmth . . . which causes people to give things away. Not that Clare does not give things away, for she has made many and substantial gifts. Curiously, however, few people seem able to identify the motive as "love and affection." . . . It may be that the legend needs a new casting director to take her out of the typed role of shrewd commercialism.[27]

Clare read the text in galleys and telephoned Henle to say that she supposed biographical subjects got the book they deserved. "It'll all come out in the wash, you little so-and-so."[28]

She could do nothing about negative assessments of her character and motives, but factual mistakes belittling her honesty and professionalism were another matter. John Billings could help with at least one of these, so she called him to say she was in trouble. He wrote in his diary, "A nasty book is coming out in which she is accused of palming off on us photos from Burma as her own whereas they were really taken by George Rodgers at the risk of his life." He was able to come to Clare's rescue and get the erroneous attribution excised.[29]

When *Au Clare de Luce* duly appeared, it received much adverse criticism, of both writer and subject. The *Birmingham News* called it "the outline of a good biography by a poor biographer." A *Chicago Sun* critic felt that Clare was portrayed as a "composite of Theda Bara, Joan of Arc, Helen of Troy and Cato the Younger." The *Bridgeport Herald*, seldom kind toward her, agreed with Henle that Lillian Hellman was a better playwright, Edith Nourse Rogers a superior Congresswoman, and Dorothy Thompson a more accomplished journalist. Another Connecticut newspaper, the *Hartford Times*, wrote that readers were left with the impression that Clare Boothe Luce was shrewd, calculating, audacious, egocentric, and opportunistic, as well as facile, witty, and clever. "She doesn't like people, except a few, chiefly Clare." However, she had "made a career of knowing the right ones."[30]

The *New York Post* took the long view. "Books will undoubtedly be written about Clare and Henry Luce that will one day tell us just what they stood for in American life. Just now we are a little too close to them to measure their merit or lack of it with any accuracy."[31]

Clare sought solace in her oft repeated maxim, "Even bad publicity is better than none."[32]

On Tuesday, November 23, the Luces commemorated their eighth wedding anniversary with an exchange of gifts. Harry gave Clare a jade Kwan Yin.[33] She presented him with an extraordinary piece of needlepoint, designed by herself and embroidered over the span of several years, mainly while he read aloud to her after dinner. Six feet wide and three deep, it was a complex, basket-weave composition showing his accomplishments in multicolored yarn: covers of *Time*, *Life*, *Fortune*, and the *Architectural Forum*, a newsreel camera recording *The March of Time*, and an aerial perspective of Rockefeller Center, headquarters of the Luce publishing empire.[34]

More personally, a corona of sharp red pencils and zigzagging radio waves signified the communicative reach of husband and wife, and a curving globe and soaring airplanes their international travels. Clare's own career was represented by graphic symbols of three of the plays she had written since 1936—*The Women*, *Kiss the Boys Goodbye*, and *Margin for Error*—as well as her book *Europe in the Spring*. A Willkie presidential campaign button and a view of the Capitol bespoke her political

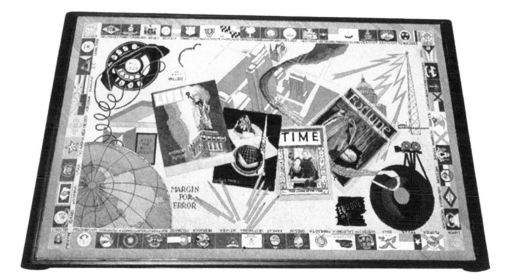

Clare's needlepoint gift to Harry, November 1943

interests. The tapestry was bordered by the flags of the American states and territories, meticulously rendered.

Originally, she had conceived it as a representation of the unity of their lives, "a Penelope's job . . . while my Ulysses was on his great journalistic journeyings." But finding herself unable, as their marriage fractured, to execute the last few icons, she had asked a professional to complete the work. In a letter to Harry, significantly cast in the past tense, Clare wrote, "It was for a long time a labor of great love, the proof that once at least we were a very happy couple. . . . I have never ceased to regret the circumstances which kept me from finishing it myself."[35]

▽

Thanksgiving came two days later. Never keen to celebrate with Harry's relatives ("the only thing worse than having no family," she joked, "is having family"), Clare stayed in Greenwich. "I've spent two days at a job of war work," she wrote Ann, "investigating for the Military Affairs the termination of contracts and renegotiation. Yes, it's as *dull* as it sounds."[36]

As she set off on another committee chore—to inspect Ford's Willow Run bomber plant in Detroit—the "Big Three" were meeting in Tehran. This was Roosevelt's first encounter with Josef Stalin. During their initial tête-à-tête, they discussed the war in Eastern Europe and China and, in particular, Indochina. Clare the anti-imperialist would have been pleased to hear Roosevelt say it was time to prepare that region for postwar independence from Britain, France, and the Netherlands. But Stalin's additional suggestion that India needed total reform "somewhat on the Soviet line" was not what she or Nehru had in mind for the subcontinent.[37]

On her return to Washington, she found that Faye Henle's book had done little to damage her reputation. A local letter saluted Representative Luce as "one of the zippiest citizens that has hit this town in a long while." Another, from Kansas City, urged her to throw a vice presidential hat into the ring for next year. A third of her fan mail came from women. One wrote: "I prophesy that your name will stand out in this country as Madame Chiang is outstanding in China, if the men will but give you the chance."[38] There were many requests for photographs. "Imagine me, a pin-up at 40!" she gushed to a reporter.[39] Her celebrity seemed to spread to fashion pollsters. At the beginning of December, Clare Boothe Luce tied with the Duchess of Windsor as the best-dressed woman in the world.[40]

Simultaneously, a "Draft Mrs. Luce Committee" was formed by Connecticut constituents eager to win her the number two spot on the GOP ticket in 1944, whether it was headed by General MacArthur, Governor Thomas E. Dewey of New York, or Governor John W. Bricker of Ohio. Clare affected humility. "What have I ever done to deserve such high office, outside of having a burning desire to serve my country? There are plenty of Republicans who are better equipped . . . the whole idea is too fantastic."[41]

Nevertheless, it was she, on December 15 in Fairmont, West Virginia, who launched the Republican presidential campaign with an attack on FDR and the New Deal. She praised her congressional colleagues for being united on foreign and domestic policies, while Democrats were "wracked by internal strife." Whomever the GOP chose as its standard-bearer, she went on, was bound to be, in contrast with Roosevelt, "a man not given to impulsive experimentation, to self-whims, and love for personal power."[42]

Talk of Clare Luce as a potential nominee continued. Even the quintessentially British Noël Coward, on a visit to New York, was asked what *he* thought about Mrs. Luce's vice presidential prospects. Tactfully, he said, "I think she's a very good playwright."[43]

As it happened, Coward and Clare knew each other. They had first met backstage in a London theater when he was twenty, and she seventeen, and vainly infatuated with him. In the early 1930s, she had been his editor at *Vanity Fair*. Just after the fall of France in 1940, they had run into each other unexpectedly at Lisbon airport, and shared their mutual horror of Fascism and Nazism over glasses of red wine. Coward had then been one of several entertainers, including Cary Grant, Leslie Howard, and David Niven, who had been recruited to sound out foreign opinion as to Hitler's intentions.[44]

Now they were to be reunited. On December 20, Clare attended a dinner party for Coward in the New York apartment of the producer Gilbert Miller, and lectured him on British foreign policy, as she had with Freya Stark. Later he wrote in his diary, "She became rather shrill over the Indian question, about which she knows only a little more than I do." He had taken her on to the Stork Club, where the discussion continued, with the American travel writer John Gunther supporting Clare.

> I was feeling tired and ill, and I resented being made a sort of show-off target for the Luce shafts at the British Empire. I let [them] talk

for ages and remained quiet. Then I upped and said that although they doubtless knew a lot about the Indian question, it was none of their damn business, and if in fifty years they had successfully settled the American Negro question, by which time our Indian problems would have settled themselves we should be perfectly prepared to let them [talk more]. . . . All rather tedious and obvious.[45]

▽

In the last days of 1943, Congresswoman Luce could look back on a voting record liberal enough to please even Helen Lawrenson. It included support for infant and maternity care appropriations for the wives of enlisted men, as well as higher allotments for all military dependents. She had further enhanced her reputation as a public speaker, showing herself willing to travel the country and spread the Republican credo.[46]

On December 25, after broadcasting a Christmas Eve message to occupied France, Clare left New York for California with Harry and an assistant, Virginia Blood. The latter was to accompany her on her postponed lecture tour for the Republican National Committee. It was scheduled to begin in Los Angeles on January 6, and continue through ten other Western states.

But first, the Luces were due to meet Ann in Palm Springs, to celebrate the new year.

7

IMPACT

▽

It is required of a man that he should share the passion
and action of his time at peril of being judged not to have lived.

—OLIVER WENDELL HOLMES, JR.

J ust before joining her parents at the Ingleside Inn in Palm Springs,
Ann Brokaw told her test pilot boyfriend, James Rea, that she had
lost interest in study. "I don't really honestly care very much *what* grades
I get . . . ten years hence what difference will it make?" Her routine at
Stanford, she said, compared unfavorably with "the stimulating life"
available back East.[1]

It was not just there that she was proud to be the daughter of such a
famous person. On Clare's last visit to the West Coast, Ann had been
taken to 20th Century-Fox to meet Orson Welles (then playing Mr.
Rochester in *Jane Eyre*). She had also been introduced to Claudette
Colbert, Tyrone Power, and Joan Bennett over lunch, and to Budd
Schulberg and David and Irene Selznick over dinner.[2] Everywhere they
went, the Congresswoman-elect had been respectfully received as a
bona fide screenwriter.[3]

Ann had not noticed a tension between her mother and the elegant
and epigrammatic Mrs. Selznick. Irene resented being treated as a Rolo-
dex card, the "accessible, available, useful" wife of a legendary Hollywood producer. She was never taken in by flattery, and would recall that
Clare was "always on the verge of being very fond of me."[4]

But Ann struck her as different. Irene's first impression was of "a bell pealing, clear and crisp with a beautiful smile." Although Harry was gentle and loving toward his stepdaughter, Irene sensed that the girl was "starved" for signs of maternal affection and approval.[5]

Ann was also frequently frustrated and depressed by her inability to love any of her boyfriends. "It is a terrible thing how very often the idea of suicide occurs to me," she wrote in her diary. "I long to know the beyond—to see Granny again."[6] Like Clare, she was haunted by memories of the first Ann, killed in a car crash in January 1938.

Walton Wickett remained her emotional anchor in California. One day she felt "very much in love," the next disdainful of the way he looked in swimming trunks.[7] "There just isn't the feeling in my heart."[8] Walton admitted to Clare that his attraction to Ann was materialistic as well as romantic. Although he loved her for her "sublime" self, "the idea of [your] having a plantation in South Carolina, a country home in Connecticut, and an apartment at the Waldorf Astoria intoxicates me."[9]

Perhaps a love of the lavish life was what primarily linked the young couple. "A question I have asked a thousand times," Ann said, "is—what weight does my 'brilliant setting' have compared to the true me."[10] She accused Walton of using her to impress his Pan Am business associates.[11]

He sometimes recoiled from Ann's less appealing traits. She could be imperious, frivolous, and snobbish. "I was not born to ride on streetcars."[12] She was also acquisitive. "Did you see that ring?" she said to Walton, eyes blazing, after they ran into Henry and Frances Fonda at the Beverly Wilshire Hotel.[13] "Did you see the solitaire diamond? That belongs to me, and she'll have to give it to me." Bizarrely, Frances had succeeded Clare as the second wife of George Brokaw, and was therefore Ann's stepmother at the time she acquired that family heirloom. Walton had seldom seen Ann so exercised.[14]

He learned that she had once visited Frances and Henry in their Brentwood mansion, and tried in vain to befriend her much younger half-sister, "Pan" Brokaw, as well as the Fondas' own children, Jane and Peter.[15]

After toasting the arrival of 1944 *en famille* in Palm Springs, Ann accompanied her mother to Los Angeles for another round of socializing with Hollywood luminaries, while Harry took a train to New York.

Longing to be done with college so that she could rejoin the world of adults that she preferred, Ann wrote Greenwich friends, "July doesn't seem so far away. And then—whee—I'm coming back to help win the war—to do my bit to bring the end closer."[16]

On the evening of January 5, Clare was feted by cinema moguls in the Thalberg Executive Dining Room at Metro-Goldwyn-Mayer. One participant was the studio's chief story editor, Sam Marx, who found her both regal and remote.[17] The following night, with Ann looking on, Representative Luce gave the first speech of her Western tour. She denounced the administration's handling of foreign policy, and said that domestically conditions were deteriorating: America had become a nation of "hypochondriacs, introverts and psychotics" in the "tragic era of Franklin Roosevelt."[18]

Her next engagements were a radio talk and evening lecture in San Francisco. Ann preceded her north to Palo Alto to register for Stanford's spring semester. They arranged to spend three more days together at the Mark Hopkins Hotel on Nob Hill in San Francisco, where Clare had reserved a suite. She meanwhile remained behind to see Irene Selznick again, telling her that she thought raising children was the chief reason "for living and loving and learning . . . for being born and growing old." All her difficulties with Ann were over, "the childish troubles and adolescent misunderstandings had all been long forgotten." They now understood and loved each other "about as perfectly as a child and mother ever can." [19]

Reunited on Saturday, January 8, Ann and Clare posed together for a publicity photograph. Ann wore one of her mother's dresses in blue-and-white-striped silk with large buttons. On Monday evening, their last before college classes began, they dined with a former schoolmate of Clare's. Ann excused herself early to have a drink with Walton at the Top of the Mark bar.

▽

The two young people sat looking out at the nightspot's panoramic views of Golden Gate Bridge and San Francisco Bay, dotted with warships that would soon be embattled in the Pacific. They talked little, though Walton felt there was much to say. Their intimacy had mel-

Clare and her daughter, January 8, 1944

lowed into friendship, and Ann acknowledged that the last two years had been her happiest, that her fondness for him had "stood the test of time." Not long before, she had waxed nostalgic over their shared love of music. "I've just been listening to the waltz from *Der Rosenkavalier*. It sent the usual tingles up and down my spine and now I'm enjoying for the umptiest [sic] time the Album you gave me—Yehudi's rendition of *Symphonie Espagnole* by Lalo." They agreed to see each other in Palo Alto the following evening. Before saying good night, Walton promised Ann he would listen to her mother's radio talk.[20]

Clare returned to the suite at about eleven o'clock, finding Ann prone and already asleep. She smacked her bottom. "Lazybones, why aren't you out enjoying yourself?"

Ann opened her eyes and groaned, "Mo-*ther*."[21]

▽

The next morning, Tuesday, January 11, Ann crept out of the hotel without waking Clare and took a lift back to Stanford in the 1941 Mercury Club coupé of a friend, Virginia Lee Hobbs. By approximately 9:45, the two students were traveling southeast through a residential district of Palo Alto, just minutes from their destination. Virginia kept to the twenty-five-mile-an-hour limit along Byron Street, slowing slightly as she entered the intersection of Everett Avenue. She was about halfway across when, out of the corner of her eye, she saw a car approaching on her right. Sensing that its driver may not have seen her, she gripped her steering wheel and accelerated—too late to avoid being hit on her rear fender and wheel hub. She braked, but her car was already spinning. Both doors flew open as the vehicle circled 180 degrees onto the left sidewalk. Ann was flung out, and her door, swinging wildly on its hinges, smacked her body toward a roadside tree. Her head bore the brunt of the impact, which was compounded by the force of the chassis as it wedged her torso against the trunk.[22]

Virginia, thrown with less velocity, landed more gently on the pavement. Finding that she had only minor leg scratches, she rushed to Ann and found her crushed half shapeless. Feeling her pulse, Virginia thought she detected a faint throb. Within minutes a policeman appeared, along with a doctor from a nearby clinic, and declared Ann Clare Brokaw "dead at the scene."[23]

▽

At the Palo Alto Hospital, another physician noted that Ann's face was unscathed, except for a small cut at her mouth's right corner. But her other injuries were extensive: a fractured skull and pelvis, twenty-four broken ribs, lacerations of the liver, spleen, lung, and brain, and a pancreatic hemorrhage. The police report stated that had her door not broken open, she could have survived with minor or no injuries. Even so, the crash had been violent enough to strew the contents of her suitcase, and to splatter a bottle of lotion from her toiletry bag on the upper reaches of a house twenty feet away.[24]

Ann's briefcase, retrieved from the debris, revealed the seriousness and breadth of her interests, as well as the promise of a fruitful life. It contained notes on Eino Holsti's *International Relations* and library call cards for three books on the life and philosophy of Ralph Waldo Emerson. There was a list of works she had recently studied: *The Taming of the Shrew*, *Of Human Bondage*, *The Last Puritan*, and *Portrait of the Artist as a Young Man*, as well as others to be read—*The Scarlet Letter*, *The Ambassadors*, and Nehru's *Autobiography*. She had kept three articles, including the flattering piece about her "perliteness" that Clare had sent from Washington. Another, on foreign policy, was from a recent issue of *Time*, and had been assiduously underlined. There was also a page of Spanish vocabulary, a map of Iberia, a pamphlet on Indian symbols as used on silver-and-turquoise jewelry, and an invitation to meet Madame Chiang Kai-shek at the Palace Hotel in San Francisco on March 29.[25]

Most poignant of all was a paper tissue with a dark red kiss. In one of her last communications with her daughter, Clare had advised Ann to "study the effect of too darn much lipstick."[26]

▽

Shortly after 10:00 A.M., Virginia Hobbs's father, who worked as a sales director at a department store near Byron Street, assumed the unenviable task of reporting the accident to Clare. Her assistant, Miss Blood, took the call.

"Ann is seriously hurt but I don't know the details," Mr. Hobbs said. "They are calling me just as soon as they find out."[27]

Miss Blood told him that her employer was still asleep, and that it would be best not to disturb her until they knew how severe Ann's injuries were. Some ten minutes later, Hobbs called with the final news, and asked her to break it.

"Wake up! Wake up! Your daughter is dead!"[28]

Clare, barely conscious, tried to absorb what the hysterical woman was telling her. Miss Blood knew only a few flimsy facts, and the tragedy she tried to describe made no sense. Nightmarishly, it seemed to Clare a duplicate of another collision—the one that had dismembered her mother. Two Anns, born in August and dying in January.

The supreme irony was that Clare had always been terrified of car accidents. At Ann's graduation from Foxcroft, she had refused to give her the customary convertible, because she thought it unsafe.[29] In another macabre foreshadowing, Ann had bumped lightly into a car some months before, while also approaching Palo Alto's main street, and Clare had written her a warning note: "Please please please drive more cautiously. It is such an irretrievable thing . . . to have your pretty face all bashed up, or be crippled for life, for a silly moment of speed or inattention . . . for my sake, be careful. It would be a stupid meaningless world without my Annie in it."[30]

Now just such a world confronted her, and she struggled to comprehend it.

Further items of information arrived at the Mark Hopkins suite. The coroner had released Ann's body to the Roller and Hapgood Funeral Parlor in Palo Alto. A college friend had dressed Ann's hair, knotting it strand by strand, and artfully arranging it to conceal the cracked skull.[31] One side of her body was so badly mutilated that the undertaker advised no viewing until that evening, giving the mortician time to make the corpse look as natural as possible.[32]

Charles Hobbs called again to speak to Clare. She was still in a dazed state, making his task especially awkward. He had once reprimanded her for writing too infrequently to Ann, who "admires and adores you," and she had answered with veiled sarcasm that unlike Mrs. Hobbs, who wrote to Virginia daily, she had a career to maintain as well as correspondence.[33]

Now he did all he could to spare the stricken mother. Offering to complete the death certificate on her behalf, he asked for biographical details, and requested a change of clothing for Ann's laying out. Miss Blood contacted the university to schedule a funeral service in the college chapel, and spoke to the chaplain, who suggested that part of Ann's last class paper, on Oriental religions, might be read at the service. He knew it had received a high mark, and contained some of her own philosophy.[34]

Seeing Clare succumbing to hysteria too, Miss Blood asked a West Coast *Time* employee to help her cope. He had worked as a police reporter, and saw at once that the Congresswoman was a typical "survivor in shock." She kept trying to talk through tears and gasping groans, as he tried to console her. A doctor sent by Irene Selznick gave Clare a sedative. This calmed her enough to be able to place a call to Harry.[35]

He had arrived back in New York just that morning, but could not be reached either at work or at home.[36] It was left to his secretary to tell him once he got to the office. John Billings noted how ravaged Luce looked, as if Ann had been his own child.[37] Yet when sharing the news with another confidant, Harry seemed oddly unsympathetic toward Clare, saying that any grief she might feel would be out of guilt, because she had treated Ann "abysmally" in earlier years.[38]

After booking an overnight flight for his return to California, Harry wired Clare to expect him in San Francisco the next morning, Wednesday, January 12.[39] He would be traveling in a DC-3 propeller plane, stopping every 250 miles or so to refuel. Knowing that she was due to make a speech at the local Press Club the evening of his arrival, he offered to deliver it in her stead.[40]

Before he left, Harry gave instructions that the announcement of Ann's death in *Time* must identify her as the daughter of Mr. and Mrs. Henry R. Luce. "That's the way it goes in." West of Chicago at 12:50 A.M., he radioed his wife: "Thoughts ever with you and our darling."[41]

Clare was in no condition to travel to Palo Alto anytime soon. Nor did she seem ready to contact Virginia Hobbs to hear exactly what had happened. Instead, she reached out for sympathy, calling Bernard Baruch, Maggie Case at *Vogue*, and her New York physician, Dr. Milton Rosenbluth. She asked her assistant to telephone Walton Wickett and read a dictated message: "Even under the influence of dope, I know in a cockeyed sort of way that my Annie loved you and I know that you loved my Annie."[42]

Reeling with disbelief, Walton managed to muster a few lame words about his good times with Ann and their "little spats," which, he stressed, had meant nothing.[43] Now, of course, they meant everything. The violence of his bereavement left him feeling naked.[44]

Close to nervous collapse as the day ground on, Clare distracted herself with correspondence, some of it official. She sent a message to the family of a soldier captured on Corregidor, informing them that she had heard from their son, now imprisoned in a Japanese camp. She wrote David in New Guinea, sure that he would promptly tell Charles Willoughby of Ann's death.

As the news spread by radio, two emergency switchboards had to be installed in a room adjoining Clare's suite, to cope with condolences from America and around the world.[45] Norman Ross, another of Ann's friends, took calls from Winston Churchill and the Chiang Kai-sheks.[46] Isabel Hill reported that Luce offices in Washington and New York were similarly bombarded with letters and telegrams of sympathy.[47]

To escape the incessant ringing of phones, Clare went for a walk with Colonel William Cobb, an aide to a general she had known in Burma. She was grateful to him for having delivered Ann's funeral outfit to Palo Alto, and for bringing back details of the accident.

Not far from the hotel, they came upon Old St. Mary's Cathedral of the Immaculate Conception, and went in. Clare had been fighting surges of bitterness all day, as the reality of her bereavement took hold. Keeping despair at bay required more spiritual strength than she could muster on her own. Though she thought of herself as Episcopalian (rather than Lutheran like her mother or Baptist like her father), she had long lost the habit of praying. Now she needed to reconcile herself to her pointless loss, and maintain her equilibrium through the coming obsequies.

Cobb sensed Clare's struggle, and marveled at her determination to surmount self-pity. He stood at the back of the church as she sat motionless in a pew halfway along the nave. Shafts of colored light from stained-glass windows beamed on her. A priest went up and said a few words. On the way back to the hotel, she seemed more at peace.[48]

▽

Late that night, Clare received a platitudinous, self-exonerating telegram from Kurt Bergel, the driver who had killed Ann. He was a thirty-two-year-old German refugee working as a language instructor in Stanford's Army Program. Clearly dreading a manslaughter lawsuit, he claimed not to have been at fault. He said that he had devoted his life to the education of youth, felt the tragedy deeply, and conveyed his "heartfelt sympathy."[49]

It transpired that Bergel was wholly to blame. His landlady testified that he had been late for breakfast, and left her lodging house in a hurry. She said that he had only recently learned how to drive, and was fast as well as erratic behind the wheel. Police investigators discovered that he had mislaid his driver's license several days before, and not applied for another. Incredibly, they dismissed this as "a technicality."[50] A garage inspection revealed that the brakes of Bergel's 1934 Buick sedan had frozen cables and oil-soaked linings. Subsequent road tests proved that in such a vehicle, travel at any speed over 15 mph was dangerous. Even at the 20 mph he had professed to be going (tests showed that his speedometer was faulty), he would have skidded twenty-five feet before coming to a standstill.[51] His only injury was a bruised knee.

Several people who had been walking in neighboring streets said they had heard a car engine racing, followed by the clang of colliding metal. But there were no eyewitnesses to confirm that Virginia Hobbs had entered the intersection before the Buick appeared. Bergel could therefore claim right of way.[52]

▽

A weary Henry Luce appeared on Nob Hill at lunchtime on Wednesday. His wife's near catatonic state brought out the executive in him. First, he canceled the rest of her speaking tour. This was a blow to the GOP, because thousands of tickets had been bought to benefit local party organizations, and the money would have to be refunded. Next, Harry contacted the Palo Alto Police Department and heard that they had decided not to prosecute either driver. Clare raised no objection. Litigation could not bring her daughter back.

She let Harry answer Bergel's telegram. In an astonishingly forgiving letter, he wrote that his wife was wholly absorbed in living memories of Ann, not in details of her death. "The time will undoubtedly come when she will want to know everything that can be known—for it is characteristic of her to face facts and to wish to know the truth as exactly as possible." Once she did, "you may be sure that you will have all her sympathy in the sorrow which this tragic event has brought you."[53]

In another gesture of compassion, Harry contacted Walton Wickett and proposed that they go to see the Hobbs family. Virginia might need consoling. Walton agreed, and they made the pilgrimage together.

Overawed by Luce's eminence, Walton let him do the talking.[54]

▽

74

As Harry's voice droned in the background, Walton's thoughts ranged back over his long courtship of Ann. He recalled that two years before, he had motored with her to an out-of-town football party, and she had locked his car door, telling him about her grandmother being flung from an automobile at a railroad crossing in Florida.[55] After the party, he had escorted her to her sleeping quarters in an old school on the coast, and was perplexed when she failed to say good night. Later, he had gone to her room and found her lying in the dark, staring at the ceiling.

She seemed to be in a strange state, not responding when he told her he was going down to the beach to listen to seals barking in the moonlight. But then, as he made his way through pines and cypresses toward the water, a figure in a long white dress had stumbled past him and fallen. He recognized Ann, and rushed to take her in his arms.

"I know how I'm going to die," she wailed. "It will happen to me very soon."

Desperate to divert her, Walton had suggested that they continue to the shore. But she had risen and, brushing away tears, said, "This is silly," before abruptly returning to her bed.

The incident—not improbable in a gothic novel—plagued Walton. Had Ann's behavior that strange night betrayed "a sublimated yearn-ing . . . for high romance"? Had her sexual frustration peaked with a premonition of death, before she was fulfilled as a woman? He thought of Goethe's line "Stay, for thou art blissful," fearing he had lost an op-portunity to consummate their relationship at its most intense, by merely offering his love a walk on the sands.[56]

Ann Brokaw's funeral service, conducted by the university chaplain, took place in Stanford's Memorial Church at 4:00 P.M. on Thursday, January 13. The undertaker had offered to deliver the coffin into the chapel on a gurney, but James Rea objected to strangers carrying his dead friend any part of the way.[57] In spite of having one leg weakened by polio, James joined Walton Wickett and Norman Ross as pallbearers. None of them knew the fourth man, a shy Southerner in naval uniform who seemed extremely distraught.[58]

Harry had ordered the casket closed for the ceremony, with a blan-ket of gardenias on top. He sat with his wife and other dignitaries on a platform at the front of the chapel. Clare was partly screened by potted plants, but at one point during the service, Walton heard a loud sob from behind the shrubbery.[59]

The texts, chosen by Harry, were from Psalms 46, 91, and 130: "God is our refuge and strength," "He that dwelleth in the secret place of the most High shall abide under the shadow of the Almighty," and "Out of the depths have I cried unto thee, O Lord." There were also verses from chapter 14 of Saint John's Gospel, "In my Father's house are many mansions . . . I go to prepare a place for you," and from chapter 8 of the Epistle of Paul the Apostle to the Romans: "Nor height, nor depth, nor any other creature, shall be able to separate us from the Love of God."[60]

Illuminating for Clare were lines from Ann's own thesis, read by her Oriental philosophy professor.

The more we learn, the more we realize how little we know, for at those times we seem to feel the great and sometimes terrifying mystery of everything about us . . . the way lies in broadening our consciousness to the maximum so that it might better grasp . . . the most limitless and infinite reality that is God.[61]

8

AFTERMATH

Becoming famous creates a fortunate remedy against utter despair, but it does not cure suffering.

—Czesław Miłosz

Photographers swarmed around as Norman Ross escorted Clare to a limousine after the ceremony. He raised an arm to protect her, thinking how often *Life* cameramen had intruded on similar moments of private sorrow.[1]

After she was back in seclusion, Harry completed plans for the complicated rail journey to Ann's final resting place. The girl had expressed a wish to be interred at Mepkin in South Carolina, where the family had spent many blissful days before Pearl Harbor. But for as long as the plantation remained closed and unkempt—most of its personnel were at work in wartime factories—Clare preferred to bury her at the nearby graveyard of Strawberry Hill, where the ashes of her grandmother and namesake already lay.

She and Harry left San Francisco on Friday, January 14, at 4:30 P.M. They occupied separate bedrooms on the Union Pacific streamliner, and Ann's coffin rode in a third. When they reached Washington, Clare met briefly with her aide, Al Morano. "I don't know why this happened," she said, still uncomprehending.[2]

At 6:40 on Monday evening, the Luces began the last segment of their trip South. They traveled now in a private parlor car, with a small ·

group of fellow mourners riding in the attached train. Waiting to pick them up in Charleston the next morning was Harry's ever-dependable factotum, Wesley Bailey. He had selected the burial plot, planned the service to be held in an eighteenth-century chapel adjacent to Strawberry Hill, and arranged for lines from Psalm 45 to be etched on Ann's headstone.

HEARKEN, O DAUGHTER
AND CONSIDER
AND INCLINE THINE EAR
FORGET ALSO THINE OWN PEOPLE
AND THY FATHER'S HOUSE
SO SHALL THE KING
GREATLY DESIRE THY BEAUTY
FOR HE IS THY LORD
WORSHIP THOU HIM

The last rites for Ann Clare Brokaw took place on Wednesday, January 19, at 11:30 A.M. An Episcopal priest officiated.[3] Joining the Luces at the graveside were a few of Harry's relatives, including his sister Elisabeth Moore and his nineteen-year-old elder son, Henry ("Hank") Luce III, a Hotchkiss and Yale alumnus, about to be commissioned as a naval ensign in the Pacific.[4] Other mourners included Maggie Case, Clare's decorator Gladys Freeman, John Billings, and Bernard Baruch, who saw how distraught Clare was and offered her his nearby estate, Hobcaw Barony, as a place to begin recovery. Harry said he would keep her company for a day or two.

A week later, he was still there. The crisis they had shared eased their estrangement of the past year. Clare wired after he left for New York, using a nickname from the early, romantic days of their marriage: "The day is bright again but I fear darling I am not and yet I was so very glad to have found 'Mike' for a little while."[5]

Harry's efforts to console Clare and shake off his own sadness affected his attitude toward the outside world. When Billings asked what editorial position Luce periodicals should take in the coming presidential election, he said it was not important. "The country has gone to hell anyway."[6]

It was clear to a top Luce aide, Allen "Al" Grover, however, that the boss had "swung far to the right in his hatred of Roosevelt." Executives at Time Inc. would have to control this phobia during the campaign, lest the Editor in Chief alienate millions of readers, and "ruin himself and his magazines."[7]

▽

Clare's return to the Hill in early February was preceded by a major profile of herself in *Look* magazine. Written by Maxine Davis, an experienced correspondent, it began by saying that Representative Luce was "not a great woman" but might well become a force in national and international affairs. She had "a consuming ambition . . . to direct the destinies of nations." No veteran legislator was "in more deadly earnest" about the business of Congress. But Davis was skeptical regarding her idealism. "In her eyes the nation's interests and Clare Boothe Luce's are identical."[8]

Among the stack of condolences awaiting the Congresswoman were notes from Franklin and Eleanor Roosevelt. Clare replied that she hoped the future would hold "no such irremediable sorrows" for them, and hinted that personal tragedy had revived her dormant spiritual side.

> The terrible *pain* of it is not one bit lessened by the knowledge that I have been held lovingly, or sympathetically in the hearts and minds of many friends, but that knowledge has, most strangely, assuaged my anguish. And then, too, I have been helped by the great communion of grief which I find myself sharing with thousands of others all over the country who have lost their beloved sons, the bravest and finest of America's boys, in this war. What a crowding and a jostling and a milling there is of young people at the gates of Paradise these days.[9]

To Laura Hobson, Clare wrote, "I shall never be truly happy again, I know . . . agony reaches down to the depths of the heart."[10]

Another sympathy letter came from Lieutenant John Fitzgerald Kennedy, Ann's occasional escort. "I thought I had become hardened to losing people I liked but when I heard the news today I couldn't have been sadder."[11]

David wrote from New Guinea: "I cried. For the first time in many years, not even when mother went. How can a man believe when people like . . . myself have continued on and a kid like Ann is snuffed out. If there's a God in Heaven it's high time he gave you a break."[12]

▽

Perfectly coiffed, but with strands of gray visible at her temples, Clare resumed her seat in the House on February 15.[13] She was soon her old acerbic self, airing her preconvention views to *The New York Times*. Franklin Roosevelt, she said, would be the most desirable Democratic nominee, since he was indisputably qualified to "answer for the last twelve years." If he chose to campaign mostly on foreign policy, she thought General MacArthur or Wendell Willkie would be ideal Republican opponents, and if on domestic issues, Governor Dewey of New York, an honest and efficient administrator.[14]

She suggested no vice presidential candidates, perhaps in tacit acknowledgment that the boom for her had abated. Now she was being touted only as the keynote speaker at the Republican National Convention.[15] Before that, she faced a crucial decision: whether to run for reelection in the fall.

Harry, who had always been more enthusiastic about her career as a politician than as a playwright, urged her to commit to a second term.[16] It was a prospect, in her current emotional state, that filled Clare with more dread than joy.

▽

With six weeks to go until the Easter recess of Congress, Clare continued grieving. "She didn't eat and was consumed by a terrible restless energy," a friend noticed. "I did not think she would survive. She took long furious walks."[17]

Some legislative agenda absorbed her, particularly questions of immigration reform. But her chief interest remained the progress of the war—particularly the Fifth Army's fight against tenacious German resistance at Anzio, Italy. Most of General Mark Clark's troops who had fought in the baking deserts of North Africa were now deployed in the freezing Italian midsection, suffering from high rates of exhaustion and disease. Many thousands were already dead, captured, or missing. Soldiers trying to advance along valley roads were being bombarded by enemy redoubts in the mountains. The historic monastery of Monte Cassino had just been devastated by Allied bombers, in the mistaken belief that Germans were sheltered there. Clark was at last poised to take Rome, but before he did, more than sixty thousand Wehrmacht and Allied servicemen would be killed, and countless more wounded in one of the harshest campaigns of the war.[18]

Allegations of military mismanagement in Europe and the Pacific circulated in American political and publishing circles. Clare and twenty-two other Republican Congressmen signed a letter to Secretary of State Cordell Hull, asking for an elucidation of the administration's current war and peace policy. He responded evasively, and Clare had no luck trying to get him to say more in a follow-up interview. She concluded the White House had no overall strategy.[19]

Contrary to her misgivings, the Pentagon was shipping legions of men and hundreds of thousands of tons of matériel to both war theaters. American manufacturers were hiring millions of unenlistable men and women, and producing vast quantities of armaments. Training camps were turning out lean, fit recruits for all services at breakneck speed. Ill equipped and undermanned only three years before, the United States military was benefiting from a productivity unprecedented in the annals of warfare.[20]

▽

Clare remained hypersensitive about the manner of Ann's death. Unable to forget how brutally her assistant had woken her on that bleak January day, she announced in early March that Miss Blood would leave her employ to work for the GOP in Connecticut.[21] She had many sleepless nights, and at times contemplated suicide.[22] Ann, she wrote Irene Selznick, had been "all my hopes for the future, all the justification for the past." Though she managed to put up a good enough show in public, "grief has shortcircuited the mechanism of me rather badly. Perhaps time will restore and repair this strange and deep disorder." She doubted it ever could.[23] "Where else shall I plant the hopes of my heart, what else encompass with so much love. Where else give or get such gay, tender, unquestioning loyalty and companionship. Motherless, fatherless, childless—and in my forties! How odd for 'the woman who has everything.'"[24]

Debilitated and gaunt, she lost interest in her appearance, a sure sign of clinical depression. At the end of the month, she checked into a New York hospital for a thorough examination, and remained there ten days.[25] It was whispered around Time Inc. that Clare had become "a heavy secret drinker."[26] But no reports of that appeared in print. Dependency on drugs was another matter. A lifelong insomniac, Clare often needed sedatives to sleep, and occasionally seemed frail at early morning appointments. She wrote to Alice Basim, "I go places, do my work, laugh and talk with people. But inside me is . . . a grief too deep for words."[27]

9

CAMPAIGN '44

Truth is what your contemporaries let you get away with.

—Richard Yorty

T he Wisconsin primary on April 4, 1944, made plain that Thomas E. Dewey was far ahead of all other GOP candidates. Of twenty-four delegates to the convention, he won seventeen, Harold Stassen four, Douglas MacArthur three, and Wendell Willkie none, leading to his withdrawal from political life.[1] Dewey's victory was a rebuff to both Luces. Harry had been pushing for Willkie in his magazines since 1940—an advocacy complicated by his more recent infatuation with MacArthur.[2]

Though impressed and charmed by the latter, Clare felt that he was too old at sixty-four to undergo on-the-job presidential training. In addition, there was the important question of character. Whatever his virtues, the general was hugely self-enamored. "He wasn't conceited, he was vain," she said, meaning he was unaware that military expertise did not necessarily guarantee political acumen.

In view of Dewey's apparent lock on the nomination, Harry and Clare transferred their allegiance to him. The GOP Arrangements Committee formally considered a proposal that she should be keynote speaker at the convention in June. This would "not only constitute recognition of the part women have taken in politics, but would also assure the brilliant delivery of a forceful speech, and would bring to the convention and the party unprecedented attention."[3] Dewey, however, felt no need to ingratiate himself with either of the Luces, and gave the honor to Governor Earl Warren of California.[4]

In compensation, the Connecticut GOP elected Clare as one of its delegates, and the national committee asked her to introduce former President Herbert Hoover.

▽

A keynote speech she did give was to a meeting of the United States wing of the Revisionist Zionist movement in New York City on April 23. She was prompted to do so by a reading of Pierre van Paassen's *The Forgotten Ally*, which argued the right of oppressed European Jews to settle in Palestine without restriction. Taking up the cause in typically bold language, Clare castigated British authorities in the Mandatory for turning back ships of would-be refugees. She blamed them for the fact that "Jewish blood stains the blue Mediterranean red."[5]

The executive director of the Revisionists, Benzion Netanyahu, acclaimed her address as historic, "one of the great expressions of the American conscience." He distributed tape recordings of it to radio stations around the country, and reprinted excerpts in large newspaper advertisements.[6]

Clare continued to beat the same drum in an article for the journal *Zionews*. "As a well-fed person can never truly understand the sensation of starvation," she wrote, "so it is impossible for most of us to . . . grasp the plight of a people who have neither a roof over their heads nor even a homeland they can call their own." In May, she introduced a House resolution urging the creation of temporary havens in the United States for displaced Jews. "For eleven years now . . . while we deplored and lamented, millions of refugees were savagely murdered. Others escaped death only to wander . . . across the face of a world which was sympathetic but coldly inhospitable. They have life but no place to live."[7]

▽

A personal task she now had to brace for was the disposition of her daughter's possessions. Ann had left no will. The lawful beneficiary of her share in income from Brokaw trust funds, worth some $200,000, along with her share of two Fifth Avenue mansions, was her half-sister, Frances "Pan" Brokaw. As next of kin, Clare received just $60,000 in bonds, cash, and jewelry.[8]

She sent mementos to Ann's suitors and pallbearers: a gold filigree ring for Walton Wickett, cuff links for James Rea, and for Norman Ross a black jet ring with a secret poison compartment, a gift from Madame Chiang Kai-shek. The Curtis Institute of Music in Philadelphia received Ann's 1860 Vuillaume violin, and Georgetown University her Baldwin grand piano.[9]

It was too soon, Clare felt, to decide on a memorial. But she commissioned a posthumous portrait of Ann by Boris Chaliapin, a *Time* cover artist, and made the first of several interim donations to Stanford, suggesting the creation of a campus music room with a library of records and listening facilities.[10]

With fewer resources, Walton Wickett gave the university $100 annually to buy books and sheet music "in memory of Ann Clare Brokaw . . . whose incomprehensible death I regard not only as a personal loss . . . but as a loss to the thousands of people with whom she would have come in contact and whose thinking she would have stimulated."[11]

▽

Fighting sorrow with frenetic activity, Clare gave eight further speeches up and down the East Coast, on topics ranging from America's relations with Indochina to legislation of consequence to women. She rattled Democrats in Philadelphia by saying that the United States should return to the coherent foreign policy of the President's Republican cousin Theodore Roosevelt.[12] She published several articles on themes such as "Why We Should Have a Woman at the Peace Table" and "How a Woman Can Get Along in State Politics."[13]

Back in Washington, she sat for a portrait by the famous Canadian photographer Yousuf Karsh, impressing him as "a person of great presence and decisiveness."[14]

Less apparent, when Clare was not posing or performing, was the degree of debilitating introspection that afflicted her in depressive moments. She suffered recurring images of her bleak youth, guilt over her neglect of Ann, and remorse for her betrayals of Harry. David Boothe hinted at his sister's trials in a letter to Isabel Hill: "I don't believe anyone apart from myself can realize the tremendous obstacles, pitfalls and snares she's overcome and side-stepped in her life."[15]

During periods when she felt sorry for herself, she had no tolerance for what she saw as the derelictions of others, such as General Willoughby's inability to cross the Pacific to attend Ann's funeral. Her letters to him became less frequent and their tone chillier. He chided her for withholding news and love: "I need some sign occasionally."[16]

He explained that his hope for leave had been dashed by battles for the Japanese islands fringing Australia. "The action was important, though, since we had the Grand Fleet for a few days, to stand between us and the Jap fleet, ex Singapore . . . hovering hyena-like to jump on us." The navy was indispensable, Willoughby wrote.[17] Japan's empire now stretched four thousand miles, mostly across water. Its soldiers had taken seventy-eight thousand Americans and Filipinos on the island of Bataan alone. To help marines and infantry recapture territories, U.S. battleship cannons were positioned to shell the caves and jungles of innumerable hostile islands, in an attempt to make transport landings safer. Naval pilots, leaving flight decks every few seconds, helped intercept kamikaze bombers, and provided cover for men negotiating mined beaches.

David Boothe was performing his own risky role, flying supplies to the lines. Like many peacetime misfits, he found his element in war, and loved the unpredictability of the air. He kept Willoughby informed of his activities, and also unburdened himself about Clare's emotional state. "That sister of mine has me good and worried . . . I know her General and when Ann died so did most of Clare."[18]

To ensure that America would be a congenial place for her brother and other veterans to come back to after the war, Representative Luce supported the GI Bill of Rights. Sponsored by President Roosevelt, the legislation passed unanimously in the House on May 18. It promised career help, government-assisted college education or vocational training, unemployment insurance, and loans for servicemen or -women to buy homes, farms, or businesses.[19]

▽

On June 4, 1944, General Mark Clark at last captured Rome. It was a partial victory for him, in view of the intransigence of German resistance northeast of the Eternal City. The news of his triumph was overshadowed two days later, when the biggest armada ever assembled crossed the English Channel and deposited an invasion force on Normandy beaches.

As the post-D-Day battles raged, Clare wrote her address introducing former President Herbert Hoover to the Republican National Convention. Although its purpose was clearly procedural, she could not help dwelling on the sacrifices of America's fighting men. She sent the twelve-page first draft to Hoover, telling him that it would take about twelve minutes to deliver "without applause."[20]

He replied that he would not change a word of her "powerfully affecting" speech. Moreover, he modestly proposed, in view of "the beauty of it and its high emotional pitch," that *he* speak before *her*. He would cover such ponderous subjects as foreign affairs, freedom, and totalitarianism, then end with a paragraph that would herald Congresswoman Luce as "the Symbol of the New Generation." Reversing the order of their presentations, Hoover said, would give a "high lift to the whole convention" and "add drama to the occasion."[21]

Clare welcomed this idea, asking if he would tell the arrangements committee of the switch. She knew members were unlikely to reject a suggestion from the party's senior statesman.[22]

It had been twelve years since Clare Boothe Brokaw, managing editor of *Vanity Fair*, had attended her first political convention—as a Democrat—in company with Bernard Baruch. Together they had witnessed the nomination of Franklin Roosevelt, and rejoiced at his subsequent defeat of Hoover.[23] Now, after remarrying and switching her party affiliation, she had Harry as her escort to Chicago, and her feelings about FDR were radically altered.

The convention opened at the Chicago Stadium on Monday, June 26. In a listless, ill-attended session, delegates adopted the campaign platform, pledging postwar international collaboration for peace, and restoration of prosperity at home.

On Tuesday, the pace of politicking heated up, and by evening the hall was packed. Hoover preceded Clare to the rostrum and predicted that the United States, Britain, the Soviet Union, and possibly China would emerge as the dominant world powers after the fighting ended. A general assembly of nations, he said, would be necessary to moderate or circumvent potential conflicts, but it must not become a mere "debating society." Referring indirectly to the World War I aid program that had made his reputation, he added that America should share its prosperity after the war by giving food to starving populations of countries ravaged by the enemy.[24]

Throughout Hoover's address, Henry Luce, wearing a white suit with a red rose in his buttonhole, sat with his feet on the gallery rail, reading a newspaper. But when his wife stepped up to the podium, he focused on her intently.[25]

The temperature outside had been in the nineties for most of the day. Inside the hall, under the klieg lights, it approached a hundred as Clare, in a short-sleeved blue dress, took the microphone. She was greeted with prolonged and loud applause from thousands of delegates, alternates, and guests. After it died down, she said that she supposed party leaders expected her to speak about the millions of American women doing war work in the armed services, industries, canteens, hospitals, and Red Cross. But the timbre of her crystal-clear voice became forceful and her words incendiary as she embarked on an anti-administration diatribe.[26]

She attacked the "inefficiency, abusiveness, evasion, self-seeking, and personal whim" that were steadily "distorting our democracy into a dictatorial Bumbledom." President Roosevelt had sent some twelve million United States citizens to fight abroad, with no long- or short-term plans for victory. War could have been averted by "skillful and determined American statesmanship."[27]

The main body of Clare's speech, long and meandering, aimed to stir patriotic as well as partisan feelings, and was often more heated than coherent. Resorting to allegory, she evoked a symbolic figure, "GI Jim," killed in battle and buried in an unmarked grave, a victim of his country's unpreparedness. "Jim was the heroic heir of the unheroic Roosevelt Decade: a decade of confusion and conflict that ended in war." Republicans owed it to that young man to undo years of Democratic mismanagement, and ensure that his sacrifice was not useless. "For a fighting man dies for the future as well as the past, to keep all that was fine of his country's yesterday, and to give it a chance for a finer tomorrow." She went on to cite Jim's equally allegorical buddy, "GI Joe," who would return one day via Berlin and Tokyo to a "greater, freer America," built by the Republican Party.[28]

The response was a tumultuous standing ovation. Clare smiled and held her arms high, while Hoover and other party dignitaries flanked her. Theatrical to the core, she lingered onstage, even though she was spent and soaked with perspiration.[29]

Undoubtedly, her unique aura—the combination of apparent delicacy and forcefulness that *Vogue* once described as "analogous to being dynamited by angel cake"—had much to do with her oratorical success.[30] Her words alone, broadcast nationally and around the world on Armed Forces Radio, aroused varied reactions. John Billings wrote that she "put on a magnificent act—her voice was perfect and I was really proud of her."[31] The journalist Murray Kempton, serving in the Pacific,

Clare addresses the Republican National Convention, July 1944

considered her attack on the President so "unseemly" as to put his morale at hazard.[32] Critics suggesting Adolf Hitler might be responsible for more war casualties than Franklin Roosevelt decried the speech as unpatriotic as well as demagogic. *The New Yorker* put its objections simply:

> To hint that the American war dead died because the majority voted wrong in the last three elections is a palpable misstatement of fact as well as a staggering breach of taste, and we must in charity assume that the lady did not understand the implications of what she was inspired or advised to say.[33]

But inside the GOP, Clare had scored a rhetorical coup. Even isolationists chose to hear her riff on GI Jim as proof she agreed with them that non-intervention would have been best for America.

The following night, Dewey was nominated on the first ballot, and confirmed Governor John W. Bricker of Ohio as his running mate. Douglas MacArthur received only one vote. Clare was photographed in the hall's press section, looking all business in front of a typewriter. She seemed at home in the proximity of a disheveled reporter chomping on a cigar.[34]

She returned East to find that the left-wing press was already gearing up to punish her for berating the President. The *Sunday Worker* accused her of being absent from Congress for twenty-three of seventy-one important roll calls, four of them concerning the passage of war appropriation bills. It took a lone defender on a Connecticut radio station to point out that most of Representative Luce's absenteeism had been in the six weeks following her daughter's death.[35]

Harry, meanwhile, traveled to California to give an address at Stanford on the day Ann Brokaw would have graduated.

He returned to his office feeling weary and jaded. Now forty-six, Luce had for some time appeared "rushed and distracted" to his colleagues. A rumor spread that the boss had "heart trouble"—Al Grover's euphemism for infatuation with someone other than Clare. The fact was, Harry's publishing empire had grown too big for him to run single-handedly. Acknowledging this, he handed over the job of editorial director to John Billings.

It was a huge promotion, rewarding the Southerner for having helped raise *Life*'s circulation to four million.[36]

With less to occupy him, Harry began to regret his ban on coverage of Clare, and wrote a rambling memo to senior staff about "the human aspects" of her situation.

> Other publications—both newspapers and magazines—are not over eager to give strong favorable publicity to the wife of Publisher Luce. Meanwhile for many years one of the main smears against her has been the thousand-time repeated allegation that she owes practically everything to the enormous press build-up she has received in the enormously powerful Luce press.
>
> It is, I think you will agree, a bit tough on her. . . .
>
> She is, of course, far more in demand as a speaker than any Republican except the Presidential Candidate himself. The "pros" recognize her as one of the few speakers who can *influence* votes. Gradually she is getting a better press. She is getting it the hard way. Maybe that's the best way to get things.[37]

Democrats drafted Franklin Roosevelt for a fourth term as President at their convention in late July. He took the advice of party leaders to drop Clare's bête noire, the controversial Henry Wallace, from the vice presidency, and in a startling bid toward bipartisanship sounded out Wendell Willkie as his potential running mate. But Willkie declined, sure that Democrats would not accept him.[38] FDR chose Senator Harry S. Truman of Missouri instead. He then left for a conference with his Pacific commanders in Honolulu, where General MacArthur was shocked by his appearance.[39]

Roosevelt had been in abject physical and mental condition all year, suffering from high blood pressure, acute bronchitis, and cardiac disease. He was "just a shell" of the man MacArthur remembered.[40] Winston Churchill was also "alarmed by the state of the President's health" when he met with him later at Hyde Park.[41]

Insiders, with the election in mind, tried to conceal his condition. Truman had lunch with him and told reporters that he had eaten well, while privately informing aides that FDR was so "feeble" and shaky that he poured more cream into his saucer than into his coffee cup.[42]

Although he continued to be charming in social situations, Roosevelt had difficulty concentrating, and was less and less able to handle the war pressures climaxing that summer. His doctors advised him to cut back his workload to no more than four hours a day, prescribed digitalis for his irregular heartbeat, put him on a low-fat diet, and recommended fewer cocktails and a maximum of five or six cigarettes a day instead of his usual twenty to thirty.

Nothing about the President's rapidly failing health appeared in print—even "the enormously powerful Luce press."[43]

▽

In Connecticut for the state GOP convention on August 9, Clare announced her intention to run for a second term. She took the opportunity to vilify the Soviet Union, saying that Communism was "the most deadly blight that has ever hit the spirit of man." Clearly, her abhorrence of colonial imperialism had spread to include the ideological empire building of Josef Stalin. Galvanized by the Congresswoman's invective against a U.S. ally, state Democrats nominated Margaret Connors, a twenty-nine-year-old attorney, to run against her. Deceptively low-key, with a pleasing voice, Connors was a Roman Catholic from an affluent Bridgeport suburb, a graduate of Wellesley and Yale Law School, and the first woman to serve as Connecticut's Deputy Secretary of State. She had wide experience, having also worked at the Department of Justice and as counsel for the American Civil Liberties Union.

Despite a promise to campaign on issues, she started off with a personal attack. Clare, she said, had done nothing in Congress except oppose the President and his administration. "Mrs. Luce is perfectly charming, lovely to look at, puts on a wonderful show—you can see the actress in every gesture—but I have long considered her a menace."[44]

Connors had met Clare only twice, on public occasions. In recalling those encounters for a *New Yorker* reporter, she again patronized her rival's theatrical qualities. "What a performance! She looks at you in that sweet earnest way, and it's awfully hard not to think you're the only person of *real* intelligence she's spoken to in years." But she saw that Clare's celebrity worked to her advantage. "People . . . come up to me and say, 'You know honey, I'd love to vote for you, but this Luce woman has really written some damn good plays.'"[45]

It was evident that Connors was a formidable candidate in one of the most closely watched contests in the country.

▽

Clare asked William Brennan, the beefy, blue-eyed Irishman who had served as her campaign manager in 1942, to do so again. She also rehired Wes Bailey to handle publicity, radio broadcasts, and speech schedules.

Knowing that she was in good hands, Harry left for London in early September.[46] He was responding to an invitation from Lord Beaverbrook, owner of the *Daily Express* and *London Evening Standard* newspapers. "Max" Beaverbrook was now Minister of Aircraft Production in Winston Churchill's government. Two weeks in a fellow press mogul's company, discussing affairs of state, was more to Harry's taste than tracking Clare around the hustings of Fairfield County.[47]

He had been gone barely a week when she cabled him: "Darling hurry home. It's getting pretty grim without you to argue with."[48]

In his absence, she indulged in an epistolary flirtation with another of the endless number of military officers who lusted after her. This time it was Colonel Stephen Mellnik, a colleague of Willoughby's. He mailed her risqué letters. "Making presidents doesn't substitute for a warm and sympathetic pair of feet in bed on a cold night. . . . To my naïve eye you were designed by nature to kiss and make love to—NOT to worry about Prexys or military affairs."[49]

Mellnik also gave Clare insights into Japanese strategy for winning the war. In "Nip opinion," he wrote, the United States would win a protracted conflict, so Japan was determined to make the cost of such ultimate victory prohibitive. If leaders in Tokyo were willing to lose ten million more soldiers, did those in Washington have the stomach to match that figure?

▽

Meanwhile, "Luce v. Connors," the only all-woman face-off that fall, got under way, to the delight of journalists anticipating a bitchy fight. George C. Waldo, Jr., Editor in Chief of the *Bridgeport Post* and *Telegram*, was besotted with Clare and favored her in his columns, while Leigh Dannenberg's *Bridgeport Herald*, an organ of the extreme Left, accused her of being anti-labor, anti-Semitic, and anti-Negro.

The last was an egregious claim, given that Representative Luce had introduced a resolution calling for equality in the armed services, and had condemned the Daughters of the American Revolution for refusing the use of its Washington hall to the Negro soprano Marian Anderson. On the trail, she won warm welcomes from black audiences, and did not flinch when one committee chairman hailed her as "the Honorable Clara Boothey Lucie."[50]

Her outspokenness vis-à-vis Soviet totalitarianism elicited the wrath of America's Communist Party leader, Earl Browder. He railed against Clare at every opportunity, and encouraged his chief mouthpiece, the *Daily Worker*, to malign her as "the lady with the dry ice smile, and an aristocratic contempt for the people who work for a living."[51]

In Connecticut, operatives of the labor leader Sidney Hillman's highly organized Political Action Committee handed out pamphlets, bellowed vituperations through loudspeakers, and broadcast hourly propaganda spots, assailing Clare's looks, age, clothes, and husband. She was accused of being an isolationist, interventionist, and imperialist.[52]

Time magazine adhered to its policy of not mentioning Clare. In a way this helped her, because the ban included her detractors, notably President Roosevelt. He stopped his campaign train in Bridgeport to endorse Margaret Connors, and called Clare a "sharp-tongued glamor girl of 40."[53] Vice President Wallace, who had not forgiven her "globaloney" gibe, spoke at no fewer than seventeen Connors gatherings. Other big-name Democrats attacking Clare included Secretary of the Interior Harold Ickes, Orson Welles, and the authors Edna Ferber, Max Lerner, and Rex Stout. The tart humorist Dorothy Parker, who had once worked for Clare at *Vanity Fair*, charged her with visiting her own state only at election time. Most vituperative of all was the writer and broadcaster Clifton Fadiman, a resident of Connecticut. Mrs. Luce, he said, was a political "refugee from a Park Avenue fox hole."[54] Fairfield County had no need of this "photographer's delight" as its representative in Congress. Her speeches convinced Fadiman that no woman of the time had "gone further with less mental equipment."[55]

Clare countered by campaigning doggedly in every corner of her constituency, with its blend of plush "bedroom" communities, blue-collar industrial towns, and remote farms. She made more than one hundred appearances at rallies, factories, country fairs, firehouses, restaurants, and private homes, and shook hands with some twenty thousand people. Taking Roosevelt's bait, she denounced the twelve years of his administration as a period "of humiliating failure," and derided the "carpetbagging celebrities" rounded up to distort her record.[56]

Alarmed by the numbers of eminent Democrats touring Connecticut and railing against Clare, the Republican National Committee offered to send in big names of its own. But she said she preferred to "slug it out single-handed."[57]

As in 1942, Bill Brennan drove her hard. On some days the candidate had no more nourishment than a cup of hot milk, because he would not stop at roadside diners unless he saw a sizable number of cars parked outside. Clare seldom arrived home in Greenwich until the small hours.[58]

One potentially formidable campaigner for her died on October 8. Wendell Willkie, only fifty-two, was the victim of fourteen successive

Congresswoman Luce campaigns for reelection in Connecticut, 1944

heart attacks. His loss stunned both Luces. Al Morano was at their house when the telephone rang. He noticed that Harry, who took the call, asked Clare to issue a statement for him. It was evident to Morano, as she wrote eight or ten quick lines for the Associated Press, "who the writer in the family was."[59]

Evidence of Clare's literary talent infused her epigrammatic campaign speeches, although the most quotable lines were usually the most aggressive ones. She also had the disarming gift of spontaneity. One reporter noted that she frequently "talks straight at you, either from memory or extemporaneously. At such times she removes the harlequin glasses that she wears when reading, and gestures gracefully with them. . . . She is as pretty with them on as with them off."[60]

In her capacity as one of the party's oratorical stars, Clare spent four weeks out of state. She stumped in St. Louis, Indianapolis, Philadelphia, Newark, Worcester, and Boston, pulling in greater audiences than any but the nominees themselves.[61]

On October 13, appearing for Dewey in Chicago, she leveled her most devastating accusation yet against FDR. History would never forgive him, she said, for being "the only American President who ever lied us into a war because he did not have the political courage to lead us into it. . . . The shame of Pearl Harbor was Mr. Roosevelt's shame."[62]

This indictment caused an uproar among Democrats. The left-wing journalist Quentin Reynolds, addressing a "Broadway for Roosevelt" gathering, said, "Representative Clare Boothe Luce's charge that President Roosevelt lied us into war is not the first time a person named Booth treacherously assaulted the President of the United States."[63]

▽

One typical campaign day late that month, Clare stood in a biting wind on a truck outside the Bridgeport Brass Company. She played down her glamour image by wearing a black coat and sweater, with a simple shoulder bag. Speaking into a microphone to no audience at all, she defended her labor record in Congress. As workers streamed out of the factory, nineteen out of twenty passed her by. A group of girls paused briefly. One said, "Her hair is a lot lighter than in her pictures." A freight train roared past. Drowned out, Clare climbed down to shake hands with stragglers. Then Brennan, smiling determinedly, whisked her off to a conference in Stamford and a rally in New Canaan.[64] She was still in her daytime outfit after dark, appearing at Darien High School. A large crowd welcomed her and sang "Let Me Call You Sweetheart." Clowning for them, she took out a mosquito gun and mimed an attack on Sidney Hillman and his Communist committee.[65]

Despite powerful opposition, Clare remained optimistic and intent on continuing as the first woman to represent Connecticut in Congress. She wrote her uncle Charles Boothe that she looked forward to "seeing quite a bit of that Dome in Washington during the next two years."[66]

But she was not sanguine about the electoral prospects of her party as a whole. Earlier in the year, she had thought the country was veering away from a fourth Roosevelt term. Now she told Harry that the young and able Dewey would probably lose to the old and ailing incumbent. She said that the GOP was running a "well-planned and efficient" campaign, but had failed to show that it liked people as well as power.[67]

On October 31, Margaret Connors sought to score a knockout blow by sending Representative Luce an open telegram that asked six tough questions. Each was likely to lose Clare votes, no matter which way she answered. Did she stand on the record of the Republican Party in foreign policy? Did she support its pledge to end rationing and price control next January? What agricultural program did she propose to replace incentive payments, crop insurance, and soil conservation? What alternative to the Home Owners' Loan Corporation, which she voted against, did she recommend? And why had she been absent from the roll call vote on the GI Bill?

Clare hedged for time, saying she had already addressed these subjects, and would do so again in a series of radio broadcasts in the week remaining.[68] This lame response did her little good. Fairfield County's so-called station-wagon voters began to desert her. She redoubled her courtship of Bridgeport factory workers. On Wednesday, November 1, she took Bernard Baruch's advice and held a dinner for six hundred Connecticut women who had published an advertisement supporting her. "Hundreds more wanted to sign," she wrote Baruch, "but there just wasn't room."[69]

Yet her polling numbers continued to languish, and the outcome remained in doubt through election eve. President Roosevelt, speaking at Hyde Park, gloated that Clare Luce was way behind his candidate, and declared that her defeat would "prove a mighty good thing for the country."[70]

All Clare's grinding days on the trail paid off on November 7, when she defeated Margaret Connors by the narrowest of margins: 102,043 votes to 100,030. The rank and file of Hartford, Stamford, and Bridgeport labor unions ignored the advice of their bosses, and the apple growers of upstate supported her, as in 1942, with another crucial bloc of votes. She became the first Connecticut member of Congress to recapture the Fourth District since 1930.[71] Four out of six other state Representatives running for reelection lost.[72]

Magnanimous in victory, Clare telephoned reporters to say that she bore no "rancor or malice" toward the President for his efforts to oust her. On the contrary, she would support the administration in working for peace, and hoped that all in government "may be given greater wisdom and courage to meet the task ahead."[73]

She was also gracious with her opponent: "I wasn't running against Miss Connors but against the New Deal and the PAC." To her mind, she said, the latter was short not for Political Action Committee, but for "Party of American Communism."[74]

Clare received a congratulatory telegram from former President Hoover: "That was a grand victory. I wish we had more men like you."[75]

10

TO THE FRONT

Great men, great nations, have not been boasters and buffoons but perceivers of the terror of life.

—Ralph Waldo Emerson

Henry Luce was in good spirits when he returned to work the day after his wife's two-thousand-vote win. He told staff members it was a "personal slap at FDR," and proposed that *Time* end its taboo and do a story on her campaign.[1] An article duly appeared, noting that "in two years Clare Luce [has] risen from the position of an interesting novelty ... to an eminence as a main target of the Roosevelt administration."[2] Dewey's defeat by three million votes showed how closely divided the country was, as she had foreseen.[3] The President had benefited from wartime fear of leadership change.

Still tired two weeks after her reelection, Clare had curiosity enough to embark on something new in congressional history: a foreign junket. The House of Representatives authorized seventeen members of the Military Affairs Committee to visit the battlefronts of Western Europe.[4]

It was known on Capitol Hill that General Mark Clark's five-hundred-thousand-man Fifth Army in Italy felt neglected after the June D-Day landings in France.[5] Clark had the onerous task of fighting alongside British forces in order to secure airfields from which to bomb Germany, while also pinning down thousands of Hitler's soldiers on another front. But after the fall of Rome, General Dwight D. Eisenhower, the

Supreme Allied Commander in Europe, had shifted his priority to ousting the Wehrmacht from France, and then taking Berlin. Clare and her colleagues hoped that by focusing most of their fact-finding mission on the Italian Front, they might draw attention to Clark and his struggling contingent. They also intended to tour bases in England and France, and assess what might be done to improve conditions and boost morale among American servicemen.

▽

The committee delegation took off in a C-47 transport plane from Andrews Air Force Base at noon on Thanksgiving eve, Wednesday, November 22. Representative John M. Costello, a California Democrat, acted as chairman for the trip. Clare was the junior member, but as press reports noted, she had more battlefield experience by far than her fellow members.[6] She wore a forest-green traveling suit and WAC-style matching beret. Honoring a sixty-five-pound luggage limit, she had packed a pair of fleece-lined boots, battle pants, an evening suit, and six scarves that she could alternate on her head or around her neck, waist, and shoulders to give the illusion of multiple outfits.[7]

The C-47 flew south and then east across the Atlantic, with refueling stops in Bermuda and the Azores, before landing in London on Saturday. An official from the U.S. Embassy met the group, and all members except Clare were dispersed to hotels. She and a female military aide assigned to her by the War Department were treated to luxurious accommodations in Lord Beaverbrook's well-appointed apartment, with servants to run them hot baths and serve drinks. Almost ten years before, Bernard Baruch had urged Max to meet "America's most fascinating beautiful and intelligent woman," and they had bonded.[8] Beaverbrook was now Lord Privy Seal, but was best known for having been the Minister of Aircraft Production, who built a third more planes than the Luftwaffe in 1940, ensuring victory for the RAF in the Battle of Britain.

A *Time* writer, Noel Busch, was in town and invited Clare to dine at the Savoy. Hearing that she was going on to France, he warned her she would find Paris short of food, cigarettes, transport, and heat.[9] The last was particularly bad news. She felt the cold intensely, and was already shuddering in England's penetrating damp.

Beaverbrook sent a car and driver the next morning to show her the extent of London's destruction. What she saw was a city sadly different from the one preparing to protect itself with sandbags that she had described in *Europe in the Spring*.[10] Some twenty of the East End's financial and residential districts had fallen to air attacks, and the severity of the raids was compounded by the Nazis' latest diabolical weapons, the V-2 rocket and V-1 flying bomb, locally nicknamed "the Doodlebug." Clare came across a site where diggers were looking for bodies, and she expressed admiration for the stoic Britons, beleaguered not only by blackouts and bombing, but shortages of food, clothing, furniture, and housing.[11]

After seeing enough of London's destruction, Clare went in search of Julian Simpson, the handsome British Army officer she had fallen for in her late teens. In her lingering fantasy, he remained "the only man I ever loved."[12] As far as she knew, he had not married and would be fifty now. Attempts to locate him at his club were unsuccessful, so she had to postpone her search.[13]

▽

The delegation was assigned a luxury train for a two-day journey around American bases in England. Fleets of cars were on hand for side trips at Bristol, Liverpool, and Cambridge, as well as secret locations where GIs were stockpiling ordnance for shipment to the fronts. Clare and her colleagues inspected depots, hospitals, training bases, and prison camps.

Her overwhelming impression, she wrote Harry, was of "the vast prodigious *power* of the USA, its men [and] matériel being flung in unbelievable quantities and with great order to every corner of the globe." But what she saw also buttressed her long-held suspicion that most American servicemen were bewildered by the war. "They do not quite know what we intend to accomplish . . . beyond beating the enemy to a frazzle, with that power."[14]

Reporters in London quickly sensed Clare's headline potential, only to find she had little to say. Committee members were under orders not to give individual opinions. However, she could not prevent newsmen from following her as she toured servicemen's camps, laughing and photogenic in the dreariest of weather. At one air force base, while her less enterprising companions plodded through mud, she took off for an hour-long flight in a B-17 bomber, tucking herself into the co-pilot's seat and the belly gunner's bay. She got back in time to see a squadron land after a raid over Germany.[15]

Unable to control her natural tendency to voice her opinions, Clare forgot about the delegation's press ban. "Every civilian ought to give up smoking to let the GIs have cigarettes," she announced one day. "And the women ought to be the first to do it . . . I'm a heavy smoker my-self."[16] Colleagues, peeved at her penchant for the limelight, attempted to muzzle her but failed. Upon arriving in Paris on December 1, Clare gave an interview. It took place in the same room at the Ritz Hotel she had occupied in May 1940, as Germans neared the city.[17] She urged the United States government to give more aid to the long-suffering Brit-ish, and accused the Roosevelt administration of "not making the su-preme effort to finish the war soonest."[18]

This was hardly a fair indictment of her country's cornucopian in-dustrial and military outpouring, now reaching its peak. In the last three years, sophisticated machinery coupled with government expenditures of $300 million a day had sent United States productivity soaring be-yond the most optimistic predictions. The first quota of one hundred thousand airplanes had taken 1,431 days to build, the second 369 days. All of this brought an end to America's ten-year Depression far more effectively than the President's faltering New Deal.[19]

▽

By December 6, Clare was in the Saar Valley, perilously close to the German border, to keep a committee appointment at Third Army head-quarters with the most controversial of all U.S generals, George S. Pat-ton. He had been assigned this new command by Eisenhower, after apologizing publicly for having slapped shell-shocked GIs in Sicily and calling them "cowards" in front of fellow servicemen.

Patton was waiting as the delegation's transports drew up, with his splendidly uniformed, six-foot-two charisma on full display. Newsreel cameras began rolling as he chivalrously removed his shiny black hel-met to shake hands with the radiant Congresswoman. He then posed for a series of photographs with individual members. Predictably, only the one with Clare would appear in newspapers across America. The general, an obsessive manager of every detail, even supervised seating arrangements at a lunch he had organized. He noticed that Clare's name had been mistakenly left off the guest list, and announced that in that case he would sit with her at a separate small table.[20]

A visit to an army hospital followed. Clare managed to attract at-tention among the seriously sick and wounded by complaining of a sore throat and having it swabbed. The congressional group then climbed into a convoy of muddy cars for a tour, conducted by Patton, of military installations immediately behind the lines. Again Clare delighted re-porters by seizing the chance to fire a round from a 155-millimeter howitzer directly at a German position. She yanked the lanyard so vigorously that she accidentally knocked Representative Matthew Merritt (D-NY) to the sodden ground.[21]

On December 10, her spartan traveling wardrobe was mysteriously augmented by a luxurious fur coat as she posed for photographs with General Eisenhower outside Supreme Allied Headquarters near Versailles. Inside, Ike received the lawmakers in a large room hung with detailed maps of the Western Front, and accepted a bottle of bourbon and a jar of his favorite dish, pork sausage and hominy grits. Asked about rumored shell shortages, he blamed fluctuating conditions of warfare, and confirmed he needed more ammunition fast. He also wanted Congress to increase combat pay for medics serving with fighting battalions. Already looking ahead to peacetime, Eisenhower volunteered the information that the defeated French would share with other Allies in the eventual occupation of the Reich.[22]

Reporters accosted Clare afterward and asked her how she found the war fronts. "Oh," she said, "I knew where they were."[23]

After flying to Naples and proceeding to Rome on December 14, the delegation checked into the Grand Hotel on the Via Veneto, where high-ranking Fifth Army officers were also billeted. Sergeant Bill Mauldin, a twenty-three-year-old cartoonist for *Stars and Stripes*, dropped in "looking for something to satirize." He was famous for his mordantly humorous sketches of dog-faced grunts, which had swelled the service newspaper's daily circulation to half a million copies in Italy alone. But the only potential tableau he saw down one corridor was unpublishable: a portly Representative in underwear and socks, attempting "a frontal assault on a chambermaid."[24]

Early the next morning, Clare covered her head and joined her colleagues in an audience at the Vatican with Pope Pius XII. They sat in a crescent as the Pontiff, speaking extemporaneously, declaimed, "At this critical moment in human history, the legislators of the nations of the world carry a particularly grave responsibility." He said that they must decide questions of "more than a passing political significance," reaching down to "those inalienable God-given rights that are antecedent to the State and that no State dare infringe without jeopardizing its own existence."[25]

When Clare's turn to speak came, she told Pius that "women believed less than men, perhaps, in a peace by force and brute strength."

They put their trust more "in a peace of charity and understanding."[26] At the end of the ten-minute meeting, he gave each of his visitors two strings of rosary beads, one black and one white.[27]

Meeting with the Pope seemed to affect Clare in some fundamental way. She chose not to accompany the delegation on a tour of the Sistine Chapel, and went instead to an orphanage where hundreds of young refugees were being housed by the Vatican. One titian-haired, eight-year-old boy named Augusto appealed to her thwarted motherly instincts. He was eating a chunk of bread with water for breakfast, and his fingers and toes were swollen and purple from the cold. She found herself unable to walk away, and persuaded the authorities to let her borrow him for the day.[28]

Back at the Grand Hotel, she fed and bathed him, and taught him to say a few English phrases: "How do you do?," "Good-bye," and "Give me a kiss." She bought him wool shirts, shoes, socks, mittens, a scarf, and underwear. Employing all her military and diplomatic authority (as a traveling Congresswoman, Clare ranked as a two-star "assimilated general"), she found a church school for him.[29] She arranged with a priest to give Augusto music lessons after he rushed across the reception room to a piano marked with a card reading, "Last Played by Franz Liszt." In effect, she adopted the boy, and for the next ten years would pay for his keep and tuition.[30]

▽

Lieutenant General Mark W. Clark, the delegation's host in Florence two days later, was a tall, sharp-nosed West Point graduate in his mid-forties. With his fellow commanders, Eisenhower, Patton, and Omar Bradley, he was one of the crucial men chosen for the Western theater by General George C. Marshall, the U.S. Army Chief of Staff. For the last two years he had conscientiously led the Fifth Army, appearing at the Apennine Front daily, even in the foulest weather. Rivals blamed the slow advance of the Italian campaign on his desire for glory as the captor of Rome.[31] But his superiors rated him highly for strategic vision.

He had just been promoted by Eisenhower to lead the 15th Army Group, made up of all Allied ground forces in Italy. Clark's challenge now was to mold separately trained Americans, Canadians, Frenchmen, Poles, Brazilians, Indians, New Zealanders, South Africans, and Welsh Guards into a homogenous fighting force. The logistics of communicating in so many languages, providing religious services, and catering to the food restrictions of multiple faiths—such as having to keep a herd of goats behind the lines to feed the Punjab Brigade—were formidable.[32] Nevertheless, it was with some relief that he handed over command of the Fifth Army to Lieutenant General Lucian K. Truscott, Jr.

Truscott's task was equally daunting. In a little more than six weeks that fall, the Allies had suffered almost thirty thousand casualties. As a result, they were critically short of combat-ready men, and also of supplies, which since D-Day had been diverted in large part to France. Alarmed by the deteriorating situation, Winston Churchill had asked the United States to send two more divisions to northern Italy, but General Marshall refused, preferring to keep the greater pressure on what he considered the primary war theater.[33]

As a result, Truscott now found himself facing Clark's old dread: a static winter campaign in the north of the peninsula. The Fifth Army and its British counterpart, the Eighth, held a line that stretched across Italy from the Ligurian Sea in the West to the Adriatic in the East. Some of Hitler's best divisions were heavily fortified beyond it, in a parallel deployment across the Apennine Mountains between the river Arno and Bologna—the so-called Gothic Line.[34]

The retreating Germans had blown up all the bridges across the Arno, sparing only the Ponte Vecchio in Florence, because it would not support tanks. If Truscott could push them north to the Po Valley, he might be able to march over the Alps and through the Balkans to Austria. On the other hand, he might not.

A gruff, no-nonsense Texan one month short of fifty, Truscott was generally acknowledged to be the best American combat officer in Europe. On his second day in Sicily, he had won the Distinguished Service Cross for valor in action. His men revered him as a soldier's soldier, so fearless that he coolly studied maps on Jeep hoods in the midst of enemy fire. Yet Truscott drove them hard. "Every good commander," he said, "has to have some son of a bitch in him."[35]

▽

When Clare met the new commander, she felt an instant sexual attraction. He was burly, with blunt features and penetrating blue eyes. His voice was husky from accidentally swallowing carbolic acid as a boy, and exacerbated by heavy smoking. He wore cavalry breeches with high boots, a russet leather jacket, and a black-lacquered helmet reminiscent of General Patton's. There the similarity ended. In Bill Mauldin's opinion, Truscott could have "eaten a ham like Patton any morning for breakfast."[36]

Clare rides in a Jeep with General Mark Clark (center), December 17, 1944

Aware of his qualities from a recent cover story in *Life*, Clare saw at once that Truscott was "the real thing." She resolved to see as much of him as possible in the days ahead.[37] But it was Clark who gave her and the other delegates their first look at the Fifth Army Front.

Early on Sunday, December 17, they left the comforts of the Excelsior Hotel and assembled for a publicity shot in battle clothing. They wore steel helmets with their names painted on them, and winter camouflage outfits that were brown outside and pure white inside. "Just before the photographers snapped," an army public relations officer recalled, "Mrs. Luce, with perfect timing, suddenly reversed her jacket, and there was our Clare, a gorgeous laughing snow bunny, surrounded by a dozen drab nobodies who were obviously out of her league at this sort of thing."[38]

Clare took her turn riding with Clark in a procession of thirty Jeeps along twisting, sludgy, rock-strewn chamois trails The mountain terrain was half-familiar. She had surveyed it from the air a few days before, and noted that its countless shell and bomb craters swollen with slime made the earth look as if it had "a hideous case of smallpox."[39] Now she found herself bumping through the ravaged landscape for more than eight frigid hours, traveling as far forward as Loiano in the center of the last massif before Bologna.[40]

At one point the delegation was deposited in ankle-deep mud only four miles from the Gothic Line.[41] As Clare tramped about in her bulky outfit, a German 88 shell dropped less than a thousand yards away.[42] Bill Mauldin rode with the press attachment, observing Clare closely. "She was as bright as a bird through the whole trip, taking notes and talking to soldiers."[43] At an evacuation hospital, he noticed that few other Representatives shared her interest in amputees and other casualties, unless the patients hailed from their own states. Coming upon a wounded German captive, one member wondered aloud what kind of care "the krauts" were giving American POWs. When reminded that Germans usually abided by Geneva Convention rules, he said that all the same, he hoped that this one would not get the ward's last bottle of plasma.[44]

Mauldin caught Clare's eye when another Congressman draped his arm around a GI and said, "Gee, we sure would like to share Christmas with you fellas. But we have to get home to be with our families." No words could have more demoralized the soldiers standing around.[45]

The delegation was scheduled to fly back to Naples from Florence on December 18, departing the following day for Washington. Clare went to General Truscott.

"Look, can you fix it up for me to miss the plane?"

"Oh yes," he said. "I think I can arrange that."[46]

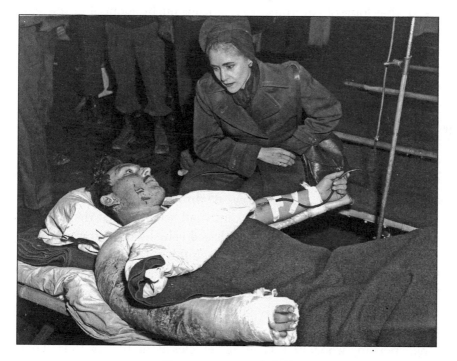

Clare visits a wounded GI

Telling her colleagues that she wanted to make a final visit to Twelfth Air Force headquarters, she took herself off. When, in due course, they left without her, she told a reporter that fog and an earache had prevented her from joining them.[47]

▽

Married, but starved for female companionship, Truscott was as attracted to Clare as she was to him. He later admitted, "I was drawn to you as iron is drawn by a magnet and was almost as helpless."[48]

He had a suite at the Anglo American Hotel in Florence, and offered it to her for as long as she wanted it.[49] Since he himself was going to be quartered in a grand tent at the front, he invited her to join him there for Christmas.

Clare not only accepted but went a step further and decided to stay in Italy for another ten days. She let Harry's office know that she would be unable to spend Christmas with her husband in Florida, as planned. Harry had already made the trip South, and he reacted angrily.[50]

On the evening of December 22, Clare spoke at a forum for several hundred servicemen at the Red Cross Club in Rome. The weekly event was officially "off the record," so she was even franker than usual. When asked what form of government Americans might adopt after the war, she said the administration was "headed towards some form of national socialism." But so were "governments all over the world." She inveighed against "economic trends" at home similar to those that had led Europe to Fascism. A reporter in the audience sent a summary of her remarks to Eleanor Roosevelt.[51]

▽

Clare went again to the front the next day. This time she traveled with General Truscott's personal driver.[52] Their journey from Florence followed the notoriously perilous Route 65 through the Apennines. Trucks loaded with ammunition, rations, and mail accompanied them northeast, while a steady stream of camouflaged vehicles came toward them, bringing battle-fatigued troops south for a three-day break. As the Jeep bounced and skidded on the frozen road, soft snow swirled in icy blasts. The temperature fell to 25 degrees Fahrenheit. Clare tried to keep warm by zipping her body into a sleeping bag and covering her head with an "Ernie Pyle" knit cap. Even so, she was recognized by GIs who were digging, chopping wood, and repairing vehicles along the roadside. They smiled and waved as she called out, "Merry Christmas."[53]

She made several impromptu stops, including one at a field hospital. For lunch she ate the same C rations as the soldiers: sausages, Spam, potatoes, beans, and bread, washed down with an unpalatable powdered lemonade drink. Clare observed that troops in foxholes or pup tents boiled canned meat and vegetables in their helmets, then put soap in the remaining water to shave and wash socks.[54]

As the Jeep climbed higher, the landscape of trees, hedges, corn-stalks, walls, and farmhouses became a scene of wintry beauty. Every

General Lucian K. Truscott, Jr.

valley was dotted with black tents, their ropes festooned with icicles. Stovepipe chimneys emitted plumes of dark smoke that were carried off by gusts of wind. At last they found the Fifth Army command post. In a huge tent, with shadows lighted by a roaring fire, Truscott stood waiting.[55]

That evening, Clare put on her black silk suit for dinner with the general. He told her what she already knew: that most Americans had the impression Italy was a secondary front with not much fighting. Some of his men had received letters from home saying how glad the family was that their boy was in "sunny Italy," not in France, "where all the shooting is." The truth was that the Fifth Army had been battling the Wehrmacht nonstop for four hundred days, keeping some of Germany's best divisions "off the necks of the fellows in France."[56]

The conversation turned to literature and politics, and Clare found that Truscott, a former teacher who carried Tolstoy novels in his kit bag, was as much at ease talking of these subjects as he was of military matters. She countered by showing off her knowledge of Homer Lea, the hunchbacked American military strategist who at the turn of the century had helped Chinese rebels overthrow the Manchu monarchy.[57] General Willoughby had interested her in Lea in the aftermath of Japan's 1938 invasion of China, and she had published two long articles about the little man's life and work. She had also written introductions to reprints of two Lea books, in which he had accurately predicted the rise of Germany and Japan, and the methods both would use to attack Britain and America.[58]

Truscott was impressed. Waxing confidential, he invited her to sit on his regulation cot. Used as Clare was to men making passes, she was not surprised at this development. She warily settled at one end, with him at the other. Soon he reached out, grabbed her knee, and said he was going to tell her something.[59]

The most beautiful thing in this world is an American division! There's nothing my division can't do. You want somebody to put on a show, sing a song, fight a battle, build a bridge, pull a tooth, deliver a baby, my men will do it. An American division is a beautiful thing.[60]

The following morning, Christmas Eve, Clare set off in freezing mountain air "to find out what war is all about." Dressed in a parka, fur cap, and galoshes, she went to tour a nearby encampment. Some soldiers had decorated a small fir tree with a pack of cards, and strewn shreds of toilet paper along the snowy branches in lieu of tinsel. For her exclusive use, they had also erected a powder-room tent, and teasingly attached a placard reading, "THE WOMEN."[61]

She had a long visit with the "Blue Devil" Eighty-eighth Infantry Division. Several of the men confessed their long-term worries, such as a potential lack of jobs when they got home. Others wondered if America might resort to totalitarianism in any postwar chaos. One GI, hopeful that she would report on her trip, described what local warfare was really like: "You fight your way up that blankety-blank mountain, and you get to the top, and ahead of you is another mountain, and then you are up and you think you can relax and fight your way down easy, and ahead is another mountain, and the Jerries [are] on top of that one, too, and another one behind that one . . . Wonder if I'll make the last mountain in Italy. Think of this perspective when you write."[62]

On Christmas Day, Clare rose early, put on her parka, and headed off in a Jeep, this time with Truscott himself as her escort. She told him she wanted to go to forward post areas, "where there is no Christmas." He asked how good she was at walking. Blue eyes twinkling, she said she walked fine.[63]

"What security restrictions are there on you and me?" she inquired later, seeing they were headed to unprotected positions. The general grinned, saying there were none on him and only those that he imposed on her. Clare coquettishly let him know that "Uncle Joe" Stilwell had taken her close to the action in Burma. In that case, said Truscott, he would do likewise.[64]

After hurtling through the Futa Pass, the Jeep stopped beside an icily shining field, where Clare saw a spectacle that would stay with her. Kneeling in the snow was a congregation of GIs at Mass. The priest held up a wafer that seemed whiter than the surrounding snow. She found herself thinking, with a humility that surprised her, "Dear Christ, have compassion on those kids . . . and if it's all the same to You, let me share their sacrifices."[65]

Even though the Jeep bore the general's three stars, the servicemen paid it and her no attention. As the last Eucharist bell rang and Truscott's driver pulled away, Clare looked back and saw breath from the soldiers rising like small puffs of incense curling toward the altar.[66]

▽

As they arrived at the line, Truscott ushered her so close that she could see German troopers on a distant hillside emerge from a foxhole, and tipsily perform handsprings in the snow.[67]

Lunching with enlisted men at a rough table in the kitchen tent of an armored infantry battalion, she quizzed a sergeant for over half an hour about trench foot and other painful consequences of extended service in the field. She returned in the afternoon to Florence and shared Christmas dinner with the general at the Thirty-fourth Division's 168th Regimental headquarters.[68]

On December 26, Clare left at last for Rome. Truscott was not the only officer who regretted having to bid her farewell. General Clark noted in a diary entry that the Congresswoman's presence and understanding of what his men endured had given him "a great lift."[69] In appreciation, he gave her a white silk "escape map" scarf, used by paratroopers in Sicily. It had been autographed by several generals, and was particularly precious to her because Truscott wore one just like it.[70]

By now she understood that the fight in Italy would drag on well into the next year. It was a depressing prospect, but as one of Clark's aides wrote her, in the grimness of war, she had brought cheer to homesick men as a symbol of what they were fighting for: "the beauty of home, freedom, democracy, wholesomeness."[71]

▽

In Rome, Clare told newsmen that of all the impressions she had gained from her visit, the most urgent was the need for troop rotations from the combat lines, such as pilots were allowed after a number of missions. As things stood, an infantryman had only medical reasons for a break, and that carried "a shell-shocked or yellow taint." She also advocated combat pay not only for medics, as Ike had suggested, but also for reconnaissance cavalry units attached to infantry divisions. Since Truscott had started his career as a cavalry officer, she might have heard this recommendation from him.[72]

On Wednesday, December 27, she broadcast to the United States a fifteen-minute summary of her visit. She said the American Fifth Army infantryman was "the proudest and bitterest" of all fighters—proud because he had "borne the hardest brunt in these endless mountains," and bitter because he felt that his countrymen thought he was serving "on an inactive Front."[73]

She sent a transcript of her talk to Truscott, with a letter enclosed. "I wonder if you know what a joy it was to know you," she wrote, "how proud I am we have generals like *you* running our show—and I wonder if you guessed the real regret with which I said goodbye to you . . . Or rather, let us call it, as the Ityies do, *Arrivederci!*" Flirtatiously, she added "La Belle" to her signature.[74]

He replied that her speech had brought tears to his eyes, "hardened soldier that I am!" He said he had never expected a Congressman, let alone a woman, to capture the great spirit of his soldiers as she had done. "You are a wonder!"

Mimicking her flirtatiousness, he added, "The war effort was greatly advanced when you were 'fog bound,' and suffered an 'earache.'" By postponing her departure, she had given him "the nicest" of the three Christmases he had spent abroad.[75]

Two days later, it was announced that Clare Boothe Luce had been elected Woman of the Year by an Associated Press poll of American newspaper editors. The margin was 98 to a crushing 18 for Eleanor Roosevelt. The *Herald Tribune* writer Dorothy Thompson, Clare's former antagonist, came third. One voter said that the Congresswoman had been chosen because no legislator had won greater renown in a single term.[76]

Back in New York on New Year's Eve, Clare gave an interview to the *Bridgeport Post*. The unsung hero of the war, she said, was "the doughboy." After five weeks in Europe she had changed in her attitude, and now had no criticism of the war's conduct. American soldiers she had come to know in Italy were superb. The Fifth Army infantry had sustained 93 percent of peninsular casualties, and had fought long and hard "under the most appalling difficulties."[77]

She sounded as if she had adopted an army as well as a refugee.

11

WANING DAYS OF WAR

Sorrow keeps breaking in.

—Samuel Beckett

Wearing a black suit, white blouse, and trademark red flower, Representative Luce entered the House on January 3, 1945, a few minutes before the noon gavel signaled the convening of the 79th Congress. Some members applauded, and other onlookers nodded and smiled. Apparently, Clare had gained in popularity over the last two years. One Congressman had brought his two-and-a-half-year-old son to the opening ceremony. Clare bounced him on her knee, let him rummage in her bag, and playfully dabbed her lipstick on the end of his button nose.[1]

Her seat was directly opposite the recently elected Democrat from California, Helen Gahagan Douglas.[2] Reporters noted that the newcomer, wife of the movie star Melvyn Douglas, looked striking in a svelte black dress that contrasted starkly with her chalk-white face and crimsoned lips. But women in the galleries thought Clare "the snappiest looking" female on the floor.[3]

The following day at the National Press Club, Mrs. Douglas decried the coverage given her debut, saying she resented the competitive position into which the press had "jockeyed" her and Mrs. Luce. Work was surely more worthy of comment than clothes, and she would not "put on a show, to vie with the gentlewoman of Connecticut." At this, Clare, sitting one seat away, reached out and clasped Helen's hand reassuringly. Ever since her public spats with Dorothy Thompson during Wendell Willkie's 1940 campaign, she had avoided perceived "catfights" with other women.[4]

▽

One week later, a telegram arrived in Clare's office from the United States War Department. It said that Second Lieutenant David Boothe had been seriously wounded in action on Morotai Island in the Pacific. There were no details yet of the injuries.[5]

Al Morano saw his boss turn deathly white. She knew from childhood that David could be both brave and foolhardy. Just last summer in New Guinea, he had been awarded a Bronze Oak Leaf Cluster for "meritorious achievement" during reconnaissance missions in the Driniumor River Campaign, one of the bloodiest battles so far in the Pacific war. His citation mentioned flights "at low altitudes, often at night, in an unarmoured L-4 airplane, over territory where enemy fire was encountered."[6]

Clare had long seen complicated consequences from her brother's military service, the only occupation that had ever suited him. He was bound to find a return to civilian life, with no opportunities for adventure, unbearably dull. From the tone of his recent letters, she had sensed that David neither expected nor wanted to survive the war. He had even sent her his medals for safekeeping, and expressed a desire to see her "once again," a phrase that could be read in two ways. More strange, he had said he wanted to spend time with their mutual friend the decorator Gladys Freeman, "before my ultimate demise."[7]

David never begrudged his sister her success. He proudly wrote that no day went by when "some officer doesn't show me your picture in some local US paper," and noted with approval that her publicity was "veering from the Blonde Bombshell to dignified status."[8] She, in turn, loved him (though she wrote him infrequently) and, for his amoral tendencies, despised him in near equal measure.

The distressing news about him came at a bad time. It was the eve of the first anniversary of Ann Brokaw's death, and Clare was about to set off with Harry on a grim pilgrimage to her daughter's grave site in South Carolina.

Upon returning to Washington, she was confronted with a report in the *Bridgeport Post* that Democrats on the Military Affairs Committee were furious with her for having "staged a one-man show" during their trip to Europe, and had pressed for her ouster. But the ranking Republican, Joseph W. Martin, Jr., had blocked the move. He was friendly toward Clare and considered her too important a party spokeswoman to be purged.[9] She was slated to reiterate her value to the GOP and the war effort in a speech to the House about her European trip.

▽

Clare entered the chamber on January 18 with a battle-green Fifth Army scarf around her neck. In the crowded gallery was the mother of the man who had given it to her, General Mark Clark.[10]

She took pains not to sound naive about military tactics, or to misrepresent the aims of those commanders she had interviewed, but simply spoke of what she had learned firsthand at the battlefronts, aiming her remarks directly at War Department officials.[11] In more than two and a half years, she said, American forces in Italy had suffered a colossal 98,366 casualties, 90 percent of those being infantrymen. Citing the four hundred consecutive days Truscott's Thirty-fourth Division had spent in wretched conditions, holding down a far larger enemy, she urged yet again that combat ground troops be allotted the same recuperative leave that airmen enjoyed after a set number of flying missions. Currently, the only hope GIs under fire in the South had of being replaced was to be "killed or wounded."[12]

Few Democrats bothered to attend her forty-five-minute address, notably Helen Gahagan Douglas. Later, Vice President Truman objected to Clare's plea for troop furloughs, saying war policy was "none of her business."[13]

▽

David Boothe, recuperating from multiple shrapnel penetrations in his left leg, received such a depressed letter from Clare about the majority's reaction to her speech that he responded with alarm. "I don't know what I'd do if anything happened to you."[14] He suspected she was suffering from the cumulative effects of bereavement, marital spats, and her seemingly endless separation from Willoughby. Days spent "without the desire to love and be vital to someone," he wrote, could turn everything "flat and sour."[15]

Actually, Clare's present desires concerned another general, stationed antipodally from Willoughby. Lucian Truscott was suffering, too—or at least his men were, in health and spirits as they waited on "the Forgotten Front" for a spring offensive still more than two months away.[16] She longed to see him again, and be back in Europe before the Red Army, sweeping west and south, met up with Eisenhower's armies swinging east and north in the race to take Berlin.

By late January, Warsaw had already fallen and the Battle of the Bulge was over, Allied troops having stopped Germany's last desperate drive across the Ardennes, at a cost of ten thousand American lives.[17] Events on both war fronts were speeding to a conclusion. For Clare to see any more European action, she needed to arrange transport straightaway. Fortuitously, a flattering invitation came from the Supreme Commander of the Allied Forces in the Mediterranean Theater, Field Marshal Sir Harold Alexander, whom she had first met in Burma in 1942. He said that since her visit she had been doing "a superb job for the Fifth Army" vis-à-vis publicity, and he hoped that she might do the same for his Eighth.[18] Clare accepted, and planned to leave as soon as President Roosevelt returned from his current meeting with Churchill and Stalin at Yalta.

▽

Encouraging though war news from Europe sounded in February, that from the Far East was still grim, as was obvious in a letter from Charles Willoughby to Arthur Vandenberg. The Senator passed it on to Clare. Written on February 4—two weeks before seventy-five thousand marines would battle twenty-one thousand enemy holdouts on the island of Iwo Jima—it conveyed MacArthur's determination to reassert himself in the Philippines:

> Today our leading columns are 15 miles from the northern suburbs of Manila. The arrogant conqueror of Singapore, General Yamashita, has been defeated from Leyte to Luzon. We have driven the Jap into the hills and utter confusion. The MacArthur cycle, Manila-Melbourne-Manila, is complete, and in comparison with the abattoir of Europe, at astonishingly little cost in human lives.[19]

Willoughby went on to complain that he had recently submitted an account of MacArthur's return for publication in the United States, only to have a chapter documenting Japanese barbarism censored by the War Department. The reason, he suspected, was the inclusion of gruesome photographs of the enemy beheading captured American aviators. "Apparently they still want to stifle the emotions of our people, and divert them from this theater of war, to the witches' cauldron of Western Europe."[20]

In a later letter to Clare, Willoughby told her he was again quartered in the capital where they had become lovers. "Every street crossing spells death." Eighty percent of the town's buildings and infrastructure had been destroyed, and one hundred thousand Filipino civilians slaughtered by the Japanese in advance of MacArthur's return.[21]

> Yesterday, as on other days, I flew into the smoky haze of the burning city. A Stalingrad, a blitzed London, like all the cities of this war, that are defended house by house by a desperate enemy. . . . All the bridges are out . . . the Cavalry and paratroopers are hacking their way up Dewey Boulevard, past the Polo Club (tiens—le revenant, in the midst of this depressing recital: the dance, in which I asked to accompany you back to your Hotel and paced wakefully through the night, in a nightmarish, fantastic hour of anguish that has left its mark).[22]

On Thursday, March 1, 1945, Clare joined her colleagues in both houses of Congress to hear the President's report on the Yalta summit. She shared the communal shock as the President rolled into the chamber in a wheelchair, instead of walking on the arm of one of his sons, as he usually did.[23] Aides helped him onto a red plush chair at the center table.

He began by asking members to excuse him for not standing. Only two days before, he had completed a fourteen-thousand-mile journey from the Crimea. "I know that you will realize that it makes it a lot easier for me not to have to carry about ten pounds of steel around on the bottom of my legs."[24]

Congressmen sat in grim silence as the gaunt Commander in Chief proceeded with his speech. Once a powerful and assured orator, he now followed his script with a finger, stumbling over words. When he reached for a water glass, his hand shook. He outlined the Allies' plan to divide Germany into four occupation zones once hostilities ended. Their agreed policy of unconditional surrender, he said, did not mean the "enslavement" of the defeated enemy, only the destruction of the Nazi Party and the militarism that had "shattered the peace of the world."

Ideally, what victory should bring in the postwar period was an end to unilateral action, exclusive alliances, spheres of influence, "and all the other expedients that have been tried for centuries—and have always failed."[25]

Representative Luce was unimpressed by this accommodating postwar vision. She complained to reporters that the President had mentioned nothing about war reparations. Granting that Germany's bombed-out infrastructure would be unable to produce payment in kind, such as tractors or machinery, she said, "Why not ask for cash?"[26]

12

A GLORIOUS WOMAN

*Pacifism is a tenable position, provided that you are
willing to take the consequences.*

—GEORGE ORWELL

Two days later, Clare left Washington for her second tour of the European battlefronts, this time traveling as the guest of Field Marshal Alexander. A huge British flying boat, courtesy of his command, flew her to London via Bermuda, where the movie magnate Sir Alexander Korda came aboard.

A wistful letter from Harry followed her.

> It's been so long this war, five years that we have known that we each had to do our own job but tonight I know that it's you and you alone I'll always be missing—and that when my life has no room for missing it's because you're there filling up all the room. . . . I should always be telling you I love you. I try tonight to catch up with you across the waves to tell you now. God bless you my darling, Harry.[1]

On her first evening in London, Clare dined with Max Beaverbrook, a gnomish-faced, permanently tanned widower in his mid-sixties. Clare quizzed him relentlessly about military and political matters and deduced that he disagreed with Churchill's pessimism about the long-term intentions of the Soviets. But she was sure the Prime Minister was right.[2]

Clare flew to Italy on Thursday, March 8, just as General Patton and his Third Army momentously reached the Rhine in Germany. Her seat was again secured on a British plane. In return for Alexander's generosity, she knew he expected her to publicize the achievements of the British Eighth Army, just as she had Mark Clark's 15th Army Group. She had accordingly contracted to write a series of syndicated articles for the *New York World-Telegram*.

Upon arriving that afternoon in Naples, she found a note from the field marshal, assigning her his guest quarters in the Villa Content, and inviting her to dine with him in his hunting lodge, where they could "discuss what you would like to do and where you would like to go. I shall put everything at your disposal."[3]

Sir Harold was the epitome of an aristocratic British military commander, with his aquiline nose and clipped mustache, immaculate dress and highly polished riding boots. He was so well-practiced in the art of diplomacy as to conceal his military ineptitude and intellectual deficiencies.[4] Fortunately, he had in his orbit the astute Harold Macmillan, Britain's Minister Resident in the Mediterranean.

"Alex" proved as susceptible to Clare's charm as other men in uniform, and gave her a privileged identification badge to facilitate her movements.[5]

She spent her first two days in Naples being briefed on military and intelligence operations by high-ranking officers and diplomats.[6] En route north after the weekend, Clare stopped by Allied headquarters at Caserta, a palace as big as Versailles. Alexander had converted its huge glass orangerie, lush with palm and fruit trees, into his mess.[7] About twelve hundred British and American uniformed men and women crisscrossed the courtyards daily. It was, she said, an "Italian Pentagon, a bewildering labyrinth of incomparable galleries and rooms," most of them boxed in by beaverboard partitions to create countless offices and cubbyholes. At one end of the building she found groups of British officers with windows wide open, nursing cups of tea, and at the other, Americans drinking coffee, their windows tightly shut.[8]

By Wednesday, March 14, Clare was at the Excelsior Hotel in Florence, her base for visiting three commands—Clark's 15th Army Group, Truscott's Fifth Army, and Sir Richard McCreery's Eighth. Beginning with medical facilities for the first, she inspected penicillin laboratories, toured traction, amputee, and hepatitis wards, and sympathized with soldiers crippled with trench foot.[9] It was a relief that evening to dine with the man she most wanted to see.

Clare needed a drink, and Truscott's mess had plenty of gin, brandy, Scotch, and rye whiskey—"medicine," Truscott said, for his raspy throat. That night, and over the course of several evenings they spent at his field quarters in the Po Valley, or his villas in Florence and Rome, the tough warrior exulted in what he afterward described as "golden hours" snatched between his military duties and her fact-finding mission. He invoked "blonde halos," eyes as clear blue as the sky, and "loving fingers through soft and beautiful hair." The Allies were about to begin their spring offensive, and he dreaded having to leave, even while insisting there could be "no separation from that which is in one's soul."[10]

Enclosing a sprig of edelweiss in a note for Lucian, Clare set off for the headquarters of General McCreery on the Adriatic coast. Soon, she regretted making the long trip by road. "General Truscott's chauffeur doesn't drive a Jeep too fast," she joked, "he flies it too low." McCreery, a stiff and flinty knight, did not detain her long, and she continued to Cantoniera, where some young enlisted men let her fire on a German-occupied house eight hundred yards away.[11]

Turning south, she had tea with a Jewish brigade, more proof of how polyglot the forces in northern Italy were. A blond, blue-eyed sergeant named Levi told her he had been born in Berlin and lived in Palestine before joining the British Army. Though German was his native tongue, he chose to speak only Hebrew or English now, and after the peace, he wanted to farm in Tel Aviv.[12] He was one of many "displaced persons" Clare met in subsequent weeks, and made her see the dimensions of what Europe and the Middle East would face after the war, with millions more uprooted and facing relocation.

At Castrocaro, she encountered a company of Poles in an old prison. They gave her flowers and serenaded her with national songs. Some, rendered homeless after the 1939 Hitler/Stalin pact sliced off east and west parts of Poland, expressed rancor over being "betrayed" by Roosevelt and Churchill at Yalta.[13]

Clare watched the Tobruk Battalion in a dive-bombing exhibition at Castel Bolognese. One of her dinner companions that night was Major Julian Beck of the 79th Wing, RAF, who had bombed Berchtesgaden, Hitler's mountain hideout in Bavaria.[14] Something masculine in Clare relished the harshness of war, and her versatile mind embraced all the details of strategy, logistics, and technology thrown at her in briefings. Yet at the same time, her outward femininity disarmed her military hosts, who did not realize from her calm and apparent impassivity how much she absorbed.

Next morning, she talked to pilots who had just returned from a mission in the north. One plane was riddled with flak holes, so it was with some trepidation that after lunch she accepted McCreery's offer of a ride back to Florence in his private aircraft, only to find herself escorted by a flight of Spitfires from the 244th Wing that "kept stunting around" until she was "well beyond the bomb line."[15]

▽

A letter from Truscott, addressed to "La Belle," awaited her in the city. He thanked her for the sprig of edelweiss ("I shall carry it always") and enclosed an itinerary for her pending Fifth Army visit. When not on tour, he wrote, she could stay at his villa or his hotel suite. In either place they could dine together, "Just the two of us . . . I will devote myself to you . . . for as long as you and the war effort will permit it!"[16]

But Clare did not let the general monopolize her time. The following night, she was photographed playing billiards at the Robertson Club with British servicemen half Truscott's age. This made news in her constituency and sparked a letter to the *Bridgeport Herald*, complaining that Mrs. Luce was elected to represent the Fourth District, not to play games with soldiers. "She is not a war correspondent. She is not an entertainer. She is not a Red Cross worker. She is a Congresswoman."[17]

Clare hit the road again on Wednesday, March 21, traveling west to inspect Fifth Army positions near the Ligurian Sea. The weather was at last warm, and she broke her journey to chat with GIs from the Tenth Mountain Division. During a lull in enemy gunfire, they had stripped off their shirts to get a tan. She noted that their mental and physical caliber was "extremely high."[18] Unable to resist a 75mm pack howitzer, Clare took aim and fired it. In the process, she broke all her fingernails and almost a knee. She wisecracked that the gun had "more kick than the mules which carried it there."[19]

Her curiosity about military life extended to whether the new rations supplied to Allied troops were appetizing. After quizzing men about their preferences, she concluded that a soldier's ideal meal would include British sardines, Indian mutton and chutney, Italian guava jelly, and Brazilian coffee.[20]

By Thursday afternoon, she was back on winding roads with a new escort, Major Vernon A. Walters. Multilingual, he was a born intelligence officer, and became a lifelong friend. At an expeditionary en-

Clare beguiles Fifth Army Group troops, 1945

campment just north of Pisa, an Associated Press reporter, Stan Swinton, was on hand to witness the arrival of their mud-spattered Jeep. "Mrs. Luce, a steel helmet covering her blonde hair and clad in an olive-drab uniform cut to her trim figure . . . somehow managed to look as if she had just stepped from a beauty parlor."[21] On her left lapel she wore a strange Asian medal. Somebody asked her what it was, and she replied, "Order of Chastity Second Class." The men roared.[22]

▽

Another letter from Truscott awaited Clare in Florence. Could she dine with him on Sunday? "What a glorious woman you are! Never before have I experienced the peace in the soul that I feel today. My only cloud . . . is the knowledge of days that I must pass without you. . . . I envy all who are seeing you. God bless you and keep you. Lucian."[23]

Opportunities for them to meet were diminishing, so he asked Clare to come on Tuesday to the Roman villa that he had first occupied after the Allies captured the capital. "It's nice, it's private." He had it all planned. They would have an afternoon stroll, or sit in the sun and talk. At dinner, he would quietly contemplate her "and think how beautiful are the lilies of the field." On Wednesday they would take a Jeep trip to Anzio, and picnic there while he told her "stories of heroism." Afterward, he would show her the now infamous beachhead where superior

German forces had stalled his army's advance. Until he met her, he had thought "there could be no adequate reward" for those "122 days of misery."[24]

Clare knew enough military history to understand that Truscott's reveries were those of the archetypal soldier, imagining a few hours of bliss before what might be his last battle. She went ahead of him to attend a dinner in her honor hosted by the British Ambassador, Sir Noel Charles, at his lavish apartment in the Orsini Palace.

She arrived late and last, incensing the wife of Myron Taylor, Roosevelt's personal envoy to the Holy See. "I wouldn't have her in my drawing room in New York," she said to a fellow guest, Harold Macmillan. "Why should she keep me waiting here?"[25]

Macmillan sat next to Clare at dinner, and was intrigued afterward to see the military contingent zeroing in on her "like bees round a honey pot. She 'turns it on' in rather a marked fashion. But that goes very well with the sex-starved soldiery."[26]

▽

Clare then disappeared for a couple of days, staying incommunicado with Truscott. Meanwhile at the Pentagon, aides to the Chief of Staff began questioning her whereabouts. She had not bargained for the fact that since her House speech on the Forgotten Front, Marshall was now paying more attention to the Italian war. The Allied spring offensive was due to begin in less than two weeks, and he needed General Truscott's full tactical attention.

Dr. Morrison C. Stayer, the Surgeon General of the Mediterranean theater, was ordered to track Clare down and send her to the "ZI" (Zone of the Interior, i.e., the United States) without delay. She was affecting morale with her "somewhat inappropriate behavior" and "had to be saved from her own indiscretions."[27]

Dr. Stayer was a practical rather than a prudish man. Having observed Clare's alcohol intake and flirtations in Caserta, he suspected her mysterious absence was due to a drinking binge, a liaison, or both. To avoid publicity, he asked a recuperating soldier, Arthur B. Dodge, Jr., to handle the "sensitive and delicate mission" of finding Mrs. Luce. "General Marshall wants her out of here."

Furnished with the address of a certain villa in Rome, Dodge and a driver set off there in an army staff car. He announced his mission to a maid who answered the door. Clare appeared in a tweed suit. When Dodge informed her that he had been assigned "to escort you to your transport home," he was struck by a look of mixed relief and reluctance on her face.

After changing into army fatigues for the drive to Rome's airport, Clare climbed into the waiting car. Even now, she had to be coquettish with the attractive, mustachioed young officer. "Why don't you sit in the back with me, Lieutenant, and we can talk?"

Dodge rode with her, but resolutely put her on a flight to Naples. He then called his superior with a discreet message: "Sir, the package has been dispatched."[28]

▽

Clare risked Marshall's wrath by delaying her departure for Washington. Instead, she brazenly returned to Rome on March 29 for another audience with Pope Pius XII. The Holy Father remembered seeing her four months before, and said that he believed American women would be a great influence for world peace after the war.

She then visited Anzio with Truscott. It seemed to mean a great deal to him that they spent their last Italian hours together there, so much so that he wrote a poem for her entitled "Anzio Revisited."

> Sit here and drink this glass of wine with me,
> Dear lady. Do you hear the springtime song
> A bird is making in that tree? That tree . . .
> Now how the memories begin to throng!
> That pine's the very one which death once sought
> Me under while I watched a dog-fight there.
> Today, the sky is sunlit—like your hair.
> Then sky and sea were wintry as we fought
> Up the beach to this cover deep in mud.
> Men crouched against the naked bark, and shell
> Came screaming at us—thirsting for our blood.
> This quiet wood was once the home of hell.
> I'm troubled by the ghosts that haunt this place.
> They mock the skull beneath your lovely face.[29]

▽

On April 7, Clare arrived in Paris. She wanted to see how the benighted city had recovered from the occupation. Reporters lay in wait, and were not disappointed. With the European conflict winding down, she said, American troops must be informed of their immediate future. "Many of them think a boat will be waiting to take them home as soon as the war is over. I think a large number of them are likely to be sent to the Pacific."[30]

Lieutenant Colonel Ray J. Stecker, commander of the "Hell Hawks" 365th Fighter Group, was on hand to squire her around town. He had performed a similar function in Italy during her first trip and described those "ten days in December '44 [as] the most precious of my life."[31] A former champion jock with a Distinguished Flying Cross, Bronze Star, and Croix de Guerre, he was tall, blond, thirty-five, and married. Clare was drawn to such young men who daily risked death, and she offered them solace, which they sometimes took more seriously than she did. Next day, just as Mark Clark's offensive began in the south, Stecker flew her to Cologne and Marburg.

Clare marked her forty-second birthday near the French lines on April 10, while Allied forces—three out of four of them American—raced toward the river Elbe. Simultaneously, the Soviets took Vienna, depriving Truscott of his dream to capture the capital of Hitler's homeland. At dusk, he wrote Clare a "commemorative" letter, saying that in her company he had been "truly and completely happy" for once in his life.

> Without hope, this would indeed be a dreary world. Therefore like Cinderella I shall await the wand of the fairy godmother to do for me what I cannot do for myself—bring us together again. Meanwhile, be it one year or twenty, I shall not be sad ever, only joyful and thankful for the one complete and perfect association of my life. Do you recall that in the garden at Villa La Speiga I railed a bit at the fate that had delayed our meeting until the afternoon of my life? I am over that. I am only grateful to whatever kind fate brought us together even for such a brief period.
>
> Thus I shall be a better man and a better soldier than ever before because there is again serenity in my soul. The battle is on as you know and in just forty eight hours this Fifth of yours will be on its way to Berchtesgaden, and in its commander's pocket a bit of edelweiss will spur him on and bring him luck, and in his heart a great love, always.[32]

13

OPENING OF THE CAMPS

For there is nothing covered, that shall not be revealed;
either hid, that shall not be known.

—Saint Luke's Gospel, 12:2–3

C lare heard of Franklin Roosevelt's death near the German battle lines on Thursday, April 12. In Moscow, the news stunned even Josef Stalin, who clung silently for a time to the hand of Ambassador Averell Harriman. And in Tokyo, to a background of solemn music, a radio announcer proclaimed "the passing of a great man."[1]

Leaving Heidelberg for Paris three days later, on what she assumed would be the first leg of her journey home, Clare suddenly suffered a gastric disorder and checked into the American hospital in Neuilly for a few days.[2] While there, she had leisure to absorb news reports, coming thick and fast, of the nightmarish conditions that Allied troops were finding in German concentration camps. She recovered just in time to seize on an invitation from General Eisenhower to join a British-American political delegation that would visit some of these Nazi labor and extermination facilities and publicize the horrors found there.

The delegation's first stop on April 21 was Buchenwald, a five-hundred-acre compound in East Germany.[3] Named incongruously after nearby forests of beech trees, the camp sat on the north slope of a hill, over-

126

looking the exquisite city of Weimar, where Bach, Goethe, Schiller, Liszt, and Nietzsche once lived. Recent Allied air raids had wrecked the eighteenth-century houses of the poets (hitherto preserved as national shrines) as well as the architecturally fine main square.[4]

Clare and her companions—Representative John Kunkel of Pennsylvania and Leonard W. Hall of New York, as well as ten British members of Parliament—learned that Buchenwald could accommodate a maximum of 120,000 prisoners at a time.[5] But over a four-year period, 51,000 of Hitler's "undesirables," among them Jews, Communists, Gypsies, Fascist resistance fighters, convicted criminals, and homosexuals, had died from overwork, starvation, or disease.[6] Thus, it was a greatly diminished population of some 60,000 all-male inmates, including Poles, Hungarians, and Russians, that the Sixth Armored Division of Patton's Third Army had found on April 11. By far the greatest proportion were Jews. Clare learned that they were the only people in any camp with numbers tattooed on their wrists.

A guide met the delegation at an iron entrance gate embellished with the words *Recht oder Unrecht—Mein Vaterland* ("Right or Wrong—My Country"). Inside, along a main avenue aptly named Blood Street, Clare was startled to encounter a bunch of skeletal figures in blue-and-white-striped prison garb, staring at her dull-eyed.

It was a hot, dry day. As she followed the guide through the ill-kempt grounds, whirling winds blew dust into her eyes and coated the walls of wooden huts and brick housing. The gusts also brought odors of rotting bodies and human waste. Although press gangs of German civilians from outside the complex were supposed to have cleaned up for a week under American supervision, Clare's chief impression was of "intense general squalor."[7]

One of the first dormitories the delegation saw consisted of small rooms with windows and cement floors. Four of these, Clare learned, had been used as a camp brothel, where non-Jewish prisoners employed in supervisory jobs were allowed to have sex for twenty minutes at a time. Female inmates, brought from other camps, had become "prostitutes" under duress. The same verminous huts were now a makeshift medical facility, treating men in advanced states of emaciation. About one hundred a day had been dying when the Americans took over. The rate had already dropped by almost two-thirds, but doctors expected few of the survivors to last. Clare understood why, when she noticed that the thighs protruding through scanty cotton garments of men still barely breathing were no thicker than normal wrists.[8]

Clare in Buchenwald barracks, April 1945

Among the younger prisoners was Elie Wiesel, a seventeen-year-old Romanian. He had gone down with food poisoning three days after liberation, and was hovering between life and death.[9]

About eight hundred children remained in the camp. They had been forced to work alongside adults, on eight-hour shifts seven days a

Clare with Buchenwald survivors, April 1945

week, in nearby quarries or at a large munitions factory. Their basic daily ration had consisted of a bowl of watery soup and a chunk of dry bread.

Clare and her colleagues moved on to the white-walled basement of the mortuary block. Its ceiling was eight feet high, and according to the guide, more than a thousand inmates had been hanged from it on hooks. Those dying too slowly were finished off by executioners with clubs shaped like potato mashers. One of these was still stained with blood.[10] A large electric lift carried the dead from the basement to a yard above, where SS guards, anxious to flee the advancing Allies, had stacked them on the ground or in carts. Some piles were still there. Clare scrutinized the naked, decomposing bodies. None bore obvious marks of violence.

Off the yard stood the camp's crematorium, a row of capacious arched ovens. Many of them, she noted, were "still full of splintered, charred remains and blackened skulls of corpses."[11]

Near the end of the tour, a camp official briefed the delegates on the sterilization experiments that had continued in Buchenwald's laboratories even after "the policy of exterminating Jews had long superceded that of castrating them." They then heard about Ilse Koch, wife of the camp's commandant, who had collected articles made of human skin. The members of Parliament took one of her lampshades and other samples for forensic analysis.[12]

A reporter heard Clare muttering repeatedly, "It could happen to us in twenty years." After he told her that army camera crews had shot copious footage of the camp's atrocities for public distribution, she voiced her approval. "Everyone should see these films and never forget them." She brushed aside a cameraman's suggestion that some scenes were too horrible for popular viewing. "No one wants to believe such things could happen. But they have happened here."[13]

Her own comprehension was strained further, as some inmates of Buchenwald told her they had been transferred there from an even worse facility in southeast Poland, Auschwitz-Birkenau.[14] Auschwitz was reportedly an extermination center (Treblinka being another) so efficient that between May and July 1944 alone, it had eliminated four hundred thousand Hungarian Jews, disposing of them at the rate of twelve thousand a day.[15] Women, children, and men unfit for work were routinely herded into a mammoth shower-bath, stripped naked, and sprayed with Zyklon B, a nerve gas comprising amethyst-blue crystals that was routinely used in pest control. More than a million people had died at Auschwitz, most of them under the authority of Adolf Eichmann, head of the Jewish Office of the Gestapo. His obsession was to destroy "every single Jew he could lay his hands on."[16]

Every day of her tour, Clare learned more about Nazi torture and annihilation policies. The delegation's next stop was Buchenwald's sub-camp, Ohrdruf, a little to the west near Gotha. Generals Patton, Eisenhower, and Bradley had already visited and the last had vomited at the sight—no longer available to her—of shallow graves filled with more than thirty-two hundred naked, emaciated bodies, lice crawling over them.[17]

Ike reported to Churchill that the Burgomaster of Weimar and his wife, forced to confront what their nation had wrought in that camp, had gone home and hanged themselves.[18]

▽

Revelations of a different kind awaited Clare at Nordhausen, a town fifty miles north of Weimar, in the Harz Mountains of Thuringia. As a member of the Military Affairs Committee, she was intrigued to discover that it was here, in late 1943, that Hitler's armament czar, Albert Speer, had established Dora-Mittelbau, a subterranean slave labor factory for the manufacture of secret experimental weapons. Thirty sub-camps on the perimeter of Dora were built aboveground for thousands of workers, to replace the spent or dead from the main facility. Troops of the 104th U.S. Infantry Division had found only two survivors among three thousand scattered bodies in one of these interim shelters. Allied air attacks were responsible for some of the fatalities.[19]

As for Dora itself, a camouflaged work site carved out of old gypsum mines on the side of a green mountain, Clare at first thought it was a disused salt mine. Inside the unobtrusive entrance, there was a network of well-lit, air-conditioned tunnels, the central one about a mile long. It took the visitors fifteen minutes to travel to the end in a Jeep. Along the way, Clare saw transverse corridors housing a variety of up-to-date machine tools and assembly belts. All the equipment had been installed by Speer to make the V-1 and V-2 pilotless guided missiles—the "V" standing for *Vergeltung,* meaning "retribution." In retaliation for the bombing of Germans by the Royal Air Force, Hitler had hoped, before D-Day, to obliterate the British capital with them, but many of the pilotless bombs ran out of fuel or malfunctioned. Others were destroyed by antiaircraft fire or shot down by fighter planes. Nevertheless, three thousand Londoners had been killed by rockets in the last year of the war.[20]

For eighteen months, the delegation was told, sixty thousand men had worked here continuously, in an underground temperature no higher than 59 degrees Fahrenheit. They had been given no water for washing, had only truncated oil barrels for toilets, and slept in neighboring warrens on tiers of makeshift bunks. Short of sunlight and proper nourishment, twenty thousand had died, taking many German technological secrets with them.[21]

As Clare marveled at the assembly lines, still gleaming with rows of incomplete rockets, she concluded that such destructive inventions "can only be hatched secretly by nations which limit interior freedom."[22] What she did not yet know was that her own country was working on an even more devastating war product.[23]

▽

Still wearing the khaki tunic and slacks she had at the outset, Clare arrived at Bergen-Belsen, near Hanover in Lower Saxony. By the time it was freed on April 15, it had become a dumping ground for sixty thousand sick inmates from other prisons. Anne Frank and her sister had been transferred there from Auschwitz at the end of October 1944. Both lived only four more months, succumbing to typhus a few weeks before the camp was liberated.[24]

The Franks were buried, but Clare saw corpses "stacked like boards, thumbs and ankles interlocked fifteen and twenty deep," awaiting interment. For the first time, she understood the import of the word *stiffs* as applied to gunned-down victims by hoodlums in Hollywood gangster movies. She tried to make conversation with a few survivors, reminding herself that some of them may have been among the finest minds in Europe. "*Sprechen Sie Deutsch? Parlez-vous français?*" Unthinkingly, she reached into a breast pocket for a cigarette, whereupon a few prisoners rushed at her and grabbed for the packet. Beating them off, she screamed, "Get away from me!"

Her reaction was instinctive, and she felt shamed by it. "I realized in that moment what it was like to be a Nazi. I was treating them like animals, too."[25]

14

VICTORY IN EUROPE

▽

Being on the move is no substitute for feeling.

—Eudora Welty

When Congresswoman Luce broadcast an account of her tour from London on April 26, she was pessimistic about the likelihood of Germany's bombed-out cities being rebuilt. "They had better salt the streets the way they did in Carthage and forget them." As for the concentration camps, "It's hard for ordinary people in the democracies really to believe that torture can be . . . state policy." Responsibility for the Nazi atrocities fell squarely upon Germans. Until they acknowledged their guilt, they should not be admitted "into the decent family of nations."[1]

Clare flew home two days later, hearing en route that Italian partisans had captured and shot Benito Mussolini, then hung his body upside down in Milan's Piazzale Loreto. When her clipper landed in Miami on May 1, she exited the plane to news of Adolf Hitler's death. "Golly golly!" she exclaimed to reporters. "It's like the end of a dreadful nightmare." Her language was trite, but she promised that on Capitol Hill she intended to advocate "a hard peace for the Germans."[2]

On May 3, Clare rose in Congress. "Mr. Speaker, I wish to address the House briefly on the subject of the Buchenwald and Nordhausen camps." But first she asked that the report of her British parliamentary colleagues be inserted into the *Congressional Record*. She could testify that it was "in no sense exaggerated." It was as if she hoped that British understatement would balance the dramatic rhetoric of her own findings.

> No American ... can imagine what grisly tortures were visited upon some of the prisoners for the smallest infraction of the camps' inhuman disciplines. No words can describe them or evoke the ghastly sights and sounds and the unutterable smells that day and night afflicted all the occupants of these infernos, two among many in Germany. Existence for human beings at Buchenwald, Nordhausen, Bergen-Belsen, Ohrdruf, Langenstein, Dachau and other extermination centers was a descent into the bowels of hell.[3]

From what she had seen and heard, the "beatings, burnings, hangings, clubbings, foul mutilations, and massacres practiced in these charnel houses" were merely part of a larger Nazi policy of "death by slow starvation." The dead and dying, she went on, "were difficult to tell apart at the hideous barracks of Nordhausen." She gave a detailed description of the underground facility, where the Nazis had not flinched at "using the blood and fat of men as one uses fuel to stoke secret furnaces and fire secret weapons." When the fuel was exhausted, the human containers had been scrapped.

> Torture for torture's sake is nothing new. ... The Coliseum at Rome had witnessed even more senseless orgies of sadism than those intermittently practiced by the jailers of these camps. But carefully calculated starvation of hundreds of thousands of human beings in the building of a modern aggressive war machine—this surely is something new and terrible in the world.

What most struck her was the creativeness of Nazi cruelty. Nordhausen had produced "the most ingenious and devastating weapons yet tried on earth," which "already challenged the supremacy of the heavy bomber as a strategic weapon." She foresaw the development of "radio-guided, motor- and jet-propelled missiles, with tremendous warheads," that "can be hurled thousands of miles with great accuracy." Ending her address with an appeal to the international peace organization currently forming in San Francisco, she said that if it hoped to prevent future wars, it must first guarantee the liberty of individuals and do away "with the imprisonment of men anywhere in the world for their political convictions."[4]

▽

Newspaper typefaces documenting the last hours of the war in Europe grew larger and bolder in the days immediately following Clare's speech. On May 4, the *New York Herald Tribune* announced:

NAZI SOLDIERS SURRENDERING BY THE THOUSANDS
ALLIES BOMB MILITARY EXODUS TO DENMARK
DOENITZ'S AIDE HOPES TERMS WILL BE "GENEROUS"

On the same day, *The New York Times* ran wrenching photographs of a leveled Berlin, now in Russian hands. It was "one great tombstone," wrote a *Stars and Stripes* reporter. The only signs of life in the city, once home to four million people, were a few dispirited shovelers clearing remnants of toppled masonry and dead bodies. Clare would not have recognized the beautiful capital she visited as a nineteen-year-old. The Hotel Adlon had vanished, as had the State Opera building. Even the elegant Unter den Linden boulevard was obscured by layers of gray powder and reportedly reeked of sewage and death.[5]

At 2:41 A.M. on May 7, 1945, in a schoolhouse near Rheims, General Walter Bedell Smith, Eisenhower's Chief of Staff, watched General Alfred Jodl and Admiral Hans-Georg von Friedeburg sign an unconditional surrender of all German land, sea, and air forces. For the Western Allies, Victory in Europe, henceforth known as V-E Day, came into effect officially a minute before midnight. For the Soviets it began a day later, with a signing ceremony in the Berlin suburb of Karlshorst.[6] And so, one week after the death of its instigator, the most ferocious war the Continent had ever seen came to an end.[7]

▽

New Yorkers were jubilant at the news. Half a million crowded Times Square, laughing, dancing, waving flags, tooting horns, and kissing strangers as ticker tape floated down.[8] But in Washington, government employees were ordered to keep working, and the streets of the capital stayed relatively empty when President Truman announced on the radio the "solemn but glorious hour" of peace.[9]

At sixty-one, he had only just moved into the White House and felt unprepared for the onerous task that faced him. He now had to ponder a state secret that Roosevelt had not shared with him as Vice President. "Within four months," Secretary of War Henry L. Stimson wrote, "we shall in all probability have completed the most terrible weapon ever known in human history, one bomb of which could destroy a whole city."[10] The prospect of being pressured by his own and Allied military leaders to end the Pacific war with this new weapon, coupled with the task of wheedling money from Congress for postwar recovery programs, compounded Truman's anxieties, as did a cable from Churchill about the Russians: "An iron curtain is drawn down upon their front. We do not know what is going on behind."[11]

Clare echoed the Prime Minister's concern in a speech at Columbia University on May 27. She warned that Stalinism was "rushing over Europe and Asia at a greater speed than Nazi ideas did ten years ago," and that thirteen nations in Europe were already controlled by local or Muscovite Reds. "Germany is the battleground where either democracy or Communism will win."[12] Two days later, in a broadcast entitled "Shall It Be One World?" for NBC's Blue Network, she took up again the subject of burgeoning antidemocratic threats, an obsession that she would trumpet for the next forty years.

During the war, she noted, America had given the Soviet Union $8 billion in matériel, buttressing what was now the "the strongest military and industrial power in Europe." Since Stalin might now turn to help the West defeat Japan, he could become the most formidable force in Asia. There were already strong Marxist organizations in Belgium, the Netherlands, France, Spain, Mexico, Central and South America, the Near East, and China. It was also no secret that Indian intellectuals were "looking toward their near and mighty neighbor . . . for guidance in the technique of revolution." Meanwhile, "we have our own Earl Browder"— an allusion to the Stalinist head of the Communist Party USA.

She drew a parallel between Communist and Nazi totalitarianism, saying that it was as murderous to throw a farmer off his land, or send him to a Siberian gulag, as to incarcerate a Jew in a concentration camp.

> This cannot long remain two worlds, as it is today—the world of totalitarianism and the world of liberty. Indeed, as our conflict with Nazi totalitarianism proved, these two worlds are doomed to come into conflict. It must, and will be one world sooner or later.
>
> Shall it be one world in which all mankind crawls and cringes in the darkness of slavery? Or shall it be one world in which all the great nations of mankind love and live in the light of freedom?[13]

15

FRAGMENTATION

If we want things to stay as they are, things will have to change.

—GIUSEPPE DI LAMPEDUSA

Clare experienced a letdown as she settled once more into the humdrum duties of congressional life. It had been the same after her last trip to the front, but this time she felt worse. Peace in Europe, and probable peace in the Pacific later in the year, would bring to an end her thrilling involvement with commanders in the field. For the most part, her attraction to men-at-arms was visceral and intellectual rather than merely sexual, and they were beguiled by her understanding of their missions, as well as by her extraordinary personality and looks. Generals in both theaters were confessedly in love with her—Lucian Truscott in Europe and Charles Willoughby in the Pacific, not to mention Ray Stecker and the long list of officers, American and British, who at least found her irresistibly beautiful. It had been that way with Clare ever since her teenage flings with the White Russian Alexis Aladin and Julian Simpson—career soldiers both, and in the case of the latter, a man for whom she still yearned.

She was enough of a femme fatale to encourage current beaux in their fantasies of marriage, but doubted such dreams could survive the war. Willoughby, certainly, was both handsome and free, but none of them had a chance of competing in peacetime with Henry Luce's wealth and power. It was true that since 1939 she had gotten no sexual satisfaction from her husband, and frustration on that score mounted now that she was back in Washington and had to watch her social behavior.

She had to be particularly careful right now, because Stecker was in town, having left Europe at about the same time she had. He was staying at the Wardman Park Hotel, while going through the process of demobilization. Following that, he would resume his career as a "dealer in wool and animal hairs" in Massachusetts. Harry, who had briefly visited the capital to welcome Clare home, embarked on a lengthy trip to Asia, leaving his wife and her air ace free to continue their liaison through mid-June. Before going north, Stecker wrote her a farewell note.

> My Darling: The time has finally arrived when we must part. Each time it gets worse but each time we leave each other more of ourself. It is not right for a person to be as happy as I have been these last six weeks. . . . I love you deeply, Clare, for the fine beautiful woman you are. Your talents are legion, but darling they are overshadowed by your talent of a loving kind pure woman. . . . I can make you so happy, so much wanted, so much needed you would love me always as you do now.[1]

The effect of this was somewhat negated when he wrote again to say that his wife had agreed to a divorce. He plainly expected Clare to get a similar release and marry him. But she promptly squashed this fantasy by not responding and not being available for his calls.[2]

▽

A mutual acquaintance reported to Willoughby that Clare looked taut and restless that spring, glancing constantly at her watch, as though anxious to be somewhere else. The general was not surprised: he knew her susceptibility to strain and tendency to be depressed out of the limelight.[3] His own feeling of pity for her was sharpened by resentment that she had not written to him since February, except for a casual wire at the end of her European trip.[4]

He sent a jealous letter that accused her of wasting her "great talent and charm" on Field Marshal Alexander's "second-rate professional outfit." Clearly suspecting her of dallying with other officers, he felt shunted aside. He quoted a "stiletto" passage in one missive from her that had pierced his heart: "Time has delivered its soft, imperceptible, lingering mortal blow just as we foresaw it would. You know when you come back, I shall be deeply fond of you, and yet many things have happened to both of us, that will make us strangers."[5]

She also received a wistful letter from General Truscott. "I did not reach Berchtesgaden . . . I'm told the Air lads laid the place flat." He was establishing new headquarters on the west shore of Isola di Garda. "Of course I shall dream a bit of other villas and other associations."[6] He was coming home soon on leave, to be feted in his native state of Texas. "The great American public must have its spectacles."[7] After that, he would visit Washington and hoped to see her.[8]

While awaiting this reunion, Clare spent solitary nights at the Wardman Park, finishing an outline for a novel. She mailed it to Truscott for his opinion. He recognized himself as her thinly disguised protagonist and responded tactfully, writing that he did not think "a fictional hero on a forgotten front" was an appropriate vehicle for her views on postwar American foreign policy.[9]

Their subsequent reunion, circumscribed by his Pentagon and family commitments, consisted of cocktails and dinner at the Wardman Park on Sunday, June 24.[10] More than two months had passed since they had last seen each other. They felt the awkwardness of a couple whose romance had flourished in an alien, dangerous environment and could not survive transposition to native soil. Their paths must now diverge. Lucian not only had a wife of twenty-six years and three children to consider, but was slated for an administrative position in occupied Germany.[11] Clare had to confront the specter of Henry Luce, back in New York that evening from his extensive Far Eastern trip and hoping to see more of her now that the war in Europe was over.

Truscott summed up their relationship in a letter permeated with regret:

> It is perhaps just as well that we were both too old, too wise, too devoted to the task in hand, too conscious of duties to be done, and books to write and lives to be lived—to fall in love—or I might have written you a love letter. I might have cried against fate that so arranged history. I would certainly have devoted pages and pages to saying what a glorious person you are. Since we are old, I must write drivel like this and sign off
>
> Yours L.[12]

As the summer progressed, Clare began to show signs of sexual frustration. One night she dropped in on Isabel Hill's son John, a soldier in his early twenties, who was staying at the Wardman Park Hotel. He was already in bed, and she embarrassed him by ruminating on what the consequences of leaving her husband might be. "Would it be awful to have a romance, John?" she asked, pulling at his bedsheets. But he did not encourage her.[13]

Harry meanwhile was telling everybody who would listen, including thirty-three Senators and an uninterested President Truman, about his thirty-thousand-mile trip to Pacific battle stations. He spoke of a four-hour interview with MacArthur, his dislike of Admiral Chester Nimitz, the huge development of Guam, and how Japan's surrender might be brought about politically, rather than by more fighting.[14] Not knowing, or not caring, that such fulminations were tolerated because of his media power, he seemed unaware, until he saw Clare in mid-July, that she was on the verge of a nervous breakdown and in need of rest and recuperation. Congress had just adjourned, so he got his secretary to book rooms at an inn in the White Mountains of New Hampshire, starting the following Wednesday.[15]

Before committing to it, Clare sought the soothing company of George Waldo, her editor friend at the *Bridgeport Post*. He was fifty-seven, recently widowed, and shyly besotted with her. A perceptive man, he had been aware of strains in the Luce marriage ever since watching Harry proudly show Clare a new issue of *Time*, only to receive what amounted to an editorial kick in the teeth. Harry "just can't take it from you above all others," he had warned her.[16] Luce struck him as a sensitive, humorless man, and she, right now, as a troubled woman, "hemmed in, bewildered and bitter."[17]

Clare turned down Harry's offer of a vacation—not altogether to his disappointment, since that week Truman, Churchill, and Stalin were discussing postwar policy at Potsdam, in the Russian sector of Berlin, and the news flowing daily into Time Inc. fed his addiction to world affairs. The main purpose of the summit was to discuss the future of Germany and Poland. But Stalin had plans for invading Manchuria and was angling to be part of peace negotiations in the Far East as well as in Europe. This alarmed American diplomats. GIs had, after all, done most of the fighting in the Pacific. Had Luce known what the President secretly knew—that scientists at Los Alamos, in the deserts of New Mexico, had just successfully tested a superdeadly nuclear fission bomb— he might have been too distracted to notice his wife's bleak mood.[18]

In an attempt to humor her, he summoned Billings to say he wanted to end the ban on references to Clare in *Time*.[19] She should be given the degree of attention she deserved as a public figure in her own right. The result was a staff memo that Billings complicitly wrote as if coming from himself and addressed to Luce. It stated that the moment was opportune "to straighten out *Time*'s treatment of Clare." Any newsworthy things she did in Congress, or significant foreign trips she took, should be noted in appropriate sections of the magazine. Keeping in mind that readers knew she was married to the Editor in Chief, she should be treated fairly, with "no snide adjectives, no unnecessary puffs." In a final line, Billings disingenuously asked for his boss's "O.K.," and Harry scrawled on the document, "Very okay, HRL."[20]

As if on cue, "hot" news about Clare circulated through the office on July 23. She had accepted the leading role in a summer stock production of George Bernard Shaw's *Candida*. The general reaction of staff was, "My God, what next?"[21]

Her casting had come about by chance. She had been fretting in Greenwich that her literary talent was being harmed by having to draft too many political speeches. "Congressionalese will get me. And that's death to a writer." She had asked Al Morano and Isabel Hill to sit with her and read scenes from one of her unproduced plays, *The Happy Marriage*.[22]

Fortuitously, Gus Schirmer, Jr., manager of the Associates Theater Company, was in the neighborhood looking for material, so she offered her script to him. Schirmer rejected it as too technically demanding for the venue he had in mind, Stamford's Strand Theatre. He suggested that she switch métiers and star in Shaw's play. "The perfect Candida would be someone who looks and talks and acts as nearly as possible like yourself." Clare had always loved the works of GBS, and *Candida* was her favorite. Although her last appearance as an actress had been in the late 1920s at an amateur comedy club in New York, she did not hesitate and said to Schirmer, "Why not?"[23]

▽

The show was to run for just one week, opening on August 6, so Clare memorized her part in time for a rehearsal on her porch with the rest of the cast.

Her partiality notwithstanding, *Candida* is not considered one of

Shaw's best plays.[24] Shorter and less preachy than much of his work, it has amusing, even iconoclastic, lines about love, marriage, domesticity, class, politics, shady business practices, artists, creativity, and religion. Set in northeast London in 1894, all three acts take place in the drawing room of a parsonage, where the Reverend James Morell improbably conducts all his business and interacts with seven other characters. The most important of these is his wife, Candida, a statuesque, even-tempered, but controlling woman of thirty-three. Morell is seven years older, a handsome, virile, and somewhat complacent Anglican cleric.[25] Together they charitably "rescue" Eugene Marchbanks, a tormented eighteen-year-old poet whom they find sleeping on the Thames embankment. He turns out to be wellborn and affluent, but emotionally demanding. Soon, both priest and poet are vying for Candida's affection. As a quintessential nurturer, she condescends to both males as if they were boys and feels an obligation to teach Eugene the value of the love "of a good woman" before he degrades himself with a bad one.[26]

Marchbanks, it transpires, is wise beyond his years. "We all go about longing for love," he says to Prossy, Morell's spinsterish assistant. "It is the first need of our natures."[27]

That was a line with which Clare could identify, if not Shaw's stage description of Candida as "like any other pretty woman who is just clever enough to make the most of her sexual attractions for trivially selfish ends."[28] Forced in the play's final moments to choose between Marchbanks's effeminate ardor and Morell's pomposity ("I have nothing to offer you but . . . my authority and position for your dignity"), she elects to stay with her husband in a display of insufferable condescension, saying that he is "the weaker of the two," because he would find his altruistic life empty without her beside him.[29]

Schirmer recruited a formidably experienced cast to support Clare. Morell was played by Paul McGrath, who had starred opposite Gertrude Lawrence on Broadway, Marchbanks by the movie actor Dean Harens, and Prossy by Brenda Forbes, who had once appeared with Katharine Cornell. Connecting the production to Clare's best play was the director Robert Ross, who was married to Margalo Gillmore, originator of the role of Mary Haines in The Women.

Five days before opening night, the company arrived for a partial rehearsal at the Strand and was encouraged to hear of a great demand for tickets. Electricians were already putting up marquee lights as Clare stepped onto the stage in gray slacks and a shirt, her hair combed back in pompadour fashion, with a blue ribbon tucked in over tight ringlets.

At forty-two, she was nine years older than Shaw's heroine, but her scarcely lined face and lithe deportment enabled her to look the part.[30]

▽

On Monday, August 6, a stylist arrived at 11:00 A.M. to fix Clare's hair for opening night. At that precise moment, as heavy rain and high winds thrashed against the windows of Rockefeller Center, an AP flash came in to John Billings's office. A United States Air Force B-29 had dropped the unheard-of "atomic bomb" from thirty-nine thousand feet on the Japanese city of Hiroshima. Set to explode at two thousand feet, the weapon had created a mushroom-shaped blast that had devastated everything below across an area of four square miles.[31]

In spite of the appalling news, Billings managed to approve a *Time* item on Congresswoman Luce's new venture, while at the Strand Theatre the *Candida* cast went ahead with a final three-hour afternoon rehearsal.[32] Ross had allowed Clare to choose her own costumes. For the first two acts, she picked a green taffeta traveling dress with a tight bodice, leg-o'-mutton sleeves, and a full skirt. Her third act selection was an ice-blue crepe satin gown with a net jabot.

The rehearsal was followed by a two-hour rest at the nearby Roger Smith Hotel. Rain was still cascading down as the company returned to the theater to make up and get back into costume. Already the lobby entrance was mobbed with a mix of local patrons and New Yorkers, some in black tie and floor-length gowns, others in raincoats and galoshes. Flashbulbs popped. Bobby-soxers looking for autographs clustered around celebrities: the musical performer Mary Martin, the movie stars Jean Arthur, Margaret Sullavan, and Fredric March, the producers Lee Shubert, Gilbert Miller, and Max Gordon, the director/playwright Moss Hart, the superagent Leland Hayward, Governor Raymond Baldwin of Connecticut, House minority leader Joe Martin, Brigadier General Elliott Roosevelt, Clare's ever-faithful Bernard Baruch, and Henry Luce.[33]

A group of political protesters added to the premiere's publicity by mingling with the crowd and trying unsuccessfully to distribute pamphlets critical of Henry Luce, his magazines, and his wife. "Stop playing, Clare," they shouted. "These are serious times."[34]

By 8:40 P.M., all thirteen hundred seats in the narrow auditorium were occupied, and the late curtain rose to a recording of "The Star-Spangled Banner." It was underamplified to the point of being barely audible, which was just as well, as the words *bombs bursting in air* suddenly seemed inappropriate. Clare could not complain about the dialogue Shaw had written to prepare for her entrance fifteen minutes into the first act, a glowing speech by Morell touting his wife's virtues and a jealous outburst from Prossy: "Candida here, and Candida there, and Candida everywhere! It's enough to drive anyone out of their senses to

Clare as Candida, August 1945

hear a woman raved about . . . merely because she's got good hair and a tolerable figure."

When Clare at last appeared, clad in her green dress and a black chapeau trimmed with feathers, an outburst of applause stopped further action for almost a minute. She showed no signs of nervousness and managed to speak her first lines in a firm voice, while struggling without success to find a pin anchoring her headgear. It had to stay in place until the scene's end.[35] This made it difficult for her to display what Shaw prescribed as Candida's characteristic expression, "an amused maternal indulgence." But even with the hat off, as the play proceeded, Clare failed to persuade the acerbic *New Yorker* critic Wolcott Gibbs that she could convey any side of her stage personality at all.

"She moved," he wrote afterward, "somehow as if she were on wires, like a marionette, as if at any moment she might sail up and away into the flies. Her delivery was tranquil and monotonous, the lines clear but not seeming to mean anything in particular." Gibbs admitted that Clare looked beautiful, was "letter-perfect," and so composed that she was able to glance sharply at Paul McGrath when he fumbled a line. But all in all, Representative Luce was seriously miscast, and he advised that in future "her country's call must always take first place."[36]

Clare needed all her aplomb to get through to the end, because Dean Arens did his best to upstage her, going so far as to wave a fire poker during one of her speeches.[37] The final applause was, in the words of a *Variety* reporter, "distinctly mild."[38]

▽

George Frazier, who had the unenviable task of reviewing the production for *Life*, was one of the throng of critics awaiting the midnight train back to New York. He stood next to Jean Meegan of the Associated Press. She looked around the crowded platform and said, "Never have so many traveled so far for so little."[39]

Preparing his notice, Frazier wondered how to be tactful "about a performance as dreadful as Mrs. Luce's."[40] Billings tried to make it easier for him. "Clare wasn't very good, and *Life* isn't going to say she was." Frazier's solution was to quote as many other negative notices as possible, but the editor balked. "Good *God*. After all, Clare's the boss's wife!"

Billings suggested Frazier just report only that seasoned critics had found Mrs. Luce's performance lacking in credibility. At the same time, *Life* would print high-quality photographs of scenes from the play and audience, to give the impression that the evening's "glitter" was comparable to that of many a Broadway first night.[41] At the bottom of the piece, he gave Clare space to exonerate herself.

"It took me a little while to get over the first stage fright," she wrote. "But I had a lot of fun." Any playwright could benefit from such an experience. But there was a touch of wounded pride in her subsequent announcement that "despite heavy demand for tickets," she did not want a longer run.[42]

Her performances—another of which coincided with the August 9 dropping of a second A-bomb, this time on the town of Nagasaki— improved with repetition, and she never flubbed a line.[43] Loyal friends came and dined with her afterward. They included Joseph and John F. Kennedy, Madame Chiang Kai-shek, Buff Cobb Rogers, Mark Sullivan, some of the Luce family, and Gypsy Rose Lee, who said that Clare had done better by Shaw than his limited play had done by her.

The leading lady herself boasted, "We played to the very end to standing room only!" But by then the critics had had their say.[44]

▽

On Sunday, August 12, the day after *Candida* closed, John Billings sat close to his home radio, waiting to hear Japan's response to Allied calls for surrender. He was interrupted by a telephone call from his boss, who wanted to know if he had "checked" the text of Frazier's article. Billings said he had, whereupon Harry angrily wondered why the reviewers hadn't given Clare a break as an amateur. "What do they think she is— an actress?"[45]

That night at 7:00 P.M., President Truman announced that the Japanese had surrendered unconditionally.[46]

16

BLACK HOUR

The mind is its own place, and in itself
Can make a Heaven of Hell, a Hell of Heaven.

—JOHN MILTON

The specter of civilization blotting itself out compounded Clare's dis-enchantment with public life. She had been furious over Truman's concessions to Stalin vis-à-vis the Poles at Potsdam, but these paled in light of reports from Japan that survivors of the atomic blasts were found to be suffering from exposure to massive amounts of radiation that winds might carry to other shores. This poisoning of the earth was further cause for her hopelessness.

Since the military committee Clare served on would be less rele-vant in peacetime, she was unlikely, as a junior member of the House minority, to influence a Democratic administration emboldened by its cache of nuclear weaponry—to use an adjective that had only just en-tered everyday speech. No matter how soaring her oratory, or far-seeing her essays on rebuilding countries in upheaval, her views were unlikely to impress the White House.[1]

In addition to her new sense of political irrelevance, compounded by the savage critiques of her *Candida* performance, was fear that her creative gifts had atrophied. She no longer felt able to write satirical and mordantly witty plays. Personal voids, too, proliferated in her life. She had no children, few close friends, and no religious faith. During

her most ambitious years in the 1930s, Clare had often been accused of
selfishness. Seeing this as a "cancer of the soul," she had grown moody,
fickle, and distracted.[2] Now she felt adrift in her marriage and bereft of
her relationships with Truscott, Willoughby, and Stecker, forcing her
one bleak night in mid-September to admit that her life was closing
down.

▽

Alone in her Waldorf apartment, at a "black hour" sometime after midnight, Clare could no longer tolerate her feelings of emptiness and insecurity. Confronting these twin demons, she searched for clues in her
past and recalled her mother's constant plaint, "I live in my children."[3]
This was not an option for her with Ann gone. Nor did she see, amid
myriad dogmas and doctrines, any that enlightened her. She mistrusted
all religious and scientific orthodoxies. Of the many left-leaning reporters, novelists, publishers, producers, directors, and actors she knew, few
believed in God. The patron saint of this liberal elite was Sigmund
Freud. They naively believed that through psychoanalysis, "the individual could achieve health, wealth, wisdom and of course popularity,
by hauling away at his subconscious bootstraps."[4]

After divorcing George Brokaw, she had undergone a few sessions
of therapy with a Viennese analyst. He had diagnosed that she had a
father complex, saying that the motivating force for all her ambitions
was that she "wanted to be 'masculine' in order to spite Papa." The jargon of the couch had irritated her. Instead of using such simple words as
sin, lust, hate, and *laziness* to acknowledge that most failings were moral,
the doctor had spoken pseudoscientifically of *inhibition, libido, superego,*
and *id.* She had decided he was a "soul quack" and walked out on him.[5]

Her subsequent remedy for psychological problems had been to pursue a career packed with incident. But now, her professional achievements seemed of slight import, in a bloody and violent universe. She
was tormented by visions of catastrophes she had witnessed: the German bombing of Brussels in May 1940, the Japanese air attacks on
Chungking, the horrific sight of dead babies "bobbing like apples" in a
Mandalay moat, the head of an old Englishwoman protruding from a
pile of V-2 wreckage, row after row of mutilated soldiers in Italy, the
gruesome lime pits of Nordhausen, and skeletal figures wandering dazed
and aimless about Buchenwald.

She also brooded on the prewar suicides of four talented friends: the
beautiful actresses Rosamond Pinchot and Dorothy Hale, the artist

Ralph Barton, and her lover and editor at *Vanity Fair*, Donald Freeman. All had sought solace in work and sex, until they realized that happiness was elusive. Before each death, Clare had noticed a desperate "smouldering in their eyes." That look haunted her now that she herself was challenged by the enigma of existence. If she failed to cast off the pall of meaninglessness that enshrouded her, might she, too, be on a path to extinction? Echoing the anguish of Charles Ryder in Evelyn Waugh's new novel, *Brideshead Revisited,* she deemed herself to be "unloved, unlovable and unloving." This brought her to a spiritual nadir. She felt "a vast sour tide" sweep over her, leaving her stranded.[6]

▽

As the night wore on, Clare continued her search for existential answers. She circled the room, picking things up and laying them down in a panic of tearful indecision. She thought of the "isms" she had studied in her search for a pertinent creed—Capitalism, Socialism, Communism, Freudianism, Isolationism, Interventionism. Not one had sufficed. Terrified she might be going mad, she knelt and recited the Lord's Prayer. The familiar words, which she had seldom uttered in the long period of desolation following her daughter's death, consoled her somewhat. She resumed pacing, then stopped at the sight of an unopened letter.

It was from Father Edward Wiatrak, a Jesuit priest who a few years earlier had been impressed by an article she had written about war orphans and had become an intermittent correspondent.[7] He had never tried to convert her to his faith or asked a favor of any kind. He merely expressed concern for the state of her soul and gave the impression that God was waiting to do *her* a favor.

When she read the letter, it spoke directly to her current confusion. Wiatrak asked if she was familiar with the passage in the *Confessions* of Augustine that described the saint's spiritual crisis in a Milanese garden at the age of thirty-two. Apparently, he had despaired over his own and the world's "vileness." Clare knew nothing of Augustine's anguish, nor of his youthful reputation as a libertine, but she was experiencing such extreme torment herself—what Wiatrak called *cruciatus miserabile,* the agony of the cross—that she dialed the number of the New York mission where he lived.

Somebody who picked up the phone offered in a sleepy voice to rouse him. As the sound of footsteps impacting on a bare floor grew louder, she realized that it was two o'clock in the morning and was about to hang up when Wiatrak came on the line. She blurted out, "Father, I am not in trouble, but my mind is in trouble."

"We know," the priest replied, using the plural pronoun affected by Catholic clergy. "This is the call we have been praying for." However, he said, he was too simple a cleric for her. "You think you have intellectual difficulties. They are spiritual, of course." The man to deal with her malaise was Monsignor Fulton J. Sheen, who lived in Washington. "No doubt you have heard him on the radio. I will make an appointment for you."[8]

17

CONVERSION

The powers of the soul are commensurate with its needs.

—RALPH WALDO EMERSON

Clare had not heard the radio programs that gained Monsignor Sheen his reputation as an erudite, persuasive, and witty preacher. Nor did she know his academic credentials: a PhD in philosophy from Belgium's University of Louvain, a professorship in theology at St. Edmund's College in Britain, and currently the same position at Washington's Catholic University. He had published such books as *God and Intelligence in Modern Philosophy*, *The Divine Romance*, and *Victory over Vice*, but it was his pioneer broadcast, *The Catholic Hour*—soon to have four million regular listeners—that prompted the thousands of letters he received daily. In 1940, Sheen had conducted the first religious service ever to be telecast, and the following year narrated a documentary for Henry Luce's newsreel *The March of Time*, entitled "The Story of the Vatican." Soon he would achieve even greater renown with a network television series, *Life Is Worth Living*.

On hearing that Congresswoman Clare Boothe Luce was in extremis, he telephoned and invited her to dinner.

Monsignor Fulton J. Sheen, c. 1946

Clare had never dined with a priest, let alone a monsignor, and was not sure what to expect. As it turned out, she was agreeably surprised. The fifty-year-old Sheen and two other clerics shared a large, white brick house, with an impressive curved staircase, two studies, white lacquer furniture, and a private chapel.[1] The first glimpse she had of her host was of a slender man of medium height, moving lithely toward her in an immaculate cassock and cummerbund. He had prominent blue eyes that glowed beneath thick eyebrows, and his long upper lip accentuated a warm smile.[2] Sheen was "lace curtain" Irish out of Illinois farm country, but she got the impression that he was as comfortable in sophisticated society as in a pulpit. He loved creature comforts and dressed well on the grounds that "the ambassador of Christ should always present himself as a gentleman."[3]

After a few pleasantries, Sheen said that they would not discuss religion at the dining table. Instead, he launched into secular topics that demonstrated the depth and speed of his mind. He made graceful gestures as he spoke in a melodious baritone with a faint burr. An eight-thousand-book library embellished his formidable intellect, and he quoted readily from Roman poets, Thomas Aquinas, H. G. Wells, G. K. Chesterton, C. S. Lewis, and Anatole France.

After dinner, Sheen ushered Clare into his study and they sat down facing each other. "Do you know about the philosophy of Yin and Yang?" she asked.

"Oh, yes," he replied, and explained it as the Chinese perception of the dual nature of things.

Sensing that she was trying to intimidate him, and that she liked to hold the floor, the Monsignor laid ground rules for their discussion.[4] He would speak for five minutes about God, and she would have an hour to state her views. But when, after about three minutes, he mentioned the goodness of God, Clare bounded out of her chair and shook her finger under his nose.

"If God is good, why did he take my daughter?"

Sheen tolerated the interruption. "Perhaps it was in order that you might believe. Maybe your daughter is buying your faith with her life."[5]

Reflecting on the moment later, Sheen felt that it was a turning point in her quest for religious enlightenment. She was clearly a candidate for conversion. In her heart, Clare realized this, too, and saw that he would be the ideal catechist for her. Yet she was loath to commit at once to an intellectually taxing process that would challenge all her preconceived ideas about God and morality, and also require many months of instruction and study. Her hesitancy was fine with Sheen. "We do not allow a leap of faith," he said. "Before everything else there must be conviction."[6]

▽

Visiting Roman Catholic cathedrals in Europe before and after her first marriage, Clare had felt no compunction to take part in the rituals. She aesthetically admired monumental architecture and sculpture, craftsmanship in stained-glass windows, lavish flower arrangements, and sonorous organ recitals. Only when witnessing the sacrament of the Mass had the playwright in her responded to its theatricality—the ceremonial robes, the clouds of incense, the ancient liturgy, the symbolism of wafer and wine. At the same time she had felt "an ineffable peace, that was also a Divine uneasiness. I had taken great art for the Great Artist."[7]

During World War II, Clare had occasionally dropped into New York's St. Patrick's Cathedral, and in the gloom her eyes had sought something "that hung like drapes of black over the dull golden glow of the high baldachin." This was the altar canopy, acting as a kind of shroud for the host at Communion, and for some reason it fascinated her.[8] Then had come that Christmas of 1944, when in Italy's Futa Pass she had seen the congregation of soldiers at Mass, kneeling in deep snow. She thought often and with envy of the simple devotion of those worshippers and regretted her own religious vacuum.[9]

Chronic guilt also plagued her. "I feel crumby every night of my life. It comes of falling short of my own ideal of conduct."[10] The prospect of her own death and whether she would merit an afterlife were other arguments for her to accept Sheen's instruction, as was a desire to honor her marriage vows and "stick by Harry."[11] But ultimately she acknowledged that the chief reason was "to rid myself of my burden of sin."[12]

Maisie Ward, a Roman Catholic writer and publisher, described Clare's spiritual state at this time as exemplifying "the sharp cry of hunger when a diet of stones is set upon the table."[13]

▽

When Clare told Isabel Hill of her encounter with Sheen, the secretary was vehemently against the idea of her becoming a Roman Catholic.[14] Most Americans at the time were similarly biased, unaware that the Anglican Creed included the line "I believe in the Holy Catholic Church." Buff Cobb, her classmate from St. Mary's Episcopal School in Garden City, remembered that Clare had been confirmed there in her early teens and also disapproved of the change. She came all the way down from New York to protest.[15] Expecting equally strong objections from Harry, Clare postponed telling him until he returned from yet another trip to China.[16]

Al Morano was puzzled when Clare invited him to supper at her apartment and in a tentative voice asked him, "How would you like to go with me to Mass tomorrow?"[17]

By late September, Clare had committed to taking instruction from Sheen. His teaching tool was the Catechism, an interrogatory method established in the sixteenth century, whose chief purpose was to instill the two fundamentals of religious practice: faith and morals. She was also required to learn by heart statements of faith in the Apostolic Creed, of hope in the Lord's Prayer, and of ethics in the Ten Commandments. As "homework," Sheen recommended studying the New Testament, especially the 36,450 words of Christ.

This assignment coincided with the arrival on Clare's desk of a mound of briefing documents about atomic weaponry. Reading them, she saw the prospect of global obliteration. Religion was already impinging on her political thought, so her first reaction was to conclude that mankind's ultimate hope of controlling the bomb was to obey "the law of our Lord, to love one another as He loved us."[18] But the realist, not to say the pessimist, in her impelled her to push in the House for legislation to create a nuclear arms control agency.[19]

On November 14, Representative Luce presented a concurrent resolution, HR 101, proposing that Congress create appropriate machinery, within the framework of the United Nations, "for international control and reduction of armaments and weapons, especially those involving atomic power."[20]

▽

A problem for Clare was when and how to tell Harry of her religious plans. When he came back from China, he was in an especially good mood, having been the only foreigner present at a dinner in Chungking for Mao Tse-tung, the denim-clad chairman of the burgeoning Communist Party.[21] That her husband had been invited to such a momentous event reminded Clare of how much clout he had, and that the international journalism he financed had more resonance in the world than anything she did, in or out of politics.[22]

As the autumn days shortened, both Luces craved sunshine, so they accepted an invitation from Bernard Baruch to spend Thanksgiving at Hobcaw Barony. The seventy-five-year-old financier still adored Clare. He marveled at the enduring beauty of her face, her Venus-like figure, her braininess, and caught himself beaming with pride. "If I were only sixty again I would swoop down on you and bear you away. Harry better keep a sharp look out or some gallant knight will snatch you."[23]

The Hobcaw estate was refreshingly peaceful, with no telephones and everybody in bed by ten o'clock. Harry shot quail and slept a lot,

Bernard Baruch shooting at Hobcaw Barony

while Clare read and did congressional paperwork. On November 26, they visited nearby Mepkin, where they were met by their decorator friend Gladys Freeman. She agreed that the neglected plantation badly needed refurbishing, yet remained "the prettiest place in the Southland."[24]

That evening, Clare at last told Harry of her pending conversion. He was speechless. All his entrenched Presbyterian hostility to the Church of Rome surfaced. He was chagrined at not having been informed sooner, and went onto the terrace to unburden himself on Gladys.

"Why didn't she talk to me? Why did she go off and do this?"[25]

▽

Her husband's disapproval notwithstanding, Clare resumed Catechism sessions with Sheen. Some lasted as long as three or four hours. She concluded that no matter how heavy her workload on the Hill, or how fraught her home life, soul-searching was more arduous and often more painful than either. To weigh the claims of comparative religions was purely an intellectual exercise and not difficult for her. But reconciling the history of an ancient church that she felt "had not always been marked by sanctity or unmarked by violence, prejudice and scandal" with its present calls for love and charity was a challenge. The most intractable question she asked herself was, "Can the existence of God be proved?" Gradually, she realized that no priest—even Sheen—had answers to all her doubts. He could only prepare her for conversion "as a farmer prepares soil for seeds."[26]

Digging up old beliefs for close inspection proved as demanding as her attempt to open like a bud to new ones. Another problem was accepting the divinity of Christ. If He was divine and eternally alive, why did He not perform miracles, so badly needed in a war-torn world? Sheen convinced her that God did use His power daily in man's interest. The Sacraments were another enigma, even if she agreed that a degree of imagination was necessary to accept transubstantiation in the Eucharist. She took the priest's word that to ingest the Body and Blood of Christ at Communion was to purify "the secret places of the heart."[27]

As their dialogue continued, Sheen marveled at Clare's mastery of *sorites*, the Greek use of logic in extended argument, leading by polysyllogism to an inescapable conclusion. "Clare," he said long afterward, "used *sorites* better than any other person I ever met."[28] At the same time, he marveled at her intuitiveness. "It has something to do with light. . . . She is scintillating. Her mind is like a rapier. It bursts foibles in a second. . . . She sees things all at once. It would take a man six or seven steps to arrive at the same conclusion."[29]

He also delighted in her humor. One day his St. Bernard jumped on her. Pushing the dog off, she said, "You remind me of someone. Who is it? Oh I know—my first husband."[30]

They talked one night about Hell. Clare sat on the floor and said she could not accept it. For the next hour, she argued that the mercy of God preempted such punishment. How could it be worse than the hell she had passed through on earth, after losing Ann?

"Only those who walk in darkness," Sheen said, "ever see the stars."[31]

He took equal time to argue the reason and logic of Hell, so persuasively that at last she leaped up and threw her arms in the air. "Oh God, what a protagonist You have in this man!"[32]

The Monsignor's apostolic zeal astonished her. Like an instrument conveying "the sudden and unfamiliar sight of Truth and Love and Life eternal," he was also "at once so patient and so unyielding, so poetic and so practical, so inventive and so orthodox."[33]

Between sessions with her catechist, Clare read books by scientists, philosophers, and historians, seldom finding that their authors could accept the Divinity of Jesus. Yet they often told readers to hold on to Christian principles and virtues, while doing away with religious belief and practice. In her view, these thinkers might just as well advocate keeping "our streets and houses well lighted, but do away with power plants."[34]

▽

The new year of 1946 presented Clare with the prospect of a visit to Washington by General Willoughby. He was now stationed in Tokyo's Imperial Hotel, having gone from one shattered capital—Manila—to another, in order to help MacArthur begin the process of bringing democracy to Japan. A priority for the Supreme Commander was to oversee the prosecution of local war criminals. To assist him in this, he had made Willoughby his chief of counterintelligence, investigating some ninety-five thousand Japanese repatriates from Russian POW camps. The suspicion was that they might have been indoctrinated by the Soviets, in order to form the nucleus of a Communist Party in Japan.[35]

Willoughby's decision to remain in Asia had not sat well with Clare. On January 5, she wrote him to convey her feeling that their long-thwarted romance would not survive the peace. "So long as the battle was on, I had faith and patience. I no longer have either, for I think that what you do where you are is more clear and fruitful . . . than what you might be doing if you left." She was deliberately vague about her own future. "I have begun to write new dramas of my own, and cannot indefinitely wait for leading men who are playing run-of-the-mill contracts elsewhere."[36]

Her warning was in vain, since Charles was already on his way. In a letter that crossed hers, he said that he planned an extensive stay. After tending to business at the Pentagon, "I shall be free to wait on you. . . . There is so much to tell, so much to do."[37]

Visiting Mepkin on the second anniversary of Ann's death, Clare at last had the revelation for which the Catechism had prepared her. She described it as the "Coming of Faith," a melting of the heart into love for God, elusive yet unmistakable as the moment when dawn breaks or ice thaws. She still had questions to ask Sheen. But this was undoubtedly an epiphany, forced upon her by the totality of her experience. "It finally took two world wars," she wrote in an account of her conversion, "the overthrow of several dozen thrones and governments, the Russian revolution, the swift collapse, in our own time, of hundreds of thought-systems, a small number of which collapsed on me, the death of millions, as well as the death of my daughter, before I was willing to take a look at this extraordinary institution, the Catholic church."[38]

She was back in Washington by January 14 for the opening of the 79th Congress. Determined to stamp her ideas on it immediately, she introduced a resolution calling for research into profit sharing as a tool for American businesses, and for complementary legislation to give workers "the security of a vested interest in their corporate places of employment."[39] Once again, she revealed herself to be more left-of-center than most of her Republican colleagues.

A week later, it was reported that Willoughby had reached San Francisco. Clare's office promptly announced that the Congresswoman had influenza and was recuperating in Florida. To avoid publicity, she stayed at a friend's house in Hobe Sound.[40] This enabled her to invite two guests to stay with her separately, Father Sheen and Willoughby.

She received the Monsignor first, apologizing for having asked him to make the long trip. It was a characteristic of hers to want people to make inconvenient gestures on her behalf. One day she took him for a long walk on the beach. Sheen wore his black cassock, which struck Clare as comical in the bright sun and warm breeze. They spoke at length of God and the universe. Clare recalled her girlhood in Old Greenwich, where she had courted danger by swimming out far into Long Island Sound, as if to defy the sea's immensity. These forays had made her aware of her own insignificance, futility, and finiteness. Sheen countered by picking up some of the shells abundant on that stretch of sand, pointing out the microscopic intricacies of their shapes, sizes, and patterns.

After he left, she wrote asking him to choose an especially human saint to look out for her, one not too good or too clever. "What about this St. Helena you spoke about today? I rather liked the vigorous way she set about building churches."[41]

▽

As if Willoughby's pending arrival were not distraction enough, Clare now received a letter from Ray Stecker, to whom she had recommended a study of Catholic doctrine. Ardent as ever, he wrote that he missed her "like the devil" and loved her "as I will never love again." He was annoyed that she never made promised phone calls.

> If you think I love you as I do because you beat your gums, get your picture in the paper, can write plays, save the nation, do all these things better than anyone else, then lambchop you have been reading your press clippings too frequently. And if I were to treat you any differently our marriage (if it ever happened) would not last a year. . . . Once and for all, you are just a woman to me and once in bed, at home, and by ourselves, your accomplishments won't get you by, only your ability to be a woman, and my darling you are not superior at that.

He confessed that he could not figure out what she wanted from life. As far as he could gather, her current alternatives were:

A. You are going to get out of politics.
B. You are going to live in your house by the river.
C. You are going to divorce Harry.
D. You are going to marry me.
E. You are going to become religious.

Stecker thought she would do A, B, and E, while C and D were only remote possibilities.[42]

Her reunion with Charles turned out to be heart-wrenching for him. Straining to be poetic afterward, he wrote of an intimate evening "in the restless flicker of the hearth fire" as a descent into "the valley of shadows," because it lacked consummation. He recalled a maddening glimpse of her "lovely body, iridescent, ivory-like—gleaming in a half-light," and the feeling of something warm draped about him "like the mantle of the Madonna." Her perfume lingered in memory, as did the profile of her "pale, noble face, the face of a saint delineated as thru a transparent veil."[43]

Clare could be inaccessible emotionally as well as physically and was especially preoccupied at the moment. Charles tried to be sympathetic and supportive, but felt excluded and told her he was baffled and hurt by her immersion in matters of faith and doctrine. Everything now seemed "so far removed from the time when we were lovers." [44] He was so wretchedly frustrated at one point that he crouched before her, while she laid a sympathetic hand on his head.[45]

▽

After a few more emotionally turbulent days, Charles went north to stay with friends in Bronxville, and Clare headed for Washington. While she was in transit, her office released a bombshell statement, datelined January 30:

> I feel I must make it quite plain and definite to the people of Fairfield County, Connecticut, that I do not intend to be a candidate for reelection in 1946.
>
> My good and sufficient reasons for this will become abundantly clear in time.

Some commentators took the "will become abundantly clear" phrase to be an arch reference to pregnancy.[46] Others guessed the Congresswoman was quitting out of disappointment. The Kansas *Emporia Gazette* stated unequivocally that "boredom and a sense of frustration" had overtaken her in the House.[47] A rumor circulated that Mrs. Luce wanted Senator Thomas C. Hart's Connecticut seat.[48]

▽

Clare decided she would be ready for her still-secret conversion ceremony in New York by the first week of Lent. On Sunday, February 10, she flew to Johnson City, Tennessee, where she was due to deliver a speech at a dinner in honor of Lincoln's Day. Her views on race relations had so startled fellow Republicans at a similar dinner in Washington that some of them had walked out on her. "As Christians," she said, "we know that there are no such things as 'Negro rights' or 'white rights.' There are only human rights."[49]

Upon arrival, Clare learned that Walter Winchell had heard about her religious intent and was about to broadcast the news on his ABC radio show. She urgently telephoned him to ask if he would drop the report, since it would make it doubly difficult for her, in the anti-Catholic South, to attack the Truman administration's race policies. Winchell reluctantly consented, if only because Clare had occasionally substituted for him in his newspaper column.[50]

Before leaving Johnson City on Tuesday, she was confronted by, of all people, her husband. He was en route to a two-week tour of California, coincidentally timed to absent him from New York on the day she was to be received into the Church of Rome. Clare sensed he wanted to tell her something, but for whatever reason he changed his mind.

Puzzled, but used to Harry's mysterious spells of reticence, she returned East to meet up with Willoughby in the capital. They had no more than three days together before she must go to New York and he return to Tokyo. For him, at least, those final hours turned out to be so disillusioning that he left his bed at the Wardman Park Hotel to write an anguished letter to Clare headlined simply "In the night."

First, he recalled his last "glorious visit" to the West Coast in 1943 and the understanding they had achieved there, after which he had considered her his "wife, and friend and confidante." He said he sympathized with her struggle for peace of mind, believing she would attain it, and that Father Sheen would approve of him. But as a man deeply in love, he wanted her to know that she was making him suffer the "torture of humiliation," which could not be assuaged until he possessed her again.

> That is why I have been insistent. To stop this corrosive poison that is planted in my mind. To restore my self confidence that has been shattered. You chide me of little faith? You have dealt me a mortal blow, that will emasculate me forever—except that it is in your power to restore to me my pride, my confidence and my hope.

He needed to recapture the talisman that during their separations had protected him from temptation and forgetfulness. "Do not let me

Clare and General Willoughby
with Japanese mementos, January 1946

go, I implore you, without this solace and this strength, so that I can carry with me, once more, the golden image that has kept us together so long."[51]

Willoughby left partially satisfied, since his notes written en route to Japan were affectionate and optimistic. But once he reached Tokyo, he found Clare's cold letter of January 5. He returned it with a scribble on the back, asking if it was "an adieu."

For her it was certainly a rite of passage. Charles's visit and her change of faith had complicated her life to such an extent that she finally grasped what G. K. Chesterton meant when he wrote that "the process of conversion involves turning yourself inside out."[52]

Completing that scrutiny had taken almost five months of intense discussion and argument. Summing up her Catechism, Clare concluded that Sheen had presented the whole body of Catholic doctrine to her "in a form that [had] the solidity of a pyramid, the progression of a symphony, and the inevitability of a mathematical equation."[53]

For the Monsignor, it was the longest period of instruction he ever undertook.[54] He gave his student and God the credit. "No man could go to Clare and argue her into the faith. Heaven had to knock her over."[55] Only those who had witnessed the transformation could "realize the depth of her, the spectacular sublimity of her motivation."[56]

Sheen was willing to perform her conversion service, but not to serve as her confessor afterward. When he offered to find her one, she self-mockingly asked him to choose "someone who has seen the rise and fall of empires."[57]

On the afternoon of Saturday, February 16, 1946, Clare Boothe Luce entered St. Patrick's Cathedral in New York City to be received into the Roman Catholic Church. Since Harry had conspicuously absented himself in California, only a handful of friends and a lone reporter witnessed Father Sheen perform the rites of Conversion and Baptism, in an otherwise deserted side chapel.

18

OTHER ARENAS

No one ever has enough power. Power will not overcome one's
inferiority. . . . Power increases the person's narcissism
and reinforces the underlying insecurity.

—ALEXANDER LOWEN

The conversion of Congresswoman Luce was front-page news in newspapers across the country. She had issued a formal statement, saying she had wanted for some time to become a Roman Catholic. But cynics had tried to inject her choice into a state campaign, even though tolerant people of all faiths surely did not want religion to obscure important political issues. "Therefore, I have chosen to be unavailable by design or draft for elective office."[1]

This did not stop further speculation that she wanted to succeed Senator Hart, an appointee incumbent who had no desire to run for election. A *New York Journal-American* columnist went further. Commenting on press predictions of a woman president by 1952, he said his bet was on Clare Boothe Luce.[2]

Tere Pascone, the *Bridgeport Post* reporter who had been at St. Patrick's, might place the same wager. The more she saw of Clare the politician, the more impressed she became. After spending Saturday night at the Luces' Waldorf apartment, she became infatuated with the private woman, too. Next morning, on her way to Clare's Confirmation and First Communion services at the cathedral, she met Father Sheen in the elevator. He assumed that she knew some of the reasons for her friend's

163

conversion and added one of his own: "Great people have great problems and they need the Divine."[3]

During Mass in the Archbishop's Chapel, the communicant knelt on a velvet prie-dieu to receive the host from Bishop Francis McIntyre. Pascone thought she looked thin and forlorn, yet had a profile "as beautiful as a saint."[4]

Sheen marked the ceremonies with a gift to his most brilliant convert. "I am more proud of you than any child I ever begot in Christ. I thank God daily that He used me as His poor instrument."[5] A framed photograph of himself carried the inscription "To my darling Clare, an arrow shot from the bow of God." She placed it on her bedside table.[6] In return, she commissioned an oil portrait of Sheen by Gerald Brockhurst, who had once painted her. It showed the Monsignor seated against a Lourdes background, dressed in clerical garb, his hair perfectly groomed and his piercing eyes looking straight ahead.[7]

After the momentous events of the weekend, Clare felt a step nearer to the spiritual state of Saint Augustine when he wrote: "God created us for Himself, and our hearts will always be restless until they rest in Him."[8]

While Clare had been on her knees making her Catholic vows, Harry was on his at the Beverly Hills bedside of his mistress, the theatrical agent and producer Jean Dalrymple.

For the past three years, he had managed to keep their relationship—which Jean would always insist was platonic—a secret from his wife and from the eagle-eyed gossips at Time Inc.[9] One night in 1943, Harry had gone alone to a party given by the journalist Elsa Maxwell and had met Jean, a blond, hazel-eyed, amply bosomed divorcée about six months older than Clare. She claimed to have discovered both James Cagney and Cary Grant in vaudeville. Now she represented the opera singer Grace Moore and the pianist José Iturbi, who was also her lover. Professionally and sexually content, with homes in both New York and Los Angeles, Jean had not encouraged Harry's first attempts to woo her. One reason was she had known and admired Clare since the early 1930s and retained a lasting memory of the managing editor of *Vanity Fair* at a Condé Nast penthouse party, wearing white and carrying a white rose. Only when a copy of Clare's autobiographical first play, *Abide With Me*, came her way had Jean been horrified "that anybody would expose her tawdry life to the world that way."[10]

Jean Dalrymple, c. 1947

All these years later, she found herself in danger of involvement in a melodrama of her own. But Harry's power and intellect fascinated her, and she had gotten into the habit of wining and dining with him—sometimes in his apartment when Clare was out of town—and even tolerated his occasional attempts at a pass. His intensity and palpable loneliness intrigued her. She was also touched by his clumsy compliments ("If Betty Grable is the legs, you're the mind") as they slowly attained an intimacy just short of total commitment. Harry had gone so far as to install Jean in a house not far from the Waldorf.[11]

His current posture before her was one not of supplication but of necessity, because she was flat on her back with influenza. She had been reluctant to see him, but he insisted, wanting to tell her about Clare's conversion. "Now I can ask you to marry me," he said.

Jean shook her head and burst into tears. "You never will."

More concerned about Clare's emotional fragility than Harry appeared to be, she warned of dire consequences if he asked for a divorce. "If she loses you, she loses everything. She'll never, never, never give you up."[12]

Still smarting over his wife's second life-changing move in little over two weeks, Harry called John Billings to say brusquely that he did not want to know the content of any "Clare-Catholic" item in *Time*. Billings's own reaction to her conversion was more colorful. "Fantastic! Yet logical for a half-crazy woman who must always be doing the bizarre to attract notice."[13]

The disapproval of both men paled in comparison with that of Harry's mother. As the widow of a Protestant missionary, and part of a team that had competed vigorously with the Roman Church for Chinese souls, Mrs. Henry Winters Luce frowned on her daughter-in-law's defection. In a note to Clare signed, "All my love, Mother," she wrote, "The glorious Faith . . . which generations of my forebears have lived and died by, is of such surpassing worth that I am filled with wonder and sadness that anyone should deliberately exchange it for another."[14]

Caustic remarks from skeptics who knew Clare were plentiful. Brock Pemberton, the Broadway producer of *Kiss the Boys Goodbye*, worried that Clare's preoccupation with religion would hinder her creativity. "There's a brilliant woman, and all she does is run around proselytizing people!"[15]

Jack Kennedy said to her, "You're still young, my God. Why strap the cross on your back? I never thought that the Catholic religion made much sense for anyone with brains."[16]

Martha Gellhorn, the veteran reporter, was appalled and saddened to hear of Clare's capitulation to "Mother Church." She predicted that politically, it would steer a minor, fairly liberal player in the House toward the "dangerous machine" of the Far Right. Psychologically, Gellhorn felt that the move signified deep unhappiness. If Clare had embraced "that consolation, that shutting of the eyes and cowardice of the mind, and means really to renounce all else, then I am terribly sorry for her. Life must have been too much . . . having worked so hard and singlemindedly to be given the apple, [she] found it tasted sour and had a worm."[17]

The screenwriter Lamar Trotti took Clare to a party and was irritated by the way she dropped the names of monsignors, archbishops, cardinals, and even the Pope. "I got the impression that she's not so much joined the church as affiliated with the hierarchy."[18]

Helen Lawrenson, too, scoffed at Clare's top-of-the-ladder approach to religion, noting how quickly she ingratiated herself with Cardinal Francis J. Spellman of New York. She was amused to see Clare wearing a floor-length crimson cape, and hanging a glittering crucifix over her bed. "My first impression was that it was covered with sequins but I must have been mistaken."

When Clare invited Helen and her husband, Jack, a left-wing union official, to dinner, they were disappointed to find her with Fulton Sheen instead of Harry. The Monsignor tried his best to recruit the couple for instruction but failed, not least because he gave Jack "the creeps." This did not stop Sheen from later dropping in on the Lawrensons when they were sick and sending them rosaries, religious tracts, and even a foot-high statue of the Madonna.[19]

Undeterred by all the opprobrium, Clare attended daily Mass, either at St. Thomas Apostle in Washington, St. Patrick's when she was in New York, or a small rural church, Our Lady Queen of Peace, during visits to Mepkin. In response to letters asking why she had converted, she began to write "The Real Reason," a three-part account for *McCall's* magazine of the spiritual crisis that had led her to Father Sheen and the long path to belief that followed.

With publication many months away, she used her powers of persuasion to convince friends that faith had steadied her intellectually and emotionally, deepened her sympathies, and quickened her sense of humor, as in her mock complaint, "Freedom from worship prevails everywhere."[20]

On March 5, President Truman escorted Winston Churchill to the small town of Fulton in his home state of Missouri. The former Prime Minister was to deliver one of the most important orations of his life there, at Westminster College. Entitled "The Sinews of Peace," it would soon be known by a more graphic name. A crowd of thirty thousand watched the statesmen drive to the college gymnasium in an open limousine. Two thousand more waited inside, while across the nation, multitudes of radio listeners gathered around their sets to hear Churchill's oratory.

He began by saying that America currently stood "at the pinnacle of world power." This primacy brought with it "an awe-inspiring accountability" to protect vulnerable nations from future war and tyranny. To do so required an end to the current precarious counterbalance of East and West, as well as a need to cement the "special relationship" between English-speaking peoples, and a United Nations that would become "a force for action, and not merely a frothing of words."

To be effective, he said, the peacekeeping body must be armed. For the foreseeable future, the technology of the atom bomb ought to be shared solely by the United States and Great Britain. "It would be criminal madness to cast it adrift in this still agitated and un-united world," Churchill said as Truman and the crowd applauded.

Then, in words that resonated around the globe, Churchill praised the Soviet Union's wartime achievements, but not its subsequent aggrandizement. "From Stettin in the Baltic to Trieste in the Adriatic," he said with orotund portentousness, "an iron curtain has descended across the Continent." Behind that line lay the capitals of Central and Eastern Europe, now in Moscow's sphere of influence, and many already under "totalitarian control." He expressed doubt that the Soviets contemplated war. But they did want "the fruits of war, and the indefinite expansion of their power and doctrines." Western democracies were unlikely to be molested so long as they stood together. But if they became divided, "catastrophe may overwhelm us all."[21]

▽

Eight days later, Churchill and his wife and family were entertained to lunch by Clare at the Waldorf-Astoria. Others attending were Bernard Baruch, the John D. Rockefellers, and the Charles Scribners.

Crisscrossing the country had tired Winston. His eyes were rheumy, his back stooped, and he shook hands limply, with his fingers only.[22] His son, Randolph, too, showed signs of wear. Now in his mid-thirties, he was no longer the bright, handsome youth of twenty-three whom Clare had captivated in 1934, first at Chartwell and then at the Ritz in Paris. Randolph had written afterward to say he thanked God for the passions they shared.[23]

The ravages of dissolute living, and an unhappy, brief marriage to Pamela Digby (currently having an affair with Averell Harriman), had turned the former Adonis into a pugnacious, puffy, and veined satyr. He continued to lust after Clare, still smitten with her looks, wit, and intelligence.

By now, world reactions to the "Iron Curtain" speech had proliferated. Stalin predictably denounced Churchill's criticisms of the USSR, and even Truman declined to endorse the address, saying untruthfully that he had not known of its content in advance. The socialistic George Bernard Shaw complained that Churchill's words at Fulton had been "nothing short of a declaration of war on Russia." Leftist protesters planned to disrupt a New York ticker tape parade in his honor.[24]

That evening, it was Harry's turn to host an all-male banquet for Winston at the Union League Club. After chomping on terrapin and pheasant, and downing six glasses of champagne, the old warrior gave a toast: "To Time, Life, Fortune—and any others I don't know about." At ten o'clock, he and Harry left the club and walked to their limousine to boos from Communist pickets.[25]

▽

Clare joined Herbert Hoover on March 16 for a WNAB broadcast entitled "World Famine." In support of the administration's food relief program, she urged American housewives to reduce their purchase of wheat products by 40 percent, so that twenty million starving people worldwide might at least have a daily ration of bread.[26] She then requested a few minutes of Oval Office time to discuss the issue further, along with the possible gradual assimilation of some fifty-five hundred Jewish refugees into the United States. But word came back that she was "blacklisted from the White House."[27]

Truman apparently bore her a grudge going back to his Senate days, when she had publicly called his wife "Payroll Bess" for taking a salary of $4,500 a year to handle her husband's business mail and edit committee reports.[28] Clare had also gibed at Truman's claim that his mother had not reared him to be a statesman. "His mother will not be disappointed."[29]

Peeved at being rebuffed, Clare asked her House colleague Joe Martin to intervene on her behalf. He agreed to do so, saying he had "never heard of a President refusing to see a Representative on national business." But Truman told Martin that as long as he was Chief Executive, "that woman" would not be welcome at the White House.[30] When he ignored a second appeal from Clare, she wrote to say she was entitled "as a duly-elected Representative of 418,384 citizens of the State of Connecticut, to transact business with you officially in their behalf." She explained that the wisecracks that irritated him had been made in her parody of a Walter Winchell column. Truman regarded even this excuse as "a mortal insult" and still refused to see her.[31]

▽

By now Clare was by far the most sought-after public lecturer in the House of Representatives, unable to fulfill a tenth of the speaking requests that came to her office. But as her retirement from Congress neared, she accepted more of them.[32] Martha Gellhorn's prediction that conversion would make her an oracle of the anti-Communism Right came true on May 21, when the Congresswoman took part in an *American Forum of the Air* radio debate aired by the Mutual Broadcasting

Clare, Theodore Granik, William Z. Foster, and Harry F. Ward debate
on *The American Forum of the Air*, May 21, 1946

System. The topic was "Are Communism and Democracy Mutually
Antagonistic?" and her fellow panelists were William H. Chamberlin, a
conservative writer, William Z. Foster, chairman of the National Committee of the Communist Party USA, and Dr. Harry F. Ward, professor
emeritus of Christian ethics at Union Theological Seminary. The mod-
erator was NBC's Theodore Granik.

Clare had shone in debate since her school days, gathering experience through a decade of arguing contemporary issues with Harry, followed by more than three years of congressional give-and-take and five
months of intense philosophical and theological dialogue with one of
the best intellects in the Roman Catholic Church. Although she
sounded impatient on the air, interrupting and making too many barbed
remarks, she outdid the two leftist members of the panel, particularly
Dr. Ward, an ill-informed ethical "expert."

In her opening statement, she provocatively quoted Foster as proof
that the answer to the debate question was yes. In the early 1930s, he
had claimed before an investigating committee of Congress "that a belief in God and loyalty to the American flag are wholly opposed to
Communism." He shot back.

FOSTER: Communists learn as they go along. I would like to ask
Mrs. Luce whether she believes in this statement, which she
wrote in 1930. *Lying increases the creative faculties, expands the
ego, lessens the friction of social contacts. It is only in lies, whole-*

heartedly and bravely told, that human nature attains . . . the idealism that, being what it is, it falls so short of in fact and in deed.

CHAIRMAN: Do you want to let her answer, Mr. Foster? Go ahead, Mrs. Luce.

CBL: The article of which you speak was a parody—a society satire—clearly so marked, for *Vanity Fair* magazine, written in the year 1931, in a series of other café society satires; and if Communists had a sense of humor—which they obviously haven't or they would laugh themselves to death at themselves—they would have seen that. . . . For a belief in lying as a high art, for subterfuge, and all sorts of evasion, I will be very happy to supply you with a quotation from your own left-wing Communist magazine, quoting Lenin on the subject. *It is necessary, says Mr. Lenin, to be able to agree to any and every sacrifice and even, if need be, to resort to all sorts of devices, maneuvers, and illegal methods, to evasion and subterfuge, in order to penetrate the trade unions, to remain in them, and to carry on Communistic work in them.*

At this point, Ward questioned if Clare regarded capitalism as a moral ideal. "Mr. Ward," she replied, "our capitalist economy has many faults. . . . I am the first to acknowledge them, and the first to say that we must improve them. But the fact that capitalism has faults does not prove that Communism is virtuous; nor does it prove that Communism is a cure, except as a guillotine might be called a cure for a case of dandruff."

Chamberlin, supporting her, asked Ward if, "as a more or less prominent Christian," he saw any inconsistency between the ethics of his faith and "such Soviet practices as executing people without trial and keeping millions of human beings in slavery in concentration camps?" Ward was dismissive. "I should think those extravagant statements of yours by this time had become too hoary for any respectable man to use." If Chamberlin would "read a little history," he would find that from early times it had been agreed "that the ethical base of the Communist ideal and the ethical base of early Christianity were the same."

The first burst of audience laughter occurred when Ward blustered that the gulags Chamberlin spoke of were "constructive rehabilitation programs."

CBL: Lenin, in his pamphlet, entitled "Lenin Speaks to Youth," said, *Our morality is entirely subordinated to the interests of the class struggle.* . . . Now, Dr. Ward, do you think that this belief, which you have referred to as a high ethical principle, explains why, after twenty-five years of Communist education, the thing that the Soviet armies will be remembered for best by the women of Europe is rape?

WARD: You have not a shred of proof. Not one shred of proof can anybody produce that there has been any more rape by the Soviet armies than by the capitalist armies.

When Foster defensively accused America of "an imperialist campaign designed to dominate the world," Clare pounced.

CBL: I consider it nonsense of the most egregious sort for anyone to try to pretend as you do, that the United States is out to start a war with anybody. . . . We have not asked for a foot of territory in Europe or Asia. We have not taken a piece of loot. To call this an imperialist, aggressive country is just shabby nonsense. [*APPLAUSE*]

CHAIRMAN: Please hold the applause. You are taking the time of the speakers.

Chamberlin gave Ward some of the proof he had demanded of Clare's accusation of Russian rape. He quoted a congressional report that cited "the wholesale raping of Polish women" by Soviet soldiers, and testimony by the author John Dos Passos saying that the Red Army was "allowed to rape and loot and murder at will."

Ward continued to bluster that there was "not a shred of proof" of these accusations. He even denied there was any such thing as OGPU, the Kremlin's secret police. Clare suggested that the best way to learn the truth about the workings of Soviet Communism was "for Uncle Joe to let down the iron curtain and let us all go in and have one good, big look at it. . . . What goes on there that he is so ashamed of?"

"Mrs. Luce," said the exasperated Ward, "I have lived enough in the Soviet Union to know that that iron curtain is in part a figment of Mr. Churchill's rhetoric and imagination, and in part a necessity of the situation."

Foster reverted to his charge of American imperialism, claiming that the nation's armed might around the world was such that "trigger-happy" reactionaries in Washington wanted to drop the atomic bomb again at the first opportunity.

Clare joined in audience cries of protest and insisted on interrupting.

> CHAIRMAN: I have to give the mike to Mrs. Luce.
> CBL: Mr. Foster, are we the ones who marched into Poland and took half of it over? . . . Have you ever at any time publicly before, during, or since the war, condemned, criticized, or found fault with anything that Stalin has ever enunciated from Moscow? If so, what? Take all the time you want.
> FOSTER: The Soviet policy is the correct policy, and why should I criticize it?
> CBL: Oh, dear! I wouldn't if I were you. Remember what happened to Trotsky. [LAUGHTER]

When the time came for her to sum up, she spoke directly to him.

> The charge that Mr. Chamberlin and I have made to-night is that you and the American Communist Party . . . are loyal to an antireligious foreign system and government which has been characterized by torture to obtain confessions, executions without trial, falsification of the record, floggings, beatings, shootings, slave labor, and the suppression of all minority and individual opinion. I would rather die than live under such a system and, incidentally, I think Dr. Ward would, too, though I am not sure. In any case, like many liberals of his ilk, Dr. Ward is a self-deluded man. He is fighting against our system of Christian democracy, a system which he does not in his heart wish to destroy, and defending a system that he could not bear to live under.[33]

A private worry for Clare at this time was whether her brother could bear to return to civilian life from the army, where for once in his errant existence he had found purpose. Shortly after V-J Day, she had received a poignant letter from him.

> It is with deep regret that we bid goodbye to the phantasmagoria of World War II. So while the entire world celebrates there remains

173

but one, an obscure 1st Lt., who is sad, for in his selfishness he can see no further than the fact that his only sweetheart is irrevocably gone.[34]

That David had seen combat as his one reason to exist plagued Clare. At the time he wrote, David was based at Clark Field in the Philippines, and complained of being harassed by black marketeers and pimps.[35] Clare suspected he was drinking heavily, being forty-four years old and afraid that his services as a transport pilot would not be required much longer.

Charles Willoughby had stopped by to see him, at Clare's request, en route to Japan and wrote to reassure her that David looked well and seemed reasonably happy. He had given him lunch and—unwisely— a bottle of scarce Scotch. Not only that, he had offered him a desk job in Tokyo, working on Korean intelligence directly under his supervision.[36]

David had agreed, but the description Charles sent Clare of life in the tumbledown capital did not convince her it was an ideal destination for David. "Unrest. Poverty. Blackmarket. The fellow travellers are right in Headqrs."[37]

▽

Summer found Clare still in Washington, unable to be free of Congress until the long session ended, with luck by August. She needed weekend escapes, but the house in Greenwich was no longer available. The government was building an airport nearby, so she and Harry had sold it. She found a temporary rental in Far Away Meadows, a weather-beaten old farmhouse in Newtown, Connecticut, owned by a friend, the opera star Grace Moore. Harry could have joined her there but for some unstated reason chose to vacation in Snowville, New Hampshire. As a possible guilt gift, he sent a bouquet of red roses.

Clare knew he was depressed, but not why. Missing his advice on her career, she wrote to tell him that formal overtures had been made for her to run for the seat that Senator Hart would be vacating in November. "I cannot tell you with what repugnance I view all this, and how I shrink from it, really. . . . At best the Senate can only involve me in noble futilities."[38]

Harry wrote to assure her that government work was not futile. "It is, on the contrary, a high calling. You have only to ask: is it your calling? It certainly *looks* as if it is!"[39]

This letter belied Clare's fond belief that he wanted her out of Congress because he missed her.⁴⁰ In the absence of total honesty, husband and wife remained at cross-purposes, neither sure of the motives, ambitions, and emotional needs of the other. To Clare, Harry's recurring malaise was harmful to their well-being.

> "The lover," says Thomas a Kempis, "desires always the *good* of the beloved."
>
> As I do love you very much, I do desire your *good*, tho' the trouble is, of course, I am not wise enough to know what that good really is. Nor have I ever been able to figure out, since you ceased to be "in love" with me, whether or not it should include me. . . . My very presence seems a reproach and a burden to you, very often. What, oh what can I *do* to make you a happier—or as you sometimes put it—a more useful man? To accomplish this would be more important by far than "going to the Senate," or even writing books. For myself, it is remarkable how little I really care about doing this or that, or being this or that, anymore. . . .
>
> It is *wrong*, terribly, horribly *wrong* that a man as gifted as you, as powerful, as successful, as fortunate, should be miserable within himself.⁴¹

On July 17, Clare made her last important speech in the House. She spoke for thirty minutes in favor of establishing an Atomic Energy Commission, which would put the atom under civilian control, while including two military advisers. It was a subject that aroused passions, and she tried to be a voice of reason. Energy and matter, she pointed out, were amoral, as opposed to human beings, whose only choice was morality or immorality. If all world leaders were good men, the development of atomic energy "would not require such totalitarian legislation as this."⁴²

She claimed to have prepared for her address by talking to fifteen physicists and military experts and reading twenty technical reports. But Representative John Elliott Rankin (D-MS) disparaged it as "the powder-puff argument of the delightful gentlewoman."⁴³

Another item on the late July agenda was aid to China. Republicans made the case that the Democratic administration was not providing the Nationalist leader Chiang Kai-shek with enough funds to beat Mao and his Red Army. Truman, on the advice of General George Marshall, who was in China to assess the situation, wanted to limit aid and have American officials supervise its distribution. Marshall said that the amount of money should be dependent on the Generalissimo's regime getting rid of corruption and being more inclusive in its political base, by trying to form a coalition with the Communists. Two months before, on the House floor, Clare had praised the fruits of Marshall's statesmanship and the "extraordinary diplomatic job" he had done in China.[44] Now she opposed his recommendation to limit aid and had a letter of protest signed by thirty-eight Chiang supporters put into the *Congressional Record* of July 24, 1946.[45]

▽

Clare took the floor of the House on Wednesday, July 31, this time to give a summary of her two terms in office.

She admitted to few legislative successes in her first year, and to being absent for much of her second, due to depression after the death of her daughter. Between October 1943 and March 1944, she had sponsored only two bills of note, to do with redistribution of service and civilian manpower. Both measures had become the basis for legislation passed by the House, but were rejected by the Senate.

She spoke with more pride of her current term. It was already impressively documented in the *Congressional Record*—almost two hundred fine-print pages of speeches and legislative proposals. Careful not to sound boastful over the variety of her initiatives, she merely recited them in chronological order, and refrained from expressing disappointment at the failure of many of them, just using the simple phrase *No hearing was given this measure.*

For a rich Republican, still assumed by many to be an elitist, Clare had demonstrably promoted the rights of minorities. At home these were oppressed workers, women, unemployed veterans, and blacks. Abroad they were the starving and stateless victims of war. She noted, too, that her proposal to amend the immigration law to authorize the admission and naturalization of Indians had become law, albeit under the sponsorship of a majority member.

Sounding the first contentious note of her address, Clare recalled that in February 1945, she had futilely asked the House to "assume national responsibility" for the acquiescence of the United States in the partition of Poland at Yalta. Her idea had been to admit as immigrants Polish soldiers who had served with the Allies and who were forced "to choose between persecution at home or becoming men without a country." At the end of that year, she had further proposed that United Nations passports be issued to hundreds of thousands of displaced persons in Allied occupation zones. The State Department had unofficially approved this scheme, but no congressional committee had followed through.

She had also called in vain for a cabinet-level Department of Children's Welfare, to combat an alarming postwar rise in juvenile delinquency and malnutrition. Democrats had included the essence of her idea in their call for a general welfare agency. But the Ways and Means Committee had declined to consider another measure of hers, allowing tax deductions to doctors and dentists volunteering their services to clinics for the poor. Clare's most nearly successful proposal had been to establish a Housing Bureau that would help veterans procure homes, farms, and bank credit. It had gone nowhere in committee, but its major features were now incorporated in Public Law 388.[46]

Rounding off, she noted that she had called, again without success, for the formation of a Department of Science and Research; for the popular election, rather than presidential appointment, of American representatives to the United Nations; and for a Congressional Medal of Honor to be awarded General Jonathan M. Wainwright, the defender of Bataan and Corregidor. Her only hint of reproof came when she noted that Congress failed to act on this last request, but that President Truman had bestowed the medal anyway.

Altogether, Representative Luce could take credit for eighteen major initiatives espousing the causes of human rights: equal pay for equal work, racial and sexual fairness, profit sharing, and rehabilitation of veterans. She closed her account on a partisan note.

During the 79th Congress, now presumably passing into history, 4,748 bills were introduced for consideration by committees of the House. Of this number, 675 reached actual debate on the floor. Senate and House together were presented with a total of 6,647 bills, and only 293 of this total became laws of the United States—a vast and overwhelming majority of which bore Democratic names, for the simple reason that the Democratic Party controlled the House, the Senate, and, therefore, the committees.[47]

▽

The day after her marathon presentation, Clare appeared in the House dining room as the guest of her staff for a farewell steak lunch. Joe Martin also attended, as did the chairman of the Republican National Committee. Congress disbanded the next afternoon, and the soon-to-be former member for Fairfield County headed north.

Representative J. William Fulbright remarked years later that Clare Boothe Luce had used her sex appeal "twenty-four hours a day" on the Hill. "But she was the smartest colleague I ever served with."[48]

19

IN LIMBO

▽

Everyone can be measured by his adaptability to change.

—ROBERT RAUSCHENBERG

For the first time in almost four years, Clare had the luxury of untrammeled days to write and reflect. But Harry seemed to want her to continue in politics. On August 15, 1946, he escorted her to a conference in Connecticut with Governor Raymond Baldwin, Republican State Chairman J. Kenneth Bradley, William H. Brennan, and George Waldo. The purpose of the meeting was to decide once and for all whether Clare should run for the Senate in November. She was adamant she would not.[1]

Apart from the frustration of the legislative life, the malice of the press, and the tedium of evenings alone at the Wardman Park, there was the narrowness of focus.[2] In Congress, she remarked, one had to be a piccolo player, "stick to one note and hit it all the time."[3] *Her* one note had been the war. She had run for office because of it, vowed to leave when it ended, and kept her word. Now theological and literary interests preoccupied her. Six more years on Capitol Hill would starve her intellectually, she felt. "Politics is the refuge of second-class minds."[4]

Unable to persuade Clare to run, the GOP strategists turned to Baldwin, who was stepping down after four terms as Governor.[5] He agreed to be a candidate, much to the disappointment of at least one

Washington stalwart, Alice Longworth, the politically savvy, sixty-year-old daughter of former President Theodore Roosevelt. "She is a lady of quality, highly intelligent. I regret deeply that she has decided not to seek reelection."[6]

Harry, reconciled to his wife's desire for private life, wrote a footnote to *Time*'s summary of her congressional career for the August 26 issue.

> The story of Clare Luce, though told in nearly every other publication in the land, has been told hardly at all in the pages of *Time* or its sister publications. *Time* editors, beginning with Editor-in-Chief Henry R. Luce (husband) fumbled the story, because they were too fearful of being damned if they told it or damned if they didn't.

In spite of this gesture, it was evident to his staff that there was disharmony in the Luce marriage. Charles Douglas Jackson, a vice president, known around the office as "C.D.," had been Harry's personal assistant since the early 1930s and now became, in Billings's words, "a repository for his troubles with Clare."[7] Al Grover, visiting the Luces at Far Away Meadows, reported that they "had nothing in common."[8] They were barely civil to each other, competing to be the focus of his attention.

At work, Harry was increasingly dour and ill-tempered, ordering Communist sympathizers in his employ to be fired. One Monday, he came into the office disheveled and cross. His adoring secretary, Corinne Thrasher, blamed "the weekend with his wife."[9]

▽

Captain David Boothe seemed settled in his desk job in Tokyo, reading copious military, political, economic, social, and psychological reports about Korea. He edited them for entry in an intelligence summary and liaised with other sections of the MacArthur administration.[10] His association with General Willoughby brought him perks, such as a chauffeured pickup when they dined together.

But now he said he must leave his job to have a "nervous ailment" treated in the States. Willoughby urged him to return, offering a "brilliant spot" in counterespionage, with activity on "risky frontiers." But David turned it down, on the grounds that he detested dreary Tokyo.[11]

The truth was more complicated. He wrote Clare that he found himself "bereft of emotional ties."[12] Although he claimed to be reading

Kant, Voltaire, Spinoza, and Plato to get a philosophical aspect on life, his true taste was for the semicriminal night owls in Damon Runyon stories. Having actually known characters just like Harry the Horse and Little Isadore as a young man carousing on Broadway, he had come to identify with them, and when binge drinking, he sometimes shared their murderous impulses.[13] He found it difficult to erase from his mind enemy barbarism in the jungles of New Guinea and feared, with his short temper, that he might take violent revenge. One night, when stopped by a Japanese official and asked for his name, rank, and serial number, David had to restrain himself from choking him.[14] He admitted to Willoughby that his heart was filled with hate for "the hypocrisy and thieving, and lying and indolence" of Far Easterners, and he told Clare that "as sure as the sun rose I'd destroy myself in that environment."[15]

She dreaded his return. Earlier that year, when applying for his captain's commission, David had given as his address 398 Beacon Street, Boston. This was a house that Clare had bought clandestinely in case she ever walked out on Harry. Was he imagining that it might one day be his? If he left the military, what would he do? At various times he had tried to be a stockbroker (losing in the process a large amount of her money), run a chain of movie theaters without success, and worked briefly for a Canadian airline. His latest notion was that she should get her friend Sam Pryor to appoint him manager of Pan American Airways in Melbourne, Australia, where he had a girl he was keen on. She advised him to "sweat it out" in the army and stop fantasizing about becoming rich overnight.[16]

Another reason for David to remain abroad was that he faced some twelve years of federal and state income tax troubles. Harry's lawyers and accountants, working with the Internal Revenue Service, calculated that he owed somewhere between $10,000 and $20,000. Since he had few assets, the Luces would probably have to help him yet again.[17]

David, however, insisted that he needed medical treatment in America. Clare resignedly told him that in that case, he could hitch a flight home on the plane of a congressional delegation that was about to visit Japan on an inspection tour. She planned to be among the group. But then, inexplicably, she dropped out.

Her decision was all the more mysterious given that General Willoughby had personally arranged for her to meet Japanese dignitaries not readily accessible to Western visitors. These included the Empress and ladies of her court, as well as female members of the Diet, the democratic parliament MacArthur had installed.[18]

Possibly Clare was annoyed by news David had relayed that Charles, "in lieu of your presence," had been seeing a thirty-two-year-old Spanish woman.[19] Whatever the case, she preferred to remain in Connecticut throughout the fall, while David made his way across the Pacific by boat. It turned out that his "nervous ailment" was venereal disease that required treatment at a medical facility in San Francisco. He sailed on September 5, and Clare braced for his eventual appearance in New York.

▽

In spite of her protestations, the politician in Clare could not help being caught up in the midterm election campaigns. For the first time in sixteen years, the GOP had a chance of regaining control of Congress and many statehouses. Much of the electorate was tired of the Democratic Party's obsession with foreign aid, and President Truman's approval rating had dropped to the low thirties. Her own seat seemed safe for a Republican candidate. Al Morano aspired to it, but she suggested he wait four years, saying that Fairfield County voters would disparage him as her stand-in. In any case, she had decided to support John Davis Lodge (grandson of the famous Senator Henry Cabot Lodge), even though he had lived in Connecticut less than a year. She told Morano that Lodge would probably run for Governor in 1950, and he could then try to replace him in the House of Representatives.[20]

On November 5, Republicans gained fifty-five seats in the House and twelve in the Senate, taking Congress for the first time since the 1920s. Clare's old friend Joe Martin became Speaker.

"The twenty-four hours after the elections were bad," she admitted to an acquaintance, "because it would have been fun to have been in on the big victory. . . . But now I am *completely content* with my retirement. I have already set to work, on what may become a book and two producable plays!"[21]

▽

On arriving in San Francisco, David Boothe entered Letterman General Hospital. He was loath to tell his sister he had VD again, particularly since she had paid for a previous treatment of gonorrhea. So he confided in the sympathetic George Waldo, whom he knew from years back. "Many a man," he wrote, "has been placed beyond misery, when the doctor finally diagnoses that strange and lingering sore as syphilis."

He attributed his bad luck to having had sex while drunk, promising that henceforth he would stay sober.[22]

After being released by his doctors, David had fifty-two days of leave before reporting for a medical examination in Florida. His new hope was to qualify for a pilot's commission in the U.S. Army Reserve.[23] Before that, he planned to drive around the South and Southwest and work for a while on the fruit farm of a pilot friend in Arizona, getting extra fit for his physical.

Clare realized that her brother was again embarking on a nomadic existence of dependency and let him know she had less income now, and higher liabilities. "I've read your letter several times," David wrote on November 11. "All I can say is this sister dear, currency circulation in '29 was about 5 billion; now stands at 30 billion."[24]

On December 22, he showed up at his sister's apartment in New York. She affected "great joy" in seeing him, but he immediately felt under scrutiny. He told her she looked well, her gray wisps "not unbecoming." Prematurely grizzled himself, he dyed his hair jet black and claimed to have "the health of an ox."

In spite of Clare's apparent warmth, David intuited that he was still marked "caution" in the Luce household. This annoyed and saddened him, for he believed that his war service and medals should exonerate his delinquencies.[25] But he was frank enough to admit he had a personality disorder. "It just ain't right to be so inconsistently put together & disturbs me no end."[26]

Within twenty-four hours, eschewing a family Christmas, he was back on the road, heading south.

▽

A week after his brief glimpse of Clare, David wrote to say that he saw the United States as "a big fat rich nation, utterly without integrity . . . ploughing along, dog eat dog." That was why he hoped to stay in the army and "not get chewed up myself." But he felt somewhat less disillusioned after receiving a surprise check from Clare and a $1,000 Brooks Brothers credit from Harry.[27]

In early January 1947, David sent alarming news. He wrote that he had met a Phoenix woman he wanted to wed. Fearing a repetition of his disastrous earlier marriage, Clare replied, "This is an immoral thing for a man like you to do." He had surely taken advantage of "some little girl who doesn't know the truth about you." She told him that she and

Harry would not subsidize the relationship. What he needed, she said, was "spiritual guidance."[28]

He responded defiantly. "Immoral—why? Because I'm guilty of the crime of having no money—apart from a few hundred? . . . Because a man such as I has no right to love someone? I'm not too obscene to embrace a Faith am I? . . . Don't you think I know truth when I encounter it? Me a guy that has skirted the fringes of pimpdom, thievery, gangsterdom, connivers, schemers, bums, touts, et al."[29] As for Mary Jane Haskin, his potential bride, she was not a "girl," but a college-educated, thirty-six-year-old former naval lieutenant who now worked as a clerk in a department store.

Suspecting that Clare wanted to convert him to Roman Catholicism, David said he was willing to listen to "whatever wisdom or knowledge" she could impart that did not insult his intelligence. He reminded her that at age ten, in an Episcopal ceremony of confirmation at Racine College's military school, "some huge pontifical hulk crossed my forehead with his fingers and established eligibility for Holy Communion. As my voice was not adaptable for choir work the Church had no need of me nor I of them. Since then my incursions into sanctuaries have been infrequent."

He posed a few questions that he would like her to answer before he even considered religious instruction.

> How did you first conceive of the infinite in terms of the finite?
> What do they the Atom boys say to your creeds?
> How does a man like Einstein view the Church as the true faith?
> What about life or intelligence elsewhere in the universe?
> And the justice of Infinite Wisdom that so eagerly took your
>   Ann? And passed me up?
> What crime or series of crimes could a person commit that
>   renders him throughout Eternity beyond recall or
>   redemption?

He ended ingratiatingly, telling Clare that he was reading G. K. Chesterton's *The Everlasting Man* and eschewing hard liquor. "Thinking and alcohol conflict, so of necessity I go for beer. No sister, your brother isn't getting ready to sprout wings, he's just getting accustomed to the fact that his tail has sort of shriveled and almost disappeared."[30]

Later that month, David reported to army authorities in Washington, D.C., who told him that at almost forty-five he was not eligible for a reserve commission. He wrote Clare that he was soon to be separated from military service, "the only endeavor in which I've ever been successful."[31]

Before leaving the capital, he was startled to receive a call from a man with a purring, syrupy voice. He quickly identified it as that of his sister's favorite priest.

"I can help you," said Monsignor Fulton J. Sheen.

"Lord love a duck, one of us is nuts," David thought to himself. "Here I have 39 months overseas and a gink I've never seen is going to help me. Help me to do what? Join his outfit? I should send him a bill for keeping the Japs off his back."[32]

After successfully evading Sheen's overture, David proceeded to Morrison Field in Florida to register for demobilization, effective June 1. Clare invited him in the meantime to visit her at Mepkin, where she aimed to stay through April. He asked if he could bring Mary Jane. She wrote back to say that he could hardly expect her and Harry to welcome them as a couple. "You . . . we shall admit, but you only." David hastened to explain that he was only thinking of remarriage. "Enactment and contemplation, in this instance, are poles apart, for the hurdles are obvious even to me."[33]

The chief of these was "a big balance sheet staring me smack in the face, no net worth & all on the debit side."[34] He accepted her terms for his visit to the plantation, assuring her he would not arrive "cloaked in a pall of gloom nor as a martyr. I shall be as I am."[35]

▽

"I have not done one blessed thing since I have been down here," Clare wrote her literary agent, George Bye, from the plantation on February 4. One excuse for her lack of productivity was that she was entertaining numerous guests. Another distraction was her seventy-two-hundred-acre estate, where she had not spent any length of time since 1941. The main house, aptly named "Claremont," and cottages of whitewashed brick in the Modernist style (for which Edward Durrell Stone had won the 1937 Silver Medal for Architectural Excellence) had been extensively refurbished by Gladys Freeman.[36] But circumnavigation of the grounds, which took four hours in a buggy, revealed many signs of neglect, and frost had killed the budding camellias. Then, on Sunday, February 9, her brother arrived.[37]

Her welcome to him was warm, given their recent acrimonious correspondence. "There is nothing to worry about," she said. "Stay here the rest of your life."

David was not deluded into thinking he was suddenly the beloved prodigal. But Clare could be beguiling, and when he learned that he was to have her to himself for a few days before Harry came, he was as agreeable as he could be. Clare described him to Maggie Case as "the handsome Captain Boothe, who is in great form and, as the French say, *en grande beauté*."[38] At the same time, she had long realized that his flawed nature was incurable. Though he could be ingratiatingly genial, his mood was capable of sudden change, and a "fleeting saturnine expression" that she found particularly disturbing would signal that Jekyll was about to become Hyde.[39]

Harry's arrival on St. Valentine's Day was ironic—had Clare but known it—because his intent was to ask her for a divorce. He had been encouraged to make this drastic move by C. D. Jackson and even had a lawyer lined up in New York to handle the details of separation.[40] But once he was ensconced at Mepkin, something dissuaded him. Whether it was for lack of an opportune moment, or David's dark presence, the potentially wrenching confrontation did not take place.

For the next five days, he had to share Clare with an emotionally starved soldier who was possessive of her to an almost pathological degree. David's envy of her husband's professional success was exacerbated by disappointment in himself.[41] At times Harry felt that the misfit might be mad. One day, the two men were duck shooting and David, gun at the ready, trailed him along a rice bank. He seemed to exude such venom that Harry feared for his life.[42]

▽

David left for Florida in early March to complete paperwork for his departure from the military, leaving Clare with the quiet she claimed to crave for literary projects.

On the twelfth, the President went before both houses of Congress to announce a foreign policy initiative—soon to be known as the Truman Doctrine—in response to Soviet penetration of Greece, Asia Minor, Africa, and Western Europe. "I believe it must be the policy of the United States to support free peoples who are resisting attempted subjugation by armed minorities or outside pressure." To that end, he asked for financial aid to Greece and Turkey, moving closer to what Clare had advocated in the House: a plan to prevent Russian aggression, and another to rescue Europe from insolvency and joblessness. The new doctrine, aimed at containing Soviet expansion by means other than armed conflict, marked the onset of what would become known as "the Cold War."

Harry, probably annoyed with himself for failing to ask for a divorce, took his frustration out by grumbling about his wife's extravagance. Clare was now running three households, including a new property in Ridgefield, Connecticut, that Al Grover had found. She had already spent some $64,000 of Harry's money renovating it, but kept the figure from him when he started complaining that Mepkin cost $40,000 a year to maintain, much more than before the war. He suggested they economize by not using the estate next season, and she reluctantly agreed. Then he switched his attack to her current lack of employment, asking what her "real ambition" was.[43]

She replied that she still wanted "to write books and plays." As for domestic costs, she offered to take a smaller apartment at the Waldorf. The discussion ended inconclusively, and Harry asked himself what he, "a missionary's son, was doing with a plantation, horses and guns when all I should be doing is work."[44]

His mood was not improved by a facetious letter from Clare, offering to cancel magazine subscriptions, forgo flower arrangements, eat homegrown vegetables, and give up shooting. "You'll drop dead when you see the bill for bamming away at skeet."[45]

David returned to the plantation with an honorable discharge in time to celebrate his forty-fifth birthday on March 30. It at once became clear that Clare had an agenda other than pampering him.

"I have a secret for you, I really shouldn't tell you but I must," she said. "Do you know that when Father Whitey's mother died last week, her dying words were a prayer for your conversion?"[46]

It dawned on David that Monsignor Sheen's purring phone call of a few weeks earlier had been a precursor to Clare's plan to lure him into her church. But he knew he must humor his sister, on whom he would soon again be financially dependent. Even though he felt he was watching the approach of a "buzz saw," he agreed to read two preparatory books, Pierre Lecomte du Noüy's *Human Destiny* and A. Cressy Morrison's *Man Does Not Stand Alone*. In dialectical sessions with Clare, he showed signs of susceptibility to her theological arguments. But she was unable to satisfy him on all of the moral questions he had mailed her in

January, particularly his last conundrum: "What crime or series of crimes could a person commit that renders him throughout Eternity beyond recall or redemption?"[47]

In spite of all her efforts, David was slow to commit. Showing signs of self-delusion, he protested, "I am no psycho, or possess a mind degraded by alcohol or drugs or a body weakened by sexual excesses. . . . The answer for me is not to be found by embracing a Faith nor a wife, it must come from within."[48]

▽

The April issue of *Look* featured a laudatory cover story entitled "The New Clare Luce." The author, a Roman Catholic named Gretta Palmer, noted that in a recent poll of American women, Clare came second behind Eleanor Roosevelt as the woman they most admired. Unlike any other finalist, she also made the "Ten Best-Dressed" list.[49] The latter accolade was belied by an airbrushed full-color photograph of Clare in a green silk brocade Chinese blouse with mandarin collar, over which hung a double strand of pearls and fob. Oversize gold rings ornamented each hand, and her right wrist sported a jumble of clunky gold bracelets. Around her curly, gold-tinted hair was a narrow white scarf studded with gold clips near the ears, anchored on top by a bow and two red flowers with five leaves. Her gaze was as direct as in person, but she seemed ill at ease and less confident than in portraits taken by great photographers during her *Vogue* and *Vanity Fair* years.

Helen Lawrenson recognized Clare's lack of chic, unless dressed by designers or fashion magazine editors. Left to her own devices, "she was always too fond of ruffles, bows, frills, dowdy hats, too many jewels at one time."[50]

▽

Clare had a contract with the New York publisher Alfred A. Knopf for a memoir of her congressional experiences. Unable or unwilling to bestir herself to do this, she offered instead a compilation of already written essays and speeches. "The material is interesting," Blanche Knopf wrote her, "but I do not believe that it adds up to a book that would do you any good now."[51] Clare then suggested an expanded version of "The Real Reason," whose last installment had just appeared in *McCall's*, but Knopf also rejected that.[52]

Due to various factors, including her disparagement of psychoanalysts, scientists, and literati in the articles, as well as anti-Catholic sentiment in the country at large, Clare's stirring account of her depression, instruction, and conversion would never appear in book form. The Catholic house of Sheed & Ward later expressed interest, but by then she did not want to see the account of her spiritual crisis between hard covers.[53] This was unfortunate, since Maisie Ward drafted a penetrating foreword.

> There is in her an almost miraculous clarity—few people are named with such precision. . . . Externally she had all the means of happiness. But a mind of that clarity could not be happy in meaningless activity. Happiness is complexion, not cosmetic: it cannot be laid on from outside, it must start at the center of one's being: and she had only darkness at the center.[54]

Before leaving for New York in the last week of April, Clare asked David to stay on at Mepkin until Gladys Freeman arrived to close the house and cottages for the summer.[55] His nomadic impulse was stirring again, and he was notoriously light-fingered, so the decorator had to make sure he did not take off with silver, or guns, or anything else portable. As it was, when he left the plantation in early May, he got away with a typewriter and eight bottles of liquor.[56]

20

A TERRIBLE MAELSTROM
OF TROUBLE

▽

The abandoned becomes the abandoner.

—Clifford Odets

In the early spring of 1947, the Luces moved into Sugar Hill, a twenty-room, redbrick Georgian-style house on Limestone Road in Ridge-field, Connecticut. Its servants' wing had space for a butler, chauffeur, cook, and maids. Elsewhere on the estate was a guest cottage and a su-perintendent's quarters. They had paid $220,000 for it, the same amount realized from selling their place in Greenwich. Clare hired landscapers to improve the hundred acres of gardens, lawns sloping down to a grove of silver birches, and woodland overlooking Fox Hill Lake. Builders added a pool, tennis court, and outdoor terraces.

Gladys Freeman decorated the large formal rooms and bedrooms. A small white foyer with an alabaster bust of Clare gave on the right to a drawing room with dark green walls, rug, and couches. Over the man-telpiece hung Gerald Brockhurst's portrait of Clare in her green manda-rin tunic. Chinoiserie, extending even to bamboo curtain rods, filled the room: tables and chairs in Chinese Chippendale style, Asian bride chests, a rare Tang camel, Manchu quartz, a collection of blue-and-yellow porcelain, and a life-size figure of the Goddess of Plenty.

The Oriental theme continued in the dining room. Against a cream

190

wall stood intricately carved cabinets and cloisonné vases, and around the teak dining table were arrayed high-backed, lacquered chairs with yellow cushions. The library had parchment-colored walls, beige curtains, a yellow Chinese rug, curving coral sofas, and a Segonzac landscape. French bow windows, facing south, overlooked flowering dogwoods and roses.[1]

After a week or two Clare heard from David, who was now traveling in the Deep South looking for an outdoor job and staying, wherever possible, in accommodations his sister had arranged for him. Some of his stops were with Roman Catholic clerics. He wrote to say that he preferred their company to that of "insipid and watery Protestants," but felt obliged to tell them that "I am violently anti-Communistic, dislike Jews which is most unChristianlike, am a heretic . . . and never enter a Church."[2]

On June 12, Clare checked into Doctors Hospital in New York to prepare for a hysterectomy. Her decision to do this was so sudden that Harry had to curtail a business trip in Latin America to be at her bedside. Her recovery was slow, and she remained incapacitated for two weeks. At age forty-four, she had to accept that youth and motherhood were at an end, leaving her "psychologically and physically deeply diminished."[3]

Harry dropped in rarely and struck Clare as being "in a strange, unhappy mood."[4] At the office he was noticeably tense and miserable.[5] Learning the reason for her indisposition, Billings said, "Boy, that's not going to make Luce's life any easier."[6]

As Clare recuperated at Sugar Hill, David reappeared to keep her company. He had found no work in the South. One reason for his return was that he hoped Clare would honor a recent promise to launch him in business with $5,000, followed by a $100,000 operational bank credit. But she failed to follow up, burying herself in C. S. Lewis's polemical book *The Screwtape Letters*.

This pithy work of fiction, written at the war's onset, consists of thirty-one letters from an elderly devil, Screwtape, to his nephew, Wormwood. The one-sided correspondence contains profound theological argument and witty analyses of the strengths and weaknesses of Christianity, as well as showing how easily even regular churchgoers might be won over to the side of evil.

In the insidious corrupting of human beings by a pair of devils, Clare saw passages of relevance to her brother, who at times seemed under satanic influence. She worried that by indulging him, she abetted his curse, noting how Screwtape tutored the inexperienced yet malevolent Wormwood in how to seduce a recent convert. These tactics were instructive for Clare, still a novice in her struggles with daily temptations. Screwtape also gave tips on how to ensnare those who denied the existence of Satan as well as God.

She also found parallels in the book to herself and Harry, as Screwtape gleefully explained how dullness and despair might lead to "a permanent condition" of melancholy. In this state, believers or atheists often sought numbness in alcohol and extramarital sex, especially if they inclined, as she did, to pessimism.[7]

Screwtape pointed out that a persistent longing for change, often characteristic of the rich and feckless, conflicted with the natural desire of men and women for permanence. "Horror of the Same Old Thing," he observed, "is one of the most valuable passions we have produced in the human heart." It often led to a craving for novelty—excessive spending on personal adornment, overindulgence in food, drink, sex, and consorting with lowlifes. God, whom Screwtape always referred to as "the Enemy," countered by offering people variety as well as stability in everyday life. "The rhythms of the seasons, the church calendar and its feasts, and domestic routine" replaced the arrhythmia of restlessness and lack of discipline.[8]

Screwtape made at least one observation relevant to both Luces. "Wherever a man lies with a woman, there, whether they like it or not, a transcendental relation is set up between them which must be eternally enjoyed or eternally endured."[9]

▽

Clare was beginning to regain strength when one day in mid-July an attorney representing Harry arrived at Sugar Hill on an astonishing errand.[10] The lawyer, Bruce Bromley, told her that she "owed it" to Roman Catholicism to divorce her husband. He argued that their marital situation could be interpreted in only two ways. Either she was deceiving her church by sleeping with the previously married Mr. Luce, or she was holding on to him while "denying him the rights of a normal man."[11]

Still physically and emotionally frail, Clare was outraged by the cruelty, cowardice, and mendacity of this approach. The truth was that for some eight years, Harry had denied *her* sexual rights. His excuse for his impotence, oft repeated, was that she had long ago "deeply wounded his masculine pride." He cited two ludicrous examples as reasons for having cooled on her. The first was that on one of their initial nights together, when he had boasted of earning $1 million a year, she had said, unimpressed, "That's fine." The second occurred when she had been dismissive of his membership in Yale's secret society, Skull and Bones, which he considered one of the most important achievements of his life.[12]

Clare insisted that her husband drive out at once and join them. He did, and admitted to wanting an end to their marriage. A stormy scene ensued as he tried to put the responsibility for its failure on her. After she converted, Harry said, he had assumed a breakup "would certainly follow," because in the eyes of her new faith, he remained pledged to Lila.[13] Bromley backed this up, contending that as a Catholic she was now in an invalid and sinful relationship, which she mitigated by denying Mr. Luce sex. At a minimum, this gave his client grounds for an annulment.

Clare, determined to enlighten the lawyer, said Harry had been impotent with her for many years, so she was "not denying him anything." If, on the other hand, he had been lying and was in fact capable of sex with "some other woman," he should simply ask for a divorce rather than threaten one. At this, Harry crumbled, stuttered, and paced around the room. He said he and Bromley would have to talk more, and the two men returned to New York.[14]

Left alone, Clare mulled over Harry's specious logic. "If I had not been a Catholic," she wrote in a memo of their confrontation, "I would probably have committed suicide because of the 'double-header' loss of my female capacities . . . and loss of the love of the only man who was in any human sense responsible for my security and well-being."[15] She realized that he had been cynically supportive of her conversion, seeing that it could invalidate their marriage vows. Still reeling, she turned to her brother for consolation.

"Now I really will kill him," David said.[16]

▽

When Clare committed her thoughts to paper in times of crisis, she did so with lawyerly logic. On July 26, the Feast of Our Lady of Mercy, she wrote a summary of events for Harry that showed him not only how well she understood his predicament, but how much more lucidly she could express it than he, in spite of his boast that he was always the smartest person in any room. She exposed how hypocritical, ungallant, and shameful his behavior had been, without even hinting at how often she had betrayed him.

Her handwritten, ten-page letter began with a one-line paragraph: "The storm is passed." She meant that she had been in a suicidal state of mind.

> My fierce bout with Mr. Screwtape—for that is what it was—is over. And I'm limp but still alive. And once again I have seen the last terrible shape [devilish] temptation always takes: the death urge. It always begins in the same way. First there comes the appeal to my feminine pride, and vanity. Then all the pleasures and tendernesses and indulgences that I think *ought* to be mine, simply because I am a normally attractive and loving woman, are dangled before my eyes like a lovely lost empire.

Evidently, she considered Harry to be as evil as Screwtape, in telling her periodically, "But I *do* love you," only to prove that he did not. Time and again, she had been seduced by the magic of his words and rushed forward with open arms to find that "what was gone is still gone." This left her with just one temptation, "the wish to die."

She saw that it was this suicidal desire that had taken her four times to war zones, each time after marital squabbles had made her suffer "the cruel drama of humiliation and frustration of senses and emotions." As she had written him from Europe in 1940, "I just don't want to live in a world where you are not."[17]

His continuing false claims of love had caused her much heartbreak. But none had been as dishonest and unforgivable as "the aid and 'sympathy' you showed towards my conversion!" At first this had saved her reason and probably her life. But after his and Bromley's visit, she saw that in *not* trying to prevent her from becoming a Catholic, he had betrayed all the canons and mores of his own church and marriage vows.

> As an honest Presbyterian, you believe, I assume, that there is essential evil in Catholicism. And yet, you offered no arguments, made no efforts, brought no witnesses to prevent me from falling into what (I assume) you believe to be a false faith. . . . Secondly, you realized (I know now) that it meant the end of any real husband and wife relationship. You realized too, that I accepted that, not as a condition if I became a Catholic, but as a condition that was inherent in our, or rather, your disability [professed impotency], rather than confirmed disinclination. Thirdly, the "mores," mere modern sportsmanship, required at that time that

you lay the true facts of your non-celibacy before me, as I was laying the true fact of my intended celibacy before you.

I know now why you failed your religious conscience, your
marriage, and even the modern "code." Partly because you figured
Catholicism would bring me comfort and surcease. . . . But mostly
you aided me into the church . . . because you believed my conversion would mean *your* legal freedom.

Clare accused him of flagrant hypocrisy in conspiring to rid himself
of her in a manner that left him standing on high moral ground. He
wanted to be able to say, "Ah! The Catholic Church broke up our marriage! Nothing else could have parted me from her!" That was why he
had let her proceed so unsuspectingly to her Baptism. "As you said,
when Bromley was here, you *assumed* a divorce would certainly follow. I
know now, that when you came to Tennessee that night, you *intended* to
tell me just that, but lost your courage."

She called him "a moral leper" but acknowledged there was little
she could do, except offer him friendship, sympathy, and freedom to "go
where you will . . . lie where and with whom you can. That is the best
way. . . . I would with the utmost joy die for you this or any other night.
For I never loved another, except my Ann, so deeply."[18]

▽

Harry saw the truth of Clare's indictment of his behavior, and began to
weigh the traumatic consequences of divorce. On the first Monday in
August, gazing out of his office window, he told Billings he needed a
vacation. "You know Clare isn't too well and we've got this new house
now and I don't want to go too far off or for too long." The editor
thought, "There's no place he really wants to go and nobody he really
wants to go with. A strange lonely fellow who doesn't know how to
have fun."[19] For the next two days, Luce was remote and cranky. Something apart from publishing matters bothered him.[20] Time Incers deduced further domestic discord, since Clare was in town. They guessed
right.

One morning that week at the Waldorf, Harry assumed Clare had
gone to Mass, so he telephoned Jean Dalrymple. Being somewhat deaf,
he tended to shout on the phone, especially when distraught. Clare, as
it happened, had not yet left the building. Through the wall, she heard
him say, "I tell you, I've done everything I can. She refuses to give me a
divorce."[21]

Although she had given Harry permission to stray, Clare returned to confront him. He was mortified, then contrite, and finally begged forgiveness, confessing that he had been seeing Jean for the past four years. Staggering her further, he owned up to many one-night stands. As she listened to him almost brag about these, she saw a pathetic man with "excruciating emotional and mental misery," who was tormented not only by having betrayed her, but by a perverted sense of moral obligation to his mistress, coupled with religious guilt.[22]

Clare said again that she was ready to give him his freedom, knowing he would continue to be unhappy, whether he left her or not. Harry's response was to go down on his knees and beg her forgiveness. He said he no longer wanted to marry Jean, but to stay with her, "the one great love of his life." There would never be another, for only with her had he ever felt "like a whole man."[23]

Perplexed, she went to David for comfort and advice. He had never seen her at such a low ebb. She told him she was inclined to "chuck" her wrecked marriage and would need his support. "I can't do this alone, you must promise to stick by me."[24]

David pledged to stay close, seeing himself as potentially the main male presence in his sister's life.

▽

On August 11, C. D. Jackson found his boss "in a terrible maelstrom of trouble." It transpired that he was being blackmailed by Jean Dalrymple.

"The little bitch really has Harry by the short hairs," Jackson told Billings, "and every time she pulls 'em, it costs Harry another $100,000." Luce was calling him at all hours to unburden himself, saying that he felt like "a fool to get into this mess, but also like a heel." His sister Elisabeth and her lawyer husband, Tex Moore, had been informed of Jean's demand for money, and Bromley was doing damage control to prevent the scandal from leaking. "Now Clare has gotten wind of it— hence a fresh crisis."[25]

Billings, who had a love-hate relationship with Harry, was not sorry to see him suffer. "I hope his private dirt doesn't splatter on the company and therefore on me."[26] When he told his wife that Harry was "deep in woman-trouble," she laughed and said she was glad to see "his high and mightiness brought low." Billings felt the same. "What a hypocrite he is—preaching great Christian virtues and then practicing just the opposite!"[27]

Clare sought the seclusion of Sugar Hill to digest the reality of her fractured relationship with Harry. In mid-August, relishing the sound of robins in the apple trees, the sun shining on the pool, and a cool wind sweeping in from the foothills of the Berkshire Mountains, she wrote him a querulous yet strangely optimistic note.

> I no longer hope that you will ever be in love with me again. Nor would such ardors be seemly at our advanced ages! . . . I expect that what depresses us, in one another's presence, is that *we* see the dead body of our love lying between us, and we cannot decide whether we murdered it separately, together, or if, after all it did not die a natural death.
>
> And yet, somehow, I think it's going to be alright, don't you?[28]

She had been attracted to Harry initially for conventional reasons: his good looks, editorial brilliance, power, and enduring interest in the world. But above all it had been "just something mysterious. I wished to confide in him."[29] In extremis, the need was as urgent as ever.

Their apparent rapprochement left David Boothe feeling useless again, if not outright rejected. "Now that your marital difficulties have proven surmountable," he wrote her, "it behooves me to start getting my own house in order." He said he was going away for a couple of days, "for reflection, not devilment."[30]

Borrowing the Luces' Chrysler, he drove to Massachusetts with the intention of stopping off in Boston, where Clare suggested he look over the house she owned on Beacon Street. She told him, "I bought it for you." Skeptical, David did some local sleuthing and heard that she had acquired the property a couple of years before "in contemplation of a 3rd marital try."[31]

At work, a distracted Harry spent hours closeted with C. D. Jackson. After Clare returned to town, he started shuttling agitatedly between the office and the Waldorf. Finally, he declared himself incommunicado. Miss Thrasher said, "There's something terribly wrong with Mr. Luce. . . . I'm afraid he's going to turn Catholic."[32]

On August 17, Billings sensed the approach of "a climax of some sort." Harry became incensed after discovering that Clare had asked Roman Catholic officials if there were grounds for annulling his first marriage, in order to validate hers in the eyes of the Church. Lila would be deeply hurt if she found out about this, not least by having Rome rule her two sons illegitimate. When Harry told Clare he resented being "closed in on," she knelt and grabbed his legs, wailing, "It's all because I couldn't give you a baby that you don't love me any more." Embarrassed, he ordered her to "get up and stop that nonsense."[33] At this Clare said *she* wanted a divorce.

Out of his depth with such histrionics and vacillations, Harry went to see his mother at the Cosmopolitan Club. He told her of Clare's request and his own wish for "a bishop" to advise him. Elizabeth Root Luce, fanatical in her disdain for Catholicism, said, "No one can tell you what to do, *you* will have to decide it."

Harry sensed that his mother would not mind if Clare left him. "You don't like her," he said.[34]

She did not deny this and reminded him that from the start she had deplored their union. After he left, she concluded that Clare brought her son only trouble. *"I hope he will let her go!"*[35]

Thinking that distance might lend perspective, Harry set off on August 22 for a ten-day vacation in New Hampshire. While gone, he asked Clare to decide if she really wanted a divorce, and if so, on what terms. Jackson bet fifty-fifty on a permanent split and a big cash settlement for the wronged wife.[36] Rumors flew around Manhattan: Clare had demanded $4 million and 51 percent of company stock. Harry had said no, and the result was a stalemate.[37]

Incredible though such gossip was, Clare behaved during Harry's absence as if she already had influence at Time Inc. She called Billings and asked why Eliot Janeway, a friend of her husband's, was "representing himself as the mastermind of company policy." Billings told her Janeway was not popular among the staff, but advised Harry on "high politics." When Clare found out the man was paid $12,000 a year, she said she would like a "a snap job like that."[38]

"The damn bitch," Jackson growled after hearing about the exchange. He then went on to provide salacious details of Harry's infidelity. The boss's relationship with "Mrs. X," he said, had been platonic until Clare joined the Church. Only then had Harry "popped into bed" with her.[39]

That night Billings was shaken by a call from Harry. "Did you tell Clare that I kept Janeway on against the advice and wishes of all my associates?" Billings could not believe that she had acted so quickly and exaggeratedly betrayed his confidences. "No," he replied, "though she may have drawn that conclusion."[40]

Aware that Harry was in doubt about what she intended to do,

Clare felt a twinge of sympathy for him. "I reached my wretchedly low point several years ago," she wrote him, "when you perhaps were hardly aware of it. You reached yours in the recent past. . . . I fear one or the other of us has to try to be a saint."[41]

Harry, writing from his mountain retreat, took responsibility for their estrangement.

> I keep thinking of you wanting a window into my heart—and of how to give it to you . . . to me it seems that my heart and most of the rest of my innards are wide open to inspection. . . . You are the incomparable person in my life. I loved you without reservation and in the dearest hope of happiness for us both. I failed in my love for you and yet I deeply believe I would not fail again because if there is an "again," it would be a most precious gift—and would be cherished more seriously and less selfishly. You ought to have perfect love because with perfect love you are, not perfect (no, that can't be) but in your beauty and gaiety a very remarkable resemblance—and that near perfection I should certainly know is worth any kind of effort in "little things" and in great. It was a terrible thing that I should ever have lost the vision.[42]

Back at work by September 2, Harry was no wiser about Clare's intentions. Over lunch, he asked Billings what he knew about his "crisis with Clare." To avoid implicating Jackson and Grover, the editor said, "Nothing." Harry probed further. What were the survival prospects for his marriage? Billings said he doubted Clare would want to make a go of it.[43]

During the afternoon, the pace of office gossip picked up. Al Grover inadvertently dropped the name of "Mrs. X" to Billings and Jackson, who, not to be outdone, let on that Eliot Janeway was a friend of Jean Dalrymple—hence Clare's vindictive phone call. In a further revelation, C.D. said Luce was expecting his wife's decision on divorce that day, but she still had not made up her mind.[44]

"What a whirl of events, ideas and emotions," Billings wrote in his diary. "Sex makes more damn fools out of more people than liquor."[45]

Grover announced the next day that there would be no divorce. Clare would soon leave for Hollywood, to write a movie script for Darryl Zanuck, and Harry would probably go with her.[46]

Shortly afterward, Clare summoned Billings to the Waldorf for a late afternoon highball. He was surprised to find the front of her hair gray and her figure plumper. She said her screenplay was going to be an adaptation of C. S. Lewis's *The Screwtape Letters* and suggested he assign a *Life* "close-up on the Devil." As she rambled on about a group called Young Christian Workers, he was intrigued by her strange, ramrod-straight posture, as if she were making a speech. "She is clearly a woman under considerable stress, and religiously obsessed."[47]

These assumptions were confirmed when he heard from Grover that Clare was "again on the rampage, and giving Harry hellish trouble." She was now at a Catholic retreat and had disposed of many worldly belongings. They included her collection of five thousand books on drama and theater, many of them rare, donated to Georgetown University.[48]

▽

For some time, David Boothe had sensed that he was outstaying his welcome with the Luces. Clare understood his dilemma. If he left their orbit for some unknown terrain, he would resume drifting, with slight chance of finding a decent job. She had reneged on her offer to set him up in business, promising instead an outright gift of $50,000. But when he announced his intention to leave soon, Clare again disappointed him. She knew that once on the road, he was bound to dissipate his cash on booze, betting, and women.[49] During his last fruitless attempt "to find a spot," he had spent all $3,000 of her gift money.[50]

On the evening of Friday, October 3, the atmosphere at Sugar Hill curdled when David rejected her final entreaty to join the Church. At first she appeared hurt and disappointed, and then she accused him of being anti-God. "I don't intend to do business with unbaptized people."[51]

Had he converted, she said, he could have stayed near her and looked for work in New York City. But he sensed her reluctance to support him if he had done that. In a letter to George Waldo, David showed how well he understood his sister. "When Clare is in trouble she is quite human, she's a little girl and every man's heart goes out to her. When she is out of trouble, it's a different deal and I was getting conditioned for the end of our honeymoon."[52]

The significant word was *honeymoon,* indicating that David had felt virtually married while living with her for seven months. He had nurtured Clare when she was ill and commiserated during her bleak moments over Harry. Sensing, however subliminally, that his emotional as well as fiscal dependence on her had become unhealthy, he said he must leave, although he had no long-term plan in mind. She said that if he was determined, all she would give him was $2,800 and her Studebaker.[53] On Monday, David packed his bags and used the car to drop her off in Manhattan.

They drove there in a tense atmosphere. Clare resented the hours wasted on his instruction. For an intelligent man, she said, his rejection of Catholicism was incomprehensible. He agreed that he was beyond the spiritual pale, but asked, "Who is the Authority that determined whether my mind preferred evil to the Faith?"

"I am," Clare snapped.

Smarting over the diminution of her financial assistance, David reminded Clare of the night at the Waldorf when he had promised to stick with her should she divorce. He had also "performed a mission of service" after her hysterectomy and the painful encounter with Harry and Bromley that followed.

Clare said that his objective had not been merely to help her survive those traumas.

"What was it?"

"Examine your conscience."

At this, they pulled up in front of the Waldorf. Clare stepped out.

"Get in touch with me, *when* you get in trouble."

"Thank you," he said.

It occurred to David, as he wound his way uptown through heavy traffic, "that all the swarming and teeming Jews crossing our path have loads in common with me, we all deny Christ."[54]

21

HOLLYWOOD

*What the American public always wants is a
tragedy with a happy ending.*

—William Dean Howells

K ay Brown of the Leland Hayward Agency negotiated a $75,000
contract with 20th Century-Fox for Clare's *Screwtape* screenplay. It
called for delivery of the script in thirteen weeks, including time for
revisions, and promised payments in three installments: $25,000 each
on signing, completion, and movie release. In addition, the studio
promised a $10,000 accommodation allowance and two round-trip air-
line tickets to Los Angeles.

With the arrival of the first check for *Screwtape*, Clare again became
an active member of the show business community. As if to confirm
this, she entertained Noël Coward and Gertrude Lawrence on October
6 (the night of David's departure) for dinner and a private preview of
John Ford's *The Fugitive*. Adapted from Graham Greene's novel *The
Power and the Glory*, it starred Henry Fonda in the role of a whiskey
priest. Coward panned it as a vehicle for "ardent Catholic propaganda."[1]

Clare left for Hollywood on November 18, leaving Harry to follow.
As a farewell present, he fired Eliot Janeway.[2] Al Grover had only one
word to describe Luce's concessions to his wife: "infatuation."[3]

En route to Los Angeles, she pondered a letter from *Screwtape*'s author about the task ahead of her. C. S. Lewis wrote that "those who

know" had told him he was lucky to have the adaptation of his comic novel entrusted to her. "It wd [sic] be absurd of me to intrude any *advice*," he wrote, before telling her how to ensure Hollywood moguls kept faith with his intentions.

> That the Devils be represented as having no sense of humor whatever. The audience may laugh *at* them but never *with* them. The popular picture of the mocking or mischievous sprite wd be fatal to the whole story. . . . My devils ought to look like what are called "undertakers" in our country and (I think) "morticians" in yours.
>
> If the angels [mentioned near the end of his book] are to be shown at all I implore that they shall not be *female*. . . . Make them—by whatever means—unearthly, severe, and beautiful in a rather terrifying way. Masks, if you have a good man to make them, might be far better than real faces. I couldn't bear them to be the angels of modern church windows i.e. elongated consumptive schoolgirls with wings. And music to suit—something sharp and shrill and vibrant: nothing sentimental.[4]

At her first story conference with the studio head, Darryl F. Zanuck, Clare realized that he had no comprehension of the subtleties or meaning of Lewis's book. He had made one mistake already, casting Clifton Webb in the title role, mainly because he had him under contract. Clare tactfully pointed out that Webb, being a suave and elegant actor, was unsuited to play either of Lewis's devils. Zanuck, as Lewis had anticipated, wanted the angels to be female and played by established stars. His idea of showing satanic wickedness was to have Wormwood politely offer to escort an old lady across a street and midway shove her under a truck. Clare argued that the point of Lewis's satire was not to demonstrate the infamy of devils, since that was understood. What her script had to show was their wily determination to coax human beings into committing sinful acts. She told Zanuck how his suggested scene should ideally play out.

The nephew and heir of an elderly woman is helping her cross the street in heavy traffic. A devil appears and whispers in the young man's ear, "Give her a push." He recoils. "No, I can't do that, I'm too fond of her." The devil persists. "She's going to die soon anyway and, after all, you will get the inheritance."

Clare explained, "The devil's work is to tempt *us* to do evil."

Zanuck made a lame joke about his father being a rabbi and warning him that if he went to Hollywood, he would end up doing Satan's bidding.

"Now's your chance to do *God's* work," Clare said, "and get this story straight."[5]

Harry joined Clare in her rented Bel Air house on December 10 and stayed through Christmas. His present to her was a Madonna triptych by Adriaen Isenbrandt.[6] She entered it on her art acquisition list. "This picture, given to me after the 1947 'settlement' . . . my most sentimental possession." The adjective would not have appealed to C. S. Lewis.[7]

Over the festive season the Luces immersed themselves in Hollywood society, giving a party for more than three hundred members of the movie community that cost $12,000. Adherents of the Left and Right in West Coast politics met for the first time since the House Committee on Un-American Activities (HUAC) had begun to investigate alleged Communist subversives in the picture industry. They mingled uneasily, conscious of the ideological schism that divided them, yet united in their eagerness to cultivate the goodwill of the most powerful publisher in America.[8]

In his fiftieth year, Henry Luce had reached a new peak. The editorial opinions expressed in his magazines were largely his own and resonated around the globe. Many policy mavens considered them to be more influential than those of the President of the United States. Even as Harry cavorted with movie bigwigs, a member of his staff was editing Churchill's memoirs for serialization in *Life*.[9]

Clare, in contrast, was dispirited. Stalled on *Screwtape*, she felt in decline as a writer of dialogue.[10] Her 1942 script about China, *The 400 Million*, had gone nowhere. Now, just as she resumed screenwriting, there was panic over a decline in movie attendance, largely attributed to the growth of television.

▽

Leaving Clare to fulfill the final weeks of her Fox contract, Harry returned to New York on January 3, 1948. An advance copy awaited him of a new novel by Ralph Ingersoll, who had worked alongside the Luces on the first layouts of *Life*. It was an unflattering lampoon of them both. Entitled *The Great Ones*, the book portrayed Sturges Strong, the owner-editor of a fabulously successful magazine called *Facts* (Harry's original name for *Time*), as a dull egocentric. He was saddled with a money- and power-hungry wife named Letia Long. After multiple careers as a designer, painter, and bestselling author, she had become a war correspondent and politician. Early on, Ingersoll wrote, Sturges had had visions of his queenly spouse as co-runner of his company and tried to ingratiate her with his employees. "He wanted, for her, the satisfaction of their acknowledgment of her status."[11] But his dream failed to materialize. Incidents of betrayal and adultery proliferated, until all ended badly.

Clare, meanwhile, had a surprise encounter in Los Angeles with Julian Simpson, the World War I hero she had fallen in love with at twenty.

Having failed to see him in London during the war, and after fantasizing for more than two decades about what might have been had he been bold enough to run away with her, Clare was shocked by his appearance now. At fifty-four, Julian had lost the dark good looks she had kept in her mind's eye, and much of his quiet charm and charisma. "He was beefy," she recalled, "with a veined, whiskey nose, and he was a little pompous."[12]

How he found her in Los Angeles remained a mystery, as did his purpose for being in the country. He also elected not to tell her that in 1934 he had married an Australian heiress. She had died four years later.[13]

On February 2, from the house in West London he still shared with his mother, he wrote Clare that during their reunion he had "formed the impression" she was withdrawing into herself. Even so, he hoped for another chance to get to know her again and "to understand" what had kept them apart.[14]

In spite of Clare's promise to look him up on her next trip to London, they never met again. Julian returned to New South Wales after the death of his mother in 1950, and he died two years later at fifty-eight, in the homosexual quarter of Sydney. He was heavily in debt despite family inheritances, yet in his will he left £200 "to my friend James Maxwell Ramsay, a Commander in His Majesty's Royal Australian Navy."[15]

Lack of money had been a crucial obstacle to proposing at the height of their youthful romance. But perhaps the real cause of his marital misgivings—his bisexuality—had eluded her, and for the rest of her life would keep her from achieving a wholly satisfactory romantic attachment. A poem expressed her feelings.

The mind has a thousand eyes
And the heart but one;
Yet the light of a whole life dies
When love is done.[16]

▽

In the third week of January, Zanuck turned down Clare's 150-page screenplay. His accompanying note proved that he had not read C. S. Lewis's book. All he could deduce from the script was that Screwtape and Wormwood were "unpleasant characters" who talked "over the heads" of the average moviegoer. He said he had hoped for a story "about a lad who seduces a girl," after which nobody went to hell or heaven. What people really liked to see, he said, are "not devils, or for that matter angels, but Betty Grable and Hedy Lamarr in a passionate scene."[17]

Attempting to explain her failure in a five-page letter to Lewis, Clare said that her producer, Samuel Engel, had doubted her belief in Satan's existence. After realizing that she was sincere, Engel was "torn between dreadful alternatives: that I might be daft, or that he might be doomed."

She likened the making of movies to an automobile assembly belt. She had hoped "to lick the system" and be faithful to the intent and spirit of the book, even counting on Hollywood's ignorance of Christian theology as an advantage. But she had been wrong in thinking that Fox executives had no ideas on how to portray Screwtape. On the contrary, some saw him as an Al Capone type, "brutal and thuggish," or "a sadistic, paranoic manic depressive, first cousin to Frankenstein's monster." To others, he was a diabolically charming seducer.[18]

Clare tried to rationalize her failure to a fellow Catholic playwright, Donald Ogden Stewart: "Oh well, I had no business, in the rash pride of my new found faith, to think I could succeed where so many better men and women have failed—getting a touch of God into a movie!"[19]

▽

To honor her contract with Fox, Clare sketched out a fresh synopsis for Zanuck.[20] It was inspired by the recent box office successes of two Bing Crosby vehicles with pious themes, *Going My Way* and *The Bells of St. Mary's.*

Fifteen months before, addressing a religious audience in her home state, she had told the true story of Reverend Mother Benedict Duss, an American nun who, imprisoned in a French convent during the war, had been liberated with her fellow sisters by a troop of GIs. In gratitude, Mother Benedict and a French nun had traveled to the United States with $20 between them and, using an old factory and fifty acres of land donated by a local businessman, had built the Abbey of Regina Laudis in Bethlehem, Connecticut. Clare had predicted that this Benedictine community would last as long as the one the order had established at Monte Cassino around A.D. 529.[21]

Intrigued by the narrative possibilities of this story, she had asked her Catholic friend Gretta Palmer to gather more recent information from Mother Benedict. The journalist had obliged with a seventeen-page history. From this, Clare now conceived a scenario in which two young and attractive nuns, one a crack tennis player, arrived in Bethlehem to found an abbey similar to Regina Laudis. They received a warm welcome from a songwriter and, among others, an artist (based on Lauren Ford, a painter of religious subjects) who—in an act of biblical symbolism—allowed them to stay in her stable. But a few local commercial interests opposed the construction scheme. Clare's synopsis ended with the nuns using determination, guile, and charm to overcome obstacles and achieve their sacred goal.

She sent her outline to Zanuck and he responded with flowers and an encouraging note. "There is jubilation in heaven to-nite. Consternation in Hell, and great joy on earth—certainly in my heart. Your ever lovin' producer."[22]

Before continuing, Clare had conferences with a veteran script writer, Oscar Millard, who combined their ideas into a detailed treatment. Then, feeling full of energy and optimism, she checked into Arrowhead Springs Hotel, a mountain resort popular with actors, and began a screenplay tentatively called *Bethlehem*. Working with a Fox continuity expert, she completed a draft in three weeks.[23]

Harry came back to California for a few days in late February, and put off his return to New York when Clare became mysteriously ill. Her symptoms were exhaustion, nausea, and stomach and joint pains. She was diagnosed as suffering from "Virus X," a disease that had been prevalent in America for more than two years. It was later discovered to be not viral at all, but DDT poisoning, due to the chemical's near universal use in agricultural and household sprays.[24]

"I wish she'd croaked," Miss Thrasher said.[25]

22

CROONERS OF CATASTROPHE

A demagogue is a man who makes a dangerous highway look smoother than it is.

— ANONYMOUS

When a recovered Clare traveled back East in the first week of March 1948, she heard that the first annual international Gallup poll had ranked her the fourth most admired woman in the world. Only Eleanor Roosevelt, Madame Chiang, and Sister Kenny, the polio therapist, were ahead. For the next fifteen years, she would remain on the list, never falling below number six.

On April 10, Bernard Baruch held a forty-fifth birthday party for Clare at Hobcaw Barony in South Carolina. She did not feel like celebrating, because Harry had told her the day before that he had been offered $250,000 in cash for Mepkin—$100,000 more than he had paid for it in 1936—and was inclined to accept. He asked if she was ready to part with the property. She was not but said, "Dear, *you* decide."[1]

As early as 1933, Clare had been prompted to search for a winter retreat near the old rice fields of the Cooper River, after reading "The Marshes of Glynn" by Sidney Lanier. It was a poem about faith and redemption through pain and conversion.

As the marsh-hen secretly builds on the watery sod,
Behold I will build me a nest on the greatness of God:

I will fly in the greatness of God as the marsh-hen flies
In the freedom that fills all the space 'twixt the marsh and the skies . . . [2]

Curiously prophetic of her own spiritual progress, the verses had haunted her until she found Mepkin, an Indian word meaning "serene and lovely."[3] She had seen its potential as a paradise on earth, and Harry had agreed to buy it.[4]

The plantation was still not perfected, and this made losing it doubly hard for Clare. She persuaded Harry to sell only four thousand outer acres to a local lumber merchant and to give the buildings and remaining thirty-two hundred acres to the Trappist monks of the Abbey of Our Lady at Gethsemani, near Louisville, Kentucky.[5]

Luce's generous donation would enable the silent Trappists, Cistercians of the Strict Observance, to establish their third foundation in America, subject to Vatican approval. The plan, which Clare brokered, called for the transfer of a small number of monks from the Mother House to Mepkin, near the aptly named village of Moncks Corner. The plantation's existing house and cottages would serve as their base, while they built a chapel and agricultural facilities to make a self-sustaining enterprise. The site was initially to be called Our Lady of Mepkin and with more inmates might one day become an abbey.

One member of Harry's family who looked askance at losing Mepkin to a Roman Catholic order was his sister Elisabeth. A Wellesley graduate, fervent Calvinist, and supporter of Nationalist China, Beth was a huge influence on her brother. He talked to her so often that he had a direct telephone line from his office to her apartment.[6] Unlike their mother, she was warm toward Clare and had spent many happy days at the plantation, where her two boys had learned to fish, shoot quail and wild turkey, and play Monopoly and mah-jongg with their glamorous aunt. But now she felt Clare had put Harry seriously off track.

Beth Moore put her objection in writing, hoping to divert his philanthropy in a direction more palatable to the Luce family. In an extended nautical metaphor, she likened him to a "powerful battleship" surrounded by his mother and siblings—"your cruisers and even the lowly tugs," who nosed him into harbors, albeit of his own choosing. As he maneuvered, they served as lookouts, since it was impossible for a larger vessel "to have sufficient perspective, at all times, to steer a straight course."

While ready to admit that America needed more places of prayer,

Clare reading under a live oak at Mepkin, 1947

she regretted that when he was in a position to make a "truly princely gift" to one of the Protestant causes dear to his heart and hers, he was ceding an estate to Papists.[7]

But Harry's mind was made up. In mid-April, Mepkin was shuttered for the summer, and the long process of transfer began.

▽

Despite Clare's desire to put electoral politics behind her, she was chosen by the GOP convention in Hartford on May 17 to be one of six delegates to represent Fairfield County at the Republican National Convention in Philadelphia. Two days later, she announced her support of Senator Arthur Vandenberg as the Republican candidate for President, even though he denied wanting to run.

At sixty-four, Vandenberg was tall, white-haired, majestically deep-voiced, and egotistical. He had been a power in Congress since 1929 and was now its leading internationalist. For this reason if no other, Harry also favored him and undertook to promote his candidacy in *Time* and *Life*. It was rumored that Luce nursed a fantasy that if the Senator was elected President, he might become his Secretary of State.[8]

Isabel Hill was unhappy that many of the speeches she typed that spring were, however, not political, but for the Catholic lecture circuit. She was approaching fifty and did not want to spend the rest of her working life focused mostly on religious activities. So she quit the job she had held for fourteen years and went to work for John Hay Whitney.[9]

Her departure was a major crisis for Clare, who thought it "*far* easier to get along without a maid, or even a husband! than a secretary."[10] Fulton Sheen came to the rescue, offering her one of his part-time assistants, a Georgetown University graduate and ardent Catholic, Dorothy Charnley Farmer.

At their interview, Mrs. Farmer was captivated by her prospective employer, who struck her as looking amazingly young in a gray blouse and red waistcoat with matching turban. She felt herself swept up by Clare's theatrical persona and would remain enthralled for thirty-five years.

Plumply small (she snacked on butterballs), Dorothy was efficient, gifted at keeping unwanted callers at bay, and always cheerful. This last, along with humor, proved a crucial trait for coaxing Clare out of dark moods. More and more mutually dependent as the years went by, Dorothy and Clare formed a bond to be broken only by death.

Clare in a fashionable turban, spring 1948

In a commencement address at Creighton University in Omaha, Nebraska, Clare coined a graphic expression when she chastised modern man for being "a moral muttonhead." A strong faith in God, she went on, "is necessary to the preservation of national life, the enlargement of political liberty and the successful attainment of private happiness."[11] She continued her sharp coinages on June 21, the first day of the Republican National Convention in Philadelphia.

It was the hottest summer in the City of Brotherly Love since the Constitutional Convention of 1787. But this did not stop young people from jitterbugging in the streets, while inside the Convention Hall their elders were fanning themselves and sucking on elephant-shaped Popsicles. Sixty large fans, and ice hauled six flights up onto the roof, made little difference to the temperature in the baking Art Deco auditorium. Immense television lights beaming down on the proceedings intensified the heat.[12]

It was the first time a national political convention had ever been broadcast visually. An estimated ten million viewers watched in thirteen Eastern states. NBC, the biggest and richest network, had done something unheard of in awarding a single sponsor, *Life* magazine, broadcast rights to all three presidential conventions—Republican,

Democratic, and Progressive. This meant that the year's most important journalistic undertaking was controlled by Henry Luce. All commercials at each gathering would advertise Time Inc. products, and every display feature—down to reporters' badges and door signs—was labeled "LIFE-NBC." The coverage included everything from press conferences with the eventual nominees to interviews with delegates in barbershop chairs and a segment on hats worn by women on the floor. For all this Harry paid a bargain $250,000.[13]

It was unfortunate that he consequently financed the airing of an event that caught his wife looking so unprepossessing, and making a speech so overwrought, that Brock Pemberton wondered if she had lost her mind.[14] The columnist H. L. Mencken observed that "La Luce had not bothered to take lessons in television makeup." As a result, the harsh lights made her look ghostly, and the humidity flattened her hair.[15] Clare's choice of outfit was a disaster: a steel-gray taffeta dress with a sweat-inducing tight bodice and an ankle-length tiered skirt, unbecoming with low-heeled shoes.[16]

She followed the keynote speaker, Governor Dwight H. Green of Illinois, to the podium and berated Truman as a man "of phlegm not of fire," whose party was held hostage by the "lynch-loving Bourbons" on its right wing. Democrats as a whole were "less a party than a podge" and "a mish-mash of die-hard warring factions."[17]

Clare went on too long, and her alliterative invective distracted from valid political points. FDR and Truman were castigated as "troubadours of trouble, crooners of catastrophe," who could not win elections except "in a climate of crisis." It followed that they had "a vested interest in depression at home and war abroad."

What particularly exercised her was their capitulation to Stalin at Tehran, Yalta, and Potsdam. To show how much they liked "old Joe," she said, they had given him "all Eastern Europe, Manchuria, the Kuriles, North China, [and] coalitions in Poland, Yugoslavia, and Czechoslovakia." For this dereliction alone, voters must render President Truman "a gone goose."

Pre-nomination speeches traditionally expressed no direct support for any candidate. When Clare, to the ire of GOP officials, praised Vandenberg's work in creating a bipartisan approach to the new threat of Soviet Communism, pandemonium broke loose. The Michigan delegation, seizing on her remarks as an endorsement for their man, crowded the aisles, cheering and converging in a wild demonstration in front of the platform.[18]

She went on to throw barbs at Jim Crow Southerners who would shrink from going to heaven because it "isn't 100 per cent American," and at the "buckle-brained fringe" led by Henry Wallace, consisting of "economic spoonies and political bubbleheads." Even they were harmless compared with "labor racketeers, native and imported Communists, and foreign agents of the Kremlin." Her final tirade was hurled at the Democratic Party's "Pendergast wing run by the same city bosses who gave us Harry Truman in one of their more pixilated moments." How, she asked, could the President "rule with, and in, such political bedlam?"[19]

Clare soon discovered that a penalty of television exposure was a mound of abusive letters. She was accused of using "the expressions of a gutter woman," thereby letting the world know "how deadly the female of the species can be." One anonymous writer recommended that she be investigated by the House Committee on Un-American Activities for deriding Henry Wallace and "promoting a war between this country and Russia for the benefit of the Pope."[20]

Others were favorably impressed. William F. Buckley, Jr., a Yale undergraduate and member of the university's Political Union, was struck by her "marvelously animated" performance. Lord Beaverbrook cabled from aboard the *Queen Mary:* "Your speech in Philadelphia is a fine piece of oratory. You have spoken wonderfully well in and out of Congress but this is the high water mark."[21]

Governor Dewey of New York, the party's candidate in 1944, unanimously won renomination over Senator Robert Taft of Ohio. The most votes Vandenberg managed to attract were 62 on the second ballot. Earl Warren, Governor of California, was nominated for Vice President.

The whole extravaganza filled John Billings with mixed emotions. He acknowledged that it was television's year as far as politics was concerned, just as 1924 had been radio's transforming moment. Awed by the immediacy of NBC's camera coverage and commentary, he felt pessimistic about the new medium's effect on print and picture journalism.[22]

▽

Clare was interviewed in Ridgefield on July 1 and said again she was through as a politician. The Dewey-Warren ticket was "as good as elected" and did not need her help. Instead, she would go back to Philadelphia for the Democratic National Convention later that month, as a reporter for the United Features Syndicate.[23]

But she could not entirely forsake the limelight nor resist issuing another statement that made headlines and infuriated Truman. Knowing that he and Eleanor Roosevelt did not get along, Clare mischievously suggested he campaign for reelection with the former First Lady as his running mate. It would be highly practical politics, she said, because Mrs. Roosevelt was not only the best-known and -loved woman in the world, but the only Democrat "who could take back from Wallace the Negro vote, the labor vote, the underdog minority vote, and, as a mother of four boys in the service, the pacifist vote." It was essential for such a ticket to succeed, because its defeat would set back for a hundred years the chance for women "to be truly equal with men in politics."[24]

Newsweek quoted this on Monday, July 12, the day the Democrats convened. Philadelphia was still in the throes of a heat wave when Clare checked into her hotel. She occupied a deluxe air-conditioned suite, and for an extra $22 a day got a television set. It would spare her having to go to the stifling Convention Hall to hear the opening night speeches. She invited some friends to watch with her, including Randolph Churchill, who was covering the event for a British periodical, the journalists Stewart and Joseph Alsop, and Laura Z. Hobson.

Laura was now famous for having written the novel *Gentleman's Agreement*, the source for last year's Oscar-winning movie of the same name, starring Gregory Peck. The flickering screen afflicted her with a headache, and she went to the bathroom to look for an aspirin. On her way back, she caught sight of two crystal flasks beside Clare's bed. They were respectively filled with bright blue capsules of sodium amytal and red Seconals. Laura deduced that religion had not brought her friend peace.[25]

The chief reason for Clare's dependency on barbiturates was the febrile nature of her constitution. She had always had abundant physical and mental energy and wanted to keep both working at full capacity. As an overworked editor at *Vanity Fair*, she had depended on large quantities of cigarettes and brandy. People often commented on the dark semicircles under her eyes and the overall appearance of frailty. She was aware now of some midlife attrition in body and mind and sometimes overdid consumption of alcohol and tobacco, after which she needed sleeping pills. She knew this seesawing was bad, but the illusion of herself as a superwoman had to be fed one way or another.

The Democratic National Convention lacked drama for Clare, since the renomination of Truman was a foregone conclusion. One line that caught press attention was delivered by the Mayor of Minneapolis, Hubert Horatio Humphrey. He urged his party to "get out of the shadow of states' rights and walk forthrightly into the bright sunshine of human rights." This reference to Negro emancipation drove furious Southern delegates to the exits. They subsequently chose Governor Strom Thurmond of South Carolina as presidential nominee of a States' Rights Party known as "the Dixiecrats."

On July 14, Truman and Alben W. Barkley of Kentucky became their party's nominees.[26]

▽

While Clare was in Philadelphia, Harry spent time with his mother at her home in nearby Haverford. Elizabeth Root Luce had liver cancer and shortly after the visit sent her son a nine-page letter inscribed *Swan Song*.[27]

"There is some unfinished business between you & me," it began, "and though it will hurt you to read it & me to write it, yet I must clear it up while I may, for I think the time is short." She followed with a series of grievances that showed her and her daughter-in-law to be antagonists from the day Clare married Harry and failed to invite her to the wedding.

At their first meeting, she had been in awe of Clare's braininess and sophistication. But the elegance and hauteur of the younger woman had made her ill at ease in her plain black suit. "She froze the very marrow of my bones." She was further repelled by Clare's courtship of reporters and photographers. "Every one who could wield a pen . . . sprung up to write about her—her beauty, her wit, her brilliance. . . . They never seemed real to me." In her opinion, the "lurid and vulgar publicity" surrounding *The Women*, and press coverage of Clare's run for Congress, had demeaned Harry's image as a media giant. Pictures of him dunking doughnuts on the campaign trail had appalled her. "Must the good name of Luce be dragged around like this?"

Recently, she had been bewildered to receive a marital advisory from Clare: *I have had such happiness as has been given to few. But now a cloud has arisen no bigger than a woman's hand.* The implication of adultery was plain. "A chill of foreboding came over me. 'Whose hand?' I thought. 'What woman's hand save your own?' My son—my son, would that I had died for thee—my son—my son!"

Mrs. Luce could not comprehend Harry as a philanderer, but even this incident had been of slight import compared with the "stunning blow" of Clare's conversion. She was glad her missionary husband had not lived to see it. Her worst fear was that Harry was doomed to live in "a Roman Catholic atmosphere . . . open to every art of persuasion and flattery" that such clerics as Fulton J. Sheen might apply. "They will leave not one stone unturned to capture your famous self, or to weaken your own Faith, for which they have not an iota of respect, contemptuously counting it as rank heresy."[28]

That summer Clare, along with two other eminent converts, Evelyn Waugh and Graham Greene, was asked by the publisher Harcourt Brace to read and comment on galley proofs of a spiritual autobiography by Thomas Merton, due out that fall. She read it with special interest because Merton was a monk at the Gethsemani monastery, now taking over Mepkin. He was thirty-two, a poet and scholar. His book, *The Seven Storey Mountain*, gave an astonishingly frank account of his youth in prewar France and England, where, as a student at Cambridge, he had joined in drunken brawls, performed a mock crucifixion, and fathered an illegitimate child. After continuing to carouse for some years at Columbia University, he had begun attending Catholic Mass and was transformed by the peace it brought. In 1938, he had been baptized into the Catholic Church and then entered Gethsemani.[29] He now combined monasticism with literary work, dealing with the alienation of contemporary man and the need for a visceral relationship with God.

All three reviewers responded enthusiastically to the memoir. Waugh said it "may well prove of permanent interest in the history of religious experience." He remarked that Merton's colloquial style "should prove popular with readers who are repelled by formal theological language." Greene wrote that it had "pattern and meaning valid for us all." Clare predicted that readers would turn to *The Seven Storey Mountain* "a hundred years from now to find out what went on in the heart of man in this cruel century."[30] Sooner than that, the book would sell more than three million copies worldwide. In the words of *Time*, it "redefined the image of monasticism and made the concept of saintliness accessible to moderns."[31]

Intrigued by Merton's spiritual journey, Clare sent the monk a letter on August 12, the Feast Day of Saint Clare. As if in the confessional, she wrote, "I am in the world more deeply embroiled and entangled with these living dead who hold my wrists, and pour flattery into my still greedy ear, and puff up cushions for me to sit upon." She also described

Mepkin and its "long green enchantment" in winter, acres of azaleas in spring, and "summer's drugged damp heat . . . enormous woods whirring with mosquitoes where snakes slip through to the black ooze of the river." These last two were discouraging enough to potential inhabitants, but another sentence would have repercussions: "Berkeley County, SC is the most illiterate, most disease-ridden county in the USA."[32]

As her admiration for Merton increased, she sent him gifts, replacing his old typewriter, and gratifying his thirst for music with a recording of Handel's *Messiah*. She envied the dedication and discipline that he had for his double vocations, the cloister and the pen. Though she was free to implement the numerous ideas for articles and books that she claimed to have, her mind went blank whenever she sat at her desk.

Her fears of a permanent block had increased when the Catholic publisher Frank Sheed told her that a number of his authors complained of a creative blackout following conversion. She asked Sister Madeleva, a poet at Saint Mary's College in Indiana, to pray that she might again write "with the bounce and joy that I once knew."[33]

▽

As she settled in for what remained of summer at Sugar Hill, nagging worries about David plagued her. She had not seen him since their frosty parting at the Waldorf curbside the previous fall, but she heard from George Waldo that he had been roving about the South and Southwest. Having let him go with just a car and a token amount of money, she felt uneasy and was now in the middle of a thirty-six-day novena for him, asking God to let her bear all the evils David might have to endure, so he could have a new chance in life.[34]

Hope of that was interrupted on Tuesday, August 31, by a telephone call from her brother that disturbed and irritated her. He asked for money to pay a life insurance premium, making his Phoenix girlfriend, Mary Jane, the beneficiary. When Clare refused, he asked her to say a prayer for him and hung up.

Later that day, he wrote his "Dear Sister" a note so awkward and truncated as to indicate extreme stress.

> It was nice speaking with you this evening even tho you declined
> to advance the twenty-one [dollar] insurance premium.
> During the war years the beneficiary was you. . . . In good
> time we shall me [sic] of that I am sure. Love David.

In a strange postscript, he said that he was enclosing a two-page letter to Regina Foote, a flight instructor with whom he had been living for about a month in Burbank, California. The tone of the note was recriminatory, and he asked Clare to use her judgment about forwarding it. Apparently he owed the woman $55 in rent and $75 for a personal loan. Before decamping, he had left her a typewriter in settlement, but she was insisting on cash and had asked a credit agency to collect from him.[35]

Clare knew her brother hoped she would pay these debts. His letter was postmarked Los Angeles, September 1. Four days later, just as her novena for him ended, word came that Mr. David Franklin Boothe had been reported missing on the West Coast, and was presumed dead.[36]

23

OUTSIDE THE PALE

Man is not what he thinks he is, he is what he hides.

—ANDRÉ MALRAUX

After leaving Clare in Manhattan nine months before, David had driven north and checked into the Smith Hotel in White Plains, New York. That night, October 7, 1947, he had written a summary of his recent experiences for George Waldo, with a copy for Clare, "while details are fresh of mind." He said it was not "a gripe nor crying letter," but an assessment of why his reunion with the Luces had gone so awry. He felt his sister's mercurial personality had something to do with it, so he began by analyzing her character, abilities, current situation, and prospects.

> To me, Clare is a tragic figure. She is not a genius; a clever writer, brilliant & smart, yes, otherwise typed as having intellectual power. . . . Reading press notices and hearing the plaudits of secondary & fawning characters has taken toll. You realize, George that in this temporal world she has but two and a quarter friends, you, self, & [Isabel] Hill. A husband that hates her & in addition is probably the most disliked (among her acquaintances) female in the USA. Currently is approaching the convent door and glancing heavenward, for a sign not to enter. Here is a life that could pro-

duce much & today is motivated by indecision and uncertainty. Why? Simple. Because she can't make a louse come to heel.[1]

David's hatred of Harry had been palpable ever since the divorce lawyer had shown up after Clare's hysterectomy. He went on to cite the times he had vainly solicited help from her, and quoted one of her excuses: "I have no rich men that love me any more, & besides when you got through with me there was nothing left."

This last was a reference to his disastrous prewar attempt to be a Wall Street stockbroker, resulting in heavy losses from her Brokaw alimony portfolio. Moving on, David did not excuse his own inadequacies. "I am not productive, not creative, am devoid of friends and most of all my sister regards me as an expatriate." As he once said of himself, he was a man outside the pale. His hope of starting a business with Clare's financial help had been "shot to hell" when he quit the conversion program she mapped out for him.

He feigned optimism about his prospects, saying that he had "tried a bit of psychiatry" on himself and concluded that he was still mentally sharp, "despite association with psychopathics the past seven months."

David gave Waldo the General Post Office in El Paso, Texas, as his next address.[2] For the moment he was flush. He had not only Clare's car and parting gift of $2,800, but $2,000 "borrowed" from Waldo, having cultivated the latter's friendship for the same reason he had Willoughby's. Both men adored Clare, and he felt that if he encouraged their courtship, they would speak well of him to her, as well as grant him favors. In the process, he had come to regard them as confidantes, to be kept informed of his whereabouts, health, and state of mind.

Replying to David, Waldo sharply observed that although it was "natural and right" for brother and sister to be close, he should not think that Clare had any "legal, moral or implied financial obligation" to him. Whatever money she had given him in the past was out of affection. Rather than wait for "vague financing that may never come," he should do something practical for himself.[3]

David preferred to be self-indulgent. En route to Texas, he checked into a two-bedroom cottage in Panama City, Florida. From there, he wrote another letter to Waldo that sounded like a farewell.

I am glad that I got away & yet am quite sad, for no one knows better than I do that life without responsibility, direction or purpose is futile. And so I rush madly across the country much in the same fashion as the common eel who departs his fresh water streams & unaccountably pursues a hegira to the bottomless Bermuda Bay.

When I say a prayer, and on occasion I do, it is with the hope that all peoples who believe in a Creator will not have prayed in vain. I am certain that as surely as Clare will meet her Ann, so it is inevitable the Jews will reach their promised land & the Jap, who so heroically and foolishly died in battle, will rejoin his ancestors. The nuances of faith are of human invention, be they divinely inspired is beyond my ken. A hundred years or a hundred hours from now possibly, I shall know the answer.

So in passing I say, if I should die before I wake, I pray the Lord my soul to take, and likewise yours, Clare's, Harry's, black men, yellow men, and all men. Sincerely, David.[4]

▽

By early 1948, he had reached Arizona and was still writing to Waldo, complaining that the Luces ostracized him because he "knew too much" about their marital problems. There had been a time when David had claimed that Clare was the only person who counted in his life, and that he would gladly die for her.[5] But now he berated her as being devoid of feelings, "a cold hard intellect in a beautiful, womanly body."[6]

Waldo detected incestuous leanings in David, a subject that he had touched on with Clare.

> If the trouble with David is what you and I think it is, there is no more use in getting angry and repeatedly asking "Why does he do this, or why does he do that?" He does what the unnatural compulsion in him makes him do. The big question is "How can we rid him of his compulsion?"[7]

Little more was heard of David until August 12, when he wrote from a hotel in San Diego to tell Waldo he had "no intention currently or in futurity of asking for anything. Excepting, of course, your best wishes."

Nineteen days later, he spoke by phone to Clare for the last time, about his life insurance premium. Evidently he had spent the last of the money she and Waldo had given him. On September 5, he rented a red-and-yellow Aeronca two-seater plane from Grand Central Airport and flew six miles south and two miles west of Santa Monica, before plummeting into the Pacific Ocean. A party of Sea Scouts saw the crash and later noticed aircraft cushions and pieces of propeller floating on the surface. The Coast Guard patrolled the area for two days and came upon no more wreckage, while the Los Angeles Sheriff's Office dragged the sea floor to a depth of 120 feet. Neither group found David's body.[8]

The most poignant line in one obituary, and an appropriate epitaph for a man who had made so many futile attempts to get rich, was that at the time of his death, "Mr. Boothe lived in Ocean Park, Calif., where he was planning to set up his own business."[9]

24

THE TWILIGHT OF GOD

*Mysticism . . . is bound to be inviting to the person who is
afraid of the deep emotions.*

—Diana Trilling

David's end left Clare with an acute sense of guilt.[1] She knew that
her brother's soul had been "sick . . . unto death. And only great,
great love and patience would have healed it." Those she had shied
from giving. "I did not love enough."[2]

One of her recurring nightmares was that David wanted to murder
her. Now she dreamed with extra vividness that she had gone to look for
him, in a place that seemed like hell. Suddenly he was chasing her, trying to pull her "through a sea of black mud, mixed with gobs of blood."[3]

Dorothy Farmer helped wrap up David's affairs. Since his savings
account had a balance of only $13.02, she sent an outstanding $100
doctor's bill to Harry and asked Al Grover to find out if George Waldo
wanted Clare to repay David's $2,000 "loan," adding that Mrs. Luce
would not, however, settle gambling debts.[4] After retrieving a suitcase
of personal effects from Regina Foote, Dorothy discovered that David
and the young woman had a mutual interest in aviation, and had
planned to marry on Christmas Day. Miss Foote had last seen him just
one hour before he took off on his fatal flight. He had left, she said, "terribly discouraged by financial troubles."[5]

One of those had been Clare's refusal to pay his small life insurance premium. This did not stop her from hurriedly settling the bill now and claiming to be David's sole beneficiary, in case any of his girlfriends had expectations.[6]

▽

That September, Clare read an article in *Atlantic Monthly* entitled "Man Against Darkness" by Walter T. Stace, a Princeton philosophy professor. The essay drew special attention in religious, academic, and other circles, because of its author's pessimistic tone and admission that he had no religious belief.

> Since the world is not ruled by a spiritual being, but rather by blind forces, there cannot be any ideals, moral or otherwise, in the universe outside us. Our ideals, therefore, must proceed only from our own minds; they are our own inventions. Thus the world that surrounds us is an immense spiritual emptiness. Nature is nothing but matter in motion . . . governed, not by any purpose, but by blind forces and laws. . . . The life of man is meaningless too. Everything is futile, all effort is in the end worthless. A man may . . . still pursue disconnected ends, money, fame, art, science . . . but his life is hollow at the center.[7]

This paragraph in particular affected Clare, as she continued to wrestle with David's similar nihilism. Since her conversion, she had aspired to the heights of spiritual ecstasy, usually attained only by the most devout monks, nuns, and saints. She was so thrown by Stace's bleakness that she found herself harboring the same suicidal thoughts as during her dark night of the soul at the Waldorf exactly three years before. To dispel them, she set to work on a rebuttal, hoping *Atlantic Monthly* would publish it.

But she underestimated the breadth and depth of reading needed to counter such a scholarly piece. Among the books and articles she selected were Arnold Toynbee's *Civilization on Trial*, Robert C. Hartnett's "The Religion of the Founding Fathers," Adrienne Koch's *Philosophy of Thomas Jefferson*, the prose works of Heinrich Heine, F. S. C. Northrop's *The Meeting of East and West*, Lenin's *Collected Works*, Fulton J. Sheen's *Communism and the Conscience of the West*, as well as *The Communist Manifesto* and *Das Kapital* of Marx and Engels. She even perused Josef

Stalin's *Problems of Leninism,* not to mention Lincoln Barnett's "God and the American People," William J. McDonald's "The Religion of Communism," and an 1846 encyclical of Pope Pius IX.[8]

Months went by before she had amassed enough material to begin her essay. The writing took many more weeks, and the result was a lucid examination of what she saw as the struggle shaking the modern world, between the "Godfearing power of Democracy and the God-hating power of Communism." After dividing her sixteen-thousand-word manuscript into four sections, she realized she had something too long for an article and too short for a book. She called it *The Twilight of God,* and when it was published the following year as one of Regnery's Human Affairs Pamphlets, she could take pride in having produced an impressive polemic.[9]

Section I, "Is the United States a Christian Nation?," began provocatively. "That Communism hates God is a matter of official record. But that Democracy—American Democracy—fears God is a matter not easily proved." Citing Toynbee, Clare supported his view that Western civilization had been "living on spiritual capital," in that society clung "to Christian practice without possessing Christian belief—and practice unsupported by belief is a *wasting asset.*" She pointed out that of all the fifty-six signers of the Declaration of Independence, only Jefferson had claimed to be a deist, believing in the teachings of a mortal Jesus, but not in revelations from the Son of God. If Jefferson lived now, he might fear for the fate of the nation upon learning that an educator as prominent as Stace trumpeted atheism and asserted the worthlessness, futility, hollowness, and amorality of human existence.

More worrisome, to her mind, was that others in academe were passing on fewer and fewer Christian precepts to future leaders. The effect of this spiritual neglect showed in the breakup of one in three American families by divorce, the uncharitable reluctance of the country to take in more displaced persons from war-ravaged Europe and Asia, and the abuse of nature by overconsumption of raw materials. This led Clare to conclude that the Christian spirit in the United States was withering, and to question if it was dead in the USSR, "as we so commonly suppose."

Her second section, "Is the Soviet Union Irreligious?," granted that the Communist concept of man was that he is an animal without a soul, and that religion, as Marx said, was merely an opium that bourgeois capitalist institutions had used to stupefy and exploit the working class.

Lenin, in consequence, had declared atheism an integral part of his cultural revolution.

Clare suggested that the Soviet Union's postwar socialistic creed was, paradoxically, "more *religious in spirit*" than that of the United States. This was due not to any supernatural aspect of Communism, but to its ability to inspire the kind of devotion, fidelity, and fanaticism once found in adherents of traditional faiths. While Marxist tenets might appeal to the poor and disenfranchised on a materialistic level, she thought that, "strangely enough, its deepest appeal is often to the talented, the rich and the famous, and is experienced by them as an emotion, or a *mystique*." They were drawn to it by idealistic appetites or spiritual needs that craved satisfaction. Most of all, and most dangerous, it appealed to intellectuals.

In using the words *religion* and *religious* in connection with Communism and its followers, Clare was imputing a supernatural character not to Communism, but to the *religious a priori* that Communism taps in man, inspiring a devotion, fidelity, rigidity, fanaticism, and apostolicity generally associated with religionists.

She noted that Reinhold Niebuhr had called Communism a Christian heresy. She thought it "a political perversion of the Golden Rule, that primary law of natural theology which has manifested itself in every great religion." Would America's failure to find Christian solutions to global economic and political problems lead distraught people to accept Communist solutions? If man did turn to an alternative set of beliefs, in crisis or not, he must be a "religious incurable," looking for salvation not through the Cross but through the Hammer and Sickle, with Lenin the Messiah of the new religion, Marx and Engels its prophets, *Das Kapital* its Bible, and the likes of Trotsky its heretics.

In fact, Clare went on, Marx had invented nothing new. He carried atheistic materialism to its logical conclusion, making a faith out of man's lack of it. What alarmed Christians was not just that Communists wanted a more equable share of material goods. After all, early followers of Jesus had voluntarily shared lives and goods, as those in convents and monasteries still did. She said that the Soviet system disturbed the faithful because it saw man purely as an animal with no soul or spirit. Like a pig, he was born to "root, and rut, and rot," with no hope of existence beyond.

Heine, a German Jew and friend of Marx, had anticipated her bleak assessment a century before. He saw the spread of Communist ideology as the arrival of "wild gloomy times," heralding the smell of "Russian leather, blood, godlessness and many whippings." Acknowledging the subhuman aspect of that fear, Clare saw a more insidious threat in socialism's donning of some of the emotional trappings of religion. Could this new "faith" be the transforming power that some sought in order to unify East and West? Was it the only alternative form of worship for America and the world?

In her third section, "Christianity or Totalitarianism?," she tackled the position of atheists who were not Communists, in particular the eminent British scientist Sir Julian Huxley. He did not deny the metaphysical impulse in man, but he believed that science, logic, and psychology had brought human beings to a stage where God was no longer "a useful hypothesis." Huxley put the Almighty in the same category as pagan gods, angels, demons, "and other small spiritual fry"—a human product, arising from ignorance and the neurosis of helplessness.

Clare said that while Marx offered mankind what he believed to be a superior creed, Huxley and Stace wanted no belief at all. The latter thought moral self-control would not save man from doing evil. In the future, only educators, and doctors and psychiatrists with their pills and injections, might do what Christ and the prophets had failed to do. The professors claimed that men without faith could live decent lives. Clare countered that they could do so only "in an atmosphere where *other men do believe*." Atheists were parasites on the Christian tradition, and it was of interest "to see them try to live their 'decent' lives in the godless environment of a Nazi or Communist America!"

In her fourth and final section, "Must We Have a 'Holy War' with Russia?," she argued that all major conflicts tended to take on the character of a crusade. World War I's shibboleth had been "Make the World Safe for Democracy."

> A real crusading title for the second World War was never found. The press and the people continued to call the conflict "World War II," although nobody liked that. It contained the dreadful suggestion that we were engaged in what was to be a series of world conflicts. . . .
>
> The very fact that in World War II the USSR fought on our side rather than on the German side (which ideologically was so much closer to the Soviet position) did help in a measure to keep us from indulging in too much self-satisfied and self-commendatory praise of the utter purity of our own political and religious motives.

There would be little, except the grace of God, to prevent us from wallowing in hypocrisy once we found ourselves fighting against the sons of Marx and Lenin. For this reason, if for no other, we should regard the impulse to wage a "holy war" with Russia as *a great temptation to the growth of an un-Christian spirit in the nation.*[10]

She noted that an awareness of the fundamental conflict between the Soviet Union's material and the West's spiritual interpretation of the nature of man had caused Stalin to write in *Problems of Leninism*, "It is inconceivable that the Soviet Republic should continue to exist for a long period side by side with imperialist states—ultimately one or the other must conquer."

At the end of *The Twilight of God*, Clare speculated how Soviet expansionism might be contained. The atom bomb gave America protection for the time being. Washington had already asked the world to accept joint stewardship of its nuclear arsenal and was helping diffuse Marxist-Leninist propaganda by reconstructing Europe with Marshall Plan funds. But in order to resist being conquered by the "dynamic false faith of Communism," she warned, "we must resolutely refuse to yield the liberties of those we have promised to safeguard. We must keep sufficient military strength to discourage any sudden use of force to which Russia might be impelled by what [the Kremlin] considered tempting evidence of our physical or moral weakness. *To defend the truth and to save their souls, Christians must be just as ready to combat the world as to renounce it.*"[11]

25

COME TO THE STABLE

$$\triangledown$$

The practice of an art demands one's whole self.

—Delacroix

For the first time in eight years, Clare did not campaign for herself or anyone else in the fall of 1948. While recognizing that Thomas Dewey had been a highly competent, racket-busting Governor of New York State, she disliked him. She was especially offended when one of his aides told her she was not welcome on the stump. They were running a "peace and national unity campaign," he said, and she was "too aggressive and controversial."[1]

Dewey was so confident of success that he took a week off the trail in the final month before voting. Meanwhile President Truman traveled thirty-one thousand miles around the country in a bulletproof train, giving 350 speeches. Luckily for him, the season brought such a huge harvest of corn and wheat that people felt prosperous and turned out in great numbers to shout, "Give 'em hell, Harry!" Nevertheless, polls continued to show the GOP ticket way ahead. Clare's political instinct told her otherwise, and she accepted a friend's thousand-dollar bet that Truman would win.[2]

After the polls closed on Tuesday, November 2, the Luces walked through Times Square and saw a running caption display on the New

York Times Building: TRUMAN COMES OUT OF BRIDGEPORT WITH A LARGE PLURALITY. Clare said, "Dewey's had it, because you can go back through all history, and whichever party came out of that town ahead won the national election." Harry looked annoyed. She went to bed at midnight, and he stayed up waiting for results that he hoped would prove her wrong. At 3:00 A.M., she returned to the sitting room and found him close to the radio, just as news came that Truman had won the electoral college vote. After breakfast, it was announced that the President had had a popular margin of two million. Clare joked that she "shed no bitter tears," because she had won lots of money betting on the victor.[3]

Four days later, the most distinguished literary stylist to be published in *Life* arrived in New York, and was driven to the Plaza Hotel for dinner with the Luces. Clare had managed to enlist Evelyn Waugh to write an article on Catholicism.[4] Waugh assessed the evening in a letter to his wife, Laura.

> It was not a great success; caviar, dover soles flown in that day from England etc., but neither aware of what they ate or drank. He handsome, well-mannered, well-dressed, densely stupid. She exquisitely elegant, clever as a monkey, self-centered. She came back with me and sat in my suite talking about religion for a long time but complained later that I had no heart.[5]

Clare rumbled Waugh's determination to exploit and intimidate Harry by ordering the most expensive items on the menu and wine list. "I ate very little," she recalled of the four or five courses served, "to show up his vulgarity."[6]

Though keen to become a fixture on the Catholic lecture circuit, Clare hesitated to address the National Council of Catholic Women in New Orleans, when she heard that four Negro delegates had been denied seats on the grounds that it was state policy. "All I can say is—it's a lousy law," she told reporters.[7]

Her speech sounded surprisingly anti-feminist. She warned that women who married for security without fulfilling the obligations of "motherhood, wifehood and domesticity . . . might pay the penalties of frustration, neurosis and physical disorders." Those who went further, as she had, and pursued disparate careers that took them away from home should brace for "loneliness and fatigue."[8]

At her own local church, Saint Mary's in Ridgefield, Connecticut, she gave a speech entitled "The Dramatic Perfection of the Mass," a topic that suited her own theatricality. Appearing at Maryland's College of Notre Dame, she was introduced by Monsignor Sheen. "Woman was just a side issue at the time of creation," he joked. "Tonight she will be the whole show." The speech that followed was a postconversion mix of religion and secular affairs, "Christianity in the Atomic Age."[9]

Clare again invoked the prime ritual of Catholicism on November 13, at Convent of the Sacred Heart in Overbrook, Pennsylvania, in an address entitled "The Playwright in the Pews." As soon as the doors opened, an enthusiastic crowd stormed in and ticket sellers were overwhelmed. At 8:30 P.M., the stage curtains parted and Clare, in a dark blue dress, stepped forward to thunderous applause.

In the audience was a forty-year-old lapsed Catholic named Constance O'Hara. A sometime playwright herself, she was curious to see how the author of *The Women* performed in her new role as inspirational orator. She was expecting to scoff but was disarmed by Clare's seemingly surprised smile, as though the wild reception was unexpected. O'Hara's next impression was of a "brittle blonde with a thousand-voltage charm," yet the eyes in the exquisite face were sad.

Clare spoke for two hours. O'Hara noticed how she moved about the platform with the ease of a dancer, gesturing gracefully. At times she resorted to humor, captivating the audience with charm and sincerity. She remarked on how rapt congregations were at Mass. This was especially true during Communion. But after the Benediction, the dramatist in her always felt a need for catharsis. "I want to hear the crash of cymbals."

The audience gave her a standing ovation. Nuns escorted Clare to a neighboring parlor for a reception. Schoolboys clamored for autographs, clergymen bowed over her hand, old ladies offered Saint Anthony's medals. They had read about a $65,000 burglary in her apartment the week before and said the image would protect her remaining jewelry.

Waiting in line, O'Hara noted that Clare's forceful stage presence had disappeared. There were bruises of exhaustion under her eyes, and her extended hand looked frail. She spoke in a gentle voice, but her demeanor changed when O'Hara stood before her. Apparently, she sensed the proximity of an apostate as well as a disillusioned competitor.

A look that was steel and flame bored into me.... This woman was capable of unleashed power and fury. I tried to stare her down, interested in what I had aroused. I sauntered from the room, feeling that stare going through to my spine.[10]

▽

In January 1949, Thomas Merton felt that Clare was struggling too hard to be a good Catholic. He suggested she try to do nothing for a while and learn "to submit completely to the idea of loving God."[11] An opportunity to follow the monk's advice came when Lord Beaverbrook invited the Luces for an extended stay at Cromarty House, his winter mansion in Montego Bay, Jamaica.

They arrived there on January 13, and Clare quickly established a vacation routine. She rose early and rode in Max's car to daily Mass at a local church. Harry began to accompany her, and a fellow worshipper noticed that he made all the correct liturgical responses.[12] For the next three weeks, husband and wife swam and walked on the beach, acquiring deep tans, something they had rarely done since their Cuban honeymoon in 1936. They also ate heartily, and Clare gained seven needed pounds.[13]

Beaverbrook's other guests included his twenty-year-old, peachy-complexioned granddaughter Lady Jeanne Campbell. At one dinner, attended by John B. McNair, the Prime Minister of New Brunswick, Clare monologued so relentlessly that Max was reminded of Ernest Bevin holding the floor at Churchill's wartime cabinet meetings. McNair was nevertheless captivated and invited her to fish in his province, promising a guard of honor when she arrived.[14]

Clare was disinclined to do any writing in Jamaica, having heard that *Bethlehem*, the screenplay left so confidently with Darryl Zanuck a year before, had been extensively restructured by Oscar Millard and others. It was now in production under a new title, *Come to the Stable*, and the only credit she could expect was for her original story.[15]

More discouragement came in a cable, reporting that Fox had declined her latest script, *Saint Anthony and the Gambler*.[16] It was a spiritual, antic melodrama about a New York gambler finding a sweepstakes ticket in front of a statue of Saint Anthony, tracking down the ticket's owner, an Italian Countess, and being hired as her butler in reward. Among other improbable incidents, a young girl accidentally swallowed the ticket, and the gambler discovered he had a twin brother who was a Catholic priest.

This farce demonstrated that Clare had lost her gift for plausible comedy. Sam Engel sent copies of the script to Fox colleagues, only to report that it had elicited "a unanimous and resounding *NO* from everyone."[17]

▽

Back in New York, Clare took on a new confessor and spiritual adviser recommended by Monsignor Sheen. He was Wilfrid Thibodeau, a forty-five-year-old Frenchman and a member of the Fathers of the Blessed Sacrament, based at the fashionable church of St. Jean Baptiste on Lexington Avenue. With his wiry hair above a strong face, he looked like an ascetic. There was a sternness about him that signaled he had no time for nonsense.[18] Yet his large eyes were full of compassion, and he proved to be so understanding and sympathetic in the confessional that Clare was soon baring her soul to him in letters as well.

She wrote Thibodeau on February 16 to say she had experienced what she had prayed for since her conversion: a religious rapture. It had come the minute she opened her eyes that morning. As she lay in bed alone, enjoying the benign emotions enveloping her, life suddenly seemed as simple and pure as it had when she was eighteen. "I feel young in my soul, and eager to walk in the sunshine with my Beloved . . . if I should have the good fortune to meet Him."[19]

But the serenity was fleeting. By the end of the month, Clare was

Father Wilfrid Thibodeau, c. 1949

234

telling Father Thibodeau that the city looked bleak, its dark streets and unlit rooms conjuring "spoiled and wasted" days of her youth.

Gazing west from her twenty-eighth-floor apartment at the neon glow of Broadway, she remembered the first night of *The Women* and felt wistful for "the lights of fame that no longer spell my name." The only theater connection she had at the moment was an off-Broadway one-acter by Gertrude Stein called *Yes Is for a Very Young Man*. One of its central characters, a woman living in Vichy France, was said to be based on her.

Depressive images proliferated in letters to Thibodeau. She told him that she felt alone as if in a jungle. Even familiar sounds such as laughter, the ring of a telephone, or the rattle of a cocktail shaker seemed as menacing "as the snarl of wild beasts."[20] A climax to her gloom came one day during Lent, as she knelt in church. Unholy thoughts buzzed in her head like wasps, leaving her confused and discouraged. She lit a candle for David and, emerging into daylight, wanted to cover her face. "It felt like a taut mask that didn't quite fit around the eyes. I had been praying so hard my *face* felt naked!"

Even in her despair, she had flashes of caustic humor. Reluctantly preparing an address to the National Conference of Christians and Jews in Washington, she groused to Thibodeau, "The whole thing is so phony. Some Christian always gets up and coos at the audience, 'And after all, we must *never* forget Jesus was a Jew,' and I think, rather rudely, 'You *might* add, only on His mother's side.'"[21]

She returned to Sugar Hill before the onset of spring and found nothing in bloom. Wandering through the house, she no longer got pleasure from its jades, porcelains, silver ornaments, and rare books. There was a time, she wrote Father Thibodeau, when she had tried to compensate for the ebb of Harry's desire by amassing objects, desperate to believe that "gleaming furniture or oriental splendor helped to *prolong* love." Now, excess felt like a burden to be shed, in order to experience "the calm of surrender, and the passion of prayer."[22]

Her closeness to Thibodeau grew as a result of these confidences. Within weeks she was addressing him as "my darling Father T" and insisting he call her Clare, because "Mrs. Luce" reminded her "of most of the things that make me sad."[23]

No matter how nurturing her confessor was, he could not protect Clare from the sycophantic strangers whom she wowed in the briefest encounters. It took a fellow convert to point out that her compulsion to charm people indiscriminately was like "patting strange dogs on the head." Before long they wanted to jump into her lap with muddy paws.[24] But the art of seduction—called vamping in her mother's time—was genetic, inherited from both parents. It was a drive more for devotion than sex. She wanted to conquer all comers, even though her interest in them could be short-lived.

As her fame as a Catholic speaker grew, a number of women became acolytes, their admiration bordering on the erotic. A prospective devotee of this ilk was Constance O'Hara, who gushed over her as a personality and performer in a letter to their mutual friend Brock Pemberton. The producer forwarded it to Clare. Intrigued by its candor and perceptiveness, she invited O'Hara to meet her in Philadelphia, where she was to participate in a forum in late March.

In advance, she read O'Hara's play, *Years of the Locusts*, about nuns offering succor to the wounded during the Battle of Ypres in World War I. It had been produced in 1938 at the prestigious Birmingham Repertory Theatre and praised by its renowned director, Sir Barry Jackson, as "the most beautiful—and most satisfying" play he had ever put on. O'Hara had for a while thereafter been dubbed a "successor" to the author of *The Women*.[25]

But then her career had stalled, leading to a suicide attempt. She had turned to journalism and lectures, yet continued to dream of wealth and fame as a playwright. Clare personified this ambition. "Mentally," O'Hara wrote in her autobiography, *Heaven Was Not Enough*, "I had pitted myself against this woman who had everything I had ever wanted."[26] She felt they had similar gifts, but "she wants more from them than they are able to give. I have had less than they deserve."[27]

At 9:00 A.M. on March 24, she found Clare in a luxury suite at the Warwick Hotel, wearing an austere gray dress and smiling. The smile, she surmised, was that of a sophisticate trying to put an inferior at ease. Over a formal breakfast, Clare talked about being overextended. Constance had a twinge of sympathy for her as someone seeking her identity in too many disparate spheres.

Clare, for her part, perceived O'Hara as a lapsed communicant, ripe for recapture, and hard up.[28] "I know what you're going to do," she said. "You're coming with me to Sheed & Ward." She had just become an editorial board member of the London-based religious publishing house. It had been founded in 1926 by Frank Sheed and Maisie Ward, a husband-and-wife team eminent on both sides of the Atlantic as proponents of progressive Catholicism. They had scored a public relations coup by adding Clare to their directorate, and while flattered by their desire to publish anything she cared to write, she did not want to be burdened with more work for them. She accordingly offered Constance $1,500 to dramatize the Catechism for an audiovisual project that she herself had no desire to tackle. The cash-strapped journalist was delighted.

> Breakfast over, she pushed me down in a big red chair by the fireplace, and curled up opposite like a college girl. The telephone shrilled. Bellboys knocked and handed in telegrams and letters. Flowers came. She glanced briefly at the cards, the floral tributes. I loved the symbols of success so intensely that my Achilles heel was throbbing. . . .
>
> She pushed me down in the chair each time I attempted to leave. We talked about many things, of dramatizing Bernanos's *Joy* together, of her book *Europe in the Spring*, which she defended against my jeers.
>
> "Don't make fun of that book. It's as sound as the day I wrote it."[29]

Four hours passed, Clare confiding many of her life's difficulties and disappointments. Constance, infatuated, was left with the impression the convert had discovered that "bitterness is based on *nothing*, sorrow on *something*."[30]

▽

By her forty-sixth birthday, Clare noticed her hair was thinning at the temples. At that time she had a dream, in which all her teeth crumbled and fell out "like bits of corn."[31] Alarmed, and starved for companionship, she invited Constance O'Hara (already in New York, working on the audiovisual project for Sheed & Ward) to join her for Mass.

Kneeling beside her, Constance felt the stares of fellow congregants.

> I realized that Clare Luce's personality was dominant, dwarfing those around her. As a companion she was fascinating and exhausting. There was no peace with her, no quiet moment. And yet there was that sweetness in her nature that made it easy to become excessive, even to worship a little . . . out of her sight you missed her; granted that she was disturbing and possessive and impossible,

you looked toward the silent telephone and wanted to hear that voice.[32]

And hear it Constance did, most often around midnight. They talked into the small hours about the Council of Trent, St. John the Baptist, and the neglected Spanish dramatist Jacinto Benavente.[33] During Holy Week, they attended daily Mass together. At breakfast one morning, Clare was withdrawn.

"We will all die alone in hotel rooms in twenty years or so," she said, "or in some hospital with a paid nurse beside us, because we have no children."

Constance tried to temper her morbidity. "You won't get lost," she said. "For the first time in your life you've found something big enough to hold you."[34]

On Maundy Thursday, Clare hired Constance as a temporary assistant to handle mail. While the younger woman drafted messages and telegrams and cables, she sat with her feet up, absorbed in Robert Sherwood's *Roosevelt and Hopkins.*

"You'd think from this book," she said with some irritation, "Roosevelt won the war single-handed. I guess none of the rest of us ever did a thing."

Constance was soon exhausted, since Clare never let secretaries relax for a second. One night in her sparse hotel room, Father Sheen telephoned.

"How do you like Clare?"

"I like her very much, and it scares me to death."

Over the line, she sensed his embarrassment at her frankness.

"Ah! She's marvelous."

Constance felt duped, realizing that Clare was using Sheed & Ward, daily Masses, secretarial intimacy, and now Sheen in a concerted effort to round her up as a lost sheep. This was confirmed by a call from her ensnarer, saying that the Monsignor had reserved scarce places for them at the Good Friday service he would conduct in St. Patrick's Cathedral.

The following day, Constance was disconcerted to find herself seated some distance behind Clare, who was seated with Harry. Did Clare's crusade now include her famously Presbyterian husband?

Over the weekend, Clare kept up her inducements. On Easter eve, she gave Constance a luxurious traveling case and took her to meet Father Thibodeau in a fortresslike building attached to St. Jean Baptiste. When he appeared, she peremptorily ordered her, "Go to confession."

Constance was unprepared, but followed the priest. She had difficulty enumerating her sins, but he was so profound in advising her how to atone that she felt "as if the struggle for faith were over instead of just beginning."[35]

Clare rewarded her with an invitation to the seven o'clock low Mass conducted on Easter Day by Sheen in the Lady Chapel of St. Patrick's. Breakfast at the Waldorf with the Monsignor would follow. "I'm always alone on holidays. Harry goes to visit his children. . . . We'll have some fun."

Thrilled, Constance sent Clare two of the most ostentatious orchids she could find. Next morning at the service, she decided to take Communion. Afterward, they joined worshippers flocking around Sheen, and Constance checked with Clare about their rendezvous at the Waldorf.

"We're not meeting," Clare said airily. "Harry's going with me to [High] Mass. Isn't it terrific?"

Overhearing, Sheen wheeled around. His face was taut with anger, and his eyes turned from blue to piercing coal black. Clare put on a naughty-girl pout, while Constance started for the door. A sympathetic Sheen called her back and proffered a card for the same service Clare and Harry would be attending. It was to be celebrated by Cardinal Spellman.

Leaving the cathedral later, Constance caught sight of the Luces on the other side of Fiftieth Street with Elsa Maxwell between them. Clare wore a sable coat, and Elsa's outfit was ornamented with a pair of orchids. Looking more closely, Constance recognized them as her Easter gift to Clare.[36]

▽

Henry Luce left New York the next day for five weeks in Europe. Clare was to have gone with him but begged off at the last minute. She meant to spend the next six months writing at Sugar Hill.[37]

Although Harry was traveling ostensibly on business, his letters showed that a good part of his tour amounted to a spiritual quest. He visited cathedrals, attended Masses, and lunched with clerics. Most important of all, Clare arranged for him to meet Pope Pius.

In her letter to the Pontiff, she reminded him of her own three audiences: in 1940 with a group of tourists, in 1944 with the House Military Affairs Committee, and in 1945 alone. "During that third interview did Your Holiness see what I did not know myself: that I yearned for the Light and the Truth that were nowhere to be found in this melancholy world except in His Church? And did you then, while we talked of large impersonal matters, say a little prayer for my conversion? Oh, I do believe that you did!"

She requested the Holy Father's help in persuading her husband, who "will shortly arrive in Rome," to become a Catholic. "For he is longing in his heart—as I once did in mine—for the ineffable riches of Christ, the fullness of the Faith. He is not wholly aware of this." She closed with a request that the Pope "say a prayer for his conversion just like the one you may have said for mine," and signed off, "Your obedient daughter in Christ."[38]

When not working in her study or running the house, Clare was diverted by the beauty and lushness of spring on her hillside. She reveled in a splash of hot-gold daffodils, apple and dogwood blossoms, and budding maples. At night, she educated herself in classical music, listening to records of Bach's Mass in B Minor, Beethoven's *Appassionata* sonata, and Stravinsky's *Le Rossignol*, interspersed with Gregorian chants.[39]

By the end of April, however, she felt isolated, and summoned Constance O'Hara for a long weekend, installing her in Harry's suite. During the day, both women read and walked. After dinner, they "went on a spree of confidences." On her return to New York, O'Hara had few misgivings about the intimacy that had developed, in spite of warnings that "rained down on me like hailstones."[40]

The next visitor was Elsa Maxwell, who was pleased to find that Clare's change of faith had left her sense of humor intact, along with "a greater sense of humanity."[41]

If so, it did not help write the play Clare had planned. But she did complete "Under the Fig Tree," an essay on personal travails and religious epiphanies. Encouragement was not lacking for her to start producing dialogue again. A letter praising *The Women* came from Moss Hart. He and his frequent collaborator, George S. Kaufman, had given her professional advice before the satire opened on Broadway. He now confessed that he had not admired it at the time.

> It's a first-rate job, and to my mind a highly under-rated play. . . . It's a highly civilized and biting comment on the social manners and morals of our society, and women's place in it. I had no idea it

was so good a play—I don't think you ever got the credit you deserved for it—and I just thought I'd write and tell you so.[42]

As if in proof of Hart's judgment, there was renewed interest in *The Women* among regional companies such as the Little Theater of Walla Walla in Washington State and another in Reno, Nevada. Both productions sold out.[43]

▽

For a while Clare flirted with politics again, agreeing to see a group of local Republican officials who wanted her to run for the Senate in 1950. They assured her that having a better grasp of foreign affairs than anyone in Connecticut, she was "the only possible candidate" to challenge the state's Democratic senior senator, Brien McMahon.[44] "Do you suppose God could *possibly* want me to do any such thing?" she asked Thibodeau. "My puritan streak makes me imagine sometimes that He might want it *precisely* because it would be such a horrible penance."[45]

Representative John Lodge, who had won her House seat, was reported to hanker for the nomination, as did former Governor James C. Shannon. The eagerness of two qualified rivals further discouraged Clare, who wrote Lord Beaverbrook that the more she was pressed for a decision about returning to politics, "the less appetite I have for it."[46]

She retained, however, her avid interest in world affairs and began to write an article for *Plain Talk* magazine entitled "The Mystery of Our China Policy." Questioning the State Department's doctrine of Communist containment in all areas vital to American security, she asked why the United States was allowing a free China to collapse, while permitting Stalin to expand in the Pacific. The rationale was that Chinese Communists were nothing more than "agrarian reformists." But she pointed out that Mao and his revolutionaries "never made a secret of their Soviet orthodoxy." In fact, "agrarian reform is their platform promise. Communism is their party principle."

Of course, Clare went on, corruption—"mostly a product of war's tyrannies and tribulations"—existed among Chiang's Nationalists, as it did elsewhere. "The European black marketeer in his black Rolls Royce is a familiar figure today on the lush, unbombed French Riviera." Yet corruption was the excuse Washington made for not giving further aid to Chiang. Meanwhile, Mao's Reds had an official policy of mass murder and genocide.

She warned that America must be willing to tap its resources to the limit to defend itself. "A budgeted war is a lost war. If our desire to contain Communism in Asia or Europe is conditioned by how much it will cost—we are defeated now."[47]

▽

On May 17, Clare rounded up about forty people in a New York cinema to see a preview of *Come to the Stable*. They were mostly friends such as Bernard Baruch, as well as Catholic magazine editors, intellectuals, and clergymen. She seated herself between Constance O'Hara and Father Thibodeau. It was her first chance to assess what Oscar Millard and another screenwriter, Sally Benson, had done with her story.

The movie was directed by Harry Koster, known for his work on early Deanna Durbin pictures, and starred the Oscar-winning Loretta Young and Celeste Holm as the two nuns. It looked as though it had been shot in and around Bethlehem, Connecticut, but in fact derived almost entirely from a sixty-thousand-square-foot lot, the largest at 20th Century-Fox. Only the tennis-playing scene had a real locale, Henry Fonda's court in Brentwood. Young played Sister Margaret, and Holm Sister Scholastica, while Elsa Lanchester was the artist Amelia Potts, and Hugh Marlowe the handsome popular-song composer Robert Masen.[48]

Few of Clare's original lines survived, but her plot was largely intact, allowing for an overlay of slapstick humor and religious sentimentality. The movie represented the two sisters as belonging to a fictitious nursing order, for the obvious reason that contemplative Benedictines were unlikely to exchange feisty dialogue. Nor would they be inclined to drive a Jeep down Fifth Avenue in New York, importune land from a gambler, and lustily pound stakes through water lines. A not unwelcome commercial addition was to have a pretty chanteuse sing a song called "Through a Long and Sleepless Night," based on a Gregorian chant. It was composed by Alfred Newman, with lyrics by Mack Gordon, and was catchy enough to become a huge hit when it was recorded by Dinah Shore, Peggy Lee, and Vic Damone.

The screening came to an end with the triumphant dedication of the abbey and hospital of St. Jude. As the lights came up, there was applause and cries of "Author!" Clare stood and told the true story of the struggles of Mothers Benedict and Mary Aline to build the Abbey of Regina Laudis in Bethlehem.

On leaving the theater, Baruch said that *Come to the Stable* had made a "moving picture fan of him again."[49] But Constance thought it "no more than pleasant," and Gretta Palmer accused Clare of "marring the spiritual lives" of the real nuns whose adventures she had researched for her. Fathers Thibodeau and Wiatrak both expressed disapproval of the shenanigans of the screen Sisters.

When Clare and Constance took Thibodeau home to St. Jean Baptiste in the Luces' chauffeur-driven Cadillac, he sheepishly asked to be dropped off across the street, so his fellow priests would not see him step out of a limousine. As he walked away, Constance remarked, "He's a very holy man."

"He's too nice to see through us," Clare said with a knowing grin.[50]

Discomfited by the reactions of orthodox Catholics, she reconciled herself to Stable being "a commercial success but a mild spiritual failure."[51] But then she heard that Cardinal Spellman had been seen "rocking with laughter" at another preview.[52] Not quite truthfully, she wired Darryl Zanuck that "without exception all present" at her screening had found the movie "happy, inspiring and rewarding."[53] In his reply, Zanuck apologized for "some rather extensive alterations from the original version."[54]

The changes evidently paid off. Hollywood's trade papers hailed Come to the Stable as "inspiring," "tremendous," and "irresistible," predicting big grosses for the "charming original story by Luce."[55] Variety added that the movie had moments of poignancy and was directed with sensitivity. Clare proudly sent Beaverbrook a newspaper clipping trumpeting the picture's general release in late July. "It threatens to be a big box-office success," she wrote, "and these days . . . that makes my stock high in Hollywood."[56]

Thomas Merton—henceforth to be known as "Father Louis"—was ordained on May 26, 1949, in Bardstown, Kentucky. Clare missed the ceremony to welcome Harry back from Europe. But she left the following day to see the new priest conduct his first Mass. He used a chalice consecrated by Cardinal Spellman and told her afterward that she had been "explicitly remembered" in his prayers, and would be at every future service he conducted.[57]

She now had at least four clergymen concerned with her spiritual welfare, and recorded a dream she had about potential rivals for her attention and affection.

I am in a room. Fr. Wiatrak and Monsignor come in. I am very tired. I go to bed. So is Monsignor. He curls up alongside of me, and goes quietly to sleep. Fr. Wiatrak leaves the room, angry.[58]

June was unusually hot, so Clare retreated to her country study to work on the final draft of *The Twilight of God* and write a pile of letters to Catholics. She thanked Evelyn Waugh for sending her a copy of Ronald Knox's *Sermons*.

"A conversion is not easy in mid-stream, as Knox says. I had thought when I first became a Catholic that the feeling of strangeness that it brought into my relations with non-Catholics must soon wear off. . . . Does it sound most awfully bigoted and intolerant to say that I feel comfortable . . . only in the company of Catholics who are aware that Catholicism is the central fact of their lives?" Eager for more exposure to Waugh's nuanced mind, she invited him to visit Connecticut on his next trip to the States. Perhaps in the tranquil surroundings of Sugar Hill, he might be less "cruel" in arguing theology with her than he had been in New York.[59]

One particularly scorching day, Clare called Constance O'Hara and asked her to take some time off from her job for Sheed & Ward for some last-minute research help on *The Twilight of God*. "I'll want you to telephone all sorts of people . . . check every one of my quotes from Communist authorities. I have to be exact. I'll work you like a dog, and of course I'll give you a credit line, and a percentage of royalties after publication. O.K?"

As soon as Constance started work in the Russian room of the New York Public Library, she realized she had signed on for a formidable task. Clare had misattributed some words of Lenin to Trotsky and others of Marx to Stalin. Old Bolsheviks helped her authenticate quotations in vast Cyrillic tomes. One day she went to track remarks of Earl Browder at the *Daily Worker* offices on West Sixteenth Street.

A female archivist asked her, "Are you workin' for Mrs. Luce? Want to see somethin' about your lady friend?"

The file was copious and included a number of unflattering photographs of Clare at the Lido in Venice and in Hollywood. There were two particularly vicious examples of trick camera work, one superimposing her head on the near naked body of a bathing beauty, the other giving her a bogus mouth uttering incitements to class warfare.

The archivist asked, "You still want to be her friend?"[60]

Constance's participation in the Catechism project neared its end in late June. She did not care to stay in New York as a researcher and gofer, and Clare said nothing more about collaborating on a play.[61] No sooner had she announced her intention to leave than Dorothy Farmer called.

"You mean you're going back to Philadelphia without a word to Clare? It isn't fair. Don't throw away her friendship."

"Dorothy," Constance said, "I'm a realist. Women like Clare don't want friends. They don't need them. This time next year she'll have forgotten I ever lived."

"We haven't helped you at all," Dorothy conceded. "If only you hadn't left the church and gotten yourself all mixed up."

Constance called Clare to say good-bye, half hoping to hear regrets and further blandishments. But there was only a sudden aloofness at the end of the line. In a few adroit words, Clare established the fact that they did not know each other well.[62]

The younger woman never heard her dulcet tones again, except on the radio and television.[63] She blamed the split on their both being so self-centered that they "created Hell for themselves."[64] This was more true than she knew, for soon she had to write Clare and warn her that gossip about their suspected lesbianism was "emananting from the Convent of the Sacred Heart. . . . The Church broke up our friendship, as I had an excessive affection."[65]

This she candidly admitted to Gretta Palmer, whom she saw as a rival for Clare's love. "I thought she had great sweetness, even simplicity, and that she like myself was lonely. Her treatment of me was unbearably harsh. The pain is deep. . . . And even if it hurts butch—she liked me the best."[66]

In a letter to Father Thibodeau, Clare graphically described her own capacity to upset people "without knowing it." She felt that a Daliesque artist would portray her as "tripping thru salons like the *Eisenmadchen* of Nuremburg turned inside out, my delicate spikes tipped with blood, as I trailed blue chiffon, and passed out bunches of red roses. But I DON'T mean to wound, I just must have porcupine blood in me."[67]

Whatever her disappointment with Constance, she had a residue of feeling and at Christmas sent her a strange present, stuffed in a shabby box marked "Shaving Kit, $40." Inside, with layers of old newspaper and *Life* covers, lay a small porcelain lamb.[68]

The consequence of this gesture was a bombardment of letters from Constance that eventually so disturbed Clare that she wrote to a mutual acquaintance, the Catholic psychiatrist Dr. Karl Stern, that it had become clear to her that the woman was "both mentally and physically ill." Constance was now casting her as an "icy-hearted arch-fiend . . . whose lack of charity had achieved her final spiritual undoing," and was also sending venomous letters about her to mutual friends. Claiming to be baffled "when our 'friendship' was so slight," Clare said what bothered her most was that Constance might do herself physical harm. She asked Dr. Stern if he could help her, without the risk of being added to Constance's list of demons if he failed.[69]

Behind the communication with Stern lay Clare's dread that she might be prominently featured in the autobiography she had heard Constance intended to write. It was important, therefore, for him to have her version of their relationship.

▽

In July, Clare took in a young houseguest. He was Wilfrid Sheed, the eighteen-year-old son of Frank and Maisie. Recently crippled by polio, he had a well-stocked mind, droll wit, and equable temperament that endeared him to her. In turn, he developed an adolescent crush on a fellow Catholic who treated him without condescension toward his handicap.

> Her face was as clear as Harry's was clouded, with a radiance that was not simply sexy but . . . like lights going on in a dark house. It was almost as if she had chosen Luce as a foil to emphasize her own good qualities, which included manifest ease, friendliness, and uptake: you didn't have to tell her you were tired or hungry or, as you might with Harry, that you'd just fainted.[70]

Clare planned every detail of Wilfrid's stay. After a late breakfast, they usually read on the patio until lunch. In the afternoon, since he was an avid baseball fan, it was Dodgers games on an outdoor television set or laps in the pool. Clare, who had tried out for the 1920 Olympics, remained an excellent swimmer, but when they raced, she let the disabled youth win.[71]

Most of their talk, however, centered on religion. Clare spoke of her favorite saint and role model, Saint Thérèse of Lisieux, and said she was trying to emulate "The Little Flower's" simple aim to be unspectacular and "sanctify the small things in life."[72] But Wilfrid was already shrewd enough to see that Clare could never hope to match a divine who was "virtually the patron of anti-celebrity."[73]

Clare and Wilfrid Sheed at Sugar Hill, summer 1949

During one of their discussions, Clare marveled at Wilfrid's observation that "evenness of temperament is the true mark of spirituality."[74]
It was only a mirage for her, as she continued to battle extremes of ela-
tion and melancholy. He saw a manifestation of the latter when she fell
into "a cold, inexplicable burst of silence . . . which lasted two days and
disappeared as strangely as it came."[75]

One reason for her black moods, she told him, was her pitiful failure
to write a worthy play. She complained that since becoming a Catholic
she had lost her talent to compose anything with bite.[76] Instead, she was
writing a book on religion and politics, in yet another attempt to fulfill

her contract with Blanche Knopf, and laboring on a sleep-inducing section called "The Congressional Investigation on Atheism in the Scott Decision."[77]

An aspiring writer himself, Wilfrid understood her frustration. Yet at times she was so calm and ethereal as to be almost spectral. "She was in the process of recovering from Politics, but it didn't show. In fact, her breezy serenity suggested she had never had a bad day in her life."[78] Teasingly, she said she had taken him up because he "looked like a bright sort of chap who might have an idea every now and then." He suspected a more likely reason was that he "satisfied a deep passion in her, which was simply to instruct."[79]

Their "seminars" usually lasted until the early hours, often in her bedroom, under the gaze of Chagall's *Blue Angel*.[80] In a memoir of Clare written when he was in his early sixties, Sheed raised the question of whether their intimacy was comparable to the delicate attraction between the wife of a professor and a sensitive student in Robert Anderson's play *Tea and Sympathy*.

> I can only pass on my hazy impression that she was too courteous to rule out the possibility. One evening, she reclined on my bed in a way that was over too fast to be called an invitation by anyone short of Harpo Marx, but which suggested the possibility: in a different time and circumstance, perhaps.[81]

Expanding her generosity, Clare arranged for Wilfrid to have driving lessons in her capacious blue Buick. He practiced on the grounds and on quiet surrounding roads, becoming proficient enough to acquire a license. Then, to his amazement, Clare told him on August 22 that an Oldsmobile Series 76 was on its way to him from Detroit. It was her habit, she said, to give a surprise present to someone on that date, the anniversary of Ann Brokaw's birth. This gift came with the proviso that no one outside his family should know who gave it to him. The new automobile had been custom-fitted with the same special mechanisms as that produced for Franklin Roosevelt.[82]

Clare admired how well Wilfrid walked in heavy metal leg supports. He even managed to kneel when they recited the rosary, unsnapping his braces and dropping them to the floor.[83]

Weekends at Sugar Hill were more formal, with Harry arriving from town and talking almost exclusively about current subjects: a rise in tranquilizer drug use, the peptic ulcer boom, how many trucks it took to deliver his magazines. Wilfrid's predominant impressions of him were that his real life was elsewhere, and he had an "unflickering distaste" for his wife.[84] For her part, Clare made no secret of the fact that their marriage had cooled.[85]

Social life seemed to consist largely of a steady stream of slow-thinking businessmen and politicians, of the kind Clare had satirized in her book *Stuffed Shirts*. Wilfrid, hearing her pontificate, concluded that she settled for "slightly dumb company in order to shine the more." Only when friends like George Waldo or the amusing, raspy-voiced, and exceedingly plain Buff Cobb Rogers dropped by, did she relax her effort to impress and was "as girlish and funny as she was one-on-one."[86]

While Wilfrid profited in countless ways from proximity to his multifaceted benefactor, he would never forget a warning she gave him that summer. It related to his prodigious knowledge of sports lore, literature, theology, publishing, and American musicals.

"Watch out for envy," Clare said.

He was taken aback. "I don't see why anyone would envy a guy with polio."

"Yes, I guess that might slow them down some. But they'll find a way."[87]

Wearing an ill-fitting dinner jacket, Wilfrid escorted Clare to the New York premiere of *Come to the Stable* at Broadway's Rivoli Theatre on July 27. The street and sky were flooded with rays from a fifty-thousand-watt electric lamp, highlighting the marquee and numerous stage and screen stars entering the foyer.

The following day, the *New York Telegraph* reported that the movie was so full of sweetness that it "tended to become, on occasion, somewhat sticky." In contrast, the *New York Herald Tribune* found the picture humorous, tasteful, and sometimes moving, "with the same blend of faith as *Going My Way*." Bosley Crowther of *The New York Times* wrote that the film "dishes up . . . an assortment of happy conceits which not only tax credulity but verge on the absurd." He cited the scene where Celeste Holm played tennis in her long black habit and wimple, trying in vain to win a bet that would help finance the abbey hospital. Furthermore, Loretta Young kept flashing a beatific smile even in adversity, making the experience of watching her "exhausting, even to the most romantically inclined."[88]

Nevertheless, nationwide audiences made *Come to the Stable* a box office hit. Clare received countless laudatory letters from nuns, and when the list of the year's ten best movies was released by *Film Daily*, hers came in at number six, behind *The Snake Pit*, *The Red Shoes*, and *A Letter to Three Wives*, and ahead of *Home of the Brave*, *Command Decision*, and *The Heiress*.[89] It would receive no fewer than seven Academy Award nominations—for Young as best actress, for Holm and Lanchester as best supporting actresses, for cinematography, art direction, best song, and, in a huge compliment to Clare, for "Best Writing, Motion Picture Story."[90]

26

PILGRIMAGES

*We are so accustomed to disguising ourselves from others
that we end up disguising ourselves from ourselves.*

—LA ROCHEFOUCAULD

S oon after the launching of *Come to the Stable*, Clare was besieged by
national and local GOP leaders, begging her to run again for office.
The fact that she listened to them, and showed some interest, proved
that for all her newfound spirituality, she still missed public life. Evelyn
Waugh might well have said of her, as he had of the similarly diverted
Cyril Connolly, that "the cold dank pit of politics [was] the most insidious of all the enemies of promise."[1]

With the United States in recession, Mao Tse-tung's Communists
displacing Chiang Kai-shek's Nationalist government in China, and the
Soviet Union pursuing nuclear parity, the prospect of returning to the
capital daunted Clare. By a freak coincidence, both of the state's Democratic Senators would be on the ticket that year. William Benton was an
appointee incumbent seeking a two-year extension of his current tenure, and the senior Senator, Brien McMahon, intended to run for another six-year term. Clare had no interest in the "short term" junior
alternative and suggested that Republicans nominate Representative
John D. Lodge. If so, she might consider running against McMahon.[2]

She said nothing further until mid-September, when she was on
vacation at the Greenbrier Spa in West Virginia and Senator Margaret

Chase Smith issued a statement: "The party that nominates a woman for Vice-President or President will win the 1952 election." In response, a *Hartford Times* editorial suggested that "Mrs. Luce would make an excellent choice" for either.[3]

A reporter from the *New York Herald Tribune* asked Clare to comment. "A woman on the ticket would be an asset to either party," she said, "if one could be found twice as good as the average male vice-presidential candidate. This shouldn't be too difficult."

She reminded him of her suggestion that Eleanor Roosevelt be President Truman's running mate in 1948. When he asked if voters might be worried at the prospect of a female heir apparent in the White House, she quipped, "A President might of course die of heart failure if a woman were elected Vice-President."

Coyly, she suggested that if the Republicans were short of a good vice presidential candidate in 1952, they should nominate Senator Smith "or an equally able woman."[4]

From other quarters calls came for her to run for Governor of Connecticut, while a Dallas banker announced he was forming an organization to nominate and elect Clare Boothe Luce as President of the United States. Quoting statistics from her speeches, he noted that women were already a formidable power in American life, with 51 percent of the vote, and 70 percent of private wealth, owning 40 percent of real estate, and spending 85 percent of family income. Why not, he asked, have a former Congresswoman of superior intellect, who was well versed in foreign and military policy, as Chief Executive?[5]

On September 23, President Truman announced that "we have evidence that within recent weeks an atomic explosion occurred in the USSR." Despite his careful avoidance of the word *bomb*, it was clear that America's four-year monopoly of nuclear weaponry was at an end. This chastening development inaugurated the age of mutually assured destruction between the two superpowers. Clare scrapped a speech about free enterprise that she was scheduled to give to the Bridgeport Chamber of Commerce three days later, and instead delivered an apocalyptic oration on nuclear war policy.[6]

When she rose to address the gathering, her simple gray dress with white collar and cuffs and black felt beret made her look, to one reporter, "like a French student headed for school." But she quickly revealed her mature command of defense strategy. Stalin's acquisition of the atom bomb made war "more and more likely," she warned. Congress therefore must enact a "push-button plan" to mobilize and deploy servicemen and civilians—women included—where they could effectively respond to a Russian atomic attack. The United States should also offer "every diplomatic concession possible, short of appeasement," to Stalin to induce him to accept Bernard Baruch's plan for a global nuclear control agency, stymied in the UN since 1946. She would support "any other similar plan of atomic control, which calls for penetration of the Iron Curtain by an international fact-finding or inspection body with power to punish a nation illegally hoarding fissionable material or making bombs." Loud applause followed her remarks.[7]

Within three weeks, congressional advocates of an accelerated American nuclear arms production program, led by none other than Senator McMahon, put such pressure on Truman that he authorized the Atomic Energy Commission to expand all nuclear bomb manufacturing plants.[8]

Clare's speech, and a passionate article by her in *The New Leader* appealing for a "second emancipation of the Negro," led commentators to speculate further that she was contemplating a return to politics.[9] At issue for the GOP was the possibility that in 1950 it might be able to gain control of the Upper Chamber.[10] An even more exciting scenario was that General Dwight D. Eisenhower might be the Republican candidate for President two years later.[11]

▽

Clare left for a five-week tour of Europe in mid-October with her latest convert, Buff Cobb. Italy took up much space on their itinerary, giving the trip a spiritual cast, especially since it included a meeting with the Pope. They were assured of a particularly receptive audience, because Clare had recently heard that Pius XII and Monsignor Sheen had been corresponding about her.

Sheen had passed on a startling remark of hers, that she had a "desire and intention of some day abandoning the world." It was unclear if by this she meant to enter a convent, but Sheen felt the Holy Father should be informed. Pius had responded in terms unusually complimentary of a layperson. The Monsignor had shared these encomiums with Father Thibodeau, who in turn had forwarded them to Clare.

The Pope described her as "a great apostle and a great orator," one of the most intelligent, eloquent, and "truly great women of the world" he had ever met. But apparently he did not see her in a wimple. With such attributes, he wrote, it was a pity she had given up Congress. She should consider returning to Washington, where she was needed "in these tragic and critical times, to write, give talks and illumine the public on moral and spiritual issues."

Thibodeau told Clare that her papal audience could be a turning point. "This is quite an assignment, quite a mission the Holy Father is giving you."[12]

Clare and Buff traveled south from Rome on October 21 to the Pope's country residence, the old gray Castel Gandolfo. Its ambience was of the sixteenth century, with clerics in crimson and spear-carrying guards in multicolored baggy trousers.

Far from instructing Clare as to how she could be a lay evangelist for the Church, Pius seemed more interested in talking about current political and diplomatic concerns. He launched into a review of the repercussions of World War II and noted that the United States had been magnanimous in victory. "This is the first time in history that conquerors have won a war and bound up the wounds that they have inflicted." Looking ahead, he hoped that "the difficulties of the time and the burdens placed upon Americans will not be so great that they will forget the children of less fortunate lands."[13]

He then flabbergasted Clare by suggesting that now that Myron C. Taylor, the longtime American representative to the Holy See, was about to retire, her husband would be a welcome successor. The Pope seemed to like the idea of a Protestant in that position. He suggested that Mr. Luce could serve without having to resign from Time Inc. and would be free to spend every other two months in America, if he chose.[14]

The audience lasted twenty minutes, confounding Clare, who had expected Pius to speak more about her.

After an excursion to see Rome's pagan ruins and churches, she told a Catholic journalist that it felt like "coming home."[15] She knelt in the crypt at St. Paul's Outside the Walls and prayed for her husband over the bones of the Apostle.

On Sunday, October 30, Clare and Buff attended an early Mass in the catacombs, where early Christians had buried their dead. This vast labyrinth of narrow galleries beneath the Appian Way stretched six hundred miles in various directions. In one vault, equipped with a rough wooden altar, iron crucifix, and flickering candles, Clare became aware of a yellow skull in a niche above her left shoulder. "Its sexless, sightless stare held my liquid, living glance. . . . I was face to face with *my own secret face*."[16]

Before leaving the city, she went to see Augusto Marchesi, the red-haired boy whose school fees she had been paying for several years. She learned from his teachers that he had an aptitude for machine work, so she arranged for him to be trained as a mechanic.

▽

On November 2, at the Uffizi Gallery in Florence, Clare sauntered ahead of Buff into a room of Italian Renaissance paintings. She paused in front of Botticelli's *Birth of Venus* and became aware of a man in a bright red shirt standing beside her. He began speaking knowledgeably about the picture in a Latin American accent. She turned toward him, and her glance was met by the flashing dark eyes of a swarthy Creole, his mixture of Spanish and Indian blood showing clearly in his rugged facial features. He had thick black hair and brows and seemed to be about her own age.

Just then, Buff caught up and was alarmed to hear Clare giving the stranger her name and that of her hotel. Buff was filled with dread at the prospect of "all that beautiful jewelery, and more particularly her beautiful person," falling prey to this attractive foreigner.[17] But Clare had sensed the stranger's quality and breeding. He turned out to be Carlos Chávez, the internationally distinguished Mexican composer, conductor, and founder of the Orquesta Sinfónica de México.

For two decades the fifty-year-old Chávez had been well-known in New York music circles, having lived in Greenwich Village in the 1920s, befriended the composer Aaron Copland, produced concerts for the Museum of Modern Art, and deputized for Arturo Toscanini with the NBC Symphony Orchestra. Had Clare not been tone-deaf, and until recently biased against music (on account of her father's incessant violin practicing), she might have heard of him. As it was, the Uffizi encounter would flower into a twenty-eight-year relationship.[18]

The last three weeks of the tour demonstrated her range of acquaintance with Europe's international set. She and Buff dined with the art connoisseur Bernard Berenson in I Tatti, his villa in the Tuscan hills northeast of Florence. At eighty-four, he was in physical decline, his tiny hands bony and his skull so thin that it looked crushable. Peevish at first, he soon warmed to Clare's charm and preferred exchanging spicy gossip to discussing paintings.[19] In Paris, Clare shopped at Dior and dined, unaccompanied by Buff, with Chávez. She also saw André Malraux, who had written articles for her at *Vanity Fair*, and the political philosopher Raymond Aron. Charles Murphy, a *Time* Incer who was writing a biography of the Duke of Windsor, arranged a dinner with His Royal Highness and the Duchess at their mansion on Boulevard Suchet.

Buff was impressed by their cuisine and couture. "But oh!" she wrote in her diary, "they are a frail, lost unhappy little pair of might-have-beens!"[20]

The two women went on to London, where on November 17 they attended the British premiere of *Come to the Stable*. That same night, Evelyn Waugh gave a dinner for Clare at the Hyde Park Hotel and introduced her to several prominent Catholics, including Ronald Knox and Father Martin D'Arcy, who had converted him in 1930.[21] Waugh later complained to Nancy Mitford that his "great party for Mrs. Luce" had cost him a lot of money, and he thought it odd that everyone followed up with thank-you notes except the guest of honor.[22]

Before flying home, Clare heard Winston Churchill, now leader of the opposition, make a major speech in the House of Commons, and later had tea with him. Winston was about to turn seventy-five and had recently had a stroke, but it had not stopped his work on the third volume of his magnum opus, *The Second World War*. Afterward, Clare asked Harry to send the old man a thousand newfangled plastic paper clips, because he was "*nuts* about gadgets."[23]

▽

While Clare was in London, twenty-eight Trappist monks left the Gethsemani monastery in Kentucky by charter bus and traveled more than six hundred miles to establish a new commune, Our Lady of the Immaculate Heart, at Mepkin. The move was the culmination of eighteen months of complex negotiations involving the Luces, the order, and the Vatican, which had to sanction the handover of the plantation's structures and remaining grounds.

Clare had almost compromised the deal with her indiscreet letter of the previous August to Thomas Merton, stating that Berkeley County was "the most illiterate, most disease-ridden" in America. This had given the Abbot of Gethsemani pause. He was reluctant to send his monks to such an insalubrious spot. "I have the responsibility, dear Mrs. Luce, of the pioneer community on my soul and I [fear] whether we could keep our Rule under these conditions."[24]

She had tried to rectify matters by pointing out that air-conditioning, refrigeration, and DDT spray had made Mepkin tolerable year-round.[25] In further encouragement, she donated original maps of the area, landscaping sketches, and blueprints of the main residence and three guest cottages. An advance party of surveyors reassured the Abbot about the terrain, flora, and fauna of the county, so the transfer went ahead, and the monks—six priests, twelve novices of the priesthood, and ten lay brothers—settled in without mishap.

Half of them were World War II veterans, including a dentist, a tailor, a cook, and others with special skills. Until they could build a chapel and dormitories, they used the main house to dine and worship, and the cottages for sleeping.

On their first full day, they followed their Kentucky routine. At 2:00 A.M., after little more than five hours' sleep, they rose from their straw mattresses and prayed for the first of seven times. Then, dressed in white tunics and black scapulars, with hoods over their shaved heads, they attended High Mass, meditated, and worked silently at indoor chores or outdoor laboring jobs. At noon, they ate a lunch of soup and vegetables in Clare's former sitting room, with its huge window overlooking the river. After further menial duties, they attended Vespers and Compline, the last office of the day. Having no radio or television, they read before retiring.

Little was needed to improve the beauty of the formal gardens or wild surroundings. "If this place doesn't lift a man to God," the Superior said, "then he's hopeless, because nothing will."[26]

27

CARLOS AND CLARITA

▽

The more human beings can learn about other human
beings, this side of nausea, the better.

—T. S. MATTHEWS

As the new year began, Drew Pearson, in his widely syndicated column "Washington Merry-Go-Round," said that "the most significant political battle of 1950 will be fought in Connecticut." The state
GOP was desperate to find candidates to run against the formidable
Democratic trio of Chester Bowles for the governorship, and William
Benton and Brien McMahon for the United States Senate. Clare remained the party's first choice to oppose McMahon, but she again declined and in a surprise move suggested her husband. She knew that
Harry was bored with his job and talked with him about pursuing a new
career in politics. He was guardedly agreeable, but only to run for Benton's temporary seat. Before making any commitment, however, he and
Clare paid their first visit to Mepkin monastery, marking the sixth anniversary of Ann's death.

Harry was moved by the simplicity and dedication of the men from
Gethsemani. "The happy 'peace of soul' or whatever of the monks," he
wrote his son Hank, "has to be seen to be believed."[1] Abruptly switching subjects, he asked Hank's advice regarding the senatorial run. "Businessmen seem to think I am not the kind of fellow to get votes."[2] A
college friend had warned him he would dislike working in the capital,

and Tom Matthews, *Time*'s newly appointed editor, passionately insisted he could not be spared.[3]

For the rest of the month, Harry was undecided. "I shouldn't have gotten into this," he told Billings, "I feel miserable." After a sample poll of voters confirmed he could not win, he let the politicos know he was not available.[4]

This redoubled the pressure on Clare, especially when Harry told Al Morano that if she won, he intended to take a house in Washington and spend half his time there so she would not feel lonely as she had as a Congresswoman. But on February 13, she gave "definite and final notice" that she would not run.[5]

▽

That evening, Clare left for a vacation in Mexico in a heavy snowstorm. Since meeting Carlos Chávez in Florence last November, she found herself drawn to him intellectually and physically. In addition to his other distinctions, Carlos was founding director of the National Institute of Fine Arts and Literature, and had sent her some handsome books on the modern Mexican art renaissance that affected her with a sense of a country "throbbing with artistic vitality and even genius."[6] She cabled coquettishly that she was "looking forward to art gallery visit with Uffizi guide." He wired back that the guide would do more than that. He would be at the airport to greet her.[7]

Looking down as the plane approached the Central American isthmus, Clare made notes for a *Vogue* article about her travels. The topography of Mexico seemed to rise "tawny-flanked from the sea, like a vast sprawling lion, lying on a lush carpet of verdant banana and coconut palms and golden henequen, spread between the Pacific and the Gulf." The hot winds of the Sierra Madre, a double mountain range stretching from the United States border to Guatemala, visibly kept the air dry and dusty, and sparse rains made the earth look "as if it had sweated."[8]

Meeting her as promised, Carlos took Clare to the Hotel Del Prado in Mexico City. He had arranged a Valentine's Day gathering of friends to welcome her that evening, at the house he shared with his wife of some twenty-eight years, Otilia Ortiz, a classical pianist, and their three children.[9]

At sunset Clare set off for the party. Her limousine cruised northwestward past elegant villas that reflected French and Spanish influences and concrete public buildings aping Mayan pyramids. Climbing the hills—*lomas*—that overlooked the capital, they entered the exclusive outreach of Chapultepec. Designed and landscaped by *norteameri-canos* in the 1920s, it consisted of spacious houses and gardens and a large Olmsted-like park. Soon they arrived at Avenida Pirineos 775, the Chávez villa.

Carlos had assembled an impressive roster of guests, at least three of whom Clare already knew. Seeing the artist Miguel Covarrubias brought back memories of the marvelous caricatures he had done for her at

Carlos Chávez, 1950

Vanity Fair, including one of her as an angel hovering over FDR's first inauguration. The others were the muralist Diego Rivera and his wife, Frida Kahlo. In 1938, Clare had bought for $600 *Between the Curtains,* a Kahlo self-portrait depicting Frida in Spanish colonial dress, holding a piece of paper that dedicated the painting to her lover and fellow Communist, Leon Trotsky.[10]

Carlos invited Clare to visit his Pacific retreat in Acapulco, after she completed a three-day sightseeing tour for her article. Wanting to absorb as much as possible of Mexico's history, culture, and folklore, she traveled east to Chichén Itzá in Yucatán and noted the impressive size of the Mayan Temple of the Warriors, with its hundreds of headless columns, and the pyramid of Kukulcan, a profusion of opalescent blocks stretching up to the "burning turquoise sky."[11]

In arid hamlets, she saw people stacking their dead on shelves to dry like prunes in the sun. Occasionally, Clare noted, they took them down to pat them affectionately. She interpreted the constant laughter of the villagers as a defense against "the underlying harshness and sombreness of life."

On Saturday, February 18, Clare reunited with Carlos in what he called his "high mirador" with spectacular views of the Pacific.[12] Over the next forty-eight hours, she learned more about him. Though his manner was quiet and dignified, he had a raw vitality and such an appetite for spending long hours writing music that he was known as a "work machine." But he was also a bon vivant, with an appreciation for society, good food, wines, and beautiful women.[13]

As they talked of life and work, she sensed that Carlos was not entirely satisfied with his career. Two years before, he had quit as principal conductor of the Mexican Symphony, mostly because he wanted more time to compose and to perform with major American and European ensembles. But his other jobs as director of the National Conservatory of Music and the National Institute of Fine Arts and Literature took time from creative work. His compositions were respected by international peers such as Copland and Stravinsky, and his excellence as a conductor was universally acknowledged.

Clare, knowing little about his vocation, asked him how he composed. Without being too technical, Carlos said that he liked to use "a full palette" of orchestral sound.[14] As he described and demonstrated his native sources of inspiration, she began to understand how ingeniously he allied ancient Mexican traditions with progressive musical modernism.

Impressed by his passionate artistic temperament, fluency in languages, frankness, and decency, Clare found herself falling in love. That Chávez was agnostic with no metaphysical philosophy, she saw as a challenge to her powers of persuasion. She was relieved to discover that though politically liberal, he was not a Communist like the Riveras.[15]

That night Carlos took "Clarita," as he now affectionately addressed her, onto his rooftop, which seemed to touch the heavens. He turned oceanward, and she had a chance to admire and later rhapsodize about his profile silhouetted against the dark sky and stars, "your black hair tangled in them, your solid shoulders wearing the midnight-blue like [a] royal mantle. . . ."[16]

As the hours slipped by, they fantasized about what could unite them, were they not tied to other people and places. This did not prevent them from talking, against sense, of running off together. But eventually Carlos the realist brushed aside such vain speculation. "We cannot marry. We cannot be lovers."[17]

Clare the pragmatist proposed that they could at least continue seeing each other and bring into being a permanent musical creation that would bind them in perpetuity. She tore the end off a page of newspaper and scrawled in the margin: "I want to commission a piano concerto for Ann Clare Brokaw, the most beautiful and sad and gay thing you ever wrote that has her lovely face and my broken heart in it." She dated it and signed it with her full name. In another margin, Chávez wrote, "Yes I would love to write a piano concerto for you," and signed it, "Carlos."[18]

No fee was discussed. He was too polite—or too infatuated—to raise the subject of money just yet.

Attending Sunday Eucharist in Acapulco's ancient cathedral, Clare noticed how especially devout the packed congregation seemed to be, and wondered why the church hierarchy had not supported them in their revolution to overthrow the autocratic regime of Porfirio Díaz. "Had *they* come to the defense of the masses twenty years ago," she wrote Father Thibodeau, "there would be no Communism [in Mexico] today." Though the country's extreme leftists were anti-clerical, they were "*not* essentially anti-religious." She saw their politics as a justified reaction to American economic imperialism. "We talk high ideals about human rights coming before property rights, but our government backs, still, all the millionaires and exploiters of the Mexicans who bought

Clare commissions a musical memorial to her daughter, February 18, 1950

their human rights from the 19th century dictators and imperialists. And the people resent that, properly, I think."[19]

Summing up America's southern neighbor for *Vogue*, she admitted being stimulated by the "exciting and challenging blend of Catholicism of the passionate Spanish variety, and Marxism, and Capitalism, and Indian mysticism. . . . Time and reflection will tell whether I like it better than Italy."[20]

Bidding Carlos good-bye, she invited him to visit her in America soon. This prospect made parting less of a wrench. On February 20, she headed home, night-stopping in Mérida. The next morning was Shrove Tuesday, and Mardi Gras was under way in the small, hot town. Truckloads of painted children happily scattered confetti. Clare, in contrast, was in a tumult of emotions that precluded joy. How could she explain her latest moral lapse to Father Thibodeau?

Early on Ash Wednesday, she attended Mass and found herself passionately saying the liturgical words *"Salvum me fac, Deus, quoniam intraverunt aquae usque ad animam meam"* (Save me, O God, for the waters have come in even unto my soul). She was humbled by a vision she sometimes had of the heart's corruption. As the priest marked her forehead with the penitential ashes, he said, *"Memento, homo, quia pulvis es, et in pulverem reverteris"* (Remember, man, that you are dust, and shall to dust return).[21]

Lingering in the church after Communion, Clare prayed before a black statue of Christ. "For you, my love, and for myself," she wrote Carlos, "that you would be given the grace *and* the will to cut free from the tentacles of that modern monster, mediocrity, who comes so often these days, disfigured as some form of social service. . . ." She understood his frustration over extracurricular duties, and urged him to have the courage to *"be* what you are." When he composed great music, he attacked "the disorder which afflicts us at the *roots.*" She advised him to leave organization to second-rate talents.

Writing from the Colonial Hotel in Miami, she lamented how fast their days together had gone. She consoled herself with the thought that "love's intensity gives time some of the quality of eternity." In vivid memory, she saw his gestures, heard the inflections in his voice, and brooded over everything he had said.

> "We cannot marry. We cannot be lovers." That is true. Not only do I agree I insist. It *must* be this way. There is peace, of course, in accepting what is *right.* . . . That's the way it *is,* and unless God (who else?) wills it otherwise, it will, all our lives stay that way. And yet do I love thee. *Je t'aime, tu sais.*
>
> You know how much I want to see you again. And yet, if, I never do—*je t'aime!*[22]

▽

Harry, meanwhile, awaited Clare at Yeamans Hall Club in Charleston, where, as often when he felt solitary, he wrote to a woman his wife knew nothing of.

He had met Mary Bancroft four years before during a business trip to Europe. She was now forty-six, the twice-divorced Boston Brahmin daughter of the publisher of *The Wall Street Journal.* Though she worked in Geneva for the CIA, she periodically visited New York, and always managed to spend some close but chaste time with Harry. Politically, she was far to the left of him, but they enjoyed arguing issues, and like Jean Dalrymple, she had become an indispensable confidante.

Harry's twelve-page letter said that he was disappointed that after the conviction of Alger Hiss she had joined "the choir of sentimental unreason headed by Eleanor Roosevelt." Why did she not get exercised instead by the brutalities of the Communist doctrine Hiss espoused?

Then, sounding lost, he asked Mary to tell him what to do with the rest of his life. She had scoffed at his flirtation with a senatorial run that he saw as his last chance to satisfy a craving for public office. He complained that she had also cruelly accused him of editorial bias in his magazines, but he still had warm feelings for her.[23]

▽

When Clare joined him for a three-week vacation at the club, she wrote a letter to Father Thibodeau, bemoaning her lack of spiritual growth. She confessed that after all her aspirations to purity over the past four years, she had succumbed to a magnetic artist and free thinker, and was overcome with guilt. She lacked the evenness of temper that sanctity demanded. By not showing enough of either in Mexico, she said, she had failed to convert any skeptics and atheists, although she had made some impression on the iconoclastic Communist Diego Rivera, "and a great one" on Carlos. Everything had seemed to conspire "to make me feel very much like a woman, and not at all like an apostle. I was—and am—badly shaken."

She dreaded having to start writing again, even though she had plenty of ideas. "Why I don't just sit down and BEGIN I just do not know," she wrote. "It is a major and painful mystery. I suspect it has something to do . . . with a lack of incentive . . . I am no longer interested in making money or achieving fame." [24]

Though often conflicted in choosing between seclusion and society, chastity and sexuality, faith and agnosticism, Clare had no lack of industry or vitality. To the contrary, she had an unquenchable desire to go everywhere, see everything and everyone of substance, probe the depth of psyches, and understand the consequences of choices and actions. Writing plays involved the re-creation of the milieus, motives, and emotions of imaginary characters. That meant limiting her own extramural activities. The isolation necessary to perfect her craft required a discipline she could no longer summon at will.

Even a recent glowing reappraisal of her talent as a playwright failed to break her block. It came in a book, *The American Drama Since 1930*, by Joseph Mersand, an academic critic. He allotted a chapter to Clare Boothe, giving her equal prominence with George S. Kaufman and Clifford Odets. Praising her wit, clarity, judgment, and brilliance, Mersand wrote that she was a social satirist fearless enough "to admit her hatreds." This willingness to offend came from not having to depend on box office income "for her daily sustenance."

He cited the critic Richard Lockridge's ranking of Clare as one of eight leading contemporary playwrights, and quoted Burns Mantle's praise of *The Women:* "the most brilliant social satire of its time." Mersand went further, comparing the gossip of the bridge-playing socialites in the first scene of that play to the village small talk in Jane Austen's novels. Both writers "make the commonplace interesting."[25]

At least Clare could still produce travel prose. When she delivered "Thoughts on Mexico" to *Vogue* for its August issue, Maggie Case said it was the best article the magazine had received in years.[26]

▽

Carlos Chávez appeared in New York soon after the Luces returned from Charleston in mid-March. Clare took pains to treat him to the best of Manhattan. On Monday the twentieth she took him, Maggie, and Tiffany's design director Van Day Truex to dinner at Le Pavillon, moving on to the latest Rodgers and Hammerstein musical, *South Pacific.* The following evening, Maggie held a cocktail party for Chávez, also inviting Igor Stravinsky, Arthur Rubinstein, Aaron Copland, Ezio Pinza, Rudolf Bing, Sol Hurok, and Gian Carlo Menotti, whose opera *The Consul* was playing to acclaim in New York. Harry and Clare honored Carlos further at a black-tie dinner in their Waldorf suite, to meet such friends as Irene Selznick and the former British spymaster Sir William Wiseman. On Wednesday night they attended Menotti's opera, and the following day had lunch with Nelson Rockefeller at Louis XIV. That night they saw Anita Loos's *Gentlemen Prefer Blondes,* and on Friday afternoon Carlos and Clarita drove to Sugar Hill for the weekend.[27]

There, they walked around the still-wintry estate and had long talks in the plush sitting room, its mantelpiece still dominated by Gerald Brockhurst's portrait of Clare in her green mandarin tunic. They again examined their relationship. Carlos said that before becoming inextricably linked, they must face the practical questions of their marriages and separate nationalities and occupations. "To act in time," as Clare grandiloquently put it, "and to believe that the consequences will reverberate in eternity!"[28] Whether only she would suffer from those cosmic shudderings went unsaid.

A few days later, Chávez left for a professional engagement in Los Angeles. Clare telegraphed his train, slightly misquoting lines from

Shelley: *Music when soft voices die vibrates in the memory; / And odours when sweet violets sicken / Live within the sense they quicken.*[29]

She followed up with a long love letter to "My darling Carlos." He obsessed her like no one since Julian Simpson, perhaps because it was he and not she who was circumscribing their intimacy.

> Well, if lovelessness is a foretaste of Hell, then surely being loved and loving (I speak of the heart, you understand?) is a foretaste of Heaven. I contemplate your gentleness, and tenderness, and good-ness, and suddenly I am suffused with a desire to bring all that is real and good in me to your service, and all that, then, floods my being with sweetness I have never before needed to describe! For it is now the *joy* of loving that I have come to know. And that is something quite different (though not always unrelated!) to the pleasure of desiring or being desired! It is a *blessed* thing to have known you, Carlos. You are not really like any other man. . . . It is not that you are more intelligent, more candid, more sensitive, or more or less anything, than other men. It is simply that you are different.

With his mix of Spanish and Indian blood, he even looked unlike anyone she knew intimately. He seemed nearer to her "than anyone else in the world," even though he was now far away.

> I had thought I would be much more unhappy than I am when you left . . . I daresay that is because I have accepted *in my will* the fact that insofar as anything you or I can do, our problem is insolu-ble. . . . Shall I complain that I cannot have *everything* as I would wish, when I have so much more than I had dreamed of?[30]

▽

To learn more of the classical repertory, Clare started attending musical events. One Carnegie Hall concert featured Toscanini conducting De-bussy, and she shared the experience with Chávez.

> I have always felt that one's appreciation of art is inescapably tan-gled up with one's appreciation of the *prestige* of the artist . . . so she [*sic*] is not sure whether it was good or not. . . . I awfully much wanted you to be there last night . . . conducting *La Mer* . . . because it was music that spoke to my deepest heart, and . . . how

nice if you were speaking to that, in a manner at once so public and private—as thru a symphony orchestra![31]

She dreamed of Carlos appearing with New York's great Philharmonic Orchestra, gaining prestige for herself as his local patron. One day, perhaps, he would conduct "her" concerto for Ann in Carnegie Hall. To that end, she donated a large check to the New York Philharmonic Society. In consequence, she was unanimously elected to its board as a trustee and director. On April 5, hoping to secure Carlos a guest conductor post with the orchestra, she had a three-hour talk with its manager, Arthur Judson, ostensibly to find out "what the real problems of the Philharmonic are."[32]

When she referred to Chávez as an underused performer, Judson agreed that he had great talent. But he had the reputation of never wanting to be away from Mexico for long. In fact, Carlos had once turned down the music directorship of the Houston Symphony. "He wants periodic engagements," Judson said. The best musicians were always in demand, and those who were too "whimsical" about where and when they appeared were not so likely to be courted.[33]

This reminded Clare that when she had discussed more northern exposure with Carlos, he had been evasive, saying any offer must fit in with his Mexican commitments. But when he later announced that he was contemplating a European tour, she objected to the idea "just now!" If he was to travel anywhere, better for it to be in her orbit. Flattering herself that she was his creative equal, Clare added, "Artistic people (like you and me) . . . *are* sometimes more obscure and difficult than we think."[34]

On April 26, she spent the whole afternoon with the producer and orchestra executive Bruno Zirato. Without any nudging, he said that Carlos Chávez was "one of the best conductors in the world," and would be his choice for director of the Detroit Symphony. Reporting to Carlos, she wrote that a "Jewish" donor in Michigan was lobbying for Leonard Bernstein. "But Zirato and Luce, they want Chávez. And Chávez, I suppose, will do exactly as he pleases, no matter who wants what."[35]

Clare's meeting with Zirato was not entirely altruistic. In the excitement of having bewitched a composer, she had sent Carlos the synopsis of a ballet, *Saint Francis in Manhattan*, expressing the hope that he would collaborate with her on it. He had composed music for at least five ballets, including one for Martha Graham, but did not immediately reply. Now Zirato offered an avenue to the greatest ballet composer alive, his close friend Igor Stravinsky. The Russian had money worries, having spent two and a half years writing an opera, *The Rake's Progress*, and failing to find anyone with the $100,000 needed to mount it. Clare volunteered to look for an investor. Zirato conveyed her offer to Stravinsky, who promptly appeared at her apartment.

"I absolutely adored him," she wrote Carlos. "I know you do not like me to mention such matters. But it was *wonderful* and consoling to find that this great musician is also an exceedingly devout and prayin' man. And very well read too. Nietzsche, Kierkegaard, Dostoevsky, my favorite European prophets." Pointedly, she let on that Stravinsky had asked to see *Saint Francis* and had recommended Vittorio Rieti, composer of scores for *Le Bal* (1929) and *La Sonnambula* (1946), to write the music.[36]

Rieti soon telephoned to say he would take a look at her synopsis. Clare informed Carlos that she guessed his silence meant that the ballet's theme, the appearance of a saint in the fleshpot of Gotham, might have put him off, being more sacred than profane. But she hoped that his respect for her intellect would persuade him of its merits.[37]

▽

In pursuit of her new identity as a patron of the arts, Clare had lunch on April 28 at Le Pavillon with Salvador Dalí. She wanted him to design a stained-glass window for a chapel she had decided to build in memory of Ann Brokaw. She was surprised to see that he had lost his upcurling, waxed mustache, which she had always disliked. He had once told her that if he ever converted to Catholicism, he intended to shave it off. Now, she wrote Carlos, the surrealist was transformed into "*un trés beau garçon* without that silly antennae."

> He insisted that he had worn it because it helped him to get ideas out of the air, as a butterfly does from its feelers! And that now he is a Catholic again, he no longer *needs* reach for ideas: he has enough for the rest of his lifetime.[38]

Stimulated, she began to buy art again, acquiring from the Knoedler gallery a "rather violent" painting of the ongoing eruption of the volcano Parícutin in Michoacán. It was the work of Rufino Tamayo, an esteemed Mexican Indian and friend of Chávez. "Did I ever tell you," she wrote the latter, "that the only thing I ever really wanted to be besides a writer was a vulcanologist?"[39]

Trying to impress him with a list of other famous people she had seen recently, even though she knew he disliked name-dropping, she went on, "I realize how strange and remote and even distasteful many of my interests and preoccupations are to you."[40] But Carlos saw her incessant traveling, socializing, shopping, and starting new writing projects before finishing those under way as proof of a pathological need for change and stimulation. Clare's fear of failing was in itself a failure, a reluctance to wrestle vestigial ideas into a coherent whole, and to concentrate on the fundamentals necessary for a satisfying existence. He voiced his polite disapproval of activities that sapped her essence and vitality. "I see from your letters how tremendously hectic schedules you impose on yourself. Please make stations; isolate yourself; contemplate. It is only this way how you can really live, and not feel yourself a stranger from me."[41]

But she remained constitutionally unable to stay still for long. Thinking of ways to reunite with Carlos, she sent him details of her forthcoming speaking destinations, should he be in or near one of them. And he might keep in mind that Harry would soon leave for another lengthy business trip. "I wish you could be in New York at that time. . . . It's very strange, you know, how much I miss you."[42]

Clare's relationship with Carlos seems to have given her a new sensitivity toward sound and lighting effects enhanced by music and dance. Her synopsis of *Saint Francis in Manhattan* begins promisingly, indicating that she still had enough imagination to embrace a fresh way of writing for the stage.

> The opening scene is set just before dawn in the square opposite the front of the Plaza Hotel. A small group of young people emerge, from a debutante ball, and whistle for taxis.
>
> A drunken bum lurches out of the black pool around the fountain, into the light. He collides with two young men in tails. They, too, are swizzled. But they are young and hard: they shove him so rudely he falls by a stone bench, rolls under it, and lies there still. A woman with a thin red scarf about her throat, and a ratty fox fur, whisks out of the dark and accosts the young men. But she is cut out by a debutante who is just as willing . . . much prettier, and costs nothing. They hail one of the old coachmen who sleep in their victorias at the entrance to the park, hoping to pick up romantic fares for the buggy rides from midnight to dawn.

The dance orchestra gives its final raucous blare, but in the ballroom, someone, who can't bear for the party to be over, begins to play the piano with harsh frenzy. Alone now in the plaza, the woman with the red scarf goes to the bench, starts back in disgust as she stumbles over the fallen bum. He rolls out of the way.[43]

At this point Clare's inspiration begins to flag. The prostitute, for no apparent reason, decides to commit suicide. Her initial impulse is to strangle herself with the red scarf, but then she whips out a pair of scissors "as though she would cut the throat she dares not choke." Just as inexplicably, she loses her death wish. Dawn comes, illuminating "a slim, brown figure of a monk," kneeling by the fountain. He rises with upreached arms to the sound of an offstage chorus singing "The Canticle of St. Francis."

> Praised be Thou, my Lord, with all Thy creatures,
> Especially the honored Brother Sun.

Unintentionally hilarious episodes follow, as St. Francis levitates in his ecstasy to the third tier of the fountain and is distracted by the bum falling into the pool below. He descends, takes off his robe, wraps it around the shivering man, and makes him dance until he warms up. The monk then permits the prostitute to cry on his shoulder, and wipes her tears and nose with her red scarf. This makes all three of them laugh, and they join in singing along with the chorus.

By now, the suspicion that the author is not in her right mind is reinforced when the blonde star debutante emerges on the arm of her fiancé, and is identified as "Saint Clare." They are taken aback by the sight of a half-naked man with a shaven head cavorting with "queer-looking characters." A policeman finds the spectacle strange enough to charge onstage and attempt to club the trio with his nightstick.

Clare's synopsis then becomes as crazy as a Marx Brothers farce.

St. Francis explains (to the cop) that while he was praising Brother Sun and Brother Wind, Brother Bum fell into Sister Water, and because Brother Fire was not there to dry him off, Brother Francis had to give him his cloak.

The debutante is, despite herself, attracted to St. Francis as she watches him feed scraps of bread to "Brothers Pigeons and Sparrows." The stage then fills up with a cast of tormented characters—drunks, drug addicts, beggars, and "a young Negro, in a sweat shirt, with a bleeding bandaged head." St. Francis, undulating back and forth, encourages them to join him in prayer. He is helped in his ministrations by St. Clare. Debutante and monk join in a joyful pas de deux. A frenzied riot of the entire ensemble ensues until, "to a wild shrieking of police and ambulance sirens," cops and paramedics from Bellevue arrive to cart everybody off. But St. Francis calms them with comforting words: "They now go willingly with the police and the attendants to their alcoholic and insane wards."[44]

▽

As Clare feared, Chávez disliked her ballet's religiosity. "Carlos is so bitterly against my beliefs how can he like me if he dislikes what I believe?" she complained to Maggie Case. "If I told him I hated music, it was nothing but sounds, would he be offended?" Maggie reported this remark to Chávez, warning him, "She is a child in many ways, certainly an endearing erratic brilliant hypnotic one!"[45]

Bruised and melancholy, Clare unburdened herself to Carlos in a poignant letter written on May 8 from a hotel in Detroit. She was there for a series of lectures in satellite towns, motoring long distances in weather that changed abruptly from heat and hurricanes to cold and damp. Between times, she researched the possibility of Chávez being appointed music director of the Detroit Symphony, a once great ensemble still struggling to restore itself after near collapse in the Depression.

But she soon concluded that the automobile capital was "a cultural desert" unlikely to welcome a Mexican modernist. Tycoons who might be tapped for financial support were bereft of artistic and aesthetic values, she wrote Carlos. As for local audiences, their favorite music was *The Nutcracker Suite*.

"I think you would *loathe* this city if you had to live in it," she went on, noting significantly that the museum's contemporary collection was poor, and its murals by Diego Rivera badly placed.[46]

If only he were doing her ballet, there would be a reason for him to come to New York "to see the choreographer and me!" She appealed to his sympathy.

> Carlos you do not know how I have suffered because of you. Time and distance *are* very potent enemies. . . . But what is devastating is misunderstanding, or rather *non*-understanding. No doubt it is one of love's saddest—and bravest—illusions that "two hearts can

beat as one," or that there are twined souls, and mated minds. Each of us, in the end, is so appallingly *alone*. . . . We attach quite different values to things, and that's why I suspect we are strangers.[47]

He tried to be positive in his reply. "You make up ghosts and then you scare yourself with them. We are not negative, and that is where we find one another. There are problems, yes, but after all you and I do not like easy things."

Hoping she might visit him again soon, he wrote that fall in Mexico was a beautiful season. He had ideas for the Ann Brokaw concerto, and planned to start composing it then. As for Detroit, he said that despite her dismissiveness, resurrecting a fine orchestra was exactly the kind of challenge he liked. If the directorship was offered, he would take it. "Good music and good work will do the rest."[48]

▽

The inability of Carlos to fill her romantic void elicited a cri de coeur in mid-June, after Harry had been away three weeks. "It matters so greatly that I should see you again, and when I do, you should be just as happy to see me as you were in spring. . . . As the poet says, 'hope deferred maketh the heart sick.'"[49]

As summer approached, Clare thought of a chance to meet Carlos in Colorado, at the August gathering of the Aspen Institute of Humanistic Studies. The theme was "Great Books, Great Men and Great Music," and seemed a perfect one for a double appearance by Clare Boothe Luce as writer and Carlos Chávez as musician. To her disappointment he declined, saying he was not comfortable with "theoretical discussions" onstage. He would, however, be agreeable to appearing as a distinguished guest near the end of the month, when Stravinsky would be in residence, the Juilliard Quartet performing, and Clare speaking on St. Thomas Aquinas.[50]

Overjoyed, she booked spacious private quarters for them to share, and promised to join him afterward for a vacation in New Mexico. He had long wanted to attend the annual festival of Indian dances performed there by troupes from the reservations.

In the interim, Carlos accepted an invitation to conduct in Washington, D.C., in July, and Clare canceled a trip to Argentina to finally see him on the podium. But he then advised that due to bureaucratic bungling, the engagement in the capital was off. It occurred to her that he never put himself out to see her, unless he had professional reasons to be in her vicinity. As so often, when inconvenienced or rejected, she lashed out in a curt note.

I don't think Aspen will work out too well, as Harry has become very interested and has secured himself an invitation to join in one of the seminars. I had taken a pretty cottage with several guest rooms, but he now has decided to come along, so that is *that*.[51]

28

A RED VELVET TUFTED SOFA

Private faces in public places
Are wiser and nicer
Than public faces in private places.

—W. H. AUDEN

Harry joined Clare in Aspen on August 16, 1950, in time to hear her engage in a middlebrow discussion of St. Thomas Aquinas's "Treatise on Law" with the philosopher Mortimer J. Adler. In the eleven days that followed, she also took part in panel debates on Thucydides's *History of the Peloponnesian War*, Jonathan Swift's *Gulliver's Travels*, and Henry David Thoreau's essays "Civil Disobedience" and "A Plea for Captain John Brown."

Speaking to a reporter about the conflict that had broken out that spring in Korea, she said she saw no more than a fifty-fifty chance that the United States and the Soviet Union could resolve their differences in the region. "We may as well settle down on a total war footing now. We should build up our strength and force a backdown in Kremlin policy."[1]

The week that Harry spent in Colorado was not the tranquil break he had hoped for. Clare was distant, still annoyed by the absence of Chávez. Her behavior was in contrast with that of Mary Bancroft, who had recently enjoyed a happy time with him in Munich. Mary had never seen Luce so unbuttoned. They had attended a carpenters' ball in a *biergarten*, where he had quaffed copious steins of lager, and whirled around the floor with red-faced Frauen, pinching their bottoms and tickling them until they squealed.[2]

After he left, Clare wrote him to say that she had fallen into a depression so deep that it was "sheer hell," and made worse by knowing she was "IRRATIONAL."

> The blackness just closes down, like a cold midnight on my spirit, and I am lost in a suicidal fog of searing melancholy. I really feel my heart *bleed*, and my spirit seems to be dying. I hurl cries for help into the black night, and no help comes. Only the knowledge that it *will* pass keeps me from . . . [sic] because if I didn't know that, I couldn't bear this anguish of meaninglessness, this horror in which I seem utterly abandoned by love and life. It is too huge and all embracing a thing to have much to do with self pity. . . . All I know is that what is not pathology is demonology, and a terrible temptation as well as a trial.

She said she was bored with the seminars—"Too much Adler"—and missed him greatly. She signed off with just her name.[3]

▽

When she returned to New York on September 6, she found awaiting her the inaugural issue of a lavish style magazine called *Flair*. It was financed by Gardner Cowles, founder of *Look,* was edited by his wife, Fleur, and ran an essay by Clare called "It's About Time."

Her piece was the first in a series giving eminent writers the chance to sound off about anything that bothered them. Among those enlisted for future issues were George Bernard Shaw, Simone de Beauvoir, Margaret Mead, and Ogden Nash.

Clare described three kinds of time: organic, psychological, and mechanical. Neither of the first two categories, she wrote, had anything to do with the clock, which represented mechanical dead time, "the totalitarian tyrant over all our technological 'progress,' over everything that ticks, cranks up, takes off, turns over or—as in the case of The Bomb—goes off on schedule. In the end the clock may destroy us all." She pointed out that when "the hypnotic hands on the dial" seemed to move too slowly, people tried to "kill time." Or, when the hands moved too swiftly, they attempted to "steal" it. But in the end, though memory might mitigate or try to stall time's passing, it could not "avert its last lethal stroke."[4]

The essay was illustrated with a black-and-white photograph of Clare, sporting a short, wavy hairstyle and wearing a lace dress reminiscent of the Victorian era, plus a double strand of pearls.

Her uncertain sense of style was called into question again, as she began decorating a new duplex apartment that Harry had bought at 450 East Fifty-second Street. It was located across from the River House, where they had rented in the early years of their marriage, and had tenth-floor views of the East River and the rapidly rising headquarters of the United Nations. Clare estimated that renovating and furnishing the apartment would take several months and cost $50,000.

Spurning Gladys Freeman, her decorator for almost twenty years, she hired the coming man of American interior design, Billy Baldwin. Lean and immaculately dressed at forty-seven, he relished the prestigious assignment. But what transpired was an experience so galling that in a memoir written a quarter of a century later, he recalled every exasperating detail.

Clare came crisply to the point at their preliminary discussion, saying the space should be practical as well as beautiful. "I care how it looks, but I do not want to sacrifice efficiency to aesthetics." She stressed that she liked to act quickly, assumed he did, too, and invited him to spend a day at Sugar Hill to get an idea of her taste.

Mutual friends had told Baldwin it was "pretty awful," so he welcomed the chance to see for himself. Even so, he was unprepared for what ensued. Admitted to the Luce mansion by a butler who spoke in whispers, he soon discovered that this was customary with other servants as well, and wondered if they were reverential or simply terrified. In a bleak upstairs office, he met two cowed secretaries. They gave him a batch of typewritten requirements pertaining to the duplex. It struck him as "a veritable thesis on the gadgetry and mechanics of the new apartment," including wiring for indirect lighting, a totally rebuilt kitchen, and a complex electronic intercom for summoning Clare's staff, husband, or guests. A special note informed him that since most of the Luces' books were in the country, he must buy only ones with false spines for the city. This affectation was a pet aversion of Baldwin's, and compounded the dubious feelings he already had about the enterprise.

Clare entered the room wrapped in a becoming beach robe.

"It's time for you to swim with me," she announced, not bothering to indulge in the usual exchange of greetings. She led me to the pool and proceeded to do some systematic lapping while I puttered about in the delicious coolness. After about fifteen minutes, she stopped, took a long satisfied breath, and instructed me to get dressed and go tell the secretaries it was their time to swim with her. When I delivered the orders, one of the ladies burst into tears.

"How can she ask us to swim with her?" wailed the other in anguish. "Before you arrived, she was unspeakably cruel to us." But they obeyed.

When their swimming session was over, I was again summoned and we all had a good rich lunch outdoors on the terrace. Madame, I noticed, was having something different—a health salad.

"I hope you all realize," she lectured, "that what you are eating is as nourishing as poison." She was packed with all the facts. But she was extremely dogmatic and wholly lacking in humor, which made conversation with her no great pleasure. Every so often, after a certain amount of concentration, she managed to produce some cheap wisecrack; that was the extent of her wit.

Baldwin's post-lunch house tour failed to allay most of his fears. Since he preferred to create spare, modern interiors in neutral palettes, he recoiled at Sugar Hill's profusion of heavy, multicolored, antique Oriental furniture and objets d'art. But he had come to discuss the urban environment of New York, where he hoped to have influence. This dream was quashed when Clare singled out two rooms in the apartment that needed special consideration. One was a combined sitting room and office off her bedroom, to be furnished with a large desk, book-shelves, and a chaise longue from which she could dictate. "I want the room to look like *South Pacific*," she said. Appalled, Baldwin facetiously suggested sand-colored walls, a blue ceiling, and lots of tropical plants. Clare was jubilant. "You understand perfectly!"

Her second space with specific requirements was the two-story drawing room. Since it was to be used primarily for large parties, she said, a grand piano was essential, as was a U-shaped, capacious sofa for Harry, who liked to be surrounded by listeners when he held forth. Baldwin knew that the monster seating she envisaged would have to be custom-made and, along with the piano, hoisted up from the street and swung through the windows. That would be a huge expense, probably not in the budget.

Going against his own preference for sleek lines and subdued colors, Baldwin suggested the drawing room be predominantly Venetian in style with red and pink hues. Clare was ecstatic, and insisted on being involved throughout the restoration, demanding face-to-face weekly progress reports from the chief electrician, plumber, plasterer, and painter. This did not go well with them. They could barely conceal their disdain when summoned one by one to stand before her.

In spite of the size and scope of the job, everything was finished on time. Baldwin looked forward to walking his client through—previously an exciting ritual for him. Twenty-four hours before, however, a call came from one of Clare's secretaries. "I know this is less than discreet of me," she confided, "but Madame visited the apartment yesterday—and she hates the big room." Baldwin was speechless. In spite of its bright hues, he considered it spectacular—"quite a feather in my cap." Clare had approved in advance every paint and fabric sample, including a four-yard length of wall damask, and all the furniture, fixtures, and fittings.

When she arrived to confront him, she was trailed by two assistants. Glaring about her, she dispensed with pleasantries. "I loathe everything about this room, and I wish you to remove all the furniture by tomorrow."

Struggling to keep his composure, Baldwin said he supposed all could be taken out by that deadline, except for the sofa, which would require scheduling with the crane company.

"I will not pay for any special equipment," Clare snapped. "Saw the thing in three—it is only suitable for the city dump anyway."

At this the decorator lost his temper. "You knew exactly what the room was going to look like. You had the floor plans, you saw and approved every single thing in the room, and you loved it all!"

Clare strode around. "Everything is vulgar and absolutely tasteless," she said. Pointing to a red velvet tufted sofa she had personally chosen, she thundered, "This looks like Mae West. I came to you because of your professional reputation. But sir, you are an amateur."

Her subdued employees stood to one side, recording the entire exchange as Baldwin completed the tour with his dissatisfied customer. In the *South Pacific* study, he was surprised to encounter a tall, handsome young priest.

Clare's countenance softened. "Isn't it marvelous," she cooed. "He comes and winds all my clocks—it's therapy."

After the dismantling, Baldwin received a note: "Madame would like the bill as soon as possible, and of course the entire contents of the drawing room should not appear on it." Though he had Clare's signature on the estimates for everything purchased on her behalf, he decided not to sue.

"I just couldn't face the tedium and expense of a long court battle," he wrote. "I took my loss."[5]

29

PILATE'S WIFE

No creative artist ever contracted a religion without a
concomitant atrophy of his talent or genius.

—BERNARD GUILBERT GUERNEY

The Luces' annual trip to South Carolina in January 1951, marking
the seventh anniversary of Ann Brokaw's death, had a special poignancy. Clare had decided to move the remains of her daughter and
mother from the nearby Strawberry Hill Cemetery to Mepkin.

Ann's body, encased in a large metal vault, and Ann Austin's ashes
in an urn, were brought to Mepkin by two monks. Mass was sung in the
icy chapel, which was so frigid that breath from the chanting Trappists
misted the glass doors.[1] Clare noticed that a niche by the altar, which
had once been the plantation's gun cabinet, now housed a statue of the
Madonna. She saw it as symbolic of what the world needed: to replace
armaments with religion.[2]

The spot chosen for the burial was a landscaped flower garden beneath a stand of great live oaks, with a view of the river. Frosts had
burned the camellias and withered the azalea bushes. During the ceremony, which was marred by the monks' coughing, wintry rain dripped
from the Spanish moss.[3]

The two headstones commissioned by Clare showed that both interes had been born in August and died in January. She intended one
day to join them, so that the three Ann Clares might lie close together.

If Harry agreed to be buried there too, they could all spend eternity side by side, as anticipated in the words of the marshlands poem by Sidney Lanier that had first inspired her to live in the South.

Wildwood privacies, closets of lone desire,
Chamber from chamber parted with wavering arras of leaves,—
Cells for the passionate pleasure of prayer to the soul that grieves.[4]

Afterward, Clare half-teasingly asked Harry if one day he would like to help her "fertilize the camellias." He muttered something noncommittal and turned away.[5]

Her jocularity concealed a deep seriousness. Until, or if ever, Harry converted, she shied from raising the subject of his grave site again. But the prospect of him lying beside her at Mepkin never left her mind.

Years later, she would write him to say that it was strange to think of a Presbyterian endowing a Trappist monastery that had formerly been their romantic retreat.

I am happy to know that I will one day lie in ground that once knew the height of my love for you. I will rest well in the place where we were once so good for each other. It is as though the hand of God had stretched forth to touch the hand of the missionary's son, so that everything *his* hand touched, even the breast of a fond & foolish & passionate woman, should work to the Glory of God & in the future of time, to the love of Him.

Though you will not be there, in the end, I suppose, and I will, Our Lady of Mepkin Abbey is more a monument to your faith, your generosity, your love than to mine. . . .

Thank you Harry—for myself, for Ann, for mother, for the dear monks, for all *this* you have wrought.[6]

▽

Carlos Chávez visited New York in early February with exciting news. He had at last begun composing the music in memory of Ann, but instead of a concerto it was to be a symphony—his third, and he hoped to conduct the world premiere in the United States with his patron in attendance.

Still working to promote him, Clare had him dine with the president of the New York Philharmonic, and with Rudolf Bing, manager of the Metropolitan Opera. In gratitude, Carlos invited her to Mexico in spring.[7] Clare said she would try, although for the next three months she would be on a cross-country speaking tour booked by the Columbia Lecture Bureau.

In Oklahoma City on February 24, she spoke on "The Quality of Greatness" at the Men's Dinner Club. Her lecture was more like a sermon, reflecting her current religious, social, and political preoccupations, as well as her belief that in spite of the country's apparent prosperity, all changes were not for the better.

The *Daily Oklahoman* ran a report next day headlined A LONESOME VOICE VALIANTLY CALLING. It lauded her for startling and significant views on the state of the nation and the soul of man.

> This frail-appearing woman seemed to radiate an inner fire—a zeal that carried far beyond her hearers into the space of universal understanding. . . .
>
> At times she seemed to be a strange combination of Joan of Arc and John the Baptist, for she exhorted the people to struggle for the liberty that is being slowly strangled by the materialism of the welfare state and by general selfishness. She pleaded for the recovery of God's own pattern for the human race, as contrasted with the current political prescription which deals with appeals to personal greed on the basis of "let's get ours while the getting is good."
>
> There was a note almost of desperation in her voice, for she seemed to be watching precious things gradually being lost to American life, and yearning for some powerful leverage for rebuilding the great strong beams and timbers of our national house—a structure that has become a house of confusion.[8]

▽

Carlos had been hoping that Clare would be in Mexico City by April 19, to attend his ballet *The Four Suns*, designed by Covarrubias. She would also be able, for the first time, to see him conduct at the Auditorio Nacional, with Claudio Arrau at the piano. In anticipation, he reserved hotel rooms for her and Harry, and planned a dinner in their honor, to be attended by the U.S. Ambassador.

But at the last minute, she pulled out, leaving Harry to go alone. At first her excuse was that she had to attend the funeral in Grand Rapids,

Michigan, of her colleague and friend Senator Arthur Vandenberg, who had died of lung cancer.[9] But since the service was held three days before her scheduled departure for Mexico, there had to be another reason. She asked Dorothy Farmer to explain to Carlos that she had to go on to the West Coast, where she was due to start work at RKO Studios on her latest movie project.

It was a religious-historical drama called *Pilate's Wife*. She had been thinking about the subject for years. "Almost from the day of my conversion," she wrote Father Thibodeau, "I knew I had to do this picture in Hollywood. (Isn't it strange: the name means Holy rood—the wood of the Cross). . . . My mind teems with ideas and thoughts. What is clearest, just now, is that this *must not* be a 'Spectacle'—a technicolor orgy of camels, palms, desert sands, and bearded Jews. It must be pitched at the *psychological* level—for its interior rather than visual impact."[10]

Her notion was to tell the story of Christ's arrest, conviction, and crucifixion, as seen through the eyes of Claudia Procula, the beautiful eighteen-year-old stepdaughter of Emperor Tiberius. Claudia had married Pontius Pilate just before he became governor of the Palestinian province of Judea.

When Clare first called Howard Hughes to discuss it, he sent an executive aide to see her. After a follow-up conference with the producers Norman Krasna and Jerry Wald, RKO contracted to purchase all rights to her "original, unpublished, unproduced story," and assigned her to write "a stepline continuity" (outline) by May 11, for an initial payment of $11,250.[11]

Even before Clare's arrival in Los Angeles, word leaked that Hughes planned to make a "mammoth spectacular" from her story. Already the name of René Clair was being mentioned as director, and Laurence Olivier and Vivien Leigh as stars. But Clare knew that Leigh, at thirty-seven, was too old for Claudia. She favored another British actress, the twenty-two-year-old Jean Simmons, who was about to start filming *Androcles and the Lion*.

Among the sources Clare claimed to use for her script were the Apocrypha, *The Works of Flavius Josephus*, and the New Testament. RKO Research also found a 1929 novel by Mary Granger entitled *Wife to Pilate*, and recommended, "It may be best to have the Studio consider buying the rights—to avoid a lawsuit for plagiarism."[12]

Clare's initial outline was enthusiastically received by RKO, and on May 29 she was told to proceed with a full treatment, preparatory to writing actual dialogue. She completed it on June 7, and decided to work on the screenplay at Sugar Hill during the summer.

▽

Reestablished in her country study, she set the first scene of the movie in A.D. 26.

> Pontius Pilate is standing on the deck of a Roman vessel approaching the port of Caesarea. It is to be the site of his main residence. Beside him stands his new wife Claudia. She is sensual, impetuous, wilful, and amoral, like most privileged young pagans of an empire and civilization in decline. As the ship nears shore, the young woman reacts to the sight of her provincial future home town in words intended to reveal her mores as well as her priorities.

> CLAUDIA: It's a pile of whitewashed sand!
> PILATE: Augustus Caesar found Rome made of clay and left it marble.
> CLAUDIA: I do not care a fig what you leave Palestine made of, provided you leave it with a fortune made.
> PILATE: Will you never tire, Claudia, of trying to make me into another Julius Caesar?
> CLAUDIA: Should I not be ambitious for you? Is not that a virtue in a wife?
> PILATE: Not the greatest.
> CLAUDIA: What then?
> PILATE: (*A pause*) Fidelity.
> CLAUDIA: But fidelity is no longer the fashion in Rome.

Clare proceeded to switch the scene to Jerusalem, and dramatize the familiar story of Pilate washing his hands of Christ's trial and crucifixion, followed by the less familiar story of Claudia's conversion. But soon she had doubts that cameras would ever roll, "for reasons which have nothing to do with my script," she wrote a friend, "and a good deal to do with the panic that television has caused in Hollywood."[13] Besides, she had a creative problem, in that she wanted Jesus to be an off-screen character only.

"I could show Christ in my story," she said to a reporter, "but who would play Him?" H. B. Warner had portrayed the Savior successfully in

Cecil B. DeMille's 1927 epic, *King of Kings*. That, however, had been a silent picture. "He did not have to talk." Now the actor would have to be heard, "and I feel that Christ spoke more to the heart than to the ear. Also, the accent would be hard to manage. No, I won't show him."[14] This meant that *Pilate's Wife* would lack the most desirable Hollywood commodity: a charismatic, handsome, heroic male star.

Setting the script aside until she was next in Hollywood, Clare switched to writing a play. In six weeks she completed a three-act melodrama entitled *Child of the Morning*.[15] It was based on the true story of Maria Goretti, a young Italian village girl whose priest believed her to be a mystic. She had died in 1902 of fourteen stab wounds, while resisting a sexual predator. Subsequently, miracles had been attributed to Maria's interventions, and in the Holy Year of 1950, she had been canonized a virgin, saint, and martyr, "who gave her innocent and most pure life in order to prevent a sinful act against the virtue of Christian purity."[16]

Clare transferred the mise-en-scène of her play to Brooklyn, and reimagined her heroine as Cathy O'Connell, a guileless sixteen-year-old in a family of mostly lapsed Irish Catholics. The girl aspires to be a nun, but settles for charitable work. Her good intentions are cut short when a reefer addict breaks into her bedroom, bent on rape. As Cathy struggles to preserve her virginity, he shoots her multiple times, killing her.[17]

The actor Eddie Dowling, with whom Clare had appeared onstage in her brief Broadway career, offered to produce and direct *Child of the Morning*. He said he would first stage it in the provinces, with the hope of an eventual transfer to Broadway.

▽

That summer, Charles Willoughby visited Clare at Sugar Hill. Now in his sixtieth year and recently retired from the army, he was weary and confessedly "deteriorating," after more than four decades of active service. He wanted to discuss his grand plan to write an account of Douglas MacArthur's long career in the Pacific, ending with the general's recent dismissal by President Truman, due to a disagreement over Korean War tactics. Having not seen Charles for almost five years, Clare was disappointed to find him in a plain gray suit, lacking his former bemedaled military glamour. To Dorothy Farmer he was "handsome in a gross Germanic way, with a chip on his shoulder."

Divining that he was still more obsessed with McArthur than with her, and that his biographical project was likely to be a tome, Clare recommended John Chamberlain as an ideal collaborator. He thanked her, and once again walked out of her life.[18]

Clare returned to Hollywood in mid-September to resume work on *Pilate's Wife*. Notwithstanding her earlier skepticism about its prospects, she found Wald and Krasna touting the project as "one of the most ambitious" they had ever planned.[19] Location filming in the Holy Land, they announced, would start in early 1952. Curtis Bernhardt, their current choice as director, was all set to scout sites. He intended to ask government and labor leaders in Tel Aviv and Jerusalem how much cooperation RKO could expect from them.[20]

Soon, however, news leaked from the producers' casting service that Krasna and Wald "would have to wait" until Olivier and Leigh were available. The actors had current Broadway commitments to appear together in *Antony and Cleopatra* and *Caesar and Cleopatra*, which were due to begin in late December and would run well into the new year.[21] This delay did not prevent the producers from promoting both Clare and her script at every opportunity. In an interview, she claimed to be working twenty-hour days, and had 120 pages done.[22]

Clare in Hollywood

But she privately realized that becoming a Catholic had affected her creativity. That was the reason she had redirected much of her energy into articles, religious tracts, and speeches.[23] As the weeks at RKO dragged on, her powers of invention continued to wane.

▽

Carlos Chávez suspected that Clare had failed to come to Mexico because she did not want to share him with his family or her husband. Perhaps she was also punishing him for his non-appearance at Aspen. "Of course, you had other things to do," he wrote, "but more than that, I know you wanted it that way."[24]

Having been the victim several times of her flightiness over the last seventeen months, he had his secretary draw up terms for his symphony in memory of Ann. The fee was $3,000, with half to be paid on signing. He ceded to her the live and broadcast performance rights for three years, while keeping for himself publication and recording rights, as well as copyright ownership in perpetuity. Delivery of the complete score was promised for January 1, 1952, except for "causes of *force majeur.*"[25] Clare always disliked being asked for money, and was in no hurry to reward him.

The third week of October saw the fruition of another enterprise in her daughter's memory: the dedication of a chapel named for Saint Anne designed by the San Francisco architect Vincent Raney. It was situated not far from the crossroads in Palo Alto where the deadly accident had occurred. Funds for the construction of a box-shaped Modernist building of red brick, complemented by a white-faced rectangular tower, had been supplied mostly by Harry and Clare. They both attended the ceremony, timed so that Stanford students back from vacation could take part.[26]

An inscription on a plaque to the left of the entrance read:

+ + + + + THY BEAUTY, NOW,
IS ALL FOR THE KING'S DELIGHT:
HE IS THY LORD, + + + + + +
AND WORSHIP BELONGS TO HIM.

IN MEMORY OF MY DAUGHTER
ANN CLARE BROKAW

CLARE BOOTHE LUCE + OCTOBER 21, 1951

Determined to make the chapel a work of art, Clare had hired the New York sculptor Janet De Coux to carve a symbolic Tree of Life on the teak entry doors. For the facade above, she had placed a bronze statue by Frederick C. Shrady, depicting Saint Anne in a flowing gown, a gold halo encircling her head, reading to her child Mary from a tablet. Its inscription read, *Ante Saecula Creata Sum* (Before the Ages, I was created).

Moving away from traditional stained glass, she had commissioned André Girard to paint four twenty-five-feet-high windows along the right side of the nave, and suspended Stations of the Cross opposite. Louisa Jenkins, a mosaicist in Big Sur, made a baldachin to hang over the altar, consisting of a large oval frame of black lattice metal, with tiles worked into Picassoesque angels playing heraldic musical instruments. In addition, Jenkins had made a shrine in an alcove to the left of the chancel, using lapis lazuli, gold leaf, shells, and ceramics to embellish a statue of the Blessed Virgin.

Clare had recruited noted craftsmen even for smaller objects. A set of sterling silver candleholders were by Victor Ries, and a silver crucifix by Louis Feron. She said her aim in using Modernist artists was to dem-

Interior of Saint Anne's Chapel, with paintings by André Girard

onstrate that "Christianity is a religion of Resurrection and Renais-sance."[27]

Looking around her now, she felt a sense of accomplishment. Sun-light filtering through five small blocks of multicolored glass in the left wall softly illuminated the nave. The thirty-foot-high ceiling dropped to eight feet at the point where the Stations of the Cross formed a pro-gression of overlapping oblique segments, each lighted by an exterior aperture. Girard's four painted windows on the other side represented the teaching methods of Jesus, including his parables, Sermon on the Mount, and last instructions to his disciples.

Although Clare was tone-deaf, she could not fail to notice the sub-lime resonance of the organ, an effect brought about by the chapel's great height, narrow length, and rounded apse, making the acoustics resemble the sonority of a Romanesque church.[28]

She boasted of her architectural achievement to Evelyn Waugh, who had grown fond of her since she converted. "It is a splendid thing to be a church builder," he replied. "I do congratulate you. I wish you would rebuild the Holy Sepulchre at Jerusalem."[29]

▽

Clare traveled to Springfield, Massachusetts, in mid-November for the first tryout of *Child of the Morning*. Near to curtain time in the Broadway Theatre, she appeared backstage, wearing a red coat and dark dress with a rose corsage. She instructed the gifted ingenue Margaret O'Brien, who was playing her heroine, on how to hold a missal correctly. Now almost fifteen, Margaret had costarred at age seven with Judy Garland in Vin-cente Minnelli's movie *Meet Me in St. Louis*. She turned out to be an equally talented theater performer.

Out front, Clare mingled with the audience, and warned a mother with two young children that the last act was violent. During the inter-vals she eavesdropped on audience comments at the rear of the orches-tra.[30] She had reason to be nervous, because many influential people were backing her play. John D. MacArthur (Helen Hayes's brother-in-law) had invested $22,800, Henry Luce and Bernard Baruch $5,000 each, Dorothy Farmer $3,000, Bishop Sheen $2,000, Mother Mary Judge $1,000, and Father Thibodeau, Al Morano, Maggie Case, and Tere Pascone $500 each. The production was capitalized at $60,000, and included $5,000 from Clare, who had never before put money into her own productions.[31]

After the final curtain, there were plentiful cries for the young lead, gratifyingly followed by eight resounding cries of, "Author! Author!"[32] But reviews next day, and after the play transferred to Boston's Shubert Theatre on November 19, were mixed. The *Springfield News* praised Clare's talent for line and phrase, but said that in dramatizing mysticism and murder, she had "placed too large a subject on too small a canvas."[33] The *Boston Post* commented, "Some of its scenes have the high excitement of great drama; some others are just plain silly." Other critics said that Margaret O'Brien's performance was "inspired, but that the melodrama was clumsily crafted, repetitious, and long-winded, with poorly developed characters."[34] Ticket sales flagged, and after the last Boston performance on December 1, Eddie Dowling canceled a pending transfer to Philadelphia.[35]

A letter from Charles Willoughby, dated December 23, surprised Clare. He began by spelling her name with an *i*, which always irritated her. What followed was strangely curt and clumsy, a farewell of sorts.

> Against the background of the holidays, I count on the benevolent understanding of an old and trusted friend.
>
> I hope that you appreciate that my erratic silences are due to a curious psychological adjustment, which I had to solve or adjust personally.
>
> Needless to say I remain appreciative of your friendship and understanding.
>
> I married Mrs. M. Pratt in a civil ceremony, Nov. 20th, a friend from Tokyo and sister-in-law of the American Minister.
>
> I expect to go abroad shortly for an indefinite stay in Spain.
>
> I send warm holiday wishes.
>
> Fondly Charles.[36]

Clare was in California again in late January 1952, staying at the Beverly Hills Hotel for ten more weeks on *Pilate's Wife*. RKO assigned the veteran screenwriter William Cameron Menzies to help her finish.[37] This seemed to signal that the producers had lost confidence in her ability to fully implement her idea. She felt at first disillusioned, then bored.

On March 20, she appeared as a presenter at the annual Academy Awards ceremony at Hollywood's RKO Pantages Theatre. It was small compensation for not having appeared as a winner two years before. *Come to the Stable*, despite seven nominations, had won no Oscar. Dressed in an oyster-white satin gown with a diamond pendant, Clare handed the screenwriting award to Paul Dehn and James Bernard for *Seven Days to Noon*, misstating the title as *Seven Days to the Moon*. According to the screenwriter Philip Dunne, she then seemed not to recognize famous names, pronouncing that of John Huston "with a short 'u,' as in 'hut,' and [my own] with a long one, as in 'dune,' both with a questioning note in her voice, and the look of one who has bitten into a sour apple."[38]

Announcing that the first-draft screenplay of *Pilate's Wife* was finished, Clare left on March 22 for New York and soon after accompanied Harry to Europe. He was to gather material for a special issue of *Life* on Spain. In Seville, she was intrigued to find an old villa called La Casa de Pilatus. It was a replica, built in A.D. 1200 by a Holy Land crusader, of Pontius Pilate's seaside house in Judea—where Clare had set the early scenes of her screenplay. She described it to Dorothy Farmer as a "delicate Moorish building with a large patio in the middle, balconies, garrisons for troops on the ground floor etc. Not so different from what we imagined at Caesarea!"[39]

At the end of the month the Luces reached Paris, and Clare went to Rocquencourt to see General Eisenhower. Now head of SHAPE (Supreme Headquarters Allied Powers Europe), he had recently informed President Truman that he was resigning his command, effective June 1, in order to run for the Republican presidential nomination. Clare wanted to let him know that she and Harry were supporting his candidacy.

Before showing her into the general's office, an aide told her that Eisenhower had "a stinker of a problem" with reporters asking about his religion. He belonged to no church and felt faith was a personal matter. His handlers, however, feared that some paper might print that he did not believe in God.

Risking Ike's ire, Clare raised the subject of religion, stressing how necessary it was for a presidential candidate to practice one. He assured her that he believed in the Almighty. His German immigrant grandparents had been Mennonites, but had found no house of worship for those of their persuasion when they settled in East Texas. His parents had therefore not been churchgoers. This had not stopped them from reading the Bible to him every morning and evening, and he knew its contents well. Claiming a denomination now, just to get votes, was not something he cared to do.

Clare said that nevertheless a Chief Executive must be seen as a symbol of the highest ideals. She asked if Mrs. Eisenhower was a practicing Christian. Ike said she was a Presbyterian.

"Then why not accompany Mamie to her place of worship in Paris on Sunday?"

The general took her advice, and for the time being silenced press speculation.[40]

▽

Clare returned to New York on May 13, and ten days later found time for a reunion with Carlos Chávez. She had at last paid him half of his fee for Ann's symphony. Despite his promise to deliver early that year, it was still far from finished. She put no pressure on him, and in a grateful letter tinged with regret, he said that he was unable to express all that he saw, and felt, and loved in her.

> I have been telling you these last two or three days that you have been a revelation to me . . . Yes, I *do* want to [put it] in words, but however objective I would like it, I know I can better say it in my own more subjective medium, in my music.
>
> I miss you. It is incredible what your presence does . . . I hope to see you very soon, my love.[41]

30

BACK TO THE HUSTINGS

Each indecision brings its own delays
And days are lost lamenting o'er lost days.

—Johann Wolfgang von Goethe

At the Connecticut GOP convention in Hartford on May 26, Clare again succumbed to her fascination with politics. She agreed to represent her old district, Fairfield County, at the Republican National Convention in Chicago that July. By the time she left the arena forty-eight hours later, all twenty-two delegates were committed to Eisenhower.

On June 9, they met with Ike at his Morningside Heights residence in New York. Clare asked him what he thought of General MacArthur warning against the election of a "military man" to the presidency. Ike said that he did not recall MacArthur objecting when *he* had been proposed for that position in 1948. Speaking to the press afterward, Clare praised Eisenhower as "a most astounding combination of humility and confidence," who spoke with "equal authority on many subjects." To her husband, however, she remarked on the general's platitudinous oratory, comparing him to the cornpone poet Eddie Guest, of whom Dorothy Parker wrote, "I'd rather flunk my Wasserman [syphilis] Test / Than read the poetry of Edgar Guest."[1]

Harry planned to throw the resources of his magazines behind Eisenhower's candidacy. He met with Ike in Denver on June 19, and said it was imperative he make "at least one statesmanlike speech"—preferably on world affairs—before the Chicago convention. Time Inc. would send ninety-six staffers to cover the proceedings, and donate a substantial sum to the nominee.[2]

Mary Bancroft encountered Harry at a dinner party at Al Grover's, and ridiculed his support of Eisenhower. She accused him of hoping to be a behind-the-scenes presidential adviser. Blood drained from his face, and he screamed, "You've been for every catastrophe of the twentieth century—from FDR on."[3]

▽

When Clare appeared at the Chicago convention on Monday, July 7, she found that Dwight Eisenhower and Senator Robert A. Taft, an Old Guard conservative, were close in delegate counts. They were trailed at a distance by Governor Earl Warren, former Governor Harold Stassen of Minnesota, and Douglas MacArthur, now conveniently retired from the army and hoping to secure the number two spot on a Taft ticket.[4] But after a tedious, bitter keynote speech by "dugout Doug," and an anti-Red harangue by Senator Joe McCarthy of Wisconsin—also a Taft supporter—Ike's momentum accelerated. Clare worked the floor on his behalf and, under pressure from some party members, floated Margaret Chase Smith's name for the vice presidency.[5] But the lady from Maine withdrew to preserve party harmony, and nobody proposed Clare Luce in her stead.

In the first roll call of states on Friday, Eisenhower registered 595 votes to Taft's 500. Then a last-minute switch of Minnesota votes put him over the top, and he was nominated with a final majority of 845 to 280. MacArthur's support shrank from 10 to 4.

On the advice of GOP stalwarts, Ike chose Richard Milhous Nixon, a thirty-nine-year-old Senator from California, as his running mate. A smart lawyer, Nixon had first won nationwide recognition by nailing Alger Hiss as a Communist subversive, and was recognized in Congress as being well versed in both foreign and domestic issues.

Many years later, Nixon speculated that if the idea of women in high office had been more advanced in 1952, Clare Luce could well have been nominated instead of him.

> She had the brains, the drive, the political acumen, the judgment, and she was the first really interesting woman to make a major mark in American politics. She also had a well-honed ability to

engage in the cut-and-thrust of political conflict and she was identified as a strongly-committed anti-Communist—two of the specific qualities for which Eisenhower chose me.[6]

▽

Oratorically, the Democrats did better at their Chicago convention in
the last week of July, where Adlai E. Stevenson, the witty, intellectual
Governor of Illinois, became the nominee, and chose to run with Senator John J. Sparkman of Alabama. Harry recognized the verbal superiority and message of the opposition, and stepped up his support of
Eisenhower. He reacted in fury when T. S. Matthews, a Princeton classmate of Stevenson's, took advantage of his absence to run an adulatory
Time cover story on the Governor.

In the course of the campaign, Luce magazines relentlessly portrayed the Democratic ticket negatively. While Eisenhower was described as purposefully striding into a room, Stevenson merely
"shambled." Picture editors featured unflattering photographs of the
Democrat's disheveled clothes and balding head, even snapping a hole
in the sole of his shoe. Nixon was described as good-looking, modest,
and smart, while Sparkman was caricatured as "a Southern connoisseur
of cough drops."

Thousands of letters poured in complaining of extreme bias, and
canceling subscriptions. Harry defended his pro-Ike stance. "A political
campaign is not a sporting event requiring polite neutrality," he told his
staff.[7] A disillusioned Matthews concluded that Luce "had come to the
point of believing that the Republic was in danger whenever the Republicans weren't running it."[8]

▽

After returning to Hollywood Clare worked on studio revisions for *Pilate's Wife,* but soon became "disgusted and depressed" over them.[9] On
July 28, she was presented with a possible way out. News came from
Connecticut that Senator Brien McMahon had died of cancer at age
forty-eight, only two years into his current term. Newspapers reported
that Governor Lodge was expected to appoint Clare Luce to the seat
until November, when she would have a good chance to win the unex-
pired four years of McMahon's term.[10] She called Lodge, and said she
was interested only if he did not want the seat for himself. Lodge discon-
certingly replied that before making the temporary appointment, he

needed to consult with party leaders. He would then wait to see who emerged as the nominee of the state convention in September.

A week later, Clare went to Los Angeles Airport to greet Eisenhower, who was to make the opening speech of his campaign. She bumped into Al Morano, who had at last followed her as Representative of Fairfield County "You've got to come back, Sis," he said, insisting that the Senate race in Connecticut "is wide open."[11]

Clare at once told reporters she was available for McMahon's vacant post, "if the people want me."[12] On August 11, she wrote the Governor. "I think as a Senatorial candidate I could help Ike with various groups of voters—most especially the women, since in the national picture there are so few women running for important office." She repeated that her availability depended on "your not wanting to fill the vacancy yourself."[13]

Those familiar with Lodge's patrician background knew that his burning ambition was to emulate his brother, Senator Henry Cabot Lodge, Jr., of Massachusetts, and his esteemed grandfather of the same name, who had represented the state in the same capacity for thirty-one years. The main dilemma for him now was that if he ran for the Senate and won, he would be succeeded for the next two years by his Lieutenant Governor, a Democrat, thus incurring the wrath of Connecticut Republicans. He could avoid such ire only if the state convention drafted him. Speculation was rife that secretly this was what he hoped might happen.

Clare received many letters, telegrams, and phone calls urging her to run. She announced that having turned down two chances in the past, she was about to exercise a woman's privilege to change her mind and fight alongside General Eisenhower.[14]

Her RKO contract came to an end on August 20, and she returned East with only sixty-six pages surviving of her original script for *Pilate's Wife*.

Three days later, the *Bridgeport Post* reported that the Governor was hoping for a deadlock at the convention between Mrs. Luce and Prescott S. Bush, a Greenwich banker, so that delegates would turn to him. But *The New York Times* stated that Clare had "moved into the lead" for McMahon's seat. Simultaneously, an aide close to Eisenhower asked certain Connecticut GOP leaders to support her candidacy.[15] Three Republican caucuses, irked by this outside interference, pressured Lodge to make his temporary appointee William A. Purtell, a forceful-speaking

Clare and Richard Nixon, c. September 1952

Catholic from Bridegport, who, confusingly, was already the party's nominee for the junior seat held by Senator William Benton.[16]

On August 26, Clare met in New York with Eisenhower and then Nixon. Both meetings proclaimed the national campaign's desire to have her back in Washington, now that Ike was widely seen as the next President. Clare issued a statement confirming that she had asked Lodge to back her for the nomination, and he "flatly and finally told me he would not extend me any support, so I must believe that he is supporting Prescott Bush under the guise of neutrality." She refused, at least publicly, to believe whisperers who claimed the Governor surreptitiously sought the nomination for himself. "An honorable man must be taken at his word."[17]

Lodge's outraged response was to appoint Purtell to hold McMahon's seat through the end of the year.

▽

Politicking among party leaders continued as Clare trekked around every Connecticut county, advertised widely, and made radio and television speeches. On Thursday, September 4, she joined hundreds of delegates at Bushnell Memorial Hall in Hartford for the two-day Connecticut State Republican Convention. Richard Nixon gave the keynote address, his presence reaffirming the Eisenhower campaign's support of Clare's candidacy. But as she canvassed the floor, her optimism faded. Prescott Bush was obviously favored to win in the next day's ballot, unless a movement to draft Lodge succeeded.

At that night's reception, Clare, dressed in the same navy-blue polka-dot crepe outfit she had worn all day, ate nothing. She was the only candidate who continued pleading her case after the function ended at midnight. Going on to the Bond Hotel where delegates congregated, she traipsed from room to room until 4:30 A.M. Cheerful despite rejections, she was gratified when at least one Fairfield County delegation said it would vote for her.[18]

Friday's proceedings began ominously for Clare, as Lodge was duly drafted to run for Senator McMahon's seat. But the Governor garnered a mere five votes. Four main candidates remained on the ballot: Clare, Bush, J. Kenneth Bradley of Westport, and John Lupton of Weston. At the last moment, Congressman Antoni Sadlak of Rockville, Joseph Talbot of Naugatuck, and Mansfield Sprague of New Canaan put their names forward. In the subsequent polling, with 616 delegates voting, Clare was chastened to receive only 50 votes (most from her old constituency) to Bush's 412 and Sadlak's 54. The other five candidates got 100 among them.

With the roll call complete, Lodge went to the rostrum and said that the ticket comprising Bush and Purtell would "command great support" on Election Day. Clare followed to make the nomination unanimous. "I stand before you as a defeated candidate, but no battle is worth fighting that is not worth losing." She appealed for party unity to elect

Eisenhower and Nixon in November, and in a hint of personal disappointment quoted lines from an ancient English ballad.

I am hurt, Sir Andrew Barton said; I am hurt but I am not slain.
I lie me down and bleed awhile, and then I'll rise and fight again.[19]

Apparently, her dithering over a Senate run in previous years, when she could have won handily, had lost her the support of local party leaders and most delegates. Another reason for her defeat was the reluctance of Governor Lodge and the state party chairman, Clarence Baldwin, to have two Roman Catholics—Clare and Purtell—run for the Senate at the same time, especially when a third, Al Morano, was up for reelection to the House.

Harry, who had been standing in the wings during the voting, made only one comment to the press about his wife's part in the proceedings: "I am proud of her today as I have always been proud of her." As they drove away, he turned to her and smiled. "Look at all the money we've saved." Two weeks spent vying for the nomination had cost them $6,000, with little more than $1,000 coming from others. Two months of further campaigning would have been vastly more expensive.[20]

Lord Beaverbrook wrote sympathetically to say he had hoped to see "Senator Luce" continue "the most brilliant career" of his female acquaintance. "Oddly enough," Clare replied, "I was responsible for getting Lodge into politics." He had been a movie actor, hardly an obvious qualification for Congress, but she had supported him for her own House seat when many said he had no chance, and later urged him to run for the governorship.

"No good deed," she concluded, "goes unpunished."[21]

▽

By now, Carlos Chávez was resigned to Clarita and himself living in different worlds. He had telephoned her just before the convention, but she had cut him short, sounding rushed. He wrote later to say he did not resent her lack of time to talk.

I love your intensity in things you take up and your definiteness. . . . At our age, you and I have to grow; and not only that, but grow together, how together and apart? Bah! That is our particular characteristic, and don't you think that is what we have been doing for the last three years?[22]

Sadly for him, Clare no longer felt as intensely as during their idyllic days in his Acapulco aerie.

▽

Taking a short break before the Republican presidential campaign began in earnest, Clare compiled and edited a book for Sheed & Ward called *Saints for Now*. She persuaded twenty eminent authors to contribute short biographical essays—in effect hagiographies—of a saint they admired. Among them were Thomas Merton writing on John of the Cross, Robert Farren on Thomas Aquinas, Paul Gallico on Francis of Assisi, Sister Madeleva on Hilda of Whitby, Whittaker Chambers on Benedict, Wyndham Lewis on Pius V, Rebecca West on Augustine of Hippo, and Evelyn Waugh on Helena, mother of Emperor Constantine. Clare also commissioned illustrations by André Girard, Jean Charlot, and Salvador Dalí.[23]

In her introduction, she cited Augustine, among her favorite saints, for abandoning a life of "lust and sophistry" for one of religious devotion. She also admired Thomas Aquinas for "the glory of his intellect" and Joan of Arc for dying in defense of political principles. Most of her choices had a spiritual ideal that eluded her. "Saints give little thought to changing the world around them. They are too busy changing the world within them."[24]

The book would go on to win the Christopher Award, and sell thirty thousand copies in its first weeks. It was also published abroad, despite mixed American reviews. The *New York Herald Tribune* found the efforts of an ostensibly all-star cast of authors "ragged." The *Voice of Saint Jude* said that the best pieces were by women, except for Clare's pedestrian introduction, which "did not succeed in matching the high quality" of the rest.[25]

▽

Clare kick-started the GOP presidential campaign in Connecticut on September 11, before a huge crowd at Bridgeport's Stratford Hotel. She concentrated most of her energy thereafter on lectures, radio talks, and television speeches, ratcheting up an eventual total of over a hundred appearances. She focused on inner-city, blue-collar Catholic Democrats, as the most likely part of the former New Deal vote to be lured away from Stevenson. Al Smith had done just this in his New York gubernatorial races in the 1920s. Many of these Catholics were Poles who had been angered when FDR ceded their homeland to Stalin at

Yalta. Ike, too, took up the Catholic anti-Communist cause, berating the "tragic blunders" made at Tehran, at Yalta, and in the postwar negotiations at Potsdam, where the West had traded "overwhelming victory for a new enemy and for new oppressions and new wars which were to come."[26]

Nixon adhered to the anti-Soviet theme, alliteratively accusing Stevenson of being "a Ph.D. graduate of Dean Acheson's cowardly college of Communist Containment." He had been incensed during the first Alger Hiss trial, when the Governor appeared as a character witness, and swore to the loyalty and integrity of the defendant.

The hapless Stevenson played further into the hands of the GOP by saying he would not appoint an envoy to the Vatican, because "it constitutes an official recognition of a religion incompatible with our theory of the separation of church and state." He followed this with an impolitic boycott of the annual Al Smith dinner hosted by Cardinal Spellman, leaving the floor to Eisenhower to capture yet more Catholics with his pro-Poland remarks on foreign policy.[27]

Clare was not at her best on September 28, when she debated Senator Hubert H. Humphrey in an *American Forum of the Air* broadcast. She attacked the Truman administration for being careless of the safety and resources of the United States Treasury. "We are in a bloody war in Korea. And certainly it hasn't given us solvency. Every American citizen owes the government $1,800 . . . our national debt is $655 billion." What was more, the Democratic-dominated Congress, with Humphrey's approval, now wanted to pour taxpayers' money into a wasteful, "high-minded" irrigation scheme in Asia.

Humphrey effectively replied that the scheme was part of a foreign aid program to advance democracy, not just drainage. Clare continued to protest that after having spent "billions and billions of dollars" abroad, the United States saw "nothing in return."

The Senator was not about to be steamrolled by allowing her to monopolize the conversation. "With all the charm on the other side of the table," he said, "I still want my moment." He repeated a mantra of his own campaigns. "Freedom is not free . . . $500 million for a continent that embraces over a billion and a half people is a small price . . . to wage a war for peace."

Drawing attention to the contrasting platforms of the presidential candidates, Humphrey damagingly cited Eisenhower's tolerance of the ranting anti-Communist Senator Joseph McCarthy of Wisconsin. At this Clare seemed at a loss for words. Recovering, she accused him of being "violently opposed to Mr. Truman" in the 1948 election. When he corrected her, she became uncharacteristically flustered. "Well, I don't see why we should labor all these points, of what you said or didn't say." Humphrey replied, "I don't either."[28]

▼

Meanwhile, Harry, riding along for two days on Eisenhower's campaign train, was unimpressed with some of the acolytes he encountered on board, calling them "90 percent self-seeking chiselers."[29]

His remark gained credence when Richard Nixon was accused of making personal use of a campaign trust fund. Eisenhower was appalled when this became public, and told aides that Nixon should quit. The GOP's crusade against unethical practices in Washington would lack resonance "if we ourselves aren't as clean as a hound's tooth."[30] Nixon was cleared by an audit, but Ike believed that even the rumor of malfeasance had tarnished his value as a running mate.

Afraid of being dropped, Nixon appeared on prime-time television to exonerate himself before a record sixty million. With his stony-faced wife, Pat, beside him, he righteously pleaded his modest financial status, and asked viewers to let the Republican National Committee know whether he should remain on the ticket or not. Eisenhower was furious, but in more than four million responses to party headquarters, 200 to 1 said the answer was yes.[31]

▼

Hoping to redeem her Humphrey debate performance, Clare agreed to stand in for Joseph McCarthy in a television broadcast on September 30. Increasingly virulent in his diatribes, the Senator had been accusing Roosevelt and Truman of "twenty years of treason," for not having been sufficiently anti-Communist. Posed against a stark background in a black rhinestone evening gown, Clare gave her apocalyptic views on the Sino-Soviet threat to Western democracy. John Kenneth Galbraith, a speechwriter on Stevenson's team, derisively noted her "taut, high-pitched, frantic tones" as she condemned domestic tolerance of Bolshevism.[32]

Since Clare always made a point of speaking in a low register, Galbraith was likely objecting more to the content of her remarks than to any lack of mellowness. Eisenhower, in contrast, complimented her for "bringing into sharp focus the Communist infiltration of our America."[33]

Encouraged, she gave a substantial address to a capacity audience at the Executive Club Ladies' Day lunch in Chicago, eleven days before the election. She said that the number one issue before the world was the problem of Communism, and until it was solved no nation could know peace or security. Defending McCarthy's "blunderbluss, bile and brimstone" style of fighting the Red menace, she said it was harmless compared to what President Truman had been saying about Eisenhower. He had accused the general of wanting to start an atomic war against the Soviets, as well as being anti-Catholic, anti-Semitic, callous to Negroes, and prone to the Nazi theory of a "master race." No Democrat, she observed, had reprimanded Truman for *his* "hysteria, slander, smear, or of whacking away at the Bill of Rights . . . all of which things are by their own definition, 'McCarthyism.'"

Leavening her onslaught with humor, Clare caused much laughter by deriding the President's lack of inches. "Just last week Mr. Truman rose to his full height . . . stretched his neck looking way up, and shouted, 'Moral pygmy!'" She granted that many people did not like McCarthy's language. She had been a victim of it herself. "I am not here . . . to pat McCarthy on the back or sock him in the nose, though it is my private opinion that it would be a good idea for the Senator's soul if both were done calmly and with regularity." This got applause as well as laughter. But, she went on, his desire to oust Soviet sympathizers from the United States government was sincere, as was his "relentless exposure of their sinister influence on New Deal foreign policy."

She accused Secretary of State Dean Acheson of bringing into the State Department a cadre of "arrested adolescents whose minds stopped growing somewhere in the Thirties, at the time when they first experienced the fine raptures of liberalism." The reverence of these immature bureaucrats for Soviet ideology had caused the loss of China, and the present war in Korea. "Young people are often like blackberries. When they are green, they are red."

In the brief question period that followed, she went after Stevenson for having chosen a white supremacist as his running mate. She also pointed out that the Governor, who had been a reporter in Russia twenty-five years before, had never spoken of the million or more citizens liquidated by Stalin. A prolonged ovation followed as she returned to her chair.[34]

Within hours of Clare's Chicago address, Eisenhower made a major announcement on television about America's military involvement in

Asia. He had been appalled to learn that in the past two years the United States had incurred more than one hundred thousand casualties in Korea, twenty-five thousand of them fatal. Truman was at fault, in his opinion, for failing to devise a withdrawal plan when Chinese reinforcements made it impossible to defeat the Communist North. The President, in response, had challenged Ike to propose an immediate exit strategy of his own.

Taking the bait, Eisenhower said he would make ending the stalemated conflict his priority as Commander in Chief. In honor of that intent, he vowed that as soon as he was elected, "I shall go to Korea."

These words from the five-star general were immediately seen, by Democrats and Republicans alike, as certain to assure him victory in November. Clare, asked to comment on CBS's *Longines Chronoscope* show, said that Eisenhower would be especially able to evaluate what he saw and heard at the Korean Front, "because he has been a great modern soldier." As for those who feared that his military background would incline him to wage war, she said, grinning, "Did you ever hear of a fireman that wanted to start a fire?"[35]

In the campaign's final week, as Stevenson's support dropped precipitously in the polls, Clare appeared again on national television to blast the administration's record on Communism. She illustrated her remarks with newsreel clips and phonograph recordings of testimony by Whittaker Chambers and other witnesses to Red perfidy. Her broadcast turned out to be among the most effective of that electoral season, with a rating second only to Nixon's apologia.[36]

To the last hours of his eight-week countrywide tour, Eisenhower, at sixty-one, showed a degree of energy that Stevenson, nine years younger, could not match. He traveled 51,376 miles through forty-five states, spoke in 232 towns, and held many more press conferences than his rival, who sometimes showed signs of fatigue.

Ike's stump work paid off. On November 4, he won the election by 55.1 percent of the vote to his opponent's 44.4 percent, and a resounding 442 electoral votes to 89. Republicans also gained a majority of eight in the House, and tied for seats in the Senate, which meant that in a deadlock, Vice President Nixon would cast the deciding vote.[37] Ike also took all but nine states, including "doubtful" Connecticut, sweeping Bush, Purtell, and Morano into office with him—the last with the highest plurality ever recorded by a Congressman in the Fourth District.

Cutting into the traditional Democratic hold on the South, Eisenhower carried Texas, Tennessee, Virginia, Florida, and Oklahoma. Two

Clare filming a television spot for Eisenhower, October 1952

of the nine states he lost were Kentucky and West Virginia. The others were in the Deep South. Clare had correctly bet a dollar on six for Stevenson: Alabama, Arkansas, Georgia, Mississippi, North Carolina, and West Virginia.[38]

One statistic that especially gratified her was the GOP's overwhelming success with Catholics (particularly of Eastern European descent). No longer the religion of a select number of rich elite and poor immigrants, the Church of Rome had finally exercised political clout through the ballot box rather than the pulpit, and was on the verge of becoming a force in American life.[39]

The Democratic Party thus found itself out of power for the first time in twenty years. Clare and Harry were ecstatic, having contributed not only her oratory and his editorial support, but a whopping $48,500 to Ike's coffers. The question now was whether either of them would be rewarded with a plum post in the new administration.

31

THE HEALING DRAUGHT

We are what we repeatedly do.
Excellence, then, is not an act, but a habit.

—ARISTOTLE

Two days after the election, Clare addressed a dinner for Jesuits in New York. Her subject was the mission of St. Francis Xavier to China, and she laced her remarks with references to the same Red villains she had castigated in the presidential campaign. She told her audience that exactly four hundred years before, Emperor Kia Tsing had issued a xenophobic edict refusing the Spanish monk admission to his country. Now, she said, the door to China was more firmly closed against Christian envoys than ever, but it was Communist imperialism that kept them out.

Harry, whose desire to spread the values of American capitalism abroad was as zealous as Xavier's evangelism, arranged a five-week business trip to the Orient. Since Eisenhower was about to visit Korea, he wanted to update himself on the strategic prospects for the United States in the region.

No sooner had he left than a summons came for Clare to meet the President-elect at his transition headquarters in the Commodore Hotel at 3:00 P.M. on November 28.[1]

En route to her appointment, Clare fantasized ways she might play a part "in the world and in history." When she arrived at the hotel, she found a warren of offices swarming with job seekers, and chatted with an aide for twenty minutes. Then Eisenhower emerged and strode toward her, smiling broadly with outstretched hand. He ushered her into his room and closed the door.

She was impressed, as often before, by the "sheer vitality of the man, and his essential simplicity and goodness . . . with that warmth and cheerful heartedness and self-possession that inspire love and confidence in everyone."[2]

Their conversation began with pleasantries about Harry's role in the campaign. Eisenhower then changed the subject, saying he would like to appoint a Catholic as his Secretary of Labor. What did she think about that? Not knowing how to respond, Clare said he would need someone of "tremendous capacity" for such a demanding job.

"There is *no* job so tough *you* couldn't do it," Ike said.

While she digested this compliment, he remarked that she was "certainly smarter and abler" than Frances Perkins, the first woman to hold that or any cabinet post. Clare was even more flattered, but knowing from congressional experience that she had no propensity for dealing with unions, said she felt unqualified.

Eisenhower asked if there was another job she would prefer. Clare suggested tentatively that she could be a successor to Eleanor Roosevelt as chairman of the United Nations Commission on Human Rights. He looked surprised, and said that would not be "much of a thing." In any case, the post was filled.

Edging closer to candor, Clare said she "fit no where except into the field of foreign affairs." Before Ike could reply, she added, "And with London gone to Aldrich—"

"*Who* told you that?" he snapped.

"Everyone in New York knows, because the Aldriches have leaked it."

He laughed and said Winthrop Aldrich was "the brainiest man with the least wisdom" he had ever encountered. It was true, however, that the former banker had been appointed to the Court of St. James's.

Continuing to press, Eisenhower asked, "What would *you* like best?"

As his question—perhaps the most momentous ever asked of her—hung in the air, Clare knew there was only one answer. Mysteriously and often over the years, Italy had summoned her, first when she had been a correspondent for *Life* in the spring of 1940, then twice more, visiting American and British troops in 1944 and 1945. It was there that she had first met Pope Pius XII, and adopted little Augusto. Since the end of the war, she and Harry had been as concerned over the threat of Communist expansion in Italy as in China. They had helped orchestrate the successful fund-raising visit to the United States of Alcide De Gasperi, Italy's postwar architect of Christian capitalist democracy. He was still in power, and deeply grateful to them both.[3] Over the years, she had returned to Italy for cultural and spiritual refreshment, even finding love in the Uffizi gallery.

But Eisenhower was waiting to hear what reward she wanted. Clare took the plunge.

"Naturally, what I can't get. Rome."

"Who told you you can't get it and why?"

"There are so many others to whom you are obligated."

At this point, she cast aside false modesty, and cited three benefits he might gain in choosing her. First, he would gratify the millions of Catholics who had voted for him, second, her appointment would save him from having to send another of her faith to the Vatican—something Stevenson had found out was a sore point with Protestants, and third, every female in the electorate "would be pleased that a woman had finally got a number one diplomatic post."[4] She felt she could handle the vexed question of how much further aid to give a country that was making a remarkable economic recovery from the war. Left unspoken was her own dismay at the growing presence of Communists in Italy's government and industries.

Eisenhower hedged. He wondered if she might have a second choice, such as Mexico. "You could do a splendid job for me there." Clare said lamely that it would be an easier commute. Still probing, Ike asked how her husband would feel about her going to Rome. She admitted they had discussed it, and Harry liked the idea. Time Inc. had a bureau in the Holy City, so he could visit her and run his business from there. She did not have to remind Eisenhower that with their combined wealth, they had ample means to finance the entertaining expected in a prime ambassadorial spot.

He brought the discussion to an end without committing himself, but gave her a caution that sounded like encouragement. "Please don't discuss this with Foster." John Foster Dulles, as Clare knew, was his choice as Secretary of State.

"Let me wrangle it, and be patient," Ike said.

As if on cue, Dulles entered. After a brief chat, she left with the impression that if Dulles (a former adviser to Senator Vandenberg) agreed to have her in his diplomatic corps, she would get her heart's desire.[5]

▽

Outside, she faced reporters and cameramen, telling them nothing about her conversation with Eisenhower. But in a letter that night, she shared every detail with Harry, seeking to assuage whatever disappointment he might feel at not having been favored himself.

She told him that she disliked the prospect of their having to pursue separate careers on different sides of the Atlantic. "The awful apartness . . . fills me with panic, vertigo, anguish beyond reason when I contemplate it." They must thrash it out as soon as he returned from Asia—the implication being that she hoped Harry would reassure her their marriage could stand the strain. In the meantime, "my poor, thirsty little (no, big) ego has had the healing draught it needed most."

Clare wished that he could have shared the moment when, after offering her a cabinet post, Eisenhower had agreed to consider her for the position she hankered for all along. "I am so happy because I feel *recognized, appreciated, wanted* . . . by the one man whose recognition and appreciation matter most in politics." In a dozen ways, she added, Ike had made it clear that "in honoring the wife, he sought to honor and please the husband!" She reminded Harry, in a postscript, of his importance around the globe. "Gosh darling, in the tragic environs of Korea and Formosa, does all this sound—trivial and selfish? And irrelevant?"[6]

Her true excitement showed in a note to her friend at *Vogue*. "Maggie, I want Italy more than anything in my entire life."[7]

▽

The day after seeing Clare, Eisenhower flew to South Korea. He met in Seoul with President Syngman Rhee, who wanted to unify the divided country by forcing the Communists back to the Yalu River. General Mark Clark, now commanding the United Nations forces there, had even bolder hopes, suggesting air and sea assaults on China, and even proposing that "serious consideration" be given to the use of the atomic bomb. Ike refused both men. "I have a mandate from the people to stop this fighting," he said. "That's my decision."[8]

Clare was not sure how long confirmation of her appointment would take, so she decided to spend the next few weeks in the Bahamas. As she settled into Nassau's Cable Beach Manor, she yearned for Harry's company and counsel. But he was unlikely to join her until Christmas.[9] After years of marital crises and exhausting reconciliations, their mutual support of Eisenhower and shared interest in Cold War politics boded salvation for them both. They were now in a position to try to influence policy as well as comment on it.

▽

Far away in Mexico City, Carlos Chávez felt increasingly isolated from Clare. He was hurt that she had sent only perfunctory replies to his many letters in the last couple of years. He did not understand that foreign policy, not religion, was her latest obsession. At any rate, it certainly excluded him. "I really should not be keeping on this correspondence without correspondence," he wrote in a note tinged with sadness. "But I am not expecting any answer to these lines anyway."

Carlos added that he had finished only the first movement of Ann's symphony, and half of the second. Completion of the whole four-movement work, his most complex and ambitious yet, was going to be a long process. He now aimed for its world premiere in "the winter of 1953–54." To that end, he was about to take the score to his Acapulco studio, "where you once were in a starlitten [sic] night."[10]

▽

On December 17, Clare received a phone call from C. D. Jackson, now a senior aide to Eisenhower. He confirmed that she had been appointed Ambassador Extraordinary and Plenipotentiary to the Republic of Italy. The nomination would be announced in the new year, and if approved by the Senate, she would soon find herself at the center of the Mediterranean world.

Harry got back to New York four days later. Stopping only long enough to report on his travels to the President-elect, and at greater length to his editors, he flew to Nassau on December 23, bringing Clare an engraved Cartier gold circular pill box, decorated with a cabochon sapphire.[11]

Reunited after more than five weeks apart, the Luces attended Christmas Eve Mass in the island's small cathedral. Clare, ecstatic at her elevation, felt that the service was one of the most beautiful and inspiring she had ever attended. She wrote to tell the Abbot of Gethsemani about "a great golden-throated choir of Negroes—and all the parishioners, most of them colored—singing the responses in Latin . . . from memory."[12]

32

GAL FOR THE JOB

*The art of diplomacy is to get other people
to want what you want.*

—MADELEINE ALBRIGHT

B y the time Clare left Nassau with Harry for New York on January 2, 1953, the FBI had begun background checks in anticipation of her Senate confirmation. Its grilling of friends and acquaintances was extensive and intrusive. One agent even barged into George S. Kaufman's bedroom, where he was working on a play, simply because he had helped Clare with third act problems in *The Women* seventeen years before.[1] The Luces were alarmed when they discovered that their apartment telephone wires were tapped.[2]

Clare's new status as the first woman ever chosen to head a major U.S. Embassy abroad, plus Harry's now undoubted status as the most powerful publisher in America, with presidential access, placed the couple at the height of sociopolitical eminence.

Harry felt exalted to find himself, or imagine himself, as a counsel to the powerful. He advised Secretary Dulles on how to handle the Korean stalemate, gave Ike a further briefing on his tour of the Far East, and had lunch with Winston Churchill. Returning to Time Inc. from the last encounter, in "what Billings called a delirium of happy excitement," he treated his editors to impressions of the last two leaders. Ike, he said, had given Churchill "unshirted hell" for failing to do more on

European unity. But the President-elect did not understand the full nature of Communism, and thought Japan should be free to trade with Red China. Struggling, as so often, to express himself in metaphor, Harry said Winston was "like a great symphony orchestrating fixed themes." Yet he was unable to quote the exact words of either great man.[3]

▼

The weather for the Inauguration of Dwight David Eisenhower on January 20 was cold but clear. Before dawn, crowds gathered in front of the east face of the Capitol. Men wearing top hats or homburgs mingled with Indians in full tribal regalia, and a California woman held up a live turtle that waved a small flag wired to its right front leg. Just after 10:00 A.M., the U.S. Marine Band struck up beneath the swearing-in platform. As noon approached, the VIP stands began to fill. Clare, a guest of her old colleague Joseph W. Martin, Jr. (now Speaker of the House), took her place near, but not among, members of the diplomatic corps, since her appointment had not yet been announced. Finally, to the sound of ruffles and flourishes, Eisenhower followed President Truman and Richard Nixon to the front row.

The invocation was given by Monsignor Patrick O'Boyle, the Archbishop of Washington, as an obvious sign of Republican gratitude for the Catholic vote last November. A black soprano, Dorothy Maynor, sang "The Star-Spangled Banner." Nixon was then sworn in as Vice President. At 12:30 P.M., Eisenhower stepped forward to take the oath. Before beginning his Inaugural Address, he acknowledged cheers with the wide grin and upstretched arms that had become so familiar in the campaign.

His speech was notable for its spiritual fervor and frequent references to foreign affairs.[4]

> My fellow citizens, the world and we have passed the midway point of a century of continuing challenge. We sense with all our faculties that forces of good and evil are massed and armed and opposed as rarely before in history. . . .
>
> Are we nearing the light—a day of freedom and of peace for all mankind? Or are the shadows of another night closing in upon us?

Eisenhower was referring to the totalitarian threat of Communism, which he did not mention by name. But he clearly saw the ideology as more than the domestic ogre that obsessed Senator McCarthy. It was a worldwide phenomenon that all lovers of democracy must combat together.

> To produce this unity, to meet the challenge of our time, destiny has laid upon our country the responsibility of the free world's leadership.
>
> So it is proper that we assure our friends once again that, in the discharge of this responsibility, we Americans know and we observe the difference between world leadership and imperialism; between firmness and truculence; between a thoughtfully calculated goal and spasmodic reaction to the stimulus of emergencies.

Clare was already aware of a problem facing her in Italy that had the potential of becoming just the sort of emergency the President had in mind. It was a territorial dispute with Yugoslavia over the Free Territory of Trieste. Eisenhower seemed to be saying to her and his other foreign service appointees, on the basis of his experiences as Supreme Allied Commander, that diplomatic solutions were preferable to military ones. The United States should use force only when diplomacy failed to prevent the subjugation of a free people, as in Korea. That was its moral imperative. "A soldier's pack is never as heavy as the chains of a slave."

After enumerating nine rules of conduct for future American domestic, foreign, and trade policy, Eisenhower closed with a rousing peroration.

> The peace we seek . . . is nothing less than the practice and fulfillment of our whole faith among ourselves and in our dealings with others. This signifies more than the stilling of guns, easing the sorrow of war. More than escape from death, it is a way of life. More than a haven for the weary, it is a hope for the brave.

For the five-hour parade that followed on Pennsylvania Avenue, Clare was prominently placed in the viewing pavilion immediately behind Eisenhower. She sat between Speaker Martin and General Marshall, and narrowly escaped being lassoed by a cowboy corralling the President. That night, at the Inaugural Ball, she wore a gold-sequined Hattie Carnegie gown with a long emerald stole that drew special press attention, as did her chat with the Eisenhowers.[5]

Any satisfaction Clare enjoyed from her prominent participation in

General Marshall, Clare, and Speaker Martin (behind Ike)
witness the "corralling" of the President. Mamie Eisenhower
and Vice President Nixon, far right.

the inaugural was clouded by Italian reactions to the announcement of
her ambassadorial appointment on February 7. Though Prime Minister
De Gasperi's government expressed approval, many popular newspapers
did not. They treated the prospect of a female envoy with sarcasm, rib-
aldry, or outright scorn. A cartoon in the weekly Monarchist publication *Candido* (edited by Giovanni Guareschi, author of the popular *Don
Camillo* books) showed the United States Embassy flag in Rome fringed
with negligée lace.[6] Clare became the butt of such street vulgarisms as,
"The Ambassador doesn't tote a fountain pen"—the last noun in Italian
being a double entendre for "penis."[7]

Il Mattino, a conservative Naples newspaper, questioned why President Eisenhower had not picked "an American who knows how to talk
and listen to us," while left-wing commentators disparaged her as "a
friend of the Pope."[8] One magazine, *Il Giorno*, mistakenly—or
mischievously—published a photograph of the actress Claire Luce onstage in a Shakespeare play, swooning in the arms of a swarthy Mark
Antony. She was identified as "Cleopatra Ambasciatrice."[9]

This especially annoyed Clare, who for some twenty years had been confused with her near namesake. Both had been born in 1903, shared careers in the theater and movies, converted to Catholicism, received each other's mail. Clare's own name was constantly misspelled, as in "Claire Booth Lewis" and even "Mrs. Boots Loose." One humorous Christmas card caricatured her wearing antlers as "Clare Boothe Moose."[10]

In the United States, reactions to Clare as Ambassador were mostly tolerant, although some members of Congress received outraged mail from constituents. Senator Herbert Lehman of New York got a telegram from the advertising executive William Esty saying, "Please vote against confirming that well-heeled Torquemada Claire [sic] Luce." Another objected to her having lampooned Truman as "a stuffed pig," calling it "hardly the language of a diplomat."[11] A letter to the chairman of the United States Commission on Foreign Relations suggested that since Mrs. Luce was such an excellent propagandist for the Vatican, she should be sent instead to Korea, where her "glamor and histrionic ability" would be appreciated by soldiers starved for entertainment. "But keep her out of Rome!"[12]

Friends were more positive. Evelyn Waugh wrote that he could not conceive "of a more attractive post or of a more suitable incumbent. . . . You will find me often on your doorstep."[13]

Harry flaunted his pleasure and pride, strutting around the office with a white carnation in his buttonhole. He gave Clare a lavish Valentine's Day party at the Carlton Hotel in Washington, D.C. Speaker Martin and half of the new cabinet were among the 150 guests, and the new hit singer Rosemary Clooney, about to appear on the cover of the next issue of *Time*, performed.[14]

On Tuesday, February 17, Clare braced for her confirmation hearings before the Senate Foreign Relations Committee. Inevitably, she was asked about her ideological ties to the Luce magazines. She assured her interrogators that only her husband was responsible for the content of *Time*, *Life*, and *Fortune*. Denying rumors that she might try to exert influence with the Papacy, she said that as a supporter of "the American tradition of the separation of church and state," she would have no relation with the Vatican in her new role, "formal or informal, open or secret."[15]

After a few innocuous questions from committee members as to whether her arrival in Rome would be seen as an attempt to influence Italy's imminent general election, the Senate confirmed Clare's appointment without objection on March 2. The following day, wearing a black suit with a large red rose in her left lapel, she appeared at the office of the Secretary of State to be sworn in.

The tall, stoop-shouldered, sixty-five-year-old Dulles struck her as being "a great Bull of Bashan," powerful in physique and forthright in his opinions. These were influenced by the staunch Presbyterian faith he shared with Henry Luce. Both men believed that "any serious moral issue is at bottom a religious issue." Critics of Dulles disagreed. Jawaharlal Nehru thought him a religious bigot, while Harold Macmillan derided his intellect. "His speech was slow, but it easily kept pace with his thought."[16]

The Secretary's main support came from church groups, Wall Street lawyers, and the China Lobby. Eisenhower had come to depend on his passionate anti-Communism in formulating a foreign policy based on Soviet containment. For this reason if no other, Dulles and Clare were ideological soul mates.

Before Chief Justice Fred M. Vinson administered the oath to her, Dulles addressed a few remarks to the reporters, photographers, and television and newsreel cameramen in attendance. He said that never before had a woman taken on a post of such responsibility in the diplomatic corps. Turning to Clare, he went on, "The President and all who know you realize that you will not only discharge your new responsibilities well, but will go even beyond that." Her appointment would "open up a great vista for women in some countries who are subject to prejudice."

After being sworn in, Clare said it was an honor to serve at a time when Italy's decisions "count so heavily in the world's scales." She hoped to strengthen the economic, political, and spiritual bonds between America and the still-new Republic across the ocean, "which have knit us so closely together since the time of Christopher Columbus."

A large crowd vied to congratulate her. Alberto Tarchiani, Italy's envoy to the United States, informed her that his countrymen would address her simply as *Ambasciatrice*, the feminine version of "Ambassador." She replied, "I hope it's the worst I'll be called."[17]

Two days later, Josef Stalin died. Already, before Clare had planted a foot in Europe, the world had changed dramatically, and no one could be sure if it was for good or ill.

Over the next six weeks, Clare underwent a cram course at the State Department on the history, politics, and possibly troubled future of the California-sized country to which she was accredited. Its population of some forty-seven million was almost exclusively Catholic. Unified by an ancient culture, but torn apart by two world wars, the nation remained divided in fundamental ways. Geographically and economically the arid, hardscrabble south contrasted with the fertile north, the location of most of Italy's heavy industry. Tillable land amounted to only one-fifth that of France. Farm and factory workers in Lombardy and the Piedmont earned about double the wages of those south of Rome. Two-thirds of industry ran at a loss, and oil, coal, iron, copper, lead, zinc, and bauxite had to be imported.

Politically, modern Italy was not quite seven years old, the still-uncertain product of a referendum in 1946 that had rejected both Mussolini's Fascism and the Royal House of Savoy by a margin of less than 8 percent. Monarchists, predominant in the south, still formed a large and influential minority. Their reactionary views were challenged by a leftist bloc of Socialists and Communists, mainly representative of the northern working classes. The centrist mechanism by which these extremes were kept in balance was that of the Christian Democratic Party, led by the formidable Alcide De Gasperi.

Clare already knew and liked the Prime Minister. She had met him during his visit to the United States in 1947, and recognized him as a fervent anti-Communist, strong enough to turn back the alarming rise of his country's Marxist-Socialist parties. Largely as a result of her efforts, De Gasperi had gone home with a $100 million loan from Washington, plus many private contributions from like-minded Americans— including both Luces—toward his reelection campaign the following year. The result had been a historic triumph for the Christian Democrats, with 48 percent of the vote, and a 50 percent drop in support for the Communists.[18]

De Gasperi was now hoping to form yet another government in early June, about six weeks after Clare's expected arrival in Rome. But even if he won the election handily, she might be confronted in the long term with a major diplomatic challenge: how to reshape United States policy toward Italy, should the Republic's immature economy— hampered by having to pay war reparations to the Soviet Union—fail to keep fourteen million rural and industrial workers permanently employed. She was encouraged to hear that the discovery of oil and gas in the Po Valley and Sicily was firing industrial production, and fueling trucks and machinery to rebuild Italy's war-devastated infrastructure. Even so, she believed that further American military and economic assistance was essential, to keep the country safe and solvent, especially if Soviet funds continued to flow into union coffers and those of other Communist-infiltrated organizations around the country.[19]

Awkwardly for Clare, the Eisenhower administration was not as generously disposed toward struggling Western European states as Truman's had been in the days of the Marshall Plan. Since the end of the war, the United States had given $4 billion to Italy alone. Ike and Dulles believed that once native economies and democratic political systems improved, after the paralysis of the immediate postwar period, they ought to become less reliant on foreign taxpayers. Yet the State Department expected Ambassador Luce to warn Washington at once, if she saw Communists taking advantage of any anti-American feelings that reduction of aid might engender.

▽

Much of Clare's tuition concerned protocol. Perhaps most sensitive, given her Catholicism and personal acquaintance with the Pope, was the fact that the United States maintained separate relations with the Vatican. She was not accredited to that sovereign state, which had lacked an American "representative" since 1951. Fortunately, a vestigial diplomatic corps remained that was independent of her own embassy staff, and was not allowed to mix with her or them socially.

Clare underwent further briefings at the Departments of the Treasury, Economics, Agriculture, and Immigration. A five-hour strategy session at the Pentagon was more to her liking, and amplified the expertise she had acquired on the House Military Affairs Committee. Between appointments, she prepared for administrative and domestic duties. This involved perusing floor plans of two splendid buildings in which she would spend most of her time.

One was the U.S. Embassy in the Palazzo Margherita, located on the fashionable Via Veneto. The United States had bought it in 1946 for the enormous sum of $1,252,000, thriftily using money from the sale of surplus war matériel to the Italians. The other was the Villa Taverna, the Ambassador's residence on Viale Rossini, abutting Rome's exclusive Parioli district. It had been built by a Cardinal in the sixteenth century, but took its name from Count Ludovic Taverna, who owned it during the Mussolini era. In World War II, the mansion had served as a government hospital, before being taken over by General Mark Clark's Fifth Army, and then in 1948 acquired by the State Department for $752,757.[20]

Clare learned that twelve servants were employed at the villa. A residence allotment of $13,000 a year paid for a chef, butler, housekeeper, footman, and two kitchen boys, as well as utilities, repairs, and upkeep of the grounds. A gateman and chauffeur were on the embassy payroll. For some inexplicable reason, she would have to fund an assistant chef, extra footman, and two wardrobe maids out of her annual salary of $25,000. In addition, she would need a social secretary to organize the marathon entertaining expected of her, from formal receptions and banquets to more intimate lunches and dinners with Italian ministers and American visitors. That salary too must be paid by the Luces, as would that of Dorothy Farmer, whom Clare had persuaded to take an apartment in Rome, away from her husband and beloved priests, to work on personal correspondence and finances. In addition, Dorothy was to keep in touch by phone, cable, and mail with secretaries and domestics in New York and Ridgefield.

Italian law limited structural alterations to ancient buildings, so Clare could do little to reconfigure some of the cramped formal rooms at the Villa Taverna. But there would be other hefty expenditures—mainly out of Harry's pocket—including new carpets, furniture, and upholstery, as well as replacement of art and objets d'art that did not meet their taste. Time Inc. accountants estimated that the boss would have to pay a supplement of $5,000 a month for Clare to live as graciously in Rome as in the States. On the plus side, she would receive two months' paid vacation a year, and a single allowance of $7,000 to cover both entertaining in Italy and trips to America for conferring with Dulles and Eisenhower.[21]

Her first such meeting was held in the White House. A few minutes of newsreel footage showed her looking relaxed as she chatted with Ike and Dulles, and when she emerged alone from the East Wing to face more cameras. She appeared to be radiantly happy at this climax of a life that had begun in humbler circumstances than the reporters crowding around could imagine.

▽

The days before her departure for Italy were spent in New York packing outfits, selecting artworks and ornaments to ship to the Villa Taverna, and continuing Italian lessons. Clare's fairly good French made the latter task less difficult, and soon she was fluent enough for conversational purposes.

On March 26, she attended an Overseas Press Club luncheon in her honor. Addressing the three hundred attendees, she spoke of the "tremendous significance" of Italy's forthcoming election, and predicted that the course its voters took, either toward or away from state socialism, would be "followed by all Europe in the years to come." She added reassuringly that after weeks of cramming at the State Department, she knew a good deal about her destination—its trade, defenses, political parties, personalities. "They laughingly refer to it as a 'briefing session,'" she said, "but I can assure you there is nothing brief about it."[22]

Sounding somewhat undiplomatic as the date of her sailing neared, Clare told the America Italy Society on April 8 that while she was lucky to be appointed to an embassy as glamorous as the one in Rome, hundreds of her fellow envoys were less fortunate. Some had to work in missions as remote as Tinwa, China, a town that had only one bathtub, or Jiddah with its Red Sea sandstorms, or Accra with its sewage flowing in open ditches along the streets. A typical U.S. consul in South America must face the prevalence of malaria, syphilis, and tetanus. She sardonically noted that the song "Home, Sweet Home" had been written by a Foreign Service officer stationed in Tunis. "It is not pleasant," she said, "to serve one's country by accepting exile from it."[23]

She sounded more positive speaking to the New York Newspaper Women's Club at the Biltmore Hotel on April 10, her fiftieth birthday. Flattered by the presence of Eleanor Roosevelt among the special guests, she paid tribute to the former First Lady's "prodigious capacity for work in many fields," and for giving hope, inspiration, and desire to her sex "to be useful in activities outside the home." Clare seemed to have in mind how far she and other women had advanced professionally from the days when among the few paying positions open to them were those of domestic servant, nursery school teacher, seamstress, governess, or prostitute.[24]

For all that, she gave the impression to one perceptive reporter, Eleanor's friend Lorena Hickok, that "here was a woman almost at bay. . . . There was a trace of defiance in her manner as she replied in her light, pleasing voice to the speeches they made about her, something that suggested she was not at all sure they had meant what they said or that she could command the backing of newspaper women in general."[25]

Mrs. Roosevelt was characteristically more circumspect in her column, "My Day."

They say the Italians were uncertain about accepting a woman as ambassador, for it was a somewhat new departure in their part of

Mutual admirers: Clare and Eleanor Roosevelt

the world. But in Mrs. Luce they will find not only a beautiful woman, but an able ambassador, with brains which any man might be proud of. I feel Mrs. Luce will represent us well. Her powers of observation and analysis, sharpened by her training both as a writer and as a member of Congress, should make her very valuable.[26]

Clare celebrated that night at the Ritz ballroom in Bridgeport. Senators Bush and Purtell were among the thousand guests wishing her bon voyage. Governor and Mrs. Lodge presented her with a silver stand bearing American and Italian flags.[27]

Perhaps the most personal of the countless au revoirs Clare had to exchange was with Father Thibodeau. Their intense spiritual relationship was drawing to an end, because in the excitement of her new worldly responsibilities, Clare's religious fervor had waned. She could hardly admit this to herself, let alone to him. "You must never never never doubt my deep devotion," she wrote. "Not time, not circumstances, not distance, can separate me from you."[28]

He felt even more strongly about parting from her. For the rest of his life, he would revere the memory of Clare Boothe Luce.

> She possessed a combination of qualities seldom found in man or woman. A keen intelligence and great simplicity . . . a great sense of humor; deep spirituality and a simple childlike devotion to Christ and his blessed mother; a holy terror when dealing with evil and evil doers; hated and vilified by many, yet seldom if ever did she retaliate. She is one of the most wonderful and noble-minded women it has been my privilege to know.[29]

A lighter tribute to the new Ambassador was published as an eight-verse popular song.

> *In gown of puce Mrs. Henry Luce*
> *Will have her say on the Appian Way*
> *Machiavelli in a Schiaparelli*
> *Clare's the gal for the job.*

33

LA LUCE

A perfect Woman, nobly plann'd,
To warn, to comfort, and command;
And yet a Spirit still, and bright
With something of angelic light.

—WILLIAM WORDSWORTH

On Tuesday, April 14, 1953, Ambassador Luce set off for Pier 84 on the Hudson River in time for a noon sailing of the new liner *Andrea Doria*. The State Department had suggested that it would be diplomatic for Clare to travel to Naples on this sleek symbol of Italian prestige. Harry and his sister Elisabeth Moore were with her, having agreed to spend six weeks in Rome organizing the household at the Villa Taverna.

Warmly dressed in a camel coat over a gray check suit, Clare encountered a bevy of reporters at the dock. One asked her if Julius and Ethel Rosenberg, who had just been sentenced to death for leaking atomic secrets to the Kremlin, were in fact guilty. She said evasively that officials had not briefed her on the case, prompting a fusillade of follow-up questions. Their aggressiveness startled her. Was it a harbinger of what she might encounter in Rome?[1]

Near collapse from fatigue, Clare told Harry she wanted to be alone for much of the crossing. To that end, she had coaxed the purser into giving up his own capacious stateroom, low down in the ship. She found it already suffused with the scent of seven dozen bunches of roses from well-wishers. Annoyingly that first night out, an unlatched door kept banging somewhere, so she slept fitfully, even after taking Dramamine.[2]

For the next week, while Harry and Elisabeth amused themselves on the promenade deck, where they had luxury cabins, Clare continued studying Italian with the help of a Linguaphone course. She also perused reams of papers concerning the seventeen major diplomatic tasks she had been assigned. The three most important of these were, first, to help Italy become a major partner of the Western Alliance by committing fully to NATO, and endorsing the European Defense Community, a French-inspired plan to permit West Germany to rearm under supranational authority. Second, she was to make clear that American "offshore procurement" contracts would no longer be given to factories dominated by Communist unions. Third, she must encourage the Italian government to settle what was known as the Trieste problem.[3]

This vexed matter, concerning Italy's claim to sovereignty of the most important port in the eastern Adriatic, had come up during her farewell meeting with Eisenhower. She had told him then that resolving the argument between Rome and Belgrade might be the most urgent issue during her tenure. It was more than a quarrel over a few square miles of waterfront, still administered by the wartime alliance of the United States, Great Britain, and France. Potentially, it could trigger an epic conflict between democracy and Communism.

The President understood Clare's concern only too well. In May 1945, a few days before the end of the war, he and General Alexander had faced the unbearable prospect of having to take up arms again—this time to prevent Yugoslavia's new Prime Minister, Marshal Josip Broz Tito, from gaining Trieste as his strategic outlet to the Gulf of Venice. Tito was, ironically, their former comrade-in-arms against the Nazis. But he was also a committed Marxist, pursuing only a semi-independent line from Moscow. If he accomplished his goal in Trieste, the Soviet Union might gain access through the Balkans to the western Mediterranean.

A temporary solution had been found by the tripartite occupying powers: to divide the land north of the port into "Zone A," a mainly Italian enclave controlled by Allied troops, and to cede the southern and inland region, mainly Serbo-Croatian, to Yugoslavia as "Zone B." This had not satisfied either side as a long-term fix, and Clare sensed that the simmering ethnic tensions would boil over on her watch.

On the third day out she wrote Father Thibodeau, wondering how best she might help a country unsure of its future. "I *must*, somehow, go to the *people*, and be *with* them, if I am to do any good at all. Italy is a political and moral invalid, choking on . . . three centuries of man-centered errors." She cited in particular "the negative Christianity of the Reformation" and "the positive atheism" of Communism. Despite her campaigns in Connecticut, she still felt awkward about talking with field and factory workers. "How my *nature* shrinks from it!" But she must overcome this, "if our world is to be saved from the Commies."[4]

When ascending to first class for sea air and deck-chair chats with Harry, she found that she was already a celebrity among Italians on board. Stewards addressed her as *"Eccellenza,"* and fellow passengers, watching her precise skeet shooting on the rear deck, admiringly called out, *"Brava Donna Clara!"*[5]

One day she found time to write an overdue letter to Carlos Chávez. It was in answer to an appeal for financial help. As a woman of private means, invested now with ambassadorial power, she would have to deal with such mail tactfully but firmly. Carlos had been asked by organizers of the Venice Biennale to conduct a new work of his own there in September. He naturally thought of presenting his Symphony No. 3 in memory of Ann Brokaw. The only problem, he wrote, was that the festival declined to pay expenses. "Now this is just an idea: would you be able to provide the fifteen hundred dollars for the trip? (This would be aside from the fifteen hundred dollars that I am to receive as balance of the commission when I finish the work.)"

He discreetly intimated that it would enhance her public status to be patron of the first performance of music she had commissioned. "I would regret not premiering the work in Italy while you are there."[6]

Clare replied, "I think you know that I am not personally a rich woman, though I've always before had enough for not only what I need, but all the luxuries. However, since I've taken on this job in a major post it has become increasingly clear that I simply could not carry it alone." She told him that her husband must bear much of the expense. If Harry discovered that she was subsidizing Carlos, he might "attach an importance to it which would be quite wrong."[7]

The weather was fair on the morning of Wednesday, April 22, as the *Andrea Doria* steamed past the island of Capri toward Ischia, where a welcoming party in a launch approached. Six men came aboard, all senior members of Clare's embassy team. Elbridge Durbrow, whose title was "Minister Counselor," greeted her first. He was a stocky, fifty-year-old career officer wearing an old-fashioned, dark, diplomatic suit. The others were Admiral Robert B. Carney, Commander in Chief of NATO forces in Southern Europe, General James Christiansen, her army attaché, John McKnight, her press relations officer, Joseph E. Jacobs, her economic adviser, and Gerald Miller, a Yale graduate in his late forties, listed as "Personal Assistant to the Ambassador" but actually chief of the CIA Rome station.

Durbrow gave Clare an initial briefing on the perils of Italian politics. He said that the city of Naples had readied a welcoming ceremony for her ashore, with the Mayor, Achille Lauro, on hand. But Lauro was a member of the conservative Monarchist Party. If she posed for photographs with him, before presenting her credentials to the President of the Republic in Rome, he would gain kudos for the next general election in June. Furthermore, some leftist newspapers were bound to say that she was signaling approval of the restoration of the Royal House of Savoy.

No sooner had the liner docked and thrown down its gangplank than at least a hundred reporters and photographers rushed aboard and surrounded Clare. She made a statement in front of newsreel cameras on deck, speaking slowly in Italian, but with amazing confidence. "I am proud to come here as the Ambassador of a President and country that wants what Italy wants most—to help build for all of us the house of security on the rock of justice and liberty." Toward the end, she dispensed with the notes in her white-gloved hand, took off her spectacles, and said with an enchanting smile, *"Buon giorno, salute, e arrivederci."* Cries of *"Brava, Brava!"* rang out.[8]

Carrying a bouquet, she disembarked on the arm of Admiral Carney, with Harry a few deferential steps behind. The biggest crowd ever to greet an American Ambassador awaited her on the pier, as a band played "Anchors Aweigh." She was again besieged by journalists shouting questions. Harry was ignored in the melée. After speaking a few words, Clare moved on to meet Signor Lauro, who had assembled an honor guard of *carabinieri*, resplendent in blue suits with cocked hats, white belts, and sabers. She kept pleasantries to a minimum, avoided the cameras, then quit the dock through a side door, leaving behind the crestfallen Mayor.[9]

Outside, two limousines awaited her and her party, with a pair of police motorcyclists to escort them all the way to Rome. As the mini-motorcade got under way, about a thousand mostly female Neapolitans clapped and cheered. Clare regally waved a handkerchief.[10]

▽

She sat beside Durbrow in the back of the embassy's Chrysler Windsor, while Harry rode with the chauffeur. Scrupulously, whenever the Minister Counselor began discussing classified information, she closed the glass partition. Her husband understood that they must avoid creating any impression that Time Inc. was privy to significant or secret data.

The 150-mile journey to the capital was a nostalgic one for Clare, passing the palace at Caserta, which she had inspected during the war at the invitation of General Alexander. Her entourage soon left the coastal road to cross the ridges astride the peninsula, enabling her to revisit the devastated terrain she had last seen in April 1945. Farm laborers paused to acknowledge the speeding convoy. She was surprised how few scars of war remained in a countryside that had endured so much heavy artillery fire.

Stopping for lunch in Cassino, Clare was astonished to find that the ruined place she remembered had become a reconstituted modern town. Even Monte Cassino, its hilltop monastery bombed to a skeleton nine years before, had been partially rebuilt with American funds that she and Mark Clark had helped raise. The slopes below were stippled with a thousand white crosses, marking the graves of Allied soldiers she may have met in hospitals or at the front.[11]

▽

In the early evening, the cars arrived at the seven hills of the Roman Campagna. A golden glow suffused the Eternal City's honey-colored buildings, and church bells pealed. In the distance soared the dome of St. Peter's. Then the Parioli district opened out about three miles from the Capitol, and Clare's motorcycle escort led the way along the Viale Rossini, past the Borghese Gardens. As they approached the Villa Taverna, a crowd of Italian well-wishers slowed their progress.[12] Gates opened ahead onto a driveway lined with olive and elm trees. Clare found herself cruising through a stone-walled, seven-acre park, with stands of cypress, intertwining ilex, and orange trees in blossom. She noticed a group of a dozen pines, which to the estate gardeners represented Christ's Apostles. The last one, out of alignment, symbolized Judas Iscariot. Elsewhere, marble statues, a fountain, and a campanile circled by swallows graced the grounds.[13]

The Villa Taverna, Rome

As the three-story villa came into view, fading sunlight bounced off its mellow, cinnamon-tinted stones, and picked out the Stars and Stripes hanging from the facade, along with an ecclesiastical escutcheon inscribed: IN CONSTANTIA ET FIDE FELICITAS.

Clare had enough school Latin to translate it as "Happiness lies in perseverance and faithfulness." Something told her she would need both these qualities in the days ahead. "It's not going to be easy," she said to herself.[14]

The limousine deposited the travelers beneath a portico ornamented with Corinthian capitals and two ancient sarcophagi. A butler ushered them into the villa's vaulted lobby, where they were greeted by other servants in starched white gold-buttoned jackets.

The Ambassador's ensuing tour of the eighteen-thousand-square-foot house was necessary but wearying after her long drive. It disclosed three reception rooms to the right of the entrance. First came the Piccolo Salon, decorated with frescoes and furnished with large antiques. Adjoining was the Galleria, its stucco ceiling vaulted and its walls mostly bare, crying out for pictures or tapestries. Beyond was the Grande Salon, dominated by a monumental red marble fireplace, a grand piano, huge Venetian mirrors, and two Canaletto paintings. The dining room, on the opposite side of the main floor, had a Murano glass chandelier over the table, and Pope Gregory XIII's coat of arms over the mantel-piece, but was otherwise empty.[15] All floors had multicolored Vietri tiles. Clare could see that her Democratic predecessor, Ellsworth Bunker, had cared little for art or luxury; room after room was sparsely and indifferently equipped. It was a boon to have Beth's help with refurbishing.

The villa's second floor, reached by a winding staircase, had five bedrooms, the largest of which went to Harry. Clare chose a boudoir with four high windows, green-and-white tiles, and a terra-cotta-beamed ceiling painted with white roses. One disadvantage was nocturnal noises from a zoo in the Borghese Gardens behind the house, and she was kept awake much of the night by trumpeting elephants and roaring lions.[16]

▽

Preparing to leave for her first day at the office, Clare kept in mind a farewell letter from Bernard Baruch.

> Please be most conservative in your dress. Always *bien soigné* but play down jewels and ornament except on grand occasions and not then. Get around among the people. See how they live—keep away from the rich big spending Americans. Visit our graves the places our boys died in. Study Italy's needs—material and spiritual. Talk of the grandeur that *was* hers and must be there still in her people. You have brains, beauty, personality character and a heart—use and show the last. Go on in there little game chicken. Bernie.[17]

Shortly before nine, she stepped into her chauffeur-driven car wearing a simple black suit with her signature red rose in a vial pinned to one lapel. Traveling along the Via Veneto, she passed the Excelsior Hotel, where she had stayed during the war, and arrived at the U.S. Embassy a block farther on.

The four-story, terra-cotta-pink Palazzo Margherita, once the residence of King Victor Emanuel's mother, was the largest diplomatic headquarters in Rome. But it was far from constituting the entire complex that Clare would administer. It stood in a lavishly restored park—originally the gardens of a Renaissance grandee—with an elegant central pond and white marble Triton blowing spray through a conch shell. The lawns were dotted with classical statuary. In the northern part of the compound, twin villas housed the consulate and United States Information Service. East and south of them were two adminis-

trative buildings, the Piombino Wing, and an American-constructed
New Wing, matching the nineteenth-century architecture of the rest.

Clare entered through the Palazzo's west-facing archway, flanked by
palm trees. A soaring, semicircular marble stairway took her to the second floor, or *piano nobile*, its corridor decorated with Roman statues and
lined with grand salons. Grandest of these was her enormous, northwest
corner office, once the royal drawing room. This square, cream-and-
gold chamber had a Venetian glass chandelier hanging from its lofty,
gilded ceiling. An Oriental rug covered the floor, and world maps in
pale blue enhanced a series of wall panels. A rococo writing table, set in
front of tall windows overlooking the main street, stood ready to serve
as her desk. Only after she presented her credentials to President Luigi
Einaudi could it be flanked by her flags of office: the Stars and Stripes on

Ambassador Luce at her desk in the Palazzo Margherita

the right, and to the left her blue-and-gold ambassadorial banner. Directly opposite was a long table with a gleaming patina, used for weekly senior staff meetings.

During the next eight hours Clare went from floor to floor of her domain, introducing herself to as many officers as possible. Five counselors reported to Durbrow and his principal assistant, John Shea, administering, respectively, the Political, Labor, Agricultural, Public Affairs, and Embassy Departments. Other officials handled such programs as Mutual Defense Assistance, Treaty Claims, Navy Purchasing, Veterans' Affairs, and Cultural Exchange. In addition to these Foreign Service units, Clare was responsible, as Chief of Mission, for thirty-two separate agencies, including a twelve-man CIA team under Gerald Miller, a Narcotics Bureau, the Agricultural Service, and the American Battle Monuments Commission.[18]

In all, she had authority over fifteen hundred employees—five hundred in the embassy compound and a thousand more stationed elsewhere at eight consulates and other posts throughout Italy, as well as the U.S. Representative in Trieste. Most were holdover Democrats appointed by Truman after the war. Some went back further: her press relations officer referred to himself as "a howling New Dealer."[19] Their impassive, even glum, demeanors revealed how much they disliked having to defer to a Republican envoy. More than a few were skeptical of Clare's diplomatic acumen. Mutterings behind her back demonstrated insecurity as well as querulousness. "Will she have a purge? Will she be difficult? Will she run a social rather than a substantive Embassy?"[20] Italy had enacted female suffrage only six years before, so a concern widely shared was, "Why the heck send a Latin country a woman?"[21]

Given the hostile press that had preceded Clare's arrival in Naples, it was a surprise that the majority of that day's newspapers seemed disposed in her favor. They quoted her broadcast remarks from the *Andrea Doria*, and featured her picture on many front pages. She was described as "one of the most beautiful women in America," and "a writer and journalist of the first rank." Only the Communist *l'Unità* disparaged her as an "elderly lady" who spoke Italian with a Brooklyn accent.[22]

That night, Durbrow asked the Luces to his house for a buffet supper, so that top aides and their wives could get to know them socially. Harry was at ease in his new role as "Consort." Durbrow had looked into the delicate question of Luce's protocol ranking, and decided it should be only slightly inferior to that of a minister plenipotentiary. This allowed him to be seated in any formal situation below *Sua Eccellenza*, but ahead of the chargés d'affaires.[23]

When Clare returned to her office the following morning, much of the earlier frosty reception had thawed. She was further gratified by an extraordinary gesture on the part of the Italian Foreign Office, housed in the Chigi Palace. Custom required her to pay a courtesy call there on Barone Michele Scammacca, the Chief of Protocol. But Scammacca instead came to the Palazzo Margherita, and was photographed gallantly kissing her hand.[24]

Before getting down to work in earnest, she put on her desk a framed copy of Lord Astley's prayer before the Battle of Edgehill:

Lord, thou knowest I shall be verie busie this day.
I may forget Thee—
Do not Thou forget me.[25]

Soon to supplement this, on a side table, was a cautionary motto by Talleyrand: "Above all, not too much zeal."[26]

▽

Clare could not function officially as Ambassador until the President of Italy received her. But Einaudi was on a visit to France, so on April 28 she presented a copy of her credentials to Prime Minister Alcide De Gasperi, in his subsidiary capacity as Minister of Foreign Affairs. Their meeting was cordial, since he gratefully remembered the financial support he had received from her and other Americans.[27]

Tall and slightly stooped at seventy-two, De Gasperi remained vigorous and intensely serious, with blue eyes that could be chilly. He was internationally respected as the most distinguished Italian statesman since Cavour. Yet he was not guaranteed reelection when his countrymen went to the polls on June 7 to choose a new Parliament from multiple parties. Even at the height of his power in 1948, De Gasperi had never managed to amass more than 48.5 percent of the vote for his Christian Democrats. Effectively, he maintained control only by virtue of his skill in building coalitions from moderates on both the right and left sides of Italy's bewilderingly wide political spectrum.

This juggling act, which excluded extremists in the Monarchist Party, as well as Socialists and Communists constituting the Popular Front, had enabled him to preserve a working majority through seven different governments since 1945. However, his chance of forming an eighth was threatened by an escalation of political tensions, with the Popular Front growing in power, and former Fascists arguing that only a military dictatorship could keep Italy from going Red.

De Gasperi and Clare were therefore linked at the outset of their official relationship by a dread that the coming election could bring about a disaster for democracy. The Italian Communist Party was two million members strong, by far the largest in any country beyond the Soviet Union, making Italy the weakest link in the Allied chain of defense against Soviet expansionism.

The Prime Minister had another electoral liability. Moderate Monarchists, whom he relied on for coalition support, were traditionally against social reform, and a fanatically nationalist minority blamed him for not governing like Il Duce. Clare was no admirer of Mussolini, although in 1940 she had met and been charmed by his son-in-law Count Ciano, one of the principal architects of the Fascist State.[28] But she feared totalitarianism on the left much more than autocracy on the right.

De Gasperi was not as convinced as she that the Monarchists were less dangerous than the Communists.[29] Clare emphasized that President Eisenhower and Secretary Dulles shared her concern about the danger to the vote in June posed by the brilliant and shrewd Communist leader, Palmiro Togliatti.[30]

▽

The following day, Ike's Secretary of Defense, Charles E. Wilson, arrived in Rome for a meeting with his Italian counterpart, Randolfo Pacciardi. At the embassy, Ambassador Luce chaired a preliminary discussion of Italy's role in NATO.

Besides Wilson and Admiral Carney, there were several attachés and aides from her staff. Clare initiated the proceedings by saying that having been in her post only one week, she would like to hear opinions on the "salient points" of NATO policy in Southern Europe.

The Italian Republic had been a member since March 1949—a reluctant one at first, because De Gasperi had needed to persuade both his nationalistic right wing and the anti-American Socialists and Communists that Italy would not lose its sovereignty by joining. Since then the pace of American-assisted rearmament had been rapid, and NATO bases were already established along both coasts, much to the disgust of Togliatti. Italy was now firmly integrated into the Western Alliance's Mediterranean defense strategy, to the chagrin of Monarchists as well as

Clare holds a staff meeting in her Embassy office. Gerry Miller, CIA
representative, far left; Elbridge Durbrow, chief of staff, fourth from left.

Communists.[31] One of Clare's assignments would be to persuade at least
the former that NATO was not detrimental to national pride.

Some attendees at the meeting tried to impress her with an excess
of bureaucratic detail, as Carney later recalled.

> Well, she stood it for a few minutes, and then she let go with a
> resounding sailor man's oath, and said this was not the kind of in-
> formation she wanted, and let's get down to brass tacks and confine
> it to facts. There was a silence around the table that you could
> have cut with a knife, and it suddenly dawned on everybody who

was the boss man at the table, and it was Mrs. Luce; and she did a superb job at chairmanship . . . bringing these people down to factual viewpoints and statements. I was highly amused, and I must say that Mrs. Luce's stock went up with me very considerably when I saw her take charge.[32]

That night, with a fur cape over a long gown, Clare arrived at the Villa Madama to dine with Wilson and Pacciardi. Bystanders were so struck by her glowing looks that they called out, *"La Luce, La Luce."*

▽

While his wife went about her business, Harry did, too, setting off daily in his black Lancia to an old building on the Corso d'Italia. After entering a dark hallway, he deposited a five-lire *gettone* into a coin box, rode an elevator cage to the second floor, and entered a door marked "Time Inc." At the end of a carpeted space, he sat at a small Venetian desk, among the bureau's other five employees.[33]

But supporting and escorting Clare was his main priority. Thus on Monday, May 4, Henry Luce became the first consort in Italian history to squire a female Ambassador to her presentation of credentials at the Palazzo del Quirinale. Shortly before noon, he donned striped trousers, cutaway coat, and top hat, while she put on a dark dress, two strands of pearls, a hip-length mink coat, and a robin's-egg-blue beanie hat.[34]

As they alighted in the courtyard, *Bersaglieri* in cock-plumed helmets saluted, and Baron Scammacca stepped forward to shepherd them inside. Lining the stairway and long marble corridors were cuirassiers of the presidential guard, in horse-tailed headgear and shiny breastplates. They raised sabers in salute as the Luces passed.

Harry waited in a side room while Clare proceeded to the chilly Salon of Kings, keeping on her hat and coat.[35] The Chief of Protocol announced her as Signora Clare Boothe Luce, Ambassador Extraordinary and Plenipotentiary of the United States. "Extraordinary, *yes*, but plenipotentiary—*no*," she was tempted to say as she approached President Einaudi, an elderly man with rimless glasses and a cane. He welcomed her in a soft voice and in a manner distinctly democratic, despite the regal trappings.[36]

Divested of her formal papers, Clare now officially represented her country, becoming the junior member of Rome's diplomatic corps, outranked by at least two dozen others.[37]

▽

Her principal responsibility, more important than ingratiating herself with Italians or entertaining eminent compatriots passing through Rome, was to implement American postwar policy toward Western Europe, as laid out in a 1947 State Department paper.

> The staff does not see Communist activities as the root of the present difficulties in Western Europe. It believes the crisis in large part results from the disruptive effect of the war on the economic, political and social structure of Europe. . . . The planning staff recognizes that the Communists are exploiting the European crisis and that further Communist successes would create serious danger to American security.

In recognition of this situation had come the Marshall Plan and the Offshore Procurement Program, which awarded defense-related manufacturing contracts to equip NATO. Now that the basic needs of the Italian populace for food, housing, and work were being satisfied, largely by the improving economy, Clare could concentrate more on the precarious political situation. "I can already see that it is going to be a fascinating experience," she wrote in a progress report. "Especially just at the outset, with the Italian elections approaching in less than six weeks."[38]

She made it a goal to encourage moderate politicians to resist, and if possible defeat, Communist efforts to dominate the ideological conversation. At the same time, she aimed to help nurse a still-struggling democracy with a weak parliamentary system that until recently had known only monarchical or totalitarian rule. The extreme Left was doing its utmost to upset the frail alliance of the centrist parties, De Gasperi's Christian Democrats being the strongest of those. Moscow was covertly giving financial support to the Italian Communist Party (PCI), led by the canny Togliatti, and by extension to its ally the Italian Socialist Party (PSI), led by the equally adroit Pietro Nenni. These two had been partners in underground wartime efforts to unseat Mussolini. Imprisoned together in Nazi concentration camps (Nenni's daughter had died at Auschwitz), they had forged a political bond.

Clare knew that secret Soviet funding of the Popular Front had a destabilizing potential for the governing coalition. In communications with Washington, she implied that Togliatti and Nenni were ideologically of one mind, and referred to them as "Socialcommunists."[39] Gerald Miller shared her views and her faith, and quickly emerged as a close confidant. His main mission at the CIA was to counter the influence of Moscow by clandestinely funneling millions of dollars to democratic center parties, non-Communist labor unions, Catholic youth groups, and other anti-Red organizations.[40]

On May 10, Clare had a second meeting with De Gasperi. Foremost on his mind was how the Trieste issue might affect the coming election. If it was not settled soon, he said, it could lead to his defeat or, even if he won, jeopardize his ability to form another coalition. Trieste, De Gasperi emphasized, was an emotional subject for his countrymen of whatever political stamp. Ever since the port's annexation at the end of World War I, they had seen it as the final jewel in the symbolic crown of their unity. "Trieste is for Italians," the Prime Minister kept insisting. "More than a city and a harbor: it is a national feeling."[41] This was particularly so for the Monarchists, whose support was essential to De Gasperi's political survival.

Just a day after Clare's arrival in Rome, he had been at a NATO meeting with Secretary Dulles in Paris, and had told him that the large Italian population of the so-called Free Territory of Trieste (FTT) wished to "return to the motherland."[42] He had rejected Dulles's suggestion that Yugoslavia's Slovenes and Croats, having fought bravely with the Allies during War World II, were surely entitled to at least one point of access to the Adriatic. They had enjoyed that privilege since the earliest days of the Austro-Hungarian Empire. In technical diplomatic terms, that meant that De Gasperi was not only demanding the repatriation of some 286,000 Italians in Zone A north of Trieste, but objecting to a significant presence of 93,000 Slavs living just south of the city in Zone B.

The problem, as De Gasperi saw it, was that the Allied governments of the United States, Great Britain, and France seemed undecided how and when to partition the two zones of the Free Territory. He asked Clare if the United States, in view of the comparative apathy of its partners, would make a final effort to honor the Tripartite Declaration of March 20, 1948, which had hastily committed the Allies to supporting the wholesale return of the FTT to Italy.

Yugoslavia had been offended at not being made party to the terms of that announcement. Tito was particularly angry at the apparent Allied impression that he was a Soviet stooge. This misperception had

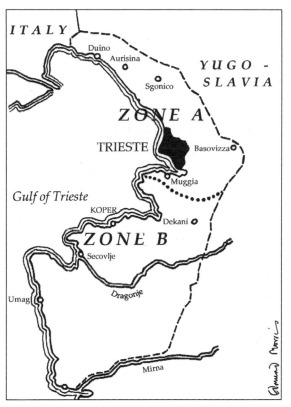

Map of the Free Territory of Trieste, 1953–1954

long ago been invalidated, when only three months after the Tripartite Declaration, Yugoslavia had been expelled from the Soviet defense bloc (Cominform) for not being sufficiently malleable. The Truman administration had thereafter recommended granting the Yugoslavs at least those parts of the Istrian peninsula where they were in the majority. It saw advantages in wooing Tito closer to the West by also giving him economic aid. In 1949, the State Department had done just that, urging that Tito's feelings be considered whenever Trieste's return to Italy was discussed. This amounted to a watering down of the pro-Italian Declaration, and a furious De Gasperi had made it clear that his country intended to keep the Allies "nailed to their moral engagement."[43] Echoing him, Clare reproved the State Department, saying the contradiction between America's ideological war against Communism and its support of "renegade Communist dictator Tito" was morally indefensible.[44]

Now the Prime Minister told her that Italy would hold direct talks with Yugoslavia, but only if the United States arranged an advance agreement, based on the Tripartite Declaration, that also included "at least one half of Zone B."[45] Parrying, she replied that her government would require a quid pro quo for any such favor: a speedy acquiescence, "immediately after the election," to the expansion of U.S. military facilities in Italy.

De Gasperi avoided a commitment on that score. He warned that his time as senior statesman was nearing its end, and that with him gone, some "hotheads" in Parliament might take it upon themselves to solve the Trieste problem violently.[46]

▽

To increase rapport with her senior staff, Clare began to hold informal discussions with them each Monday morning at the Villa Taverna. She thrived on lively debate, and ran the sessions as she had editorial conferences at *Vanity Fair,* asking for ideas and opinions so that she could make informed decisions. If tempers flared, she tamped them down with a joke or witty anecdote.[47]

The embassy's economic adviser, Joseph Jacobs, who had contemplated retirement from his post rather than work for her, admitted, "I came to scoff, but I stayed to praise."[48] Francis Williamson, head of the political section, marveled at her ability to repeat hour-long diplomatic conversations "with the fidelity of a tape recorder." Durbrow singled out her powers of absorption and reasoning. "She thinks things through using a lawyer's logical method," he said, comparing her sharp mind to a "diamond edge."[49]

Clare took her first official trip out of the capital on May 12, leaving by air for a three-day car tour of Apulia, the southeasterly heel of the Italian boot. Her purpose was to assess the effectiveness of millions of dollars of American aid for land reclamation. Covering some 250 miles, she was pleased to see farms and villages thriving, and a good number of war-damaged roads, bridges, houses, and schools rebuilt. She surprised a group of farmhands by climbing onto a reaping machine and riding across their fields.

Another reason for visiting the impoverished province was to measure the support of southerners for the Communist Party. Again Clare found reason to be encouraged. In the main square of a small town near Bari, a thickset man elbowed his way through the crowd, brandishing a pasteboard that proclaimed his intention to renounce Communism. He turned out to be the president of a local cooperative, and wanted to give

The Ambassador tours southern Italy

Signora Luce his party membership card. Laughing, Clare accepted it. "I hope Senator McCarthy won't investigate me for this."[50]

Rome's leftist newspaper *Il Paese* accused her of traveling through Apulia merely "to carry on electoral propaganda in favor of the center parties."[51]

Clare planned to visit all Italian cities in due course, and chose Milan for her first major ambassadorial speech on May 28. She had to be careful not to sound partisan two weeks before the general election. It was a "period of tension and verbal violence," as *The Reporter* magazine warned.[52] Any controversial remark might affect her relationship with the contending parties. The situation was made more delicate by a controversial move on the part of De Gasperi. Confident of victory for his Christian Democrats, he had pushed through a new election law that gave any party winning over 50 percent of the vote an automatic working majority in Parliament.

It was normal procedure for the embassy's Press Relations Office to write an envoy's formal addresses, with various department chiefs contributing. Clare read the draft and showed it to her husband. "Harry, look, you know all the briefing I got in the State Department about the sensitivity of these people. There's a phrase in this speech that might make a little trouble." The words that bothered her intimated that if extremists on either side of the centrist coalition gained too much power, America might have to reexamine its foreign policy toward Italy. "I don't think the speech would lose anything if we left that out," she said, and blue-penciled it.

Durbrow objected to the excision. "No, the time has come for us to get a little tough. We have to tell them where we stand. Put it back in." Clare understood that the words represented the policy of the Eisenhower administration, but did not know that her staff had intended them to combat erroneous rumors that Washington favored a neo-Fascist victory in the polls. After restoring the remark, she sent a text mimeograph to the Italian Foreign Office.[53]

When she arrived for her dinner engagement with the Milan branch of the American Chamber of Commerce for Italy, she wore a plain black dress and a pair of horn-rimmed spectacles. Evidently, she was still following Baruch's advice to play down glamour. She began her speech ingratiatingly, with the promise of $22 million in new American aid. As Italy progressed "along the ancient highways of her natural greatness," Clare said, its people could depend on the goodwill of the United States. "We should—we Americans—be very sad to see that forward march

Clare delivers her provocative Milan speech, May 28, 1953

checked or diverted." Then came the passage Durbrow had insisted she deliver.

> But if—and I am required in all honesty to say this . . . the Italian people should fall unhappy victim to the wiles of totalitarianism of the right or the left, there would follow—logically and tragically—grave consequences for this intimate and warm cooperation we now enjoy.[54]

She sat down to enthusiastic applause. Next morning, there was little comment in the Milan press. The Ambassador proceeded to Genoa, where she blasted Russian expansionism, and reminded transportation executives that since the war, the United States had given Italy $650 million in direct aid, and another $300 million as part of the Offshore Procurement Program.[55]

Within days, Rome-based Monarchist, neo-Fascist, and Communist editorials condemned Signora Luce's rhetoric as interference in Italian affairs. They said that her Milan threat might have an explosive effect on the coming election. In *Candido*, Guareschi suggested she was deranged.[56] Adverse criticism spread to other countries. In France, *Le Parisien libéré* said her "well-meaning statement" had been "as unfortunate . . . as it was conspicuous."[57]

Emilio Taviani, the Italian Under Secretary of State, reassured Clare that her oratory would probably not affect the outcome of the election. But he said that diplomacy bent on making Communists "look like devils" might have a counterproductive effect on the labor vote.[58] He and De Gasperi privately felt that some of her judgment was questionable, such as the way she equated "socialism and marxism with nazism." Yet they recognized that Clare's ardor could be useful for their policy purposes, especially concerning Trieste.[59]

▽

After six weeks in Rome, Harry announced that he needed to go to America for hospital treatment. He was suffering from neuritis, but with his usual stoicism did not complain.[60] He set off on Saturday, June 6. Fortunately for Clare, Maggie Case had arrived three days earlier, for a prolonged stay.

That night, election eve, the two women attended a reception at the British Embassy "on the occasion of the Coronation of Her Majesty Queen Elizabeth II." For Case, at sixty-one, it was also a crowning moment. She and Clare had known each other for twenty-four years, going back to their days at *Vogue*, Maggie as the short, plain society editor, Clare as caption and then essay writer. Maggie had been smitten. In December 1936, she had gone to Philadelphia to see the curtain go up on the first tryout of *The Women*. Later, in rapid succession, she had rejoiced in Clare's success as war correspondent, book author, and politician. In November 1942, she had heard the radio announcement that the votes of Connecticut apple farmers had sealed Clare's election to Congress. Now she was in Rome, sharing in the achievement of her adored one.[61]

The following morning, Italians went to the polls. De Gasperi's Christian Democrats lost forty-five seats in the Chamber of Deputies and fifteen in the Senate, with a vote drop from 48.5 percent to 40.1 percent. More alarming to Clare was that 22.6 percent of voters backed Togliatti's Communist Party, and 12.7 percent Nenni's Socialists— a combined total of well over a third of the electorate. More disturbing still, the Popular Front had bettered its share of the vote by 4.3 percent. This was counterbalanced, to some extent, by an even bigger advance scored by the Monarchists and neo-Fascist Movimento Sociale Italiano, which together got 12.7 percent of the electorate, a joint increase of 7.9 percent.[62]

Nevertheless, De Gasperi's center, with the support of Republicans, Liberals, and some Socialists, maintained control of Parliament—albeit by a margin so slim that it was doubtful he would be able to form a viable government. If not, the election would amount to a sad defeat for the Prime Minister, who had built Italy's postwar democracy.

In her seventeen-page report to the State Department, Clare wrote, "His task is certain to be a hard and exhausting one. He will have to be prolific in expediency and yet fertile in prudence to prevent his own party from splitting towards left and right in some new coalition."[63]

As she dictated this, her Milan warning of punitive withdrawal of American aid was being blamed, on both sides of the Atlantic, for at least some of De Gasperi's misfortune. Togliatti declared that Ambassador Luce had "brought bad luck" to the Prime Minister. The British left-winger Michael Foot agreed.[64] Red newspapers exulted that Washington would soon have to recall the "Old Woman with the Evil Eye," a folklore epithet implying the Ambassador had witchlike powers.[65] However, a majority of Italians felt that De Gasperi had suffered because of his manipulative election law, as well as overconfidence.

"There is no shadow of doubt in my mind or in the mind of any thoughtful person in Italy," Clare wrote, "that if America had not supported De Gasperi and the CD party in 1948 and until now, all of Italy would have been Communist." It was more imperative than ever for the center parties to find a solution to the diplomatic and military question of Trieste, otherwise the NATO concept in Italy would crumble. "The grand lesson of the election," she went on portentously, "is that [Italy] is slowly but steadily moving—towards the Kremlin."[66]

As if in proof of her words, local Communists, enraged by the execution on June 19 of Julius and Ethel Rosenberg, began bombarding the U.S. Embassy with hundreds of threatening phone calls and letters. Rumors of a plot to blow up the building spread, and Jeeps full of armed police appeared to protect it. Security officers arrived at the Villa Taverna to walk the halls and hide in the bushes. The two *carabinieri* on guard at the gate were reinforced by a defense patrol in the Viale Rossini. Suddenly, the walled residence felt like a citadel.[67]

34

CRISIS AT SEA

The absence of alternatives clears the mind marvelously.

—Henry Kissinger

For fifty-seven days after the election, the Italian government remained in a state of suspense. De Gasperi tried to form a new coalition, but with his reduced number of seats he found it impossible to win a governing majority in the Chamber. On July 28 he admitted defeat, and amid left-wing jeers his historic premiership came to an end. Emboldened, Togliatti insisted on a role for Communists in any future cabinet. President Einaudi was left with the difficult task of finding a Christian Democratic leader who could ignore this demand and yet succeed where De Gasperi had failed.

In the meantime, calm returned to the Villa Taverna and U.S. Embassy, and Clare resumed her daily diplomatic routine. She usually had a light breakfast at 8:00 A.M. and on arrival at her office at 9:00 or 9:30 went over cables and dispatches from Washington and notes and *démarches* (position papers) from the Italian government. Consultations with heads of embassy sections followed. She regularly quit her desk for meetings at the Chigi Palace, where she had to demonstrate an informed familiarity with European politics, economics, commerce, labor, transportation, communication, science, and religion.

The fall of De Gasperi had left the Italian Foreign Service leader-less. Ranking diplomats in the Chigi were essentially ideological heirs of Count Ciano, though lacking his *tono fascista*. All were rich, well-bred men from titled families of conservative and nationalistic bent. Conveniently for Clare, who was still not fluent in diplomatic Italian, almost all spoke English.[1]

Since there were sixty other embassies and legations in Rome, she had to attend about 300 cocktail parties and 150 dinners each year, let alone host entertainments of her own. Each weekday, she found time for "grip and grin" encounters with American politicians and businessmen visiting Rome. On Sundays, she found that if she went to Mass in local churches, she was invariably mobbed, so Pope Pius gave her permission to celebrate the Eucharist in the Villa Taverna, or any "fitting and properly appointed home in Rome."[2]

At about 9:30 P.M. most nights, a U.S. Marine guard arrived at the villa, carrying a dispatch case full of late-breaking documents. He would wait while the Ambassador plowed through them. Often it was midnight before he returned them to the embassy.[3] Only after his departure could Clare tackle a few of the hundreds of letters a week she received from people around the world.[4] Some asked for money, a loan, or help in publication of enclosed manuscripts. Others sent gifts, ranging from a Sicilian shawl to a model boat made of mother-of-pearl.

Most acknowledgments were left to Dorothy Farmer, now working at the embassy, importantly styled the Ambassador's "Executive Secretary for Official Matters." A fierce protector of her boss from predators, she joked that she could be more accurately called "the anti-social secretary." This was a dig at Clare's new recruit to manage Villa Taverna events.

Twenty-eight years old, blond, and six feet tall, Letitia "Tish" Baldrige was from a more exclusive background than Dorothy. She had been educated at Miss Porter's School and Vassar College. Since graduating, she had traveled widely in America and Europe, including Yugoslavia, and was well tutored in diplomatic etiquette, having worked at the U.S. Embassy in Paris for the supersophisticated David and Evangeline Bruce. Just before coming to Rome, she had heard allegations that Clare was "a bitch." But after arriving at the Villa Taverna one Sunday afternoon, for what was supposed to be an interview with the Ambassador, she was quickly disabused. "I came in terror, and remained to adore."[5]

The meeting took place in Clare's boudoir.

She was wearing blue bedroom slippers and a pale blue *peignoir* over her blue nightgown. . . . I sat down across from her on one of the pale blue satin *bergères*. An oversized square inlaid marble coffee table separated our chairs. The table was covered with magazines that had been airmailed by *Time* as well as straw letter baskets full of embassy work and writing projects. The table was littered with almost every electronic gadget that had been invented: dictaphones, minirecorders, tape recorders, record players, and . . . generators to transform American electrical voltages and watts into Italian.

All her life, Clare had loved gadgets for work and entertainment. She enjoyed the mental challenge of mastering the latest technology, but complained that none of the transformers functioned in Rome.

For the next two hours, the Ambassador did most of the talking. As early evening shadows began to creep across the grounds, Baldrige experienced one of Clare's most disconcerting characteristics: a tendency to be overly confiding with strangers.

She told me about her daughter Ann, who was killed during her college years at Stanford in an auto accident. A great cloud seemed to lower itself over her. The voice changed, becoming lower in volume and tone, and her eyes were now half shut. She explained that she welcomed working like a demon at this embassy job because she did not want to give in to the grief she felt.

Clare said nothing formal to indicate that Baldrige had passed muster, only warning, as the young woman took her leave, that tomorrow she would be plunged into pandemonium. "Hell has been waiting impatiently for your arrival."[6]

▽

With horselike energy and strength, Tish endured eleven- or twelve-hour days during the week and six hours on Saturdays. Speaking fluent French and serviceable Italian, she handled the press, and helped with the Ambassador's wardrobe, steering her toward Italian designers such as Fabiani, Simonetta, Irene Galitzine, and Sorelle Fontana. She even cared for her boss's silver-gray and black poodles, Scusi and Prego.[7]

Her biggest challenge was planning large formal entertainments. "I don't know one pasta, veal dish, or *tiramisu* from another," Clare told her, "and I don't want to know, so just decide."[8] Harry picked up the tab for everything over the State Department allowance, including new china, crystal, and linens.

Typical functions ranged from working lunches to elaborate dinners. Eminent artists such as Leopold Stokowski, who came to Italy to conduct a production of Gian Carlo Menotti's opera *Amahl and the Night Visitors*, meant lavish parties with great numbers of guests.[9] Roman socialites complained that Clare associated mainly with politicians and top industrialists.[10] So she used the maestro's visit as a reason to invite them to an evening reception in the rose-scented garden, illuminated by antique iron oil lamps on fragments of antique wall. Showing a twinge of guilt, she wrote to tell Carlos Chávez that she might likewise fete him, if he managed after all to premiere Ann's symphony in Italy.[11]

She also had to take notice of American citizens living in Rome, as well as tourists. She spent $3,000 out of her own pocket for a Fourth of July party, with truckloads of chicken, ice cream, and Coca-Cola set on tables in the villa's verdant grounds. Dressed in a patriotic outfit of white dress, blue hat, and red rose, she received all her guests individually. Standing for hours, flanked by U.S. Army and Navy officers, she posed for snapshots in front of a Greco-Roman statue. One young woman in the reception line awkwardly told her, "I'm over here to study the romantic old ruins—and I'm so glad to have seen you."[12]

▽

Back in New York, Harry had been treated for his neuritis, but was still in pain. Recuperating in his apartment, he felt wistful for the stimulating new life he and Clare had in Rome. John Billings stopped by one evening, and found him alone in the huge pink-and-crystal living room overlooking the river. Post–Billy Baldwin, it had been refurnished with French pieces. There were ugly marks on the walls, since many of the major paintings—works by Delacroix, Fragonard, Pissaro, Redon, Renoir, Goya, Van Gogh, Matisse, Monet, Rouault, Sisley, and Chagall—were now hanging in the Villa Taverna. Harry had begun amassing paintings because he thought that was what rich men did, but he had little judgment as to their aesthetic worth, leaving the choice largely to his wife or dealers.

Other art and *objets* had been sent from Sugar Hill, including sixty Japanese prints, Ming horses, busts of both Luces by Jo Davidson, and the Brockhurst oil of Clare.[13] Before the year was out, Time Inc. would have spent approximately $100,000 for the purchase or shipping of everything from furniture to tableware.[14]

In spite of his stripped surroundings, Luce was in an expansive mood. Clare was "doing fine" in Rome, he said. *Time* was making heaps of money, and seemed likely to have its best year on record. Perhaps it was an opportune moment, he mused, to start a sports magazine, and maybe buy the *New York Herald Tribune*.[15]

The next day, struggling to hold a pen, Harry wrote Clare. He commiserated over the fall of De Gasperi, and in a self-mocking reference to his status as consort signed himself "your devoted servant." Clearly missing his wife, he added that at a recent viewing of the movie *Moulin Rouge*, he had kept an empty seat for her.[16]

On August 13, President Einaudi invited De Gasperi's former Finance Minister, Giuseppe Pella, to form a provisional government and take Italy through the fall season of budgetary deadlines in the Chamber of Deputies.[17] An austere, fifty-one-year-old economics technocrat, Pella assumed not only the premiership, but the portfolios of Budget and Foreign Affairs. He was known to be cautious, courteous, and frugal. Italians referred to him as *uomo di equilibrio*, man of balance.[18] On one subject, however, he was anything but balanced. Like his Monarchist backers, he was an extreme nationalist on the subject of Trieste.

By midmonth the Luces were reunited, and ready for a vacation. Harry rented the *Niki*, a 190-foot, Greek-owned yacht with three offi-

The yacht *Niki*

cers and eighteen crew. They planned to explore the west coast of Italy, sailing south from Civitavecchia to Capri, Ischia, and Naples, then returning north via Livorno, La Spezia, and Portofino.

Needing to keep abreast of clerical work and events, Clare invited a few diplomats and several of her staff to come aboard at various ports of call to talk shop. Her most important guest was Dr. Remigio Grillo, who handled American affairs at the Italian Foreign Office. He was smart, spirited, and flirtatious. During stretches at sea, he and Clare had such illuminating talks about international affairs that she asked him to stay until the end of the cruise. Grillo was equally impressed with her.

"Don't worry about your Ambassador," he said to Maggie Case, who joined them ten days out. "I believe before she's through she will be hailed as our Joan of Arc."[19]

Throughout the voyage, Clare assiduously kept in radio-telephone contact with the mainland. Maggie realized that she hated to be inactive or solitary. At various times, they were joined by Secretary Dulles's brother Allen (Director of the CIA and a Catholic favorite of Clare's); the British Ambassador to Italy, Sir Victor Mallet; her air attaché, Colonel Emmett B. Cassady; and Admiral William M. Fechteler, Carney's replacement as Allied Commander in Chief in Southern Europe. Elbridge Durbrow was holding the fort in Rome, but his wife and children appeared, as did Dorothy Farmer and Jack Shea, loaded with documents, letters, and cables.

Clare held court, ebullient and tanned in stylish shorts and dark glasses, sunbathing on the afterdeck, playing with her poodles, and outswimming everyone who dared to plunge off the gangway into the blue water with her. At mealtimes, informality vanished. Place cards, strictly observant of rank, were routine at formal lunches and dinners in the *Niki*'s stuffily furnished, wood-paneled salon.[20]

▽

After the yacht dropped anchor off San Stefano on the evening of August 27, a crewman hailed Clare aloft to take a radio call. She was unable to make sense of anything on the crackling airwaves, so she took a launch to shore. Maggie, Harry, and Grillo accompanied her, and sat outside a trattoria eating gelati while she went into a telephone booth in the smoky interior and asked to be connected to "Rome 414." None of the men drinking at the bar, or boys banging away at automatic table games, recognized the lady in overcoat and slacks as the American *Ambasciatrice*.

The following morning, Friday, she was back on deck, sporting a tasseled, multicolored Sorrento cap on the back of her golden hair, when Durbrow, wearing a dark city suit and carrying a briefcase, came up the gangplank. Clare went below with him, and they talked for an hour.[21]

After he left to return to Rome, Maggie deduced that something critical was brewing on the international scene, even though the cruise continued. Then, at noon, a storm warning forced the party to disembark again. The ambassadorial limousine, which had been following their progress along the coast in case of emergency, was ready to take them to Livorno. Harry ordered the *Niki* captain to proceed there, once the inclement weather cleared.

Livorno was a U.S. Army and Navy base, and Clare was scheduled to review the local troops on Saturday morning. Jeeps, trucks, and other field supplies stretched for miles around the headquarters, kept in reserve for American forces in Austria. In an emergency, this matériel would be transported through the disputed Free Territory of Trieste.

By late afternoon, the *Niki* passengers were back on board in the Bay of La Spezia, once Italy's chief naval harbor. The yacht was dwarfed by the massive U.S. battle cruiser *Juneau* anchored nearby and preparing for Tyrrhenian Sea maneuvers. Its presence emphasized the barrenness of the dry docks along La Spezia's embankments. Grillo, standing at the rail with Maggie, pointed out the ghostly, half-sunk, and gutted battleship *Vittorio Veneto*, and told her it was named for the last decisive World War I battle that had led to the collapse of the Austro-Hungarian Empire. As a spoil of war, Trieste, long owned by the Hapsburg dynasty, had then been annexed to Italy.[22]

He made Maggie understand, just as De Gasperi had Clare, what a fraught issue the Allied partition of the FTT was for Italians, uniting all of them "except the Communists." He called Trieste "the Martyred City," and remembered how in childhood he had been taught to sing an ode to it: "Our heart, we will come and liberate you."[23]

Even as he spoke, Clare received another sputtering radio call from Rome. Durbrow reported that he had just been informed by Prime Minister Pella that the standoff between Italy and Yugoslavia over Trieste had escalated to a "most serious" state of crisis. Pella had not ventured any specifics, but the wire services in Rome were spreading news that Italian troops, guns, and tanks had been ordered to the border of Zone A, and were prepared to cross it at any provocation.[24] The flint that had sparked this mobilization was a Belgrade press release stating that "Yugoslavia has lost patience with Italy on the Trieste question and is considering changing its moderate and tolerant attitude."[25]

Later that day, however, the U.S. Embassy learned that the release had been "entirely untrue." Nevertheless, Pella kept his troops in place, and Clare continued her cruise, pending developments.[26]

▽

On Sunday, August 30, the *Niki* proceeded north toward the Italian Riviera. From the deck, as it cruised past the distant Apennine range, Clare could see the slopes where she had taken her hair-raising drives with Truscott in the last months of the war, visiting the mountain's muddy battlegrounds. Now, eight years later, the peace pacts of 1945, meant to end all of Europe's armed conflicts for good, seemed in jeopardy just because of a territorial dispute that, in essence, devolved down to twelve hundred yards of Trieste's commercial waterfront.

To patriotic Italians, such as Grillo, reclamation of that prize port was a matter of national honor. To the occupying Allies, even a partial cession of it to Yugoslavia augured the possibility that the Soviet Union would woo Marshal Tito back into the Comintern fold, thus gaining strategic access to the northern Adriatic—in opposition to NATO's emplacements in the southern Mediterranean. To Clare's fertile mind, this meant that World War III could conceivably break out less than 250 miles from where she was currently sailing.

Despite the negation of the Belgrade press report, that day's world headlines were ominous. *The New York Times* blazed, ITALY ALERTS ARMY: FEARS TITO PLANS TRIESTE COUP.[27] All Allied furloughs had been canceled, and the Italian navy was ordered to the Adriatic.

Everyone aboard the *Niki* made the best of the last hours of the cruise, as the steward passed gin and tonics, and the yacht docked in the small harbor of Portofino. Above its cobblestone piazza and colonnaded houses, a castle nestled in the precipitous cliffs. Noël Coward appeared in a Jeep, and escorted the Luce party to call on Rex and Lilli Harrison. But first, Clare had to make yet another mysterious phone call, this time from the Hotel Splendido. For once, she was able to share her news, reporting that she had been summoned back to Rome to confer with the Italian government. Tomorrow morning a plane would come to collect her. "So, Madame Ambassador," said Coward, "those Jugs are at it again."[28]

That evening, Clare hosted a champagne-and-caviar farewell dinner in the *Niki*'s salon. She and Noël exchanged jokes and reminiscences. At fifty-three, he was still captivating, especially when he sat down at the piano, a red carnation in his buttonhole and a glass of white wine above the keyboard. He could have been performing at the Café de Paris. Listening to him play and sing songs such as "Tea for Two" was enough to temporarily banish Trieste from Clare's mind.[29]

35

PATIENCE AND COURAGE

*The insane fear of socialism throws the bourgeois
headlong into the arms of despotism.*

—Alexis de Tocqueville

Clare arrived back in Rome on Tuesday, September 1, to find the city
buzzing over reports that Yugoslavia had accused Italy of inciting
war. In fact, the Foreign Ministry received an official note of protest
from Belgrade, pointing out that Italy's deployment of troops on the
border of Zone A represented "a gross violation of the rules of conduct
among states maintaining regular diplomatic relations." Pella's government countered with a truculent declaration that Italy had "the full and
indisputable right to take . . . any measure it judges necessary in given
circumstances."[1]

These developments made Clare's hour-long meeting with Pella on
September 3 urgent. It was their first encounter since he had become
Prime Minister, but he was already an admirer of her work in Italy, telling the Supreme Allied Commander, General Alfred M. Gruenther,
that he hoped she would "remain on this assignment for a long period."[2]

Pella plunged straight into the current crisis. He said he would not
consider withdrawing his troops from the FTT frontier until he heard
what Marshal Tito might say in a speech scheduled for September 6,
provocatively close to the manned border. Nor would he let Monar-

chists in Parliament force him to take more extreme measures, even though his coalition government depended on ultra-nationalist support.[3]

Confidentially, Pella told Clare that an acceptable solution could be "one based on a plebiscite." But any settlement must be in the spirit of the 1948 Tripartite Declaration. He needed the backing of the signatory powers to help consolidate his regime, and unless the United States, Great Britain, and France exerted their diplomatic muscle, they might lose Italy as a friend and ally.[4]

Clare pressed him, as she had De Gasperi, on whether the Chamber of Deputies would in response approve expansion of American military facilities in Italy. Pella insisted that this and other issues of mutual concern could be addressed only after a satisfactory Trieste outcome. If not, the United States might continue to endure "the daily fatigue and frustration" of diplomatic inaction.[5]

Clare found herself largely in agreement with the Prime Minister about Trieste. In her report to the State Department, she said that any attempt by the Allies to persuade Italy to withdraw its troops from the border would weaken the Christian Democrats and "only strengthen extremist elements."[6]

That same day in Washington, John Foster Dulles held a press conference that undermined her concern. He said that the United States "has been exploring other alternatives" to the promise of the Tripartite Declaration to return Zone A to Italy.[7] There were immediate press and street protests in Rome, forcing the Chigi Palace to put its own protective spin on the Secretary's statement. Dulles, it said, was merely suggesting that there might be a negotiable way of implementing the Declaration. But Ludovici Benvenuti, the Italian Under Secretary for Foreign Affairs, privately subjected Clare to a twenty-minute tonguelashing on Dulles's "disastrous" remark. Tito, he said, was bound to take advantage of it, unless the United States issued an immediate clarification.[8]

Clare conceded that the situation approached emergency. She cabled the State Department that "failure to clarify the Secretary's statement at once, and to seek a rapid resolution of the question . . . [would] endanger not only the future of a moderate pro-American government in Italy, but might crack open [the] NATO system in Europe." Following up with a rare call to Dulles, she sounded so worried that he sent her a consolatory wire: "Was glad to talk with you on phone and have since discussed our conversation with President. . . . Please feel free always to send frankly your views. You can be sure we here do not minimize importance and danger in situation."[9]

This assurance was too noncommittal for Clare, who took it upon herself to go over the Secretary's head to Eisenhower. She used as an intermediary C. D. Jackson, who now had the unusual title of Special Assistant to the President for Psychological Warfare. If Pella's government fell as a result of American emasculation of the Tripartite Declaration, she told him, it would be a moral, diplomatic, and strategic blow to the West. "I wish I were in Washington now. . . . I could then thrash all this out vigorously with Foster and Ike." She asked Jackson to pass on to Ike her syllogistic summary of the dilemma:

> For the want of Trieste, an Issue was lost.
> For the want of an Issue, the Election was lost.
> For the want of an Election, De Gasperi was lost.
> For the want of De Gasperi, his NATO policies were lost.
> For the want of his NATO policies, Italy was lost.
> For the want of Italy, Europe was lost.
> For the want of Europe, America . . . . ?
> And all for the want of a two-penny town.[10]

In response, the State Department instructed Clare on September 5 to ask Pella to withdraw at least some of the troops he had placed on the border of the FTT. But she refused, saying the Prime Minister would consider such a request "highly offensive," because he had promised not to make a forceful entry unless provoked.[11]

She met with Pella again. He saw her by now as "our friendly mediator."[12] Neither divulged the content of their conversation. But *The New York Times* reported that Ambassador Luce had shown the Prime Minister a full transcript of the words of Secretary Dulles, and convinced him that "the deductions made from them were exaggerated." In Washington, Dulles assured Ambassador Alberto Tarchiani that he anticipated no alternative to the 1948 Tripartite Declaration.[13]

Clare urged the State Department to consider allowing Tito to annex Zone B, so that in fairness the Allies could at once transfer Zone A to the Italians. Such a simple double handover "would constitute all [the] satisfaction that Italian public opinion would demand to continue to support the government." It was a solution that might have been adopted years before, if both sides had not been intransigent over the question of equal rights in the port of Trieste itself. She asked that her proposal be given "fullest consideration" at a meeting of all five powers concerned—the United States, Great Britain, France, Italy, and Yugoslavia. She suggested that the British Foreign Secretary, Anthony Eden, might be flattered if London became the conference locale.[14]

The State Department was impressed and, in a potential major shift of policy, agreed to "urgently" consider her plan.[15] Its appeal was threefold: the Allies would be relieved of their longtime administrative burden in the FTT, a grateful Italy would remain aligned with the West, and Tito would understand that he might negotiate with, but not browbeat, representatives of democracy.

On the eve of the Marshal's tensely anticipated speech, Clare advised that even if it was inflammatory, and Yugoslavia massed troops on the frontier of Zone B, Pella intended to take no countermeasures, so long as the border was not breached. He would be making a new policy statement of his own a week later.[16]

Despite her calm tone, she and her entire staff remained in a state of high alert over the Labor Day weekend. The Yugoslav Legation in Rome had already delivered no fewer than four notes to the Italian government, threatening that if "the abnormal situation at the frontier" was not ameliorated by diplomatic means, Yugoslavia would "be forced to take corresponding measures."[17] As a result, warships of the Italian navy were proceeding at full steam toward Venice.

On Sunday, September 6, President Tito appeared in a dazzling, bemedaled white uniform before thousands of Partisan veterans and workers at Okroglica. While he spoke, peasants lit bonfires that could be seen by Italian soldiers across the border.[18] In Trieste, British police patrolled the city, fearing violence, and all leaves were canceled for Allied troops in the FTT.[19]

Tito, a lifelong Marxist, had been persona non grata at the Kremlin since his expulsion from the Comintern in 1948. He kept a bust of Lenin on his desk but not of Stalin, whom he referred to as a *"Schweine."*[20] He had risen to power as the leader of Yugoslavia's anti-Nazi resistance in World War II, and in 1943 had been overwhelmingly elected Prime Minister. By January 1953, he had become his country's all-powerful President, and seemed destined to be its dictator for life. Deeply disillusioned with the collaborationist role the Yugoslav Roman Catholic Church had played during the war, he was still holding Cardinal Aloysius Stepinac in prison, and said he would never allow him to serve as

Archbishop again. For this Tito had been excommunicated by the Vatican, and was despised by Italian conservatives, not to mention Clare Luce. She persisted in seeing him as a once and future Soviet lackey, when in fact he lived in fear of a punitive attack by the Red Army. As a beneficiary of the Marshall Plan, he was flirting with the idea of joining NATO, if invited.[21] Being half Slovene and half Croatian, Tito passionately identified with Trieste's Slav minority.

Sounding conciliatory at first, he told the crowd at Okroglica that Trieste should be a free, international city. But he insisted that its hinterland—Zone B—be incorporated into his Slav Republic. Addressing the Italian government directly, he went on, "The Yugoslav peoples wish to have the last morsel of their national territory, and you must bear this in mind if you want peace." He called for bilateral negotiations with Italy and, as a show of faith, promised not to retaliate militarily for the time being.[22]

The Chigi Palace reacted to this statesmanlike speech by accusing Tito of "megalomania" and devious opportunism. Clare's own reaction was less apprehensive than wry. Noting the United States had supplied arms as well as dollars to both squabbling countries, she wisecracked, "At least, if Italy and Yugoslavia go to war, we'll find out what American tanks can do against—American tanks."[23]

Maggie Case saw her that afternoon, and found her preoccupied. After a while, Clare said, "I should talk to Ike."

She weighed her options. "If I telephone him, these lines are listened in on. Should I fly over . . . ? That might cause speculation."[24]

Maggie said, "What do you care if everybody in Italy does hear you this time?"

She imagined, as did many Italians, that Ambassador Luce and the President talked often. In fact, Clare had not yet phoned Eisenhower about anything. But she needed to know directly from him what ultimate course he advised on Trieste. So she went into her bedroom and placed a call. All she would say on emerging was that Ike had promised "to look into the matter immediately."[25]

On Wednesday, September 9, Pella separately summoned Clare, the French Ambassador, and the British chargé d'affaires. He told them that Tito's proposal was not a suitable basis for negotiations, and that Italy still demanded a full execution of the Tripartite Declaration. But he promised to withdraw his troops as soon as he could do so without ap-

pearing to yield. Clare told him that her "double handover" plan to resolve the whole question was currently being considered in Washington.
That satisfied Pella, who emphasized, as De Gasperi had, that he did not
want to negotiate with Tito directly.[26]

Some five thousand people gathered in the square outside Rome's
City Hall when the Prime Minister arrived on the thirteenth. Inside,
two thousand packed the main salon, ostensibly to honor all those who
had fought in wars to defend *la patria*. The salon was decorated with
flags, and its walls were painted with scenes depicting national victories.
After paying tribute to Italy's veterans, Pella said he wished "with reason and without passion" to propose a plebiscite to settle the future of
the Free Territory of Trieste. He asked the Allies to meet as soon as possible with Italy and Yugoslavia at a neutral site, to discuss a procedure
for such a vote. As a prior condition, he demanded that Tito withdraw
his soldiers from Zone B. The audience cheered repeatedly, and as Pella
stepped onto a balcony to wave to the street crowd, he received another
ovation.[27]

Unknown to Italians, Clare's plan for Trieste had received administration endorsement at the highest level.[28] This news must have leaked,
because when Maggie Case returned to the Villa Taverna after hearing
Pella speak, she received a call from an excited friend at the Chigi Palace, telling her to read a front-page Trieste story in *Il Messaggero*. The
government itself had secretly and unprecedentedly worded one paragraph:

> The report sent to Washington by Ambassador Clare Luce on the
> Italian point of view and on the situation created in Italy by Tito's
> threats is complete in its information and precise in its conclu-
> sions. The text of this important diplomatic document has not
> been made public. . . . But Italian journalists in the United States
> have indicated the tenor of the report and have justly expressed
> the satisfaction and gratitude of Italy for the wise and energetic
> move on the part of Mrs. Luce. By this step she has again given
> new proof of the sensibility with which, while loyally and intelli-
> gently serving her own country, she also serves our common cause
> and demonstrates the greatest friendship for the nation in which
> she is such a welcome guest.[29]

A chorus of praise followed from other once-mocking Italian newspapers. "Perhaps never in the whole of history has a great nation owed

so much to so small, fragile and gentle a woman," remarked *Corriere della Sera*. Even Giovanni Guareschi conceded in *Candido* that the Ambasciatrice had "great tact and intelligence," in contrast with Secretary Dulles, who had "acted with the delicacy of a hippopotamus."[30]

The following evening, Clare gave Maggie a farewell dinner à deux in the Villa Taverna. Close to tears, the older woman raised a champagne glass and muttered something about leaving her "on a note of triumph." After a quarter century of watching Clare's inexorable ascent, she felt she had witnessed the conquest of another pinnacle. "It had not come through beauty, ease and facility," Maggie wrote in her diary. "She had worked hard every step of the way."[31]

▽

Steeper and more perilous steps confronted Ambassador Luce in the weeks and months immediately following. She left Rome on Thursday, September 17, for an American Chief of Missions meeting in Luxembourg on "Top Secret Security Information." Attending were Charles E. Bohlen from the USSR, C. Douglas Dillon from France, Winthrop W. Aldrich from Britain, James B. Conant, Special Envoy to Germany, John C. Hughes, the U.S. Representative to NATO, and David Bruce, Representative to the European Defense Community (EDC). For the first time, she was to be at close quarters with a group of her more experienced American diplomatic peers, some of whom did not look favorably on her.[32]

Dillon was particularly prejudiced. "She hasn't got anything except *Time, Life* and *Fortune*."[33] Bohlen resented Clare's constant haranguing of Communism over the years, which made it more difficult for him to maintain amicable relations with Moscow.[34]

The first session at the two-day gathering was a briefing by Bohlen entitled "The Soviet Scene." This was a critical topic since Stalin's death in March and the succession to the premiership of the colorless Georgi Malenkov. There had been lethal power struggles within the Presidium, marked by the June arrest of Security Chief Lavrenti Beria, less than seven weeks before the surprise detonation of his main project, the RDS-6s hydrogen bomb. Designed by Andrei Sakharov, and twenty-six times more powerful than the Hiroshima bomb, it was the most terrifying weapon yet in the international nuclear arms race, giving the Soviets defense parity with the United States.

Just four days earlier, Nikita Khrushchev, Beria's dynamic nemesis, had been appointed First Secretary of the Communist Party. Churchill was trying to persuade Eisenhower to meet the Kremlin's new leadership, since the only senior bureaucrat in the regime known to the West was a Stalinist hard-liner, Foreign Minister Vyacheslav Molotov. One of his bon mots was that he mistrusted free elections, because "you never know how they are going to turn out."[35]

Next came Bruce, who gave a briefing on the status of the still-unformed EDC. This embryonic organization envisaged a common European military force composed of units contributed by six member states, including West Germany. Bruce saw it as more likely to constrain the Germans than allowing them to rearm under the American-dominated NATO umbrella. Eisenhower was even more ambitious for the EDC, hoping that it might lead to the economic and political unification of the Continent, a proposition soundly opposed by the gallocentric Charles de Gaulle.[36] Churchill, too, was dubious, calling the proposed EDC treaty "a sludgy amalgam."[37]

In the afternoon Clare, as the junior envoy present, spoke last. Her subject was how Italians felt about the EDC and the Trieste problem. Simply put, she said, they were lukewarm about the former, and red hot about the latter. If Stalin's death had eased East–West tensions, Chigi officials were asking, why should Europe arm itself further, since it already had the protection of NATO? Pella saw the EDC mainly as a bargaining chip, and was pushing for a settlement of Trieste before he would even consider signing the treaty. Her task was to "unlink" the two issues, "so that each may be seen on its own merits." As for the United States, it surely wanted to lighten its foreign military burden, "in the cold face of Europe's unwillingness to integrate its own defense."[38]

David Bruce was impressed by her analysis of the Trieste situation, saying later it demonstrated "an experienced diplomatic mind." In his opinion, she was "smarter than any man present."[39]

That night at dinner, a weary Clare unwound with alcohol, and shocked her colleagues with loud remarks about Alfred Kinsey's new report on women's sexuality. She said she had been asked to write a review of it, but in light of her current position felt the assignment inappropriate. Had she accepted, she said, her voice rising, she could have pointed out that a 480-page study was not needed "to prove that all men are dopes."

The dining room went quiet. "After all," she went on, "women are not interested in sex. All they want is babies and security from men. Men are just too stupid to know it."[40]

▽

The following day's discussion topics were psychological warfare, and American foreign and economic policy. All the envoys lauded the recent West German reelection of Chancellor Konrad Adenauer, who strongly favored European integration. Concerns were expressed about the health of the aging Winston Churchill, and that of his likely successor, Anthony Eden. Another problem cited was Britain's need to reduce its defense commitments abroad, especially by removing troops from Suez.[41]

Clare flew on to Frankfurt for briefings on strategy at the United States European Command headquarters, and returned to Rome on September 22.[42] A week later, Tito formally rejected Pella's plebiscite proposal. However, he still expressed a desire to hold a dialogue with Italy. Wild rumors circulated in Rome that the Italian Ambassador in Moscow was seeking Soviet backing of the Tripartite Declaration, in exchange for a refusal by his country to join the EDC. Meanwhile, the Italian press speculated that the Allies were about to make a decision unfavorable to Yugoslavia.[43]

▽

At 9:15 on the morning of October 8, Clare and Sir Victor Mallet met with Pella and read him the text of a momentous new Anglo-American declaration, to be released to the press later that day. Simultaneously in Belgrade, their counterparts delivered the same text to Tito. The crux of the statement, replacing the Tripartite Declaration of 1948, was that the Allies were "no longer prepared to maintain responsibility for the administration of Zone A." Therefore, they intended to withdraw their troops immediately from the Free Territory of Trieste, "and having in mind the predominantly Italian character of Zone A," were ceding the government of the area to Italy. Yugoslavia could have Zone B, which it already administered.[44]

The wording of this statement, henceforth to be known as the October 8 Declaration, was in parts almost identical to Clare's own recommendations to the State Department. She was authorized to inform Pella secretly that as far as the Allies were concerned, the new "*de facto* settlement" was final. Should either country later wish "to initiate bilateral negotiations with a view to modification of boundaries, the U.S. and the U.K. governments would not intervene on behalf of either party."[45] Since the end of the war, America had been spending $10 million and Britain £2 million every year in Zone A, and they were tired of the financial burden.[46]

Tito balked at these unilateral and arbitrary terms, and asked that they not be made public until he had consulted his government. But the Allies went ahead and published the October 8 Declaration at 4:00 P.M. as planned. "Thanks for the skillful way in which you have handled delicate and important program for Trieste," Dulles cabled Clare, "first reactions indicate that operation will be successful."[47]

As it turned out, the Secretary was overly optimistic. Tito's formal response a few hours later was vehement. Dropping his earlier placable tone, he announced in two angry speeches that he had increased his forces in Zone B, and massed more troops along the Zone A border. He threatened that if any of Italy's soldiers marched into Zone A, Yugoslavia's would, too.

Ominously, the USSR protested the October 8 Declaration as a "gross violation" of the Paris Peace Treaties of 1947. Andrey Vyshinsky, the Soviet Representative to the United Nations, went before the Security Council in New York, and said that Moscow "would not tolerate any decision in the dispute over Trieste unless the Soviet Union has a hand in it."[48]

Demonstrations broke out in Yugoslav cities, and escalated to the vandalizing of Allied and Italian-owned buildings. Tito's Partisan veterans shouted, *"Zivot damo, Trst ne damo"* (We gave our lives, we did not give Trieste).[49]

Claire Sterling, a respected columnist, wrote in *The Reporter*, "U.S. diplomats who generously shared the credit and acclaim when their brilliant coup was first announced, have every possible reason to be worried now."[50]

Dulles, alarmed by Tito's reaction, asked Pella to be prudent, saying that Communist Yugoslavia was not likely to be bound by "restraints from the use of force inherent in a Christian society."[51]

Keen to head off Russian interference, Tito proposed a four-power conference of American, British, Italian, and Yugoslav diplomats to resolve the crisis once and for all. (France had signaled its weariness with the whole Trieste issue.) The Marshal's requirements were reasonable: guarantees from Italy that Slovene rights in Zone A be respected, and from the Allies that Italy not be allowed to expand elsewhere in the Balkans.

Clare had no objections to Tito's proposal, pointing out that she had suggested a similar conference herself. Pella informed her that it was no time to appease the Marshal, adding that if the Allies gave even the "impression" that they were reneging on their commitment, he would resign. The Prime Minister made this threat public in the Italian Senate on October 17.[52]

▽

By now Clare was fretting over the slow pace of negotiations. "I've been here six months," she told Durbrow. "We lost the election. The government spends its time fighting itself. . . . I've accomplished nothing!"[53] Yet she continued to drive herself, often putting in sixteen-hour days. Dorothy Farmer feared a breakdown, and shared her concern with her counterpart in New York, Dorothea Philp. "You are probably familiar with this mood: working feverishly, everything has to be done immediately, all that has been done has been done wrong, and the most insignificant item becoming suddenly the most important, etc. etc. . . . Her mind is 100 percent occupied with the current situation—and when she's at home she keeps the radio on."[54]

Courtesy of Dr. Milton Rosenbluth in Manhattan, Clare kept going on a daily cocktail of drugs: three doses of Dexedrine for fatigue (preferable "in every way," he said, to her usual Benzedrine); one or two Trasentine before meals and two tablets of Syntrogel after, to ease abdominal cramps; one tablet of painkilling Spasmalgin every four hours; and one or two sodium amytal for sleep.[55]

On October 27, Clare collapsed with influenza. That same day, she was humiliated to hear that Sir Victor Mallet had seen a preliminary draft of an Eisenhower-approved Trieste initiative—only loosely based on her original proposals—that had not come to her. It proposed a delay in handing over Zone A to Italy for as long as talks lasted, potentially committing the Allies to another year or more of occupation of the FTT. After getting a copy, she felt it amounted to a face-saving concession to Tito, and made her displeasure known to Dulles.

"I cannot believe that the U.S. seriously intends to back-track, weasel, welch, renege or—since the Department prefers the euphemism—to 'finesse' its decision to proceed with the transfer." Dulles tried to mollify her, saying he had not known about that particular draft either. It was merely intended for discussion by low-level staffers on either side. To avoid a similar mishap, he wrote, "I have given instructions that despite the expense involved significant working papers are to be telegraphed to you—even before they have evolved into formal shape." Trying to be conciliatory, he signed off with congratulations "on your excellent work in this difficult task."[56]

Pella also exploded, in a note to Dulles that insultingly questioned America's good faith regarding the October 8 Declaration. The Secretary refused to accept it from Ambassador Tarchiani, asking if Pella understood the consequences of such language. Tarchiani tried to explain that the situation in Italy was one of "suspicion, diffidence and despair." Dulles assured him that the Allies meant to honor their commitment, but not "in such a way as to start another war." Speaking with unusual bluntness, he added that if Italy thought it could dictate the foreign policy of the United States, the Eisenhower administration would have to make "a radical revision" of its strategic attitude toward southeastern Europe.[57]

Clare recovered enough by November 3 to send Eisenhower and Dulles an "Eyes Only Top Secret" estimate of the Italian situation, warning both that an overlong delay in implementing the October 8 Declaration would result in Pella's fall, followed by "a chaotic political situation among the weakened, strife-torn anti-Communist parties." If significant Communist gains in the next few months went unchecked, she wrote, then Italy might see a counterreactionary swing to the right.[58]

In a gloomy letter to the White House, Clare wrote, "If the Cominform left gains only 4 percent from the Center to Right parties by the next elections, the President of Italy will be required by the Constitution to call upon a Cominform leader to form the next government."[59]

Eisenhower, a voice of reason and restraint, answered in a long personal letter. "I assure you that, as far as I know, we have no intention of weaseling . . . on Trieste." Although Italy's response had been supportive, he wrote, "this unquestionably made Tito feel that he had to react adversely and much more vehemently than he otherwise would have." Accordingly, "a situation has been created where we must observe sufficient caution that we do not almost force Italy and Yugoslavia into even deeper trouble in order to save face on one or both sides."

Ike continued with an observation that could hardly have made Clare feel satisfied with her efforts, or secure in her post. "It seems odd that of all the countries in which we have been opposing Communism, we have had less success in Italy than any other." Despite growing prosperity as a result of United States aid, "every report from Italy bears evidence of an increasing resentment against us and increased respect for the Soviets." Clare could not deny the truth of this.

The President continued, "So while I accept in its general sense your argument that the United States must give to Italy increased concern and interest—to say nothing of money—I believe also that a great burden of responsibility rests upon the leaders." He suggested that Clare give him fewer exhortations about what "material, moral, and political" assistance the United States should lavish on Italy, and more suggestions as to what kind of pressure *she* could apply to make Italians help themselves.

To soften this obvious reprimand, he handwrote an encouraging P.S. "You are really going *good*."[60]

▽

When Clare awoke on November 6, Rome radio was broadcasting reports of bloody riots in Trieste. Some twelve thousand Italian nationalists, stirred by the thirty-fifth anniversary of the liberation of the city at the end of World War I, had marched into the Piazza dell'Unità and clashed with British military policemen. Pella, fearing similar violence at home, ordered city schools and universities closed.

By chance, Clare had a meeting scheduled with him that morning. She went ahead with the appointment, and presented yet another top-secret initiative from Dulles. It was that the Italian and Yugoslav prime ministers should choose a personal representative to discuss a Trieste solution with Allied diplomats in Washington or London. Their instructions would be to pave the way, or replace the need, for any multinational conference.[61]

Pella offered to discuss this with De Gasperi and leaders of parties supporting his government. Listening to him, Clare did not yet know that downtown, an estimated twenty thousand nationalist and neo-Fascist demonstrators were overturning and burning any cars that looked British. But by the time she left the Palazzo Chigi, the mob had swelled and was moving up the Via del Tritone into Piazza Barberini, heading toward the United States Embassy. When her limousine turned onto the Via Veneto, she found her way blocked by a vast crowd pushing against a thin line of *reparto celere*—a flying squad of riot police deployed just twenty yards from the Palazzo Margherita. The protesters were hurling insults, stones, and bottles in the direction of the ornamental gates, amid a defensive barrage of high-pressure hoses and tear gas. Wounded *carabinieri*, their faces streaming with blood, were being given first aid in the embassy courtyard.[62]

Having in her time dodged bombs in China, Burma, Belgium, and the Italian front, Clare was unintimidated. She elected to get out and

The U.S. Embassy gates where Clare confronted rioters, November 6, 1953

walk. Durbrow was waiting for her inside the gates, which were guarded by U.S. Marines. He said Italian army reinforcements were on their way, and begged her to hurry indoors. She insisted on finding out what had enraged the protesters. Michael Stern, an American foreign correspondent, approached.

"Who is in charge there?" she asked him. Stern indicated a burly officer in a tight uniform.

"I would like to talk with him."

Stern brought the man over and watched with amusement as, to the sound of screaming sirens, he kissed the Ambassador's extended hand.

"Ask him who the leaders are," Clare said to Stern.

"He says they are Communist agitators."

"I'm not afraid of them. Tell them I will meet a committee of their leaders in my office now."

Stern did, although the police chief said it would seem that she was giving recognition to radicals.

"I don't care. I am ready to listen to anything they have to say."

At this point, a CBS-TV man Clare recognized as a former war reporter came up, saying, "It's dangerous for you to remain here."

Stern was struck by Clare's saintly smile as she replied, "Remember, I too was a war correspondent."[63]

By now it was lunchtime, and the demonstrators had begun to move off.[64] The following day, Ambassador Luce won kudos in the press for her fortitude.

▽

The day after her encounter with the Rome rowdies, ongoing riots in Trieste reached their climax when panicky Allied MPs fired randomly at protesters, killing six people and injuring forty.[65]

Pella's government tried to present the outbreak as *italianita*— nationalist passions run amok—a result of Allied foot-dragging over the October 8 Declaration. "The sky of the Fatherland is, in this hour, covered with clouds of sorrow," the Prime Minister publicly mourned. Other politicians were outraged, and a Monarchist deputy challenged General John W. Winterton, the Allied commander in Trieste, to a duel in the square where the fatalities occurred.[66] As unrest spread to other towns, Pella blamed Winterton for having refused an offer of twelve hundred *carabinieri* to keep order.[67]

Meanwhile Tito grew more statesmanlike by the hour, compared with his Italian counterpart. In Belgrade on November 15, he suggested a peaceful solution to the whole vexed question. Yugoslavia would give up its claim to the city of Trieste, he said, since "there is no good will to give it to us on any side." All he wanted was an amicable separation of powers along the borders of the two outer zones, and he hoped Italians would not continue to spoil conference prospects by insisting on the prior occupation of Zone A.[68]

Three days later, a somewhat shamed Pella agreed to a full five-power conference. Yet he still wanted advance control of Zone A. Insulted, Belgrade replied on November 24 that in view of continuing Italian provocation, Yugoslavia was withdrawing its acceptance of Dulles's latest initiative. Pella thereupon declined to move any further, redoubling pressure on Clare and the State Department to find a way out of the impasse.[69]

▽

Although she had handled the embassy riot with grit and aplomb, Clare still felt a lack of achievement on Trieste. Durbrow reminded her that diplomacy was a slow business, and could not be forced, partly because of the need to consider local pride, traditions, and mores. "In other words," she replied, "I must take for my motto that old Italian saying, '*Pazienza e coraggio.*' "[70]

Tito came to her aid. Nudging Pella into a more conciliatory frame of mind, he declared in Jajce on November 29 that both Yugoslavia and Italy should stand down militarily, "so that the matter can be discussed without armies on the frontier." On December 5, Pella and Pavel Gregoric, the Yugoslav envoy in Rome, formally agreed to a mutual withdrawal of troops within seventeen days. The Prime Minister demonstrated extra good faith by offering to relax trade sanctions against Yugoslavia that had been in place for three months.[71]

From all points of view, especially Clare's, the agreement was a major breakthrough: the two sides at last talking, the borders of Zone A soon to be demilitarized, eight years of escalating postwar tensions mitigated, and a high-powered conference in the offing sometime later that winter.

36

EVIL EYE

▽

*A democracy which fails to concentrate authority in
an emergency inevitably falls into such confusion that
the ground is prepared for the rise of a dictator.*

— WALTER LIPPMANN

C lare spent the first week of January 1954 in Washington, D.C., having her first face-to-face meetings with the President and Secretary
Dulles since going to Rome. As she reiterated her written warnings to
them about the increasing Communist threat in Italy, a political upheaval was under way there. Prime Minister Pella's grip had been weakened by a rift with right-wing nationalists over the proposed Trieste
conference. Apart from the need to negotiate a legal formula for the
exact partition of the FTT, a sensitive question remained: protection of
ethnic minorities in both zones once the Allies withdrew. Pella was
perceived as too inflexible on that subject to survive any equable settlement. His likely successor as leader of the Christian Democratic coalition was the left-leaning Amintore Fanfani, whom Clare feared would
be susceptible to demands from the Popular Front for cabinet posts.[1]
She suspected Fanfani would fail, necessitating an election in which
Communists might gain even more votes and seats.

Dulles took her concerns seriously and had senior administration
officials meet her for what became a two-hour discussion of ways to
strengthen the bonds of Italian-American relations. Attendees included
CIA Director Allen W. Dulles, Under Secretary of State Walter Bedell

Clare and President Eisenhower, January 1954

Smith, Director of Foreign Operations Administration Harold E. Stassen, and Assistant Secretary of Defense Frank C. Nash.

An urgent subject before them was the fact that, unbeknown to the press, the Trieste Conference had already been postponed, due to renewed Italian opposition. The State Department's recourse was to ask Yugoslavia if it would commit to a round of individual, supersecret talks with Allied diplomats, in the hope of arriving at a basic set of demands that Italy might separately approve by the same covert means.[2]

The New York Times commented that there must be "an unusual dimension" to Mrs. Luce's reports. Ambassadors returning stateside for consultations rarely encountered "such a reception."[3] The truth was that Italy's problems extended far beyond Trieste and petty politicking. A major article in the *New York Herald Tribune,* headlined ITALY IS GOING COMMUNIST, reported that the Republic had an 85-billion-lire deficit. American aid, budgeted at $325 million for 1954, could hardly dent this shortfall. There were other alarming statistics. Out of a population of 47 million, 4 million Italians were unemployed, including many of the 250,000 youths who entered the labor market annually. The country needed to lose at least 500,000 emigrants a year to balance the birth of 825,000 babies.[4]

Given the tendency of dire socioeconomic conditions to drive poor people into the arms of Karl Marx, Clare and her like-minded colleagues agreed that should further democratic coalitions fail in Italy, billions of dollars' worth of American armaments given to that country since the end of the war might end up equipping a Red insurgency.[5]

Reassured by Dulles that a Communist electoral triumph in Italy would not be tolerated by the United States, Clare made off-the-record remarks to a group of journalists at a Mayflower Hotel luncheon on January 5.[6] Nevertheless, she spoke and answered questions with a frankness that, for a head of mission, bordered on indiscretion. She should have realized that reporters were inveterate note takers, and that one day her remarks might see print.

The situation in Italy was serious, she said, and if strong measures were not taken in Rome, the country could become Communist "in two or three years." It was imperative that a new Christian Democrat government be formed as soon as Pella resigned. She felt that the Catholic Church was "the only effective force" against the advance of the extreme Left. But Americans should understand that many Italians, for all their love of church rites, were anti-clerical, and not immune to a godless ideology. Should Pietro Nenni or Palmiro Togliatti ever gain power, "it is certain that the Church will become a clandestine organization." In conclusion, she announced that "Congress does not intend to throw money into Italy, if the money should serve to better the position of the Communists."[7]

Her talk with Eisenhower the next day coincided with news that Pella was resigning. Clare pressed Ike to send Vice President Nixon on a goodwill tour of Italy, in order to combat left-wing propaganda. He promised to consider it.[8] At a stag dinner soon after, he credited Ambassador Luce, "more than any other single person," with the recent defusing of the Trieste war threat.[9]

When Clare hosted a party in Manhattan for Harry's staff on January 7, John Billings thought she looked "old and tired and haggard."[10] Adding to the pressure on her was the subject of that day's front-page headline in *The New York Times*: MRS. LUCE TO RUSH TO ITALY IN CRISIS.

▽

Canceling speeches in Washington and Chicago, as well as a vacation in White Sulphur Springs, Clare flew back to her post. She arrived at Rome's Ciampino Airport at 6:00 P.M. on January 11 to find Italy essentially leaderless. President Einaudi had not yet designated a permanent new Premier. Politicians expected extremist newspapers to claim that Ambassador Luce was bringing succession "orders" to the Palazzo del Quirinale. To deflect such rumors, Clare made a radio statement. She said nothing about the current uncertainty, but hinted that a new "mutually satisfactory" aid program might be negotiated between the United States and Italy, as soon as there was a lessening of Communist influence in both Parliament and industry. The following day, just as Amintore Fanfani was charged with forming a new government, *The New York Times* reported that Washington would award no defense contracts to Italian factories that had Red-dominated unions.[11]

On January 14, Clare received a "Top Secret" cable from Secretary Dulles. He said that he and Eisenhower had been "particularly impressed" by her "vigorous" recent briefings in Washington. "The growth of Communist influence [in Italy] and the absence of any firm governmental measures to counteract it are matters of grave concern to us." The aid package she had mentioned, he said, would be forthcoming, "if the Italian people and government could decisively reverse the present dangerous trend and reject Communism."[12]

Armed with this confirmation, Clare embarked on a series of meetings with leaders of Italy's major political parties, with the exception of Nenni and Togliatti. Well versed by now in the labyrinthine ideologies of the Republic, she looked forward to dialogues that engaged her analytical faculties and love of argument.

First she lunched with Giuseppe Saragat, Secretary of the moderate Socialist Democrats and a key supporter of De Gasperi's former coalition. He was fluent in French, which was convenient for Clare, who had not yet progressed beyond "drawing room" Italian. Most of the Chigi officials she met spoke English, but when they did not she generally brought along an interpreter. Saragat surprised her by saying he had just received a letter from Fanfani, accepting two conditions the Socialist Democrats had laid down in exchange for their support in forming the new government: a formal declaration of republicanism, and the cessation of monopolistic practices by the Christian Democrat majority.[13]

This led to a discussion of the Monarchists. Clare said that despite their name, she doubted they wanted to restore the House of Savoy, because if they did, "they might disappear as a party." She asked about a rumor that the former Queen of Italy nurtured a fantasy of returning to power with Saragat as her Prime Minister. Coyly, he admitted that "there might be some truth in the story."

Getting to her main purpose, Clare said there was "a growing feeling of disillusionment in the United States" about the lack of results from the aid Italy had received to strengthen democratic trends. Since World War II, Washington's investment had totaled $3.5 billion for economic development and $1.5 billion in military expenditure. In view of this generosity, she declared that her government wanted "positive action" to combat Communism.

Clare reported to the State Department that Saragat "was content, as are many Italian leaders, in the belief that in the saying is the doing."[14]

Two days later, she had lunch with Alfredo Covelli, General Secretary of the Monarchist National Party. He refused to support Fanfani if the latter made a coalition-building deal with Nenni. The Socialist Party was completely in Communist hands, Covelli said, but a fair number of its three million voters could be wooed away, should Nenni ever step down.

Sounding him out, Clare suggested that his party, despite its name, had little interest in restoring the monarchy. Covelli said that was not true. But since his followers believed in constitutional government, the House of Savoy could be reinstated only "through the will of the people, and not through any political machinations."

She emphasized that the United States did not wish to interfere with the composition of any Italian government, but did want to see a stable regime installed, one "capable of combating Communism on both the social-economic and political fronts." If these aims were not met, she stressed (repeating her instructions from Dulles), future American aid to his country would be cut.[15]

Later that afternoon, Clare saw the septuagenarian Bruno Villabruna, Secretary of the Liberal Party and an old anti-Fascist with a lawyerly mind. He said he would probably support Fanfani, but as a believer in free enterprise he worried that any free-spending social program would worsen Italy's inflation. Clare asked why he could not cooperate with both Saragat's and Fanfani's parties to produce, at least, a program acceptable to the moderate Left and moderate Right. Villabruna replied that he could not compromise with Socialist Democrats, because they were even more free-spending than Christian Democrats. He preferred to work with Covelli's Monarchists, having voted in favor of the House of Savoy as recently as 1946— even though he had doubted it could be restored.

Clare said the Monarchist question resembled an iceberg—"little on the surface, but a great deal more . . . hidden from sight."

When she followed up with her authorized warning about cutting aid, Villabruna replied candidly. He said the United States should tell

Italian leaders that aid must be spent to achieve specific democratic ends, or it would be withheld. When Clare said that this would be seen as "intolerable interference in Italian domestic affairs," he said that Washington should not flinch at making "moves which are unpopular."[16]

At the end of the day, Clare heard that Fanfani had put together a fragile, *monocolore* government consisting only of Christian Democrats. The chatter in the diplomatic community, she was told, was that the leftist Fanfani was already "tapping the wires," and would "probably make a police state."[17]

▽

An exhausted Clare checked into the San Domenico Palace Hotel in Taormina, Sicily. Her room overlooked the bay, and had a view of the snowy bulk of Mount Etna. But a cold wave that held all of Europe in an icy grip affected the usually sunny resort as well, so after enduring five days of rain that kept her cooped up, she returned to Rome and its freezing fountains.[18]

The governmental crisis was unabated, threatening her with many challenges in the coming weeks. She was at least relieved to hear that Yugoslavia had agreed to secret Trieste negotiations in London. Tito's representative was Dr. Vladimir Velebit, a hard-line Slovene. His counterparts were Geoffrey W. Harrison, an undersecretary in the British Foreign Office, and Llewellyn E. Thompson, the U.S. Ambassador to Austria. It was probable that several anticlimactic months would pass before Manlio Brosio, Italy's Ambassador to Great Britain, would be able to make his case.[19]

On January 29, the Italian Chamber of Deputies debated whether to give Fanfani a vote of confidence. Palmiro Togliatti stood up and said acidly that the new Premier's liberal agenda was guided by a foreign power. "The things you, Honorable Fanfani, have said against us have already been said by the American Ambassador on her peregrinations. My advice is, don't run after her. She is a *porta sventura*."[20]

Everyone in the Chamber knew that this phrase, meaning a bringer of bad luck, also connoted *malocchio*, "the evil eye," a sinister power that in popular belief brought disasters, from crop failures to volcanic eruptions to the death of the Pope.

Signora Luce's Milan speech last June, Togliatti went on, with its threat of aid reduction, had weakened the Christian Democrats. And her meddling in the Trieste question had inflicted trouble on Premier Pella. "Beware of all advice that comes from that quarter," he warned.

Fanfani rose to his feet to protest such an attack on the representative of a foreign nation. As a man, "I must lament that the most elementary rules of chivalry have been so crudely disregarded." De Gasperi followed, denying that other countries had a hand in formulating Italian policy. Togliatti evidently mistook Italy "for one of the Soviet Union satellites."[21]

When the vote was taken, all the minor coalition parties that Fanfani depended on—the Monarchists, the Liberals, the neo-Fascist Social Movement, and Saragat's Socialist Democrats—withdrew their support, leaving him with 260 ayes and 303 nays. As a result, on February 10, Fanfani, after just nineteen days in office, was replaced by Mario Scelba.[22]

Scelba was the fourth man to serve as Prime Minister of Italy since Clare's arrival less than ten months before. He swore in a left-of-center cabinet, consisting of fourteen Christian Democrats, four moderate Socialists, and three Liberals. Monarchists were conspicuously lacking. For this reason he, too, was not expected to last long.

Clare nevertheless welcomed the elevation of another Christian Democrat. Scelba was an able former Minister of the Interior, and on socioeconomic issues was firmly left of center. He had been an enforcer of law and order in De Gasperi's government, and was responsible for creating Italy's *reparto celere*—flying squads that Clare had seen in action last November outside her embassy gates. Together with the PS (*pubblica sicurezza*) and the *carabinieri*, they were part of a civilian force of 160,000, the largest in Europe, and more numerous than the current Italian army.[23]

▽

As publisher of the recently launched *Sports Illustrated*, Harry, back in Rome, felt duty-bound to acquaint himself with European soccer, and went to a game at the Foro Italico, a monumental stadium built by Mussolini. Most evenings he attended social events with Clare. He was usually seated next to well-informed people, and was frustrated by having to keep to himself what he learned from them.[24]

While he enjoyed playing consort in Rome, he happily went to other capitals in search of firsthand news to file with his home office. An opportunity arose in late February, when trouble erupted in the eight-month-old Republic of Egypt. He flew to Cairo and arrived just in time to see General Gamal Abdel Nasser's troops quelling what turned out to be an attempted revolt against the regime of President Muhammad Naguib. Harry collected complaints from protesters that he thought would make lively copy, and managed an interview with Nasser himself. He found on reading the next issue of *Time* that all his best stuff had been cut. "Damn it, they were interesting quotes."[25]

Clare's own store of international information was enriched by Harry's confidences, although she could not share classified material with him. Continuing her series of meetings with powerful Italians, she received a variety of industrialists, undeterred by the warning of Giulio Pastore, president of Italy's Free Trade Union, that they were "*transformisti*—political chameleons of the first order."[26] Among these conservatives were Dr. Angelo Costa, president of Confindustria, Count Carlo Faina, chairman of Montecatini Industries, and Carlo Pesenti, president of Italcementi.

The Ambassador respected Costa as a man of moral worth, but soon divined that he did not understand problems outside business. He had come to maturity in the Fascist era, and was used to working under an authoritarian government, not a weak one like Scelba's. When she told him that Communist gains in last year's Italian elections were "a major worry" for the United States, he blustered that uninformed people were capable of voting for extreme parties while having "little sympathy" for them.

"We fell for this explanation once," Clare responded, "and the mistake cost us a) the loss of China, and b) the vast sacrifice in blood of the Korean War and imperilled all of Asia." She could hardly be expected to tell the Senate Appropriations Committee that Italians who voted Red were aid-worthy because "they are not *really* Commies."

She ventured close to interference in Italian corporate affairs in a meeting with Vittorio Valletta, managing director of the enormous Fiat car company based in Turin, and a close friend of Scelba's. Speaking in French, she stressed the State Department's reluctance to award offshore procurement contracts to any Italian plant with Communist-controlled unions. A scared Valletta later sent her a report attesting that Fiat was hiring three hundred new workers well trained in corporate values to be future foremen, while sacking "turbulent elements" and restricting suspected leftist subversives to the spare parts section.[27]

In Paris that February, Cyrus L. Sulzberger, the chief foreign correspondent of *The New York Times,* became curious about the political crisis in Rome. "I have decided to make a tour of Italy," he wrote in his diary, "to confirm or deny Clare Luce's asseverations to Washington that it is going Communist unless we intervene. I think she's nuts and merely wants to make a big name for herself as an activist in her first diplomatic job."[28]

Sulzberger decided to postpone seeing her until toward the end of his survey. He spent three weeks traveling from Turin and Venice to Naples and Calabria, meeting as she had done with a wide spectrum of Italian leaders, but including Communists as well as religious and cultural figures.

Alcide De Gasperi, he reported, was near tears when criticizing Clare Luce's "misguided" attempts to enlist the Right against the Communists. "It is difficult for us to form a government with the Monarchists, as your ambassador wants. . . . You cannot expect us democrats who fought fascism to join with fascism."[29] Nenni said that he was not bound to the Communists.[30] Aldo Cucci, an anti–Stalinist Party member in Bologna, a Communist hot spot, told Sulzberger that the peasants of Italy were "only temporary Communists." Like their nineteenth-century Russian predecessors, their aim was to own their own land, while factory workers were more drawn to Communism, because they had no illusions about ever becoming bosses.[31] Cardinal Lecaro, Bishop of the same city, said that the Catholicism of the Italian people was "shallow." Marxism-Leninism appealed to them because it was presented by the party as an alternative religion, with its own iconic images.[32]

Sulzberger, a good-looking, forty-one-year-old Harvard graduate, finally met with Clare on March 5. He was seated next to her at a Villa Taverna dinner, and for the next four hours was subjected to a monologue that was part seduction and part policy lecture.

> I was appalled. She is an exceptionally beautiful woman—quite astonishingly so when one considers her age. She had the (lifted) skin of a girl and an excellent figure. But this exterior conceals the most arrogant conceit and the most ruthlessly hard-boiled self-assurance it has ever been my privilege to come up against. Furthermore, Mrs. Luce blandly assumes that she has everybody eating out of her hand in a few minutes' time.

Clare told Sulzberger that she kept a scrapbook "filled" with his articles, apparently thinking it would guarantee his loyalty. She added that one of his colleagues had written that she imagined she could save the situation in Italy by charm alone. "If he only knew," she said with mock humility.[33]

> She then turned—for the benefit of Lily Cannon, wife of the American Ambassador in Greece (and Lily was gnashing her teeth throughout the performance)—to the subject of the difficulties of being American ambassador in Italy. One of these difficulties is entertaining the thousands of Americans who pour through. . . . She has organized a system to take care of it. The lowest category . . . are invited to the embassy chancery at four o'clock in the afternoon, and Mrs. Luce goes down the line shaking hands with them as they stand around in the hallway. The people in this category she described as persons with letters from Congressmen . . . or people of no importance who assure her they voted for her in the Connecticut elections. The second category are people who are honored by invitations to cocktail parties. These are people recommended by more important political figures back home or by friends of hers, but who have no importance in themselves. The third category is invited to dinner. These, she said, looking at me with a soupy expression in her eyes, are "friends."[34]

Listening half-enthralled to Clare reeling off facts and figures to do with the Italian parliamentary scene, Sulzberger found himself wondering how she acquired all her knowledge.

> She spoke admiringly of such strong men as Turkey's Kemal Ataturk, and Egypt's General Naguib and Colonel Nasser, who had helped overthrow King Farouk, because men like them could rule Italy with an iron hand, and turn it over to democracy when they died.
>
> At this point she interrupted her steady stream to say that her husband had just come back from Egypt. He had arrived just before the recent *coup d'état* but had stayed long enough to straighten things out and, she added with a giggle, to get Naguib back in. She said he had had a long talk with Colonel Nasser trying to persuade him to institute freedom of the press. I have not noticed any success along these lines. She also said that despite the miserable gap

between power and wealth in Italy, Harry had told her that in Egypt the "fellowhens" (here, of course, she meant the fellahin) were worse off than the Italian peasants.[35]

Growing more indiscreet as the evening wore on, Clare showed what struck Sulzberger as "the most extraordinary contempt . . . for the intellectual acuteness of apparently everybody." She said that Italians were "corrupt cowards who are unable to govern themselves by democratic means," and that "the government never passed any decent tax laws or slaps tax cases against the rich because it is bribed by the rich."[36]

When the meal came to an end, Sulzberger was amused to see that Harry, acting as "hostess," had to take the ladies and a few other guests into a separate room, while Clare settled down over brandy with himself and Arnaldo Cortesi, the veteran Rome correspondent of *The New York Times*. They were joined by Elbridge Durbrow.

As she explained the intricacies of the [political] situation and her own brilliance in handling it, she would occasionally turn to Durbrow and say, "Durby, isn't that so?" Whereupon Durbrow would nod sagely and add a platitude like, "Yes, the ambassador really handled that one well." With a claque like that it is easy to see why her self-esteem floats blandly along.[37]

▽

Clare's first audience with Prime Minister Mario Scelba was instigated by him that first week of March. Squat, bald, and bespectacled, he inscrutably refused to have an interpreter in the room, and spoke at great speed in a Sicilian accent for ninety minutes. She complained to the State Department afterward that her Italian, "while good enough to understand the sense of everything, is not good enough to get fine shades of meaning or subtle points." However, she did understand Scelba when, discussing the left-wing threat that so disturbed her, he surprisingly said, "If we must have civil war, we need to *prepare* for it."

Interrupting, she asked why he used the word *need*—did he mean that his police and *carabinieri* were currently unable to handle real trouble? Was she afraid of "the paramilitary strength of the CP"?

Not answering directly, he inquired what the United States would do "if such a situation did develop." Clare had no authority to speak on that point, she said, but believed the Eisenhower administration would, in its own interest, back his government.

She then read him her list of policy instructions, and was encouraged when he signaled assent to all of them, especially, to her surprise, ratification by Italy of the European Defense Community Treaty.[38] But she noticed, as he spoke, that he fidgeted with an ivory amulet carved in the shape of a fist with two fingers. To Italians it symbolized protection against "the evil eye."

Back at the embassy, she said to her CIA chief, "You know Gerry, I think he kept pointing that damned thing at me!"[39]

▽

By now, Clare was being harshly criticized in the American liberal press for diplomacy that emphasized the State Department's toughened offshore procurement policy. The *New Republic*'s Frank Gorrell accused her of a misguided "crusade" waged in tandem with right-wing Christian Democrats "who, in common with some important elements of the Roman Catholic Church, would like a 'regime,' if not of the Mussolini kind, then of the supposedly milder Salazar kind," as in Portugal.

Having thus, in effect, called Clare a Fascist, Gorrell went on to say that the greatest asset enjoyed by Italy's Popular Front was the failure of Christian Democrats to solve the chronic unemployment problem. It would be a tragedy if the only powerful and cohesive political entity in the country were to lose its progressive wing and "become a party of privilege and reaction, a party of resistance to urgently necessary social reforms."

In conclusion, Gorrell stated that Ambassador Luce's "psychological warfare" in Italy was helping rather than hindering the Popular Front, and suggested that the Eisenhower administration was trying to bring about a new policy of "neo-isolationism in military strategy."[40]

The latter was exactly what the President wanted. Never again, if he could prevent it, should American soldiers have to fight in European wars, hence his efforts to get Italy to join the EDC.

Pressure continued to build on Clare. Frustrating news came from London that the secret Trieste negotiations had run into obstacles—Velebit was more demanding than anticipated. This left her sounding desperate. "Any hope of a settlement in the near future seems to have gone aglimmering," she wrote Dulles. The Scelba government was still so weak that only a pro-Italian Trieste solution would save it and prevent a forced election in October. That, in turn, might lead to "an eventual Communist *coup d'état* or civil war." It was entirely possible, she felt, "that Italy could be the powder keg of World War III."

To avoid disaster, a "vast direct economic program" was necessary. Even that might not be enough to assuage the crisis. "Half the Communists in Europe are right here. . . . And their numbers are growing. What are we expected to stop them with, if not Trieste?"[41]

▽

On the evening of Thursday, March 25, when Clare was in Paris for a NATO meeting, the Italian newsmagazine *L'Europeo* published what it claimed was an eyewitness report of her off-the-record remarks at the Mayflower Hotel in Washington in January. She was quoted as saying, among many other things, that Italian politics were "confused and weak," portending a Communist government within three years, and that Latin men had "a kind of inferiority complex which gives way to a sense of superiority when they have to deal with a female."[42]

Before she had a chance to react, thirty-four Communist Senators in the Italian Parliament accused her of "unwarranted" interference in Italian affairs, and demanded her recall. In the Chamber of Deputies, Togliatti, amplifying his earlier imprecations, slandered her as "an aging witch."[43]

On Saturday, March 27, Clare issued a denial.

An article published last week in an Italian magazine, which purported to be substantially the text of a speech I am supposed to have made to American correspondents during my recent visit to the United States, twists, distorts, and utterly misrepresents my views on Italy, her problems and her leaders. The article is a fabrication pure and simple. I made no such speech.[44]

This statement was far from true. In the first place, *L'Europeo* had been careful to emphasize that "the text we publish is not a stenographic literal one, but rather an account written by one of the journalists present at the Mayflower luncheon. . . . This does not in any way mean . . . that the text is not substantially faithful to the original."[45]

In addition, nothing Clare was reported as saying differed much from what she had opined in private to American and Italian officials. She was understandably resorting to a public figure's hoary excuse that off-the-record remarks had been misquoted.

Writing a long letter to Harry that night from Fontainebleau, Clare sounded depressed and somewhat paranoid. She complained that the leak to *L'Europeo* had done "tremendous mischief," and probably came from New Dealers in the State Department. "What usefulness I had to Italy was badly damaged by the Trieste affair. This article damages it even more."

She dreaded returning to Rome, and felt the best she could do for the moment was to say nothing more. "I cannot help but take comfort from the usual question I ask: 'What is the worst that can happen?' The worst is, of course, that I could be recalled."

Even if she stayed, she despaired of seeing a permanent beneficial effect from her tenure. "In the end, there will be no Italian 'democracy' unless it is aggressive red, or neutralist pink. And the alternative is Fascist black." Such prospects made her long to be home and free of political entanglements—"really retiring, writing, *praying* again."

Then came a passionate outburst. "Please darling, think *hard* about the least damaging way of getting me home. The fact is, I've been given an impossible task. . . . I do feel that I am wasting my time, wrecking my health."[46]

On Sunday, the State Department expressed support of its beleaguered envoy. But the next morning, L'Europeo's editors insisted on the accuracy of their account, even though Mrs. Luce denied it.[47]

Back in Rome, Clare learned that buildings in many Italian cities were being plastered with posters denouncing her evil eye and diabolical scheming.[48] One, depicting her as Madame Frankenstein, appeared near Letitia Baldrige's apartment. She tore it off the wall and brought it to Clare, who laughed. "Tish, you have a lesson to learn that I learned long ago. Never take yourself seriously."[49]

In fact, she was alarmed by this graphic campaign, and felt vulnerable at her next meeting with Scelba on April 5. It was a bruising encounter. The Prime Minister, apparently emboldened by her discomfiture over the L'Europeo revelations, said that American attempts to bully Fiat by withholding contracts were "short-sighted and hysterical," and would only increase unemployment and the power of Communism in Italy. In her report to Dulles, Clare characterized Scelba's pitch as, "Put up *and* shut up."[50]

To comfort herself as her fifty-first birthday approached, as well as "to compete with the principesses" of Rome, she had a twenty-seven-stone emerald-and-diamond necklace reset by Bulgari. "And now," Dorothy Farmer wrote Harry, "what she would like 'most of all' is for you to take care of the bill."[51]

Knowing how much stress she was under, he had already bought a special gift for April 10, and arranged with Tish to surprise his wife with it during his absence. In her mail that morning, Clare found a cable from him: "Happy birthday to my Madonna of the Roses." It puzzled her, because there appeared to be no accompanying present.

"If you come downstairs," Tish said, "you'll see what he means."

Descending the staircase in her robe, Clare was overwhelmed by a Renaissance portrait of the Madonna and Child in the Piccolo Salon. Mary's gold halo glimmered in contrast with the pearly skin of the baby Jesus, against a background of trellised dark red roses.[52]

"She is hanging now where the Delacroix was, the two Fantin La Tours on either side . . . and how extraordinarily well they go," she wrote Harry, saying she had never liked a picture better.[53]

She continued to feel jittery, cranky, and miserable about her press image, and doubled her previous order of Benzedrine and Dexedrine to two hundred tablets of each. These, combined with other prescriptions for Edrisal (a concoction of Benzedrine, aspirin, and phenacetin for headaches and cramps), Carbatral (a sedative-hypnotic bromide), and two drugs identified only as "#254763" for nervousness and "#254764" for insomnia, indicated a potentially lethal drug dependency.[54] On top of them, she was taking the antacid pills Spasmalgan and Syntrogel, plus Trasentine tablets and weekly injections of Theelin hormone replacement.

Clare relied on at least three physicians for her supplies. Dr. Milton Rosenbluth wrote, "I send these [Benzedrines] to you with misgivings, because your need for them means to me that you are working at a pace beyond your physical capacity. If you keep this up, I greatly fear that you will reach a point at which even this stimulation will prove inadequate."[55]

Aware that the first anniversary of her arrival in Rome was coming soon, and that mischief-makers in the Italian Parliament might well begin to debate her recall that day, Clare sent a cri de coeur to her best friend in Congress, Speaker Joseph Martin.

My press clippings from home are beginning to show that the Democrats have started to pick up the Commie charge of "intervention" in Italy's affairs, without either giving the source or basis of the charges. A visiting fireman coming thru said the other day that they are beginning to mutter in his State (where there is a large foreign language vote) "Everything began to go sour in Italy the minute she got there. . . ."

Fact is, we now have here a government that has introduced EDC, and proposed and taken more anti-Communist measures and economic reform measures than any government Italy has had so far. And . . . I haven't had a single billion—not even fifty million with which to get this effect! IF IF IF we could get a Trieste solution for Italy, things would really begin to roll our way, over here, and we could probably chalk up for GOP foreign policy one of its first political victories in Europe!

She asked Martin if he could get Senator Homer S. Ferguson (R-MI) "or some other big shot name in the Congress" to enter this defense into the *Congressional Record* in such a way that it did not seem to emanate from her.[56]

Ferguson agreed, but was unable to get an immediate speech slot. Fortunately, on April 22, the dreaded debate on Clare's recall did not take place in the Chamber of Deputies. Foreign Minister Attilio Piccioni declared Ambassador Luce "not only *persona grata*, but *gratissima*, to the Italian government."[57] Giuseppe Pella called on her privately to say that the *L'Europeo* article had actually generated support for her, and Togliatti's attacks had "backfired."[58]

An anniversary telegram that day from Elbridge Durbrow cheered her further: "I want to express to you on my behalf and on the behalf of the rest of the staff how pleased we are to be on board with you as our skipper."[59]

But insecurity about keeping her post had taken its toll. In an interview at the Villa Taverna with William Attwood of *Look* magazine, Clare sipped vermouth and smoked incessantly, giving guarded answers to his questions. "She strikes you as fragile on the outside but flinty on the inside," Attwood noted. "Her inner tension is contagious; you don't relax easily with her." On the whole, he was impressed, although "as a diplomat, Clare Luce tries too hard and talks too much." It was time, he felt, "for her to stay out of the headlines—if she can—and let the Italians put their own house in order without too much gratuitous advice."[60]

▽

On May 3, Senator Ferguson addressed his colleagues on the subject of "a rather astounding incident that has recently taken place in Italy." He said the demand of Palmiro Togliatti that Ambassador Clare Boothe Luce be recalled had been expressed in language "unparalleled in its viciousness, untruthfulness, and lack of parliamentary courtesy." In particular, he cited the phrase *aging witch*, as well as almost daily references in the Red press to the Ambassador's appearance, sex, and motives for allegedly interfering in the internal affairs of Italy. "The fact that Mrs. Luce was merely enunciating the United States foreign policy, as repeatedly laid down by the White House, the State Department, the Congress, and every responsible public-opinion medium in America was naturally ignored by the Communists."

The Senator added to the *Congressional Record* a pair of *New York Herald Tribune* articles supportive of Clare, one of which, by the syndicated columnist Roscoe Drummond, stated "from first-hand knowledge" that *L'Europeo's* account of her Mayflower Hotel lunch was false "in substance and spirit."[61]

Even as the Senator spoke, Clare had the satisfaction of hearing Secretary Dulles, who was passing through Italy on his way back from a conference in Geneva, reiterate to Scelba's face everything she had said about the linking of American aid to anti-Communist action. Changing the subject, Scelba fell back on the Italian mantra that if the question of Trieste could be settled along the lines of the Allied Declaration of October 8, 1953, ratification of the EDC treaty would follow.

Irritated, Dulles said that if European military unity was not attained soon, "the Trieste question would disappear in the wake of far more serious international developments."

Foreign Minister Attilio Piccioni, sitting in, insisted that such unity must recognize "national claims" of member states.

Dulles came back even more forcefully. "If Western European countries continue to advance the satisfaction of individual claims ahead of the supreme need for unification to preserve the freedom of all, the price of such disunity will be either a) another war among European states, or b) their piecemeal conquest—by internal or external means or both—by the Soviet Union."[62]

Clare was further buoyed that month by having Harry back in Rome, and by the publication of a respectful but clear-eyed essay about her in a book by Eleanor Roosevelt and Lorena A. Hickok entitled *Ladies of Courage.*

She has many advantages. She can always get publicity, she has a way of speaking and writing that is easily understandable to the

American people, and as a writer she has developed powers of observation and analysis which should be helpful. . . . Whether or not she has a basic understanding and sympathy with all people, she has keen intelligence. . . .

One thing she may have to guard against: that well-developed, but at times caustic, sense of humor, as indicated in some of the widely quoted reports of her brushes with other women. In diplomacy, it is better to trust to kindliness and beware the witty but cutting phrase.[63]

▽

On May 31, top-secret news reached Clare from London. Velebit had agreed to a Trieste proposal that the Allies considered fair and were determined Italy should accept. To an impartial eye, the proposal amounted to acceptance of the October 8 Declaration, with some minor territorial adjustments, reparation of transferable assets, and guaranteed protection of minorities in both zones.[64]

But when Clare met with Scelba on June 3, the Prime Minister was furious. He had seen the text of the proposal and was inclined to reject it outright. It was, he said, "a slash in the face of Italy." By implicitly condoning Yugoslavia's demands, the United States showed it was not on Italy's side, so she could forget about speedy ratification of the EDC, or his signature on military facility agreements.[65]

Subtle signals of a willingness to proceed anyway with negotiations soon emanated from the Italian Foreign Office. Ambassador Brosio was instructed to concentrate on improving the territorial concessions when he began his round of meetings with Harrison and Thompson in London.[66] From now until whenever he fulfilled his brief, Clare knew she would inevitably be drawn back into the Trieste entanglement.

Harry left for New York on June 5. "I really did feel sorry for CBL when the car drove off," Dorothy Farmer wrote Dorothea Philp. "How quickly loneliness descends—and how visibly. She walked into the drawing room with me and said ever so quietly: 'It's so awful to see him leave.'"[67]

37

END OF THE DRAMA

The only way to make a man trustworthy is to trust him.

—Henry L. Stimson

T wo days later, suffering from what she thought was an attack of rheumatism, Clare arrived at the Hôtel Splendide-Royal et Excelsior in
Aix-les-Bains for a week of spa pampering. She found herself in the
same suite overlooking Lac du Bourget that she had shared with Harry
fifteen years before.

Benefiting somewhat from daily massages and a low-calorie diet, she
managed eight hours of unsedated sleep for the first time in months.
Between treatments, she followed press accounts of the Army-McCarthy
hearings being held in Washington and televised live to huge audiences. After seven weeks of contentious questioning, Senator McCarthy's reputation as a principled anti-Communist was ruined. Clare was
disgusted by what she considered a domestic sideshow to the "Orwellian" threat of Communism in Europe and Asia, as well as by Eisenhower's reluctance to denounce the Senator publicly. She wrote an
angry letter to Harry.

> How in the name of God and country can responsible men, Amer-
> ican men, in the year 1954, spend their time, energy, and vitality

fighting the "menace of McCarthyism," when all they have of all three should be turned to the menace of Malenkov? That a whole nation, and its journalists, and politicians, and president and educators should be [so] absorbed for weeks and weeks . . . is in itself a national scandal in which all sides, those for and against this petty tyrant, are equally blind, equally lacking in patriotism, equally foolish, equally treasonable, so far as I am concerned. Let the president . . . offer Joe [McCarthy] a fighting commission against the foe he claims to despise, and thus call his bluff—let [Ike] play the role of a fearless and honest patriot and a good soldier, which is what we elected him to be . . . and you would soon see what stuff America was made of.[1]

In spite of rest and therapy, her constitution remained far from robust. "If I can get my health ironed out," she wrote Dorothy Farmer, "I can mebbe get around to ironing out my 'spiritual life,' and get to Mass a couple of mornings a week."[2]

▽

On July 9, Clare was in Washington for four days of meetings with the President and State Department officials. She reported that Ambassador Brosio was being flexible on some minor points of the Yugoslav Trieste proposal, though not yet moving on the more intractable issue of territorial distribution. She told newsmen that she expected an agreement "in the not too distant future," prompting Paolo Taviani, the Italian Defense Minister, to write in his diary, "Clare Luce . . . is working for us."[3]

Three days later, *The New York Times* carried a special Rome dispatch by Arnaldo Cortesi (her dinner guest at the Villa with Sulzberger the previous March) headlined BASIS FOR ACCORD ON TRIESTE IS SET. He wrote that a "provisional" agreement had been reached, "with Zone A and the city of Trieste going to Italy and Zone B to Yugoslavia." This did not sound like news to the average reader, but to diplomatic experts, the words that followed were significant: "Some territorial adjustments of secondary importance will take place along the present line of demarcation between the two zones."

Each side, Cortesi reported, would insist on maintaining an ethnic foothold in the other's land. He identified these as the village of Crevatini in Zone A to go to Yugoslavia, and a strip of Zone B hinterland

390

south of San Cervolo to Italy. If this exchange was agreed on, he predicted that the United States would reap an additional benefit from a grateful Italy: prompt ratification of the EDC.

Especially pleasing to Clare was a subsequent paragraph.

> The Trieste agreement is a victory for Ambassador Clare Boothe Luce, who floated the problem off the reef on which it had foundered some years before her arrival in Italy as United States envoy and headed it toward a solution. Her achievement is the more remarkable because the agreement is, in effect, a carbon copy, with a few embellishments, of the United States–British declaration of Oct. 8, 1953. This declaration . . . was originally suggested by Mrs. Luce and was made as a result of her insistence.[1]

In a follow-up dispatch on July 17, Cortesi noted that there had been "some eleventh-hour hitches in the negotiations." But he was confident they could be ironed out.

Clare and her Washington superiors were not so sanguine. She wrote a forceful letter to Dr. Grillo at the American desk in the Chigi Palace, warning that if Italy continued to be obstructionist on Trieste and the EDC, the United States would have to make, in Secretary Dulles's words, an "agonizing reappraisal" of its Mediterranean policy, specifically in regard to defense and aid programs.[5]

▽

Having felt under par for several months, Clare entered New York Hospital on July 20 for what she insisted was a routine checkup. Aware that this would become a news story in Italy, she wrote Dr. Grillo that her physician was curious as to how, with so little sleep, she had so much vitality. "It must be either pathology or pasta—I sho' do miss the latter."

As she well knew, Dr. Rosenbluth was less curious than concerned about her chemical dependencies, and was especially alarmed by her frequent attacks of bronchitis, sinusitis, colitis, rheumatism, and bouts of fever, not to mention gingivitis and ulcers between the teeth.[6]

On August 4, Dr. Rosenbluth reported that he had found alarming evidence of "heavy metal poisoning" in her system. This perplexing diagnosis coincided with a demonstration of Clare's Red menace phobia. In Washington on August 10, she startled the White House Press Secretary, James C. Hagerty, by declaring that America needed to "do something fast" to arrest the world's drift toward Communism, by gaining either a political advantage, or "if necessary . . . a military victory."

Hagerty asked if she was suggesting an armed attack, and if so, where. Clare staggered him by saying, "Yes." She thought that the Chinese mainland opposite Formosa was the most likely spot, and offered to send him a written outline of her thoughts to give to the President. He reluctantly agreed to pass it on.[7]

Before she could complete follow-up forensic tests in New York, word came from Italy that Alcide De Gasperi had died. Clare flew to Rome with Harry on August 22 for the funeral, discomfiting other ambassadors reluctant to leave vacation resorts. After the ceremony, she made an eloquently simple statement: "All countries must have a past, a present and a future. Democratic Italy had no past. Now the memory of her late Prime Minister is her past."[8]

Maddening news awaited her at the Palazzo Margherita. During a conference of potential member nations of the European Defense Community in Brussels, the dynamic new French Premier, Pierre Mendès France, had scuttled its formative treaty. His reasoning, logical but frustrating to America, was that West Germany was no longer a threat to the rest of Europe, and that the nuclear capability of the United States coupled with NATO was formidable enough to repel any potential enemy, including the Soviets.

At least Clare no longer had to listen to Scelba link the EDC to a pro-Italian Trieste settlement. But he did startle her at a postfuneral meeting, saying that in spite of Mendès France's "act of mayhem," Italy would give "wholehearted support to any alternative American project for German rearmament." Otherwise, he feared that the idea of an integrated Europe was dead. "We can then be certain of only one thing: Russian divisions will not invade Italian soil. They will not need to, because our own Communists will ring down the Iron Curtain on Italy in the next election."

In her report to Eisenhower on this disturbing interview, Clare predicted that Scelba's government would "not last the winter . . . *unless* we can produce a settlement of the Trieste question—and immediately." She hoped that would be before October 8, the anniversary of last year's Declaration.[9] A catalyst was urgently needed to break the latest deadlock in London.

Just at this juncture, as she was dressing for dinner one night, Dorothy Farmer came in. "There is a man called Robert Low on the telephone."

The name meant nothing to Clare. Dorothy said that he claimed to have once worked for Harry. "He says he has to see you. He won't talk to anyone else."

Clare told her to hold the call while she asked Harry if he knew Low.

"Yes," he said. "Bob Low was a very smart lad who worked for us. . . . See him, find out what he has to say."

When the mysterious visitor arrived, Clare was reassured by his good looks and confident demeanor. "I have been doing some work for the CIA in Yugoslavia," he told her. "Their man in London is giving our people trouble, and I know why."[10]

At this, he took a map of the Istrian peninsula from his pocket, and showed her a red-penciled area of disputed territory. He predicted Velebit would settle for this, were it not for the chief cause of the stalemate in London—money for infrastructure reparations in Zone A that Yugoslavia was demanding and Italy reluctant to pay. "You give them that . . . you're in."[11]

Clare learned next day that the two sides were $30 million apart, and neither disposed to budge. She asked Chigi officials if a substantial cash contribution from the United States might make Italy willing to offer more—on condition Yugoslavia settled for less. The result was a beaming assent.[12]

By late August, she was back in New York, still feeling unwell, and having an extensive medical examination. It revealed that she was suffering from "symptoms of serious anemia and of extreme nervous fatigue."[13] Postponing treatment, she hurried to the capital with her new idea on Trieste.

There she was successful in obtaining an administration commitment to pay Italy at least half, if not more, of the $30 million. But first Tito must be persuaded to yield a little extra territory, if only to give Brosio a feeling of effectiveness as a negotiator. The question was, what would persuade the Marshal?

Providentially, it turned out to be *who*. At a dinner in Washington on September 2, Clare found herself seated next to Robert D. Murphy, Eisenhower's Under Secretary for Political Affairs. She knew him to be a consummate diplomat, experienced in both intelligence and military matters. He asked her about Trieste. The key to a settlement, she said, was held by Tito. "If only there were someone who knew him well enough to twist his arm."[14]

Yugoslavia, she added, was hoping for a free, four-hundred-thousand-ton wheat shipment from the United States, so all the intermediary needed to say was, "Okay, you sign or no wheat."

"I could say that to him," Murphy said. "I knew Tito in the war."[15]

The following day, Clare asked the President to let his aide go to Belgrade and "handle it" for them. Eisenhower and Dulles authorized the covert mission. As Murphy said afterward, "Ambassador Luce usually got what she wanted."[16]

▽

Twelve days later, he reached Belgrade, only to be informed that Tito was at his new palace on the island of Brioni, off the Dalmatian coast. Before going there, he learned from Vice President Svetozar Vukmanović-Tempo the true extent of Yugoslavia's wheat deficit. At 1.3 million tons, it was the worst the country had ever known, due to the failure of Marxist collective farming. Murphy postponed any mention of Clare's proposed wheat deal, and on September 16 proceeded to Brioni, where Tito welcomed him as an old wartime friend.

The Marshal was in a jovial mood, and over lunch enjoyed Murphy's joke about a hole at the Chevy Chase golf course called "Trieste," because it was about as big as the territory under discussion in London.[17] Murphy then handed over a personal letter from Eisenhower. Tito absented himself for twenty minutes to read it in his study. Ike had discreetly said nothing about money or wheat, asking only that Yugoslavia slightly extend the southern tip of Zone A. "I want you to understand that in urging this further small concession I am not blind to the great contribution you've already made."[18]

When Tito returned, he made clear that he was weary of the protracted Trieste affair, and said he would offer Italy a choice of two settlements. One was to move the interzonal boundary south of Punta Sottile, with Italy retaining a triangle of Zone B hinterland. The alternative was to move the boundary even further south, but with no Italian occupancy of Zone B.[19]

Murphy astutely sensed that it would be indelicate to say anything about Clare's wheat deal now. Instead, he returned to Belgrade and proposed it to Aleš Bebler, the Yugoslav Under Secretary of State for Foreign Affairs.[20] Leaving Bebler to discuss the matter with colleagues, he flew on to Rome on September 18, and met with Clare, now back at her post. She told him that Italy had a new Foreign Minister, Gaetano Martino, who was more flexible than his predecessor, Piccioni. This boded well for the final stage of Murphy's mission.[21]

A couple of days later, he delivered Tito's two offers to the Chigi Palace, and made it clear that Italy had to choose one or the other. He then, in company with Clare, said the same to Scelba. The Prime Minister grumbled that Italy was being required to make yet another sacrifice so that Tito might be seduced further from Moscow into the Western sphere. But he agreed to choose one of the Yugoslav alternatives, saying momentously, "We are at the end of the drama."[22]

On September 22, Italy formally accepted Tito's second proposal, thereby gaining all of Zone A, as well as the free port of Trieste. The government also undertook to pay Yugoslavia $30 million in real estate reparations, of which $18 million—the "substantial cash contribution" Clare had hinted at, on the advice of Bob Low—would come from the United States. The agreement remained classified, pending an exchange of documents.[23]

At 5:00 P.M. on October 5, the final *accordo in forma semplice* was signed in London by Italy, Yugoslavia, and the three Allies, including France. Clare called an immediate press conference. No one in the audience had an inkling of what she was about to say. Adapting a phrase from Woodrow Wilson's Fourteen Points, she announced in triumph, "We settled the Trieste problem by open covenants secretly arrived at."[24]

After a moment of stunned silence, one skeptical reporter asked, "Mrs. Ambassador, do you mean to say you didn't tell your husband about these negotiations?"

"I could not," she replied. "Under his rules, he would have to give some publicity to the matter."[25]

That evening, as church bells tolled in Trieste and an enormous Italian flag was raised in the Piazza dell'Unità, Clare went to the diplomatic gallery of the Senate and watched as cheers broke out on the floor below.[26]

The following day, Maggie Case sent a note congratulating "a diplomat come of age." She continued ecstatically, "Everybody has been dancing in the New York streets, drinking your health at parties, delighted to know you. 'Clare has done it!'" One of those toasting the Ambassador was her erstwhile critic Cy Sulzberger.[27]

In its report of the settlement, the New York Daily News noted that European commentators were giving Ambassador Luce credit "for her

The Italian flag rises over Trieste, October 26, 1954

tireless eighteen-month effort to reach a compromise in the Italo-Yugoslav dispute. Her diplomacy and tenacity paid off."

The *New York Journal* said she deserved praise for "having overcome a great many obstacles since she went to Italy, among them the Latin hostility to women in high position."

Clare celebrated with a champagne-and-caviar party for embassy staff involved in the Trieste settlement, particularly clerks and assistants who had worked many twenty-hour shifts in the code room.[28] She also attended an official lunch in her honor at the Villa Madama. Count Vittorio Zoppi, head of the Italian Foreign Office, presented her with a gold cigarette case, encrusted with the fleur-de-lys emblem of Trieste in rubies and brilliants.[29] It took a moment for her to recognize the object as an old gift from Harry. Tish Baldrige had smuggled it out of the Villa Taverna for embellishment.

Clare burst into tears, and even Zoppi brushed his eyes.[30]

▽

In bleak, windy weather on October 26, Allied troops withdrew from Trieste. After nine years of occupation, they were in such a hurry to leave that they did not wait for Italian troops to replace them. Gianni Bartoli, the mayor of the city, joyously wired President Eisenhower:

TRIESTES POPULATION GRATEFUL . . . HAIL YOU AND YOUR
COLLABORATION [SIC] MRS CLAIRE BOOTH LUCE AS CHIEF
ORIGINANTS OF THIS RESULT . . . THREATS TO PEACE
RECEDING . . . IN EVERY WORLDS COUNTRY.[31]

Whatever pleasure Clare felt at the resolution of her biggest diplomatic challenge was overshadowed by public speculation that she was about to quit her job and—more seriously—by private confirmation from a U.S. Navy doctor that her recent ailments were caused by arsenic poisoning.

The resignation rumors were denied by Harry on arrival at Idlewild Airport in New York. "Oh no, not again," he said to reporters. "We have about sixty ambassadors and I can't see her resigning in the forseeable future any more than the other fifty-nine."[32] *Time* followed up with a firm rebuttal.[33]

Harry was, however, alarmed enough to show the navy document to Dr. Rosenbluth, who immediately wrote Clare, saying he did not know the basis for the diagnosis. "But arsenic is one of the poisons which can affect the peripheral nerves and cause a neuropathy. . . . I think it is important that a test be made of your urine to determine whether or not arsenic is present."[34]

Clare had this done in Rome and the analysis showed nothing abnormal. But Rosenbluth said she could still have ingested enough arsenic to bring on other symptoms.[35] She was not entirely surprised. Over the past eighteen months she had suffered from anemia, nervous fatigue, nausea, cramps, irritability, a dragging numbness in her right foot, and most recently brittle nails, loosening teeth, and fragile hair that came out in clumps.[36]

Without delay, she scheduled an appointment with the United States Navy Hospital in Naples for "sinus" treatment.

▽

On November 2, in a double blow to the Eisenhower administration, the Republican Party lost control of both Houses of Congress. Clare's friend Joe Martin had to hand over his Speakership gavel to Samuel T. Rayburn of Texas. In the Senate, Rayburn's fellow Texan Lyndon B. Johnson became majority leader with a thin margin buttressed by the support of an Independent, Wayne L. Morse of Oregon.

Commiserating with Martin, Clare wrote that the Italian press saw the vote as a win for Achesonian diplomacy. "I wasn't called home to help in the elections," she complained. If she had been, she would have urged Ike to make more of his foreign policy successes, including Trieste. It occurred to her that in nineteen months of service, she had spent a total of only one hour with Eisenhower, and about an hour and a half with Dulles.[37]

On the plus side, she had made good on her threats of aid withheld from Italian manufacturers with Communist-dominated unions. She had recently canceled a $7.528 million warship construction project in Palermo, and an $18 million munitions contract in Milan. Fearful they might be the Ambassador's next target, 1,920 workers in the Fiat Avio plant in Turin voted against Red leadership, with only 77 in favor. As a result, she had come under renewed left-wing attack in Italy and America.

"If you've ever written a play," she told Durbrow, "you're used to criticism."[38]

Fiat shows Clare a fleet of F-86s built with U.S. aid

At least it was better than being ignored, which was how Carlos Chávez felt at her hands. She received a stiff notification from him, saying that he was attending the First Festival of Latin American Music in Venezuela. "My Symphony No. 3, commissioned by you, and dedicated to Ann Clare, will be premiered here . . . under my direction on December 9."[39]

He added that he had sent the full score to her in August, with a follow-up letter in September, and received no acknowledgment of either. Nor had he been paid the $1,500 she owed on delivery. Actually, Clare had not been inactive on his behalf. She had sent the manuscript to Robert Irving, music director of the Sadler's Wells Ballet, for his opinion.[40]

Irving replied that he had tried the symphony out on the piano, and found it "extremely strong stuff," if "almost too self-consciously 'clever.'" He went on to say, "The whole work is certainly uncompromisingly modern (grim in parts), & *extremely* difficult to play: but as a conductor, I can honestly say that, given a good orchestra and adequate rehearsals, I should certainly welcome the opportunity of performing the work."[41]

Clare still did not respond to Carlos, perhaps because she had always imagined herself attending its first performance in a great auditorium on her own turf. So the premiere, played by the Venezuela Symphony Orchestra, took place in Caracas without her presence or blessing. Chávez had to settle for the praise of his fellow composer and friend Aaron Copland, who, after reading the score, wrote, "It deserves a prize!"

Judges at the event concurred, and gave Chávez the prestigious Caro de Bocsi Award.[42]

▽

In the opinion of the president and faculty of the University of Trieste, Ambassador Luce deserved a year-end tribute. They invited her to visit their campus and accept an honorary degree for having helped to secure the city for Italy. During the Allied occupation, the school had been a hotbed of Italian nationalism, and the only local institution that had defiantly flown the state flag. So on December 17, Clare and Harry made their first visit to the ancient port.[43]

Though founded by the Romans, and only a hundred miles east of Venice, Trieste looked more Austrian than Italian—the result of having been for centuries part of the Hapsburg Empire. Turkish elements in its architecture also betrayed its proximity to the Balkans. Curving dramatically around a broad swath of bay, it was walled off from the Slovene hinterland by the Carso, a ridge of high, bare limestone hills. They belonged to Yugoslavia, an oppressive reminder to Clare that the city was connected to Italy only by the narrowest riviera—formerly Zone A. It was on those heights that Stalin and Tito had stood together after World War II and plotted Trieste's future as the westernmost warmwater port of the Soviet bloc.[44] This had prompted Churchill's historic

Clare presented with a *Bersaglieri* cap at Trieste University,
December 17, 1954

warning, "From Stettin in the Baltic to Trieste in the Adriatic, an iron curtain has descended across the Continent."

In spite of wind and rain, Clare found the city larger, more beautiful, and more prosperous-looking than she had imagined. She could see why Italians were so passionate about possessing it. As her car, flying the American flag, pulled into the vast Piazza dell'Unità, an enthusiastic crowd of Triestini rushed forward, waving, smiling, and doffing their hats. She was welcomed by a delegation of civic dignitaries including Mayor Bartoli, who told her how extraordinarily popular the American resident troops had been, and how much the citizenry regretted seeing them sail away, taking many local girls as wives.[45]

Before receiving her degree at a ceremony in Piazzale Europa, Clare donned the traditional scholar's *Bersaglieri* black-feathered cap, with a long, projecting brim and dangling silk tassels on the right side. She concluded her acceptance address with a few paragraphs of carefully rehearsed Italian.[46]

> *Grazie, Chiarissimo Rettore, per avermi invitato a visitare questa grande e giovane Università, il cui nome è già celebre nella storia della cultura italiana. . . . E per l'onore che avete voluto tributarmi e per quanto esso significa per me e per il Paese che rappresento, permettetemi di porgervi il mio commosso ringraziamento.*

Ora che Trieste è entrata in una nuova fase della sua storia, questo Ateneo avrà ancora maggiori possibilità di arrichire la vita di tutta la comunità e della Nazione Italiana. . . .

Vorrei esprimerle i più sentiti e sinceri auguri del popolo americano per il glorioso futuro di questo eminente centro di pensiero e di cultura.[47]

38

NO BED OF ROSES

There are three species of creatures who when they seem
coming, are going: diplomats, women and crabs.

—John Hay

Clare arrived at Idlewild on January 3, 1955, on an Italian Airlines flight. She had deliberately avoided taking an American plane to show support for Italy's chief carrier, which had suffered a fatal accident only two weeks before. Approaching the same airport, one of its craft had crashed, burned, and sunk in icy Jamaica Bay. Twenty-six people had died, with only six survivors.[1]

This gesture added further luster to the Ambassador's prestige, coming as it did not long after her recent show of sympathy for thousands of homeless flood victims in Salerno. For two days, she had tramped in mud and rain, distributing food and other supplies.[2]

Between routine appointments at the State Department, Clare was interviewed again on *Longines Chronoscope*. "Never underestimate the power of a woman," said its host, Larry LeSueur, regarding the Trieste settlement. She spoke, as usual, authoritatively and with phenomenal self-possession, smiling often in spite of a newly prominent incisor.[3] On Thursday, the sixth, wearing a gray tweed suit and dark red lapel rose, she returned to her old forum and sat in the center of the House of Representatives for President Eisenhower's State of the Union message. At the Women's National Press Club a week later, she gave a major policy speech, "Italy in 1955," which was published in the *United States Department of State Bulletin*.[4] Next came a mostly laudatory *Newsweek* cover story entitled "Madam Ambassador Clare Boothe Luce: Her Versatile and Crowded Years."

> Mrs. Luce has now been 21 months at her post. Seldom has anyone done such a face-lifting job on a hostile public opinion. . . . She has been a puissant influence for bettering Italo-American relations.
>
> The explanation for her peculiar success is largely personal. She is, preeminently, the kind of ambassador who succeeds in making her own personality, for a time, do double duty as the image of her country. It is a strong personality—almost too strong for its owner's good.[5]

Clare's satisfaction might have been greater had she graced the cover of *Time*—the ultimate accolade for any contemporary public figure. As it happened, the magazine's portraitist, Boris Chaliapin, did paint her for that purpose. But Harry, always leery of nepotism charges, pulled it after seeing the mock-up.[6]

Encomiums proliferated. In Philadelphia on January 17, the anniversary of Benjamin Franklin's birth, Clare became the first woman ever to win the Poor Richard Club's Gold Medal of Achievement. Earlier honorees had included Dwight Eisenhower and Douglas MacArthur. Simultaneously, a half-page article on the foreign news page of Moscow's *Literaturnaya Gazeta* accused "Kler But Lus" of "giving commands and orders to the Italian government." The accompanying illustration caricatured her as a blonde policewoman wearing a swastika and wielding a club.[7]

▽

That same day in Rome, Elbridge Durbrow wrote Clare a highly confidential letter, forwarded in the State Department pouch. He said that U.S. Navy doctors in Naples had submitted their findings of her recent urinalysis to the more sophisticated laboratories of Bethesda Naval Hospital in Maryland. For security reasons, they had given her a mariner's pseudonym. The diagnosis sent back to Italy read: "Seaman Jones is a victim of arsenic poisoning."[8]

The Reinsch test she had taken showed that the "positive common metallic poison specimen" contained "6.0 micrograms of arsenic per

The *Time* cover that never ran. Boris Chaliapin's watercolor portrait
of Ambassador Clare Boothe Luce, late 1954

100 mls of urine." This finding had so alarmed the Naples doctors that Admiral Fechteler had authorized a jet fighter to deliver it to Rome.[9]

Durbrow feared political foul play. Had Communist agents infiltrated her kitchen? "I've been trying to rack my brain to figure the thing out," he wrote Clare, "but so far nothing concrete." He said he would discuss the next step with Gerry Miller. In the meantime, it was "urgent" that she have another test. Since arsenic traces "disappeared quickly," a clear result would prove that her ingestion was taking place in Rome.[10]

Forensic evidence in New York confirmed this suspicion. Durbrow stressed the need for absolute secrecy, pending a CIA investigation. Allen Dulles authorized a covert counterintelligence intervention. Two agents hurried to Rome, on the pretext of representing an architectural firm that might renovate the Villa Taverna. They first questioned all staff members handling Clare's meals. Satisfied, for the time being, that there were no subversives on the culinary payroll, they examined the Luces' private quarters.[11]

One agent searched Clare's bedroom, even checking inside the heels of her shoes. He noticed that a Linguaphone record on a turntable was covered with a film of grayish-white dust, and asked a maid how often the place was cleaned. She said every day. Searching further, he found the same dust in crevices of furniture and drapery folds, even on the Ambassador's cosmetic jars. He brushed some into an envelope and took it to a small chemistry laboratory that had been set up in the basement of Gerry Miller's house. Analysis of the sample indicated "a high content of arsenate of lead."[12]

On January 22, Durbrow telephoned Clare to say that the investigation was now focused on the ceiling of her bedroom—specifically its terra-cotta beams, which were ornamented with clusters of white roses. Over the past hundred years, the flowers had been painted with many layers of lead-laden pigment that exuded toxic fumes in humid weather. Moreover, the paint proved to have powdered under the vibration of a washing machine, in a laundry room directly above Clare's bed, and the constant traipsing of maids—"peasant girls clodhopping around up there," as Durbrow put it.[13]

Clare returned to Rome on February 2, and wrote Harry.

Well darling—the "mystery" is solved. Nothing very melodramatic. It was—or rather *is*—the ceiling in my bedroom. Or so the toxologist thinks. There is much arsenic and lead in the *old* paint.

It has been slowly slowly flaking off since I got here. . . . The flakes have dropped into my mouth when I slept, got on objects near my bed, and the slow accumulation over months of arsenic and lead became more than my system could throw off, and—there it is—it's true I have been poisoned daily for months on end—and not even for a very *good* reason.

Exacerbating the problem was her lifelong habit of spending hours in bed after a tray breakfast, drinking coffee, smoking, reading documents and newspapers, and dictating letters. If she had no evening appointments, she often went to bed early, working into the small hours. Sometimes she spent whole weekends between the sheets, her windows shut against Rome's variable weather. While following this routine for almost two years, she had been inhaling and absorbing a deadly toxin.[14]

The question then arose, why had Clare's predecessors not suffered similarly? The answer was that they had slept mostly in the master suite now occupied by Harry. This would seem to clear up the matter, but in the weeks that followed, the CIA continued its secret sleuthing so rigorously that not a word of the Ambassador's indisposition leaked to Italian officials or reporters. The reason went beyond any petty embarrassment she might feel, should her boudoir routine and marital sleeping arrangements become public. She compounded the mystery in a second, handwritten letter to Harry.

There's a new—and rather *horrid* development on subject "A" which has completely shattered the partial serenity I felt about the ceiling. I naturally can't put it into a letter, except to say that you'd better . . . talk to Allen [Dulles]. . . . It's all miserable and confusing, and a little frightening. At this moment it's hard to say how I'll come home—in a box, or in two weeks, with Scelba.[15]

She was deliberately cryptic, but Harry got her inference: the CIA suspected that not only dust threatened Clare. Conceivably, Italian Communists, in or out of government, were plotting more stringent means to dispense with the evil-eyed witch.

Again the possibility of sabotage of her food arose. The CIA had Tish Baldrige intercept Clare's daily breakfast tray and surreptitiously exchange it for one with "secure" food.[16]

Clare's reference to Scelba was prompted by the Prime Minister's intent to shore up his shaky government by visiting the United States at the end of March. Her concern was that if any hint of "Subject 'A'" became public, the resultant news stir could irreparably affect American-Italian relations. The mere fact that Washington was investigating whether its envoy in Rome was an assassination target would cause such outrage that Scelba might fall, precipitating new elections and—in her recurrent neurosis—a Communist victory at the polls. For that reason she, Tish, Durbrow, Miller, and Harry must maintain a wrap on the story.[17]

This hardly assuaged Clare's dread that she might precede Scelba across the Atlantic in a coffin. "I'm going to get out," she told Durbrow. "I'm not coming back here until they find out what the devil this is, where it's coming from."[18]

She flew home almost immediately, saying that she had to make advance arrangements for Scelba's tour. In her absence, workmen stretched canvas over the lethal ceiling, beams and all, with the intent of painting lead-free roses on it.[19]

By April 12, having accompanied Scelba around the country for two weeks, Clare was back in Rome. Three days later, she joined Harry in Siracusa, Sicily, for a weekend with Sir Winston Churchill, who had at last ceded his premiership to Anthony Eden. He now needed money to finance his extravagant mode of living. Harry obliged, paying $200,000 for *Life* serial rights to Churchill's four-volume *History of the English-Speaking Peoples*.[20]

The former statesman, now eighty, was staying with two friends and his wife, Clementine, at the Villa Politi. He loved bright colors, and appeared at dinner wearing a red siren suit and matching slippers.[21] Clare, reporting on the visit to Eisenhower, wrote that the cold and rainy weather "was as un-Sicilian as the conversation was Churchillian." She was intrigued to watch Sir Winston painting a picture of the ancient caves above which the house stood. For years he had been a proponent of art as therapy for public people who for long periods endured "worry and mental overstrain."[22] Clare could relate to this, and told Ike, another leisure painter, that she welcomed Winston's offer of tuition.

> When I have learned the elementary art of getting the paints
> onto the canvas instead of onto myself, I will go to work on a pic-
> ture for your collection of High Ranking Amateurs, tho' the ac-
> cent I fear will be on "rank."

Winston Churchill painting in a Sicilian cave, April 1955

But there is always the hope that if my picture is bad enough, it may inspire you to give me a painting lesson yourself. I would then have achieved the really unique distinction of having been initiated into the art of painting by Prime Minister Churchill, and "finished" by President Eisenhower. And that would easily make me the world's most distinguished art pupil![23]

Churchill offered to teach her husband as well, but Harry said he would stick with his hobby of collecting Tang and Ming horses. "From what we read in the papers over here," Clare joked to Ike, "not all of Tang's horses nor all of Ming's men can put Chiang back on the mainland again."[24]

Shortly after returning to the embassy, she received a box of paints from her tutor. "Everything you need for your artistic career," Churchill wired her.[25] Rising to the challenge, she hired Beverly Pepper, an American artist living in Rome, for further lessons, and soon completed several portraits and scenes from her childhood. "It's become a new passion," she told a reporter. "It provides the most complete relaxation I've known in years."[26]

As her second anniversary as Ambassador approached, Clare seemed to have lost the fear of death that had plagued her a few weeks earlier. However, she could not help an old trauma from becoming the subject of one canvas. It depicted her as a small girl being tossed into ocean surf by a powerful male figure, while an indifferent boy looked on, and a frantic woman rushed along the beach to save her.[27]

▽

At this point, Clare was in the satisfying position of having accomplished most of her major diplomatic challenges. The journalist Luigi Barzini, Jr., in a *Harper's Magazine* article entitled "Ambassador Luce, As Italians See Her," penned a detailed description of the fifty-two-year-old envoy.

The hair is silky blonde, the eyes are water blue and worried, the pale face has something medieval and Flemish in its stiffness. . . . Her manner is "society": she is almost always extremely kind and often listens to the answers to her questions. For a well-known satirical playwright, her repartee is remarkably subdued: she rarely allows herself the satisfaction of a good biting line.[28]

"Being a playwright and casting plays," Clare remarked to another reporter, "is really excellent preparation for diplomacy. I watch a man's inflections, his gestures, his manner of speaking—and try to determine what his inner convictions really are."[29] Tish Baldrige observed that she also had an actor's need to be word-perfect whenever she spoke publicly, practicing her lines in the bathtub, recording them for playback, and rehearsing the whole text at least a dozen times.[30]

On social occasions, she differed from her predecessors in continuing to pay little attention to the Roman aristocracy, a small coterie with ancient names. Barzini wrote of their "immense *palazzi* in town and ruined family seats in the country, where dinners are still served by bewigged and powdered flunkies in eighteenth-century liveries, one for each guest, and where an empty throne, covered in red damask, always waits for the Pope's visit."[31]

Clare was in fact under instructions to favor Italy's political and professional classes. At the Villa, except for de rigueur diplomatic dinners, she could entertain whomever she chose. On these occasions, she liked to wear Balenciaga gowns and favorite perfumes, such as Caron's Fleur de Rocaille or Femme by Rochas. At other times, she would splash a mixture of Patou's Joy and *bois de santal* in her hair, behind her ears, and on her breasts and wrists. "It slayed you," Tish Baldrige recalled. "It lingered on her skin so you knew when she came into a room."[32]

The parties that gave her the most pleasure as Ambassador were attended by such celebrities as Senator John Kennedy and his fiancée, Jacqueline Bouvier, Audrey Hepburn and Mel Ferrer, Henry Fonda, Clifton Webb, John Steinbeck, William Faulkner, Maria Tallchief, and Eleanor Roosevelt.[33] One day Joe DiMaggio paid a call at the Palazzo Margherita. After introducing him to her staff, Clare slipped her arm through his. "Joe, let's go down to one of those little sidewalk cafés and have a cup of coffee." Within seconds of their taking a table on the Via Veneto, the street was mobbed with hundreds of excited Italians.[34]

As April drew to a close, so did the seven-year presidency of Luigi Einaudi. Clare made no secret of the fact that she preferred a liberal named Cesare Merzagora to succeed him. On the night of April 29, she was in the diplomatic gallery of Rome's Montecitorio Palace for the fourth ballot of the parliamentary election. Giovanni Gronchi, Speaker of the Chamber of Deputies, laboriously read out every vote in turn. Sleekly handsome at sixty-seven, with swept-back iron-gray hair and polished black spectacles, he was himself a candidate, and a formidable one. He led the Christian Democratic Party's extreme left wing, which

Clare and Joe DiMaggio on the Via Veneto, 1955

advocated Italy's abandonment of NATO in favor of nonalignment. More alarming to Clare, he wanted eventually to allow Communists and Socialists into the cabinet.

As Gronchi read his own name for the 422nd time, the room erupted in cheers and applause. The vote had elected him second President of the Italian Republic, by a last-minute combination of support imaginable only in Italy: right-wingers from the Christian Democrats, buttressed by Monarchists and neo-Fascists, had joined forces with trade unionists, Socialists, and Communists.

Gronchi rose and bowed while Clare left the gallery, a look of displeasure on her face.[35]

Count Vittorio Cini, a veteran of Mussolini's government, asked for a meeting with Signora Luce, and treated her to what she called a *"fortissimo con brio"* harangue. Reporting the encounter to the State Department, she quoted him as saying it had been "a grave mistake" for her "to give any evidence whatsoever of hostility to Mr. Gronchi." Her obvious preference for his rival had been "an insult to all Italians who have freely chosen [Gronchi] in a democratic manner." If America wanted to prevent a rise in the Communist/Socialist vote in the next election, Cini thundered, it ought to give his country aid to the tune of "some 300–500 million dollars a year for five years."

Clare replied that American taxpayers were unlikely to support such largesse, especially if Italy lagged in its own defense and anti-Red efforts.[36]

On May 21, she had her first interview with President Gronchi. Speaking forcefully but mellifluously, he accused her of being responsible for his bad image in the American press, and for hinting that aid would be cut if he was elected. He assured her that his "militant catholicity" would prevent him from "doing business" with Togliatti.

Afterward, she skeptically recalled to Durbrow and Miller that Gronchi had once been excommunicated for his Communist affiliations. It was her impression now that if his faith ever again came into conflict with his ambition, he would "without scruple choose the latter."[37]

▽

A week later, Clare crossed the Atlantic for the third time that year. On arrival, she denied rumors that she wanted to succeed Oveta Culp Hobby as Secretary of Health, Education, and Welfare, or to be reassigned to London or Paris.

In Washington, she startled the President by hinting she might be ready to resign. He said he would like her to stay on at least through the year, since he needed plenty of time to pick a successor.[38]

Clare also saw Joe Martin, and admitted that she was considering a run for the vice presidential nomination in 1956. Unfazed by her audacity, he promised to do what he could to help. When word of their private talk leaked to the Republican National Committee, party leaders declared that if any woman was to be nominated, it should be Senator Margaret Chase Smith of Maine.[39]

Coincidentally, Clare was headed on June 14 for the Senator's home state. She had a reservation there, under the pseudonym "Mrs. Farmer," for three weeks of pampering at Elizabeth Arden's Maine Chance spa in Mount Vernon. Continuing hair loss and dental problems plagued her, as did a nagging fatigue.[40]

For extra seclusion, she took over a suite in the old farmhouse that had been modernized for Miss Arden's personal use.[41] Shirley Potash, a new friend-cum-assistant on the payroll of Time Inc., was given a neighboring room. This meant that the management had to eject a client from the Midwest, named Eleanor Nangle.

"I moved out rather quickly," Nangle wrote later, "but not before swarms of telephone workers appeared." Mrs. Farmer, she was told, needed several secure lines. When she heard on the radio that the mystery guest was none other than Ambassador Luce, she understood why. Unable to resist publicity, Clare had told a radio interviewer at Augusta Airport that she was going to Maine Chance for "a brief rest."[42]

Once installed, she requested that her meals be served in her own quarters, and that the spa's salons and exercise facilities be emptied of other guests before she used them. This meant that masseuses, beauticians, and physical therapists had to work after hours to accommodate other clients. Clare's special privileges did not end there. On her first Sunday, wearing a white suit and black lace mantilla, she commandeered the limousine that routinely transported Catholics to a chapel nearby. Leaving the rest of the faithful to squeeze into a utility vehicle, she went to worship in Augusta.[43]

Soon enough, she learned that the woman she had dispossessed was the beauty editor of the *Chicago Tribune*. "I was reading one afternoon," Nangle recalled, "content in the beautiful surroundings, the marvelous air and the sunshine, when Mrs. Luce's secretary . . . sidled up to where I sat quite alone. Mrs. Luce, she said, had learned I was a 'press person' and she was willing to grant me an interview. I declined with all the politeness I could muster, emphasizing that I was not at Maine Chance as a reporter . . . and that I had been given to understand that Mrs. Luce was desperate to protect her privacy. I would not be comfortable invading it."[44]

On another occasion, a number of resident college girls were told that the Ambassador would like "to give a little talk" in the drawing room after dinner. Clare appeared in a floaty evening dress, sat on a satin-covered sofa, and implored the young women to consider careers in the diplomatic corps. Patriotic service was honorable and rewarding, she said, but it was "grueling." She cited her own annual Fourth of July ordeals, having to stand all day long in the gardens of the Villa Taverna, "smiling and smiling and smiling" at visitors as they devoured hot dogs.[45]

After she left, the students guffawed and mimicked her sonorous intonation. Nangle was amazed by the banality of Clare's address. "We had had not a taste of the well-publicized Luce wit, brains, or the fa-

mous Luce malice. She had been dull, patronizing and surprisingly unat-
tractive in the revelations of herself."[46]

▽

Before leaving Maine on July 3, Clare heard that Mario Scelba's government had fallen, as she had expected after the elevation of Gronchi. But
to her relief, the embassy reported that the new Premier, Antonio Segni,
had put together a similar coalition of Christian Democrats, Social
Democrats, and liberals with Republican parliamentary support.[47]

By the fifteenth, Clare was one of hundreds of top American officials congregating in Paris on the periphery of the first Big Four conference since Potsdam, about to begin in Geneva.

Winston Churchill had long pressed for such a "summit" (his own
coinage) to reduce Cold War nuclear tensions. He had fantasized that
an East–West détente would enhance his career and affirm Britain's
place among the great powers. Eisenhower and Dulles had opposed the
idea, believing that Western Europe should be militarily integrated first.
But after France's sabotage of the EDC, West Germany had become part
of NATO, prompting the Soviet Union immediately to corral its satellites into signing the Warsaw Pact. The consequent rise in tensions
among the four powers had been only partly abated by Moscow's willingness to join in an Allied withdrawal of troops from Austria, on the
understanding that that country would henceforth remain neutral. This
signal of goodwill encouraged Eisenhower to pursue Churchill's dream.[48]

The President arrived in Geneva with a revolutionary "Open Skies"
proposal, calling for mutual strategic inspection flights over the Soviet
Union and the United States. Clare had much to say on this subject to
Ike's adviser Harold Stassen, if only because she had attacked a similar,
if civil, idea—Henry Wallace's "Freedom of the Air"—as "globaloney"
in 1943.

The conference began on July 18 and lasted four days, by which
time Clare was back in Rome, having greatly enjoyed herself in the
company of the policy makers she considered her peers.[49] "The President's initiative at Geneva has had a tremendous constructive effect
around the world," Stassen wrote her on August 1. "Your thoughtful
analysis in Paris was extremely helpful and deeply appreciated. You succeeded in developing a perspective which Geneva has proved to be of
great value."[50]

Stassen was right in saying that Eisenhower's headline-grabbing
idea had been welcomed by free nations everywhere, especially in

America, where Ike had returned to an approval rating of 79 percent.[51] He had taken the moral high road at the outset of the talks, knowing that Anthony Eden and Prime Minister Edgar Faure of France would go along. But the proposal had been rejected by the Soviet Premier, Nikolai Bulganin, and his new strongman, Nikita Khrushchev.

On doctor's orders, Clare flew to Barcelona on August 19 for a weekend with friends at a beach house in Palamós. There, sitting under a pine tree alive with chattering starlings, she scribbled an odd letter to President Eisenhower, identifying the strenuousness of his work with her own. Addressing him as "Dear Ike," she asked, "Have *you* had 48 delicious hours yet—since 1951, without one speck of work you *could* do, and no way for anybody to get at you? No, of course, you haven't. And that's why I grieve for you."

She went on about "the cannibalism of the crowd devouring you bit by bit," and the wearing effect of public life, until "one gets to feel like an old glove turned inside out." Sounding like Queen Elizabeth I at Tilbury, she continued, "Here we are, by God's design, doomed (or privileged) to *act*, to *do*, to *be*—to commit ourselves, as we do our troops, as the battle unfolds."

Perhaps fortunately, the letter was not mailed.[52]

Back in Rome the next day, she gave an al fresco lunch at the Villa Taverna.[53] Among her guests were the Indian Ambassador and a clutch of other dignitaries, including three Italian Senators. Also present was a friend, Kay Halle, who published an impressionistic account of the event.

> Frail and ethereal with her halo of platinum hair, [Clare] displayed eyes seemingly glazed with fatigue and overwork. . . . The buffet lunch of paper-thin Parma ham, rosy melons and ripe figs, cannelloni (meat-filled pasta smothered in melted parmesan cheese), aspic of chicken, and American ice cream, was served on beautiful marble tables. We sat on beige marble benches strapped with gold damask cushions under an arch of ilex trees. I could reach out and pick ripe oranges and persimmons from the lanes of trees bordering the gravel terrace. The food was served on graceful ceramic plates designed and especially marked for "CBL" by Rome's most famous ceramist, Count Paolo Mischiatelli.[54]

The Ambassador wore a full-skirted rose dress by Eleanora Garnett, and black Ferragamo shoes. That season, she had bought a hundred Italian outfits in support of Rome's beleaguered fashion industry.[55] Each ensemble was custom-made with deep, lined pockets for her spectacles, powder compact, lipstick, small notepad, and gold Cartier pen. It was an idiosyncrasy of hers to avoid the encumbrance of a purse.[56]

On September 25, she was preparing to give a dinner for Thomas E. Dewey when a news bulletin from Colorado reported that President Eisenhower had suffered a coronary thrombosis. He had played twenty-six holes of golf before being stricken in his sleep.

Clare's reaction was to draft an indiscreet letter to Richard Nixon, whom that morning's *New York Times* had already heralded as being in the FOREFRONT FOR '56. She assured him that the President "cannot run again, and may not even be able to campaign for the Republican nominee a year from November." Any attempt by the administration to suggest otherwise would lead to worldwide uncertainty, which the Soviet Union would exploit.

> If the President does not return soon to his desk—to work there harder than ever—it will be put about a) that his infirmity is greater than it is, and that this fact is being concealed by a group of greedy politicians who desire to remain themselves in power . . . or b) that Eisenhower himself has decided to stay because reports at home and abroad have convinced him that his Vice President does not enjoy the confidence of the U.S. or its Allies. The Russians can be counted on to add plenty of fuel to this, charging that Nixon would mean war if he came into office.

If Ike remained sidelined beyond the end of the year, she wrote, he should retire "and thus permit you to become his successor."

Clare was not among the many Republican centrists and liberals who thought that Nixon, at forty-two, was too inexperienced for the top job. She favored him, she said, because as a proven anti-Communist, he would prevent the Soviets from destroying the foreign policy achievements of Eisenhower and Dulles. "You are young, intelligent, honorable, energetic," she told him. "Above all, you are courageous."[57]

▽

The President's illness set Clare to thinking again about her own future. Ideally, she would have liked to link it to that of Nixon. In a self-assessment entitled "Group Support of CBL as a Public Figure, or 'Personality,'" she laid out her political assets and liabilities.

First, she believed that she could rely on Catholics. But their good-will counted for little in a heavily Protestant nation. Republicans offered her only partial loyalty, since—unlike Nixon—she had never been popular with the GOP's ultraconservative Old Guard, personified by the late Senator Taft. The same applied to many New Deal holdovers and press pundits who regarded her as a "triple interloper: woman, Republican, political appointee." Intellectuals, she felt, spurned her because of her lack of college education and her *Time/Life* connection. So did people in the arts, owing to her "failure to join predominantly Jewish groups on Broadway and in Hollywood."

Clare was equally gloomy about her appeal to socialites, community organizers, labor unions, and women. Black Americans, she wrote, "*would* be for me if they knew very much about me. But owing to [the] fact Negro leadership is still oriented towards [the] Democratic party, they are not told." Her present post, moreover, was not making her rich. She was tired of "the oohings and ahings of visitors at the Embassy and Villa Taverna." Her health was suffering, and most Italian problems seemed insoluble. All in all, she concluded, "it's no fun."[58]

Multiplying physical problems lay behind this plethora of complaints. Tish Baldrige alerted Dorothy Farmer, who had transferred to New York, that the boss was exhausted and "back on sleeping pills & lord-knows-whatses pills."[59]

Clare told Harry that a visit of John Foster Dulles to Rome would be a chance for a "private personal talk" about her "near future."[60] The Secretary arrived on Saturday, October 22. He was on his way to a meeting of foreign ministers in Geneva. During his tête-à-tête with Clare, he praised her as a "strong" diplomat, but said he would not oppose her resignation, if her health continued to deteriorate.[61]

On Sunday evening, Clare left with Dulles for Paris, checked into the Plaza Athénée, and instantly succumbed to "grippe," which kept her bedridden for two days. After moving on to Vienna on November 5 for the reopening of the State Opera House, she collapsed with colitis, and had to return to Rome the next day in great pain. Feeling worse overnight, she entered Salvatore Mundi Hospital for emergency treatment, and spent four insomniac days there losing weight. She struck her staff as being nervous and despondent. "I wish she would give this [job] up," fretted her maid, Gretel. "She is killing herself & for what, no one will thank her in the end."[62]

Barely recovered, Clare flew to Geneva on November 12 for another meeting with Dulles, before continuing to London for a ball held by Ambassador Aldrich. She had lunch at White's with Randolph Churchill and Evelyn Waugh. "It became a press conference," the latter wrote in his diary, "with her giving full and satisfactory answers to a hostile cross-examination. She has become slow in the uptake and verbose as an American rotarian, but is as pretty as ever."[63]

On December 16, Clare headed to New York for the holiday season, and essential dental work. "My front tooth is sticking out further than ever," she wrote in a memo, appalled that she would soon look like Eleanor Roosevelt.[64]

▽

She appeared in Washington on January 9, 1956, amid a fever of speculation about whether the sixty-five-year-old Eisenhower—only recently returned to work—would run for a second term. That night, she went to the National Press Club for a celebration of Nixon's forty-third birthday. The political purpose of the event, attended by five hundred Republicans, including Ike's entire cabinet, members of his White House staff, and former Taft supporters, was to affirm the Vice President as Ike's chosen heir apparent.[65]

Clare's presence at the event, where she was seen kissing Leonard Hall, the chairman of the GOP National Committee, revived last summer's rumor that she was interested in higher office. "Mrs. Luce is widely believed to be available for second place on the ticket if General Eisenhower does not run," the *New York Post* reported.[66]

For all the talk of Nixon, Eisenhower remained taciturn about his own intentions. Republican leaders met with him on January 13 to assure him of their belief that only he could hold the party together, balance the budget, and keep alive "the Spirit of Geneva."[67] They followed up a week later in New York with a "Salute to Eisenhower" lobster dinner at Madison Square Garden. Harry bought a table for ten.[68]

The publication that month of an adulatory biography of Clare by Alden Hatch, entitled *Ambassador Extraordinary*, added to the speculation that Clare wanted the vice presidency. The book was widely if not favorably reviewed, and treated by many as a campaign document.[69] The *National Catholic Weekly Review* said it contained few character insights, and highlighted a statement by Hatch that Clare "aroused an almost pathological antipathy in many." In *The Reporter*, Marya Mannes called Clare intellectually smug, and said her fatal weakness was a lack of taste. "Short of being Pope of Rome," Randolph Churchill wrote in

The Spectator, "there is probably no other job which Mrs. Luce would more willingly discharge than that of President of the United States."[70]

On January 25, Clare saw Eisenhower, who looked encouragingly healthy. Her intuition was that he was genuinely undecided about running again. But if he did, and won, he would ask her to remain in Rome.[71] Again she told him that she was thinking of resigning, and again he insisted she must stay.[72]

"My health," she said, "has been bad ever since that little bout with the paint."

"What are you talking about?"

Clare realized with amazement that Ike had not been briefed by the CIA on her arsenate of lead poisoning. He insisted on hearing the whole secret saga.[73]

Facing reporters afterward, she announced that she was "definitely and irrevocably" not a candidate for the vice presidency. She would continue as Ambassador to Italy "as long as the President and Secretary Dulles believe I am doing a good job."[74]

▽

The following night in Manhattan, Clare and Harry hosted an early buffet dinner at their apartment in anticipation of the North American premiere of Carlos Chávez's Symphony No. 3 in memory of Ann Brokaw. Among the twenty-two guests were the music critic Carter Harman, the gossip columnist Elsa Maxwell, and Daphne Skouras Root, a friend of Ann. Others were the composer Gian Carlo Menotti, the Mozart biographer Marcia Davenport, and the artist André Girard, painter of the windows in Saint Anne's Chapel.[75] Chávez was not present. He was preparing to conduct his work with the New York Philharmonic at Carnegie Hall, where its patron had always hoped to hear it.

There was excitement in the hall as concertgoers took their seats to hear a major new work by Latin America's most esteemed composer. They discovered that Chávez was also a gifted conductor when he led the orchestra in his own curtain-raising arrangement of the Chaconne in E Minor by Dietrich Buxtehude.[76] After applause for that died, Clare at last heard live the piece that she had commissioned six years before at Carlos's mountain retreat in Acapulco.[77]

The symphony was cast in classic four-movement form, albeit in an unusual sequence of Introduzione, Allegro, Scherzo, and Finale. Lacking music education, Clare was aware only of a gradually unfolding, twenty-six-minute sequence of extraordinarily varied orchestral effects. The musical texture was not so much melodic as a perpetual contrast of instrumental timbres: mellow horn chords mixing with the astringent wail of oboes, softly rattling kettledrums punctuating the harmony of strings, and a long, melancholy clarinet solo suspended over rumbling, almost inaudible, bass tones. There was a particularly haunting moment when the first movement thinned into an extremely high, soft, broken-octave phrase in the piccolo, obsessively repeated and growing fainter, as if a life were ebbing away.

But then more vital rhythms came jumping in, full of syncopated exuberance, resembling the music of Chávez's friend Aaron Copland. This energy gave way to a series of exquisite woodwind dialogues. Overall, the symphony's most noticeable feature was the perpetual imbalance between its highest and lowest sounds, each pursuing independent courses. The final effect was an aching sense of dislocation, which may have been Carlos's inference of the geographic and temperamental gulf that had so often yawned between Clare and her daughter.[78]

Clare listens to Carlos Chávez playing

Next day, Howard Taubman of *The New York Times*, noting that the symphony had been commissioned by Mrs. Luce, described it as "a score of original and driving intensity." Carter Harman wrote in *Time* that it was "bluntly modern, enormously powerful and sometimes beautiful," and that the composer had conducted "with broad-backed muscular energy." He marveled that the themes of a work that had taken so long to write had been conceived in one day.[79]

Afterward, Clare took Carlos to "21" to celebrate. Their symphony was now part of the North American repertory, with two more New York performances scheduled over the weekend and others to follow in Cleveland, Seattle, and Los Angeles.

▽

On February 2, Senator Margaret Chase Smith predicted that, based on her own presidential poll, Richard Nixon and Clare Boothe Luce would lead the Republican ticket this year.

Clare was not on hand to face the renewed press stir this caused, having gone to Paris on a $4,645 shopping spree at Balenciaga. She asked Harry to pick up the bill for her coming fifty-third birthday.[80] After returning briefly to Rome, she flew back to New York for urgent work on an abscessed tooth. Her face was "all ballooned out," she wrote Gerry Miller. "For the first time in years I've been weeping continuously from pain."[81] She recovered enough from this latest affliction to be on hand for a state visit by President Gronchi, to begin on February 27.

Soon after Gronchi's arrival, Eisenhower rocked the country by announcing that he meant to seek a second term. Asked if Nixon would be on the ticket, he declined to say.[82] Nevertheless, Clare, traveling with the Italian delegation to San Francisco, said once more, on March 8, that she was "definitely and irrevocably NOT a candidate for the vice-presidency of the United States."[83] She could hardly say anything else, having overheard Eisenhower telling Gronchi that he insisted on her returning to Italy.[84] Two days later, in New York, she dropped out of the tour, citing an attack of "influenza and laryngitis."[85] But she was present for Gronchi's farewell reception at the Waldorf on March 13.

The next day, *The New York Times* gave him an admiring send-off. Gronchi's courteous frankness about American shortcomings had impressed many outside the administration. In remarks seemingly directed at Ambassador Luce, he had told *Look* magazine that the State Department's foreign policy was "far too rigid and inflexible" in its attitude toward Communism. "Human history is a continuing process. Revolution is invariably followed by evolution, and this applies equally to the Russian, Chinese, and American Revolutions. . . . Failure to understand this blinds Americans to positive aspects of developments in the Soviet Union and China."[86]

As if in proof, the free world was stunned that weekend by the publication of a historic speech by Nikita Khrushchev. Addressing the 20th Congress of the Soviet Communist Party, he listed and denounced Josef Stalin's crimes against humanity, in what the diehard Dulles called "the most damning indictment of despotism ever made by a despot."[87] Many Reds in the West, including those in Italy, tore up their party cards.[88] To Clare, it was ironic that the countless postwar accusations she had leveled at the brutality of Communism had been validated by none other than the ideology's current spokesman.

She was back in Rome with Harry in time for Easter, still experiencing dental discomfort and hoping her doctors were right in trying to cure it with penicillin. But on April 4 the tooth had to be pulled by a local dentist, after which she continued her scheduled meetings.[89]

Not feeling much better six days later, she met with Amintore Fanfani, now General Secretary of the Christian Democratic Party, to discuss "the confusion on the Left caused by Stalin's fall from grace." This had revived the perennial question of whether Italian Socialists could be persuaded to split from their Communist partners. Fanfani was suspicious of the Kremlin's latest offensive, a visit by Khrushchev and Bulganin to Great Britain. They would be the first Soviet leaders to tour a Western country, and he dreaded that accords might result that would strengthen rather than weaken Togliatti and Nenni in the coming municipal and provincial elections.[90]

On April 22, Clare's staff surprised her with the presentation of a medallion commemorating her three years of service in Italy. She started crying at the ceremony, and tried without success to stop.[91] Evidently, she was still at a low emotional and physical ebb. The reason she felt "so touched and so sad," she confided to Gerry Miller, was that she had just made up her mind to go home yet again—this time for a drastic medical examination.[92]

Feeling too weak for immediate long-distance travel—"I'm tired Durby, I'm tired"—she went to the spa of Montecatini in Tuscany. Depressed as well as ailing, she spent a week there without beneficial result. During her stay, she heard that Father Thibodeau—whom she had

stopped seeing for Confession and spiritual direction a year before becoming Ambassador—was leaving America for a post in the Pacific.
She reacted to the news with morbid narcissism.

> I think one of the hardest crosses I [have] had to bear was the fact
> that not even *you* could remember me after I was "out of sight."
> These three years . . . have been cruel ones indeed in many ways.
> I had the illusion—for that is what it was, that among all my
> friends I could really count on two—you and Dorothy. But when
> the time comes, other obligations and duties intervene, and I am
> left to savour to the utmost my loneliness and aloneness. I suppose
> it would all have been a little easier to bear if my health had stayed
> good. But it's been so bad—and getting so much worse that if you
> go to the Philippines or Australia—I'll probably never see you
> again.[93]

Perhaps because of the potpourri of drugs she was taking, Clare
showed signs of paranoia. "All telephone calls from me are monitored
by the government," she wrote Dorothy Farmer. "I just found out yesterday I have at *all* times 2 private dicks following me." She said that if she
called New York and began with the phrase "'Please remember the
Bishop's birthday,' you'll know I am about to talk about matters I *don't*
want you to make clear for the people on the line, so let me do the talking."[94]

▽

On May 11, she checked into Doctors Hospital in Manhattan for a
three-day series of tests. Her press office issued a statement that she was
in "a run-down condition," concealing the reality that Clare suspected
cancer. A secretary was shocked at her gaunt appearance. "My God, she
looks awful! She has lost about 25 pounds."[95]

The tests showed no malignancy, but an alarming array of other ailments. "I have a bad anemia," she wrote Gerry Miller, "not pernicious,
but I'll have to have blood transfusions for several weeks. . . . I have a
gall bladder obstruction [and] a 'white' hepatitis, colitis and periodonti-
tis (those abscesses—dormant for the moment on my teeth). All this
nice little package of viruses, poisons and what-not mean, according to
the doctors, at least two months of care and rest . . . (and every tooth
must be lanced!)"[96]

Her gums were sliced and cauterized, and her mouth stuffed with plaster of paris packing for three months. Unable to bite properly, she continued to shed weight until bridgework replaced her upper incisors.[97]

Dr. Rosenbluth qualified the diagnosis of colitis, stating that Mrs. Luce was suffering from chronic enteritis, and that "further study was needed to establish the particular infecting agent, which might be in the category of hepatitis—inflammation of the liver." After all this, he and other doctors informed Clare that her health problems derived from the "toxic encounter" in Rome. Enteritis was historically related to the ingestion of substances such as lead, mercury, and arsenic.[98]

In view of her long-term incapacitation, she again offered to resign. Dulles asked her to postpone a final decision until July, and she acquiesced, but insisted that she wanted to be "out of the trenches" by mid-November. Eisenhower wrote expressing concern for her health, and told Harry that Rome was considered "so delicate a post" that he did not want to risk a new appointment there in an election year.[99]

After numerous blood transfusions, Clare was cheered by news of the Italian local elections on May 27. The Communists, she crowed, had "lost about 15% of their voting strength."[100]

Her illness led to a spate of sympathetic and laudatory press articles. One, a dispatch from Rome by the syndicated columnist Dickson Hartwell, pointed out that before her arrival Italy's economy had been stagnant, the political outlook murky, anti-Americanism intense, and Communism riding high.

> Into this mess stepped a new American ambassador [with] a *cum laude* mind larded with the analytical capacity of an IBM calculator and seasoned with a New Yorker wit. She also possesses an indefinable honey quality which has wilted a generation of strong men. . . .
>
> Today this disarmingly fragile Mrs. Luce (here they say La Loo-chay) has emerged from a jungle of criticism, abuse and turmoil onto a quiet, almost beatific, plateau of accomplishment not outmatched in our foreign service.

Hartwell listed some positive achievements during her tenure. The economy had gone up 7 percent in 1954, and another 9 percent in 1955, "and is still climbing." Italy had joined the United Nations, affirmed its loyalty to NATO, and ratified a new West European Union to replace the stillborn European Defense Community. The young Republic's trade unions had 20 percent fewer Red shop stewards, it was at peace with neighbors, and its President had visited America for the first time.

He acknowledged that these major advances were not all due to Clare personally, but they were the result of sound and well-executed foreign policy. "Where Ike will next send La Loochay is pure speculation. Her health permitting, I suggest USSR. Our diplomatic successes there have not been notable. . . . It would certainly disgorge some of the stuffing out of Bulganin and Khrushchev."[101]

Clare recovered enough by June 11 to have lunch in Manhattan with Chancellor Konrad Adenauer of West Germany. They met at his request to discuss his country's rearmament. He was frank in his admiration for her, telling an aide that she was "one of your greatest Ambassadors." His "wish in life," he said, would be to have Clare Boothe Luce in Bonn.[102]

▽

At the end of June, Clare flew to Washington for State Department consultations. Wearing a suit that looked several sizes too big, and carrying a large briefcase, she was photographed waving happily as she arrived at National Airport. "Mrs. Luce is at last beginning to feel life's worth living," Dorothy Farmer reported.[103]

A few days later, Harry heard that a gossip magazine called *People Today* was about to reveal the still-classified story that Ambassador Luce had been poisoned with arsenic in Rome.[104] He decided to counter this scoop by publishing an authoritative account of his wife's illness in *Time*. The article appeared on Monday, July 16, and became an international sensation.[105] It not only confirmed what doctors knew about Clare's diseases, but documented other pathological symptoms, such as nervousness, nausea, and such numbness in her right foot that "she almost had to drag it in dancing." *Time* also exposed the true identity of "Seaman Jones," mentioned the CIA's part in investigating the mystery, and detailed the toxic decor of her now infamous boudoir.

In conclusion the magazine announced, "Her general health is greatly improved, and she is scheduled to leave this week for a three-week Mediterranean cruise. Then she will return to Villa Taverna (the bedroom and its rosetted ceiling have been long since redone in non-leaded paint) and to the embassy duties that she has often described as 'no bed of roses.' "[106]

39

THIS FRAGILE BLONDE

*There is a time for departure, even when
there is no certain place to go.*

—Tennessee Williams

Clare took her Mediterranean cruise aboard the *Creole*, a 190-foot, 433-ton three-masted schooner owned by the Greek shipping magnate Stavros Niarchos. It was considered the most beautiful and well-appointed yacht afloat, with an impressive art collection. Niarchos, known as "the Golden Greek," had heard of the Ambassador's illness, and invited her to join him and a party of friends. She arrived in Lisbon on July 22, in time to sail for Spain.

Meanwhile, a full-blown controversy erupted on both sides of the Atlantic, questioning the plausibility of *Time*'s poisoning story and Harry's motive for printing it. Some commentators accused him of wanting to increase circulation. The Italian magazine *Il Ore* said that the "otherwise moving story" of Clare's long struggle with ill health was diluted by "flimsy" reportage. It saw a Hitchcock movie in the making, with the heavy tread of maids upstairs becoming the stomp of a murderous Communist. "Khrushchev? Maybe. . . ."[1] Other European papers alleged that the Ambassador had "always taken a few grains of arsenic for cosmetic reasons," and therefore poisoned herself.[2]

In New York, the president of the National Paint, Varnish and Lacquer Association doubted that anyone could formulate, "deliberately or accidentally," a pigment with enough arsenic to make Mrs. Luce sick. In Rome, a Signor Ambrosi, owner of one of the city's oldest paint firms, said that arsenic had not been used in Italian emulsions for over thirty years, and that in any case "after a year . . . all toxic presence in paint has disappeared." However, Paolo Danna, the architect who had redecorated the Villa Taverna before Clare moved in, testified that he had only redone its walls. "The ceilings, as far as I know, were painted in 1931, and since then have never had a new coat." He also said it was not true that lead arsenic soon lost toxicity.[3]

Concerned for Italo-American relations, the State Department tried to dispel conspiracy theories by declaring that there was "absolutely no evidence" that anyone had plotted to kill Mrs. Luce.[4]

▽

The *Creole* proceeded along the Guadalquivir River from Seville and across the Mediterranean to Clare's "dream island" of Majorca, then to Ibiza, the Costa Brava, Sardinia, and Corsica, ending on the French Riviera.[5] There were fifteen passengers aboard, many of them tanned, bejeweled European socialites. Clare felt little affinity for the latter, and spent most of her time on deck reading under a blue awning.[6]

After a few days of sea air, her appetite returned, and she grew stronger, waxing lyrical about "the tall masts swaying against the far stars . . . the lapis lazuli of the deep sea; the eerie emerald waters . . . and at all times, the musical accompaniment of the violin-taut sail ropes, the timpani of the sails, the music of the sea (the only restless thing in the world that brings peace!)."[7]

David Sulzberger, age seven, came aboard at one stop, and was agog at the spectacle of Clare being lowered into the water for a pre-lunch swim. He watched her doing the breaststroke in a white leotard and large-brimmed hat, and would never forget that "when she reappeared dripping wet, the leotard was transparent."[8]

As she luxuriated aboard the *Creole*, Clare fantasized how delightful it would be for Harry to buy her "a ship of my own." She hinted to him that "there is nothing in the whole world I like better than yachting. Always have. Always will."[9]

On July 26, she was disturbed to hear on the radio of the coincidence of two big events: the sinking of the *Andrea Doria*, and the Egyptian nationalization of the Suez Canal. The tragedy off Nantucket was a poignant reminder that she had embarked to take up her mission on that same Italian liner. Colonel Nasser's shock action, in reprisal for the withdrawal of Western financing to build the Aswan Dam, portended trying days ahead for Anglo-American relations. "The real danger," Clare wrote Harry, "is the example he will set to the Arabs about oil royalties."[10]

One night at dinner, she had a conversation with Sir John Russel, a well-connected Londoner, and was flattered to hear that some diplomats in the British Foreign Office hoped she might replace Winthrop Aldrich at the Court of St. James's. "I was known as Ike's best Ambassador," she wrote Harry. "Had great prestige now, and was considered a real 'pro.'"[11]

Fresh from the cruise, she showed up at Èze-sur-Mer in early August to stay at the "villa" of her old friend Joseph P. Kennedy. It was actually a simple house along the railroad track, and trains kept waking her throughout the night. "Life with the Kennedys is so different," she wrote Dorothy Farmer. "No champagne or caviar. Yogurt and boiled rice. And a nice priest. . . . He says Mass for the whole household at 6.45!"[12]

On Friday, the tenth, she called another friend, Somerset "Willie" Maugham, at Cap Ferrat and invited herself over. The visit brought back memories of twenty-one years before, when she had been at the novelist's Villa Mauresque with Harry, who was then "madly courting me."[13]

Maugham, now eighty-two, took elaborate pains to entertain her. His assistant, Alan Searle, estimated that he made a dozen trips to the kitchen that morning to consult with his chef over the menu.

> Well, Clare came—so did the first course. Clare looked at it, made a dab at it, and passed it up. The second course came with the same result. I saw Willie's expression and I felt nervous. I prayed that she would do better by the next course. She didn't. "I see, Clare," said Willie, in a quiet but dangerous tone, "that you don't like my food." "Oh, no," she protested, "it's just that I don't eat at midday." "If you don't eat, why did you come to lunch?" said Willie. It was a very tense moment, I can tell you.[14]

Maugham must not have known that Clare was still having gastrointestinal problems, and had recently lost another three pounds.[15] Alarmed by her appearance, he recovered from his pique, and wrote later, "I felt you had never looked more beautiful, but dreadfully frail, as though you were hanging on to life by a thread."[16]

She spent another three days with the Kennedys, who were ambivalent at the prospect of their Senator son, John, being nominated for Vice President at the Democratic National Convention, just getting under way in Chicago. Clare and Joe agreed that it was a bad idea, because losing would spoil his chances of running for President in four years' time, when the electorate might be more receptive to a Catholic candidate.[17]

▽

Except for the simmering Suez crisis—which was primarily the problem of Britain and France—Clare had no large issues to contend with when she settled back to work at the Palazzo Margherita in mid-August. She was surrounded there by new faces, as Durbrow had moved on and the rest of the staff was going through a cyclical change.[18] Her resignation lay on Eisenhower's desk, but she knew it was unlikely to be accepted until after the election. Gerry Miller remained her chief confidant. At night in the Villa, she felt even more lonely, since Tish Baldrige had taken a job at Tiffany's in New York. There was no one to "gab" with, she complained to Harry, who would not join her for another seven weeks. "I really feel like the Prisoner of Taverna."[19]

She was irritated by not gaining an ounce, because she had to subsist on rice and tea to soothe her still-tempestuous stomach. "I just *never* will get well so long as I stay here, darling. . . . I've just never learned to enjoy this darn Italy!" Clare also fretted about Ike's bland reelection campaign. "It is just *stupid* to go on telling people how well off they are, and how peaceful the world is. . . . You have to tell them it's WAR if the other fellow gets in."[20]

Compounding her misery, the villa had become so overrun with mice that the General Services Administration had contracted "to put two cats on the payroll."[21]

▽

As things turned out, Eisenhower was the best-equipped statesman in the world to handle the multiple strategic crises that exploded almost simultaneously in late October. On October 23, Hungarian students and workers, encouraged by Radio Free Europe's habitual calls for liberation of Soviet-held territories, held a protest march in Budapest. It swelled to a demonstration of two hundred thousand, after their petition for reforms was rebuffed. The situation quickly turned to violence, when security forces of Erno Gero's hard-line Communist government fired into the crowd. At this point, soldiers of the Hungarian army amazed observers by joining the rebels, and handing out weapons. Rioters moved on to slice a sixty-foot bronze statue of Stalin off below the knees, leaving only his high boots. They spat on the falling colossus, then dismembered it and paraded parts through the streets.[22]

Battles continued the following day, until the Kremlin agreed to have Imre Nagy, a former, moderate Communist leader, reinstated as Prime Minister. An uneasy calm ensued for several days, as Nagy swore in a new, multiparty government, started releasing political prisoners, permitted a free press, and uncensored radio broadcasts. To everyone's amazement, Russian forces stationed in the country began an exodus.

On October 27, Eisenhower, reassured by these unexpected developments, informed Moscow that the United States would not take advantage of the situation to recruit new allies in Eastern Europe. His attitude contrasted with that of Secretary Dulles and other American anti-Marxists, including Clare and Frank Wisner, the Deputy Director of the CIA, who was on an inspection tour of Western Europe.

Wisner happened to be staying with Clare the next day, Sunday, when, in a show of support for the Budapest rebels, she attended Mass at Rome's only Hungarian Catholic Church. On her return to the Villa Taverna, she found her guest agitated and desperately drinking glass after glass of whiskey. As an OSS agent during World War II, Wisner had witnessed Red Army atrocities at first hand. Now in charge of all CIA covert operations, he was astounded to have had no inkling of the magnitude of desire for freedom in Hungary. His only officer in the country was as surprised at the uprising as everyone else.[23]

A highly emotional man, Wisner harangued Clare for hours about the need to help the freedom fighters, and expressed his anguish over Eisenhower's neutrality. For four days, he continued to drown his despair until she feared he was heading for a breakdown.[24]

Adding to their mutual concerns was an equally sudden outbreak of violence in the Middle East. On October 29, Israel invaded Egypt, taking over the Sinai Peninsula. This did not at first seem to be related to Nasser's seizure of the Suez Canal, but on the following day, Great Britain and France, the two major shareholders in the canal company, issued a suspiciously prompt ultimatum to the belligerents, warning that if peace was not restored at once, they too would invade and reestablish order throughout the region. Within twenty-four hours, this threat was implemented, and British and French warships began a bombardment of the Suez Zone.[25]

On instructions from Dulles, Clare began working with Vice Admiral Charles R. Brown of the U.S. Sixth Fleet to coordinate the evacuation of some twenty-eight hundred Americans from the Middle East to Italy. She also made arrangements for the evacuees to be housed and fed.[26]

With less than a week to go before the presidential election, Eisenhower was furious with the aggressors in the Middle East for having kept him uninformed about their collusion. He believed that Egypt was "within its rights" to nationalize a canal whose entire length ran through its own territory, linking the Red Sea to the Mediterranean.[27]

On November 1, Dulles presented a resolution to the United Nations General Assembly, calling for a total cease-fire in the Middle East. At the same time, Eisenhower informed Prime Minister Eden that Britain would not receive American petroleum to replace oil shipments stalled by Nasser's retaliatory blocking of the canal. He also threatened to restrict Whitehall's access to its American bank accounts.

That same day, Nagy, in what turned out to be an act of hubris, announced Hungary's withdrawal from the Warsaw Pact. Soviet troops and tanks, surreptitiously parked on the country's borders, began moving back toward Budapest in vast numbers. Their initial retreat had been a feint to persuade the West that Nagy's reforms would be tolerated, and to discourage any active outside support of the rebels.

While the General Assembly debated the United States' resolution, Eisenhower delivered the last speech of his reelection campaign. To Clare's horror, he seemed willing to accept the coming debacle in Hungary. "We cannot—in the world, any more than in our own nation—subscribe to one law for the weak, another law for the strong; one law for those opposing us, another for those allied with us." This assumption of a moral high ground in international affairs showed the President's willingness to chastise longtime allies, and his reluctance to provoke another world war by interfering in the Soviet sphere of influence. He won instant acclaim in Arab states and other nations with memories of colonialism. In the small hours of November 2, the General Assembly voted overwhelmingly in favor of the U.S. resolution.[28]

By then Clare was staying with Douglas Dillon at the U.S. Embassy in Paris, and Dulles had entered Walter Reed Hospital for emergency colon surgery. Eisenhower was therefore in sole charge of United States foreign policy when, at 4:00 A.M. Hungarian time on November 4, some two hundred thousand Red Army soldiers and four thousand tanks overran Budapest, shelling indiscriminately in a display of totalitarian fury. Nagy broadcast an appeal for Western help at 5:15 A.M., after which all communications with the outside world shut down.

It was apparent to Clare that all her doomsday forecasts over the last ten years were now reality. In a melodramatic cable to the President, she warned: "Ask not for whom the bell tolls in Hungary today. It tolls for us if freedom's holy light is extinguished in blood and iron over there."[29]

At dawn the following day, Britain and France ignored the demand of the UN for a Middle Eastern cease-fire, and escalated their assault on Egypt with a full-scale amphibious invasion at Port Said. Some two hundred warships, including five aircraft carriers and six battleships, crowded the shore as paratroopers and commandos took the city. Prime Minister Nikolai Bulganin at once sent messages to the three leaders responsible—Eden, Guy Mollet of France, and David Ben-Gurion of Israel—hinting that he was prepared to use nuclear force, if necessary, to restore peace.

Meanwhile, in Budapest the Soviets dangled the bodies of partisans from bridges over the Danube, executed Hungarian officers, and packed thousands of mostly young civilian rebels into cattle trucks for mass deportation to Russia. By late evening, the Red Army was in control of the entire country.[30] An increasingly distraught Frank Wisner, now on the Austro-Hungarian border, witnessed the first wave of escapees pouring across. He was hoping for permission from Washington to send in some locally stored CIA weaponry, but it never came.[31] Meanwhile, the death toll in Budapest mounted to 2,652 Hungarian dead and 669 Soviets. The number of refugees swelled to more than 200,000.

Late that Monday night in Paris, Clare wrote a six-page letter to Harry that had both Orwellian and Churchillian overtones.

It cannot be long now before the Big Show begins—unless all of Europe is to become a Hungary.

The Suez question has changed nothing, essentially. The struggle in the Near East and for the Near East was always foreseen. What *has* changed everything is the massacre and martyrdom of Hungary. For *that* is our Munich. . . . If we do *not* go forward resolutely now, we will begin the long shameful retreat into the final isolation, where we will fall, at last, between the Chinese and the Red masses of a Europe driven against us. . . .

Now we shall see: will the British and the French capitulate before the Russian threats? Will we? I do not dare to hope we will call their bluff. . . . These very hours witness what may be the long touted end of "Western civilization."[32]

When Election Day dawned in America on November 6, the world learned that Eisenhower had no intention of calling Moscow's bluff. A White House press release announced that the President had received a telegram from Bulganin that went so far as to suggest that American and Soviet forces unite to prevent what might grow "into a third world war" over the canal.[33] Privately, Eisenhower was sure that the Soviet Premier's communication was an effort to divert attention from the Hungarian uprising. "Those fellows are both furious and scared," he told senior aides. But his release simply stated that "neither the Soviets nor any other military forces should now enter the Middle East area except under United Nations mandate."[34] Its implication was that the Kremlin should not think of interfering militarily in any sphere of direct American interest. Nor could the British government count on White House permission for the International Monetary Fund to release dollar deposits Eden needed to continue his Suez adventure. At 12:30 P.M. Washington time, the chastened Prime Minister agreed to a cease-fire, effective midnight.[35]

By then Clare was back in Rome, her apocalyptic letter to Harry unmailed as "too gloomy." On Wednesday morning, she heard that Ike had been reelected in one of the greatest landslides in history—carrying forty-one states to Adlai Stevenson's seven.

▽

She returned to America in mid-November, and on the nineteenth saw the President, and at last made her resignation public. Ike let it be known that her job had been "superbly done." *The Washington Post* agreed: "Judged by the pragmatic test of results, her mission was extremely successful. . . . She worked fantastically hard, even to the detriment of her health, and there was no doubt of her warm friendship for Italy. She brought both dignity and intelligence to her position. Her efforts command the gratitude of her countrymen."[36]

A reporter asked her if being a female had been a disadvantage in her life. "I couldn't possibly tell you," Clare replied. "I have never been a man."[37]

On November 20, she wrote Gerry Miller, saying she had quit Rome for her own sake. But she was now feeling desolate "at the thought of leaving the task, which however hard and frustrating, nevertheless had many compensations. The greatest was the *camaraderie*, the teamwork . . . imperfect though it often was."[38]

She went on to say that while she and Dulles tended to look at issues such as Hungary and Suez parochially, the President "sees all the problems, in large *and* in detail, and if others don't know what he is doing, that is just what he *wants*."[39]

▽

Her final three weeks in Rome, with Harry at her side, were a whirl of farewell events. On December 10, she held her own white-tie dinner at the Villa Taverna for forty guests. The list, headed by "Ambassador and Mr. Luce," included many of the aristocrats she had earlier neglected: the Infanta Beatriz and Prince Alessandro Torlonia, Prince Don Aspreno and Princess Donna Milagros Colonna, Donna Diana Chiaramonte Bordonaro, Count Lanfranco di Campello, and others, as well as the Belgian, Dutch, Australian, Swiss, and Italian Holy See Ambassadors. The old house, perfumed with flowers, glowing with candlelight, and softly resonating with the sound of chamber music, was a long way from 533 West 124th Street in Manhattan's Spanish Harlem, where Ann Clare Boothe had been born more than fifty-three years before.

The Italian government's valedictory state banquet for the departing *Ambasciatrice* took place on December 18. In his remarks, Foreign Minister Martino said that she had conducted her mission "with energy and devotion equalled only by intelligence and experience." He presented her with his country's highest award, the Grand Cross of the Order of Merit of the Italian Republic, never before given to a woman. Clare, dressed in turquoise blue, felt her eyes again welling up. At the embassy, she received the Sovereign Military Order of Malta, entitling her to wear a Maltese cross for the rest of her life.

Her departing address, entitled "Italy, the United States and the Free World—a Retrospect and Prospect," was given in the upper room of the Banca di Roma to a packed audience of ministers, diplomats, businessmen, cultural figures, a Cardinal, and, in the words of the *Il Tempo* columnist Apollodoro, "elegantly-dressed women who came to honor so deserving, or rather so exceptional a representative of their sex."[40]

Wearing a black dress and double strand of pearls, Clare spoke of the American will to spread freedom around the world, and the cooperative role Italy could play "in that great project." Straining to describe her podium aura, Apollodoro wrote, "Mrs. Luce assumed the aspect almost of a figure of glass . . . compounded of precision and control." She delivered her peroration in Italian, gesticulating like a Neapolitan, and smiling "with a special sweetness."

In taking her leave, Clare used the same word as when docking on the *Andrea Doria* three and a half years before: *"Arrivederci."* As the crowd passed in front of the stage to shake her hand, they repeated, *"Arrivederci! Arrivederci!"* Apollodoro commented: "It was as though we were at the station, waving handkerchiefs, before a train slowly moving out."[41]

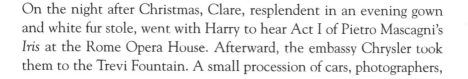

On the night after Christmas, Clare, resplendent in an evening gown and white fur stole, went with Harry to hear Act I of Pietro Mascagni's *Iris* at the Rome Opera House. Afterward, the embassy Chrysler took them to the Trevi Fountain. A small procession of cars, photographers,

Clare at the Trevi Fountain, December 1956

and onlookers followed. They watched while the Luces threw silver half-dollars into the cold water, and *ragazzi* jumped in to retrieve them.[42]

The next day, as Harry escorted his mink-coated wife aboard the 3:45 P.M. TWA flight to New York, she turned to wave good-bye to more than five hundred Italian officials, diplomats, and American well-wishers. They sang "For She's a Jolly Good Fellow" as the door closed behind her. Then the plane taxied away and lifted off.[43]

Ambassador Luce left behind an Italy strongly democratic and economically stable, in contrast with the demoralized nation that had received her with trepidation in 1953. Its Communist constituency was diminished, and its armed forces greatly strengthened by the Mutual Defense Assistance Program.[44] She had successfully completed all her seventeen diplomatic assignments, and scored a notable triumph in helping to end the long agony of Trieste. Her mission had remained controversial throughout, alienating liberals and leftists on both sides of the Atlantic.

"Clare Luce is despised and hated here," the expatriate scholar William Weaver told Christopher Isherwood. In contrast, Milan's major daily, *Corriere della Sera*, wrote: "No one will ever know how much Italy owes to this fragile blonde."[45]

40

LIQUID PARADISE

The sea has many voices.

—T. S. ELIOT

I n New York on January 2, 1957, Clare wrote a letter to a young black Baptist minister, the Reverend Martin Luther King, Jr. Avid for news in the first days of her "retirement," she had read about his leadership of the successful struggle of southern Negroes to overcome racial discrimination on public transport. Blacks in Montgomery, Alabama, emboldened by a recent Supreme Court ruling that segregated seating on buses was unconstitutional, had ended their year-long boycott of the local line and quietly resumed riding, now in whatever seats they chose. Judge Dozier DeVane of Florida declared that "every segregation act or law of any state [is] as dead as a doornail." White snipers, having already attacked Dr. King's house with dynamite and shotguns, had chosen New Year's Eve to fire on a bus, the fourth such violent incident in a week.[1]

"You know, of course," Clare wrote King, "that the race prejudice and bigotry of some of our fellow Americans have been a very strong weapon which the Communists have used against us, everywhere in the world." She cited gibes from Reds in Italy about the suppression of Negro rights in her avowedly democratic nation. "No man has ever waged the battle for equality under our law in a more lawful and *Christian* way than you have."[2]

Coming from a rich, white, Catholic Republican, these words might have surprised King, had he been unaware of Clare's enlightened record as a champion of Negro rights over the past fourteen years. As a Congresswoman, she had called for integration of the American military long before Truman, condemned the Daughters of the American Revolution for discriminating against Marian Anderson, delivered eloquent Lincoln Day speeches advocating "human rights" for all races, blasted the "lousy" segregation laws of New Orleans, appealed on radio and at the Tuskegee Institute for improvement in Negro education, and most recently, in a list of her political assets and liabilities, identified blacks as a constituency that would be for her, if they knew more about her.

King responded with a polite letter of thanks on January 14. A week later at Eisenhower's second inauguration, Clare found herself with Ike's administrative aide E. Frederic Morrow, the first black man ever to hold such a position in the White House, and the first to be seated in the presidential reviewing stand.[3]

Then, on February 18, in what was perhaps no coincidence, Harry put Dr. King on the cover of *Time*, heralding the twenty-eight-year-old civil rights leader as an American who "reached beyond lawbooks and writs, beyond violence and threats, to win his people—and challenge all people—with a spiritual force that aspired to ending prejudice in man's mind."

▽

Since the moment she left Rome, Clare had lost the tension of three and a half years of the most all-consuming activity of her life. "I felt the release so suddenly," she wrote Gerry Miller, "that like a spring uncompressed I seemed to fly apart, tangle and sprawl inside, and have been incapable almost of [making] the simplest decision!"[4]

That remained true all winter. Intermittently, she tried to bestir herself, moving between New York, Connecticut, Palm Beach, the Bahamas, and Elizabeth Arden's spa in Phoenix, Arizona. She also visited Washington, D.C., half hoping to be offered another diplomatic post— either London, Paris, or even, as rumor had it, Moscow.[5] At the same time, she announced she was at work on a play about a kleptomaniac called *The Little Dipper*, intended for the Gish sisters, and negotiated a contract with Harper & Brothers to write her autobiography, which she would call *The Dream of My Life*.[6]

John Foster Dulles, now back at work, had nothing to offer, though he hinted at the possibility of a major posting in due course. When the journalist Bob Considine quizzed Clare about her prospects, she quoted the humorist Irvin Cobb's three reasons for not going to a party. "Number one is that I haven't been invited. Which makes the other two academic."[7]

Humor aside, Considine detected a "faint aura of sadness" in her demeanor. She gave one explanation in a letter to a British diplomat friend. "The fact is, I find myself missing Rome, and certain of *mes chèrs colleagues* not less, but more as time goes by." Besides, she hungered for a purposeful routine. "I felt I *ought* to be going somewhere, doing something, in the public places. I have, I fear, contracted the diplomatic *habitus*. I do not find it as easy as I had thought to relax."[8]

To occupy her mind, she immersed herself in *The Coming World Civilization*, a recent tome by the septuagenarian philosopher William Ernest Hocking, and typed him an ambitiously intellectual, nine-page, single-spaced letter. It amounted to a survey of international affairs in terms of such symbols as the Hammer and Sickle, the Rising Sun, the Stars and Stripes.

By mid-March, she was ensconced at the Arizona Biltmore Hotel in Phoenix, relishing the warm, dry air and sweeping desert vistas. Her reading now included "great slogs of Toynbee," Pascal's *Pensées*, Camus's philosophical novel *The Fall*, Lionel Trilling's latest volume of literary criticism, *A Gathering of Fugitives*, Somerset Maugham's collected short stories, verses by Hilaire Belloc, and a second perusal of *Moby-Dick*.[9]

Harry meanwhile played golf on the hotel's adjoining course, which was surrounded by houses on the Biltmore Estates, many of them owned by multimillionaires, including Vincent and Brooke Astor. On an evening walk round the manicured circuit, the Luces came across No. 43, an appealing single-storied pink stucco, red-tiled, Mediterranean-style villa on three acres, backing onto the greens. It was owned by the much-married playboy Tommy Manville, and happened to be for sale. On closer inspection, they found it was laid out around a giant olive tree set in a grassy courtyard profuse with flowers. Inside were two salons, five en suite bedrooms, and a porch. Harry saw a spot behind the swimming pool where Clare could build an art studio. Nearby were servants' quarters and a garage. Before returning to New York at the end of the month, they bought the house as a winter retreat for $250,000.[10]

In Manhattan on March 31, Clare received an award from the Jewish Theological Seminary. Eight days later, she became the first recipient of the Mary MacArthur Memorial Fund Award at a thousand-plate benefit for a polio fund established by the actress Helen Hayes. It was held at the Waldorf-Astoria's Starlight Roof, and despite its philanthropic purpose, the evening was a celebration for the returning diplomat and playwright. The attendees, apart from Miss Hayes and her husband, Charles MacArthur, included Moss Hart, Raymond Massey, and the Duke and Duchess of Windsor.[11]

The Duke of Windsor congratulates Clare on her
MacArthur Award, April 8, 1957

Shimmering in a gold satin beaded dress and diamond necklace, Clare also wore her Grand Cross of the Italian Republic and her insignia of a Dame of Malta. The producer Gilbert Miller presented her with an engraved scroll in honor of her "outstanding contributions to the theater as well as selfless devotion to humanitarian efforts at home and abroad."[12]

In her acceptance speech, Clare joked that it was "premature" to welcome her back to the theater. "No playwright can ever be said to have come back, until after those first night notices." But clearly she rejoiced at being again in the company of show business people. Moss Hart recognized the symptom, and remarked, "She's like an old alcoholic sniffing gin through the tavern door."[13]

These spring honors were but two of a year-long succession of awards, testimonial dinners, and honorary degrees showered on Clare by various institutions. "Fame is a mayfly here," she wrote Luigi Barzini, "and dances for you only a day!"[14] With this in mind, she accepted the Gimbel "Bright Star" Award for service to humanity, Notre Dame University's Laetare Medal, Detroit's Cor Jesu Award, the Cordell Hull Award from the Committee on Foreign Trade Education, New York City's Heart of America Award, doctorates from Fordham and Temple Universities, the Gold Medal of the National Institute of Social Sciences, the International Rescue Committee's first Freedom Award "for distinguished leadership in combating Communism," and the Great Living American Award from the U.S. Chamber of Commerce, shared with nine other honorees, including Cecil B. DeMille and the breeder of a champion hen.

She also became the first woman to address New York's Union League Club, and expanded beyond her political and Catholic oratory by delivering pronouncements on such diverse subjects as problems confronting the state of Israel and peanut farming. She orated on foreign service to the Bureau of Advertising, and on international trade to executives of the Fiat Company of America. It was only a matter of time before she received a postcard addressed to "Clare Boothe Luce Foundation, Inc."[15]

From now on she would settle for celebrity rather than stardom, and pay the price in a steady loss of self-esteem.

▽

In late May, Secretary Dulles offered Clare not the major posting she had hoped for, but a temporary appointment as one of a team of delegates to the September session of the United Nations General Assembly, headed by Ambassador Henry Cabot Lodge, Jr. She considered this an indignity, having long complained to Dulles about "the inefficacy" of the world organization, and declined the offer. "The more I weigh the question the more certain it seems that I must either exclude this assignment, or exclude the book project I have so long cherished."[16]

Deeply disillusioned in mid-June by two Supreme Court decisions releasing a number of convicted Communists, Clare telephoned Sherman Adams, Eisenhower's Chief of Staff, and harangued him on what she perceived as the deficiencies of current administration policies. Adams listened with annoyance as she successively criticized the President's budget, his "confusion" on China, and his choice of Harold Stassen as disarmament negotiator. She even blamed Ike, illogically, for the Court's liberal bias.[17]

Adams asked why she was telling him "this tale of woe." Clare said she was saying it privately before speaking or writing about it. He asked if her husband was as riled as she was. When she said yes, he condescendingly told her to get Harry to come and see him.[18]

After hanging up, Clare felt that as long as Adams stayed in the White House, her views would be unwelcome there.[19]

▽

Although Harry had spent a considerable sum refurbishing Sugar Hill, Clare seemed reluctant to spend the whole summer in Connecticut struggling with "the servant problem." Instead, on July 1, she went to Bermuda to satisfy an "overwhelming desire" to learn the new technology of aqualunging, and explore the Atlantic coral reefs off the island's north shore. She was inspired by seeing Jacques-Yves Cousteau's documentary movie *The Silent World*, after which she had yearned to plunge thirty feet down to experience his "subworld of mysterious beauty."[20]

She stayed at the Mid-Ocean Club in Tucker's Town. Her instructors for the next two weeks were Park and Jeanne Breck, who ran a local company called Undersea Sports. Park, handsome and deeply tanned, was a Philadelphia Main Liner and a college swimming champion turned pioneer diver. Like Cousteau, he had been exploring the depths since the early 1940s. His blonde wife was a native Bermudian.[21]

Breck first took Clare to the local aquarium and identified all the sea creatures she could expect to see around the reefs. She seemed unresponsive, so he moved on to give her two preliminary lessons in the use of Scott Hydro-Pak diving equipment.[22]

To her consternation, this training was not in the sea, but in a cement-lined tank near the harbor. In the backwash of Hurricane Audrey, the island's weather was windy, cold, and rainy. The Hydro-Pak was so heavy that she had trouble standing. It consisted of a thirty-pound steel air tank on her back, a full-face glass mask with a button-controlled airflow valve against her right ear, and a belt of lead weights around her waist. Beneath it all she wore a clammy black rubber frogman's tunic and tights. Once in the chilly pool, she pulled on a pair of flippers, and learned how to breathe underwater, finding that she and her equipment now weighed only one pound.[23]

"There I was," she wrote later, in the first of two articles for *Sports Illustrated*, "slithering along the bottom of the pool like an eel whose head was imprisoned in a rubber-sealed pickle jar, from which little bubbles noisily escaped, while a quiet trickle of water stole in."[24] Breck signaled her to emulate him in a series of rolling, tumbling, and jack-knifing movements.

> Suddenly I was quite out of breath. I gulped for air, and swallowed water. I breathed through my nose. Water came that way too. I snorted and spat, held my breath, and sought to surface. Instead, I sank fast, arms up, legs sprawled, in a sitting position. The bottom of my tank hit the metal drain on the bottom of the pool. There was a resounding clang. It echoed through the pool like the bells on the lost island of Atlantis. It knelled doom. I sat there, not breathing, frozen with fear. *Now I will drown.*
>
> [Breck's] finger was pointing to the button on the side of my mask. I pressed it hard. Air hissed sharply into the mask, cleared out the water and escaped: gurgle, gurgle, gurgle! All around my head bubbles panicked to the top to join their own element. And mine. I gulped air deeply and found myself shooting up in the bubbles' wake.[25]

As the morning lesson progressed, Clare felt all of her fifty-four years. She trembled with cold, and something like an icicle seemed to be stabbing her eardrums, until she learned how to adjust her air pressure.[26] Later, she told Breck that she had endured bombing in London and China, and had never been more frightened than while lying on a hard cement floor in Bermuda, shivering in ten feet of water. But then she added, "I like fear."[27]

Ghastly as the initiation had been, Clare's attempt to get warm in her hotel afterward stimulated one of her funniest prose passages.

> I turned on the hot water tap in the bathroom. I bent over to peel off my frogman's shirt. It had been a struggle in the first place to get it on. It was too tight at the hips. I don't have the hips of a frogman. I rolled it up. It coiled like an enraged garden hose below my breast, which also is not the breast of a frogman. I fought it up and over, as far as my neck. I tried to pull my arms out of the sleeves. They came out of the sleeves and almost out of their sockets. I pulled it over my head. The thing turned into a devilfish. It almost smothered me before, panting, I beat it off and hurled it to the bathroom floor. It slobbered across the tiles and lay limp, like a dead man-ray. During my struggle the hot water had reached the rim of the tub. In the nick, I turned it off. I tried the water with a

tentative toe. It seemed boiling hot. But I consigned myself to it like a lobster seeking heaven in the martyrdom of the pot. I lolled like a pink jellyfish in the tub. I floated my red, unflippered toes to the top, admiring them extravagantly. "How beautiful are thy feet, without flippers, O King's daughter."[28]

Dreading the afternoon session, she wondered why she had signed up for anything so tiring and frightening, and acknowledged that she had been bewitched by photographic images of a "liquid paradise." Her ambition was modest: "to see an angelfish face to face at his own level."[29]

A hot lunch fortified her, and with the help of a Miltown tranquilizer she found her next plunge in the tank less arduous and painful.[30] Gradually, she became more adept at handling the gear. But her sleep that night was marred by a terrifying dream during which her live but severed head, "entrapped in its gurgling and roaring mask, was rolled by hidden currents on all the floors of the seven seas."[31]

A phone call from Breck woke her the next morning. He said diving was impossible because there was a sou'wester bringing high surf and sheets of rain. Clare breathed a sigh of relief. For eleven more days, the weather remained inclement. She managed only a few dives in sheltered coves, and in shallow harbor water polluted with trash. Breck taught her how to clear her mask underwater, make intelligible signals, and adjust weights for buoyancy at various depths, or for rising to the surface.[32]

Finally, forty-eight hours before Clare was due to fly home, the skies cleared, and he and Jeanne took her in a fisherman's boat to the barrier reefs, six miles out the first day and seven the second. There she made four major dives so ecstatic that in her mind they merged into one.

Dropping into a tranquil world of madrepores, polyps, rose and star corals, anemones, and sponges, she could see a hundred feet in every direction. The colors surrounding her were those of Gauguin, Cézanne, and Seurat, while others in the dark blue-green distance reminded her of Dufy and Chagall. At thirty feet, her flipper tips touched the shining ocean floor. She felt "like a bird lighting on a bough." The bubbles rising from her exhale tube no longer looked panicky, but like "little pearly parachutes seeking the far sun." A crenellated cave beckoned. She glided under a ledge, careful to skirt outcrops of poisonous ginger coral, and found herself inside an "enchanted" spot, inhabited by the myriad species she had seen in the Bermuda Aquarium. Contrary to Breck's

Clare scuba diving off Bermuda, summer 1957

impression at the time, Clare had registered every one, and was able to identify them now: a rainbow parrot fish whose white beak she tried to scratch, gold-and-black-striped sergeant majors, mauve sea fans, giant sea urchins, waving gorgonians, starfish, a bonito almost a quarter her size, two sharp-toothed barracudas, a gray squaloid shark, a shimmering cloud of small fry, silver breams, navy blue doctorfish, a speckled red hind, lolling pipefish with seahorse heads, and if not her angelfish, something even more exquisite, a jewel fish.

He is as large as two of my fingers. His body is all lapis lazuli; his brow is sprinkled with turquoise. He glows all over. I don't move, for I know now that a teasing movement will drive him away. Oh, to be a Saint Francis of Assisi among the Fish! Poor St. Francis,

445

born out of time, never to have met Brother Jewel Fish and Sister Sea Fan at their own level! What canticles you would have sung to them! What holy converse held with them about their Maker![33]

This may have been the moment when Breck saw Clare take out a lead figure of Christ, kneel on the seabed, and pray. He felt it was "a moment of privacy" and did not photograph her. "I always regretted that."[34]

In New York on July 16, Clare was hailed by one newspaper as U.S. AMBASSADOR TO NEPTUNE. Other headlines read, THE AMAZING MRS. LUCE ADDS SKIN DIVING TO HER REPERTOIRE, and SHE SWAM WITH THE BARRACUDAS. Even an Italian broadsheet noted her "*appassionati subacquei*."[35]

The long-term benefit of Bermuda to Clare was that she regained her health.[36] In the short term, she recaptured her desire to write, so much so that she could not help spilling out her impressions of deep-sea diving in lengthy letters to two philosophers and a novelist. She wrote Ernest Hocking of feeling much closer to God in the depths than thirty-five thousand feet up in an airplane. "It is a Cistercian world. All perspectives change. Your body—no longer a body, is slim, your hands attenuated, all is elongated and enlarged without losing its essential grace or form." She quoted Thomas Traherne's line "You never enjoy the world aright, 'til the Sea itself floweth in your veins."[37] For Mortimer Adler, she described the weightlessness of the depths. "It is the closest thing to *disembodiment* I've ever known."[38]

But it was to Somerset Maugham that Clare waxed most lyrical about "living in a *new dimension*." She described being able to move up the side of a cave at the flick of a little finger, and spin her whole body with the slightest movement of her chin. "You can shoot forwards, right, left, up and down with the expenditure of less effort than it takes to deal a card. You shed the terrible burden of gravity, which grows so much more painful with the passage of the years. The heaviness of head and limb, which one feels, even in bed, no longer even exists. You become *almost* a spirit."

She had found it impossible in the aftermath of her conversion, she wrote, to attain the degree of self-abnegation to which she aspired. Deep in the ocean she had experienced "ecstasy" for the first time, in the Greek sense of escape from the body.

Three immaterial things tie you to life. Keep you feeling (alas) still human—air, or need of it, cold, and—terror. How can one be so fearful, and at the same time so ecstatic, I do not know, for every second one wonders "Will this be the last? Will something go wrong with my air supply?" And in the same *breath* you think, but *this* is what death must really be like (as it is coming) and it is wonderful!

In his reply, Maugham seemed unimpressed by her metaphysics. "What is all this underwater capering of yours? I should have thought it very unwise."[39]

▽

Simon Michael Bessie, a top editor at Harper & Brothers, spent the last weekend of July 1957 with Clare at Sugar Hill.[40] A forty-one-year-old Harvard graduate and decorated war veteran, Bessie had approached her after she got back from Italy, proposing that he publish her memoirs. Clare had agreed, since "Mike" was the kind of charming and erudite cosmopolitan she sought to cultivate now that she was reentering the literary world. He wanted to discuss the project, but found that she had done little more than jot down a rough outline. At least she could tell him that she had hired a professional researcher to make a survey of the scope and content of the enormous Clare Boothe Luce archive, already deposited at the Library of Congress, minus numerous intimate and sensitive files.[41]

After Bessie left, Clare wrote Luigi Barzini. "I have begun to think about a book." Telling him she would soon be arriving in Europe to start researching it, she went on, "I am not one of those fortunate writers who can dash off a volume without a good deal of agonizing first. A lot of it will be about Italy—another reason I want to see Rome . . . through eyes that are not jaundiced with fatigue." She told a French friend, Countess Clarita de Forceville, that the book would take several years, and she must shut herself off from "contacts of all kinds until it is *done*."[42]

In August, finding she needed extra material for her diving articles, Clare returned to Bermuda for six more days of aqualunging. Increasingly confident underwater, she dove off southwest reefs to three sunken wrecks, but recouped little treasure except a hoard of five-and-ten-cent-store dishes.[43]

"God's Little Underwater Acre," her first *Sports Illustrated* essay, appeared on September 9, the same day that President Eisenhower signed the Civil Rights Act, touching off white racist outrage in the Deep South. That evening, Clare left for Rome. She was curious to see what sort of reception she would receive from old friends and associates, having left in triumph a mere nine months before. Her successor was James D. Zellerbach, a California paper tycoon, whom she had briefed in Washington. She had since heard from Italian friends that the Villa Taverna was "a gloomy place these days," and that Zellerbach was "extraordinarily dull," as well as lacking in political insight. "Before everything," Count Dino Grandi wrote her, "you are a Poet, and that's also why you have been much perfect Ambassador in this country of 'camailles and Gods.' That's also why Italians laugh now of poor Zellerbach, and call his wife *il secchio pappagallo* [the dried-up parrot]."[44]

Reluctant to ask for a room at the Villa, Clare reserved a suite in the Grand Hotel. At the airport, remnants of her old staff greeted her, but to her disappointment no Italians. Nor, with the exception of Barzini, did any visit her or send flowers. "It is almost as if I had never been to Italy," she wrote Harry, sinking into despondency. "I would not be *l'ambasciatrice* again here for all the jewels in Bulgari."[45]

After six disillusioning days, she flew on to West Berlin, where she was to represent an ailing John Foster Dulles at the dedication of Benjamin-Franklin-Halle, a cultural memorial to free speech partly financed by the United States. She stayed with David Bruce, now Ambassador to West Germany, and on her first afternoon took a nostalgic walk along Kurfürstendamm, the once elegant street where she had lived in 1923, while her stepfather studied plastic surgery at the university. She also walked through the Tiergarten, where at nineteen she had strolled daily with her mother, and was distressed to see how its former magnificence had been destroyed by war. Even more shocking was her first sight of the Communist world in the city's bleak Soviet sector. "I never realized so much what a tragedy the division of Germany is," she told a reporter for the *Berliner Zeitung*. "Those people over there, poor, sad, hopeless—I was profoundly moved."[46]

The following day, September 19, she opened the hall, a futuristic, curving concrete structure locally dubbed "the pregnant oyster," and delivered an address entitled "Berlin, Symbol of the West." Her audience included such American cultural figures as Thornton Wilder, William Saroyan, Martha Graham, Virgil Thomson, Burgess Meredith, Ethel Waters, and Lillian Gish.

Clare's remarks were State Department boilerplate, except for a paragraph unmistakably written by herself.

Who, but you, knows what courage it took to lift the offal of war from this dear ground—to lift it, crumbling stone by stone, and charred timber by timber, to untwist the twisted steel and reforge the rusted wire and iron? We who have not endured such savage destruction, who have never walked, as you have, streets more peopled with ghosts than with the living, we cannot know the full measure of your courage in the early postwar days.[47]

▽

Instead of returning home straightaway to work on her memoirs, Clare seized the chance to do some diving in the Aegean. Stavros Niarchos sent his plane to bring her from Berlin to Athens, where she boarded the *Creole* and sailed with him to Rhodes. She made several ninety-foot plunges in the island's historic waters before running out of compressed air. Seeing the U.S. Sixth Fleet anchored nearby, she put on a shirt and pink slacks ("Always pink for the Navy"), took a launch to the aircraft carrier *Randolph,* and returned with replenished canisters.[48]

While Clare swam, sunbathed, and read Homer's *Odyssey* for the third time, the Southern states of America were in turmoil over enforcement of the new Civil Rights Act.[49] On Monday, September 23, President Eisenhower signed an executive order to integrate public schools. But in Little Rock, Arkansas, Governor Orval E. Faubus vowed to oppose the order as an infringement of states' rights. A shrieking, spitting mob of white supremacists forced nine black girls out of Little Rock Central High School. The next day, an enraged Ike airlifted in a thousand regular U.S. Army paratroops to restore order, and that night addressed the nation on television. He spoke of the seriousness of the crisis, and insisted on the enforcement of constitutional law. On Wednesday morning Central High School was encircled by federal troops, bayonets at the ready. The nine girls were escorted back to their classrooms, and by the time Clare reached New York on Friday, a tense calm prevailed in Little Rock.

At about this time, Ike offered her a seat on his newly formed Commission on Civil Rights, "charged with the continuous appraisal of the status of civil rights." But Clare turned it down.[50] Then, on October 4, just as she was beginning work on a speech to be delivered at the annual Alfred E. Smith Memorial Dinner, news broke that the Soviet Union had launched into space orbit a 184-pound steel sphere named *Sputnik,* Russian for "satellite." Traveling at 18,000 mph, and visible from earth on clear nights, it resembled a steadily moving star. Its four radio antennae transmitted pulsating beeps, which Columbia University students recorded and broadcast over WKCR. Within twenty-four hours *Sputnik* had crossed the United States at least four times.

Having recoiled in East Germany at the "poor, sad, hopeless" aspects of the Soviet system, Clare was aghast at the Kremlin's ability to fund and deploy a supersophisticated technology that might lead to the militarization of space. She immediately adapted the content of her Smith dinner address, which had been mostly about civil rights, and retitled it "Little Rock and the Muscovite Moon: Challenges to America's Leadership."

On October 17, she stood at a Waldorf-Astoria podium before twenty-five hundred people in white tie and evening gowns. Among them were her host, Cardinal Francis J. Spellman, New York Governor Averell Harriman, and Mayor Robert F. Wagner. "Your Eminence," she began, "tonight my theme is the challenge to America's leadership represented by two recent symbols . . . symbols of defeat. They are the symbol of Little Rock and the symbol of the Muscovite moon."

She went on to say that she saw the first as posing a moral threat, and the second as posing a material one. "How serious is the material challenge of the Muscovite moon? Is the satellite which the mighty arm of Soviet Russia has just punched into our heavens, an insuperable one to American scientific know-how? It is not." She informed her audience that the United States had long been working on a space satellite, and conceded "the fact that our vanguard will be a rear guard is humiliating." Even so, she was confident that the country had the money, resources, and skills soon to make the *Sputnik* obsolete.

> Why, then, does the little derisive beep of the Muscovite moon, as it travels its almost hourly trajectory around the globe, sound so like a signal of doom in the ears of so many people in the world?
>
> It sounds like a signal of doom, not because it has overtaken our defenses, but because it has punctured our pretensions; not because it is a sign of the decline of the West, but because it is a symbol of that pride which since King David's time commonly "goeth before a fall."

She pointed out that after Hiroshima, Americans had flattered themselves that their way of life had "built-in supremacy." The delusion was based on temporary nuclear monopoly, and fed by the conceit that democratic government was inherently superior to Marxism.

Well, let's *listen* to the record. It will have circled our globe and be passing overhead again without mistakes and without delay, within the hour. Beep. Beep, beep. In twelve days it has clocked more than six million miles, and is good for several billions more.

There can be no doubt: the baleful beep of the *Sputnik* which is heard in every land, every hour, on the hour, is an intercontinental, outer-space raspberry to a decade of American pretensions. . . .

It is a grim portent to hundreds of millions of people that American leadership can no longer be counted on to keep even a narrow lead over its enemies.

Turning to the fallacy of America's moral exceptionalism, Clare noted that the insistence of flag-wavers that the United States was a country "utterly devoted to the equality of its citizens" was also delusive. "What have the people of the world heard on the radio, seen on their television in these last weeks to justify that contention?" she asked. "They have seen men—white men—strike children because their skins were dark. They have seen teenagers tormenting other boys and girls for the same reason. And seeing, they have understood there are hearts in America that seethe with racial hatred."

She reminded her listeners that this was the same America "which destroyed all the great cities of Germany because they sheltered men who believed in the inferiority of certain races." She cited the irony whereby American propagandists had told refuseniks living in Warsaw Pact countries that they were being persecuted for "the 'crime' of political nonconformity." These people might well think that it was worse to deprive children of their right to an education because of "the 'crime' of physical nonconformity."

In conclusion, Clare said there could be no blinking at contemporary realities.

The [Soviet] moon has exposed our material pride. Little Rock has exposed our moral hubris. And taken together, these two events have tended to destroy the image America has sought to project of herself in the eyes of the world. . . .

We implore our Southern neighbors—and those in the North who agree with their stands on segregation and integration—if they will not lift their eyes to the highest heaven, at least to lift them as high as the *Sputnik*. For that moon raises the real question:

the question *all* Americans must soon answer. The question is not whether Central High will be peacefully integrated, but whether it—and every other Central High in America—will be violently *disintegrated* by the warheads of which *Sputnik* itself is merely the pioneer.[51]

Clare sat down to cries of "Bravo!" Cardinal Spellman said it was the finest address he had ever heard. Judge Irving R. Kaufman, convictor of the Rosenbergs, felt the same, and wrote to tell her so. "Your speech, which was a masterpiece in both substance and delivery, jogged us out of our complacency." He also wrote the Cardinal. "What a talented lady she is. Our government would be wise in making more use of those talents."[52]

41

NO ONE STARED

*Only when one has lost all curiosity about the future has one
reached the age to write an autobiography.*

—EVELYN WAUGH

By late October of 1957, Clare was free to go to Arizona for her
planned six-month spell of memoir writing. Harry, still tied to his
ever-growing magazine empire (*Sports Illustrated* was losing lots of
money), could not follow her there until shortly before Christmas.[1] En
route to Phoenix on October 28, she was still in an apocalyptic mood,
and wrote her husband a note about the international nuclear threat,
urging him to take precautionary measures. "Get *your plane, your pilot*
for *your family*, and arrange . . . shelter."[2]

Settling down to work, she soon found that research and fact-
checking, not to mention the often painful honesty required for autobiographical writing, proved more daunting than anticipated. Then
there were other unfinished projects, including her play for the Gish
sisters and a fifteen-thousand-word diving book for Prentice-Hall due in
mid-December.[3] A daily distraction was what Sister Madeleva described
as "the crystal sun-smitten world" of Clare's desert retreat, with its
temptations of swimming, golf, gardening, painting in her new studio,
and being caught up in the Biltmore circle's seasonal social round.[4]

Keeping the house running smoothly was difficult, since she competed for a shrinking pool of help with equally affluent "snowbirds." A prime annoyance was that Dorothy Farmer refused to winter in Phoenix, so she had to train a succession of temporary secretaries. At least she had Arthur Little, her dependable gardener from Sugar Hill, to act as chauffeur and factotum.[5]

By November 23, Clare sounded less than wholehearted about her current occupation, telling a former embassy employee, "I have had to make a choice between applying myself to my own work—writing—or giving that up permanently and becoming a 'public figure.' Well, for better or worse, I've opted for 'English Lit.'"[6]

Yet two days later she intruded herself into politics when President Eisenhower, who had been preparing for a post-*Sputnik* NATO summit in Paris, was rushed to Walter Reed Hospital with a cerebral spasm.[7] This was the third serious illness, counting an attack of ileitis, that he had suffered in twenty-six months. At 9:00 the following morning, a parish priest, Father George H. Dunne, S.J., arrived to play golf with Clare, and found her on a sunny patio, telephone at her side.

"I just phoned Nixon," she told him. "'Dick,' I said, 'you have got to attend that meeting in Paris two weeks from now. Never mind what others advise.'" She had also called William F. Knowland and Joe Martin, the Republican leaders of the Senate and House, and commanded them to "see to it that Nixon understands that the Paris meeting must not be abandoned."[8]

Father Dunne had the impression that in rallying all Washington to Nixon's side, Clare had just taken over the management of the country. She was too busy at any rate for golf, and told one of her secretaries to play with the cleric instead.[9]

Unable to resist the lure of the dais, Clare flew back to New York in December to give two speeches. She reneged on her diving book contract, and told the Gish sisters not to expect the play she had promised. "I can't figure out a straight story line."[10] All she had managed of her autobiography was a fragmentary plan.

1903—*Born N.Y. City*

. . . (Father leaves) Chicago Flat
. . . travel Violinist Father
. . . Jersey days . . .
. . . New York flats—poverty

1934–1935—La vie libre d'une Femme du Monde

Artists & Writers
Politicians & Statesmen
People
Lovers—
The Meaning of a woman's Life—[11]

For Clare, a part of the price of fame seemed to be an inability to describe her humble origins and the ruthlessness of her ambition, not to mention the decline in her playwriting ability. Like many blocked authors, she looked for excuses.

> There's always the negative consolation the times themselves provide a writer with—that unless one happens to be a genius it doesn't matter too much what books are written or read on the eve of Armageddon. Did I say Armageddon? I don't really mean that. I'm inclined to agree with Dr. Kissinger in his analysis of the situation—that we are in the age of the creeping Munichs.[12]

Henry A. Kissinger, associate director of Harvard's Center for International Affairs and author of a new book, *Nuclear Weapons and Foreign Policy*, was, she told Nelson Rockefeller, "my latest enthusiasm. . . . I've not got around to reading him before."[13]

Her growing paranoia, incipient in her *Sputnik* speech and in her letter to Harry about preparing for nuclear attack, was yet more apparent at a dinner party that month attended and documented by Father Dunne. It took place at the house of Frank C. Brophy, Jr., a local Catholic lawyer and philanthropist. After dessert, the company of ten adjourned to the sitting room, where Clare began a monologue that accused FDR of being a Communist sympathizer, and then moved on to an anti-Semitic diatribe that reminded Dunne of *The Protocols of the Elders of Zion.*

> According to Mrs. Luce, there existed a relatively small group of wealthy Jews who met once a year in the greatest secrecy and planned the strategy of world Jewry for the future. Every major evil that had occurred in the political, economic, and social areas, dating back at least to the overthrow of the czarist regime in Russia in

1917 and the breakup of the Austro-Hungarian Empire—which breakup she deplored—and continuing through World War II and its aftermath, had been planned at and was the result of these meetings.

Clare did not say how she had managed to penetrate the secrecy of these gatherings. Father Dunne was appalled that a woman of such reputed intelligence could mouth obvious absurdities. Noticing that their host was nodding politely as she rambled on, he interrupted. "Frank, why do you agree with all of this nonsense? Simply because it comes from Clare Boothe Luce?"

At once, Clare stood up to leave. Before stepping into her car, she turned and said, "Tell Father Dunne that at least I am not anticlerical."

The next day, the priest wrote a mutual acquaintance, Father John Courtney Murray, of how disturbing he found the incident. Murray replied, "You have seen one facet of a multi-faceted woman . . . the facet which I call—and she is aware of this—the 'from rags to bitches' side."[14]

▽

Harry traveled to Phoenix on February 1 with Laura Hobson, currently working as a publicist for *Time*. She was to be Clare's houseguest. Heeding Miss Thrasher's warning, "Mr. Luce does not like to sit next to anybody he knows when he's on a plane," Laura took a seat some distance away. But when they stopped to change planes in Chicago, the boss sought her out. He was in a talkative mood, and held forth on how impossible it was to quit smoking. When Laura said she had done so, he became visibly annoyed. He also seemed irked by the current bestseller he was reading, Max Shulman's *Rally Round the Flag, Boys!* "I can't understand half the expressions in it. I suppose it's the new slang."

As the plane neared Phoenix, Laura passed Harry's seat on her way to the bathroom.

Something about the way he was sitting caught my peripheral vision; he seemed slumped sideways. . . . He was pale, waxy-looking. I knew something was very wrong; I knelt beside him, right there in the aisle.

"Harry, are you all right?" A stewardess came rushing up.

"Oxygen?" she said, but rushed off for aspirin and water.

I reached for his wrist, to try for his pulse, but he yanked his hand back. "It's nothing," he said. "I'm all right."

But I stayed there, kneeling beside him; his color began to return; he sat back, straightening himself firmly; he did look more himself. But I was glad we were approaching the airport.

As Arthur Little drove them to the house, Harry was silent. Clare seemed to notice nothing amiss when they arrived.[15]

The following day, Sunday, Harry suddenly said, "I'm dying."[16] Clare summoned an ambulance to take him to St. Joseph's Hospital. Laura was in the garden when the stretcher was carried out. He looked spent, she noted, "so unlike the powerful Henry Robinson Luce the whole world knew."[17]

Laura followed the couple to the hospital, where she found Clare crying and saying to a nun, "If anything happens to Harry, my whole life would be over."[18]

On Monday, Dr. Hayes Caldwell checked Harry's blood count and ordered an X-ray and electrocardiogram. All looked fine, but next day Clare found him in bed surrounded by bloody paper tissues. Aghast, she summoned Caldwell, who diagnosed a pulmonary embolism. He called New York to consult with a Time Inc. physician, and Dr. Rosenbluth. Both concurred with his finding, and Harry was prescribed anticoagulants.[19]

But on Wednesday, February 5, another electrocardiogram showed an alarming change. Harry had had what Caldwell called "a coronary insufficiency"—in plain language, a heart attack.[20]

Aside from her own distress, Clare was aware that the value of Time Inc. stock depended largely on the good health of its founder. Any news that Henry Luce, two months shy of sixty, was seriously ill might be calamitous, not only to the company but to themselves as major shareholders. She managed to keep his condition secret until reporters began to pester Caldwell for a statement. The doctor referred all inquiries to her. She decided to announce only that her husband was being treated for pneumonia brought on by severe influenza.[21] The story ran as a special in *The New York Times* on February 12, under the headline HENRY LUCE IN HOSPITAL: MAGAZINE EDITOR STRICKEN BY PNEUMONIA.

Not even Harry's close relatives were allowed to know the truth of his condition. Clare asked Laura to tell them only of his embolism.[22] He remained in the hospital for the next three weeks, missing a visit to his house by the Nixons and Joe Martin, who were in town for a Republican rally.[23]

▽

Harry left St. Joseph's on February 23, and felt well enough in early March to attend a dinner party at Taliesin West, the architectural school run by Frank Lloyd Wright in Scottsdale. He appeared to have lost his former glum irritability, and tolerated a couple of feisty students who criticized *Life* magazine for "talking down to the American public." At the other end of the room, Clare, in a silvery-blue gown, was surrounded by a multicultural group of young people. Olgivanna Wright heard her say, "Speaking frankly, Japan is the only important country right now."[24]

"Important to whom?" an Egyptian youth asked, eyes flashing.

Mrs. Wright, knowing him to be a fiery devotee of Gamal Abdel Nasser, tried to head off an argument. "Everybody and everything is important," she said, and the awkward moment passed.[25]

Clare's directness had already caused a frisson with the octogenarian architect himself. He had spoken of his success in melding American Southwestern and Far Eastern aesthetics and technology to produce a new style. "He was a little miffed," Clare wrote Ernest Hocking, "when I called his house Wigwam-Oriental."[26]

The Luces closed the Phoenix house at the end of April and returned to New York. Three weeks later, Clare was photographed at Idlewild Airport looking remarkably unlined, with a row of sparkling new teeth. She was on her way to the Bahamas for more skin diving. "I am fatter, healthier and more calm than I have been for years," she told Gerry Miller, "though I often feel somewhat useless."[27] The weather in Nassau was as bad as it had been in Bermuda, but she at least learned how to catch fish with her bare hands, spear a moray eel, and compile enough material for two more *Sports Illustrated* articles entitled "The Heaven Below."[28]

▽

Now that she had become proficient in the technique of "making like a fish," Clare's chronic need to conquer new disciplines impelled her into a summer of frenzied activity.[29] She seemed apprehensive that she might never do better than she had already in politics and diplomacy. A friend remarked, "She would rather dominate another field than stay in one simply for the marginal pleasure of being able to play that arpeggio a little bit faster."[30]

On June 17, she began with a course of twelve lessons at Manhattan's Helen Worth Cooking School, which at various times graduated Betty Furness, Phyllis Cerf, Pamela Harriman, and Rosemary Harris. Not knowing even how to boil an egg, she needed to learn also how to broil and bake, before progressing to *crêpes* and *court bouillon*. She took extra instruction from the chef James Beard, but was repelled by his obesity and his use of the same knife to slice onions and chocolate.[31]

Next she registered with an art teacher in Connecticut, and halfway through July flew to Big Sur to study with the mosaicist Louisa Jenkins, who had helped decorate Saint Anne's Chapel. Working with ceramics, Clare found, gave her an inner satisfaction unlike any she had experienced in public life. "I find it great therapy," she wrote Carlos Chávez, "a sort of music making in glass. One brings design and order out of a chaos of unrelated bits of stone."[32]

Later that summer, she took an advanced course in tile and pebble setting with Emmanuel Viviano at Columbia University,[33] and played bridge with the master player Charles Goren, who said she was one of his three favorite "tablemates."[34]

In September, she became a teacher herself, imparting some of her new skills to the children of her Ridgefield employees. She then returned to Arizona and worked on a 34-by-46-inch mosaic of the Virgin of Guadalupe for Scottsdale's Miracle of Roses pageant.[35]

Mosaic by Clare Boothe Luce, c. 1958

▽

In New York in early October, Clare fell into a week-long depression so severe that she felt "on the verge of insanity." Her youthful bouts of melancholy had rarely lasted more than a day, but in early middle age they became deeper and more protracted. Any perceived rejection could set them off. Recently, on leaving an elevator full of young men, she felt her loss of physical appeal when "no one, but no one, had stared at me."[36] Her low spells were characterized by fits of wild sobbing, triggered by she knew not what, and an agonizing indecisiveness, to the point that she would stand in the middle of a room, unable to make up her mind "whether to go through one door or another." Religion proved of little help when the darkness closed in. Prayer only worsened her feeling "that I had failed God, or that he had failed me."[37]

Harry was scared enough by this latest slump to send for Dr. Rosenbluth. To Clare's astonishment, he said he had been aware for years that she "needed mental treatment." He muttered something about "schizophrenia," and urged her to check into the Payne Whitney Psychiatric Clinic in Manhattan.

Unable to accept that she might be going mad, Clare resisted this advice, but accepted a medication that served only to make her jittery and sleepless. Just as she conceded she might have to commit herself, salvation came in the form of a call from the White House. Pope Pius XII had died, and President Eisenhower asked her to be one of his three representatives at the obsequies in Italy. This made her feel useful again, and her depression lifted.[38]

Secretary Dulles headed the delegation, which arrived in Rome on the morning of October 18. He was chauffeured to the Villa Taverna, while Clare and John A. McCone, the Catholic chairman of the Atomic Energy Commission, were shunted to the Grand Hotel. In a further reminder that she was no longer in the government, Clare was excluded from Ambassador Zellerbach's all-male luncheon for Dulles, and even from one for McCone. She was expected instead to attend a ladies' lunch at a restaurant, hosted by Mrs. Zellerbach. Regretting without regret, she claimed to have "private plans," and later made a pointed gibe: "I belong to the Order of Displaced Diplomats."[39] Later, Dulles and Zellerbach called on President Gronchi at the Quirinal Palace, whose gilded halls were no longer open to her. By now Clare was feeling seriously de trop.[40]

For the solemn requiem Mass at St. Peter's Basilica the next day,

Sunday, male mourners were required to wear tailcoats, white ties, and top hats. Clare put on a heavy veil and floor-length black dress with flat, sling-back evening slippers. The last caused Italian outrage. WEARS SANDALS AT FUNERAL! a local headline screamed. She did not explain that she had foot trouble.

Two weeks later, she returned to Rome, this time as Eisenhower's personal representative at the coronation of Pope John XXIII. For Clare, the most memorable part of the ceremony on November 4 was when the rotund Pontiff was carried down the nave of St. Peter's on the *sedia gestatoria*. His progress was stopped three times as, in rapt silence, a monk set fire to a bundle of flax on a gilded staff. A voice intoned, *"Pater Sancte, sic transit gloria mundi,"* reminding the Holy Father of his renunciation of worldly things. "And then," Clare told a journalist, "a hundred long silver trumpets cracked out from the balconies. It was joyful and magnificent."[41]

She attended a group audience with the new Pontiff, before flying home and proceeding to Arizona for a nonliterary six months.

By now, the Luces' Phoenix house had been redecorated and furnished. The overall impression inside was of soft whites, with splashes of red adobe, gold, and copper. Four amethyst crystal candelabra, somewhat jarring in a desert setting, served Clare as mementos of Italy. Ignoring Harry's suggestion that she make a separate study off the hallway, she reverted to her lifelong habit of working in her bedroom. She placed a desk at one windowed end of the blue-and-white retreat, and on it two blue wicker baskets marked "In" and "Out." A third, labeled "Things to Do," overflowed with notes, letters, and manuscripts.[42]

Her current interests were reflected in a French provincial bookcase packed with cookbooks, and a green-and-blue mosaic of a four-eyed butterfish. In the studio beyond the pool, she completed her mosaic "The Virgin of Guadalupe" and posed beside it for the *Phoenix Gazette*. An interviewer from another newspaper found her carrying a miniature chocolate-colored poodle and "looking strikingly two decades younger than she must be." In contrast, Harry was pale, thin, and frail.[43]

42

SERPENT'S TONGUE

$$\triangledown$$

*Life must be lived forward but
can only be understood backward.*

—Søren Kierkegaard

Early in January 1959, an ailing John Foster Dulles telephoned Clare to offer her the ambassadorship to Brazil.[1]

The proposal was unexpected, since she had turned down two other appointments from Eisenhower: a place on the Civil Rights Commission, and directorship of his People to People Program.[2] Although Rio was not London or Paris, it was a substantial post, and a chance to serve her country again. She asked for time to consider.

Running through her options, Clare acknowledged that she was enjoying life in Arizona, but often felt lonely for cosmopolitan experiences. She also had "a puritanical strain" that "creates a feeling of guilt if one is not working." A possible downside to accepting was the likelihood of being recalled should a Democrat be elected to the presidency in 1960. There was also the question of her husband's health. Since his heart attack, Dr. Caldwell had diagnosed not only angina, but urethral blockage, neither of which was conducive to long commutes to the Southern Hemisphere.[3] When she talked it over with Harry, however, he was surprisingly eager for her to go, and that persuaded her to accept.[4]

On the morning of February 20, Clare heard a radio news leak that she had been chosen as envoy to Brazil, replacing Ellis O. Briggs, one of the ablest career diplomats in the Foreign Service. Four days later in Rio de Janeiro, President Juscelino Kubitschek formally approved of the appointment.[5] Editorial reaction in Brazil, a Roman Catholic nation of sixty-seven million, was mostly positive.[6]

The official announcement in *The New York Times* noted that college girls in Italy had voted Clare their "ideal woman," over the movie star Gina Lollobrigida. But it warned that "the Democratic-dominated Senate will have to overlook some of the rough things she has said about Democrats." Alongside ran a profile titled "An Ambassador Again," accompanied by a flattering photograph. After a sympathetic summary of her earlier life, the article characterized Clare as "a tiger with sharp claws" in the political arena. It quoted her in full rhetorical flood in 1948, saying that "a Democratic President is doomed to proceed to his goals like a squid, squirting darkness all about him."

The *Times* made much of her conversion, alleging that religion had given her an "acquired warmth." It resurrected the apocryphal story of her proselytizing Pope Pius XII until he protested, "But my dear Signora, I have to remind you. I am already a Catholic."[7]

The CBS correspondent Eric Sevareid began his radio commentary on the nomination rather patronizingly.

> Mrs. Clare Boothe Luce, journalist, playwright, diplomat, skin diver and blonde, is about to make her entrance on the public scene again. And any other actors worried about being upstaged have had fair warning: the President has selected her to be the new Ambassador to Brazil, a country suffering a shortage of blondes, but an even greater shortage of new financing and technical know-how suitable to this economic age. Economics is not Mrs. Luce's strong point, but she is a "quick study," as they say in the theater, and knows how to organize a capable and loyal staff.

He went on to praise her as a "remarkable" woman, who "doesn't fit any pattern or pre-conception and never has." Sevareid was sure the Senate would confirm her "without much trouble—they just don't have a yardstick for this lady."[8]

Harry took prior endorsement by the Senate Foreign Relations Committee for granted, and telegraphed "Congratulations and best wishes all the way" to Clare in Phoenix.[9]

At noon on Tuesday, March 3, the full committee met in executive session with Senator J. William Fulbright (D-AR) presiding. Among the other ten Democrats present were Hubert Humphrey of Minnesota, Mike Mansfield of Montana, Wayne L. Morse of Oregon, Frank Lausche of Ohio, and John F. Kennedy of Massachusetts. There were only six Republicans, including William Langer of North Dakota and George D. Aiken of Vermont.[10]

Fulbright, who had apparently forgiven Clare for correcting his confusion in the meaning of the verbs *infer* and *imply* on the floor of the House sixteen years before, asked whether Mrs. Luce's nomination could be confirmed without her attendance at a hearing. Morse moved a favorable report at once to the Senate, and the committee agreed by voice vote.

Senator Langer, however, wished to be registered in the negative. This compelled Fulbright to invoke the customary rule of a six-day delay in further action. While doing so, he noted that Clare had a long record of public service, and that other nominees of her stature had been excused from testimony.[11]

At 2:40 P.M., the Senate Foreign Relations Committee's Subcommittee for American Republics Affairs, chaired by Senator Morse, met for a routine hearing on economic and other problems south of the border. An interminable report by Roy R. Rubottom, Jr., Assistant Secretary of State for Inter-American Affairs, was interrupted by an urgent UPI message, which Morse read aloud. It stated that over the weekend there had been violent anti-American demonstrations in Bolivia, prompted by an article in the Latin American edition of *Time* magazine.

Rubottom confirmed that the piece had been "quite offensive." It had quoted a U.S. Embassy official in La Paz as saying that $129 million in aid had been given to the Bolivian government, and "we don't have a damn thing to show for it." The only solution was to "abolish Bolivia and let its neighbors divide the country and its problems among themselves."[12]

The remark had been made in jest, Rubottom said, and *Time*'s decision to publish it was "patently contrary to the national interests of the United States." As a result, the situation in La Paz was grave and escalating. "Our Embassy yesterday afternoon was stoned, and a couple of cars were burned. The *carabineros* . . . apparently shot into the crowd and killed a fifteen-year-old boy, and further attacks [are] expected on the Embassy this afternoon." Evacuation of American personnel was being considered. Meanwhile, they were in hiding. Copies of the offending magazine had been confiscated or burned, but the diplomatic damage remained.

"Mr. Secretary," Wayne Morse said, "as the one who made the motion to expedite Mrs. Luce's confirmation, I am not so sure that this incident is going to help her in Brazil."[13]

▽

The Senator sounded a further ominous note on March 10, when consideration of Clare's appointment came up again in the Foreign Relations Committee. "I move we reconsider the Luce nomination without prejudice, so that we can have some executive discussion, possibly an executive hearing. . . . I think the dust ought to settle a bit before this appointment goes through."[14]

Clare was informed that she would have to testify on Wednesday, April 15, after the Easter recess. That would be three months since Dulles had offered her the job. This was frustrating for her, and an embarrassment to Harry. As Editor in Chief of *Time*, he was responsible for the Bolivian episode, which had ended with two dead, thirty-eight policemen injured, and $70,000 worth of damage to American property. Maddened crowds had stormed the embassy, shouting, *"Imperialismo Yanqui!"* and, *"Abajo Dõna Clara!"*[15] Harry issued a qualified statement of regret, but stood by his magazine's story.[16] This did little to assuage the outraged feelings of Bolivians, nor did it improve Clare's prospects for an easy confirmation. As the columnist Drew Pearson warned, *Time's* indiscretion would make it "extremely difficult" for Clare "to serve effectively in her new post," given that Brazil shared a long border with Bolivia.[17]

Nobody got more glee out of the discomfiture of the Luces than their former whipping boy, Harry S. Truman. "What a nice thing," he gloated, "to have Mr. Clare Boothe Luce in the grease in Bolivia. He spent a lot of time trying to put me in the grease, but never succeeded."[18]

In Phoenix, Clare determinedly continued her preparations to sail for Rio. She hired a professor from Arizona's American Institute for Foreign Trade to teach her the language, history, and economics of Brazil. She took a Linguaphone course in Portuguese, and found it "pretty rough" going. She read six scholarly books sent her by Allen Dulles, including Hernane Tavares de Sá's *The Brazilians: People of Tomorrow* and Gilberto Freyre's just published *New World in the Tropics: The Culture of Modern Brazil*. She asked Nelson Rockefeller to write some of his

Brazilian friends on her behalf. Using her connections at the State Department, she arranged for the transfer of eleven senior aides currently serving Ambassador Briggs to be replaced by career diplomats of her choosing.[19]

A problem Clare had to fix before appearing in Washington was to have an operation on a bursitic little toe, which prevented her from wearing high heels. On March 18, she underwent surgery, and with characteristic interest in every new experience, reported it in detail to Louisa Jenkins. "Two doctors latched onto my pinkie and split it from stem to stern, the way you slice a little sandwich pickle. Then they chiseled off a piece of protruding bone and yanked out the noisome bursa which had surrounded it like an octopus. . . . Seems I must stomp around on crutches for the next few weeks."[20]

As Clare hobbled her way into the splendid new Foreign Relations Committee room on Capitol Hill at 10:30 A.M. on April 15, 1959, front-page headlines were reporting the resignation of John Foster Dulles, who was mortally ill with recurrent cancer. It made the occasion poignant for her, since one of the Secretary's last official acts had been to put her name forward for Brazil.

Only eight of the committee's seventeen members were waiting to question her. Along with Chairman Fulbright were Senators Humphrey, Mansfield, Morse, Kennedy, Lausche, Aiken, and Alexander Wiley (R-WI). Clare was escorted to her seat by Senator Prescott Bush, from her own state of Connecticut. Introducing her, he said that her "brilliant ability" and "excellent performance" in Rome would make her a "highly effective" envoy to Rio.[21]

Fulbright asked if the nominee would like to make an opening statement. Clare had none prepared, but expressed pleasure at seeing "my old colleague of 1943 sitting in such high eminence in this beautiful room." The chairman responded with equal courtesy. He asked a few questions about possible Luce investments in Brazil, and whether her husband intended to live with her in Rio. She said they had no conflicts of interest in the country, and that Harry would stay about half the time.

"Do you speak Portuguese?"

"Senator, it is a very difficult language," Clare replied. "I can hardly say that I have mastered it, but I expect that by the time I arrive . . . I will be able to conduct an ordinary conversation in the language."

He asked if she knew of Brazil's "precarious" financial condition.

"Indeed I do, Senator," she said, and rattled off a series of its international debt statistics, relating them to "the loss of a large part of the coffee market." When Fulbright noted that Brazil was one of the largest borrowers from the Export-Import Bank, she interrupted. "About $500 million up until now."

Turning to the Bolivian riots, he asked if she thought her effectiveness would be impaired by *Time* magazine's responsibility for the violence. Clare was ready for him.

"I am not the editor of *Time*, and I am being sent as an Ambassador to Brazil and not to Bolivia."

Fulbright suddenly said, "Do you still believe that mortal enemies of the United States are growing and thriving in the organism of the Democratic Party?"

He was referring to a savage national television campaign speech she had made on September 30, 1952, and asked her if she recalled it. Her reply was both evasive and pert.

"I recall a few of yours, Senator."

Fulbright quoted her remarks for the record. "For twenty years mortal enemies of ours have been growing and thriving in the organism of the Democratic Party. There is only one way to dislodge them. . . . The tree of government must be shaken hard. Then these rotten apples, these mortal enemies, will fall out before all from the top branches."

Again she was facetious. "That is awfully good oratory."

"Well," he retorted, "it is yours."

Aware she had gone too far, Clare explained that she had not been attacking his party per se. "Where there are subversive elements in any country, they seek very hard to lodge themselves in the organism of the party in power. . . . That is the logical place for them to go. They want to be in with the 'ins,' not out with the 'outs.'"

Fulbright pressed further, saying that her use of the phrase *top branches* meant President Truman. "You don't subscribe to that doctrine, that he was a traitor to this country, do you?"

"Certainly not. I never said so."

"That is the implication to be drawn, if I may use that word. May I draw that?"

"I am glad you are implying and not inferring," Clare said.

"Well, we do learn, you know, after a long time," Fulbright conceded.

He then asked if she stood by her attack in 1944 on another Chief Executive, calling Franklin D. Roosevelt "the only American President who lied us into a war, because he did not have the political courage to lead us into it."

Clare said that history proved Roosevelt had not initially told citizens the truth about the German threat. He should have made it clear "that we were going to have to fight the Nazis . . . sooner rather than later."

"You stand by that statement, then, you think?"

"I stand by—"

"You think he lied us into a war?"

"I stand by my statement."

"I was hoping that time had mellowed your judgment a bit, but it hasn't," Fulbright said. "That is quite clear."

"Time has mellowed my language, I hope," Clare replied. "But the accuracy, historical accuracy, I must stand by."

The chairman yielded to Senator Mansfield, who wanted to place on record Clare's "commendable" service in Congress and "outstanding" achievements as Ambassador to Italy, in particular her role in the settlement of the Trieste crisis. Senator Aiken added that she "seems to stand up very well under direct examination."

"Thank you, Senator," she said.

Aiken sat back, and the chairman said, "Senator Morse."[22]

▽

Wayne Lyman Morse was a fifty-eight-year-old, hawk-nosed, mustachioed political maverick with improbably thick black eyebrows. He had been in the Senate since 1945, first as a Republican, then (in protest of Eisenhower's choice of Nixon as running mate) as an Independent, and now as a Democrat. Intellectually acute and well-read, he was considered the most eloquent, if long-winded, orator in the Senate.[23]

He began by saying that although his questions were going to be "rather pointed," he had "no personal animosity" toward Mrs. Luce, but was merely fulfilling his "public trust" as a committee member.[24]

Citing her assertion that she stood by her accusation that FDR had "lied us into a war," Morse said he was shocked by it. "I could not possibly vote for your nomination until you document [that] statement . . . because, undocumented, I would consider it subversive."

Clare apologized for her "intemperate" language, and explained that it had been in the heat of a political campaign.[25]

"What was your position, if any, on October 11, 1944?" Morse asked.

"I was a member of Congress."

"Yes. You were not a private citizen . . . you had a responsible position of public trust, and I say most respectfully you were out trying to get the American people in 1944 to believe they had a lying President, and I think you ought to be required to prove your statements."

She asked what proof would satisfy him.

Morse said he would accept any reliable authorities. Going back further, he stated that "on March 3, 1943," she had said that Harry Truman had been "handpicked by big city bosses who are ready to stuff a ballot box or steal an election before you say 'Missouri.'" Was she still of that opinion?

"I think he was certainly their candidate."

"Big city bosses?"

"He was certainly their candidate."

"What do you mean by 'their candidate'?"

"They were for him."

"You mean they supported him?"

"Yes."

"And whenever anyone supported you for your races for Congress, did that make you their candidate? Did they handpick you?"

Clare became rattled. "What do you mean by 'handpicked'?"

"I don't know. You used the word. I didn't."

"I have no idea what I may have meant by it. What does it mean to you?"

"Suppose you tell us what it means. I'm trying—"

"I have no idea."

"It is your judgment that is under examination before this committee, Mrs. Luce."

"It is not only my judgment," Clare came back at him, "but it is my memory that seems to be under observation, and I find it awfully difficult to imagine what I may have been thinking—how many years ago, Senator?"

Morse checked his notes and found he had made a mistake. "I beg pardon. This was June 20, 1948."

"Well, that is more than ten years go. I cannot always remember exactly what was in my mind about any given phrase as long as ten years ago."

"I'm only asking," Morse said, "what is in your mind today. . . ."

"You do catch me very much off base," Clare replied, "because when you ask me what was in my mind when I came here, what was in my mind was Brazil."

Senator Aiken asked Morse to yield. "I wonder if we have completely forgiven Germany and Japan . . . for what happened fifteen years ago, but still hold Mrs. Luce responsible for something she said in the heat of emotion at that time." He suggested she was being found guilty for not voting for Truman.[26]

Morse rejected this as a "non-sequitur argument."

"Is it his view," Clare asked, "that anyone who took a dim view of the election of Mr. Roosevelt or Mr. Truman is not fit to represent their country abroad?"

"Not at all," Morse said.

Clare could have reminded him that in his days as a Republican, he had himself been vituperatively critical of Roosevelt and Truman. But she refrained.

Changing the subject to her Italian mission, the Senator quoted an article in the left-wing periodical *The Reporter* of February 23, 1956. It accused her of interfering in Italian elections, favoring the "former Fascist goons" of the Monarchist Party, and using the blandishment of foreign aid to persuade the Italian government to give exclusive oil-drilling contracts to American companies. He asked her to comment on these charges, saying he was particularly interested in the third, since her husband's magazines promoted the acquisition of foreign oil by United States companies, and "Brazil is a country that operates an oil government monopoly."

Clare replied that her Milan speech of May 1953 had merely expressed the policy of her own government, as articulated by professionals on her staff. She said that her remarks had created a stir only in "the Communist and the Socialist press." As for her alleged support of the Italian right wing, "At no time ever, in any circumstances, did I or any member of my Embassy ever give aid, comfort or encouragement to the Fascist Party of Italy." She indignantly refuted the insinuation that she had used aid as "blackmail" for oil concessions. All she suggested was that Western countries of any flag should be allowed to give Italians the benefit of their extraction technology. "Because as you know, Senator, you must dig an average of seventeen wells to hit one."

To this, Morse had no reply except to say, "Are you through?"[27]

Senator John Kennedy, who had just decided to run for the presidency, asked permission to interrupt with a brief statement, before he left for another meeting.[28] Morse yielded.

"I have known Mrs. Luce for twenty years," Kennedy said. "I think personally that she could fulfill the ambassadorship to Brazil with competence and to the credit of the United States, and I have every confidence that she can, based on her public record, and I am delighted to support her nomination wholeheartedly."[29]

"Thank you, Senator," Clare said.

▽

After some forty minutes more of testimony, Clare left the hearing room close to tears. She broke down in the elevator, and an unidentified man in a trench coat tried to screen her face.[30]

Wayne Morse had continued to bludgeon her.[31] Should American Ambassadors accept decorations from foreign governments? Was arsenic poisoning the primary reason for her departure from Rome? What were her views on the relative merits of career versus political appointees to diplomatic posts? Had she asked Dulles for the job?[32]

Clare had tried to be temperate and dignified in her responses. Concerned by the overall impression she had made, she asked to be allowed to edit from the transcript of the proceedings "anything that might cause embarrassment."[33]

That afternoon, the committee met in executive session to confirm her appointment. But at the urging of Langer and Morse, the Senators decided to delay a vote until those who had missed the morning's exchanges could read a transcript. They agreed that the nominee should not be allowed to edit her own words. But she was welcome to provide "supplemental materials," including the documentation Morse demanded, as well as her *Foreign Affairs* article entitled "The Ambassadorial Issue: Professionals or Amateurs?"[34]

The following morning, the Republican Party rallied to Clare's defense, condemning Morse's "harassing action." Senator Kenneth Keating of New York recalled no such "preposterous" attack on her when she was confirmed for Italy. Senator Barry Goldwater of Arizona compared the hounding of Mrs. Luce to the tactics of the late Joseph McCarthy. Fulbright angrily countered by saying that this remark exceeded the "proper bounds" of senatorial conduct.[35]

Clare's friends among the Washington elite, including Alice Roosevelt Longworth, Perle Mesta, and General Walter Bedell Smith, gave supportive parties for her over the next few days. She was also seen at a Brazilian Embassy function wearing a black tennis shoe on her aching foot.[36]

Finally, on Thursday, April 23, the committee met to vote on Clare's confirmation. Once again, Senator Morse dominated the proceedings, saying he needed at least thirty minutes to present his "analysis" of her case. "I feel that this appointment is a great mistake, and I venture the prophecy . . . that after she is sent to Brazil, in due course of time, it will be to our embarrassment."

He attacked Clare's character and diplomatic competency. "The only role for which I believe she is well qualified is political hatchet-man. She does very well at making inflammatory and demagogic political statements." Her record did not show that she had "sound judgment and a capacity for self-restraint." Nor had she displayed much commitment to her mission in Italy.

> She was a notorious absentee, even allowing for her long illness just before she resigned. In 1955 she was absent from her job 87 days, and was on vacation for another 69 days. None of that was for sick leave or due to illness. In 1956 she was absent from her job 84 days. Plus, she took 23 days of vacation and 95 days of sick leave. . . . Her total record for those two years showed her absent 171 days of duty, 187 days of non-duty, that is, vacation and sick leave.

Turning to Clare's citation of five scholarly books to adumbrate her thesis that FDR "lied" the United States into war, Morse said he had read the first, Professor Charles A. Beard's *President Roosevelt and the Coming of the War, 1941*, and found no "specific case of falsification . . . to substantiate Mrs. Luce's charge." Nor did he see any confirmation in her second source, chapter 8 of Robert Sherwood's *Roosevelt and Hopkins: An Intimate History*.

He began to orate as if he were on the Senate floor. "Does Mrs. Luce believe that what happened at Pearl Harbor was a foreign war, one that we should have ignored? Does she think that the bombs that rained down on American ships in a peaceful harbor and upon the men, women and children in American territory were a foreign involvement that we should have closed our eyes to?"

Morse did not claim to have read Clare's other sources—two works by Basil Rauch and Edgar Robinson, and Cordell Hull's seventeen-hundred-page autobiography. But he said that Professor Rauch had wired him to complain that she had "misrepresented" his book, and that Hull's massive memoir hardly constituted a verifiable reference.

No one challenged the Senator's apparent erudition. Contrary to what he said, at least two of Clare's sources—Beard and Sherwood—amply vindicated her statement, and both had been published four years after her alleged calumny of Roosevelt. At that time, Charles Beard was regarded as "the dean of American historians," revered for his fervent patriotism and anti-imperialist philosophy. His book had challenged the received image of FDR as the soldier of freedom, and accused him of preaching peace and neutrality while secretly, through "binding agreements" with future Allies, maneuvering the United States into World War II. Sherwood's chapter documented much the same behavior, and contained a sentence that uncannily echoed Clare's words of 1944: "Whatever the peril, he was not going to lead the country into war—he was going to wait to be pushed in."[37]

Morse, unstoppable, quoted at length from three Roosevelt speeches proving, in his opinion, that before 1941 the President had been preparing America for self-defense only. Shortly before 1:00 P.M., Fulbright interrupted. "I remind the Senator he said he would like 30 minutes."

Senator Lausche chimed in. "He has had nearly 40 minutes. I think we should be permitted to go to lunch."

Ignoring him, Morse asked Fulbright if he could "take a minute" for some more quotations, but the chairman ordered the committee reporter to enter two more Roosevelt speeches as read. One, dated October 30, 1940, contained the sentence that Clare had claimed to be a lie: *I have said this before, but I shall say it again and again and again: your boys are not going to be sent into any foreign wars.*

Morse argued that Clare had taken this sentence out of context, and insisted that the rest of Roosevelt's speech proved that the President had had defense, not aggression, in mind. If other members sensed that Morse was talking at cross-purposes with Clare, they remained silent. She had merely meant to say that FDR saw the inevitability of having to stop Hitler long before Pearl Harbor, not as a result of it. They sat through a further attack on her Rome record, before adjourning for what was left of the lunch hour.

Fifty minutes later, the committee reassembled and voted to confirm Clare Boothe Luce as Ambassador to Brazil, with only one dissenting vote.

When the full Senate convened on Monday, April 27, to debate her nomination, Senator Morse again opposed it, this time for three hours and eighteen minutes. He scoffed at the appointment as "one more example of the Eisenhower Administration paying off political hacks," and rehashed his earlier condemnation of Clare for abusing Roosevelt, Truman, and Acheson. "This woman has beclouded . . . and destroyed her usefulness," he shouted. "She has neither the tact nor the diplomacy to serve in Brazil." As for honesty or reliability, "I am satisfied that Mrs. Luce does not meet either criteria."[38]

Morse's diatribe—amounting to twenty thousand words out of the debate total of sixty-five thousand in the *Congressional Record*—appeared to influence some Democratic Senators, but Clare continued to have overwhelming bipartisan support.[39] Her old friend Lyndon B. Johnson, now Senate majority leader, was for her. Kennedy, Lausche, and Thomas J. Dodd of Connecticut spoke eloquently in her behalf. Hoping to rally at least a significant bloc of nays, Morse won a postponement of the vote until the following day.

That evening, Drew Pearson, who liked to manipulate the levers of power and had actually written much of Morse's floor speech, called Senator Fulbright. Knowing that he had an aversion to unqualified political appointees, Pearson said, "Why don't you take on someone your size, such as Mrs. Luce."

Fulbright answered frankly, "I couldn't defeat her. Look at the speeches made for her by Kennedy, Dodd and Lausche."

"You know why. It's a matter of religion."

"Yes, but I can't say that publicly."[40]

Pearson then called Hubert Humphrey and warned him that if he supported Clare, it "might cause him trouble in the future." Humphrey said he would "abstain from voting for the lady."[41]

Back in New York, Clare smoldered over her humiliations at Morse's hand. The East Fifty-second Street apartment had been put on the market, and her baggage for Brazil was already at the docks. She brooded about the wisdom of agreeing to serve in South America. Through no fault of her own, the Bolivia affair had made her a controversial figure there. And Rio was not Rome. She suspected she might find it "an isolated, dull post." Brazil's economic situation was shaky, so she would probably be blamed for not getting its government the enormous amount of aid it needed.[42]

Then there was Harry. Morse seemed fixated on her relationship with him, and kept insinuating that their combined influence on the administration's foreign policy reflected the larger interests of Time Inc. She yearned for revenge on the hostile Senator, and decided to make use of a piece of biographical information that *Time's* research department had dug up for her. It read that in August 1951 he had been "walking through a stable when a scared mare let fly with both hind feet. Morse got the full blow on the right side of his face; his jaw was broken in four places and thirteen teeth knocked out."[43]

The following morning, before the Senate reconvened, Clare called Stan Swinton, her newspaper friend from Rome, now working for the Associated Press. She asked him to take down a statement and hold it until after the vote on her nomination. There was no doubt that she would be approved by a large majority, but she wanted to make it clear whom she blamed for persecuting her.[44]

"I am grateful," she dictated, "for the overwhelming vote of confidence in the Senate. We must now wait until the dirt settles. My difficulties, of course, go some years back and began when Senator Wayne Morse was kicked in the head by a horse."[45]

The final roll call on her nomination did not take place until after 2:00 p.m., due to further delay tactics by Senator Morse. The folksy minority leader, Everett Dirksen (R-IL), became so irritable that he railed, "Why thresh old straw? Why beat an old bag of bones?"

The chamber resounded with laughter, and Dirksen lamely explained that he had misused an old colloquialism. Senator Mansfield made a final plea for Clare and then, as majority whip, called for the vote. The result, tabulated at 2:15 p.m., was 79 in favor and 11 against, with 45 Democrats supporting her.

Within half an hour, Clare's wisecrack spilled out of the Senate news ticker and was delivered to Senator Morse. He rose on a point of personal privilege to read it into the record, adding that he had not expected such prompt evidence of the "emotional instability on the part of this slanderer."[46] Several of Clare's Democratic supporters declared that if they could recall their votes, they would. But she was now officially the United States Ambassador to Brazil.

Morse affected good humor at the fait accompli and said, "I wish her well."[47] Meanwhile, Dirksen alerted the White House to Clare's remark and the outrage it had caused. He also informed the *New York Herald Tribune* that Morse had gone so far as to call Mrs. Luce's physician "to see if she was under the care of a psychiatrist." The doctor had said he had "no knowledge" of this. Two more calls to the White House convinced Dirksen that the President was sympathetic to Clare. He got the feeling that she and Eisenhower had already spoken.[48]

Determined now to extricate herself from an assignment that had become distasteful to her, and feeling entirely confident in the correctness of her judgment, Clare cajoled Harry into issuing a statement that would facilitate her exit.[49] He grumpily consented, and issued it at 5:39 P.M.

> For twenty-five years, in the course of her public life, my wife has taken not only the criticisms provoked by her own views and actions but also many punches which were really intended for me or for the publications of which I am editor-in-chief. The attack of Sen. Wayne Morse is perhaps the most vitriolic example of this.

Harry went on to say that her ambassadorship "has now been profoundly compromised." It was a question of "whether she can now hope to accomplish the delicate mission assigned to her by the President in a climate of uneasiness which the smears and suspicions aired on the Senate floor have naturally created in Brazil." He revealed that Clare had already offered in vain to withdraw her nomination over the Bolivian incident. Then came his most trenchant point.

> Sen. Morse happens to be the chairman of the Foreign Relations subcommittee which has cognizance of small inter-American affairs and Brazil. As an Ambassador she will not be able to defend herself from vendetta politics at home which makes common cause with anti-Americanism in South America. Therefore I have asked my wife to offer her resignation again.[50]

At a news conference the next day, the President defended Clare. He said her comment on Morse had been "ill-advised" but "perfectly human, although she probably wished it had never been published." Reporters laughed at this. Mrs. Luce, Eisenhower added, had done "brilliant" work in Italy bringing about the Trieste settlement. Sources in Brazil had assured him that she was still welcome in the post, and despite her husband's statement, he had received no indication that she intended to resign.[51]

In fact, Brazilian reactions to her confirmation were divided along political lines. Conservatives and moderates approved it, while leftists and nationalists believed she was being sent to interfere in their domestic affairs. São Paulo's *Última Hora* accused Clare of being a "figurehead of oil trusts," and saluted "the vigilant Mr. Morse." *Tribuna do Ceará* said that "the loser is Brazil."[52]

Recriminatory debate raged on that afternoon in the Senate, reaching an extreme of anti-feminist vituperation when Senator Stephen M. Young (D-OH) read into the record a poem by Sir William Watson (1858–1935) entitled "The Woman with the Serpent's Tongue."

> *Ambitious from her natal hour,*
> *And scheming all her life for power;*
> *With little left of seemly pride;*
> *With venomed fangs she cannot hide; . . .*
> *Burnt up within by that strange soul*
> *She cannot slake, or yet control:*
> *Malignant-lipp'd, unkind, unsweet;*
> *Past all example indiscreet;*
> *Hectic, and always overstrung,—*
> *The Woman with the Serpent's Tongue.*[53]

The following evening on CBS, Eric Sevareid observed that most men did not like women in public life. "Particularly they dislike aggressive women, and when they must deal with a woman whose very appearance requires that she be treated as fragile femininity, but whose combative nature alternately requires that she be treated as a man—then, they are truly unhappy."[54]

▽

Clare arrived at the White House at 10:45 A.M. on Friday, May 1, amid expectation that she was about to be sworn in as Ambassador to Brazil. Instead, she presented a letter of resignation to the President, saying, "It is no longer possible for me to accomplish the mission which you have entrusted to me." She cited the "thousands of words of extraordinary charges against my person" made by a Senator who was chairman of a subcommittee that handled Latin American affairs. "A continuing harassment of my mission, with a view to making his own charges stick, is the natural course the chairman would follow. And the sad fact is not that I, but Brazilian-American policy would be the victim."

Eisenhower urged her not to quit. "You can't do that. A soldier fights where his commander sends him." But Clare would not be swayed.

"You need an able-bodied soldier, and I've had both my legs shot out from under me."[55]

As Press Secretary Hagerty announced her decision, she stood beside him solemn-faced in a black faille coat. Declining comment, she then left in a limousine, blowing a kiss from her white-gloved hand to the group of reporters.[56]

Clare announces her resignation as Ambassador to Brazil

43

AN UNSHARED LIFE

Adultery is a most convenient way
to rise above the conventional.

—VLADIMIR NABOKOV

Many Brazilian and American newspapers expressed sympathy for Clare in the days after her resignation. "The predominant opinion, now that we will not have her here with us, is deep disappointment," the *Jornal do Brasil* commented. The *Atlanta Constitution* said it was difficult to understand why she should have chosen to renew the row after it had been settled in her favor, yet thought her wise to resign. *The New York Times* accused her nemesis of vindictiveness. "The tactics pursued by Senator Morse of Oregon in this whole affair seem to us to have been beneath contempt." Even the Portland *Oregonian* felt that Morse had "won what may seem to him a victory over his chosen enemy, President Eisenhower. But many of his constituents are ashamed."[1]

Clare claimed that 90 percent of the editorials in a survey of 350 American newspapers were "unequivocally against the Senator." Yet a reporter from Pennsylvania's *Sharon Herald* saw two unequal stacks of mail in Morse's office and was told that seventeen hundred of them praised the Senator's performance and only eight hundred disapproved. Clare's equestrian image recurred on both sides. "If being kicked by a horse gave you your courage," one letter read, "then I'd like to see a buckin' bronc turned lose in the Senate chamber." A Luce supporter

Morse's moment of triumph: May 1, 1959

wrote, "Too bad the horse didn't finish you off." Another derided Morse as a "mental dwarf."[2]

He was far from that. Much of the opprobrium directed at him was based on the revelation that he had telephoned Clare's doctor to question her psychiatric health. In fact, Morse had correctly intuited something pathological in her behavior while testifying.[3] He had therefore telephoned Milton Rosenbluth's office, only to find that the doctor had recently died. The physician expressing "no knowledge" of Mrs. Luce's psychiatric history was Dr. Michael Rosenbluth, the dead man's son, who had not been party to the suggestion that Clare enter Payne Whitney in October 1958.[4]

Before she left Washington, Wiley Buchanan, Ike's Chief of Protocol, hosted what was to have been a bon voyage party for the new Ambassador. Clare made such an impressive entrance in a black lace dress, diamond necklace, and white mink wrap that a guest remarked, "No matter what, she is one of the most beautiful women in the United States." Dulles's successor as Secretary of State, Christian Herter, toasted her after dinner and said pointedly that he hoped "the private life of the charming lady on my left will remain private." Clare assured Alice Roosevelt Longworth, "I haven't felt so relaxed in a long time."[5]

But once she was back in New York, the enormity of the decision to forgo Brazil confronted her. She had not only put the Fifty-second Street apartment up for sale, but had reinstalled Harry at the Waldorf Towers, closed the houses in Phoenix and Ridgefield, and dismissed nine servants. Copious numbers of crates full of new outfits and personal furnishings, right down to stationery engraved with her diplomatic crest, had to be retrieved from the docks. She had even bought an air-conditioned limousine as well as cooling units for the embassy, after learning that Rio was as humid for seven months of the year as New York in August.[6]

Clare told a reporter that she was set "to resume work" on her auto-biography. The novelist Edna Ferber suspected otherwise, telling her teasingly that since she was "the Woman who Has Everything," her memoir—"the book you never will write"—was bound to be important.[7]

▽

At Sugar Hill on May 16 at 11:25 A.M., Clare took 100 micrograms of lysergic acid diethylamide. Two friends from California, the writer-philosopher Gerald Heard, and his musician partner, Jay Michael Bar-rie, supervised the dose. It was her third experience in three months with "LSD," as the new hallucinatory drug was known. The first had been in Phoenix on March 11, and the second in San Francisco on April 4, only eleven days before her Senate committee hearing—which, given LSD's known propensity to linger in the brain, might have sent an extra message to the psychologically astute Senator from Oregon. Indeed, there was something psychedelic about Clare's memory of him staring at her: "old oyster-eyed, coffin-headed Wayne Morse."[8]

By 11:55, she was gazing out of the window "with great stillness and intensity," Barrie noted as recorder. They had been listening to Sibel-ius's Symphony No. 2, and when it ended, Clare said, still staring at her lawns and flowering dogwood trees, "It's hard to tell whether the music was accompanying that out there, or that out there was accompanying the music."

Clearly the drug was taking effect. At 12:10 P.M., she protested that Stravinsky's suite *Renard*, now playing, was "a vast intrusion" on her contemplation, and should be turned off. "The trees, if they knew what they were doing, would be making their own music. . . . The colors are beginning to separate themselves into all their exquisite subtleties."

Half an hour later, she closed her eyes and said, "What a silence—but so full of noise—a paradox—an immense silence filled with a sound-less music." This remark was akin to George Eliot's observation that an artist in the rapture of creation was aware of "the roar that lies on the other side of silence." The difference was that Clare's ecstasy was chem-ically induced.

At 12:35, her mood changed, and she spoke of her recent tormentor. "If Senator Morse should come into this room at this moment—he in full possession of his faculties and I in partial possession—the thing that would surprise him would be his complete irrelevance to me. But do you think I could look at him as a brother, Gerald?"

"Perhaps not yet," Heard replied. Using one of the jargon words he favored in his philosophical talks, he added, "But in an hour, he would 'compose.'"

Clare, laughing, said, "I'm still in the state that I want him to de-compose."

Her mood changed again, and she requested that a bowl of lilacs be brought to her. "What is this great abyss between what is alive and what is dead?" She focused closely on the blossoms. "Now I'm beginning to see the flowers breathe. . . . It makes one yearn to see God."

Feeling chilly, she called for a heavy coat and said she wanted to go outside. Heard and Barrie watched her inspect a bed of vividly colored flowers, then walk into a birch grove. When she returned, she asked for another 25 micrograms. "I have one more jump to make."

Even colder after ingesting it, Clare asked for blankets. Soon she became less coherent. "Things are falling at the base of my brain. There is a blue unbending light." She closed her eyes. "I can see my own eye, even to the small blood vessels." After some moments, she said, "You're not alive, you're not dead, you're not dreaming, you're not awake."

It was now almost one o'clock, and she wrapped herself in another blanket. "I think there is only one thing God doesn't really like—and that is being flirted with. . . . *Theo logos*—does that mean the word of God or the word about God?"

The sound of an automobile horn outside announced the arrival of Harry for lunch. "I shall leave you three to wrestle with the spaghetti," Clare said. "Imagine adding all his strings to mine—it's a wonder the whole of 450 doesn't blow up!" The number apparently referred to the apartment the Luces had just sold to Drue Heinz for $175,000.

While the men ate, Clare remained on the porch, drinking a cup of broth. Then she went out, spread a blanket on the lawn, and lay down. Harry joined her at 2:45, and sat with her for the next three-quarters of an hour.[9]

▽

By 6:15 P.M., after Clare had taken a long walk, the effects of her trip wore off. She joined her husband and houseguests for dinner, and the kind of conversation with Gerald that she relished.[10]

She had first met him in 1947, while working in Hollywood on *The Screwtape Letters*, and had been captivated by his Anglo-Irish charm, erudition, and spirituality. He was now in his seventieth year, and with his bony, bearded appearance, vegetarianism, and other asceticisms reminded her of George Bernard Shaw. But in Heard's case the beard was a scraggy red Vandyke, and when light shone through it Clare noticed that he seemed to have no chin.[11] His mustache did not quite conceal the contortions of his thin-lipped mouth when he spoke in a strangely accented, hybrid voice. Yet there was something so compelling about his elocution, his haunting blue eyes under wreathing brows, and the way he repeatedly tilted his head against one long, effeminate hand that hypnotized all listeners, including such varied eminences as H. G. Wells, Aldous Huxley, W. H. Auden, Igor Stravinsky, Kenneth Clark, Dave Brubeck, Christopher Isherwood—and now the Luces.[12]

Wellborn and Cambridge-educated, a former lecturer at Oxford and BBC broadcaster in the 1930s, Heard was the author of more than thirty books on science, religion, philosophy, and Eastern mysticism, including *Narcissus: An Anatomy of Clothes*, *The Ascent of Humanity*, and *Pain, Sex and Time: A New Outlook on Evolution and the Future of Man*. He had immigrated to America with Huxley in 1937, and had encouraged Auden and Isherwood to follow them and settle in Southern California. Since then he had become a devotee of the Hindu guru Swami

Gerald Heard

Prabhavananda, and a promoter of the cult of Vedanta, whose three main tenets were that man's real nature was divine, the aim of life was to realize this, and all religions were essentially in agreement.

After World War II, Heard had emerged as something of a guru himself, founding the monastery-like Trabuco College in the Santa Ana Mountains, becoming a proponent of celibacy and six hours a day of meditation. In his extreme frugality, he eschewed having a telephone or a car. But that did not prevent him from using those of others, and enjoying the hospitality of rich friends. Nor did the apparent brilliance of his rhetoric prove, on analysis, always to have depth or coherence: "The really possible utopia is this world experienced by a psychophysique at full aperture." In conversation he would solemnly refer to "the sober certainty of waiting bliss."[13]

Heard's interest in liberating "the inner man" had led him in 1954 to experiment with Huxley in taking mescaline, a psychedelic derivative of cactus plants, which caused him to have conversations with imagined personalities. Late the following year, he had moved on to experiment with LSD, which had first been synthesized in Switzerland in 1938. Its abbreviated initials came from the original German word *lysergsäurediethylamid,* whose particle *säure* translated as "acid." Found naturally in ergot, a rye kernel fungus, the drug had become exclusively available in 1949 free of charge from the Sandoz Laboratory in Basel, but only for research purposes.[14]

Not being an accredited scientist or physician, Heard had to obtain his supplies from a friend, Dr. Sidney Cohen, chief of psychosomatic medicine at the Veterans Administration Hospital in Los Angeles. So far, Dr. Cohen had been cooperative with Heard's interest in the effect of LSD on highly intelligent, creative people, even though his own field of research focused on therapeutic treatment of psychotic cases. In exchange for limited supplies, Heard submitted reports of his sessions with people like Clare.

He was drawn to her because, as he wrote, "You and I share this struggle with melancholy." Dr. Cohen believed that Gerald had a way with "certain neurotics," and informed him that depression, rather than psychosis, was "now the mental pandemic."[15]

Clare recalled that her two previous trips had been "delicious, wonderful . . . a fantasy high," even though in Phoenix there had been some tearful episodes, moments of irritation, and tingling sensations as well as chills. Images of beauty—a dragonfly alighting on a glass ornament that turned to fire and water, a petunia whose petals seemed to undulate—

were compromised by distress at her overfurnished house with its excess of "bits and bobs and doojiggers." These were followed, as she attained what Cohen called "the upper register," by more enigmatic visions: a harp swallowed and broken, with blood surging around it. ("Where does the sorrow come from?" she asked, crying. "From the harp.") She also had memories of a lost child, of playing with pebbles on a beach, and of having her creativity questioned by an uncomprehending mother. At one point in Phoenix a maid had interrupted a session to say Vice President Nixon was on the phone. "CL says will talk later," Barrie scribbled.[16]

▽

Feeling creatively revitalized by her psychedelic intake, Clare began a three-month literary sojourn on the Caribbean island of St. John.[17] She stayed in the most secluded and luxurious cottage at Caneel Bay Plantation, a resort with beautiful beaches developed by Laurance Rockefeller. Her intent was to resume work on her memoirs, but she got no further than an opening page that drifted off into fragmentary fantasy.

> One gets born. From there on it's hell, or a little better, with a rare touch of heaven, all the way to the grave. If you hadn't been born who you were, when you were, who would you have *liked* to be? . . . There is only one answer that is not sheer nonsense: who I was. . . . So. I was born in 1903, a girl child. I wish f[ather] had not left mother. More money. A better education; not such wide hips, a smaller nose and ears. Of course, a Strawberry Duchess, England 19th Cent. a great family. A Princess, a Duchess *of course*. Doesn't every woman?[18]

A few more jottings later, she gave up in favor of writing a detective novel set in Brazil, called "The Memoirs of T. Parkington Quinn." Some of the research for her congressional hearings could be put to use. At first the prose flowed effortlessly. She told Gerald Heard that her facility must be due to the prolonged effects of LSD, and pestered Dorothy Farmer for material on Brazilian food—"some 20 good dishes for Quinn to eat at various times when he is in São Sabato."[19]

Harry joined her for a while, returning to New York for a minor prostate procedure in early July.[20] As soon as he left, she started having trouble with the novel. "I may be too old to do any creditable creative writing now." Again she fretted about producing even "a passable autobiography." Mina Shaughnessy, a Washington researcher hired to go through some of her papers, sensed her waning enthusiasm for the project, and offered to write an authorized biography instead, for an annual salary of $10,000. Clare turned her down, and continued to procrastinate.[21]

By now she was spending only a couple of hours each morning on her manuscripts, preferring to answer dozens of letters before going to the beach. She swam at least two miles a day. Her "merry chit chatterer," Dorothy, came for a few days, but disliked the sun and left. Louisa Jenkins briefly filled the void.[22]

On July 21, Clare, having not heard from Harry for several days, wrote to tell him she was reasonably at peace, and "could wish for only one thing: companionship. A presence. But my fate is my fate, and with whatever pangs I do grow every year a little more reconciled to being alone, and in your life a thing very much apart from all your most eager and passionate concerns."[23]

By way of explanation, a letter arrived at the end of the month from Father John Courtney Murray, S.J. It revealed that Harry was experiencing an unspecified emotional crisis.[24]

Murray, professor of Catholic trinitarian theology at Woodstock College, a Jesuit seminary in Maryland, had become Clare's spiritual adviser after the departure of Father Thibodeau. Having worked in Rome and Heidelberg, he was, to her, "one of the few American priests to have a real European mind."[25] During her time in Italy, he had also become a golfing buddy and confidant of Harry, and was now recruited as an intermediary to solve the problem of Clare's feeling of marital isolation.

The priest told her that her husband would return to Caneel Bay soon. Quoting Harry's typically fuzzy language when dealing with personal matters, Murray wrote: "He mentioned that . . . he did not have in mind to do any discussing or planning, since he 'wanted to let the river of time flow quietly for a while.'"

As if this were not vague enough, Murray recommended that Clare avoid "a full-dress confrontation," and "let the summer interval be dominated only by the mutual question 'What do I want to do.'" He apologized for giving so much advice. "If I need an excuse, it is that I am fond of him and I love you."[26]

Clare's reaction was a sudden frenzy of underwater killing. It began after spearing a tarpon as big as her off Hawksnest Beach, and concluded with a written mea culpa. "I am afraid of my own hate, or do I hate my own fear? All the dark unconscious things—the sea serpent, the phallus, rise. . . . There is a joy and anguish, fascination and horror about killing something which is not molesting you. . . . I shot box fish through the *skull*, ungainly fish . . . mass slaughter of the sea urchins. The little crab prodded with my spear. You can't go cutting everything in half. . . ."[27]

The following afternoon, Harry arrived.

▽

After a few uneasy days, he mumbled something about not wanting to commit to yet another apartment at the Waldorf Towers in the fall. He offered no reason. Clare lost her temper, and on August 12, he left, some forty-eight hours earlier than planned.[28]

Before she could figure out his mysterious behavior, she received another letter from Father Murray. "Harry's problem is the same as yours—the problem of loneliness, of the 'unshared life.' "[29]

In her reply, Clare asked Murray to try to "get behind the wall" of her husband's self-concealment. But after spending a weekend with Harry, and hearing little but inchoate stories of his life and religious doubts, the priest concluded that he was an enigma. "He goes in spurts and fragments and splinters of ideas." Addressing a complaint from Clare that she was having even more literary difficulties, Murray chastised her self-absorption. "Well, damn it, keep on writing."[30]

Clare was back in New York by September 1, shortly before Harry left for a "business trip" to Europe. On the eve of his departure for France, she sensed that he was already absent in heart and spirit. It dawned on her that he was having another affair. He left next day with wifely abuse ringing in his ears.[31]

Perplexed by Harry's perennial inability to articulate his needs, Clare made a summary of arguments for and against divorce. In the pro column, she listed "physical, emotional, psychological freedom," enabling both of them to find another "mate." As a single woman, she would be able to write her memoirs without having to consider Harry's personal and corporate sensitivities. She would also find out "where I belong, if anywhere, and to whom I matter—if anybody." In the con column, she mentioned financial insecurity for herself and a "loss of public respect" for him. "Couples divorcing for incompatibility in their 60s always look damn silly." Crucial for her was "the damage to me who am vulnerable—to the point of neurosis on the score of being 'rejected' and 'abandoned.' "[32]

Using the third person, she recorded a nightmare of being carried "with infinite tenderness" in the arms of a tall, strong man, who suddenly turned into a monster of sadism. "He was absolutely without pity. She realized he would now torture her to death."[33]

▽

On September 19, Harry returned to face the first of what Clare described as "agonized nights" of confession and recrimination.[34] For the past three years, he confessed, he had been seeing and sleeping with Lady Jeanne Campbell, granddaughter of Lord Beaverbrook.

Now thirty, she was a more mature version of the tall, dark-haired, peachy-cheeked twenty-year-old Clare remembered from her 1949 stay with Max in Jamaica. Since her parents had divorced when she was a child, Jeanne had seldom lived at Inveraray Castle, the ancestral home of her father, Ian Campbell, the Duke of Argyll, in Scotland's Western Highlands. Instead, she had stayed at her grandfather's multiple establishments, dabbling in acting and having a fling with the Fascist Sir Oswald Mosley. It was at Beaverbrook's villa on the French Riviera that Harry had met Jeanne again, become besotted, and admitted to Mary Bancroft his desire to seduce her.[35]

Lady Jeanne Campbell, c. 1959

But it was not until September 1956, when Clare was winding up her ambassadorship in Rome, and Jeanne was working as a photo researcher at *Life*, that Harry had seized the chance to make his fantasy a reality. That fall, he had dined with her at his Waldorf apartment a couple of times, and made tentative passes, Then, in early January 1957, after he had spent several weeks in Italy with Clare, they had what Jeanne characterized as "an explosive coming together," declaring and consummating their love.[36]

After this, Harry, naively afraid of being recognized, would visit her at night, with his hat pulled way down and coat collar turned up. He was the "cuddlyist" man in the world, Jeanne told an office colleague, "but it took him six months to get it up!"[37]

When they were apart, Harry wrote, telephoned, and sent so many dozens of roses that Jeanne ran out of vases.[38] "The most romantic man I've ever come across," she said.[39] He knew reams of verse, and could recite all of Dylan Thomas's "Do not go gentle into that good night." In return she quoted Yeats: "And pity beyond all telling / Is hid in the heart of love." Harry disagreed. "Pity has nothing to do with love."

At the height of their relationship, he often said, "If only you could get pregnant that would do it. She would have to give me a divorce." But Jeanne had difficulty conceiving.[40] Their claustrophobic assignations continued with copious drinking and talking. Jeanne discovered that Harry "had a tremendous secret love for his mother. . . . He was like a lost little boy—I've never seen such a combination of power and lostness."[41]

On March 15, 1959, afraid Harry might be happy to continue indefinitely with their clandestine couplings, Jeanne proposed marriage. Now thirty, she felt an urgent need to have children, and asked that he try to alleviate his chronic impotence—what he called his "inadequacy"—by having his prostate "fixed."[42] She then left for Europe, setting a deadline of July 15 for him to accept or reject her proposal. If the former, she expected him to begin at least separation proceedings. On that exact day, while Clare was worrying about him in Caneel Bay, Harry accepted Jeanne's proposal in writing, and had his prostate operation.

In hindsight, Clare saw that when Harry had jibbed about moving back to the Waldorf, he was about to commit to someone half his age. She now discovered that on his latest European trip, Harry had been dallying with his "girl" in Paris, on the assumption that Clare would agree to a separation pending divorce. In a further blow, Harry informed her that he had not really loved her for twenty years, was not attracted to older women, and had stuck with her primarily because he was "sorry" for her. But since she had seemed "so well, so happy, so confident," in her work on the Caribbean island, he felt that he, too, "had the right to happiness."[43]

Harry's condescension and betrayal were bad enough, but as Clare absorbed the longevity of his deceit, her fury grew.[44] For two decades the man standing before her had feigned impotence, when all along it had been a revulsion to her body that caused his incapacity.[45] He had a nerve assuming she would accommodate his current wish to dump her. This was a moment to take a cue from *The Women*, written twenty-three years before: "What has any woman got to gain by a divorce? No matter how much he gives her, she won't have what they have together."[46]

She put this now to Harry. It left him unmoved. "My girl," he informed her, "will fight for me."[47] Evidently "the Lady Jeanne," as society columns called her, was a determined young woman. Clare bounced an ashtray off Harry's balding head, and followed up with a torrent of gutter language that reminded him of the sordidness of her background.[48] His penchant for Jeanne, she said, was "all sex," in contrast with their own twenty-year lack of it.[49]

Harry denied that his relationship with Jeanne was one-dimensional, and claimed that it was "the last great love" he could expect.[50] Yet he admitted in the same breath to suffering from "post coitus *triste*." Clare attributed this sadness not only to Presbyterian guilt, but to egotistic regret that the possession of his partner had been rushed or incomplete. "Orgasm," she told him, was not "the sole and final end of sex." If it were, "prostitutes would be the happiest instead of the most miserable of women. There can be in one gentle kiss, one generous caress, one entwining of fingers more sexuality than in a whole whore house."[51]

Immersed in her own anguish, Clare saw with some pity that Harry suffered, too. In worldly and family terms, he had so much. But from long experience, she knew "how desperate is the heart's need to love and be loved." All the better for him, she charitably conceded, if, in his declining years, he had found a "sunlight love," rather than continue the chaste "moonlight love" that she and he had long settled for.[52]

This access of sympathy did not last. As the confrontation wore on, Clare suspected that Harry saw her as his jailer, and wanted her dead.[53] He intuited her misery, and in a conciliatory gesture took her in his arms. He said "a love *deeper* than love" existed between them. "I can never leave you, if you cannot bear it."[54]

The following night, Harry had a colloquy with Father Murray. He said he could not forsake "this pitiful woman," and might have to "sacrifice" Jeanne for his wife's "greater need."[55] Murray passed these remarks to Clare, and sent Harry an analysis of his difficulties.

If he was "using" Jeanne merely to prove his sexual potency, Murray wrote, "this is rather a dreadful thing." Doubtless she was sincere in wanting to marry him, but his desire to unite with her was probably a vain yearning to fill a vacuum in himself. The priest shrewdly guessed that there must be "something wrong in the woman" if, after spending much of her life in the company of an old press lord, she now aimed to have an aging substitute.

Murray deduced that Harry's attraction to Jeanne was not so much sexual as childlike. In playing the roles of nurturer and sounding board, Jeanne was acting like his much-loved mother. "Better—or a lesser evil—that she should be [your] mistress," Murray advised, adding, "Is she to be a sort of mirror in which you hope to see reflected an image of yourself that you want to be admired, and yourself to admire?"[56]

Unwittingly, he was echoing some other lines from *The Women*. "A man has only one escape from his old self: to see a different self—in the mirror of some woman's eyes."[57]

▽

On Saturday, September 26, in a state of exhausted armistice, the Luces were having dinner *à deux* at Sugar Hill when Harry was summoned to the telephone. The caller was Igor Cassini, alias the gossip columnist "Cholly Knickerbocker" of the *New York Journal-American*—William Randolph Hearst's biggest scandal sheet. Cassini asked Harry to comment on reports that he and his wife were separating.

Taken aback, Harry said, "Clare and I are here together. It is all very premature, to say the least."

After a short pause, during which he realized he had given credence to the rumor, he blustered, "There is nothing to it at all."

The result was a headline story on Sunday morning, illustrated with a photograph of a bravely smiling Clare.

The Big Topic in the Intelligentsia Set as well as in the Smart Set these days is that Henry Luce, publisher of *Life*, *Time* and *Fortune*, and his talented wife Clare, onetime playwright, Congresswoman and U.S. Ambassadress to Italy, are planning a separation—or a divorce.

Reports reaching this reporter from London and Paris, where Luce visited recently, say that the powerful publisher has admitted to intimate friends that he and his wife intend to separate.

Luce has been often seen in the company of the Lady Jean [sic] Campbell, lovely daughter of the Duke of Argyll and granddaughter of a fellow-publisher, England's omnipotent and vociferous Lord Beaverbrook.

Beside herself, Clare called Shirley Potash at Time Inc. and yelled, "You knew!" Shirley denied it, even though office gossip about Harry's affair was rife. She could not understand why Clare was so upset, after bending her ear endlessly on the subject of leaving Harry. "We have no life—he's away, I'm here!"[58]

Hank Luce, who had long known of his father's extracurricular relationship, was sympathetic to Jeanne. He phoned her in Scotland and warned her not to talk to journalists. This did not include Harry, who called her every night, and spoke at such great length that she started sleeping in the library, so as "not to disturb the house." She soon became a wreck from these monologues. Harry explained to her distress that his lawyer, Roswell Gilpatric, would not present any "papers" to Clare until Beth and Tex Moore had been consulted about an appropriate course of action.[59]

Meanwhile, it occurred to Clare that she had only Father Murray to bat for her, whereas Harry had his family, his intimates at work, and his Presbyterian pastor to protect *his* happiness, status, business, and fortune. She therefore invited the priest to spend the first weekend of October at Sugar Hill.[60]

Although she and Murray had only recently become spiritually intimate, they had first met in late 1946, when he had attended a lecture by Clare at Catholic University, and been greatly impressed. Hoping to become better acquainted, he had arranged on some pretext to meet her through Harry.

She had been struck first by his six-foot-four-inch height—"the tallest man I'd ever seen."[61] He had a deep forehead, receding hairline, all-seeing bespectacled eyes, and slight limp from having one leg shorter than the other. This congenital deformity, she later learned, had pained him in childhood, making him feel "unfinished." As he matured, he found a kinship not so much with Lord Byron as with Shakespeare's hunchback Richard III.[62]

Born in New York to upper-middle-class Scottish and Irish parents, Murray had poise, and spoke eloquently and authoritatively in pear-shaped tones.[63] Clare perceived that he was not only sympathetic, but of coruscating intelligence, with a Jesuit's logical and analytic mind. A year younger than she was, he had graduated from Boston College and taught in Italy, Germany, and the Philippines. He had lectured on philosophy at Yale before settling at Woodstock College. An avowed liberal Democrat, he had an ongoing interest in the interaction of nations with religion, tensions between faith and public life, and the morality or justness of war.

As their friendship developed, Clare had discovered that far from

Father John Courtney Murray, S.J.

being austere, Murray, like Gerald Heard, enjoyed the luxuries that came with well-off friends: a car at the airport, a bed in the city, good food and wine, country weekends with golf on the best courses, and quantities of whiskey and cigarettes. The last three guaranteed that he and Harry would form a companionable routine based on a little exercise, followed by philosophical debates that, stimulated by alcohol and tobacco, usually went on into the small hours. Harry came to admire Murray so much that when he published a *Time* story entitled "U.S. Catholics and the State," he put a portrait by Chaliapin of him on the cover.[64]

Clare was to grow more and more devoted to "Father John" as her estrangement from Harry grew, even though the priest often played devil's advocate, arguing that at her age, "a marriage of convenience" was the best she could expect. He told her it was her duty to the Catholic Church to avoid a scandal.[65]

"When I can talk with you," she wrote, "the day has meaning, it stays alive, I don't lose altitude, I can stave off melancholy and futility."[66]

As it happened, Clare could not have had a better counselor than Murray at this troubled period of her life. He would also turn out to be, in more ways than one, her rescuer.

▽

After his visit to Sugar Hill, Murray sent Harry what he called a "Report of an Honest Broker." Clare, he said, felt that the Luces were a team, without him she would be "finished," and at her age unable to build a new life alone. She also needed "someone to whom to holler for help." Strangely, for a woman of strong character who had achieved much on her own, Harry was "the hunk of reality that has always been there, when all else dissolves." Insecure, she wanted their marriage to continue, even if Harry had sex on the side, yet needed to know when and where they could be together or apart, and what "rules for communication" would apply.

According to Murray, Clare's feelings for her husband consisted of what the ancient Greeks called "Eros, Philia and Agape"—love, friendship, and goodwill. He cautioned that separation would be inhuman and dangerous, in view of her fragile emotional state.[67]

On October 10, as Harry convened with the Moores in Connecticut for further discussion of his options, the two women vying for his affection addressed urgent appeals to him. Jeanne Campbell cabled from London: "Lots of anyway [sic] love and thoughts for my beloved grumpy growly friend. Happy and peaceful weekend with Beth. Think and think hard. Your Jay."

Clare wrote him from San Francisco, where she was making a Columbus Day speech. She offered a significant concession. Though she had "a legal hold" on him, she did not wish to exercise it.

> You *are* free to marry Jeanne or not—as you choose. If this is the only way for me to prove that "underneath it all" I bear you more goodwill and love than I have ever borne anyone—you have that proof. I could not face the declining years of my life with you, knowing that you shared them with me only as a prisoner.[68]

She knew Jeanne was due back in New York on October 18 and said that since Harry would probably want to see the young woman, she would await his decision in Phoenix.

The tone of this letter was tame compared with an unsent one of the night before that expressed her true feelings. It taunted Harry as being "a man 'with all that power' who is powerless to please himself, his girl, his God, his family, his wife all at the same time." She warned him that his inability to reconcile desire and guilt would make marriage to Jeanne just as miserable as to her. "You will hate her tomorrow in proportion as you love her today." In her immaturity, Jeanne had "not yet passed the test of your rancor, and depression, and boredom and hatred."[69]

From Arizona a few days later, Clare wrote another unmailed letter, this time to her rival. Mockingly headed "Bye Baby Bunting, Daddy's gone ahunting," and addressing Jeanne as "Dear Friend," it defined the situation in one sentence: "Big Mama won't let Big Poppa go."

Pointing out that "somebody around here has to begin to act *his* or *her* age," Clare continued for eight densely scripted pages. She began by analyzing the impulsive libido of Henry Luce. "Seized by a Big Romance, he can act with a manliness, vigour, determination, boldness, that sweeps a woman off her feet—as it did me, 25 years ago." This conflicted with his moral conscience, and made him feel guilty for hurting his two wives, family, friends, and colleagues, none of whom wanted to see him "shatter" all he had built over the years.

She cited the two main reasons why "Baby *would* be bad, in fact *is* bad for Poppa." First, his health was at risk from the endless nights of drinking and smoking during their trysts. "I just can't see anything particularly *good* coming of a Romance which seems to be wrecking him physically and morally, can you?" If Jeanne really loved him, she would give him "a little less beer at 3 a.m., and a little more cheer at ten o'clock. He's *got* to have eight or nine hours sleep, and he suffers (not being thirty) when he's hung over."

> The second reason why I don't think he'd be happy (tho' *one* would do!) is that Baby herself seems—on the record—to be a bit of a case.... I have always posited that Baby *is* in love with Big Poppa—because, in the final analysis (don't look now, my Freud is going to show) she's in love with her wretched Gramp, and her poppa too—two figures who never gave her any emotional security, clear set of moral values, self discipline—and having been pushed about and shunted off (between highly unsatisfactory periods of petting and spoiling) she *feels* if she gets Big Poppa she's got *them all to herself* at last.

She ended with a stoic admission. Whatever she or Jeanne might want or say in the matter, Harry would have to choose between them. It was likely, knowing him as she did, that he would decide not to decide. In which case, Baby could "hang around, on *his* terms, whatever they are, for a couple of years, waiting for a new assault on Big Mama." Or she could find someone closer to her own age.

"Of course, to do so, is to be awful hard on Big Poppa—his long record of getting everything he wanted from women will be broken. He'll have to face *one defeat*. The awful bleak, almost intolerable prospect of finishing out his days with the one woman who has loved him more than all the others combined."[70]

▽

Shortly after putting this letter aside, Clare heard that Harry had "capitulated" to Beth and Tex Moore's insistence that a divorce was far too drastic a solution to his dilemma. It would threaten his children's inheritance, and damage his reputation as a man of Calvinist virtue. The ensuing scandal might alienate millions of Catholics sympathetic to Clare, and adversely affect the value of Time Inc. stock. They therefore recommended that Roswell Gilpatric negotiate a legal separation.[71]

Logistically, the moment for such a move was ripe, because the

Luces had sold their triplex, and were about to take an apartment on the forty-first floor of the Waldorf Towers. However they resolved the question of who might occupy it, Harry would have legal freedom to be with Lady Jeanne Campbell whenever he wanted, while Clare could depend on financial support to continue in her customary style.

Although she had promised to accept any decision Harry made, the prospect of him flying to Phoenix with actual documents for her to sign was too much to bear. While he was en route, she swallowed a large quantity of sleeping pills. As fate—or her own survival instinct—would have it, Father Murray was staying with her and called for emergency help.

By the time Harry arrived, she was recuperating. He now had to face the possibility of a recurrence, should he go ahead with the separation plan.[72] So when a newsman called on October 19, asking about reports that he was in Arizona to break with his wife, he said, "There's nothing to it, this report of divorce."

Later that morning, when he returned to the Phoenix airport, Clare was at his side.[73]

▽

In the interim, Jeanne Campbell had returned to New York, expecting that Harry would soon be free. Instead, she was confronted by the image of Clare and Harry, "a smiling happy couple in the newspapers," about to check into their new apartment.[74]

A society reporter ran into Jeanne hurrying along Fifty-seventh Street in the crisp fall sunshine. "Pink-cheeked, tousle-haired and clad in forest-green tweeds, she looked the epitome of the Highland chieftain's daughter," he wrote. But she paled when he asked if there was truth to the rumor linking her to Henry Luce. Regaining composure, she said, "I am reminded of the inscription over the gate to the beautiful flower garden of Saint Andrews University in Scotland. It's by an anonymous sage, circa 1720, and carved in stone it reads: 'They have said; they will say; let them be saying.'"[75]

Harry wanted to tell her face-to-face that he could not marry her. That night he invited her to the Waldorf, while Clare made herself scarce in a neighbor's suite.[76] After telling Jeanne about the overdose, he said that divorce and even separation were impossible, at least for the time being. "I don't know what to do." Seeing her sadness, he asked, "*You're* not thinking of committing suicide, are you?"[77]

A couple of days later, Harry called Jeanne and told her to leave

New York at once. He was afraid of his wife's fragile emotional condition. "I don't care where you go, but get out of town."[78]

Conveniently, Lord Beaverbrook happened to be visiting New Brunswick, so Jeanne went to join him.[79] Clare then swung into immediate action to ensure that she and Harry were seen lunching out and attending Broadway's new hit, *The Miracle Worker*.[80] "All is well in the Luce *ménage*," she wrote Gerald Miller on November 5. "We will have been married twenty-five years this month. . . . What's left of our lives will be together."[81]

The next day, the Luces left for a week in Hawaii, where Harry was opening a Time Inc. office. Before the war, they had been enchanted by Oahu, and he had promised to look for "a little palace by the waters," where Clare could swim and surf.[82] His search had been unsuccessful. They agreed to look again, seeing it as a fresh venture for them both. [83] Before they headed for the mainland, Harry told Clare that he "no longer wanted a divorce," and preferred to "go down the long road" with her.[84]

A heartbroken Jeanne moved on to Geneva. Her father met her with a pile of love letters from the man who had rejected her. All were written before Harry's decision to stay with Clare. In essence they said, "Wait and be patient. It will happen."[85]

▽

In February 1960, Clare published the first of a series of monthly commentaries she had contracted to write for *McCall's* magazine, under the title "Without Portfolio." She was to be paid the large fee of $3,000 for each piece, and chose for her initial subject "Could a Woman Be Nominated for the Presidency?"

The question of *could* was moot, she wrote, since three women already had been—two of them before the "Suffragette Amendment" of 1920. So was the question of *should*, because the Constitution required only that a President be native born, over thirty-five, and resident in the country for a total of fourteen years. Qualifications, she went on, were essential in four major areas: experience of practical politics, military issues, economic and financial expertise, and "a proven knowledge of international affairs." No woman currently had all four, she said, neglecting to say that she had three.

It followed that no female was fit for the Vice Presidency, either, given that seven of the nation's chief executives had died in office. The

Democrat James A. Farley had stated recently that "women are too emotional for the job." Clare pounced on this fatuity.

In the cloakrooms, I myself have seen three Congressmen who have wept tears of "feminine" rage, or pouted in "girlish" pique over some small personal affront sustained on the floor from a colleague. During the war, I was privy to the prima donna outbursts of two generals, one who felt he had been "outranked," and had been given orders he didn't *personally* like; the other who had failed to get "good reviews" in the home press for his great generalship. I have seen not a few tycoons in office tantrums a ten-year-old girl would be ashamed to throw. Indeed, I have witnessed dozens of examples among politicians, diplomats, and soldiers of behaviour so outrageously irrational and emotionally unstable that my "womanly impulse" was to shake or spank them.[86]

▽

At the beginning of that month, Gerald Heard, Michael Barrie, and Louisa Jenkins joined Clare for what Heard described as a "wonderful week" of LSD. This time the experiments were scientifically administered by Dr. Sidney Cohen, the government neuropsychiatrist who continued to supply the drug for Clare's use.

Harry now took his first dose under the doctor's supervision, and was slow to "gain orbit." But when he did, he sauntered out into the garden, where he claimed to hear beautiful music. Standing among cactus plants, he began conducting an orchestra visible and audible only to himself.[87]

Dr. Cohen was a distinguished-looking man of fifty with swept-back hair and silvery sideburns. He had a reassuring smile, soft voice, and gentle manner. But he was all business when it came to LSD, which he did not condone for mass recreational use. Nor did he have much interest in Heard's mystical, quasi-religious theories about the potential of the drug. His professional mandate was to explore LSD's possible therapeutic use with criminals, as well as psychotics and other mentally disturbed people. That psychedelics often gave users pleasurable highs was incidental, as far as he was concerned. If people wanted "to suffer for a while," he was their man. "Gerald is better to soar with," he told Clare. "The subterranean is my department."[88]

Cohen was already having doubts about the side effects and compli-

Dr. Sidney Cohen

cations that patients in many research programs had exhibited, and had just published a paper on the subject in *Journal of Mental Diseases*.[89] The bulk of data showed so far that in professionally supervised treatment, LSD could be benign and beneficial.

When he administered it to Clare on this occasion, it was not a happy experience for her. She imagined that he had "held up a mirror" to her, and she so disliked what she saw—"a rejected, jailed woman"—that she cried in front of him.

Later that day, she saw the doctor walking in the garden with Louisa. He was tanned and strong, she later wrote him, with hair "like a shining helmet, eyes dark and glowing but a little cruel." She thought of "the plumed serpent," the sign of the Mexican king Montezuma, and teasingly called him by that name. Was this, she asked, at a primitive level, "a sexual response to the sheer manliness of you?" From then on, she was "deeply concerned to have you like me. Not love me, because I always thought you saw the same face in that mirror that I saw."[90]

After Cohen left, she realized she had flirted with him, and he had not wanted to respond.[91] He did write, however, sending her a frank opinion of what he had deduced of Harry's psychological difficulties vis-à-vis her, at the same time revealing how much he understood her own need to be free of them.

What I am about to say is tempered by an awareness that I know only a fragment of the story. But fools and psychiatrists rush in with their ideas and formulations serenely unburdened by the facts. First, I'd like to repeat what I said over the phone—that he is struggling with emotional problems now which should have been resolved during adolescence—that his egocentricity is probably not easy to live near—and that your growth may have been retarded in the shadow of the Pillar.

In the light of the many things you have done and how well you have done them—the warmth of your relationships with others—and the other expressions of your creative, living potential—this release, if it comes to pass, could be the freedom which finally permits a more complete self-expression.

Still—this does not erase the loneliness—the sense of failure—somehow the humiliation—and, of course, the rejection which is your special hooker.[92]

Before returning to New York, Harry swore on the Bible that it was his "solemn intention" to stay married to Clare for life.[93] Then, on February 29, he surprised her by phoning to say he was coming to Phoenix again the following day. Despite his biblical vow, he did not love her, still loved his mistress, and wanted to negotiate a "concordat" that would enable him to have his "last chance" to sexually "dominate" someone. He said he needed to get Jeanne back from Europe, so he could "make up [his] mind." Clare saw the fatuity of this notion. Harry was in no position to decide about either of them. She had the power to refuse divorce, and Jeanne would not settle for just living with him.[94]

On the day of his arrival, she poured out anguished handwritten assessments of their relationship, past, present, and future. They were cast in the form of long letters to him, and she gave him one late that night, as he was going to his room. It stated that she would "never, under any circumstances," divorce him, or permit him to divorce her. She expected him to read it the next morning, and, as she subsequently recounted to Father Murray, was stunned to see Harry, just after midnight, enter her bedroom with a bottle of whiskey.

> It was the most extraordinary performance I have ever witnessed. . . . There was no way to shut him off, or get him out of the room. If I begged him to go, we both needed sleep, he said, "This is it, so we may as well have one last big talk." If I threatened or tried to push him to bed, he said, "From now on I'm boss." Exhausted, occasionally tearful, once "catatonic" from

sheer fatigue, I had to let him go on. His general attitude was one
of, "Well, I knew this is what you would finally do—but why
didn't you say so in September?" . . . Several times he announced
he loved me, and never wanted to leave me; wouldn't have ever
left me even if *I* had insisted, because he knew my problems better than anyone; he swore he was not going to be grim and unhappy about it; we would make the best of it. Somewhere along
the line, I got down on my knees, asking him to pray with me to
God for strength. . . . He prayed long, fervently, and even eloquently for this purpose, we kissed one another goodnight, then
he went to his room about 3 a.m., returned in five minutes to ask
me if I knew about him and Mary Bancroft—I didn't. For over an
hour he talked about his twelve year friendship with [her]. . . .
Mary, by her own account had had 43 lovers, Allen Dulles being
her favorite. She had always loved Harry madly, but he had not
wanted to have an affair with her.

Seeming to have a vicarious fascination with Bancroft's lovers, and the fact that a woman so physically unappealing could be
so promiscuous, he harped on the subject for an hour and a half.
"She's a Catholic, if she's anything," he said. "Homely. The map
of Ireland is all over her face."[95]

He then took off on his extraordinary attraction for women.
He has yet to meet one he couldn't have, if he wanted her, but
"affairs left me disgusted with myself." Only love was good
enough. On the other hand, he had always wished he could settle
"for a blonde from the chorus."

When he went to bed, he was as drunk as a stable hand. And
I was exhausted. And utterly baffled. . . . He made one final, brief
appearance to tell me that there was one thing I had never understood: sex was never important to him: proof, 12 years with
Mary Bancroft who had had 43 lovers, and *he* had never touched
her.

Clare's problem, Harry said, was that unlike Jeanne, she thought sex
was more important than love. In a telling stream of consciousness, he
talked for another hour about the torment of being a youthful stutterer,
declared that he was a genius—"undoubtedly I am"—and again boasted
about all the women he had, or could have, seduced.

By 6:30 A.M. he was still maundering on, and Clare was reduced to
stupefied silence. "Now, snap out of it," he said. "I am here, I love you.

You *belong* here; we both know it." She shook herself awake, only to hear him return to the subject of his sex life—"a matter which, at the same time," she told Murray, "he vociferously claims does not interest him. . . . There can be no question but that the poor man is demented."[96]

After five hours' sleep, she found her husband at his desk, rereading her letter declining divorce. When she patted him on the shoulder, he pushed her away, saying without apparent irony, "I am the dying Gaul. Don't expect me to be *happy* about this." Later, she saw him shambling about the garden, his large head drooping, a picture of misery.[97]

▽

Harry returned to New York still in a sulk, pursued by a taunting challenge from Clare that he be "manly" enough to go to Europe and cement the break with Jeanne. This dovetailed with Beth Moore's recommendation that her brother take a world tour of Time Inc. offices, to distract himself from domestic concerns.[98]

Clare sought her own diversion in the days that followed with yet another visit—the third in four months—from Gerald Heard and Michael Barrie. They bore a gift of LSD from Dr. Cohen. Father Murray joined them and took his first dose, a cautious one that put him, as he phrased it, "on the verge." Cohen called to ask how things had gone, and was pleased to hear that Clare had again attained "the upper register."[99]

Alone in the house after everyone had gone, Clare had time to assess on paper the man she was so determined to stay married to—and ask herself why. She found Henry Luce still handsome at sixty-two. His forehead was high and round, and his dark gray eyes looked larger than they were, being deep set and fringed with heavy black lashes beneath densely thick brows. What was left of his pale red hair was copious and curly. With her encouragement, he shopped at James Bell and Brooks Brothers, yet managed to look disheveled much of the time, with ash from three packs a day of Camel cigarettes besmirching his suits. He wore a battered felt hat in winter, or a dirty panama in summer, and bought shirts only after Clare threw out his frayed ones. Intolerant of wool, he wore black silk socks, even to the beach, and as a result suffered from blisters.[100]

Since he was indifferent to most jewelry, he sported only his father's gold watch and chain, and a platinum-and-sapphire ring on the little finger of his right hand, a wedding gift from Clare. This he never took off, less out of affection for her, she felt, than because it was carved with the Luce family crest. The blue stone had long since been cracked by his habit of pounding on the table to emphasize a point.

Though an inch short of six feet, broad-shouldered, and slender, Harry was unathletic in his movements. Tennis was the only game he played fairly well, but so aggressively that opponents had sustained black eyes from his smashes at the net. He openly cheated at golf, kicking the ball out of the rough for an easier shot. If challenged, he claimed to be "playing winter rules."

In his prime, what made him attractive to women, Clare deduced, was his aura of "relaxed power and self-satisfaction," combined with a "closed in quality." Though riches and power had given him a high profile around the globe, he remained to most "a man of mystery." He rarely talked about his personal life, or was curious about other people, caring only for what facts they knew or opinions they held. Unless Clare explained, he seldom saw the comic side of human foibles and behavior.

Careless of elementary good manners, he never opened a door or pulled out a chair for a woman, or complimented anyone's appearance. When alone with Clare, he never lit her cigarette or poured her a drink, seldom looked her in the eye, and impatiently interrupted when she was speaking.

He also butted in on general conversation. When those near him talked to each other, he would fold his arms and stare into space, until his heavy disapproval silenced them. Or he would abruptly stand up, look at his watch, announce that he had "work to do," and leave. Should he be trapped at a formal dinner, he exuded "a black brooding anger" that could be dispelled only if everyone switched their attention to him.

Clare noted moreover that Harry could be intolerant of correction, and childishly vain in playing the multimillionaire, grabbing restaurant checks even from hosts who could well afford them. It did not occur to him that this was offensive. "If I want to pay, that's *my* business."

After filling nine sheets of paper, she could no longer fathom what was so bewitching about Harry that she repeatedly humiliated herself in her efforts to keep him.[101]

On April 21, the eve of Harry's departure for his world tour, the Luces attended the annual black-tie Newspaper Editors of America dinner in Washington, D.C. Clare and Eleanor Roosevelt were billed as speakers representing Republican and Democratic points of view on the theme

"What's Wrong with the Press?" But the former First Lady had canceled, and Marya Mannes of *The Reporter* magazine was asked to substitute. Clare made the tactical error of asking to speak first, confident that Miss Mannes could not outshine her.

Glittering with diamonds, she addressed an audience that included Supreme Court Justices, Senators, high-ranking diplomats, and heads of government agencies. Her speech was serious and carefully scripted, focusing on "the debasement of popular taste" in the American press. Too many journalists, she said, were trading "their birthright of candor and truth in order to become White House pets, party pets, corporation pets, Pentagon or State Department or trade union or governor's mansion pets."

Clare was off form and received only tepid applause, while Mannes, in simple black chiffon, spoke with verve and wit. She agreed that the space given to hard news was declining in favor of pulp stories, and made the provocative point that television broadcasts, concise as they were, did "a better job" of informing the American people than print. Turning to look saucily at the Luces, she said that certain weekly newsmagazines were "the Clapp's Baby Food of the nation's news diet—especially processed for quick digestion."

The audience roared, and Mannes continued with quips that aroused ripples of laughter. Clare had not been upstaged since her appearance in *Candida*. She turned white and lit one cigarette after another, grinding out butts and expelling streams of smoke from her nostrils that one observer said "would have done credit to a jet take-off."

The result was a thunderous standing ovation for Mannes. In the receiving line, Clare was gracious to her rival, but ducked out early.[102]

After saying good-bye to Harry, who would be gone for a month, she stayed on in Washington and redeemed herself with an effective speech at the War College. At the Sulgrave Club, she renewed acquaintance with Jacqueline Kennedy, and in a letter to Harry mentioned her "big beehive hair do, baby stare, and 'baby-talk' lisp." John Kennedy was the likely front-runner for the Democratic nomination that summer, so Clare was not surprised to see courtiers already clustering around his wife. She also appeared at a state dinner for President de Gaulle of France, before spending the last weekend of the month at Brooke Astor's country place outside New York. Simultaneously, as she was aware, Harry was reuniting in Europe with Lady Jeanne Campbell.[103] But she had no inkling that he was welshing on their concordat, telling Jeanne, "We can't marry yet, but might consider setting up house in Jamaica, or Lake Louise in Canada, or even Switzerland."[104]

A few days later, Clare was mortified by another Cholly Knickerbocker item in the *New York Journal-American*. "That famous publisher and his lady friend are together constantly in Paris. Eventually everybody concerned is going to have to break down and admit a divorce is inevitable."[105]

Harry, by now in Beirut, hurriedly wired her, "My comment would be, 'There is nothing to it and columnist was evidently misinformed.' "[106]

She replied at once from the Waldorf. "I am hurt—though I said I was beyond hurting. . . . But it *is* harder to take it in public than in private." Noting he had sent her no letters and only three telegrams in almost three weeks, she cruelly quoted what Dr. Rosenbluth had said twenty-one years before: "Something is wrong, not with Harry's body, but with his mind. He is crippled by some exotic neurosis . . . and you had best leave him."[107]

On or about May 16, she finally got a letter from Harry assuring her that the "the Great Encounter" had indeed taken place, and Jeanne had shed few tears. Clare was surprised at the apparent ease with which he had accomplished what must have been a wrenching renunciation. She wrote at once to congratulate him on his "astonishing ability to get everyone to see things *your* way."

At the end of a nine-day vacation at two Rockefeller resorts in the Caribbean, Clare reunited with Harry for the Memorial Day weekend. She soon found out that he had been lying to her about breaking off completely with Jeanne in Paris. In fact, he had taken her from there for a five-day car tour of Switzerland. This revelation plus another, that he had told Jeanne he "*would* marry her" if he ever got a divorce, led to long hours of argument, with Clare yet again trying to get him to say what he wanted, and he, as was his habit, asking *her* to decide what he should do. By late Monday night, both of them were exhausted, and she went to bed. Around twelve o'clock, Harry came into her room and said portentously, "It is God's will. You are the cross I have to bear."

At the end of her tether, Clare picked up the telephone. She dialed the Waldorf's Western Union office and dictated a telegram: "Jeanne Campbell, Inveraray Castle, Argyll, Scotland. Harry says that he wishes to marry you and that he will soon be in the position to do so. Congratulations. Clare Luce." Harry, outwitted and furious, called the operator back and asked her to cancel the wire. He was told that only the sender could do that, so he fired off one of his own: "Disregard telegram from Clare."[108]

It was now almost 1:00 A.M. on June 1. Deadlocked once more, they parted to sleep. Later in the day, Clare resumed the confrontation, determined to make order out of the chaos of nine months of wrangling. Her agenda covered familiar ground. Did either of them really want a divorce? Absent a legal split, was he intending to continue his affair? What was "the right thing to do," since his family, church, and business associates were afraid of damage to their public image?

Harry asked Clare if she thought she would have a better life married to him than not. She replied that she would not want a repeat of the last four years. Wavering for the first time, he said that if they stayed together, their future would be different from the past. "Leaving 'love' out," he said chillingly, "I feel I can offer all the other things." She then asked for an assurance that he would not "reopen this question of divorce" at a later date.

"I am an old man," he said. "This is the last crisis of this kind I shall pass through."

Realizing that she was winning, Clare told him that she would start divorce proceedings next week unless he met four demands. He must convey in writing his intention to spend the rest of his life with her, notify Jeanne that their affair was over "forever" and that they must no longer communicate, and tell the Moores, in Clare's presence, that he wanted to remain married. Finally, before the month was out, he must escort her through the new Time & Life Building on Sixth Avenue, "as though you were pleased and proud to show it to me."

She typed up a five-page summary of their marathon negotiations, ending with her four demands, and in each case Harry wrote, "Agreed."[109]

▽

By now Jeanne Campbell was in Jamaica, looking for a house where she and Harry could live. She was therefore flabbergasted to receive a letter from him, telling her yet again they could not marry. He gave no explanation except to say that during his world tour Clare had made an "unserious" threat to jump from their forty-first-floor apartment.[110]

Despite having his commitment on paper, Clare still toyed with him. On June 10, as they drove to Ridgefield, she said calmly that after all she had "decided on divorce." Harry's response, after he recovered, was to insist that "we should go on for the rest of our lives together." To that end, and hoping that he might even now devise some way of continuing with Jeanne, he proposed they summon Father Murray to Sugar Hill to act as a "Qualified Witness" at another marital summit.[111]

Clare agreed, seeing a chance to get what she had long wanted from Harry: a legal division of assets, which would give her security in the event of his further treachery—or death. They set a date for the weekend of June 18. Impulsively, Harry did not wait for Murray to arrive before sending Jeanne a second letter. "Everything is opening up again. It's an extraordinary moment in our love."[112] Jeanne's reaction was to make plans to reestablish herself in New York at once, in order to "fight" for him.[113]

Father Murray was a reluctant mediator this time, because he sensed that Clare's spiritual, emotional, and material neediness was insatiable. "By what right," he testily asked, "do you demand to be loved *unconditionally?*" She was too astonished to answer.[114] At any rate, the main result of the second summit was a settlement beneficial to Clare. She was to receive "with all speed" $200,000 for the purchase of a Manhattan apartment, keep joint ownership of the Phoenix house, explore the tax consequences of becoming co-owner of Sugar Hill, and get legal ownership of whatever artworks she desired from the Luce collection.[115]

Discussing money and possessions made the weekend a "painful" experience for the two men, but to Clare it was "deeply contenting." For the first time, she told Harry, she felt "secure 'for good and always' in *your* life, and in a large area of your affections."[116]

▽

Jeanne was in the city by early July, as was Randolph Churchill, a close friend of hers as well as Clare's former lover. He had been sent to America by the *New Statesman* to cover the two presidential conventions being held that month. While Randolph was in New York, Jeanne let him stay with her in a small rental apartment.[117]

The Democrats convened in Los Angeles on July 11, and four nights later Joe Kennedy arrived at the Luces' Waldorf suite to watch his son John accept the nomination.[118] "We stand today on the edge of a New Frontier," the charismatic young candidate said, "the frontier of the 1960s. . . . Beyond that frontier are uncharted areas of science and space, unsolved problems of peace and war, unconquered problems of ignorance and prejudice, unanswered questions of poverty and surplus."

Randolph returned to New York, and on July 20 boozily inveigled himself into a dinner Clare was attending with the former heavyweight boxing champion Gene Tunney, at the new Four Seasons restaurant on Park Avenue.[119] She managed to have him seated far from her, because of his habit, going back to 1934, of loudly proposing marriage every time they met. To avoid having him escort her home, she slipped out early, on the pretext of going to the ladies' room. But when she hailed a taxi in the street, Randolph came flying out, pursued by Tunney, and jumped into the cab with her. It moved off too soon for Tunney, who ran alongside, shouting to the driver, "I am Gene Tunney. You get this lady back to the Waldorf at once, safely, or you will be hearing from me!"

At this he dropped off, and Clare became aware that Randolph was moaning. "What's the matter with you?" she asked. "I'm going to sue," he said. It transpired that in the chase out of the restaurant, Tunney had given Churchill a fourth-class kidney punch, in an unsuccessful attempt to fell him.

Saying to herself, "I'll leave this groaning object to pay," Clare jumped out at the Waldorf and headed upstairs, telling the desk clerk not to admit Mr. Churchill under any circumstances.

Randolph subsequently telephoned and asked Clare if she would be a witness for him in his lawsuit against Tunney. She assured him that on the contrary, she would be a witness for Gene.[120]

▽

Farce turned to near tragedy later that night, when Harry came home to find that Clare had taken an overdose of sodium amytal.[121] In all likelihood, she had heard from Randolph, who was known for his blunt honesty, that he was staying with Lady Jeanne Campbell. The shock that "Baby Bunting" was back in town—no doubt at Harry's urging—made Clare realize that her husband had betrayed her yet again. This brought on what she termed "a blackness," accompanied by the thought, "Nobody could love me who really knew me."[122]

She was rushed more than forty blocks to Doctors Hospital on East Eighty-seventh Street to be pumped out. Harry issued a statement from her room that she had suffered "a digestive disturbance."[123] Then, in an agony of contrition, he sent her a handwritten apologia, insisting that he did not mean to renege on his commitments of the previous month.

> I want to go on with you because I have loved you very deeply
> and I do love you. Thus by going on, we can both honor the past

and, in some measure, correct it. But most properly, it seems to me, I have mainly the *future* in mind. . . .

In the future I do not see any Utopia or glamorous "New Frontier." I do see goodness and kindness and, especially companionship. I see for both of us a chance to renew ourselves in the "things men live by, love, work, prayer, play." . . .

Of the four things, let me here speak only of love. Our love is deep—it has also suffered wounds, it has its limitations, but it meets many of the tests—not least, survival. Speaking for myself, I seek your good as you seek mine. I enjoy the pleasure of your company—no trivial test! I would share with you, more than I have, thoughts and troubles and hopes. I would hope there would be many sunny hours before the sunset and then at last a sunset hand-in-hand.

With love—and "such as I am"—

Yours,
Harry

Just then, Randolph told Jeanne that if only Clare would marry him, "Robinson," as he called Harry, might be hers. He showed up at the hospital to propose, and when told that Clare was seeing no visitors, went up and down the corridor stomping like a child.[124]

Louisa Jenkins was not fooled by reports that Clare was suffering from colitis and an ulcer. She wrote, "What are you trying to do? . . . Why don't you just go your way and let him have 50 mistresses if he wants."[125]

Randolph wrote her in much the same vein. "You may think you have had a total victory over Robinson & brought the old scoundrel to heel. But you have got the albatross firmly tied around your neck for life & it will prove a diminishing consolation to you that he will never hear the skirl of the pipes."[126]

Clare's recovery was slow, and prevented her from attending the Republican convention in Chicago, where Vice President Nixon was resoundingly nominated on July 26. His speech was pedestrian compared with Kennedy's. He pledged to wage "a campaign such as this country has never seen before," and in the course of it to "visit every one of the fifty states of this nation."

Harry's ultimate course of action came to him improbably, during a psychedelic session with Gerald Heard at Sugar Hill on August 8. This time, while Clare took 125 micrograms of LSD, he tried a mild dose of psilocybin, and heard God in the garden forgiving his sins, and ordering him to give up Jeanne Campbell. For at least the third time, he told the latter they could not wed, and in midmonth set off with Clare for the Greek islands, leaving his bewildered and wounded lover behind.[127]

The Luces let it be known that their vacation, hosted by Stavros Niarchos aboard the *Creole*, and later at his vast estate on Spetsopoula, was to be "a second honeymoon." But soon after sailing from Athens, and entering the Gulf of Corinth, Clare began to complain in her diary about the distance that persisted between her and Harry. She also felt alienated from her fellow voyagers, who included King Paul and Queen Frederica of Greece, Tina Onassis, Lady Diana Cooper, and Cecil Beaton. Their conversation at dinner consisted entirely of social gossip— "whether Pam Churchill is happy or not with Leland Hayward, or whether or not Slim Hayward got a rough deal." Nobody seemed interested in her.[128]

"Am I getting old?" Clare wrote, after seeing Eugenia Niarchos and Tina sitting around all day in bikinis. "I find them much less attractive and glamorous showing so much flesh all the time. Perhaps people are *less* themselves naked, unpainted . . . than they are clothed." She cringed at the sight of Harry ambling about the deck in old shorts that drooped from his potbelly, faded silk socks, and sneakers, with smeary spectacles perched on his nose. He was now so deaf that he needed a hearing aid, but obstinately refused to wear one.[129] The only time he paid any attention to her was at night, when he came into her stateroom to ask, as he had done for more than twenty years, "Do you want me to read to you?" If she said no, he was visibly relieved, and felt free to go off and enjoy eight hours of solitary sleep. She understood that all he wanted from her was, as he often said, "companionable silence, taciturn serenity."

Her own sleep was troubled by nightmares. In one, she dreamed in color of "the terrifying fall of the House of (Luce?!)." All that remained after it burned and collapsed was the splendid facade, and in the ashes behind, "my jewels—nothing else." In another, she was blowing out candles on a birthday cake for Harry and her hair caught fire.

> My whole face was enveloped in a blue flame like a gossamer veil.
> I put my hands tightly to my face to keep it from burning. Harry

and others poured champagne over my head, and put it out. Afterwards I was certain that my whole face had been burned away. The doctor came, and examined my hands and face, and showed them to me in a mirror. . . . There were blisters all over my hands face and nose. The doctor (to my horror) took a razor and sheared the tops of all the blisters off. I awoke sickened and heartsore, certain that even the remnants of my beauty were gone.

She saw both dreams as symbolic of the ruin of her marriage, and with it "the only security I have had for years—my beauty—which I do know now is gone, and has no 'power.'"

By August 22 they were established on Spetsopoula, in the southern Peloponnesus, mainly to shoot pheasants. The opulence of the place— "caviar coming out of the faucets"—dismayed Clare. Niarchos was indefatigable in showing off his $10 million improvements to the grounds and buildings. He was not only oppressively egocentric, she realized, but "bored bored bored. . . . He revolves about his own little doings like a dervish." Casually, he boasted to her that one night at 3:00 A.M., he had gone to the beach for sex with a girl.

Clare felt so entrapped that she thought of ordering a boat to get her off the island. Instead, she made one last attempt to ingratiate herself with Harry. On the night of the twenty-fifth, she went to his cabin, seeking "*not* passion, but comfort and closeness."

She climbed into his bed, and immediately sensed his panic, verging on disgust, about getting in with her. He paced the room in search of a drink and a sleeping pill, in the apparent hope that his "big psychological block," as he had begun calling it, would be alleviated.

Then finally he got into bed ("Why does the bed have to be so damn small?") and lay there rigid, sweating, puffing a while— perhaps a minute. He approaches it, not like a man who is indifferent to a woman, or tired, even of her, but like one who is mortally afraid of her.

I put my head on his shoulder, made some tender remark, like "Oh, now *is* it so bad to just be *cozy* with a woman who loves you?" He then made for me the fatal remark. He said, "I'm in a terrible situation. Well they say, curse God and die!" That *did* it beyond all hope of repair, beyond all hope. . . . I cannot see *how* I can stay, after this. . . . No use no use, no use.

Harry realized the extreme cruelty of his implication that blasphemy and death were preferable to having to cuddle her. He got out of bed and begged on his knees, for charity. "Let us both pray to God for help."

But Clare was beyond praying, and could do nothing for him. "I *am* the trouble. The fearsome thing. The repugnant thing. The loathsome, crucifying thing."[130]

44

A NEW ERA

Growing old is not a gradual decline, but a series of jumps down from one ledge to another.

—KENNETH CLARK

The "second honeymoon" ended in early September with the Luces parting temporarily, as Harry returned to New York and Clare stayed in Europe for the rest of the month. Since the awful night on Spetsopoula, both had wearily concluded that they were irrevocably welded. They shared too much of a past, too many interests, and too harmonious a political philosophy to divorce now—not to mention their enjoyment of social eminence in beautiful surroundings.

This did not prevent Harry from seeing Jeanne Campbell as soon as he got back. But the affair, never predominantly sexual, became even less so, metamorphosing gradually to walks in Central Park and long telephone conversations. By the end of the year, Jeanne would leave the United States for the Soviet Union on an extended assignment for Beaverbrook.[1]

Clare meanwhile enjoyed herself in Paris, staying at the Ritz and spending large sums of Harry's money at Balenciaga. She lunched with the Duke and Duchess of Windsor at their country house, and, in her role as enchantress, dined with Erich Maria Remarque. "I am crazy about you," he wrote, even though his wife, Paulette Goddard, was in town. On a side trip to northern Italy, she reunited with her old Roman courtier Count Vittorio Cini, at the Gritti Palace in Venice. George Cukor, who had directed the movie version of *The Women*, encountered her in Milan with three generals in tow. She tried to coax a Bolognese pharmacist to sell her an illegal supply of LSD, and when he declined, pursued other sources. From time to time, she and Harry exchanged assurances of undying commitment.[2]

Before leaving Paris, Clare splurged again, this time on a white satin gown from Lanvin.[3] She meant to wear it at the Inaugural Ball of whoever won the American election. By the time she got back home at the end of the month, Nixon and Kennedy had just faced off in the first television debate between presidential candidates in history. Seventy-four million of the nation's population of 179 million had watched, and most thought Kennedy had won, with his radiant vitality and youthful good looks. But radio listeners gave the victory to Nixon, because they could not see that he had refused makeup and looked pale, dark-jowled, and sweaty. This bore out Clare's prophecy in a recent *McCall's* column that with television sets in three-quarters of American homes, future candidates would have to groom and perform for the camera, rather than focus just on issues.[4]

In early October, JFK's Catholicism became a serious liability. Clare received a call from his agitated father, asking her "to do Jack a big favor." He complained that everywhere his son held a rally, swarms of nuns were settling in the front seats, "clicking their rosaries and their dentures" in excitement. Joe thought Cardinal Spellman might be able to do something about it, but could not approach His Eminence himself. "The SOB hates me. I beat him out of some real estate," he said, chuckling. "But *you* could tell him, tactfully, that if he wants a Catholic in the White House, he'd better keep those goddam nuns from hogging all the front rows. This isn't an ordination—it's an election!"[5]

Nixon, too, was concerned about the religious question, and asked Clare for advice on how to "keep it out of the campaign as much as possible." He had found that 25 percent of the voters in Akron, Ohio, were for him because they were anti-Catholic. It followed that others might be against him because he was a Quaker.[6]

As a friend and co-religionist of the Kennedys, Clare was rumored to be a JFK supporter. She did favor him, feeling that although he had less experience than Nixon, he had "more capacity for growth in office and would probably win."[7] However, on October 4 she issued a statement saying that as a veteran of Republican politics, she intended to vote for the Vice President.

Choosing a candidate was not so easy for Henry Luce. As Editor in Chief of a hugely influential news empire, his endorsement was coveted by both candidates. They vied with each other in professing strident anti-Communist views, knowing Harry's obsession with the Cold War. He felt that Kennedy was more "imaginative" on foreign policy, and was tempted to back him for that reason. He also admired the young man's social sophistication and literary bent, going so far as to write a new foreword to his book about appeasement in the 1930s, *Why England Slept*. But having given Nixon five favorable cover stories in four years, he found it hard to reject him now. So in midmonth, *Life* came out for the Republican, but so halfheartedly as not to spoil Kennedy's chances in November.[8]

Time's coverage of the campaign led to an outraged telegram from Randolph Churchill, who was still smarting from Clare's rejection of his marriage proposal. It was sent to Harry at seven addresses.

> HAVE BEEN READING TIME MAGAZINE CAREFULLY FOR THE LAST
> FEW WEEKS AND AM STAGGERED THAT A RICH MAN LIKE YOU
> SHOULD TRY TO BECOME RICHER BY PRINTING UNSAVORY
> STORIES ABOUT OTHER PEOPLES PRIVATE LIVES. HAS IT NEVER
> OCCURRED TO YOU THAT YOU YOURSELF ARE IN A MOST
> VULNERABLE POSITION AND THAT YOUR PRIVATE LIFE MIGHT
> MAKE ADMIRABLE MATERIAL FOR OTHER GOSSIP COLUMNISTS? IF
> I WERE YOU ROBINSON I WOULD HAVE A CARE OR YOU MIGHT
> LAND UP ON A MUCK HEAP.[9]

On November 8, Kennedy and his running mate, Lyndon Baines Johnson, won the election by a margin of only .17 percent of the popular vote. If the Luce magazines had been less respectful of the Democratic ticket during the final weeks, Nixon might have been President-elect.

▽

After the election, Father Murray saw signs of melancholy reappear in Clare, and wrote Dr. Cohen for help. He attributed her morbidity to several causes: a loss of confidence (after being bested by Marya Mannes, she had developed a fear of public speaking), confusion as to her identity, paralysis of will, and at the root of these an inability to do creative work. "The suicidal impulse has not asserted itself," Murray said, "though there has been the not unusual talk of it."[10]

LSD had seemed to improve Clare's mood in the past, so with her consent he asked the doctor to travel to Phoenix, administer the drug, and return periodically until her mental health was restored. Since such visits would constitute medical treatment, Clare was prepared to pay. Cohen replied that he would certainly charge for his services.[11] He flew to Phoenix on November 27, and after administering LSD stayed overnight.

On December 6, Clare wrote him to say that she was feeling much more able to cope. "While the melancholy lurks, it is background, *chiaroscuro*, without which the highlights have no meaning. The best part of it all is that I feel *almost* ready to accept my own face, with all its sadness and imperfections." She said that her experiences with Gerald as invigilator, while usually "marvelous," were "not as *corrective*" as with him.[12]

Cohen returned on the weekend of December 10, and in a letter enclosing his bill four days later wrote, "It would be just as proper for you to send me a statement for a delightful Sunday and a notable drive to the airport Monday morning."[13]

Clare neglected to have Harry send a check for several weeks.[14] She was beginning to have romantic feelings for "Sid" and, as before with Carlos Chávez, found it hard to accept that professionals she was attracted to should want to be reimbursed for services. Nevertheless, she asked the doctor to supervise further LSD trips, and on one occasion teasingly suggested that he send her "25 g. by mail pronto" in exchange for a mosaic of a lion lying with a lamb.[15]

After several months, Cohen mailed Clare a partial diagnosis of what ailed her. Most significant, to his mind, were her "self-punitive drives," which led to depressive episodes. "I think you are seeing yourself through distorted lenses. They must be removed over time and a new perception of you refitted [so that] you may come to see yourself as lovable."

Before that state could be reached, he wrote, there was "much dredging to be done" that could not be accomplished solely by taking acid. He suggested she consider psychiatric therapy, not necessarily with him, since they were often a continent apart. "I would rather be your friend," he wrote. "But if you wish, and if LSD would accelerate the therapeutic working-through, it might be possible for me to be your therapist."[16]

They tried couch sessions for a while, and Clare responded ecstatically. "I feel . . . that I am the other half of you and you of me. . . . I love you because you treat me like—a man. (By which I mean, a person.)" Their conversations made her feel entirely feminine for the first time in her life. She told him she longed "to be his slave," and please him without pleasing herself—"to serve for the joy of serving, to give without getting, to love without reward."[17]

Their mutual attraction was strong. "It would have been better for me if you had loved me sooner," Clare wrote. "And yet. No. No. For I wouldn't have believed in it, the way I do now, if it had happened in any other way." Sounding like Sylvia Plath, she went on. "I had to go down down down in the dark all by myself in order to know what a miracle could befall me. What it meant to come up up up in the light with you."[18]

In another letter addressing him as "Dearest," she admitted to exploding during an argument with Harry, because "for the last week I have been overwhelmed by the desire to *be* with you, to *live* with you, on the terra firma of real love." A handicap was that Cohen was married. "Am I being stupid not to tear down the cage? But if I did . . . there's the cruel problem of Ilse. . . . Sid, sit down right now and write me that you still love me."[19]

When apart, they set up weekly phone dates. There was much to tell him, she said, "even though all the important things have been said" about guilt in "sexual relations—in or out of marriage."[20]

Both finally realized the impossibility of a life together, given their respective marital and career commitments. When Cohen published his masterwork, *The Beyond Within: The LSD Story*, he sent her an inscribed copy.

> Clare, if "What is received is received according to the nature of the recipient"—I am both the finest and the worst of men—the finest for having known you—the worst for having lost that greatest of opportunities. It is to you—of course—to whom the book was written—a poor enough offering—but with it goes my love to the end.[21]

▽

Feeling serene after a post–Sunday Mass LSD session in Phoenix, Clare went East on January 18, 1961, to attend the inauguration of John Fitzgerald Kennedy.[22] On its eve, in bitterly cold weather, she and Harry attended Frank Sinatra's fund-raising gala at the National Guard Armory in Washington. Some women were seen protecting their minks and gowns with blankets smuggled from local hotels as they entered the vast, only half-full space. By the next morning, a blizzard had deposited six inches of snow on the capital. Attendees at the swearing-in ceremony shivered as Kennedy, wearing no overcoat, and Eisenhower, balding and muffled up behind him, announced, "The torch has been passed to a new generation."

That night, Clare climbed into an Inaugural Ball bus in her white satin Lanvin gown, and found herself sitting next to Vice President Johnson. She reminded him that when they last met, just before the Democratic convention, he had been confident of getting the presidential nomination, and had profanely vowed that even if he lost, there was "no way" he would take the second spot under JFK.

"Come clean, Lyndon," she teased him.

He leaned close and whispered, "Clare, I looked it up. One out of every four presidents has died in office. I'm a gamblin' man darlin', and this is the only one chance I got."[23]

President Kennedy greets Clare at his inaugural ball, 1961

▽

After another spell in Arizona, taking LSD under Heard's supervision and introducing her houseguest, Carlos Chávez, to the drug, Clare was back in New York by Monday, March 13. She was there ostensibly for an auction of furnishings in an eleventh-floor, twelve-room apartment that Harry had bought at 993 Fifth Avenue. Its purchase in both their names was apparently his way of fulfilling the promise he had made last June, to give her a $200,000 space of her own.[24] The limestone building, designed by Emery Roth, was opposite the Metropolitan Museum of Art, and only yards away from the Brokaw mansion, where she had lived during her first marriage.

The more important reason for Clare's return East was that she had become depressed yet again—"a cracking and breaking down interior feeling." She sought comfort from Harry, but found him equally morose. It transpired that he had been seeing Jeanne Campbell for several weeks, having summoned her from Jamaica at the end of her Russian trip. But the reunion had gone badly. Jeanne, in spite of repeated rebuffs, was expecting a marriage proposal, and when it was not forthcoming, a "ghastly row" had ensued.[25]

By Tuesday night, Harry's mood had mellowed, and he treated Clare with more kindness and affection than she could remember in years. Yet inexplicably, while preparing for bed, she felt "a ping" in her head. This was followed by what she described as "a wild flood of tears, an impulse to gallop on the nightmare of my spirit down the slippery road of death."[26]

Dr. Michael Rosenbluth was summoned at 2:00 A.M., and found she had taken another overdose of sleeping pills, her third since discovering Harry's affair. After the usual stomach pump, she woke next morning feeling so thirsty that a glass of cold water "tasted like ambrosia." Her depression had lightened, but along with it came the conviction, expressed three days later to a New York psychiatrist, "that the roses and raptures of passion are gone forever for me."[27]

It would have been supremely ironic if Clare had died on the night of March 14. As she, Harry, and all Manhattan would soon find out, Jeanne Campbell was simultaneously attending a party given by Gore Vidal and meeting the novelist Norman Mailer. Their attraction was immediate, and within days they moved in together. By November, Jeanne would be pregnant with her long-desired first child, and would marry Mailer in due course.

Untitled painting by Clare Boothe Luce

Harry's reaction to her defection was to discontinue the private phone number she had used to call him.[28] He took comfort as always in his role as America's most powerful publisher, monologuing with senior staff, putting off the day for naming his successor, reveling in the easy access he had to foreign capitals, and the Biltmore golf course adjoining his backyard.

Clare flew West to her toy poodle, her cactus garden, her heated swimming pool with its view of Camelback Mountain, her paintings and mosaics and bridge games, her socializing with wealthy, aging

"Phoenicians," and her LSD trips with the ubiquitous Gerald Heard and Michael Barrie—all conspiring to persuade her, as her fifty-eighth birthday approached, that she was heading toward retirement. This did not thrill her, as she wrote Sidney Cohen. "The snake is still hissing away under the rose bushes, but his name eludes me, except as one can call him by his family name, Despair."[29]

But her brain was too fertile and her interests too broad for her to allow herself to drop out of touch with the world of ideas and action. Aside from her monthly *McCall's* columns, which would continue for six more years, she started to write political articles and give speeches on current issues, showing a steadily more conservative bias. She also took advantage of her friendship with JFK and LBJ, as well as continuing her contacts with Nixon and her neighbor Barry Goldwater, the junior Senator from Arizona.

"The Kennedy administration looks like an exciting, vigorous and dynamic change," Clare wrote Stan Swinton. She felt that the young President would do as well as Eisenhower, while doubting he could end the Cold War, or bring about "an economic Utopia" to match that of the 1950s. "Meanwhile, the Kennedy clan is fun to watch and very easy on the eyes. What more can we ask for in the White House just now."[30]

▽

The rest of 1961 passed uneventfully, except that Clare had a long bout with pneumonia in early summer. She recuperated during a Mediterranean cruise with Harry on Bill Benton's yacht, the *Flying Clipper*, and after Labor Day moved into the Fifth Avenue apartment.

By December, she had begun to chafe over Harry's failure to act on the disposition of assets they had discussed eighteen months earlier. She decided not to make a fuss over not having been given $200,000 to buy a place of her own, since they were now together, supposedly for life. Nor was she bothered about joint ownership of Sugar Hill, and even advised Harry to donate the property to Yale or Time Inc. one day and take a tax deduction. Her main concern was that he had promised her any artworks she wanted from their collection, but had not followed through with a document of transfer. Many of them surely belonged to her, since they had been gifts from him. He had already arbitrarily deeded two paintings to his alma mater and Mepkin, as if she had no rights to either.[31]

The result was an acrimonious quarrel, in which Harry seemed puzzled and offended that she did not trust his word in financial matters.

Clare wearily capitulated, feeling she was too old to strain their marriage again by making demands about anything. She tried to be philosophical, writing resignedly, "I am here. He is here. Here we both are." Harry made amends by "stepping up to the counter" at Tiffany's and buying his wife a double-strand, cultured pearl necklace for Christmas that cost some $250,000.[32]

▽

In her February 1962 column for *McCall's*, Clare answered a reader's question: "Do you think Mrs. Kennedy should be censured for buying some of her clothes from Paris?"

Her reply began innocuously enough. "The personal activities of the President's wife cannot be dissociated from her role as First Lady." But then she could not resist parodying JFK's inaugural rhetoric. "She must not ask herself, 'What can these clothes do for me?' but 'What do these clothes I wear do for America?'"

Her remarks caused a nationwide furor, with headlines such as CLARE BOOTHE LUCE DRESSES DOWN JACKIE KENNEDY and JACKIE CENSURED? LUCE FUR FLYING. The White House announced that the First Lady's clothes were all American made, except for a Givenchy gown she had worn in Paris "as a tribute to the French people."[33]

Clare dismissed the uproar, saying, "Mrs. Kennedy would look gorgeous in a gunny sack."[34]

The President at any rate was not offended. He wrote in March to invite Clare to sit on his Advisory Committee on the Arts, whose job would be to constitute a National Cultural Center in Washington, adding that he hoped they would "meet soon." Two weeks later, on her fifty-ninth birthday, Clare accepted the appointment.[35]

She also heard from Nixon at this time. He was considering a run for the governorship of California, and sent her an inscribed copy of his new book, *Six Crises*.[36]

That spring and summer saw the apogee of Clare's quest to repeatedly attain the "higher register" of the LSD experience. More and more, she wanted to involve friends in her drug taking. Apart from Heard and Barrie (who tried without success to become permanent fixtures in her ménage), she encouraged Chávez to send a report of his Phoenix initiation to Dr. Cohen, and in early June had Father Murray watch and tape-record one of her trips in the birch grove at Sugar Hill.[37]

He told her he felt privileged to have looked "into the depths of you . . . and to have found that all was lightsome there, and full of life, with nothing of gloom or doom. You were so happy." The next day, however, there was a "switch" in Clare's attitude. She became distant, almost hostile, toward him. It was not for the first time. They had squabbled before, after the priest chastised her for wasting her literary talent on stillborn detective stories, instead of focusing on what Carlos called "the book of yourself."[38] She never took adverse criticism well, but the fact was that he had outlived his mediatory usefulness, since she and Harry had reached a state of truce.

Another reason for her estrangement from Murray was that she felt he patronized her, exemplifying a perceived bias in the Roman Catholic Church toward women as "an inferior sex." She told him she could no longer go to Confession, because "it does me *no good*," and felt herself in "deep rebellion" against the Vatican's anti-feminist theology. Murray tried to defend himself and the Church against her accusations, but admitted he was not her equal in argument. "You are far and away the most intelligent woman I have ever met—and also far superior in intelligence to most of the men I have met"—unconsciously revealing the gender bias of which she accused him.[39]

He was more effective in defining her fundamental psychological problem: "a felt incapacity to love and an equally felt unwillingness to be loved." Unease about this explained Clare's constant desire to punish herself with "the suicidal thing." In recent months, Murray said, she seemed to have shed some feelings of culpability, and he advised her to try to deal with them in everyday life, as she did successfully under LSD. But he reminded her of Dr. Cohen's warning that "the ancient emotional structures, which do indeed dissolve under LSD, tend to reconstitute themselves."[40]

Clare's next psychedelic playmate in the birch grove was a former lover from the early 1930s, the *Holiday* magazine editor William Harlan Hale. Like Randolph Churchill, he was now a bulky man eight years her junior, who had once been lean and handsome as well as promising. At twenty-two, Hale had enjoyed an idyllic interlude with Clare on the appropriately named Crotch Island in Maine, and had never forgotten it. He had gone on to publish a well-received novel called *Hannibal Hooker: His Death and Adventures*, in which an entrancing woman invited the hero to an island where she was spending the summer alone.[41]

By chance or design, Hale had met Clare again during Harry's world tour in 1960, and at a series of lunches, dinners, and theater had made no attempt to conceal that he remained in thrall. Though married with three children, he longed to recapture their earlier closeness. "In you I have staked a still unmined claim to tenderness and friendship and, if you will, passion, that makes me feel rich."[42]

On what he described as "that transcendent Thursday," they tripped on LSD, swam, photographed each other, and walked among the roses. "Dream-like as the day was," he wrote her afterward, "I remain staggered at what came up from the depths when the wraps of restraint went off. . . . I haven't known such joy except once before—on Crotch Island."[43]

On June 20, Clare left for Pollença, Majorca, where she had rented a villa for the summer. Since Harry would be joining her in July, she invited Hale, Chávez, Heard, Barrie, Tish Baldrige, and Sidney and Ilse Cohen for parts of August.

▽

Clare had fallen in love with the Balearic Islands in 1934, and had written a rhapsodic travel article about Majorca.[44] Her house, C'an Cueg— "House of the Frog"—belonged to a Baroness von Ripper, and sat in hills above the fishing village of Puerto de Pollença. It was a ten-minute walk from the ocean, and had three bedrooms besides her own, whose jasmine-draped balcony overlooked a garden full of geraniums and white oleander blossoms. The property had a freshwater swimming pool, and was screened from the road and a farm opposite by a long white wall, a backdrop for orange, lemon, and almond groves. Five servants and a cook were included in the $5,000 rental.

A highlight of Harry's visit was a sixty-seventh birthday celebration for Robert Graves on July 24. The English poet had lived for more than thirty years in the mountain village of Deiá, and had written a play to entertain his guests. It was performed in moonlight at a tiny amphitheater deep in an ancient olive grove. The plot was simple. Three travelers, searching for love, ate a magic mushroom and found instant peace and beauty in Majorca.[45]

But tranquillity once more eluded Clare, who was depressed for much of Harry's stay. Where these periods of anxieties and fears—"the God-awful dismals"—came from, she could not fathom.[46] But she was buoyed in early August by the arrival of Heard and Barrie, who brought LSD.[47] Gerald's wide range of acquaintance attracted interesting guests. Clare held court, alternating two $400 wigs from Helena Rubinstein that mitigated the effects of windy sailing on a fifty-eight-foot ketch, and swimming several miles daily. One was dark blonde for lunches and

Clare vacationing in Majorca, July 1962

sightseeing in town, the other lighter for patio dinners at a square, stone table beneath a sky ablaze with stars.[48]

Letitia Baldrige arrived on August 12, accompanied by three young American men. Tish was much in demand since the Kennedys had hired her as White House social secretary. She did not much care for Heard, skinny and garrulous in an old green shirt and slacks, or for Barrie with his extremely brief shorts and bright Hawaiian shirt. As a former CIA employee, she had made a pledge never to take mind-altering substances, so she declined to join LSD sessions. The sight of her former boss rhapsodizing about colors and imaginary music—not to mention trying to seduce her friends—repulsed her. But they did not share her scruples, and one youth had a bad trip that triggered violent, continuing nightmares. Tish remembered this druggy interlude as among the "most horrible" of her life.[49]

But to Bill Hale, who appeared on the twenty-second, Pollença was paradise. " '*Et in Arcadia ego*'—'I too have been in Arcady,'" he wrote her afterward. "I am thinking of you constantly. . . . How far off Majorca

526

seems now . . . that enchanted stillness of the flowers in the garden and of the shadows under the arches, interrupted only by a vulgar bleat from the bird-cage, or the splash of a middle-aged editor heaving himself into the swimming pool, or that wonderful bell-like call from the room upstairs, 'Oh—Bill!' "[50]

Clare had no more houseguests after Hale left, since Chávez canceled, and the Cohens were unable to travel from Germany, pleading a mysterious "predicament" on the part of Ilse.[51]

Sidney had just published an article in the *Journal of the American Medical Association* entitled "Complications Associated with Lysergic Acid Diethylamide (LSD-25)." It described the "serious complications" his researches were beginning to associate with acid. If Clare read it, she would have recognized many of them as pertaining to her own experiences under its influence and—more disturbingly—for months after taking it. Cohen listed "euphoriant abuse" (taking the drug recreationally instead of therapeutically); "multihabituation" (his own coinage, meaning simultaneous indulgence in other narcotics, stimulants, sedatives, and hallucinogens); "emotional instability"; "antisocial acting out behavior"; "dissolution of the ego" (feelings of unworthiness and a desire to be punished); and "prolonged psychotic reactions," including depression and suicide.[52]

▽

Two weeks after Clare returned from Majorca in early September, Tish Baldrige called from Washington and said, "The President wants you to come down here."

"What about?"

"I think he's unhappy about some of the things *Time* has been publishing."

Clare said she had no influence at her husband's magazines, but obeyed the summons.[53]

At 1:00 P.M. on Wednesday, the twenty-sixth, she was ushered into JFK's small dining room on the second floor of the White House. She found him still "slim, handsome, courteous, [his] graciousness concealing a great inner reserve."[54]

His first remark took her aback.

"Gather you have something on your mind."

Clare had expected him to tell her what was on his. But since he'd asked, she said, "Yes, I have."

There was a long pause, so she continued. "I woke this morning with a thought. . . . The greater a man is the easier it is to describe his greatness in a single sentence."

Kennedy seemed puzzled, and she gave him some examples.

"Does anyone need to tell you the *name* of these men: *He died to save us. . . . He discovered America. . . . He preserved the Union and freed the slaves. He lifted us out of a Depression and won a great World War. . . .* What is on my mind, Mr. President, is what sentence will describe you, when you leave here."

"I am not interested in my place in history," Kennedy said. He changed the subject to Cuba.

Less than a month before, U.S. aerial surveillance had confirmed the existence of eight Soviet missile sites on Fidel Castro's Communist island. Since then there had been mounting evidence of Soviet military shipments arriving there, most alarmingly combat troops, and several cargoes of medium-range nuclear missiles. Up to now, Kennedy had seen no need for military intervention. But he had announced on September 13 that the United States would consider it provocation if offensive weapons were installed in Cuba. The Senate had voted 86–1 to authorize the use of force if he deemed it necessary, in the face of a warning by the Soviet Foreign Minister Andrei Gromyko that any U.S. attack on Cuba or Cuba-bound shipping would mean war.

In view of these escalations, Clare was surprised to hear Kennedy say he did not think Cuba was "at present" dangerous compared with other flashpoints in the world.

"I cannot quite understand, Mr. President, why the presence of Communist power in Vietnam is a threat to our security nine thousand miles away, and the presence of it in Cuba is not."

"Would you have us give up our commitment in Vietnam? As I remember it, *Time* magazine urged us to take action there. Cuba was around at that time."

"I don't speak for or edit *Time*," she said.

"You surely have some influence."

"Such as I have—very little—I am urging them to keep their eye on Cuba now."

Kennedy asked, "Assuming Cuba *is* a threat, what is your policy?"

Clare said only that she feared the island would become a base for Communism to spread into Latin America.

"If we take action in Cuba," the President said, "it may be used as a pretext for the Russians to take Berlin."

He was clearly still nervous about the previous year's near nuclear confrontation between the Allies and the Soviets over the multinational occupation of Berlin. Just a month ago, an East German youth had been gunned down trying to escape over the wall that now divided the city.

Clare said that his argument meant that Cuba had placed the United States in a "global double bind," and asked which danger spot he thought was easier to break out of—Cuba or Berlin.

Kennedy's response was dismissive. "We can get ready in three weeks for the invasion of Cuba. We could win there, obviously."

Waiting even that long, she warned, would "be more costly in American lives."

"There are some situations you have to live with," he said.

Clare again asked if Americans should tolerate the presence of Russian military power ninety miles from Florida. "Why is the extrusion of Communism in Vietnam and the Near East more important to us than in our own sea off our own shores?"

"Your policy, then, is war with Cuba and the risk of nuclear war with the USSR?"

The Soviets had not risked it over Vietnam or Korea, Clare reminded him. She felt the United States should "call their bluff" in its own hemisphere.

Kennedy was dubious. " 'Calling their bluff,' as you put it, could lead to nuclear war."

"Nuclear war will settle nothing for anybody. But if Khrushchev really believes it will, now is the time to find it out."

"You would rather take Cuba than hold Vietnam or Berlin."

"We are holding Vietnam alone," she said. "Berlin is a multilateral commitment. If our Allies want to hold it at the risk of nuclear war, we will be in better shape to honor that commitment without Russia at our back door."

Kennedy rejected her brinkmanship. "I do not wish, or intend to be, the President who goes down in history as having unleashed nuclear war."

"Nobody—not you or Khrushchev—will go down in history in the event of nuclear war. A veil will be drawn over the history of the West. No one can benefit but China. Khrushchev knows that too."

"You have not yet said what your Cuban policy is—except that regardless of what our Allies think, we should invade."

It was up to him, Clare conceded, whether to invade or impose a naval blockade. "Militarily Cuba is more important to us than the city of Berlin. . . . Maybe the sentence by which you will go down in history will be: *He kept this hemisphere free and did not yield in Berlin.*"

"It looks easier when you are on the outside," the President said.

▽

When Hugh Sidey, *Time's* presidential correspondent, came to pick up Clare after lunch, he found her and JFK standing impatiently on the White House steps. Evidently, the meeting had not gone well. Clare had no word to say about her encounter, but Kennedy let Sidey know that he disliked having Clare Luce tell him "how to run the world."[55]

Cuba was not his only major problem that Wednesday. A black man named James Meredith had just tried to enroll as a student in the all-white University of Mississippi, and was being denied admittance by state officials, most prominently Governor Ross Barnett, playing much the same racist role as Governor Faubus had done in Arkansas five years before. Violence began to flare around the Oxford campus on Saturday night, after Kennedy signed an order sending twenty-three thousand federal troops to safeguard Meredith's registration. But there was a delay in deployment and the rioting turned bloody on Sunday night, just as JFK was prematurely announcing on television that the crisis had been resolved. Order was restored by Monday morning, and Meredith attended his first class under armed protection.

In a letter thanking the President for lunch, Clare reminded him of her "single sentence" theory of historic eminence, and could not resist adding that the recent events in Mississippi had proved it.

> *He upheld and enforced the law of the land against segregation in Mississippi.* A noble sentence! A sentence for all the world to read and applaud. A sentence which describes not only the act but the actor. We know him, not because of what he said but because of what he did.[56]

On October 15 she was back in Phoenix for the winter, completing a syndicated article entitled "Mr. Kennedy on the Hustings." Its tone was far from that of her adulatory letter. Referring to the President's current efforts to win support for Democratic candidates in the congressional midterm elections, she said that his record so far on revitalizing the economy had been unimpressive, and had plunged the country into recession. As for foreign policy, he could hardly point with pride "to his handling of the Bay of Pigs invasion, or to his success in driving Khrush-chev out of Cuba."[57]

The piece was rejected by the North American Newspaper Alli-ance as too partisan, but was in any case rendered obsolete by the rap-idly unfolding nuclear crisis of the next thirteen days. On October 16, Kennedy was shown photographic evidence of the construction of So-viet MRBM launch sites in Cuba, and told that nuclear missiles could be operational in two weeks. He had to decide between the preference of the Joint Chiefs of Staff for "surgical" air strikes upon the offensive sites, or the less aggressive option, advanced by Defense Secretary Rob-ert McNamara, to blockade further military shipments to the island. Khrushchev's argument, echoed by President Fidel Castro, was that the missiles—soon to be confirmed as numbering forty-two, though only twenty were taken from the ships—were purely "defensive." Kennedy, in contrast, regarded them as a "clear and present danger," not only to the United States, but to the whole Western Hemisphere.[58]

The situation began deteriorating rapidly on Monday, October 22, when Kennedy announced that he was ordering "a strict quarantine on all offensive military equipment" shipped to Cuba. As he spoke, the entire U.S. nuclear bomber force was on rotational high alert, with one-eighth of its fleet constantly airborne. Secretary of State Dean Rusk told a gathering of foreign ambassadors in Washington that the world faced as grave a crisis as it had ever seen.

Khrushchev responded belligerently, ordering an acceleration in shipment of installations and Soviet troops (soon to number forty thou-sand) until 10:00 A.M. on Wednesday, when the U.S. naval quarantine went into effect. Less than half an hour later, the CIA learned that So-viet ships approaching Cuba had "stopped dead in the water." After four more days of emergency, Khrushchev declared on October 28 that the Soviet Union would dismantle and remove all delivery systems and mis-siles from Cuba. In exchange, Kennedy pledged not to invade, and of-fered, as a secret palliative, to close American Jupiter missile stations (actually already obsolete) facing the Soviet Union in Turkey. War had been averted, but only just.

Castro, furious and increasingly paranoid that the United States planned an invasion to oust him, publicly accused Khrushchev of lack-ing *cojones*.[59]

▽

In the aftermath of the Cuban missile crisis, Allen Dulles called Clare and told her that in view of the President's pledge to desist from *Cuba-libre* operations, she must end her support of a "Flying Tigers" motorboat.[60] Since the Bay of Pigs debacle in 1961, a fleet of these clandestine craft, financed by Americans and operated by anti-Castro patriots, had been commuting between Miami and Cuba, gathering information for the CIA on the island's arms buildup.[61]

Clare had been recruited as a donor into this operation by William Pawley, a veteran of the original volunteer "Flying Tigers" squadron that had defended China against Japan before Pearl Harbor. His appeal resonated with her because she could not abide the thought that the ideology she had fought so ardently in Italy was now flourishing less than a hundred miles from the American mainland. Her former obsequiousness to Kennedy aside, she, like other hard-line Republican anti-Communists, felt that the administration had been maladroit, and even weak, in its policy toward the totalitarian regime in Havana.

Prevented now from giving money to any more anti-Castro activities, Clare started writing a number of articles and speeches on Cuba and other Cold War subjects that over the next two years would repoliticize her, and lead to her emergence as an oracle of Republican conservatism.[62] This did not keep her from maintaining her personal friendship with Kennedy, whose popularity had been so buttressed by the missile crisis that he seemed assured of reelection. At the same time, she challenged him publicly and privately on issues where they disagreed.

In a January 22, 1963, address to the Los Angeles World Affairs Council entitled "The Seventeen Year Trend to Castro," Clare said that the United States policy of Communist containment since 1946 had been a failure. As a result, by the time Kennedy had been sworn in, "sixteen nations and a billion people were added to the Communist empire—one third of the world's population." This was now supplemented by "Castro's Cuba—44,000 more square miles and six million more people."

She granted that the recent crisis had shown that the United States and the Soviet Union were both wise enough to have averted "a nuclear holocaust." But JFK had subsequently backed down on his demand for United Nations on-site inspections of the island. In consequence, "We have suffered a defeat in Cuba." Fidel Castro's army, the largest and best equipped in the hemisphere, outside that of the United States, was intact. There was no realistic chance now of an American invasion to topple the Kremlin's bearded puppet. "Mr. Kennedy is a brave man, but he is no hero. And like all politicians he is professionally allergic to martyrdom."[63]

Another strategic thinker expressing insecurity about Kennedy's negotiated settlement in Cuba was President Charles de Gaulle of France. He announced that 1963 would see the emergence of his country as an independent nuclear power, capable of defending itself against Soviet imperialism. This statement caused him to be attacked by American leftist commentators, and Kennedy said at a press conference that it was "peculiar logic" to infer from his accommodation with Khrushchev that America would forsake its Western European allies in the event of any aggression from the East.[64]

Clare joined the fray on the General's side. In the *Washington Star* on February 3, she wrote: "The President's remarks notwithstanding, there is much recent evidence that Mr. Khrushchev himself is now thoroughly convinced that once the 400,000 American troops in Germany are withdrawn, America's nuclear commitment will then extend no farther than its own coastline." She went on to argue that Khrushchev's brilliant "bluff" in Cuba had recast his image into that of a peaceable statesman, despite the fact that he had subsequently boasted, to thunderous applause in East Germany, that the Soviet Union would "bury" the United States with its 100-megaton bombs in any nuclear confrontation. Pointedly, she noted that de Gaulle had at least heeded Kennedy's warning, in *Why England Slept*, that "no nation can afford to wait until it is attacked to prepare its own defenses."

Senator Barry Goldwater was so impressed by her piece that he entered it into the *Congressional Record*.[65] Two days later, Clare followed up with a five-page private letter to the President, urging him to back de Gaulle's initiative. If he did not, the General would fall, and France would lose "its morale and sense of nationhood." The Left might then come into power, destroying French-German unity, and ultimately the democratic solidarity of all Western Europe.

Clare said she doubted the administration's view that Europe was safe under a nuclear umbrella "whose handle is firmly held by Washington." Nor did she accept that the United States could forever be relied on to use its atomic weapons in Europe's defense.

> I personally believe . . . that if a conflict situation arose . . . in which the Soviets gave us the choice of whether we preferred to be alive and not Red, or to be dead along with everybody in Russia

(and Europe), most Americans would opt for the former, even if it meant to abandon *all* Germany. And, frankly, the outcome of the Cuban crisis shows that your Administration holds the same view.

She told Kennedy that he could regain "the moral leadership of the West" by showing his admiration for nations like France and Britain in their desire not to be mere satellites. "The unity of Europe cannot be constructed by the United States of America. It can only be constructed by Europeans—and it *must* be based on German-French unity."[66]

A somewhat dismissive reply came from the National Security Adviser, McGeorge Bundy, who said few "important" Europeans shared her confidence in de Gaulle. Clare, provoked, fired off a three-column letter to *The New York Times* repeating her views, and unfavorably comparing the administration's enthusiasm for a "$40 billion rendezvous with the Man in the Moon" with its reluctance "to meet half-way the Man in Paris."[67]

This prompted a detailed response from the President himself. Though he claimed to find her suggestions "thoughtful and thought-provoking," he disagreed with some of them. He was not confident that "European unity and security would be assured by our enabling France to replace the United States as *the* nuclear defender of Europe." Nor did he believe that every sovereign nation should have a nuclear arsenal. "It seems to me that the objectives which you and I share, and the very real problems and European fears which you cite, can best be met by a *new arrangement which maintains the indivisibility of the nuclear deterrent while giving the Europeans real participation in its maintenance and management.*"[68]

Clearly annoyed by Clare's gibes at his leadership, Kennedy wrote, "If we are to be caught up in a nuclear war, should we not have a voice in the decision that launches it? Is it not my first responsibility as President of the United States to protect the interests of the United States in these developments?"

He then struck a conciliatory tone.

I do not despair if we agree more on ends than on means. Our views on the latter are not essentially so far apart—and the right course to achieving the victory of freedom must be hammered out, shaped and reshaped, as we go along. I know you will continue to contribute your experienced voice to the process of mak-

ing more effective the policy of our country in a changing
world.[69]

▽

Kennedy was also upset with Henry Luce that spring. He felt that recent
Time articles had been excessively critical of his administration, and
complained to Harry directly in an Oval Office interview.

"I gave it to him for forty-five minutes," he told his brother, Attorney General Robert F. Kennedy. "He says, 'Well, I've been out in Phoenix and it doesn't seem that bad to me.' I said, 'Well, listen, looks bad to
me.' . . . He's really losing his grip. Here he's in to see me, to ask me to
come up to that dinner . . ."

The President was referring to *Time*'s upcoming fortieth-anniversary
celebration on May 6. It was to be the climax of Luce's professional life.

"What did you say to him?" Bobby asked.

Kennedy said that he had hedged, but had decided not to go.
"They're just mean as hell up there."[70]

On March 12, Harry received a curt reply to his invitation: "I simply cannot see my way clear to accepting it at this time."[71]

He took the refusal with equanimity. When Clare asked him why
he had not wanted to wait and celebrate the magazine's semicentennial,
he replied, "Because I won't be here for the fiftieth."[72]

At least Vice President Johnson attended, having qualified for the
honored guest list of 284 former *Time* cover subjects. He joked that it
was evident they were selected "on a basis other than beauty." The
Waldorf-Astoria ballroom was crowded with seventeen hundred VIPs,
among them General MacArthur, Judge Thurgood Marshall, Bob Hope,
John Dos Passos, Ginger Rogers, Gina Lollobrigida, Jack Dempsey, and
Cardinal Spellman.

Clare, in a turquoise gown and Bulgari necklace of diamonds and
emeralds, said to Elsa Maxwell, "You and I, we never made it, darling."
Harry tried to make amends for this when he addressed the crowd.
"There is one in particular who has never been a cover subject, because
she married the Editor-in-Chief. With great respect and all my love,
may I introduce for a bow Clare Boothe Luce."[73]

▽

On the Fourth of July, Clare gave the keynote address at the annual
convention of the Underwater Society of America in Philadelphia. She

renewed her chiding of the Kennedy administration for its obsession with "outer" space—mocking the adjective Kennedy often used as redundantly absurd. She thought that taxpayer money would be better spent exploring the more fecund "inner space" of *mare incognitum*.

> We have by no means outgrown the superstitious attitudes acquired in the age of mythology. For thousands of years, man has positioned his gods and his supermen in the skies. *Up* and *Light* and *God* and *Heaven* are ancient emotional correlations. Most men cannot still help feeling that it is somehow more "godlike" to send a man or two barreling around and around in the empty stratosphere than to send many men to explore the mysteries of the teeming ocean.[74]

She sent her speech to the President and he again responded appreciatively, calling it "inspiring," while not mentioning her criticism of his space program. He assured her that he shared her interest in sea exploration, and had budgeted $156 million for oceanography in 1964, compared with Eisenhower's $39 million in 1960. Enclosing a couple of reports by his scientific staff, he apologized for their dullness, saying that they lacked "the sparkle and enthusiasm that punctuate your paper."

His final words were for her to share any further creative thoughts on the subject with him.[75]

▽

Clare was flying from Phoenix to New York on Friday, November 22, when the captain announced that at 12:30 P.M. Central Standard Time in Dallas, Texas, President Kennedy had been shot by a sniper along his motorcade route. At 1:33 P.M., he had been pronounced dead in the emergency room of Parkland Hospital.

She was working on a speech, and found herself crying onto the pages in her lap. More than most people, Clare had reason to weep, remembering Jack as a young naval ensign—"such a bright clever boy"—escorting her daughter to New York parties, and sending her a heartfelt letter of sympathy after Ann's death. In recent months, she had increased her public criticism of him, syndicating four articles attacking the *Apollo* moon program ("this prideful lunatic project"), blaming his administration for the assassination in South Vietnam of President Ngo Dinh Diem, and using the birth statistics of the Kennedy family to dramatize the overpopulation of the globe, predicting that by the fifth generation, "1,080 children could call Joseph Kennedy their great-great-grandfather."[76]

The best she could do now was draft a speculative tribute to JFK. "The President's death was *not* senseless. It contained the elements of both Greek tragedy and Christian tragedy. . . . His life may have been the price he paid for the Bay of Pigs."[77]

45

TOGETHER AT THE END

After the first death, there is no other.

—Dylan Thomas

In the new year of 1964, with another presidential election looming, Clare put out a tongue-in-cheek statement of her own candidacy, accompanied by a series of paradoxical platform planks. "I am for lifting everyone off the social bottom," she announced. "In fact, I am for doing away with the social bottom altogether. I am for victory in Viet Nam without any increase in U.S. casualties or expenditures. . . . I am for the sovereignty of Panama in the Canal Zone under the American flag. I am for the stabilizing of all governments of South America while allowing full scope for the natural revolutionary fervor of the people. . . . I am for putting men on Venus by 1975 or vice versa. . . . I am for a vigorous two-party system in which my party will control the White House, all the governorships and over 75 percent of Congress."[1]

Simultaneously, she contracted to write a series of political columns for the *New York Herald Tribune* that appeared as often as once a week, and were widely syndicated. One of the earliest appeared after she met with President Johnson at the White House on February 4. Referring to LBJ's biggest policy initiative, his war against poverty, she remarked that the last word should be understood relatively. "Regardless of how much we raise the living standards of those at the bottom of the economic pyramid, they will still remain poor in relation to those in the middle and at the top."[2]

In a profile of him on April 12, she noted that "Johnson has so far succeeded admirably in creating a public image of a sober, slow, and soft-spoken leader who can be relied upon to act with moderation, prudence and compassion." She doubted that any Republican candidate could beat him in the fall. A recent, well-documented report that the President, drinking beer and "driving his own car at well over 80," had nearly caused a triple collision in Texas bothered her. He was a man with a serious heart problem, she wrote, and had he been killed, "there is no Vice President to succeed him." She felt he was capable "of becoming one of our greatest Presidents." But the Texas highway incident showed that he might have trouble one day with hubris.

> History has demonstrated time and again that a man will often beat himself, where no opponent can beat him. In a moment of impulsive action or speech he strips away what in modern political jargon we call the "image," and what Dr. Karl Jung, the great Swiss psychologist, used to call "persona," unexpectedly revealing "the person," or "real man." This revelation leads to his decline in popularity—sometimes even to his downfall.[3]

▽

Clare turned sixty-one in Phoenix on April 10, and felt that it was the happiest birthday of her life.[4] One of the reasons was relief. She had at last admitted to Simon Michael Bessie that she would never write her memoirs. Having read so many life stories that she knew to be full of omissions and distortions, if not outright lies, she had concluded that the art of autobiography might more appropriately be called "alibiography."[5]

Bessie had once told her that the qualities he looked for in a writer were "a preference for solitude, vitality, and ego."[6] A problem for Clare was that she had the last two, but not the first. Also, exhuming the past did not suit her temperament. She was much more interested in the present and future. "Nothing I ever did, or felt, seems to me to be more useful or exciting than watching the scarlet cardinal who is eating sunflower seeds at this minute outside my window."[7]

Besides, she now had Harry more to herself, since he had made the decision at sixty-six to retire from control of Time Inc. He would continue to serve as "Editorial Chairman," but that was in effect an emeritus position, not requiring his daily presence at the office. He chose as his replacement Hedley Donovan, the forty-nine-year-old former managing editor of *Fortune*.[8]

Harry had suffered further heart trouble, and was so deaf that after much nagging from Clare, he had finally consented to wear a hearing aid concealed within the heavy sidebars of his spectacles.[9] But she had failed to persuade him to quit his three-pack-a-day smoking habit. The leisurely life of the Biltmore Estates bored him after a while. Golf was a poor substitute for pontificating with his editors. He played mainly because Dr. Caldwell prescribed exercise, and his demeanor on the course, where he never broke 85, was dogged and often sullen.[10]

Clare, in contrast, loved her house, garden, and studio—a new one designed by architectural students of the late Frank Lloyd Wright. Unfortunately, the space was more beautiful than practical, with no ventilation and angled clerestory windows that could not be curtained. "Now I know," she said, "why so many of his clients called him 'Frank Lloyd Wrong.'"[11]

Her major mosaic that spring was a large, iron-framed golden tiger, a gift for Carlos Chávez that she shipped COD.[12] In return, he dedicated a work for symphonic percussion to her called *Tambuco*.[13]

Her burgeoning career as a journalist kept Clare abreast of the latest issues, and gave the instant gratification of seeing her byline in print. In early May, Clare's name was linked to that of Marilyn Monroe, in a *Life* cover story she wrote entitled "What Really Killed Marilyn." She rejected the popular notion that Hollywood was to blame for the star's apparent suicide, having treated her like "a piece of meat." On the contrary, a career in pictures had saved Marilyn from poverty, made her a cinematic "Love Goddess," and brought her two famous husbands, as well as millions of adoring fans. A dread of middle age, with its attendant loss of beauty and diminishing sex appeal, was a more likely cause of Monroe's depression and overdose. "Breasts, belly, bottom must one day sag . . . her mirror had begun to warn her."[14]

As the convention season approached, Clare's rhetorical tone became more provocative. She gained headlines with a commencement address on June 14 at St. John's University, Long Island. It was titled "The Crisis in Soviet-Chinese Relations." Eleven months before, she reminded the students, the Communist monolith had split ideologically over the nuclear test ban treaty that Khrushchev had signed with Kennedy. Mao Tse-tung had angrily accused the Soviet leader of "prettifying

American imperialism" and opting for "peaceful coexistence" with the West. His view was that Communism should be warlike and expansionist, aiming for world domination by any means, including preemptive nuclear war. To date, the United States had ignored this threat by continuing (with the approval of Henry Luce) to isolate Red China diplomatically, going so far as to boycott its entry into the United Nations.

Clare ignored orthodox Republican opinion, and proposed that Washington change its policy toward Peking, as London and Paris were trying to do. She said that the things the Chinese most wanted were economic and technical aid, and the nuclear bomb. Should they ever get the last, "your generation will know nothing but endless war in the Orient." And that would moreover serve to reunite the Marxist/Leninist monolith. The answer was to deal with Mao's seven hundred million people—many of them starving—more pragmatically and generously, by means of a wheat deal. "The ways of peace—aid and trade to the Chinese people—must be explored."[15]

Walter Lippmann wrote to congratulate her on the speech, saying he had seen nothing so good on "the great schism," and agreed with her "brilliant" analysis and "wise" conclusions.[16]

The surprising reversal of Clare's militant anti-Communism was followed by an article in which she predicted defeat for Senator Goldwater, if he was chosen as the Republican candidate for the presidency in July. His nomination looked likely, despite accusations that he was a warmongering "extremist." In *National Review*, she wrote, "Barry, caught with his Conservative pants down, all his Extremities showing, will be buried (beside Alf Landon) under the Johnson landslide in November."[17]

This aroused the expectation that Clare would endorse the more liberal Nelson Rockefeller before the GOP convention opened at the Cow Palace in San Francisco on July 13. But she again surprised everyone by announcing that she was for her Arizonan neighbor, whatever his fate, and would co-chair the National Citizens' Committee for Goldwater.

"I can truthfully tell you," the Senator wrote her, "there have been few things that have so thrilled me in my life. . . . I am grateful to you beyond my ability to express it." He added that he hoped to see her on the convention floor.[18]

The Luces arrived on the weekend before the opening ceremonies, and on Sunday Harry went alone to a lunch in the hotel suite of Senator

Jacob Javits of New York. There, to his astonishment, sitting on the bed talking to John Oakes of *The New York Times*, was Lady Jeanne Campbell. She had divorced Norman Mailer the year before, and her grandfather had died the previous month, leaving her half a million in trust. They chatted for some ten minutes, after which Harry was so discombobulated that he tried to exit the room through a closet.[19]

On Thursday, July 16, Goldwater tearfully watched Clare second his nomination on television. But amid all the distractions of a raucous contest, with Governor Rockefeller of New York being booed to silence by contemptuous conservatives, her appearance attracted little media comment. Goldwater won with 883 votes, compared to 214 for Governor William Scranton of Pennsylvania and 114 for Rockefeller. In his acceptance speech, the Senator caused a stir among moderates when he said, "I would remind you that extremism in the defense of liberty is no vice!" He was interrupted by a roar of approval that lasted forty seconds, but he was not finished. "And let me remind you also—that moderation in the pursuit of justice is no virtue!" Richard Nixon, trying to make the best of the controversial line, predicted that "Mr. Conservative" would be elected President, "after the greatest campaign in history."[20]

Clare proved to be the more accurate forecaster.

Her willingness to acknowledge the validity of a Communist government on the Chinese mainland, coupled with her campaign activities on behalf of Goldwater, made Clare at once too liberal and too right-wing a conservative for Harry.[21] He would not reveal whom he voted for in November, not even to his son Hank. But the latter felt that, along with the senior editors of *Time* and *Life*, his father favored Johnson.[22]

At one stage, when Harry was still Editor in Chief of his magazines, Clare's heresy toward his venerated Generalissimo Chiang Kai-shek might have caused a major blowup in their relationship. But he was frail now, and emotionally depleted by her series of victories in his attempts to divorce her. In retrospect, she had always gotten what she wanted, with the exception of a power stake in his company: luxury apartments in New York, a plantation in South Carolina, houses in Connecticut and Arizona, consort services in Rome, a large art collection, ample funds, and all the resources of Time Inc.'s travel and research departments when writing her articles and books. He was feeling his age too acutely to fight with her anymore, or match her freelance activities, while she, still churning out articles and making television and podium appearances, seemed, with surgical help, to be getting younger and more beautiful.[23] Restless and acquisitive as ever, she pushed again for buying a house in Hawaii.

With that in mind, the Luces left on July 7 for a month in Honolulu. They checked into the Governor's Suite in the Kahala Hilton Hotel on Waikiki Beach. Bougainvillea vines grew on their private terrace overlooking a lagoon where two big dolphins played. "And beyond," Clare wrote Dorothy Farmer, "a *vast* sandy beach, edged with palms, and rolling breakers on the snorkel reef."[24]

In the mornings, she swam with the dolphins and rhapsodized over them to Louisa Jenkins: "No dog, no horse, no animal communicates love and companionship, playfulness and gaiety as does a dolphin. He is simply incomparable." At Sea Life Park and Whalers Cove, she swam with smaller, more agile porpoises. "They're thoroughly elusive—much too fast for me." But she delighted in their almost human intelligence, and got to know three by name—Haole, Lei, and Keiki. The last, a seagoing cetacean, was being trained at the oceanarium to help professional divers discover more about the submarine "inner space" around Oahu.[25]

Late that month, an old beachfront property at 4559 Kahala Avenue was put up for sale, consisting of just over two acres of palm-shaded land, 241 feet of shoreline, and a magnificent view across the bay to the volcanic cone of Diamond Head. A miscellany of undistinguished redwood buildings stood on it—house, servants' quarters, laundry, garage,

Clare with a dolphin in Hawaii, July 1965

orchid shed, and pavilion—as well as a pool and tennis court. Clare knew that if she and Harry bought the place, they would have to demolish and rebuild.[26]

They made a quick decision, as they had in Phoenix eight years before, and by July 29 "Home Hanlani" was theirs for $250,000. Casting about for a new name for the mansion she envisaged, Clare chose Halenai'a, or "House of Dolphins."[27]

At that moment, in the city of her birth, one of the most ideologically charged mayoral campaigns in New York history was being waged. William F. Buckley, Jr., was running on the Conservative ticket, mainly to get what he called an aggressive "campaign of ideas" under way against the Republican John V. Lindsay and the Democrat Abraham Beame. Buckley joked that he expected only one vote, but wanted to have serious attention paid to his anti-welfare, pro-law-and-order beliefs. Contrary to expectations, he proved to be such a knowledgeable, witty, and charming television debater that his opponents looked lackluster in comparison. Their desperate recourse was to accuse him of racism and anti-Semitism, charges that infuriated him so much that he felt he needed the support of a conservative who was as sophisticated and articulate as he was. The obvious choice was his fellow Catholic and Goldwater supporter Clare Boothe Luce.[28]

They had discovered they were political soul mates just before the South Vietnam coup d'état of November 1963, when Clare had published an article in *National Review* defending Madame Nhu, the Catholic, anti-Buddhist, de facto First Lady of President Diem's nepotistic regime. Her piece, entitled "The Lady *Is* for Burning," had brought publicity to the young magazine that might have been prolonged, but for the Kennedy assassination that same month.[29]

"I was tremendously struck by her," Buckley said. "The idea that anyone ever condescended to women in a century in which she lived is preposterous." Clare was enamored, too, and relished weekends with the Buckleys at their Connecticut house on Long Island Sound.[30] What Bill admired about her was "her relentless curiosity," along with a willingness to speak out on controversial subjects. She obliged by denouncing Lindsay's insinuations that "any New Yorker who, like myself, favors a vote for Mr. William Buckley is a bigot, or a racist, or is trying to destroy the democratic process." This was especially egregious, she said, "in a city that prides itself on its liberalism."[31]

Although Buckley did not win on November 2, his success in persuading the Eastern press that American post-Goldwater conservatism was no longer isolationist, reactionary, and unintellectual won him an unexpected 13.4 percent of the vote, depriving his Democratic rival of the margin needed to defeat Lindsay. Overnight he became a national celebrity, identified with the rising star of Ronald Reagan.

Like Clare, Reagan had been recruited in the last weeks of the Goldwater campaign to make a nationally televised appeal for the Republican ticket. He had performed so persuasively as to be seen, even before the election, as Goldwater's political heir apparent. His in-laws, Dr. and Mrs. Loyal Davis, happened to be neighbors of the Luces in Phoenix, and when Reagan visited them, he occasionally played golf with Henry Luce.

"Ronnie is going to run for Governor of California," Harry told Clare one day.

"I always thought of him as a movie actor," she said.

"I think he'll do all right."

"What makes you think that?"

"He does his homework."[32]

Clare and Reagan were both invited by Buckley to speak at *National Review*'s tenth-anniversary dinner in New York on November 11, 1965. In her remarks, she quoted a passage from Walter Lippmann's *The Good Society* that uncannily predicted the kind of hands-off leadership that Reagan would one day personify.

> It is generally supposed that the increasing complexity of the social order requires an increasing direction from officials. My own view is, rather, as affairs become more intricate . . . overhead direction by officials of the state has to become simpler, less intensive, less direct, more general. . . . The complexity of policy . . . must be inversely proportionate to the complexity of affairs.[33]

▽

In the three years since her LSD-laced Majorca vacation, Clare had undergone no recorded experiences with the drug, except to monitor a session with Hank Luce and his second wife, Claire McGill, early in 1965. The former's bad trip reduced him to sobs and befuddlement in front of his father. Perhaps not coincidentally, *Time* published an article a few weeks later on the "epidemic" of illicit LSD consumption sweeping the nation's campuses and dropout communes.[34] This had come about in the wake of Timothy Leary's promulgation of psychedelic substances to students in his Harvard Psychology Department during the winter of 1962–1963. At times he had administered LSD to undergraduates while drugged himself. An alarmed Sidney Cohen had followed *Time*'s piece with one of his own in the September issue of *Harper's Magazine*, in which he deplored the black market availability of the most powerful psychotomimetics, and lamented the consequent discrediting of their use as a scientific tool.

He shared his concern with Clare about the morality of drug-induced "escapism," whether for professional or recreational purposes. Her reply and his response showed that both had moved from the empirical to the philosophical plane of dialogue. "It seems to me," she wrote, "that it would take a moral sophist of the highest order to prove that LSD 'escapism' is more dangerous to the moral well-being of the individual and of society than, say, alcoholic escapism." Yet society treated alcohol and nicotine, which were demonstrably dangerous to health, as acceptable stimulants that constituted an integral part of the economy. Was it not unjust to regard the LSD tripper as a criminal, and the alcoholic as merely sick?

She doubted, though, that the law could handle a situation in which LSD had become easy and cheap to manufacture and distribute. "When you tell me one youth was caught with a million doses in his pocket, the difficulty and gravity of legal control becomes all too plain." Besides, she regarded the phenomenon of recreational drug taking as part of the galloping tendency of American youth to evade responsibility. "What sort of society do we have that so many young people seem eager to take flight from?" Clare felt that God, "the Absolute Good," was dying in America. "Consequently, all ethics, values, morals become increasingly relative and tend, at a certain point, to become meaningless."

It followed, she said, that fleeing from such a derelict society by way of LSD was "Escape from Escapism." From her own experience, she could testify that taking the drug could be, for a short while, "salvific." But she knew that Cohen, as an agnostic man of science, would not grant LSD any power of salvation. She could only question what standards the new generation aimed to establish in place of the old.

> For example, "Love" in our society is certainly an accepted
> value. . . . Ditto, art, beauty, music, nature. But what about work,

especially business? What about war? What about politics? And
above all, what about science and technology? . . .

I think you would find that a surprising number of LSDers
would look on science—especially in its technological applica-
tions—as the worst enemy to the happiness of man.[35]

The doctor replied good-humoredly, willing to play the role of a
scientific "strawman" for Clare to batter. He said the message of LSD
was that "God is a neurochemical event." As for what made a nation
decadent, he cited "breakdown of discipline, hedonism, failure of purpose."

In every era we find the professional escapist—the men who will
not play the game. They are of two sorts—one has retreated from
life in fear of it, or beaten. The other retreats having encountered
it fully but unwilling to continue even as a winner. What a profound difference between the two. . . . LSD is just right for the
second, just wrong for the first.

More about escapism. . . . I would agree with you that ours is
a goalless, disbelieving, undisciplined way of life. There are coun-
tercurrents, but the old people-prods of making a living, religious
faith, patriotism and the rest seem to be waning. Young people
ask me: "What's wrong with casual LSD taking, casual glue sniffing, casual copulation?" When I tell them they get what they pay
for, they ask who keeps the book? I answer that they do. They go
away, unconvinced.

Cohen concluded, "It's a bit of a shame that this most serious of
drugs has been scrubbed by the escapists who want to escape."[36]

On that note, Clare's six-year flirtation with LSD came to an end.

By early 1966, Clare was determined to do something about her place in
history. Years before, she had asked Harry to keep her letters in his vault,
saying she would take her chance with posterity if he would take his.
She did not want to romanticize her past, as Bernard Baruch had done
in the quarter century before his recent death, "sucking on the memory
of his triumphs the way a hungry baby falls to sleep sucking the nipple
of an empty bottle."[37] Nor did she need an authorized biographer who

might belittle her achievements. So she asked Stephen Shadegg, a good-looking, fifty-six-year-old political journalist and Phoenix resident, if he would undertake the task.

Shadegg was a staunch Republican and author of several books, including *What Happened to Goldwater?* He eagerly accepted, on condition he could interview Clare extensively, and be free to print, after due consultation, whatever final text he chose. "Steve, that's exactly what I want you to do," she said, "because sometimes I can't be objective about myself."

Knowing that Baruch had paid his biographer Margaret Coit $50,000, she offered Shadegg $25,000. He chose instead to negotiate a publishing contract, but did accept her offer of $10,000 to help with research expenses. "It seemed to me she was desperately seeking recognition," he recalled years later.[38]

▽

Wanting to remain relevant in political circles, Clare sought an appointment with Lyndon Johnson. He agreed to see her in the White House on June 2. This time she was not honored with a private lunch overlooking the Jefferson Monument, but offered instead a Dr Pepper in Johnson's cramped underground hideaway. She settled for a Coke, and while a photographer snapped pictures, she stared bemusedly at three Sony television sets hanging above the President's head.

To get the conversation going, Clare said how much she admired the way he had conducted the nation's affairs so far. He said he was grateful to *Time* for the "sympathetic treatment" it gave his policies. From then on, it was difficult for her to hold Johnson's attention, because his Press Secretary, Bill Moyers, kept coming in with small strips of paper that LBJ read avidly in preparation for a press conference the next day. He instructed Moyers to be sure that the columnists James Reston and Walter Lippmann were given front-row seats. "I'll face these intellectuals."

He said he wanted journalists to quiz him about Latin American affairs, and grumbled that newspapers had ignored Castro's remark that there was no hope of furthering the revolution in the Southern Hemisphere while Johnson remained in office. He complained that Robert Kennedy had told a private group that the President was so hated "down there," he would be shot if he ventured south of the border. To spite Bobby, he had done just that. "Did anyone shoot me? No. I was greeted by thousands of cheering people."

As the interview proceeded, Clare realized that although Johnson was, more than any other chief executive she had known, an enormously competent man in command of every issue, he was obsessed with his popularity, resentful of slights, and constantly looking for reassurance. This did not stop her from asking Johnson why New York liberals criticized him so much for not fulfilling "the Kennedy promise."

"Well, that's a mystery to me, too," he said. He asked what in fact Kennedy had done. "He passed the Test Ban Treaty—for whatever that was worth—he formed the Peace Corps, and that was it." He enumerated some of his own achievements in domestic and foreign policy, and noted how little credit he had gotten for them. "Looking around America there isn't much for people to complain about."

This was not a point of view shared by the hundreds of thousands of Vietnam War demonstrators currently marching in many cities, angry blacks protesting housing conditions in Mississippi, disillusioned farmworkers picketing in Sacramento, and race rioters wrecking property in Watts, Los Angeles. But LBJ focused on the small picture.

"I'll tell you what kind of a country we are living in. I got a note from my cook last night which said, 'Mr. President, I wish you would stop complaining about my cooking. You don't like what I give you, but you want to lose weight and eat at the same time. Now you eat what I give you and don't complain.' Now that's the kind of a country we live in where the cook can bawl out the President."

Talking too fast for interruption, Johnson waxed querulous about his daughter Luci's upcoming East Room wedding. "I hope they don't say that everybody's having a ball at the White House when there's so much trouble in Vietnam." He grew weepy, praising Defense Department personnel prosecuting the war as "the greatest bunch of guys I've ever seen," and looked to Moyers for confirmation. "Aren't you proud?"

Before leaving, Clare mentioned she was building a house in Hawaii. Johnson recalled his return from the Pacific war and how, when they were in Congress, he had shown her a home movie of Honolulu. "I'll come and stay with you," he said. "I'd like to do that for old times' sake."

She seized this opportunity to complain that his latest budget had canceled the Mohole oceanographic program in Hawaii.

"Clare, I'll put it back."[39]

The Luces spent most of that summer in a rented Honolulu house near their new estate, and chose Vladimir Ossipoff, architect of the Kahala Hilton and Honolulu International Airport, to design a suitable complex for them. It was to be a summer substitute for their Connecticut house, which they had finally sold for $332,000 after twenty years. Harry had always loved Sugar Hill, but Clare had come to associate the place with marital problems and illness, and was glad to be rid of it. Only the New York apartment remained of their loosening Northeast ties.

That fall in Arizona, she continued her interviews with Stephen Shadegg, and Harry persevered with a "memoir" that was more about his work, ideas, and eminent people he had liked or disliked than a comprehensive account of his life. Having never written a book before, he found sequential narrative difficult, and after about six chapters the manuscript languished.[40]

The couple celebrated their thirty-first wedding anniversary in Phoenix on November 23, and invited Gerald Heard, Michael Barrie,

Clare and Harry in Phoenix, 1966

and Shirley Potash and her husband, Richard Clurman, *Time*'s chief of correspondents, to join them for Christmas. Clare had bedecked branches of the sitting room fir tree with ornaments that she had made by stippling dozens of white foam balls with imitation jewels, scraps of velvet, and ribbons. In stark contrast with the festive scene, the Clurmans found Harry looking shockingly older than his sixty-eight years, with deep wrinkles, his fringe of hair gray against his desert tan.[41]

Clare painted a portrait of her husband at this time, one of more than thirty artworks she had completed in the past two years. This study of Harry was to be reproduced in her January 1967 *McCall's* article about famous "Sunday Painters." It showed him unsmiling and jowly in an open-necked blue shirt, gazing vacantly into the distance against a background of fiery red, as if he were about to be immolated.

By now a line in *The Women* had extra resonance for Clare: "It's being together at the *end* that really matters." During one of their now rare times apart, she added a postscript to a letter about her activities: "I *do* love you, and find life without you like being in a big, fine, interesting Italian palazzo in mid-December without any heat. The warmth, and sooner or later, the interest leaks out of everything when you are not there."[42]

Together that month, the Luces participated as usual in the Phoenix social season, hosting a Republican dinner for the William F. Buckleys. Harry expressed the hope that he might appear on *Firing Line*, Bill's successful new television interview show. He was envious that his wife had been one of its earliest guests.[43]

An exotic visitor from Clare's past was the Venerable and Most Reverend Fulton J. Sheen, now Bishop of Rochester and host of the nationally syndicated *The Fulton Sheen Program*, watched each week by an audience of some ten million. He was in town to address the Phoenix Executive Club, and Clare introduced him. Twenty years before, she had revered Sheen, and been impressed by his vow that if he ever became a bishop, he would be content to sleep in an iron cot in a mission basement. But now she realized he was "a ham at heart," and something of a voluptuary, taking daily massages and preening in his lavish vestments, among which were a pectoral cross and emerald jade ring she had given him.[44]

Harry went East in mid-February, leaving a gift for Clare of a Victorian silver-gilt, heart-shaped box engraved with her initials and inscribed, "St. Valentine's Day 1967. To my darling 'Wiff' from Harry."[45]

In New York, he attended a Time Inc. directors' meeting, where he learned that *Life*'s circulation was now 7.5 million and *Time*'s 3.5 million, making them still first and second among weekly magazines. His entire holdings, including *Fortune, Sports Illustrated,* five television and four radio stations, as well as a movie and book division, had a combined market value of $690 million.[46]

At some point, Harry took a walk in Central Park. Mary Bancroft, his friend of over twenty years, caught sight of him at a distance and hardly recognized his haggard face and blank eyes. He looked so moribund that she could not bring herself to call out to him, and let him pass by. As was his custom on solitary visits to the city, Harry went to see Jean Dalrymple, who was now married to an army officer. Walking him to the elevator, she said, "It's wonderful how you still come to see me." He replied, "My dear, it's always a joy to be with you."[47]

When he got back to Phoenix, Clare was entertaining Frank Sheed, who was surprised by how "mellow" Harry seemed. "There was a sort of sweetness in him that in all the years I had never seen before."[48]

On Friday, February 24, the Luces were in San Francisco, where Clare gave a lunchtime speech at the Commonwealth Club about the United Nations. She harshly called the organization "a dismal failure" in arms control, and "impotent" in peacekeeping. But her peroration, contributed by Harry, sounded a slightly more positive note: "The UN is still worth supporting—but not worth subsidizing."[49]

Before they returned to Phoenix, they asked a local *Time* staffer to drive them through the drug-riddled hippie community of Haight-Ashbury. Their own sedate dabblings with LSD had not prepared them for the sight of lank-haired, burnt-out young addicts in dirty jeans, nodding on the stoops of derelict houses.

"What are their goals? What are their motives?" Harry asked.[50]

Clare's address made headlines in the Arizona newspapers on Saturday. Reading them over breakfast, she complained, "I sweated over that speech for three weeks, and all they quoted was your upbeat ending."[51]

In the afternoon, Harry played nine holes of golf, riding the course with his favorite caddy. That evening, he and Clare joined friends at the Biltmore Hotel for a dinner given by a Phoenix oil millionaire. A pianist played the Yale "Whiffenpoof Song," and Harry sang along. "We are poor little sheep who have lost their way, baa, baa, baa. . . ." He was too tired to read to Clare when they got home around midnight.[52]

On Sunday morning, he ate breakfast and promptly vomited. "I have a headache," he said, and went to lie down. Clare took his temperature and, finding it to be 102 degrees, called Dr. Caldwell. When he arrived Harry was coughing blood. But his pulse was normal, and the doctor prescribed home rest overnight. He showed no improvement on Monday morning, so Caldwell ordered an ambulance from St. Joseph's Hospital. When it came, Harry brushed aside Clare's attempt to help him, and walked to the vehicle carrying his shoes. She followed him by car with the books he had been reading—a detective story, a theological study, and his Bible.[53]

All he would admit to at the hospital was, "I'm tired." Clare sat with him while he underwent tests, and stayed the remainder of the day. But he insisted that she keep a dinner date with the Loyal Davises. Feeling anxious about him, she left the party early, and called him from home. "I'm going to watch *Perry Mason*," he said.

"So am I. Do you want me to come over?"

"No, everything is going to be all right."[54]

Yet he slept fitfully that night, and kept getting up to pace the floor. At about 3:00 A.M. a nurse heard him go to the bathroom, and moments later he shrieked, "Oh Jesus!" A heavy thud brought her running, and she found him unconscious.

Clare was awakened by a phone call from the Mother Superior of St. Joseph's. "You'd better come."

When she reached the hospital, Dr. Caldwell met her and said, "Harry is dead." He had suffered a coronary occlusion.[55]

46

A DELUXE LONELINESS

*We no longer maintain that life consists in actions only
or in works. It consists in personality.*

—Virginia Woolf

When Clare reached home at 4:00 A.M. on Tuesday, February 28, 1967, the telephone was ringing. It was President Johnson, saying, "All Washington is sad. He was one of the greats." Vice President Hubert Humphrey followed with his own condolences, as did Father Murray, who said he would be with her throughout the obsequies— a memorial service at Madison Avenue Presbyterian Church in New York on Friday, and the interment on Saturday at Mepkin. Until Hank told her that his father's will decreed this, Clare had not known that Harry had wanted to be buried beside her. He had meant it, apparently, when he wrote her twenty-two years before, "It's you and you alone I'll always be missing—and when my life has no room for missing it's because you're there, filling up all the room."[1]

Tex and Elisabeth Moore came out to be with Clare, and found her outwardly calm, but with her face swollen from crying. A sign of her congenital insecurity was that she immediately asked them "where the next pay check was going to come from for the household staff."[2] Accountants at Time Inc. had always taken care of the Luces' domestic expenses.

Next day, Clare went to New York with the Moores, leaving her husband's body behind to undergo an autopsy, prior to being flown to South Carolina. The results showed advanced emphysema, chronic angina pectoris, diseased kidneys, and arthritic and urethral problems, all consistent with Harry's history of an indifferent diet, chain smoking, and a steady consumption of hard liquor.[3]

At 3:00 P.M. on Friday, eight hundred family members and dignitaries congregated at the Madison Avenue Presbyterian Church. They included Governor Nelson Rockefeller and his brothers, Laurance and David, Mayor Lindsay, Senators Goldwater and Javits, Richard and Patricia Nixon, and many media magnates, among them David Sarnoff and Katharine Graham. With the family mourners was Harry's former wife, Lila Tyng, and their younger son, Peter Paul. Simultaneously, on Sixth Avenue, twelve hundred employees assembled in the lobby and auditorium of the Time & Life Building, where an audio of the service was relayed.[4]

Clare, her face taut with grief and dark circles around her eyes, sat between Hank Luce and Father Murray. She wore a black coat, a black

Clare at Harry's funeral in New York

silk head scarf over her pale short hair, and pearl earrings. Three of Harry's favorite hymns were sung, including "The Church's One Foundation," which she knew by heart. The eulogy by Harry's pastor, the Reverend David H. C. Read, was full of conventional pieties. "There was in him a surprising amount of the 'meekness' of those who 'inherit the earth.'" When, in his closing prayer, the clergyman said, "Thy servant Harry whom though hast now taken to Thyself," Clare leaned forward and rested her head on the pew.[5]

Arriving at Mepkin cemetery at 2:20 the following afternoon, she found fifty people seated on the lawn beneath an enormous live oak that shaded the tombs of her mother and daughter. Harry's open grave was between them.[6]

The sun was shining on the banked camellias as the Trappist monks filed from the chapel with the coffin, singing Gregorian chants. The Abbot said a few words, Father Murray delivered a eulogy, and Harry's layman brother-in-law, Les Severinghaus, read from the Presbyterian Book of Common Worship, after which the casket was lowered into the ground.[7]

Soon after buying the plantation, Harry had written Clare of his "eager always wanting-wanting-wanting-you-love.... A feeble love, but one that will grow and grow until it will be stronger than the greatest oak at Mepkin."[8]

One of the first things Clare told Hank, who accompanied her back to Phoenix, was that Arizona was "meaningless" without his father. She planned to escape "that narrow circle of people on the golf links" by selling the Biltmore property as soon as possible. Although Waikiki's current development boom bothered her, she was still inclined to build the Honolulu house as planned. Returning full-time to New York had no appeal. The Fifth Avenue apartment was now too big for her, and should be sold. She dreaded ending up somewhere like the Waldorf or the Sherry Netherland. "The thought of being . . . the dowager who eats at the corner table in a hotel restaurant every night disgusts me."[9]

After Hank's departure, Father Murray was on hand for a week to administer spiritual comfort to her, and conduct a local memorial Mass for Harry before he too returned East. Left alone with her secretary, she answered a mountain of sympathy letters and telegrams from monarchs, heads of state, politicians, publishers, movie stars, and hundreds of other correspondents around the world. One note, from Frank Sheed, was especially poignant. He wrote that during his February stay, he "had an overwhelming feeling" that Harry was ready for death. "I wonder if anyone has told you of his way of quoting you—'Clare says,' 'Clare thinks'— with such appreciation of *your* mental powers."[10]

Harry had left $109 million in Time Inc stock, yielding about $2.4 million in annual dividends. Of this, he willed in trust 180,000 shares to Clare, worth about $19.5 million. She also inherited their joint real estate, and all her husband's tangible property, including art, furniture, books, cars, and jewelry. Shares worth some $14 million were to be divided between his two sons. The estate would have been twice as valuable if, in 1961, Harry had not given half his personal stock holdings to the Henry Luce Foundation Inc., a memorial to his father. Its mandate was to promote Christian values and scholarly exchanges between the United States and the Far East.[11]

Altogether Clare could count for the forseeable future on an annual after-tax income of $435,000, just from Harry's bequests. In addition, she had continuing annual payments from her Brokaw and other personal trusts of about $75,000, plus various investment dividends, freelance fees from articles and lectures, and royalties from plays and books. Her projected income for 1968 was more than $750,000.[12] Although she pleaded impoverishment to Shadegg and others, she was able to set aside $20,000 a month for living expenses, and within two years (following property sales) was flush enough to buy more than $2 million worth of Treasury bills.[13]

By the end of May, she had dealt with the immediate practical consequences of Harry's death, and braced herself for the long-term prospect of widowhood. As Louisa Jenkins warned, "Your whole life will change now, rhythm and pattern." More than that, Clare felt that "the scaffolding structure" of her whole existence had been pulled from under her. She wrote Helen Lawrenson that she found the sudden freedom to do as she wanted "ponderous and disturbing." To Carlos Chávez, she explained that Harry had been "sometimes my love and sometimes my enemy," but always her most loyal friend. "All passions spent, our last eight [sic] years were wonderfully serene and happy ones. I find myself now very much alone, and very lonely. And somewhat of a stranger to myself—and to others, too."[14]

In early July, Clare left for Honolulu, her "last port of call," as she resignedly termed it.[15] She stopped off in Los Angeles for a two-hour visit with

Lyndon Johnson. He was in an exuberant mood, having just completed a successful summit with Soviet Premier Alexei Kosygin in Glassboro, New Jersey. The leaders had agreed that no crisis between Moscow and Washington should ever be allowed to escalate into war.

She thanked the President for his solicitous call after Harry died, adding plaintively, "I have no one now."

"You have *me*, honey," he told her.

Seeing an opportunity, she said, "Well, I'd like to serve my country again—for you."

Johnson did not rise to the bait.[16]

That night, the Norman Chandlers gave a dinner for Clare, and when the conversation became critical of LBJ, she protested, "He's not perfect, but he's always been good to me."[17]

She had already asked her Democratic friend Bill Benton to find out if Wayne Morse would still oppose her should she be awarded another embassy. The Senator had been unequivocal. "I could not possibly support her nomination for many reasons."[18]

After less than three weeks in her Diamond Head Road rental, Clare was struggling with her lack of purpose and company. She complained to Dorothy Farmer, "I've met no one exciting. [The] only men are dodderers, or pansy. Same here as everywhere." She began having second thoughts about building in Hawaii, but recent race riots in mainland cities that had left 67 people dead, 3,500 injured, and 5,000 homeless scared her, and greatly modified her erstwhile liberalism. "I have so little desire to live anywhere that has a great Negro problem."[19]

Uncertainty, as well as a sense of isolation, were exacerbated on August 16 by news of the death of Father Murray from a heart attack. Clare elected not to go to his funeral, telling her secretary that she did not feel emotionally strong enough to stand by his casket alone. Yet without his mediation her marriage might have foundered, and at least once he had rescued her from suicide. As Dorothy perceived, Murray had been for more than a decade "*the* Leveler" in her life.[20]

Discussing with Vladimir Ossipoff the design and landscaping of her future house somewhat alleviated Clare's despondency. "Home is where you hang your architect," she teased him.[21] But it was not diverting enough to subdue her desire for a position in public life, even though with Democrats firmly in control of all branches of government, she knew it was unlikely.

In this, as things turned out, Clare was mistaken. Halenai'a would become her primary residence soon enough, although Ossipoff did not expect it to be ready much before early 1969. Once established there, she would be for a number of years Hawaii's premier hostess, entertaining a succession of A-list visitors, many of them stopping over as they crossed the Pacific. But she could hardly foresee that America's political fortunes, racked by Vietnam and social upheaval, would strengthen her involvement with the conservative wing of the GOP, and in time draw her more in the direction of Washington, D.C.

An early indication of this was an invitation from Johnson to attend a state dinner on September 29 for Giuseppe Saragat, now the President of Italy. Hearing that Dwight Eisenhower was staying in her hotel, Clare asked if she could stop by to see him on her way to the White House. She found Ike looking pale and shriveled, but the big grin was still there. He reminded her of the Cheshire Cat in *Alice in Wonderland*, "fading away all around that smile."

She asked him what he thought about Johnson and Vietnam. He was critical, since the conflict, now degenerating into a bloody stalemate, had been waged by the executive branch without the consent of Congress. "The President must tell the people that this is going to be a long and nasty war, and that we have to stick the course."

She asked why he did not make a statement to this effect.

"You can't," he said. "You have to support the President of the United States."

"What would you do about these draft card burners?"

Eisenhower chuckled as he recalled an experience from World War II. Some soldiers under his command had been court-martialed for stealing gasoline. He had told the court, "Give them a chance to redeem themselves." They should either accept the maximum sentence of five years in jail, or go to the front and fight. "Almost every one of them went to the front." Johnson should say to the card burners that if their consciences bothered them, they could either enlist and go to war or spend five years in jail. "They'd all pick up their draft cards."[22]

This was her last encounter with Ike. In eighteen months, he would be dead.

▽

Clare was in New York for the Christmas season of 1967, having spent a month touring the Far East with Claire McGill Luce. On December 10, she gave a "Just Everybody" cocktail party at her Fifth Avenue apartment. "Politicos, Press, Publishers, Artists, Actors, Fags, of course," Dorothy Farmer reported to her niece. "Clare is beginning to live it up."[23]

The occasion turned out to be historic, because Richard Nixon and Henry Kissinger were there. They had not met before. As Clare was aware, Kissinger did not much care for the former Vice President. She suspected, however, that with their passion for foreign affairs, and belief in balance-of-power politics, they might get along if they spent time together. Afterward, Nixon gave Clare the impression that the encounter had gone well.[24]

She spent "the Christmas that I wish never was" with the Moores surrounded by her dead husband's relatives. "I miss Harry more not less as the days go by," she wrote Helen Wrigley, a Chicago friend.[25]

After trips to Nassau and Mexico in early 1968, Clare sold her Fifth Avenue cooperative for $300,000 and bought a much smaller one with services at the Sherry Netherland Hotel for $240,000. She also sold Phoenix fully furnished for $280,000.

Meanwhile, the Vietcong's astonishingly brutal Tet offensive against South Vietnam, though not an ultimate victory, had shocked the American public, and almost overnight forced the administration to change its strategy to a search for an honorable disengagement. More than a year before, Clare had predicted that if Johnson could not "get on top of Vietnam and inflation . . . he won't run again."

Her prophesy proved accurate on March 31, when LBJ announced on television a partial suspension of the bombing of North Vietnam, and said that the United States was open to peace negotiations. He then made a personal announcement: "I shall not seek, and I will not accept, the nomination of my party for another term as your President."

Barry Goldwater saw an opportunity for the GOP in Johnson's virtual abdication. "Here we have a lame duck President, a lame duck Congress, and a lame duck General in Vietnam," he wrote Clare. "The country is leaderless at the darkest hour of its history and about the only thing the Democrats can offer is a haystack in heat." This was a reference to Vice President Hubert Horatio Humphrey, the candidate of his party almost certain to succeed Johnson.[26]

Having recently heard him make an impressive speech at the Women's Republican Club, Clare already saw Nixon (improbably resurgent since his 1960 defeat and subsequent loss in the California gubernatorial race) as the GOP's best chance for a winner that fall. "I am plunking for him now—and hard," she wrote Al Morano, and sent Nixon a campaign check with a note expressing "my great admiration and affectionate regards."[27]

Her chief reservation about Nixon as a candidate was that he was not empathetic. She explained her theory in an oral history for Columbia University at this time. "A President has to be the average man's idea of his father, his uncle, his brother, or his son." Ike could have been anybody's father, Truman easy to imagine as an uncle from Missouri, Kennedy was like "your husband, your sweetheart, your son, your brother." Dewey and Stevenson had been brother-in-law types, and both had been defeated. Nixon had the same liability—he was even cousinly: "My cousin Dick, he's done awfully well in New York."[28]

▽

The assassinations that spring of Martin Luther King and Robert F. Kennedy—the latter dying on the same day as Randolph Churchill—cast a dark cloud over Clare that she sought to escape by booking a five-week summer vacation in the Mediterranean. It began glamorously with attendance at Prince Rainier's Red Cross Ball in Monaco, but she found the oil-slicked, garbage-strewn Riviera so crowded that she was back in New York by mid-August. She had missed Nixon's nomination at the Republican convention, but found a triumphant note from the candidate awaiting her: "This year we are going to win!"[29]

Clare could believe this on the twenty-sixth, as she luxuriated in "quiet old, lovely, snobbish Newport" and watched on television the "horrid and frightening sight" of the Democratic convention opening amid violent street battles between Chicago police and antiwar protesters. The following day, chaos spread to the convention floor, as Humphrey was nominated in an atmosphere of intraparty squabbles.[30]

After Labor Day, Clare moved into her apartment at the Sherry Netherland, and found the hotel's service and food so bad that she decided almost immediately to sell. She succumbed to one of her depressions. "I seem to have dried up in every way," she wrote Helen Lawrenson, "creatively, physically and emotionally. I live in a sort of deluxe loneliness, lacking what we used to call motives, and now, for some reason, are called motivations."[31]

A proposal from Jimmy Cromwell, a former boyfriend, and onetime husband of Doris Duke, failed to cheer her up. Nor was she enthused by a first reading of the manuscript of Stephen Shadegg's biography of her. She wrote the editor, "I am curious to know on what evidence Mr. Shadegg, or anyone else but God himself, could base the assertion that 'Clare has never had a satisfactory relationship with any human being in all her life.'"[32]

Just before Nixon's election on November 5, she came down with

Hong Kong flu, and remained sickly and downcast through another Christmas and New Year's Eve with the Moores.[33] Miserable though she was, Clare now clutched at the in-laws she had once disparaged as "City Hall"—moralistic Calvinists who had, in her opinion, always tried to prejudice Harry against her. They, however, whether out of duty or, in some cases, genuine affection, embraced her in her widowhood. Beth and Tex Moore, in particular, were grateful to her for refusing to divorce Harry. Hank, perpetually struggling in his father's shadow, greatly admired his stepmother's achievements and insights.

Clare got on best with the younger generation crowding the Moores' hearth that festive season. Among them were seven youths, all "hairy and Hippy," including Michael Moore with a frizzy Afro, and Claire's sons from a former marriage, Jim and William Hurt, the latter a handsome blond eighteen-year-old destined for movie stardom. Two of the granddaughters of Harry's sister Emmavail Severinghaus particularly attracted her: the teenage Leslie Dingle, and her little sister, Libby, "blissfully undisturbed by the tinselled pandemonium all around."[34]

On January 20, 1969, Mr. and Mrs. Henry Luce III escorted Clare to Richard Nixon's swearing in as thirty-seventh President of the United States. The occasion was less joyous for Hank, a Humphrey supporter, than for his stepmother, who, in jeweled rainbow chiffon, celebrated the accession of her candidate.[35]

In mid-March, Clare moved into Halenai'a ("House of Dolphins"), her twelve-room Hawaiian house, which had taken two years to complete. High white walls and a powered security gate protected the property from Kahala Avenue's heavy traffic. The wide driveway curved past the caretaker's cottage to a courtyard, and a long, trellised loggia led to the entrance hall, guarded by two huge, dark blue Chinese temple dogs. Over the doorway was a three-thousand-year-old mosaic of a dolphin. Inside, an open-topped atrium was dominated by two large banyan trees soaring toward the sky. Surrounding them were orchids, bougainvillea, air plants, and a profusion of drooping ferns. Against one wall sat Harry's favorite artifact, a life-sized wood-carved statue of the goddess Kwan Yin, at least five hundred years old. Off a central corridor running the length of the house were two spacious sitting rooms, each with eighteen-foot ceilings, one facing the ocean, the other looking toward lush gardens, a swimming pool, and distant mountains. The twelve-seat dining room also faced the sea. At the eastern end of the corridor was Clare's

Clare's bedroom in Halenai'a

blue-and-green bedroom suite, with an adjoining skylit study, a dressing room with space for thirty-six feet of clothes, and a private patio and garden. Elsewhere in the open-plan structure was a library, a den, and a tiny guest bedroom, purposely scaled to discourage long-term visitors.

Although Ossipoff had given Clare a sleekly Modernist building with tiled floors and straight, clean lines that called for the simplest interior decoration, she had been unable to resist cozying it up with curving, padded, patterned furniture and floral rugs, as well as a variety of pottery, needlepoint cushions, shells, and other tchotchkes. A ceramic female leopard with cubs reclining on a zebra-skin rug fought with the cool beauty of Isamu Noguchi's bust of herself, and artworks by Gauguin, Magritte, O'Keeffe, and Nevelson.

Her current color preference was green, but in the carpeted dining room with a Venetian chandelier, pinks and beiges prevailed. The faux French rococo table was embellished with gilt rosettes, and the matching chairs were embroidered with pink flowers. In the south "rattan room," tubular lamps, also by Noguchi, overhung a miscellany of bamboo tables and chairs.[36]

Full-length glass doors opened onto a white-tiled, bonsai-decorated bar lanai near the pool, with mango and monkeypod trees shading the adjacent patio. Beyond stretched the largest lawn in Honolulu, surrounded by plumeria (frangipani) and sago and coconut palms. Another lawn and stands of taller palms graced the south side of the house, with velvety grass sloping down to 240 feet of beach and magnificent views across Maunalua Bay to Diamond Head.

All this design and landscaping had cost Clare almost half a million on top of the quarter million that Harry had paid for the property. But it fulfilled her lifelong desire to have a tropical, saltwater retreat. Everywhere in the house, through louvered doors and numerous floor-to-ceiling windows, she could feel Hawaii's gentle breezes, and hear the sound of the sea.[37]

▽

In May, Clare made the close to five-thousand-mile trip to Washington, D.C., for another state dinner, this time for John Gorton, the Prime Minister of Australia. The first thing she said to President Nixon was, "What about China?" He replied, "Well, yes, we have to get on with a new policy for China."[38] Before returning to Honolulu, she managed to outshine the movie star Raquel Welch on *The David Frost Show*, and sell $747,000 worth of paintings that would not do well in Hawaii's salty sea air, including Harry's gift, *Madonna of the Roses*.[39]

The way Clare disposed of her art collection did not endear her to John Richardson of Christie's auction house. She asked him for individual estimates of paintings before placing them in his hands en bloc. Richardson thought most of the collection "boring and second rate," except for Fragonard's "lovely" *Education of the Virgin by Saint Anne*. An instinctive aesthete, he also recoiled at her "hotel-like" furniture. Ostensibly satisfied with his numbers, Clare promised to ship the art to Christie's in a matter of days.[40] Yet, as a canny if not devious businesswomen, she first sought another opinion, asking William H. Kennedy, the director of the Contemporaries Gallery, to confirm Richardson's appraisal of the paintings, and the fairness of Christie's 15 percent commission.[41]

Kennedy, an attractive forty-seven-year-old Midwesterner, seized the opportunity. Years later, he remembered every detail of his encounter with the former Ambassador, even identifying her rose-scented perfume as Joy.

> I went over to her place, a big apartment on the 26th floor of the Sherry Netherland with a lot of windows overlooking the Park. The place was hung throughout with blue chip paintings and some Churchills the artist had given her, whose whole value lay

in their source. She was in a silk, peach colored peignoir and when she stood against the windows, it became transparent. She said she was 66; I said I didn't believe her, but I had to because I'd heard of her for a long time. She had the slender figure of a woman in her 30s.

Having reviewed the paintings, Kennedy assured Clare that he could get the same prices, or better, by selling to his regular customers and fellow dealers directly from her own walls.

"What's your end of it?" she asked. "Christie's takes 15 percent."

"Five percent from you, 10 percent from my customers."

"OK," Clare said. "It's Tuesday; I'm giving the whole collection to Christie's next Monday; you've got from now to Saturday."

A day or two later, between the hours of 10 A.M. and 5 P.M., potential buyers came to view the Luce Collection. Those who made purchases were asked to drop their checks in a large Chinese urn placed near the exit door. The sale was a success, and when Clare and Kennedy were left alone that evening, she poured tumblers of Chivas Regal scotch to celebrate. They talked for a while about politics, his Illinois origins, and a summer she once spent in Wisconsin.

We touched glasses and she promptly pulled up her skirt and put a leg across my lap; it was a very good leg; and she went on about her childhood and the theater of those days. After we got out of the Midwest she said, "I have to get dressed for dinner; you can help me." And I did. . . . I never got my 5 percent, but it was worth it.[42]

▽

On July 10, Clare held a formal house-opening cocktail party at Halenai'a for about two hundred people, many of them prominent in Hawaiian society. She received her guests wearing a long yellow gown decorated with orange blossoms that complemented her silver-blonde hair and still-flawless skin. A guest hung around her neck a rare 'ilima lei woven from thousands of paper-thin petals whose golden color matched the flowers in her outfit.

"I'm told these are very special—meant for royalty," Clare said.[43]

If by that she implied she intended in future years to hold court as the queen of all of Oahu society, she was mistaken. Hawaii's leading Democrats, including Governor George Ariyoshi, would never invite her. But she did entertain an ever-widening circle of other distinguished islanders, from *ali'i* princesses and pineapple and sugar barons, to the high-ranking military of Pearl Harbor, as well as artists, publishers, and faculty from the University of Honolulu. With her social, political, and theater connections, she was to host international celebrities, starting with a large event for Pat Nixon later that month.

Over the years they came in droves, and she welcomed them by draping leis of ginger, tuberose, and jasmine—*pikake*—around their necks, while kissing them on both cheeks: Ronald and Nancy Reagan, the Marquess and Marchioness of Bath, Betty Friedan, Rudolf Nureyev, Yousuf Karsh, Henry Kissinger, Diana Vreeland, Rex Harrison, Admiral John McCain, Imelda Marcos, Milton Friedman, Margaret Mead, Gerald and Betty Ford, Buckminster Fuller, Cary Grant, Ambassador Anatoly Dobrynin, Bill and Pat Buckley, Dan Rather, James Michener, Terence Cardinal Cooke, Zsa Zsa Gabor, Emilio Pucci, Edward Teller, Irene Dunne, Leon Edel, Douglas Fairbanks, Jr., Barbara Walters, Baron and Baroness Philippe de Rothschild, Chief Justice Warren Burger, Loretta Young, Mortimer Adler, Kenneth Galbraith, Sir Robert Helpmann, Marshall McLuhan, De Witt and Lila Wallace, Merle Oberon, Isamu Noguchi, Gloria Steinem, General William Westmoreland, and Gore Vidal.[44]

At the time of Nixon's election, Dorothy Farmer had remarked that Clare did not want to be rewarded with another embassy position. "She really is too old and tired for all that." So now, when President Nixon offered her a post in Paris as United States Member of the Executive Board of the United Nations Educational, Scientific and Cultural Organization (UNESCO), she turned it down, saying she did not want a job that would keep her away from her new paradise for four years.[45]

Since Clare was writing little journalism and giving few speeches these days, she spent her time managing a staff of nine, reading—Robertson Davies novels, as well as policy papers—writing letters, swimming, playing bridge, watching television or movies, and, as a penalty of her increased assets, dealing regularly with accountants, brokers, and insurers.[46] For a while she took painting lessons with a young, good-looking Honolulu professional, Edward Stasack, producing some remarkably lifelike portraits, and at least one surrealistic *Mother and Child* in oil on Masonite that resembled a fake Salvador Dalí. Under a cloudy sky, in which a giant pair of red lips floated, a pretty blonde woman with a tiny head offered an oversize bare breast to an enormous, piglike baby.

Clare and feathered friends in Honolulu, c. 1970

Shortly after completing it, Clare discontinued her instruction. "I found I could lose myself in painting," she told an interviewer, "and I was really enjoying it when my eyes starting going bad."[47]

Her teacher felt "she was frustrated because she couldn't be as good at painting as she was in all her other endeavors."[48] But the eyesight problem—double cataracts—would soon give her serious trouble.[49]

Clare spent practically all of 1970 jet-setting around the world, being toasted in bad verse by Douglas Fairbanks, Jr., at the Four Seasons in New York and hailed as "a phenomenon" by George Cukor at the Mark Taper Forum in Los Angeles, attending a rain-soaked royal garden party at Buckingham Palace and a weekend in Sussex with Fleur Cowles, cruising in the Aegean, resting up in Malaga, addressing the International Sea Frontier Conference in Malta, partying in a *petit palais* at Cap Ferrat ("all the villas of the Riviera are going full blast"), spending midsummer first in Newport and then on Fishers Island with the Hank Luces, accompanying the Bentons to Tokyo, and in November dining opposite Queen Elizabeth II at the World Wildlife Banquet in London's Talk of the Town nightclub, with Prince Bernhard of the Netherlands and Neil Armstrong, fresh from his moon walk, at the same head table.[50]

The only creative writing Clare published that year was a one-act playlet entitled *Slam the Door Softly*. A modern parody of the last scene of Ibsen's *A Doll's House*, it was intended more for reading and discussion than theatrical production, and first appeared in the October 16 issue of *Life* magazine.

Her script features just two characters, Thaw and Nora Wald, a married couple in their thirties. He is a businessman, and she has a master's degree in English. Nora enters the living room of their house with a packed suitcase and finds Thaw watching two feminists debate on television, arguing that marriage is little more than "legalized and romanticized prostitution." Thaw disgustedly bets that one is "a Lesbo," and switches off the set. Nora recommends he read the works of Simone de Beauvoir and Betty Friedan. His response is to try to carry her upstairs to bed, and she upbraids his male philosophy of "sock 'em and screw 'em." Determined to leave, she asks for no alimony, but says he owes her $53,000 for ten years of domestic labor. She plans to take a job in the research department of Time Inc., the "intellectual harem" of that corporation. Conceding that he will soon replace her with another "sleep-in" servant, Nora says that she still loves him and will therefore only slam the door softly on their marriage—and suits her action to her words.[51]

The chief point that Clare seemed to be making was that not much had changed in marital relationships during the ninety-one years since Ibsen's Nora walked out on the original Torvald.[52]

▽

Stephen Shadegg's biography *Clare Boothe Luce* was published in April 1971 by Simon & Schuster. It was the product of exhaustion on the author's part, after a four-year literary struggle in which his relations with his subject had deteriorated sharply, especially after Clare saw the second draft, which she thought was more riddled with errors of fact and interpretation than the first. She justifiably objected that he had skimped on her tenure as Ambassador to Italy. When Shadegg would not or could not rewrite the book to her satisfaction, even with the help of a ghostwriter, she had gone to his editor at Meredith Publishing and demanded that the book be withdrawn. When Michael Korda at Simon & Schuster bought the contract, she voiced the same objections to him. Unintimidated, Korda told her that everything she said made him all the more eager to publish.[53]

Under the circumstances, William F. Buckley, Jr.'s review in the *The New York Times* was remarkably equable.

It is a favorable biography, though not gushy. It obviously required a degree of cooperation from Mrs. Luce. . . . Yet the book's stylelessness suggests that [her] relationship to it was perfunctory; that she flatly declined . . . to shape the book, and so she must not be held accountable for distortions in it, and, of course, she cannot be held responsible for the principal failure of the book, which is that somehow it does not sufficiently communicate the flavor of her, and that has nothing whatever to do with the silly question whether you do or don't approve of her political views.[54]

During the third week of August, Clare received a distressing letter written on thin blue airmail paper with a thick blue marker. It was from Maggie Case.

Dearest Clare—

Forgive what I am about to do—I have cancer and do not wish to live any longer—an object of pity poor old Maggie— a care for my friends. You are the one I loved the most and regret to let down. You gave me great happiness in my life—a friend of a lifetime. Take care—and pray for my soul.
Forever

Your Maggie.
Sunday Aug. 22nd.[55]

She and Clare had become estranged in recent years, after the latter had heard that Maggie (whose airfares she usually paid when she visited) was complaining that she was no longer a generous friend. Clare might have been less upset had she known that Maggie sent an almost identically worded suicide note to Cecil Beaton. But the details of her old friend's death, related in a phone call from Tish Baldrige, were horrifying. Maggie, approaching eighty, had been dismayed by the recent firing of *Vogue*'s editor Diana Vreeland, and her own forced retirement after forty-five years at the magazine. So, feeling useless as well as ill, she had put on a raincoat and scarf and jumped from the window of her fifteenth-floor Park Avenue apartment.[56]

The almost simultaneous news that Hank's wife, Claire McGill, had died of pancreatic cancer at forty-seven, and that Gerald Heard had also expired, having suffered no fewer than twenty-four strokes, persuaded

Clare that she must live for the living, and try to remain relevant in a rapidly changing world.

To this end, she appeared in Westchester, New York, on October 16 for a weekend of "film, food and talk" centering on a screening of *The Women*. It was hosted by *New York* magazine's movie critic, Judith Crist, at Tarrytown Conference Center, on the Mary Duke Biddle estate. After the Saturday night show, Clare, Crist, and Gloria Steinem had a panel discussion of George Cukor's direction. Steinem said that it was such a parody of femininity that it should have been played in drag. Clare responded that although the cast was female, her play was about heterosexual men, because the women of that era saw fulfillment in looking after them. All the panelists favored the three characters she portrayed as amoral go-getters: Crystal (Joan Crawford), the husband stealer; Countess de Lage (Mary Boland), who uses younger men for sex; and Miriam (Paulette Goddard), the seducer of the spouse of catty Sylvia (Rosalind Russell).

It was not surprising that Steinem, at thirty-seven a glamorous icon of the new "women's lib" movement, should have such opinions. But Clare, at sixty-eight, had evolved to the point where she could be publicly tolerant of free sex and adultery. "After a long life and a long night," she told the audience, "I think [that] most men do not know what love is, because they don't ever love as equals, and the master never really loves the slave." She seemed to have in mind the theme of *Slam the Door Softly*. "To love an equal—it takes big men and big women."

The crowd enjoyed the debate so much that it lasted until 1:30 A.M. Clare had the last word: "I think Gloria and I would agree on most things. But if we didn't, we still could not air them publicly. . . . It would be announced that we had had a hair-pulling contest."[57]

▽

The year 1972 was a momentous and triumphant one for Richard Nixon. In February, he made his world-changing state visit to the People's Republic of China—an event that answered Clare's question to him of three years before, and which she rather skeptically marked during a discussion at Honolulu's East-West Center the following month.

Hewing to her late husband's line, Clare told the president of the University of Hawaii and two local Asian experts that she hoped a consequence of the China initiative would not be a rupture in America's defense treaty with Taiwan.[58]

Nixon's prospects for reelection were enhanced, in her view, by the nomination in mid-August of Senator George McGovern as the Democratic candidate for the presidency. "How did this prissy-mouthed, middle-aged, street-corner preacher from political Dullsville ever make it?" she teased Bill Benton. What particularly bothered her about "McGovernment" was its philosophy of "I'll take it from them as has, and give it to them as hasn't."[59]

Recuperation from a second cataract operation did not prevent her from attending the GOP convention in Miami, beginning on Monday, August 21. Dressed in a jade-green shirtwaist, she rode the down elevator of the Eden Roc Hotel on Tuesday afternoon, and found that her fellow passenger was the hippie leader Abbie Hoffman. They got into conversation in the lobby, and it was overheard by a *New York Times* reporter.

"Hey, have you ever dropped acid?"

"I beg your pardon?"

"Have you ever taken LSD?"

"Oh, LSD. Why, yes, as a matter of fact, I have. But I must tell you, it was only once and quite some time ago. And it was under very controlled circumstances."

"Did you like it?"

"Well, yes, I did. Oh, it didn't change my life or anything dramatic like that, but it was a good experience. I must say, though, I never was tempted to do it again."

"Maybe you didn't have the right setting."

"Oh, no. The setting was marvelous. It's just that I think once was enough. And of course it was only a hundred milligrams, and I understand people are taking something like a thousand."

"Too much," Hoffman said, shaking his head and laughing. Clare smiled back at him.

"Good-bye. It was delightful to have met you."

"So long. See you in Nirvana."[60]

Eight days later, Clare held "a whopping big party" for the Nixons at Halenai'a. Helicopters hovered as some six hundred of Honolulu's civic and social leaders thronged the giant lawn. Press photographers snapped the hostess and her guests of honor receiving in lavish leis beneath a monkeypod tree for ninety minutes, in extremely humid heat. From there Nixon went on to meet with Prime Minister Kakuei Tanaka of Japan, with the intent of launching a "new Pacifc era."[61]

Observing Clare standing next to the President of the United States that afternoon, a bystander might have thought she had happily reached the peak of her retirement in Honolulu. But the truth was that when

President and Mrs. Nixon visit
Halenai'a, August 29, 1972

not entertaining, or flying to the mainland for public appearances, she
was frequently depressed. "What are you doing these days?" a female
acquaintance asked her.

"Preparing my corpse."[62]

Although Clare's body remained strong—she was still capable of
swimming in heavy surf, and executing a perfect pike from the springboard of her pool—her eyesight continued to fade, and she braced for a
third cataract operation in October. "Hard to get my thoughts in order
when I can't *see*." Estrellita Karsh detected "a great September song sadness about her—elemental." Clare complained of old age, loneliness,
and servant problems.[63]

She thought she had solved the last before leaving Phoenix, having
sent ahead of her, as overseers of the Halenai'a construction project, the

most improbable domestic couple ever seen in Hawaii: the self-styled Prince John and Princess Jean of Liechtenstein. John may not have been a genuine aristocrat, but he was cultivated, charming, a competent accountant, and a good bridge player. His wife, however, was so bossy that Clare had been forced to dismiss them both. Their substitutes, a Chinese couple, lasted only six weeks before decamping for a better offer in San Francisco. Luckily, the faithful Arthur Little had been willing to come from Phoenix, but Clare dreaded the arrival of his boozy wife, Winnie. At least she could count on the round-the-clock service of her Pennsylvania Dutch maid, Louise Siegfried, a good Asian cook, and Ann Pearce, a devoted secretary.[64]

Clare unburdened herself to her artist friend Nesta Obermer, ten years her senior and until recently a veteran of widowhood in Hawaii. Nesta was now a contented recluse in Switzerland, and had just finished reading Shadegg's biography. "I can understand even more now," she replied, "your feeling of disenchantment, the hollowness of life, though you held it in the hollow of your hand as very few women have ever held it, grasped entirely through your own magic. You took the blows and you took the acclaim and never showed the bewilderment that must have been always with you, deep down."[65]

With decrepitude so much on her mind, Clare welcomed an assignment from Bill Buckley to critique Simone de Beauvoir's *The Coming of Age* in *National Review*. She found it brilliant, except for the author's Marxist claim that socialist societies treated their elderly citizens better than capitalist ones did. "Mao Tse-tung's Red Guard," Clare wrote, "are said to have murdered thousands of 'gray heads' in the name of the Cultural Revolution."

Her last paragraph read:

To remain intellectually involved and curious, and if the gift be given, creative, is the best way to hold senile boredom and melancholia at bay. If continuously and courageously exercised, the muscles of the mind and the sinews of the spirit are the last to decay. . . . Mme. de Beauvoir [at sixty-four] has magnificently proved her point about the durability of a well-exercised mind and spirit: she has written a masterwork in the springtime of her senility.[66]

Clare was so pleased with her last phrase that in future speeches she used it as a rueful reference to herself. Another favorite was "Widowhood is one of the fringe benefits of marriage."[67]

Clare and William F. Buckley, Jr., on *Firing Line*

She was cheered in November by Nixon's landslide victory over McGovern—forty-nine states to one—and by the announcement that *The Women* was to be revived in Washington, D.C., on December 28—thirty-six years to the day after its Broadway premiere. Its stellar cast would feature Myrna Loy, Alexis Smith, Tammy Grimes, and Rosemary Harris. If the tryout was successful, it would transfer to Philadelphia, and on to New York sometime in 1973.

As it happened, the play did not go into rehearsals in Manhattan until April, conveniently coinciding with Clare's seventieth birthday. The result was a flurry of pre-opening publicity, including a long interview in *The New York Times* and parties in her honor, climaxing in a lavish black-tie dinner for sixty-two people thrown by Hank Luce and the Clurmans at "21."[68] Wearing a blue sheik's robe shot through with gold threads and "sapphires at every pulse point," she listened while Ilka Chase, a star of the original production of *The Women*, toasted her for "the best eighteen months of my life." Brooke Astor recited an ode, and Theodore White, Harry's former Far East correspondent, incomprehensibly compared the celebration to the Chinese Tang dynasty ritual of floating candles and wine cups downstream to denote the passage of time. "Clare," he gushed, "is past and future."[69]

In response, she quoted Somerset Maugham's answer to friends who asked what he wanted for his own seventieth birthday. "Tell them it's too late for fruit, and too early for flowers."[70]

The Women opened on April 25 at the 46th Street Theatre, with two cast replacements, Kim Hunter and Rhonda Fleming, playing Mary and Miriam. As in 1936, Clare did not attend the first night. She explained to a reporter that she had been booed at the premiere of her first play, *Abide With Me*—"It abode with nobody," she quipped—and vowed never to suffer such humiliation again.[71] Instead, she gathered with a group of friends at the Waldorf, sipping a drink, nervously twirling her pearls, and chain-smoking Kent cigarettes. Hearing that Tennessee Williams was at her play, she said, "I'd love to see him laugh—do you suppose he ever does?"

Later, Teddy White burst in with a group of fellow theatergoers. "Clare, baby, it was delightful, the first play I've seen about real people all year." There were cheers and shouts of "Bravo!" and Clare, looking relieved, smiled radiantly.[72]

Most reviews praised the cast, but it was generally agreed that after thirty-seven years, her dialogue had dated. The *Village Voice* called the production "good animal fun," and John Simon wrote in *New York* magazine that *The Women*, though "still mischievous and zestful . . . remains, at the onset of middle age, somewhat immature. The wit sparkles like ginger ale rather than champagne."[73]

Audiences seemed to agree, and the revival closed in mid-June, after sixty-three performances.

▽

The satire in *The Women* may have lost some bite, but there was nothing milquetoast about Clare's language in an essay on feminism she contributed to the 1973 *Encyclopædia Britannica Yearbook*.

> In every marriage there are two marriages. His and hers. His is better. . . . What man now calls woman's natural feminine mentality is the unnatural slave mentality he forced on her, just as he forced it on the blacks. He made her the "house nigger." (Many Women's Liberationists see women as "nigger.") In the end, man dropped the shackles from woman's body only because he had succeeded in fastening them on her mind. . . .
>
> While whole psychologies have been written about the desire of one sex to possess the genital organs of the other (womb envy, penis envy), each sex is inescapably stuck with its own biological functions and cannot transfer them to the other. But roles (the parts people choose or are given to play in life) are both assignable

and transferable. Generally, they are assigned—or reassigned—according to the preferences or prejudices of those who dominate the society. . . .

The Equality Revolution is *not* inevitable. The environment includes nuclear weapons and also man's capacity to use them. The massive reduction of the population by nuclear war would once again require wide pelvises to repopulate the earth and broad backs to cart away the ruins of our civilization. Even the deepest-dyed "male chauvinist pig" must prefer the equality of the sexes to this way of reducing women to submissiveness, passivity, and dependence.[74]

As for her views on abortion, in the wake of the Supreme Court's recent decision in *Roe v. Wade*, Clare was, despite her faith, pragmatic. Responding to an appeal from James P. McFadden of *National Review* to lend her name to the Ad Hoc Committee in Defense of Life, she wrote, "It is impossible to enforce any law, especially at the national level, which is not rooted in a public consensus."[75]

In early June, she read *The American Republic* by Orestes Brownson, and told Hank that it and De Tocqueville's *Democracy in America* had taught her "more about my country, and my countrymen than any others I have ever read."[76] The input was timely, since on June 28, 1973, her seventeen-and-a-half-year hiatus from government came to an end with a prestigious appointment to the President's Foreign Intelligence Advisory Board (PFIAB), pronounced "pifiab." Nixon and his National Security Adviser, Henry Kissinger, stressed that they wanted her to serve.[77] Clare accepted, even though the position would necessitate an almost ten-thousand-mile round-trip commute between Hawaii and Washington six times a year, for a $100 per diem plus travel expenses.

The board had been instituted under a slightly different name in 1956 by Dwight Eisenhower, who needed an outside, nonpartisan body of eminent Americans to assess the information he was fed by Washington's myriad spy agencies. Its current duties were fourfold: first, to determine the impact of new technologies—particularly computer operations—upon the collection and analysis of intelligence; second, to scrutinize foreign political trends; third, to advise on crisis management; fourth, to provide the President with a "yearly, independent assessment of the nuclear threat."[78] The chairman was Admiral George Whelan Anderson, Jr., and other members included former Governors Nelson A. Rockefeller and John B. Connally, Leo Cherne, an economist, John

Clare and Henry Kissinger, 1980

S. Foster, a veteran of the Department of Defense, George P. Shultz, former director of the Office of Management and Budget, and Edward Teller, the atomic physicist.

On August 3, Clare attended her first PFIAB meeting aboard the presidential yacht *Sequoia*, as it sailed down the Potomac River. Kissinger, soon to become Secretary of State, was unusually somber as he briefed the group on the Watergate scandal's effect on American foreign policy. What had seemed, early that spring, to have been a bungled 1972 CIA break-in to offices of the Democratic National Committee had since exploded into a political catastrophe, involving top White House aides and Nixon, too.

"I think what is going on," Kissinger said over lunch, "is an unmitigated disaster in foreign policy." He explained that after the Paris Peace Accords of late January had brought the long agony of the Vietnam War to an end, American global relations had been in excellent shape. "Everyone wanted to be associated with us." But in April had come evidence of the President's direct involvement in Watergate. "Now people are holding off," Kissinger said. He was particularly worried about the effect on Nixon's rapprochement with Mao. "Let's not kid ourselves: China wants us as a counterweight to the Soviet Union. . . . But if they think we are going through *our* cultural revolution, they won't even run the ideological risk of being tied up with us. They are not sentimental."[79]

The only female member of PFIAB heard on her return to Halenai'a that she had impressed her fellow appointees. An aide to Chairman Anderson phoned to say they had been "absolutely overwhelmed by your beauty, charm, wit and intelligence." What was more, Admiral Noel A. M. Gayler, Commander in Chief of the U.S. Pacific Command at Pearl Harbor, wanted to have her at the naval base "at least once a week, for a two or three hour briefing."[80]

▽

By the beginning of 1974, it became clear that the Nixon presidency was doomed. Vice President Spiro Agnew, tarnished by evidence of corruption, had been succeeded by Congressman Gerald R. Ford. On television, the President had claimed he was "not a crook," as more and more of his aides resigned or were found guilty on criminal charges.

"Thank God for Watergate!" Clare said to Shana Alexander of *Newsweek*. "Watergate has caused a great questioning among the people of this country. It has made them ask—'How come the President has all that power?'" A free fourth estate, she went on, was all that stood between a dictator and the people. But as a result of the current scandal, it had "become full of hubris, and is capable of outrageous acts like demanding the President's resignation. If he has broken the law, he should be impeached as the Constitution provides, not tried and judged in the press."

Alexander was struck by her demeanor, "at once fierce and Madonnalike, vivid and pastel."

Clare said, "The moral consensus in this country has collapsed." Worse still, the decline of religion had created "a moral power vacuum," with nothing commensurate to fill it. Solid-state circuitry was no substitute for God. "Technological man can't believe in anything that can't be measured, taped, put in a computer. So the press, like it or not, in part inherits this moral responsibility. Newspapers and magazines have become the pulpit of the United States."[81]

Through the spring and early summer, Clare continued to propound these views, while making no secret of her compassion for Nixon. She angrily upbraided *Time* for its "overinvestment in the destruction of the President," and for "phobic Watergate reporting."[82] She published a

Shakespearean op-ed in *The New York Times* entitled "Hamlet in Congress: A Soliloquy," on the satirical theme of "To impeach, or not to impeach." She fired off nine letters to the editors of the *Honolulu Advertiser*, criticizing liberal media for their vendetta against Nixon. She sent Senator Goldwater a long and learned briefing paper on the pros and cons of a Supreme Court review of the President's possible impeachment.[83]

Urging Nixon to reject the Senate Judiciary Committee's demand for his Oval Office tape recordings, she tried to rally his flagging spirits by sending him Sir Andrew Barton's self-exhortation, "I am hurt, but I am not slain."[84]

After the President's impeachment on July 27, and his resignation thirteen days later, Clare remained outspokenly loyal, telling a Hawaiian columnist that Nixon should take his pension "and run." Yet she felt that it would be "a gross injustice if he was pardoned," writing Goldwater that the only way President Ford could honorably do that was also to absolve all draft dodgers, "thus putting in one stroke of the pen *both* Vietnam and Watergate behind us!" Ford thought otherwise, and pardoned only Nixon on September 8.[85]

▽

Fortunately for Clare, the presidential saga distracted public attention from a brutal indictment of her: a cover story in the August issue of *Esquire* entitled "The Almighty Clare Boothe Luce." A diagonal yellow banner heralded her further as "Woman of the Century." The profile was written by her old *Vanity Fair* colleague Helen Lawrenson, and came with an air of authenticity, since the author had witnessed or been part of some of the incidents described. She had also been intimate with a number of their mutual acquaintances, especially Condé Nast and Bernard Baruch, who was portrayed as a soft touch for Clare's neediness. "Poor little kid, it's hard to refuse her anything."

The opening paragraphs set the tone for much of the piece.

> When I first knew her I didn't like her. Few women do. I can think of no one who has aroused so much venom in members of her own sex. Much of it is envy. But not all. Other more talented and successful women have disliked her intensely. . . .
>
> She made real friendship impossible, perhaps because she seemed to trust no one, love no one, remaining inaccessible deep

in the malistic concept that rankled under her shield of opaque, steely self-assurance. Oddly, I was sorry for her, because I believe that despite the stunning and ineluctable procession of her triumphs, she was basically an unhappy woman, never satisfied, never content. . . . She parlayed a nimble, mousetrap mind, apodictic nerve, and a will as tough as lignum vitae beneath an exquisitely angelic façade into one of the most strategically calculated and fascinating success stories of the century. Her technique was simple: aim for the top.

Lawrenson went on to summarize the major events of Clare's life, accusing her of concealing sordid origins, being sexually manipulative, mendacious, intellectually pretentious, an insufferable monologist with "shocking" lapses of taste in oratory, cozying up to foreign dictators (such as the "unspeakable" Madame Nhu), and avid for awards and honors. Straining to be balanced, she conceded that Clare was courageous and had a "prodigious" capacity for work, quoting Winston Churchill's comment, "She's the tops!"

Clare could only surmise that her old friend's perennial financial problems had worsened. Long ago, she had helped Lawrenson when she lost her job at *Vanity Fair,* given comfort and hospitality when her husband was ill, and paid to put their daughter through high school. Just last year, when Helen asked for a $10,000 loan to hospitalize a depressive son, Clare had sent her a gift of $2,500 "for old times' sake," knowing that she would be unable to repay any amount. "As I so often must say," she wrote Al Morano after the article appeared, " 'No good deed goes unpunished'!"[86]

▽

President Ford kept Clare on PFIAB, and she and eleven other members arrived for a two-day meeting in Room 340 of Washington's Executive Office Building on October 3, 1974. Their quarters, though austere, were just yards from the West Wing of the White House, a proximity that emphasized PFIAB's status as one of the most important boards in the United States government.[87]

The Thursday session began at 9:00 A.M., with thirty minutes of "reading time," a perusal of briefing papers and intelligence memoranda that the executive secretary, Wheaton Byers, had accumulated over the last two months.[88] At 9:30, Leo Cherne presented an hour-long account of economic trends abroad. At 10:30, the Under Secretary of State for

Middle Eastern Affairs gave a briefing, and at 11:30 there was a report on special projects in the U.S. Navy. The board went to the Pentagon for lunch at 12:30 P.M. and at 2:30 was briefed on the latest status of SIOP (Single Integrated Operations Plan) and NICKELPLATE (a command and control exercise). Clare hated these acronyms, not to mention the hundreds of others that were routinely used by administration officials—COINS, CRITCOM, OXCART, IMINT, SIGINT, HUMINT, ACHDD, USCIB—and insisted on them being spelled out and spoken in full.[89] The afternoon ended with tours of the National Military Command and Joint Intelligence Centers.

Friday began with more reading, followed by highly classified briefings on Soviet antisubmarine technology and covert activities in Cyprus, Chile, and Portugal. The half day ended with lunch at Blair House, hosted by the President's young Chief of Staff, Donald Rumsfeld.

Clare attended as many sessions of the board as possible over the next two and a half years, until President Carter disbanded PFIAB in May 1977. In a terse letter, he informed all members that reforms in the intelligence community, plus permanent oversight committees created by Congress, had made their advisory roles redundant.[90]

By then, she had bought an apartment in the capital at 1106 Watergate South, expanding from that into a river-view penthouse in late 1978, and becoming a fixture of the more conservative circles of Washington society. Thanks to the generosity of Hank Luce and his new wife, Nancy Cassidy (introduced to each other by Clare in Hawaii), she also established two pieds-à-terre in New York—one in their Sutton Place duplex in Manhattan, and another at Wychwood, their country mansion on the Gold Coast of Long Island.[91] While continuing in between times to live and entertain at Halenai'a, she grew more and more disillusioned with the insularity of Oahu, but felt she could not contemplate a full-time move to the mainland for as long as Carter remained in the White House.

The former peanut farmer's presence there profoundly irritated her, and she stepped up the number and asperity of her political articles and television rhetoric to point out what she saw as his multiple deficiencies. He struck her as "a carbon copy Woodrow Wilson, reading moral lessons to the whole world, and dumping on Intelligence and the military." To Hank, a Carter supporter, she wrote, "Can the man really believe that love has anything to do with politics? What politics are about is power." She felt more in tune with Kissinger's "sophisticated defeatism" than Carter's "naïve revivalism."[92]

No longer able to advise the President on matters of the highest secrecy, she relieved her frustration by sounding off in the press on such subjects as the world population explosion, crime on television, social welfare, détente, feminism, superpowerdom, and the rising political fortunes of Margaret Thatcher and Ronald Reagan. She also became a member of twenty-six boards, including the Committee on the Present Danger, the American Security Council Foundation, Accuracy in Media, the Institute for the Study of Diplomacy, the Committee for the Preservation of the White House, and Encyclopædia Britannica.

After her seventy-sixth birthday in 1979, Clare began to complain about feeling the weight of years. "I am growing weary," she told an acquaintance. "Everything has been written—nothing is new—everything has been read, but nothing makes a lasting impression and nothing changes as a result of what is written."[93]

By now so many close friends and lovers had died: Bernard Baruch, Charles Willoughby, Lucian Truscott, Ray Stecker, Bill Hale, Gerald Heard, George Waldo, Father Murray, and most recently Carlos Chávez. Continuing problems with servants exacerbated her malaise. She had long since lost the all-capable Arthur Little. There had been a nasty incident in which she slapped his wife, blaming her for his decision to retire and screaming that he would not get a cent of the $50,000 she had promised him in her will.[94] Clare's narcissism was on occasion so out of control that it led her to see every resignation, or even a request for a raise, as a betrayal.

Feeling a need to do something drastic to allay her fears of decrepitude, she quit her half-century smoking habit, promising to give a friend $10,000 if she started again. No forfeit had to be paid.[95]

She cheered up considerably in July, on hearing she was to be awarded West Point's Sylvanus Thayer Award, presented annually "to an outstanding citizen whose service and accomplishments in the national interest exemplify the Military Academy motto, 'Duty, Honor, Country.'" There had been twenty-one previous recipients, among them Generals Eisenhower, MacArthur, and Omar Bradley.[96]

News of the award, the first ever to a woman, gave rise to several major interviews. One, entitled "Clare Boothe Luce at 76," appeared in *The New York Times* on August 18. She spoke of the amazing breakthrough of women in jobs and careers, but lamented their economic inequality. "Though we have a woman Prime Minister in Britain, I think it will be a long time before we have a woman President in this country. There are no more women in Congress now than when I was a Congresswoman thirty-five years ago." Asked which Republican candidate might have the best chance of defeating Carter in 1980, she said, "Ronald Reagan is able, but at 70, he may be too old. The presidency is a killer of a job."[97]

As it happened, she was about to entertain Reagan at Halenai'a. The former Governor was running ahead of Carter in the polls, and wrote to thank her afterward for her "most generous contribution" to his campaign.[98]

On October 7, three days before the presentation of her Thayer Award, Clare appeared on *60 Minutes* in a segment entitled "The Luckiest Woman." The opening image was a mock-up of *Time* with her face on the cover. Morley Safer, the interviewer, explained that Mrs. Luce was being presented this way because her husband had never permitted it— "though few would doubt that she'd achieved prominence enough in her lifetime to have been on half a dozen covers."

Clare was in a feisty mood, not letting Safer get away with the suggestion that she had been a ruthless careerist, isolationist, and scourge of FDR. Nor would she buy his claim that in the age of Prime Minister Thatcher, professional women were still "much bitchier about each other" than men.

> CBL: Oh, come off it! I've worked in the man's world all my life.
> And I would sit there with men in an embassy, on the floor of
> Congress, in an editorial office. What are the men doing?
> Yak, yak, yak, yak, yak, yak, yak, yak, yak.
> SAFER: About each other.
> CBL: About everything, and each other. And then, the same
> man gets home at night, and there's the poor little woman,
> who hasn't been out of the house all day, and she opens her
> mouth, and he says, "Why do you women have to talk so
> much?"

When Safer asked if she was disappointed being "born at the wrong time," and therefore unable to contemplate ever being President of the United States, Clare said no. "I was young and at my peak and serving my country when my country was at its peak in the 1950s. Now, how can you say I was born at the wrong time? I'm the luckiest of women in the time I was born!"[99]

She was not so lucky at West Point on the afternoon of October 10, when a blizzard caused the cancellation of a scheduled cadet review in her honor. "It snowed on my parade!" Clare exclaimed, but was reassured by the promise of a review at a later date. After being presented with a ceremonial saber in the officers' mess, she was escorted by the superintendent of the Academy to dinner with the Corps of Cadets in Washington Hall. A great cheer of more than four thousand young voices resounded through the enormous room, as she stood to receive her scroll and medal.

"I will thrive on this honor you have done me the rest of my days," Clare said, adding, "I am a brave woman. But I'm no heroine. . . . I suspect that the fact that this is the first year that there are women in all four classes is not unrelated to my good fortune."

Although the bulk of her speech was a serious review of the current moral, economic, and political decline of the country, she kept her listeners laughing with wisecracks. "I have lived more than a third of all the years since the signing of the Declaration of Independence," she told them. "It was the last third, in case you are wondering." She ended by saying, "My only regret is that I will not live long enough to see much of you on the long gray line become the great soldier-statesmen, soldier-scholars, or soldier's soldiers of tomorrow. Would you please remember me maybe once when you do?"

She sat down to a standing ovation.[100]

Clare receives the Thayer Award
at West Point, October 10, 1980

▽

"Mrs. Luce is thinking of pulling up roots in Hawaii and moving to either New York or Washington permanently," a secretary wrote to Clare's money manager on April 1, 1980. "Her home is now on the market, with an asking price of $4,800,000."[101]

Nobody offered this record amount, and eventually Clare would settle for much less. But now that she was, as she put it "in my anecdotage," she saw in the rise of Ronald Reagan an opportunity for rejuvenation on the mainland, as the grande dame of the Republican Party.[102] President Carter's chances of reelection in the fall had been damaged by the six-month incarceration of U.S. Embassy officials in Tehran, and Reagan had become the favorite for the GOP nomination. A failed attempt later that month to rescue the hostages by helicopter resulted in the deaths of eight U.S. servicemen, and virtually guaranteed Carter's loss of a second term.

"I hope that Ronnie will take you on for his Vice President," Clare wrote George H. W. Bush, after the latter dropped out of the race at the end of May. "It would make a beautiful ticket. And a fine spot for you, as an extraordinary number of Vice Presidents have become Presidents!"[103]

When Reagan's campaign organization, Americans for Change, listed "Mr. Claire Booth Luce" of "Honalulu" as a supporter, she acidly wrote to correct all four orthographic mistakes, saying she hoped such sloppiness was not symptomatic of how the committee would be run.[104]

Four days before the election, Clare again became the first woman to receive a major public honor. She flew to Fulton, Missouri, to deliver the annual Westminster College Lecture, commemorating Winston Churchill's "Iron Curtain" speech there thirty-four years before. Using the occasion to attack what she saw as Carter's inept foreign policy, she said: "You are all aware of the increasing relative inferiority of the United States. . . . If we didn't know it a year ago, we know it now, because no one can deny the attack on our embassy was an attack on our sovereignty and an act of war to which we were not able to respond with sufficient strength."[105]

On November 4, 1980, Reagan was elected President, carrying forty-four states to Carter's six (plus the District of Columbia). He also received the highest number of electoral college votes ever accorded a nonincumbent candidate.[106]

The following Sunday, Archibald and Selwa Roosevelt held a dinner party in their Georgetown house for the British military historian Alistair Horne. They placed Clare at his right. It was an ideal coupling, and the two talked nonstop throughout the evening. As so often in social situations, Clare, glancing around myopically, appeared to take no notice of members of her own sex. She had no idea that a young woman seated opposite at the same round table wanted to write a biography of her.

At the end of the evening, when the time came for her exit, a few guests were standing at the top of the staircase. One of them was the young woman. In a surprise gesture, Clare put both hands on her shoulders, kissed her, and said, "Good night, you sweet thing."

A flash of red cape, and she was gone.[107]

EPILOGUE

I stood absolutely still. Was the kiss a benediction?

Earlier that year, while looking through files I obsessively keep about characters who strike my fancy, I had come across Mrs. Luce's 1973 autobiographical interview with Martha Weinman Lear in *The New York Times*. I read it with deepening fascination. Here was a child actress who understudied Mary Pickford, a teenage suffragette campaigning for equal rights, a managing editor at twenty-nine of the original *Vanity Fair*, the author of two books and four Broadway plays, a war correspondent, and a Congresswoman, all before she was forty.

Most of this was fresh to me, a fairly recent immigrant from England. Before the article ended, I had learned about her conversion to Catholicism, her appointment as the first American female Ambassador to a major nation, and her 1960s experiments with LSD. I was enthralled, and the biographer in me especially reacted to her final words as quoted by Weinman: "I never thought of myself as really successful at anything. . . . I was thinking at one time of writing my memoirs and calling it: 'Confessions of an Unsuccessful Woman.'"

I decided then that I should like to research and record this extraordinary life, and expressed my interest to Daniel J. Boorstin, the Librarian of Congress. It so happened that he and his wife were friends of Mrs. Luce's. They offered to put in a good word for me. By coincidence, Dr. Boorstin called the morning after the Roosevelt party to say he had just spoken to Mrs. Luce, and that she was "receptive" to the idea of a biography. Had she somehow sensed, the night before, that the person she embraced was the biographer who wanted to "embrace" her?

Two days later, I made my first formal move by writing to Mrs. Luce at her Watergate apartment, enclosing a copy of my previous book, *Edith Kermit Roosevelt: Portrait of a First Lady*. "Sooner or later," I told her, "someone will embark on a major biography, and I should like it to be me."

The year 1980 came to an end. There was no reply. She had returned to Hawaii. I was afraid that she was no longer "receptive." Seeing her in dazzling form on *The Dick Cavett Show* on the night of Reagan's inauguration, wearing a peach-orange silk muumuu, only increased my desire to tell her astonishing story. Finally, in March, a letter postmarked Honolulu arrived. As I opened the pink envelope, I saw it was lined with seashells. A phrase written in her forceful italic hand leaped out at me: *disinclined towards working with a biographer*. Desolate, I read on. "My private life—almost all 78 years of it—has been sad, unhappy, and sometimes tragic . . . an unwillingness to deal with these unhappy and sensitive areas of my life has kept me from writing my own autobiography."

Undeterred, I sent another imploring letter. "In some strange way, the project has taken me over. Every day I find myself in the Lincoln Center Theater Collection poring over crumbling news clippings." On April 7, 1981, I heard again from Honolulu. Addressing me by my first name, Mrs. Luce wrote, "You are a very persistent—and persuasive young woman." She promised "a conclusive conversation" on her return to Washington at the end of the month.

It was the Boorstins who made that conversation possible, at a dinner in their Cleveland Park house on May 5. My husband, Edmund, and I got there first, and were waiting on the second floor when the guest of honor arrived. I heard her decline the elevator and slowly mount the stairs. Dr. Boorstin, wearing a red smoking jacket, crested the last step with Mrs. Luce on his arm. She was dressed in a sea-green silk caftan— "more Hawaiian than Halston," I thought.

Over dinner, Mrs. Luce did most of the talking. She paid little attention to the food. Her delivery was hypnotically slow as she reminisced. I noticed that whenever her monologues on politics and history were interrupted, her jaw protruded disagreeably. Sometimes she paused for a name or a date, which I could not help supplying. At one point she forgot which transatlantic liner she had taken to Europe in 1914. "The RMS *Carmania*," I said. She hesitated over a London hotel she had

4559 KAHALA AVENUE

Monday, March 9, '81

Dear Mrs. Morris,

I hope you will forgive me for not having answered your charming letter long ago. First, I wanted to read your book, but a rather sudden trip to Hong Kong & Thailand caused the postponement of that pleasure. (It is a fine book). Secondly, I thought I had sent word to you by the Boorstins, in January that I was disinclined towards working with a biographer for a number of reasons, & some

Clare's letter to the author, March 9, 1981

stayed in after World War I. "The Victoria," I said. Each time she looked at me quizzically. Our bizarre duet was interrupted by the appearance of orange blancmange. Dan said: "Well, it's time to talk frankly about why we're here tonight."

Mrs. Luce covered her head with a napkin.

"How often does it happen," he asked, "this coming together of a great subject and an ideal biographer?"

She twirled her wineglass. "I've done too many things. My life doesn't stack up."

As passionately as I could, I recapitulated her achievements. "Had you lived a little later, you might well have been President." She rolled her eyes. I said, "You should cooperate with a writer now, or someone uninformed might do a hatchet job when you're gone."

The jaw came out again. "What do I care about people's opinions after I'm dead? I'm no Madame Curie or Margaret Sanger."

Nobody could disagree with this, but nobody dared agree, either. Negative feelings hung in the air. "That's that," I thought dejectedly. "The moment has come and gone."

After dinner, we went to the sitting room for coffee. Edmund moved next to Mrs. Luce while I sank onto an ottoman opposite, wondering how to rescue the situation. She was strangely subdued, introspective even, and frowned at the ceiling. All of a sudden she gave a deep sigh, and uncertainty vanished from her face. She tapped Edmund on the knee. "What are we going to do about your bride?"

"Are you two discussing my future?" I threw up my arms in mock despair. "I have no future."

"Oh, yes, you have," she said. We both stood up and clasped hands in the center of the room. The others discreetly kept their distance. "But you understand my reluctance. My father abandoned us when I was seven [sic], my mother and daughter were killed, and my brother . . ." Her voice trailed off when she saw me nodding. I knew about *him*—that charming, misanthropic suicide.

But she still could not bring herself to say yes. "I'm going to let my secretary, Dorothy Farmer, decide," she said. "Take her for a hamburger."

"How weird," I thought. "Who is this controlling angel?"

At lunch two days later, Dorothy Farmer did not look formidable. She was a tiny, round figure who chuckled a lot. She told me that Mrs. Luce had said, "That Sylvia Morris is going to do my biography whether I cooperate or not."

Apparently Dorothy approved, because shortly afterward Mrs. Luce called to give me the go-ahead. I asked what I should do next. "It seems to me you're doing it already," she said.

With her permission that summer, I began to work my way through the restricted Clare Boothe Luce Papers in the Library of Congress. It appeared she had never thrown a scrap away. The collection—460,000 items spreading over 319 linear feet—was bigger than those of most Presidents in the Manuscript Division. And little wonder. Her life spanned twenty administrations of fifteen Chief Executives, eight of whom she had known personally. Her correspondence with statesmen, writers, and movie and theater people was vast, and included a letter written on papyrus paper from an Indian jail by Jawaharlal Nehru.

After President Reagan had reappointed Mrs. Luce to PFIAB on October 8, 1981, she spent less time in Hawaii, and I was able to schedule frequent interviews. Our first took place on the last day of that month in her Watergate penthouse. She looked regal in a long white wool dress with gold threads and lots of gold jewelry. On the coffee table was a collection of calling card cases. "They're laid out for the appraiser," she said, sitting in an armchair opposite me. "I feel a need to simplify my life."

It soon became apparent that she meant to control the subject matter of our conversation, skillfully sidestepping questions she was not ready to answer. I tried to press her. "You didn't like Mr. Luce when you first met. What did he say or do that made you change your mind? Was it his determination in pursuing you?"

She laughed, remembering the turbulent spring of 1935, when Henry Robinson Luce was trying to get a divorce from his wife in order to marry her, and she had played hard to get by going abroad. "I shook him in Africa," she said, then launched into another deflecting anecdote. "The most embarrassing story of my whole life was in Tunis. There was a toilet that had a great globe over it and a string, and any noise that you made was reverberated over all of Africa. Even pee-pee sounded like Niagara Falls."

It was not an auspicious beginning. There was another awkward moment when she said that the worst thing that happened to her was "the loss of my looks." She seemed disconcerted by my tactless response: "When was that?" But I persevered, and in the course of an hour managed to record some hard biographical material. She spoke of how she had stayed in the Weimar Republic as a girl, and how her first husband, "a golf-playing drunk," would wake her up in the early morning, strumming glee club songs on his banjo.

As I took my leave, she plucked a stem from a vase, put it in my cleavage, and recited Robert Burns's poem "My Love Is Like a Red, Red Rose."

▽

In early December, having sold her penthouse, Mrs. Luce moved to the Shoreham Apartments on Calvert Street in northwest Washington. By then we had taped many hours of reminiscences. It did not occur to me that I had begun to fill a void in her life, until I announced my departure for England to spend Christmas with my sister. A flash of anguish crossed her face, and I realized that she was going to be alone.

She resembled a cadaver when I got back in early January 1982. An aspirin-based painkiller had caused old ulcer scars to hemorrhage, and she had been rushed off in an ambulance, near death. The egalitarian treatment of the emergency room, and the balls of fluff in the corners of her private suite, had not been to her fastidious taste. "A hospital," she said sardonically, "is no place to be sick."

As yet, she lacked a full-time maid, so Edmund and I agreed to stay with her for a few days. Uneasy as I was about too much familiarity with Clare—she had asked me to call her that by now—I put aside the importance of maintaining objectivity, for she was extremely frail. Her brush with mortality had loosened her unwillingness to revisit painful memories, and when I took in her breakfast tray the first morning— fresh orange juice, a slice of whole-wheat toast with butter and jam, weak jasmine tea without milk or lemon—she launched into intimate details of her six years with her first husband, George Brokaw. He had drowned in the swimming pool of a drying-out institution some years after Clare divorced him.

I was still not bold enough to ask her about the near breakup of her second marriage in 1959. Amazingly, at this time, she received a call from none other than Lady Jeanne Campbell. Now fifty-three and twice divorced, Henry Luce's former mistress had become a Roman Catholic, and wanted to interview Clare for a book she contemplated on famous converts. As Jeanne told me later, she had never gotten over her love for Harry. At their last parting, he had said that if she ever saw his picture on the cover of *Time*, she would know that he had died. Sure enough, one day in early 1967, she had walked into a drugstore in Fiji, and seen his familiar face looking out from a magazine rack.

"There doesn't seem to be any reason not to see her," Clare said. "I'm a forgiving soul and don't bear grudges." Yet the interview never took place.

Once, I made notes on a typical day in Clare's life. She spent the first half of it in bed, reading and dictating to Dorothy and to her other secretary, Mary Leader. About 10:00 A.M. the telephone started to ring. William Safire of *The New York Times* called to ask what she thought of a report that FDR had bugged Bernard Baruch's bedroom. Bill Buckley wanted to discuss questions of conservative counsel to the Reagan administration. Both *Good Morning America* and the *Today* show invited her to appear in connection with a *Harper's* cover story by Wilfrid Sheed entitled "Clare Boothe Luce: From Courtesan to Career Woman." It was an excerpt from his forthcoming affectionate memoir about her. She declined, saying she would prefer to have gone "from career woman to courtesan."

Lunch was a scrambled egg and tea. During the afternoon, her old friend James Jesus Angleton, the former Chief of Counterintelligence at the CIA, stopped by for some "spy chat." I discovered that espionage was one of Clare's favorite subjects. Later she read a pile of position papers and magazines on domestic and foreign policy. An article on the economic and social condition of the United States put her in a dark mood. She said to me in all seriousness, "I don't see much hope for a country where you can't get live-in servants."

After a dinner of chicken salad and ice cream, we watched the shipboard seduction scene from *Brideshead Revisited*. Clare, looking over her spectacles, said, "They only allow the missionary position on PBS."

When it was time for bed, she settled down with a detective story. I kissed her good night and left, not turning out any lights, because I knew she liked to fall asleep with all bulbs burning brightly.

▽

In early June 1982, I went to Hawaii for three weeks to work with Clare on more personal and sensitive documents that she was not ready to deposit in the Library of Congress. She invited my husband too, and sent her chauffeur to meet us at Honolulu International Airport. I noticed that the Cadillac dashboard sported a brass plaque: "This car built especially for Clare Boothe Luce by General Motors Corp."

As we swung off Kahala Avenue into the driveway of Halenai'a, I could smell frangipani and see trumpet vines tumbling in profusion over a high trellised wall. Beyond lay a meticulously groomed garden with orchids, hibiscus, and birds of paradise. A swimming pool glimmered in the late afternoon sun, and mangoes, guavas, and coconuts lay scattered on the bright green lawn.

Clare greeted us with a critique of Irving Kristol's *On the Democratic Idea in America*. There was never any small talk with her. After we had a swim, she went to the bar and poured herself a large Scotch. It seldom occurred to her to offer drinks to others. In no time, her speech slowed, and the timbre of her voice grew pontifical. She had a low tolerance for liquor, and frankly admitted it bothered her quarrelsome ulcers, which she nicknamed "Qaddafi and Begin." After an early supper, we retired to sleep off our jet lag.

The next morning, a purple orchid and a copy of the *Honolulu Advertiser* were laid across our lanai breakfast table. Clare appeared at ten o'clock and took me to the library. On the desk was a large scrapbook entitled "My School Days." We looked at it together. Every picture provoked such a flood of anecdotes that I frantically tried to keep my cassette recorder going, while acting like a good listener and scribbling research leads.

After lunch, Clare's stories continued to flow in her best posterity voice. The Congresswoman was spending Christmas of 1944 at the Italian Front. In 1945, she was witnessing the liberation of Buchenwald. The Ambassador was solving the Trieste problem. . . . By now it was late

Clare and the author at Halenai'a, June 1982

afternoon, and her stories grew more intimate. "Just as I had gone to bed, someone came in and fell over the coal scuttle. It was Bernie Baruch! And I was expecting *Randolph!*"

More stories flowed at dinner. Afterward, we watched *The Lady Vanishes* on the Betamax. I sat on the bed beside her, looking up occasionally at a ceiling-hung triptych of clouds and blue sky painted by John Wisnosky, a local artist.

Twenty days passed. I sifted through a vast number of letters, diaries, and albums. Every characteristic of Clare was there from the start: beauty, charm, humor, coquetry, intellect, ambition. Sometimes she worked ahead of me in a study off her bedroom, going through boxes and trunks of papers. Once I had a fright when I heard tearing sounds, and rushed in, afraid she might be destroying important documents. "Oh no, I'm just taking blank pages out of the diaries, so they'll be lighter for shipping to the library."

In addition to having terrifying nightmares of abandonment and mutilation, Clare was an insomniac. She also had extreme mood swings. At parties, she was gracious and amusing. The following day, she would complain of the dullness of Honolulu society. After a dinner where a conservative professor made a toast to "the American dream," she moaned, "You can see why I'm so bored in this fur-lined rut." She confessed to being "low in the mind" when we said good-bye on July 3. "Seeing my life paraded before me these last few weeks has been traumatic." She hugged me with tears in her eyes.

I returned to Washington with more research to do. Those terrifying dreams and black moods hinted at repressed truths. The circumstances of her early years confused me. I tracked down her New York birth certificate, and found that she was born in March, not April, 1903, and that her place of birth was not Riverside Drive, but the less genteel environs of West 125th Street. I told her about the date, and she stared at me. "Mother always said I was born at Easter." As for her father being an aspiring violinist when he met her mother, I told her he had been a patent medicine salesman, and her grandfather had not been a Bavarian Catholic, but a Lutheran. Her response was that I was "one hell of a detective."

Over the next five years, I traveled far in search of my subject. I went to Memphis, Nashville, and Chicago to look—in vain—for her parents' wedding certificate, and with Clare to Mepkin Abbey in South Carolina, where she wanted to be buried. I crossed the Atlantic to Herefordshire and met with her oldest living boyfriend, still carrying her picture in his wallet. On the French Riviera I saw where she had dined with Somerset Maugham, and in Scotland I uncovered details about a White Russian soldier with whom she had had a youthful romance. In Newport, Clare and I toured the Bellevue Avenue mansion where she had spent her first married summer, and we had lunch at Bailey's Beach Club. In Palo Alto, I found the spot where her only child was killed in a car crash, and visited the Modernist chapel she had built in Ann's memory. Together in Rome—a trip for which she bought a set of Louis Vuitton luggage—we explored the U.S. Embassy and the Villa Taverna, and Clare pointed out the infamous ceiling that had poisoned her. We went to Bulgari, where she spent $28,000 on a necklace and matching earrings to wear at a dinner in her honor. That night, when Ambassador Maxwell Rabb toasted her "brilliance, beauty, and charisma," she rose to respond. "I despise flattery, but I do admire honest praise." The following day, we had lunch with Gore Vidal at Vecchia Roma restaurant, and in his nearby apartment afterward, he and Clare affectionately reminisced. "For once," Gore noted later, "she and I did not row about politics."

Between trips, I worked through mounds of political correspondence at the Library of Congress, and diplomatic papers at the State Department. I interviewed scores of people: members of the Luce family, relatives of the Schneiders, Fleur Cowles, William F. Buckley, Jr., Irene Selznick, Edward Teller, Yousuf Karsh, John Richardson, veterans of her congressional and ambassadorial staff, her interior designer, her confessor, her doctor, and a decaying Countess in Murray Hill. What I concluded was that few people really understood Clare Boothe Luce. Although she had the gift of apparent instant intimacy, she would distance herself at the first hint of rejection. She admitted to preferring people who asked the least of her. One of these was the devoted Dorothy Farmer, who greatly inconvenienced her by dying in 1984. "I'd hoped she'd see me out."

Although she was proud of her service as a senior member of PFIAB, she was disappointed that President and Mrs. Reagan did not pay her as much mind as she had hoped. Near the end of a dinner party she gave for them in her apartment there was a power outage, and they had to be escorted nine floors down the stairwell by candlelight.

The only state dinner she attended was for Indira Gandhi, and she had to see other, younger Republican women appointed to prestigious positions: Jeane Kirkpatrick as Ambassador to the United Nations, Selwa ("Lucky") Roosevelt as Chief of Protocol, and, most historically, Sandra Day O'Connor as the first female Supreme Court Justice. Clare said that she envied the latter most, for having risen "to the top of her particular tree," while she herself had never become the best American playwright, politician, or diplomat of her time. I noticed that her envy was mixed with awe when the Justice invited us both to lunch and a hearing at the Court.

Mrs. O'Connor launched immediately into a ten-minute history of the method of recording Court proceedings. Clare, unschooled in jurisprudence, tried to ask "clever" questions designed to bring the conversation round to her current peeve, the President's right to conduct foreign policy without interference from Congress. Throughout, she had a tight demeanor, and was at pains to impress.

Before the Court reconvened, Justice O'Connor briefed us on the

Indira Gandhi, Clare, and Nancy Reagan at the White House, 1982

case we were to hear, concerning the right of a small Texas town to prevent the opening of a nursing home for the mentally handicapped. Twenty minutes into the proceedings, Clare wanted to leave. But a note was passed to her from Chief Justice Warren Burger. It read, "Welcome, but what a sad case." Her reaction was to whisper to me, "Now we'll have to stay another ten minutes."

In February 1983, Clare's feelings of neglect by the administration were mollified by being awarded the Medal of Freedom. That spring, she was also honored as a "Living Legend" by the National Portrait Gallery, where the historian Marc Pachter interviewed her before a packed audience of Washington notables. She was on her best monologic form as she recounted her 1945 thespian stint in Shaw's *Candida*. Describing the scene-stealing antics of one young actor, she asked, "Have you any idea what it's like to be upstaged?" "No," Pachter said, "but I'm beginning to find out."

Clare and Marc Pachter at the National Portrait Gallery

In April, I gave a party on Capitol Hill to celebrate her eightieth birthday. The Boorstins were there, as were Mort Zuckerman, Gay and Nan Talese, and Richard Cohen of *The Washington Post*. Luigi Barzini happened to be in town, and stopped by to reminisce with her about their old days in Italy. After dinner, in a seductive mood, Clare sat on the couch beside Cohen, and began running her fingers through his thick hair and beard. He said to me later, "That's the only eighty-year-old I've ever wanted to jump into bed with."

To the end, she remained a practiced vamp. One evening, having sold Halenai'a for $3.6 million and moved to what would be her final apartment, at 906-907 Watergate South, she telephoned to say she had a "terrible attack of the dismals." I asked why, and she said, "It's Saturday night, and I haven't any beaus."

I asked her what kind of escort she would like. "A homosexual Admiral would be good," she said, "because at the end of the evening I wouldn't have to put out."

In November 1986, The Old Vic theater in London put on a fiftieth-anniversary revival of *The Women*, starring Susannah York and Maria Aitken. Clare asked me to accompany her to the final rehearsals and opening night. We stayed at Claridge's. Time Inc. gave a dinner for her at Le Gavroche. I saw her working hard in conversation with former Prime Minister Edward Heath. She told me afterward, "I was having no success at charming him, so I slayed him with pure intellectual superiority."

One night, after a preview, we ate alone at the hotel. Clare was contemplative. She spoke sadly of her peripatetic childhood, and Ann Clare Schneider's determination to marry her to a rich man. "Mother poisoned my life." When I remarked on how many personal tragedies she had endured, she said, "Nothing more than I could bear." Still in a retrospective mood, she said, "You know, few playwrights have their works performed after fifty years." Then, after a pause, "Possibly Shakespeare." Silent for another moment, she asked me whom I felt closest to—"not counting Edmund." Before I could reply, she said, "I feel closest to you, because you know everything."

She was now eighty-three, and seemed to be her old energetic self, doing morning exercises and running along the corridors like a gazelle. During that week in London, she kept up a grueling schedule of rehearsals and interviews. But I noticed that most untypically, she mislaid keys and itineraries, mistook the time and date, and dropped her wallet. One morning, I knocked at her door for several minutes before she answered. Looking dazed, she said, "I think it would be better if you came back in half an hour. I might have taken too many sleeping pills."

Later, I helped her zip up her dress. "The trouble with you," I said, "is that your mind and heart want to do more than your body will allow."

She nodded. "It's why I'm always so depressed."

That night I wrote on a card: "Clare's mind is going."

▽

She spent much of that winter traveling to New York to visit her stepdaughter-in-law, Nancy Luce, who was dying of cancer. We continued seeing each other, and chatted often on the phone. She complained about her appearance. "I don't go to beauty parlors anymore. My hair's so thin, and my nails won't grow." Yet she still ventured out on shopping sprees with her friend Commander Edward Koczak, once spending $8,000 at Yves Saint Laurent.

I noticed through the spring that her behavior was becoming more erratic. On her eighty-fourth birthday, she temporarily lost her power of speech and was confined to bed, unable to see visitors. I dropped off a bunch of her favorite American Beauty roses at the Watergate desk. The clerk remarked, "She must be the most popular lady in Washington. She sure receives lots of flowers."

In May, I went to Europe on a research trip. When I came back, Clare called to tell me she had a brain tumor. The growth was behind her left eye, and had been shrunk by steroids. Now she was undergoing radiation treatments. "This way, perhaps, I'll make it to December."

At the end of that month, she wrote a poignant and telling farewell letter to "Dear Friends and Family." Her penmanship no longer displayed her mastery of italic calligraphy, but had reverted to a rounded script reminiscent of childhood. Some sentences were scarcely coherent, though correctly spelled and punctuated. "I have to tell you how much I love you all, if not equally, as there is no such thing. . . . Each of you has a different place in my thoughts and memories and I leave it all to you to discover what those places are. . . . So I thank you for being part of my stage set."

Richard Nixon heard how ill she was, and wrote to cheer her up. "As I see some of the mediocrities who are running for President these days, I only wish that the Clare Luce I knew in the fifties was around today! You would be a lead pipe cinch to become the first woman President."

On July 12, Edmund and I took her to dinner. She was shaky on her legs, but ate well—smoked fish salad, broiled trout, strawberries and blueberries, and coffee. Her doctor had forbidden alcohol, but she called for a kir, poured some over the fruit, and impishly dumped petits fours in the rest. She talked as much as ever, if less sequentially, complaining of how she had lent Orson Welles $5,000 to produce *Macbeth* and never been repaid, and how the Duchess of Windsor used to rap the Duke's knuckles when he ate with his fingers. "The jury is still out on me," she reported of her eighteen radiation treatments.

On July 27, Clare gave what was in effect her own farewell party. She invited twenty-two people, mostly journalists. For almost an hour, we stood in the library having drinks. Our hostess was nowhere to be seen. At last, she made a painfully slow entrance, supported by two attendants. We were shocked at her skeletal appearance, made more macabre by a silver bob-style wig.

Guests gathered round as she sat on a low sofa, munching popcorn and drinking Perrier. Dinner was served, consisting of borscht and sour cream, pasta with shrimp, and goulash. Dessert (her final mischievous joke) was a Dove bar complete with stick, laid across fine china.

Clare never left the apartment again. By September she was confined to bed, lying beneath the Frida Kahlo self-portrait she had bought more than fifty years before, and looked after by her secretary Sybil Cooper, her maid, Lucia Fuentes, and two nurses. She was reluctant to see anyone else—"My face looks awful"—but late that month a few friends and relatives from out of town were allowed in briefly. Father Christian of Mepkin Abbey was among the last to visit. He asked about her two favorite saints, Augustine of Hippo and Thomas Aquinas, and was surprised at the lucidity with which she differentiated them. Although she had not been to church much in recent years, when the priest put on his robes and offered her the sacraments of Confession, Communion, and Extreme Unction, she said, "I want all of them."

After that, unable to read, write, or watch television, she listened to music. The last cassette in her stereo player was Bach's Mass in B Minor, stopped at the conclusion of the "Kyrie." During the night, she could sometimes be heard softly calling out to her mother and Ann.

At nine o'clock on the morning of October 9, 1987, Ms. Cooper called to tell me Clare had died. I felt a thud in my chest, such as you have as a child when you are frightened. I rushed over to the apartment, but the body had already been removed.

Just before the end, she had assured a nurse that "many important people" would attend her funeral. At a memorial Mass at the Church of St. Stephen Martyr in Washington, Senator Strom Thurmond and Patrick Buchanan were among the four hundred congregants, as was Dan Boorstin, who growled, "I feel no grief at all. I think it's because she was an unsatisfactory woman. Just wasn't interested in anybody else." Another Mass was held in New York's St. Patrick's Cathedral, attended by Richard Nixon, CIA Director William Webster, UN Ambassador General Vernon Walters, and former Secretary of the Interior William Clark. Cardinal O'Connor, Hank Luce, and Bill Buckley gave eulogies.

"Her documented achievements," the latter said, "are evidence of the lengths to which nature is prepared to go to demonstrate its addiction to inequality."

Clare was buried at Mepkin, where she had written several plays and spent some of the happiest days of her marriage to Henry Luce. The Abbot spoke of a "clear light extinguished." As she was lowered in a gleaming pine coffin into the ground near her mother and daughter and next to her husband, I heard a monk say, "There's no distance between them now: it's vault to vault." Men shoveled red soil onto the casket. A cockroach squeezed itself between two clods of earth, eager to begin the natural reprocessing of life.

So there, beneath a great oak on the banks of the tranquil Cooper River, lies Clare Boothe Luce.

APPENDIX

The Last Will and Testament of Clare Boothe Luce was signed on February 20, 1987, with a codicil added on April 23, 1987, and published on December 3, 1987. She left an appraised total of $31,625,454 in personal property, including real estate, corporate stocks and bonds, and bank accounts, but not including incoming royalties from her plays. In addition, she had power of appointment over two trust funds bequeathed to her by her late husbands, George Tuttle Brokaw and Henry Robinson Luce. From the latter, of some $19 million, she left $600,000 to Mepkin Abbey, $100,000 of which was to be set aside as a permanent endowment fund for the maintenance of her and her family's graves. Other bequests totaling $1,725,000 went to eighteen institutions, including the Heritage Foundation ($500,000, plus net proceeds from the sale of her three apartments in the Watergate complex), Saint Anne's Chapel ($250,000), the Dr. Milton B. Rosenbluth Memorial Fund for Medical Education ($250,000), the Association of Graduates of the United States Military Academy ($250,000 "to endow the Sylvanus Thayer Award for processing the selection of women candidates"), the Clare Boothe Luce Collection in the Library of Congress ($200,000 for processing and cataloging), the Eisenhower Foundation ($100,000), the Ronald Reagan Presidential Foundation and Library ($50,000), Regina Laudis Abbey in Bethlehem, Connecticut ($20,000), and the Winston Churchill Memorial in Fulton, Missouri ($10,000).

The decedent's bequests to individuals amounted to only one-seventh of her estate. The principal beneficiaries were "my longtime maid and friend, Miss Lucia Fuentes" ($100,000), and a niece, Elizabeth Severinghaus Warner ($100,000). Shirley Potash Clurman, Edward Koczak, James P. McFadden, and a personal assistant, Mary Leader, each received $25,000, and Letitia Baldrige Hollensteiner, $10,000. Bequests of varying worth went to Clare Middleton Luce ($50,000), Clare Leader ($10,000), Clare Hollensteiner ($10,000), Ann Clare Shea ($5,000), and St. Clare's Chapel in Berea, Kentucky ($5,000).

Sybil Cooper was left nothing, but a motion for default judgment filed by personal representatives of the estate granted her $10,000 for "substantial overtime performed . . . prior to decedent's death."

A codicil to the will bequeathed two portraits by Boris Chaliapin, one a watercolor of Ann Brokaw and the other a tinted drawing of Clare Boothe Luce, to the National Portrait Gallery. A self-portrait by Frida Kahlo wearing Spanish colonial costume went to the National Museum of Women in the Arts. The Luce Foundation received busts of Henry and Clare Luce by Jo Davidson.

A sale of "The Jewels and Objects of Vertu of the Honorable Clare Boothe Luce" by Sotheby's on April 19, 1988, yielded $2,163,480. Half of this came from six items: a ruby-and-diamond dome ring, a diamond brooch, an emerald-and-diamond necklace from Bulgari, and a Fabergé compact. All other property of the decedent, including works of art, furniture, and a netsuke collection, were sold at auction. The proceeds, along with her residuary estate and the balance of her Luce and Brokaw trusts, totaled some $70 million. This sum was designated the Clare Boothe Luce Fund, to be administered as an academic program by the Henry Luce Foundation. Her instructions were that it be used "exclusively to fund scholarships and professorships for women students and professors at educational institutions, a minimum 50 percent of which shall be Roman Catholic . . . to encourage women to enter, study, graduate, and teach . . . Physics, Chemistry, Biology, Meteorology, Engineering, Computer Science, and Mathematics."

Fourteen schools were designated as annual beneficiaries of the program, including Boston, Georgetown, Fordham, and Notre Dame Universities, and Marymount, Trinity (D.C.), Mount Holyoke, and Colby Colleges. Individual recipients were to be selected by a committee of six, alternately by the Henry Luce and Heritage Foundations. All scholarships and professorships were to be used exclusively for study in the United States.

ACKNOWLEDGMENTS

D ennis Ambrose, Giulio Andreotti, Robert Sam Anson, Katie Baron, Elizabeth Baruch, Sonia Bertorelle, Vernon Blunt, Daniel J. and Ruth Boorstin, Taylor Branch, Jeanne Breck, Richard Park Breck, Christopher Buckley, William F. Buckley, Jr., Charles A. Buerschinger, Dr. Hayes Caldwell, Graydon Carter, Ann Charnley, Katy Close, Shirley Clurman, Richard Sidney Cohen, Sybil Cooper, Wallace F. Dailey, Philip Dunne, Elbridge Durbrow, Nan Ernst, Amintore Fanfani, Dorothy Farmer, Edward Feulner, Joan H. Fitzpatrick, Anne Ford, Pie Friendly, Lucia Fuentes, John Gable, Matt Glover, Rosalie Noland Gumbrill, Kate Hale, Gale Hayman, Nannette and George Herrick, Kathy McLane Hersh, Jonathan Hiam, Serrell Hillman, Charles F. Johnson, Mika Kasuga, Dodie Kazanjian, William Herbert Kennedy, Edward Koczak, Rebecca Kramer, David A. Lanbart, Wayne Lawson, Mary and John Leader, William R. Leahy, Robert Loomis, Henry Luce III, Leila Hadley Luce, Clare McMillan, George J. Marlin, Lore Mika, Gerald Miller, Elsabeth Luce Moore, Albert P. Morano, Jefferson Morley, Reverend Michael P. Morris, Will Murphy, Diana M. Murray, Eleanor Nangle, Allen Packwood, Tim Page, Miranda Dunne Parry, Brother Dan Peterson, Ann Pierce, Ambassador and Mrs. Maxwell Rabb, Don Ritchie, Marion Elizabeth Rodgers, Selwa and Archibald B. Roosevelt, Daphne Root, Dr. Michael Rosenbluth, Norman Ross, Stephen Shadegg, Philip Simpson, Sally Bedell Smith, Ray J. Stecker, Jr., Michael Stern, W. A. Swanberg, Nan A. Talese, Michael Teague, Father Wilfrid Thibodeau, Calvin Tomkins, Lucian Truscott IV, R. Emmett Tyrell, Gore Vidal, Sona Vogel, Alexander Waugh, Walton Wickett, Helen Worth, Richard D. Zanuck, and above all, Clare Boothe Luce.

LIST OF ILLUSTRATIONS

Unless otherwise credited, all illustrations come from the author's collection.

PERMISSION CREDITS

G rateful acknowledgment is made to the following for permission
to reprint preexisting material:

CURTIS BROWN, LONDON: Excerpt from two letters from Randolph
S. Churchill to Clare Boothe Luce dated August 4, 1960, and housed
in a private collection, copyright © Randolph S. Churchill. Used by
permission of Curtis Brown, London, on behalf of the Estate of Randolph S. Churchill.

ENCYCLOPAEDIA BRITANNICA, INC.: Excerpt from *Britannica Book of
the Year,* copyright © 1973 by Encyclopaedia Britannica, Inc. Used by
permission of Encyclopaedia Britannica, Inc.

THE ESTATE OF BARRY GOLDWATER: Excerpts from two letters from
Barry Goldwater to Clare Boothe Luce dated July 5, 1964, and April 4,
1968. Used by permission of the Estate of Barry Goldwater.

THE ESTATE OF CYRUS L. SULZBERGER: Excerpts from *A Long Row of
Candles: Memoirs and Diaries 1934–1954* by Cyrus L. Sulzberger (New
York: Macmillan, 1969), copyright © 1969 by Cyrus L. Sulzberger. Used
by permission of the Estate of Cyrus L. Sulzberger.

HOUGHTON MIFFLIN HARCOURT PUBLISHING COMPANY: Excerpt
from *Billy Baldwin Remembers* by Billy Baldwin, copyright © 1974 by
William W. Baldwin. Used by permission of Houghton Mifflin Harcourt
Publishing Company. All rights reserved.

THE C. S. LEWIS COMPANY: Excerpt from a letter from C. S. Lewis
to Clare Boothe Luce dated October 26, 1947, housed in the Clare

Boothe Luce papers, John F. Kennedy Presidential Library. Used by permission of The C. S. Lewis Company.

MEREDITH CORPORATION: Excerpt from "The Real Reason" by Clare Boothe Luce from *McCalls*® magazine, February–April 1947. Subject to national and international intellectual property laws and treaties. Used by permission of Meredith Corporation.

A. P. WATT, LTD: Excerpts from two letters from W. Somerset Maugham to Clare Boothe Luce dated April 6, 1957, and August 15, 1957. Used by permission of A. P. Watt, Ltd.

BIBLIOGRAPHY

ARCHIVES

ABP   Alice Basim Papers, privately held
ACP   Ann Charnley Papers, privately held
AHP   Alden Hatch Papers, University of Florida, Gainesville, Fla.
AMP   Al Morano Papers, privately held
BP   Beaverbrook Papers, Parliamentary Archives, London
CA   The Citadel Archives, Charleston, S.C.
CBLP   Clare Boothe Luce Papers, Library of Congress Manuscript Division, Washington, D.C.
CBLP-NA   Records of Ambassador Clare Boothe Luce, National Archives II, College Park, Md.
CCP   Carlos Chávez Papers, Archivo General de la Nación, Mexico City, Mexico
CCPN   Carlos Chávez Papers, New York Public Library for the Performing Arts, New York, N.Y.
GFL   Gerald Ford Presidential Library, Ann Arbor, Mich.
HHP   Herbert Hoover Papers, Hoover Institution Library and Archives, Stanford University, Stanford, Calif.
HLP   Herbert Lehman Papers, Rare Book and Manuscript Library, Butler Library, Columbia University, New York, N.Y.
ISP   Irene Selznick Papers, privately held
JBP   John Shaw Billings Papers, South Caroliniana Library, University of South Carolina, Columbia, S.C.
JCMP   John Courtney Murray Papers, Georgetown University, Washington, D.C.
JFKP   John F. Kennedy Presidential Papers, John F. Kennedy Library, Cambridge, Mass.
LC   Library of Congress, Washington, D.C.
LZHP   Laura Z. Hobson Papers, Butler Library, Columbia University, New York, N.Y.
MBP   Mary Bancroft Papers, Schlesinger Library, Radcliffe Institute for Advanced Study, Harvard University, Cambridge, Mass.
NAMC   National Archives Military Affairs Committee Archive, Washington, D.C.

NASD National Archives State Department Central Files, College Park, Md.
NRP Nelson A. Rockefeller Papers, Rockefeller Archive Center, Pocantico Hills, N.Y.
SCP Sidney Cohen Papers, UCLA Library Special Collections, Charles E. Young Research Library, Los Angeles, Calif.
SJMP Sylvia Jukes Morris Papers, privately held
TIA Time Inc. Archives, New York, N.Y.
UTA University of Trieste Archives, Trieste, Italy
WWP Walton Wickett Papers, privately held

MANUSCRIPTS

Billings, John. Diary, JBP.
Breck, Jeanne. "Notes from Jeanne Breck," ca. Feb. 10, 1988, SJMP.
Breck, Richard Park. "Notes from Park Breck," ca. Feb. 10, 1988, SJMP.
Brokaw, Ann Clare. Diary, CBLP.
Case, Margaret. "Maggie's Diary, June 3rd–September 15th, 1953." Unpublished typescript, SJMP.
Chamberlain, John. Draft profile of CBL for *Life*. Unpublished typescript, 1946, CBLP.
Hatch, Alden. Interviews conducted during research for his book on CBL, AHP.
Ickes, Harold L. Diary, LC.
Luce, Clare Boothe. "The Double-Bind." Autobiographical novel (fragment, ca. 1962), CBLP.
———. "The Ghost at Westminster." John Findley Green Foundation Lecture, Nov. 1, 1980. Transcript in CBLP.
———. "Interview with President Johnson," June 2, 1966, CBLP.
———. "Caneel Bay Notebook," Aug. 6, 1959.
———. "Memorandum of Conversation [with President Kennedy]," Sept. 26, 1961.
———. "Miscellaneous Chit Chat: Items from here and there about this and that," ca. 1945, CBLP.
———. "CBL Literary Notes," CBLP.
———. Outline for an autobiography (fragment, ca. 1957), CBLP.
———. "Outlines of Italian Trip," manuscript, CBLP.
———. "Saint Anthony and the Gambler," 1949, typescript, CBLP.
———. Saint Francis in Manhattan: A Synopsis for a Ballet, April 18, 1950, CBLP.
Rogers, Elisabeth Cobb. Diary, 1949, CBLP.
Shadegg, Stephen. "It Was Never Nothing." Unpublished autobiographical fragment, 1965, SJMP.
U.S. Army Mediterranean Theater of Operations HQ. "Resume of Itinerary and Inspections for Mrs. Luce." Typescript, 1945, CBLP.

DOCUMENTS

"America in the Post-War Air World: Be Practical—Ration Globaloney," by Clare Boothe Luce, Congresswoman from Connecticut. Delivered in the House of Representatives, Washington, D.C., Feb. 9, 1943. *Vital Speeches of the Day*. New York, 1943.
Eighty-sixth Congress, First Session, 1959. *Executive Sessions of the Senate Foreign Relations Committee*, Historical Series, vol. XI. Washington, D.C., 1982.
Foreign Relations of the United States, Washington, D.C., various dates and volumes.

BIBLIOGRAPHY

Luce, Clare Boothe. "On My Record in Congress—Bills Introduced." *Congressional Record*, Seventy-ninth Congress, Second Session. Washington, D.C., July 31, 1946.

Nomination of Clare Boothe Luce. Hearing Before the Committee on Foreign Relations. United States Senate, Eighty-sixth Congress, First Session, Washington, D.C., April 15, 1959.

BOOKS

Abell, Tyler, ed. *Drew Pearson, Diaries 1949–1959*. New York, 1974.

Absher, Kenneth M., Michael C. Desch, and Roman Popadiuk. *Privileged and Confidential: The Secret History of the President's Intelligence Advisory Board*. Lexington, Ky., 2012.

Ambrose, Stephen E. *Eisenhower: Soldier and President*. New York, 1990.

Amory, Mark, ed. *The Letters of Evelyn Waugh*. New York, 1980.

Andreotti, Giulio. *The U.S.A. Up Close: From the Atlantic Pact to Bush*. New York, 1992.

Atkinson, Rick. *The Day of Battle: The War in Sicily and Italy, 1943–1944*. New York, 2007.

Bailey, Thomas A. *A Diplomatic History of the American People*. New York, 1968.

Baldrige, Letitia. *A Lady, First: My Life in the Kennedy White House and the American Embassies of Paris and Rome*. New York, 2002.

——. *Roman Candles*. Boston, 1956.

Baldwin, Billy. *Billy Baldwin Remembers*. New York, 1974.

Behrman, S. N. *People in a Diary: A Memoir*. Boston, 1972.

Bender, Marylin, and Selig Altschul. *The Chosen Instrument: Juan Trippe, Pan Am: The Rise and Fall of an American Entrepreneur*. New York, 1982.

Blumenson, Martin. *Mark Clark: The Last of the Great World War II Commanders*. New York, 1984.

Braden, Maria. *Women Politicians and the Media*. Lexington, Ky., 1996.

Branch, Taylor. *Parting the Waters: America in the King Years, 1954–63*. New York, 1988.

Brandon, Henry. *Special Relationships: A Foreign Correspondent's Memoirs from Roosevelt to Reagan*. New York, 1988.

Briggs, Ellis O. *Farewell to Foggy Bottom: The Recollections of a Career Diplomat*. New York, 1968.

Brinkley, Alan. *The Publisher: Henry Luce and His American Century*. New York, 2010.

Brinkley, David. *Washington Goes to War*. New York, 1988.

Bulloch, Alan. *Hitler: A Study in Tyranny*. New York, 1962.

Churchill, Randolph. *Twenty-One Years*. Boston, 1965.

Churchill, Winston. *Painting as a Pastime*. New York, 1932, 1965.

Clark, Mark Wayne. *Calculated Risk*. New York, 1950.

Clarke, Peter. *The Last Thousand Days of the British Empire: Churchill, Roosevelt and the Birth of the Pax Americana*. New York, 2008.

Colville, John. *Winston Churchill and His Inner Circle*. New York, 1981.

——. *The Fringes of Power: 10 Downing Street Diaries 1939–1955*. New York, 1986.

Conant, Jennet. *The Irregulars: Roald Dahl and the British Spy Ring in Wartime Washington*. New York, 2008.

Cooney, John. *The American Pope: The Life and Times of Francis Cardinal Spellman*. New York, 1984.

Cowles, Fleur. *The Best of Flair*. London, 1999.

Davy, Michael, ed. *The Diaries of Evelyn Waugh*. Boston, 1976.

Day, Barry, ed. *The Letters of Noël Coward*. New York, 2007.

Donovan, Robert J. *Tumultuous Years: The Presidency of Harry S. Truman, 1949–1953*. New York, 1983.

Dunne, George H. *King's Pawn: The Memoirs of George H. Dunne*. Los Angeles, 1990.

Eisenhower, David. *Eisenhower at War: 1943–1945*. New York, 1986.

Elson, Robert T. *The World of Time Inc: The Initimate History of a Publishing Enterprise, 1941–1960*. New York, 1973.

Evans, Richard J. *The Third Reich at War*. New York, 2009.

Eyre, David W. *Clare: The Honolulu Years*. Honolulu, 2007.

Fearnow, Mark. *Clare Boothe Luce: A Research and Production Sourcebook*. Westport, Conn., 1995.

Ferrell, Robert H., ed. *The Diary of James C. Hagerty*. Bloomington, Ind., 1983.

———. *The Eisenhower Diaries*. New York, 1981.

Frank, Anne. *The Diary of a Young Girl: The Definitive Edition*. New York, 1995.

Gaddis, John Lewis. *The Cold War: A New History*. New York, 2005.

———. *The United States and the Origins of the Cold War, 1941–1947*. New York, 1972.

Galbraith, John Kenneth. *Life in Our Times*. Boston, 1981.

Gilbert, Martin. *Churchill: A Life*. New York, 1991.

———. *The Day the War Ended: May 8, 1945—Victory in Europe*. New York, 1995.

Ginsborg, Paul. *A History of Contemporary Italy: Society and Politics 1943–1988*. New York, 2003.

Hametz, Maura E. *Making Trieste Italian: 1918–1954*. Rochester, N.Y., 2005.

Hastings, Max. *First Years: Churchill as Warlord 1940–1945*. London, 2009.

———. *Retribution*. New York, 2008.

Hatch, Alden. *Ambassador Extraordinary: Clare Boothe Luce*. New York, 1955.

Heefner, Wilson. *A Dogface Soldier: The Life of General Lucian K. Truscott, Jr*. Columbia, Mo., 2010.

Henle, Faye. *Au Clare de Luce*. New York, 1943.

Hobson, Laura Z. *Laura Z: A Life: Years of Fulfillment*. New York, 1986.

Hughes, Emmet John. *The Ordeal of Power: A Political Memoir of the Eisenhower Years*. New York, 1963.

Hyatt, Carole, and Linda Gottlieb. *When Smart People Fail: Rebuilding Yourself for Success*. New York, 1987.

Ingersoll, Ralph. *The Great Ones*. New York, 1948.

Isherwood, Christopher. *Diaries, 1939–1960*. New York, 1997.

James, D. Clayton. *The Years of MacArthur: 1941–1945*, vol. 2. Boston, 1975.

James, Sidney L. *Press Pass: The Journalist's Tale*. Walnut Creek, Calif., 1944.

Jessup, John K. *The Ideas of Henry Luce*. New York, 1969.

Johnson, Dorris, and Ellen Leventhal, eds. *The Letters of Nunnally Johnson*. New York, 1981.

Johnson, Paul. *Modern Times: The World from the Twenties to the Eighties*. New York, 1983.

Judis, John B. *William F. Buckley, Jr.: Patron Saint of the Conservatives*. New York, 1988.

Junge, Traudl. *Until the Final Hour: Hitler's Last Secretary*. New York, 2004.

Kissinger, Henry. *White House Years*. Boston, 1979.

Kobler, John. *Luce: His Time, Life and Fortune*. New York, 1968.

Kurth, Peter. *American Cassandra: The Life of Dorothy Thompson*. Boston, 1990.

Lankford, Nelson. *The Last American Aristocrat: The Biography of Ambassador David K. E. Bruce, 1898–1977*. Boston, 1996.

Larrabee, Eric. *Commander in Chief: Franklin Delano Roosevelt, His Lieutenants & Their War*. New York, 1987.

Lash, Joseph P., ed. *From the Diaries of Felix Frankfurter, May 14, 1943*. New York, 1975.

Lawrenson, Helen. *Stranger at the Party*. New York, 1972/1975.

Lewis, C. S. *The Screwtape Letters*. London, 1942.

Luce, Clare Boothe. *Slam the Door Softly*. New York, 1971.

———. *The Twilight of God*. Regnery Human Affairs Pamphlet No. 44. Chicago, 1949.

———, ed. *Saints for Now*. New York, 1952.

Macmillan, Harold. *War Diaries: Politics and War in the Mediterranean 1943–1945*. New York, 1984.

Manchester, William. *American Caesar: Douglas MacArthur 1880–1964*. Boston, 1978.

Marks, Frederick J., III. *Wind over Sand: The Diplomacy of Franklin Roosevelt*. London, 1988.

Marlin, George J. *The American Catholic Voter*. South Bend, Ind., 2004.

Martin, Ralph G. *Henry and Clare: An Intimate Portrait of the Luces*. New York, 1991.

Matthews, T. S. *Name and Address*. New York, 1960.

Mauldin, Bill. *The Brass Ring*. New York, 1971.

———. *Up Front*. New York, 1945, 2000.

Miller, William. *Fishbait: The Memoirs of the Congressional Doorkeeper*. New York, 1977.

Moore, Grace. *You're Only Human Once*. New York, 1944.

Moorhead, Caroline, ed. *Selected Letters of Martha Gellhorn*. New York, 2006.

Moran, Lord Charles McMoran. *Churchill: Taken from the Diaries of Lord Moran: The Struggle for Survival 1940–1965*. Boston, 1966.

Morris, Edmund. *Dutch: A Memoir of Ronald Reagan*. New York, 1999.

Morris, Jan. *Destinations: Essays from Rolling Stone*. New York, 1980.

Morris, Sylvia Jukes. *Rage for Fame: The Ascent of Clare Boothe Luce*. New York, 1997.

Mosely, Leonard. *A Biography of Eleanor, Allen and John Foster Dulles and Their Family Network*. New York, 1978.

Mott, Michael. *The Seven Mountains of Thomas Merton*. Boston, 1984.

Murphy, Robert D. *Diplomat Among Warriors*. New York, 1964.

Nasaw, David. *The Patriarch: The Remarkable Life and Turbulent Times of Joseph P. Kennedy*. New York, 2012.

Neal, Steve. *Dark Horse: A Biography of Wendell Willkie*. New York, 1949.

Nixon, Richard M. *Leaders: Profiles and Reminiscences of Men Who Have Shaped the Modern World*. New York, 1982.

O'Hara, Constance. *Heaven Was Not Enough*. New York, 1955.

Page, Tim, ed. *The Diaries of Dawn Powell, 1931–1965*. South Royalton, Vt., 1995.

Parker, Robert L. *Carlos Chávez: Mexico's Modern-Day Orpheus*. Boston, 1983.

Payne, Graham, and Sheridan Morley, eds. *The Noël Coward Diaries*. Boston, 1982.

Prendergast, Curtis, with Geoffrey Colvin. *The World of Time Inc.: The Intimate History of a Changing Enterprise*, vol. 3, 1960–1980. New York, 1986.

Revel, Jean-François. *How Democracies Perish*. New York, 1984.

Reynolds, David. *In Command of History: Churchill Fighting and Writing the Second World War*. New York, 2005.

Rhodes, Richard. *The Making of the Atomic Bomb*. New York, 1988.

Roberts, Andrew. *Masters and Commanders: How Four Titans Won the War in the West, 1941–1945*. New York, 2009.

Roosevelt, Eleanor, and Lorena A. Hickok. *Ladies of Courage*. New York, 1954.

Scobey, Joan, and Lee Parr McGrath. *Celebrity Needlepoint*. New York, 1972.

Selznick, Irene Mayer. *A Private View*. New York, 1983.

Shadegg, Stephen. *Clare Boothe Luce: A Biography*. New York, 1970.

Sheed, Wilfrid. *Clare Boothe Luce*. New York, 1982.

Sheen, Fulton J. *Treasure in Clay: The Autobiography of Fulton J. Sheen*. New York, 1980.

BIBLIOGRAPHY

Smith, Jean Edward. *Eisenhower in War and Peace*. New York, 2012.

Sotheby's. *The Jewels and Objects of Vertu of the Honorable Clare Boothe Luce*. Sotheby's Auction Catalogue. New York, Apr. 19, 1988.

Stannard, Martin. *Evelyn Waugh: The Early Years 1903–1939*. London, 1986.

Stern, Michael. *An American in Rome*. New York, 1964.

Stone, Hicks. *Edward Durell Stone: A Son's Untold Story of a Legendary Architect*. New York, 2011.

Storr, Anthony. *Solitude*. New York, 1988.

Sulzberger, C. L. *A Long Row of Candles: Memoirs and Diaries, 1934–1954*. New York, 1969.

Swanberg, W. A. *Luce and His Empire*. New York, 1972.

Taussig, Betty Carney. *A Warrior for Freedom*. Manhattan, Kans., 1955.

Taylor, A. J. P. *Beaverbrook: A Biography*. New York, 1972.

Veseth, Michael. *Globaloney: Unraveling the Myths of Globalization*. Lanham, Md., 2006.

Weiner, Tim. *Legacy of Ashes: The History of the CIA*. New York, 2008.

Wendt, Gerald, and Donald Porter Geddes, eds. *The Atomic Age Opens*. Cleveland, 1946.

ARTICLES

Algeo, John and Adele. "Among the New Words." *American Speech* 65, no. 2 (Summer 1990).

"Ambassador Luce Takes Over." *Life*, May 11, 1953.

"Arsenic for the Ambassador." *Time*, July 23, 1956.

Barzini, Luigi. "Ambassador Luce, As Italians See Her." *Harper's Magazine*, July 1955.

Biskind, Morton S., MD. "DDT Poisoning and the Elusive 'Virus X': A New Cause for Gastro Enteritis." *American Journal of Digestive Diseases* 16, no. 3 (1949).

"Clare Boothe Luce." *Family Circle*, Feb. 1954.

Cohen, Sidney. "Complications Associated with Lysergic Acid Diethylamide (LSD-25)." *Journal of the American Medical Association* 181, no. 2 (July 14, 1962).

Davis, Maxine. "Clare Luce—What She Is and Why." *Look*, Jan. 25, 1944.

Delehanty, Thornton. "The Devil and Clare Bloothe Luce." *New York Herald Tribune*, Mar. 14, 1948.

Dielke, Heinz. "She Is an 'Old' Berliner." *Berliner Zeitung*, Sept. 20, 1957.

Fish, M. Steven. "After Stalin's Death: The Anglo-American Debate over a New Cold War." *Diplomatic History* 10, no. 4 (Fall 1986).

Foote, Timothy. "But If Enough of Us Get Killed Something May Happen . . ." *Smithsonian* 17, no. 8 (November 1986).

Gati, Charles. Council on Foreign Relations, "Hungary-Suez Crisis: Fifty Years On (Session 2)." Transcript Oct. 24, 2006.

"Globaloney Girl." *Collier's*, Mar. 27, 1943.

Harriman, Margaret Case. "The Candor Kid." *The New Yorker*, Jan. 4 and 11, 1941.

———. "Or Would You Rather Be Clare Boothe?" *Reader's Scope*, 1945.

Herzstein, Robert E. "Five Years with Henry Luce: Second Thoughts." *University of North Carolina Historian*, Newsletter of the Department of History (Summer 1996).

Hoagland, Marjorie. "CBL." *Ave Maria*, Nov. 7, 1953.

Lawrenson, Helen. "The Woman." *Esquire*, Aug. 1975.

Luce, Clare Boothe. "Converts and the Blessed Sacrament." *Sentinel of the Blessed Sacrament*, Nov.–Dec. 1950.

———. "God's Little Underwater Acre," parts 1–2. *Sports Illustrated*, Sept. 9 and 16, 1957.

———. "The Mystery of Our China Policy." *Plain Talk*, July 1949.

———. "Thoughts on Mexico." *Vogue*, Aug. 1950.

———. "The Foreign Service as an Arm of U.S. Policy." *Department of State Bulletin*, May 11, 1953.

———. "The Real Reason," parts 1–3. *McCall's*, Feb., Mar., April 1947.

———. "Woman: A Technological Castaway." *Encyclopædia Britannica Yearbook 1973*.

Mannes, Marya. "The Remarkable Mrs. Luce." *The Reporter*, Feb. 9, 1956.

Medoff, Rafael. "Clare Boothe Luce and the Holocaust: A CT Congresswoman's Fight for Justice." http://www.jewishledger.com/2012/04/clare-boothe-luce-and-the-holo caust-a-ct-congresswomans-fight-for-justice/.

Mencken, H. L. "Decibels Hit Ceiling in Keynote-Night Din." *Baltimore Sun*, June 22, 1948.

Owens, Joseph A. "Renewing Self in Simple Ways, Says Mrs. Clare Boothe Luce." *Catholic Transcript*, Sept. 18, 1958.

Palmer, Gretta. "The Lady and the Lion—in One." *Catholic Digest*, April 1953.

———. "The New Clare Luce." *Look*, Apr. 15, 1947.

Pascone, Tere. "U.S. Doughboy Is 'Great Hero' of the War." *Bridgeport Post*, Jan. 2, 1945.

Savoy, Maggie. "L'Ambasciatrice at Home Here." *Arizona Republic*, Nov. 24, 1958.

Siff, Stephen. "Henry Luce's Strange Trip: Coverage of LSD in *Time* and *Life*, 1954–68." *Journalism History* 34, no. 3 (Fall 2008).

Smith, Beverly, Jr. "Things They Wish They Hadn't Said." *Saturday Evening Post*, Sept. 19, 1959.

Stace, Walter T. "Man Against Darkness." *Atlantic Monthly*, Sept. 1948.

Sterling, Claire. "The Mess in Trieste." *The Reporter*, Nov. 10, 1953.

Talmey, Allene. "Clare Boothe . . . in a Velvet Glove." *Vogue*, Dec. 15, 1940.

Terrett, Virginia Rowe. "The Luce Touch." *The Woman*, Nov. 1944.

Truscott, Lucian K., IV. "The Unsentimental Warrior." Op-ed article. *The New York Times*, June 24, 2010.

White, Steven F. "De Gasperi Through American Eyes: Media and Public Opinion, 1945–1953." *Review of the Conference Group on Italian Politics and Society*, no. 61 (Fall–Winter 2005).

INTERVIEWS

Letitia Baldrige, Sir Isaiah Berlin, Simon Michael Bessie, Ruth Buchanan, William F. Buckley, Jr., Dr. Hayes Caldwell, Lady Jeanne Campbell, Ann Charnley, Talbot B. Clapp (interviewed by Marion Elizabeth Rodgers), Richard and Shirley Clurman, Frances Brokaw Corrias, Fleur Cowles, Jean Dalrymple, Arthur B. Dodge, Jr., Father James Dodge, Dominick Dunne, Philip Dunne (interviewed by Edmund Morris), Elbridge Durbrow, Dorothy Farmer, Joan H. Fitzpatrick, Arlene Francis, Gladys Freeman, Mrs. John Hill, Yousuf and Estrellita Karsh, Henry Kissinger, Edward Koczak, Clare Boothe Luce, Henry Luce III, Leila Hadley Luce, Samuel Marx, Elisabeth Moore, Albert P. Morano, Elizabeth Navarro, John Richardson, Dr. Michael Rosenbluth, Norman Ross, Irene M. Selznick, John Shea, Wilfrid Sheed, Hugh Sidey, Philip Simpson, Evelyn Stansky, Claire Sterling, Michael Stern, David Sulzberger, Stan Swinton, Mae Talley, Mary Lois Vega, Walton Wickett, Helen Worth.

ELECTRONIC

Campbell, Kenneth J. "Charles A. Willoughby: A Mixed Performance." Text of unpublished paper. *American Intelligence Journal* 18, no. 1–2 (1998). http://intellit .muskingum.edu/wwii_folder/wwiifepac_folder/wwiifepacwilloughby.html.

INCOM footage, Apr. 22, 1953. Archivio Storico Luce website. www.archivioluce .com.

Longines Chronoscope, Oct. 24, 1952. National Archives Identifier 95791. https:// archive.org/details/gov.archives.arc.95791.

McNarney, Joseph T. Biography. http://en.wikipedia.org/wiki/Joseph_T._McNarney.

Mountcastle, John W., Brigadier General, USA, Chief of Military History. "North Apennines 1944–1945." U.S. Army Center of Military History website. http:// www.history.army.mil/brochures/nap/72-34.htm.

Nordhausen. http://www.jewishgen.org/ForgottenCamps/Camps/MainCampsEng.html.

Prados, John. *Lost Crusader: The Secret Wars of CIA Director William Colby*. New York, 2003, 61. "Little Outside Information." http://www2.gwu.edu/~nsarchiv/NSAEBB/ NSAEBB206/.

Rimanelli, Marco. "Italy's Diplomacy and the West: From Allied Occupation in World War II to Equality in NATO, 1940s–50s." http://fch.fiu.edu/FCH-1999/Rimanelli -1999.htm.

Ürményházi, Attila J. *The Hungarian Revolution-Uprising, Budapest 1956*. Hobart, Tasmania, Feb. 2006, 15. http://www.americanhungarianfederation.org/docs/Urmeny hazi_HungarianRevolution_1956.pdf.

MISCELLANEOUS

"Are Communism and Democracy Mutually Antagonistic?" Radio debate on *The American Forum of the Air*, Mutual Broadcasting System, May 21, 1946. Text published by the Catholic Information Society, New York.

Chamberlain, John. Unpublished profile of CBL for *Time*, ca. 1946, CBLP.

Croci, Osvaldo. "The Trieste Crisis." PhD thesis, McGill University, 1991. http://digi tool.library.mcgill.ca/R/?func=dbin-jump-full&object_id=70276&local_base =GEN01-MCG02.

Luce, Clare Boothe. *The Double Bind*. Unpublished autobiographical novel, CBLP.

———. "Eisenhower Administration." Columbia University Oral History interview with John Luter, Jan. 11, 1968. Columbia University, New York, 1973.

———, and Vernon A. Walters. *History and the Nature of Man*. Vernon A. Walters Lectures in History. United States Naval Academy, Annapolis, Md., 1979.

Willis, Ronald Gary. "The Persuasion of Clare Boothe Luce." PhD dissertation, Indiana University, 1993.

NOTES

ABBREVIATIONS

ACB   Ann Clare Brokaw
CBL   Clare Boothe Luce
DFB   David Franklin Boothe
HRL   Henry Robinson Luce
SJM   Sylvia Jukes Morris

Unless otherwise cited, all interviews were conducted by the author.

1. DELAYED ENTRANCE

1. *Bridgeport Telegram*, Jan. 6, 1943; AP dispatch, Jan. 5, 1943. (Unless otherwise cited, Associated Press [AP] and United Press International [UPI] dispatches are in CBL's scrapbooks, CBLP.) CBL was the twenty-eighth woman to be elected to the House of Representatives.
2. *Greenwich Time*, Jan. 5, 1943.
3. Albert P. Morano to SJM, Oct. 6, 1982, SJMP. In 1943, the House Office Building was not yet named after Speaker Nicholas Longworth.
4. Ibid.
5. *Bridgeport Telegram*, Jan. 6, 1943.
6. CBL to SJM verbally on several occasions. CBL also used the line to humorous effect in speeches.
7. CBL may have gone to see Bernard Baruch, her early political mentor and lover, who had a suite at the Carlton Hotel.
8. Unidentified scrapbook clipping, ca. Jan. 1943, CBLP.
9. AP dispatch, Jan. 5, 1943.
10. *New York News*, Jan. 6, 1943.
11. AP dispatch, Jan. 5, 1943.
12. Unidentified scrapbook clipping, Jan. 6, 1943, CBLP.
13. *Bridgeport Telegram*, Jan. 6, 1943.
14. Ibid.

15. Unidentified scrapbook clipping, ca. 1943, CBLP; Margaret Case Harriman, "The Candor Kid," a two-part profile of CBL in *The New Yorker*, Jan. 4 and 11, 1941.
16. Unidentified scrapbook clipping, ca. 1943, CBLP.
17. The first female Representative was Jeanette Rankin. In her first term, 1917–1919, she was the only House member to vote against U.S. entry into World War I. She was defeated for reelection. Returning in 1941, she was the only electee to vote against entering World War II. She was again beaten in the next election. At age eighty-eight in 1968, Rankin led a group to the U.S. Capitol to protest the Vietnam War.
18. An assistant at Hattie Carnegie, where CBL shopped for clothes in the early 1940s, said she was "unstylish" and "a little frumpy," but "caught on quickly" to fashion advice. Evelyn Stansky interview, Apr. 5, 1988. By 1947, CBL was also patronizing Valentina and Bergdorf Goodman.
19. Eleanor Roosevelt in "My Day," *Washington Daily News*, Dec. 21, 1938, and to CBL, Jan. 19, 1939, CBLP. Also see Sylvia Jukes Morris, *Rage for Fame: The Ascent of Clare Boothe Luce* (New York, 1997), 336.
20. Morris, *Rage for Fame*, 393–96.
21. *New Haven Courier*, Jan. 19, 1943.
22. The following account of CBL's pre-congressional life summarizes the detailed narrative in Morris, *Rage for Fame*.
23. Ibid., 42 and 51–52.
24. Ibid., 101.
25. Ibid., 114.
26. Ibid., 188–89.
27. Ibid., 3–13, 290–95, 365–68.
28. Ibid., 323–24 and 351–56.
29. Ibid., 397.
30. Ibid., 421.
31. Virginia Rowe Terrett, "The Luce Touch," *The Woman*, Nov. 1944.

2. GLOBALONEY

1. James MacGregor Burns, *Roosevelt: The Soldier of Freedom* (New York, 1970), 305; *Bridgeport Life*, Jan. 9, 1943, commented that CBL had an objective, nonpartisan attitude toward FDR, unlike Dr. Austin, who invariably opposed him.
2. Burns, *Roosevelt*, 307.
3. Ibid., 307.
4. *New York Herald Tribune*, Jan. 22, 1943.
5. *The New York Times*, Jan. 13, 1943; unidentified scrapbook clipping, ca. 1943, CBLP.
6. Ibid.
7. Letitia Baldrige, *A Lady, First: My Life in the Kennedy White House and the American Embassies of Paris and Rome* (New York, 2002), 98–99.
8. John Billings diary, Jan. 15, 1943, JBP.
9. Wes Bailey to Joe Thorndike, Jan. 28, 1943, CBLP.
10. Ibid.
11. HRL to CBL, Nov. 22, 1937, CBLP.
12. Morris, *Rage for Fame*, 388.
13. *Greenwich Time*, Jan. 19, 1943.
14. Notes and transcripts, Jan.–May 1943, NAMC.
15. During the Casablanca conference, FDR told his son Elliott that the Pacific war

was partly due to the greed of British, French, and Dutch colonists competing in Asia for resources Japan also needed.

16. *Sun Herald* scrapbook clipping, Jan. 31, 1943, CBLP.

17. The housing shortage was acute, because as many as five thousand young women a month, mainly typists, were arriving in D.C. to fill government office jobs. Since Pearl Harbor, civilian employees of the armed services had grown from seven thousand to forty-one thousand. David Brinkley, *Washington Goes to War* (New York, 1988), chapter 5. Isabel Hill was a blue-blooded Southerner. Joan Hill Fitzpatrick to SJM, Mar. 15, 1988, SJMP.

18. *Bridgeport Post*, Mar. 19, 1944.

19. Isabel Hill memo to CBL, Nov. 19, 1942, CBLP; *The New Yorker*, Feb. 4, 1943; John Chamberlain, draft profile of CBL for *Life*, unpublished transcript, 1946, JBP (hereafter "Chamberlain CBL profile"); Maxine Davis, "Clare Luce—What She Is and Why," *Look*, Jan. 25, 1944.

20. Dr. Austin lost the 1940 election by 953 votes.

21. Albert P. Morano interview, Oct. 6, 1981. William F. Buckley, Jr., said that Morano was "the most deliberate man I've ever met in my life." William F. Buckley, Jr., interview, Sept. 8, 1983. "Globaloney Girl," *Collier's*, Mar. 27, 1943, remarked that CBL "might even get to be president."

22. CBL to Alice Basim, Jan. 31, 1943, ABP. Alice married Dr. Austin in Sept. 1939. She was thirty-one, and he was sixty-two. He died in Jan. 1942, and she married Donald S. Basim in July 1949.

23. Letitia Baldrige, who worked for CBL in the 1950s, said that she could "be crying on the outside and laughing on the inside." Letitia Baldrige interview, Mar. 15, 1988.

24. Morris, *Rage for Fame*, 402–04.

25. Marilyn Bender and Selig Altschul, *The Chosen Instrument: Juan Trippe, Pan Am: The Rise and Fall of an American Entrepreneur* (New York, 1982), 375–76.

26. *Time*, Feb. 22, 1943, reported on the Democrats' expectation re China.

27. The following quotations are taken from "'America in the Post-War Air World: Be Practical—Ration Globaloney,' by Clare Boothe Luce, Congresswoman from Connecticut. Delivered in the House of Representatives, Washington, D.C., Feb. 9, 1943," *Vital Speeches of the Day* (New York, 1943), 331–36.

28. CBL to Professor Martha Weisman of the Department of Speech, City College of New York, Aug. 25, 1971, on how best to impress an audience.

29. The idea that the world would be shrunk by universal air travel was not new. Wendell Willkie, after losing the 1940 presidential election to FDR, had flown thirty-one thousand miles around the earth in forty-nine days to talk with ordinary citizens, as well as civilian and military leaders in many countries. "The net impression of my trip," he wrote in a subsequent book, "was not of distance from other peoples, but of closeness to them . . . the world has become small and completely interdependent." Wendell Willkie, *One World* (New York, 1943), 1–2. Willkie briefed the President and broadcast a summary of his travels to an audience of thirty-six million, saying, "There are no distant points in the world any longer." A chorus of listeners applauded his words, CBL among them. Steve Neal, *Dark Horse: A Biography of Wendell Willkie* (New York, 1984), 260–61.

30. The Churchill words that CBL parodied were, "We mean to hold our own. I did not become His Majesty's first minister in order to preside over the liquidation of the British Empire."

31. Eleanor Roosevelt press conference, Feb. 11, 1943, unidentified scrapbook clipping, CBLP.

32. Tim Page, ed., *The Diaries of Dawn Powell* (South Royalton, Vt., 1995), 213. In a letter to a Mr. Miller on Nov. 1, 1944, Powell described CBL as "such a dreary, totally one-dimensional insignificant creature." A copy of this letter was given to SJM by Powell's biographer, Tim Page. John Billings recorded that the main news at the Luce offices was of Mrs. Luce, and at a University Club lunch, "All the talk was of post-war aviation and who's going to get the air lanes." John Billings diary, Feb. 10, 1943, JBP.

33. Dorothea Philp memo to CBL, ca. Mar. 15, 1943, CBLP.

34. William P. Simm of Scripps-Howard, quoted in *Time*, Feb. 22, 1943.

35. Dorothea Philp memo to CBL, ca. Mar. 15, 1943, CBLP; *Saturday Review*, Feb. 20, 1943.

36. CBL to Alice Basim, Mar. 23, 1943, ABP. Notwithstanding the criticism leveled at CBL's coinage in 1943, *globaloney* entered the language, and achieved a new application in the "globalized" 1990s. See John and Adele Algeo, "Among the New Words," *American Speech* 65, no. 2 (Summer 1990), and Michael Veseth, *Globaloney: Unraveling the Myths of Globalization* (Lanham, Md., 2006).

37. Quoted in Stephen Shadegg, *Clare Boothe Luce* (New York, 1970), 68.

38. William Miller, *Fishbait* (New York, 1977), 67.

3. TURNING FORTY

1. John Billings diary, Feb. 12, 1943, JBP.

2. Ibid.

3. *Pittsburgh Press*, Mar. 2, 1943.

4. List compiled by Helena Hill Wood and presented to the House of Representatives by CBL on Feb. 15, 1943, CBLP.

5. Morris, *Rage for Fame*, chapter 10.

6. Ibid.

7. Emily D. Barringer, chairman of the Connecticut State Committee of the NWP, to CBL, Jan. 2, 1943. CBL replied, apologizing, on Jan. 4, 1943, CBLP.

8. *Bridgeport Herald*, Feb. 28, 1943, CBLP.

9. CBL to Emily D. Barringer, June 8, 1943, BLP. When CBL was asked by the Connecticut State Committee to speak in favor of the ERA, Al Morano advised against it, saying that it might be hard to arouse public interest when the legislature was in recess and people were heading for the seashore. Morano memo to CBL, June 1, 1943, CBLP.

10. CBL to FDR, ca. Mar. 4, 1943, quoted in Shadegg, *Clare Boothe Luce*, 171.

11. Ibid.

12. Steve Early to CBL, Mar. 8, 1943, CBLP.

13. *Washington Star*, Mar. 11, 1943; *Bridgeport Post*, Mar. 11, 1943; *The New York Times*, Mar. 11, 1943. "The late President Roosevelt bothered actually to dislike few people, they lacked the capacity sufficiently to hit 'home ground' with him. Mrs. Luce he apparently disliked and feared." Marjorie Hoagland, "Clare Boothe Luce," *Ave Maria*, Nov. 7, 1953. In a *People* magazine interview, July 25, 1977, CBL said of FDR: "I was very critical of him at one time, but all his lies [about not sending Americans to war] were in the interest of the United States. I owe him an apology."

14. CBL to Charles Willoughby, Mar. 15, 1943, CBLP.

15. Burns, *Roosevelt*, 363.

16. CBL, Klein Memorial speech, broadcast Apr. 17 and reported in the *Bridgeport Herald*, Apr. 18, 1943; *Ansonia Sentinel* (Conn.), Mar. 30, 1943.

17. Morris, *Rage for Fame*, 16. CBL not only continued to observe April 10 as her

birthday, but had the false date engraved on her tombstone. To avoid confusion, textual references to CBL's "birthday" in this book conform to the fictional date.

18. *Washington Herald*, Apr. 19, 1943.

4. THE MOST TALKED-ABOUT MEMBER

1. *The Boston Globe*, Apr. 27, 1943.
2. Ibid. Also see Faye Henle, *Au Clare de Luce* (New York, 1943), 195–99.
3. *New York Mirror*, May 16, 1943.
4. Joseph Lash, ed., *From the Diaries of Felix Frankfurter* (New York, 1975), 240.
5. "What's Mrs. Luce After?," *Bridgeport Post*, July 18, 1943; Harold L. Ickes diary, May 23, 1943, LC.
6. CBL to Pearl Buck, July 20, 1959, CBLP.
7. Gretta Palmer, "The New Clare Luce," *Look*, Apr. 15, 1947. House consideration of the Wayward Wives Bill took place in late Sept. 1943.
8. Congressman May was convicted after World War II of accepting bribes from military contractors. He served time in prison along with another of CBL's committee colleagues, Parnell Thomas.
9. *Newark Star Ledger*, July 26, 1943.
10. Ibid.
11. Smith Dawless, "Elegy," *CBI Roundup* ca. June 1943, http://cbi-theater-3.home.comcast.net/~cbi-theater-3/verses/dawless-09.html.
12. CBL to Charles Willoughby, Mar. 15, 1943, CBLP; Willoughby to CBL n.d., ca. Mar. 1943, CBLP.
13. William Manchester, *American Caesar: Douglas MacArthur 1880–1964* (Boston, 1978), 357.
14. Ibid., 78; and Eric Larrabee, *Commander in Chief: Franklin Delano Roosevelt, His Lieutenants and Their War* (New York, 1987), 330.
15. CBL, "What Is America's Foreign Policy?," *Congressional Record* 89, pt. 5, 6428ff.
16. *Washington Times-Herald*, June 27, 1943; *Bridgeport Sunday Post*, July 18, 1943.
17. CBL, "What Is America's Foreign Policy?"; *Bridgeport Sunday Post*, July 18, 1943.
18. *Washington Times-Herald*, June 27, 1943.
19. Ronald Gary Willis, "The Persuasion of Clare Boothe Luce," PhD dissertation, Indiana University (Bloomington, 1993), 88; Maria Braden, *Women Politicians and the Media* (Lexington, Ky., 1996), 43.
20. Shadegg, *Clare Boothe Luce*, 178.
21. Ibid.
22. John Billings diary, Apr. 19, 1943, JBP; Dan Longwell to Billings, Apr. 24, 1943, JBP.
23. John Billings diary, Feb. 18 and Apr. 19, 1943, JBP.
24. *New York Mirror*, July 9, 1943.
25. Quoted in Chamberlain CBL profile, JBP.
26. *Philadelphia Enquirer*, July 11, 1943.
27. Ibid.

5. SUMMER INTERLUDE

1. CBL's headquarters were in the Salvatore Building on Greenwich Avenue.
2. Davis, "Clare Luce—What She Is and Why."
3. CBL interview, Dec. 12, 1981. The complex relationship between CBL and DFB is fully discussed in Morris, *Rage for Fame*.

4. CBL interview, June 13, 1982.

5. CBL, "The Double-Bind," unpublished autobiographical novel, 83, CBLP.

6. Nora Dawes's list of items she wanted the Luces to pay for, dated July 14, 1940, CBLP. See *Rage for Fame*, 389–92, for DFB's problems.

7. The amounts were meticulously compiled by Harry's accountants. By his own reckoning, DFB had "borrowed" or outright stolen some $250,000 from CBL before her marriage to HRL, in the course of handling stock transactions for her over the years. The sum of $190,000 was in addition to that. Due to his mismanagement, her 1929 Brokaw alimony of $425,000 had been reduced by 1941 to just over $266,000. With gifts from Harry of Time Inc. stock totaling $58,000 and miscellaneous royalties from her writing, she had a gross income in 1941 of just over $73,000. After deducting business expenses and charity payments of $2,500, she had a net income of $40,290. In current dollars, this is approximately $500,000 for the year.

8. CBL to DFB, July 3, 1942, CBLP.

9. ACB diary, July 16, 1943, CBLP.

10. Ibid.

11. Ibid., July 17, 1943, CBLP.

12. Ibid.

13. Ibid., July 18, 1943, CBLP. CBL and Willoughby may have been sending ACB a signal in their play reading. Benavente's play is the story of two frustrated royal lovers.

14. ACB diary, Aug. 2, 1942, CBLP. "Buckey Fuller—Mother told me that he and Nehru are the two greatest minds she has met. Buckey is terribly stimulating and I feel with him that here is a mind greater than mother's."

15. ACB diary, July 25, 1939, and Sept. 5, 1942, CBLP.

16. Walton Wickett to SJM, Nov. 15, 1983, SJMP.

17. Wickett to CBL, Mar. 6, 1986, CBLP; ACB diary, Jan. 17, 1940, CBLP.

18. Wickett to CBL, Mar. 31, 1943, WWP.

19. See Morris, *Rage for Fame*, chapters 1 and 2.

20. CBL on Ann's voice, quoted in Frederick Van Ryan, "Dream Job," *Redbook*, Nov. 1942.

21. ACB to James Rea, May 2, 1943, mentions the Sorbonne as first choice, CBLP.

22. ACB diary, Mar. 4, 1943, CBLP.

23. Ibid., May 27, 1942, CBLP.

24. Ibid., July 25, 1939, CBLP.

25. ACB to CBL, undated, and May 15, 1943, CBLP.

26. ACB to CBL, July 7, 1943, CBLP.

27. ACB diary, Jan. 26, 1940, CBLP. Other examples of ACB's loneliness, ibid., Sept. 27, 1940, CBLP.

28. Ibid., Nov. 9, 1941, CBLP; ACB to Walton Wickett, Jan. n.d., 1942, WWP.

29. HRL to ACB, Nov. 24, 1943, said he was giving Ann a certificate for seventy shares of Time Inc. stock, "as much as was allowed under the tax laws," CBLP. CBL told ACB that "if Mr. Roosevelt doesn't spoil everything," she would have an income of $35,000 annually at twenty-one. ACB diary, Sept. 9, 1940, CBLP.

30. Ibid., Apr. 18, 1942, CBLP.

31. Ibid., May 23, 1942, CBLP.

32. Ibid., June 27, 1943, CBLP.

33. Ibid., Dec. 28, 1942, CBLP.

34. CBL to Walton Wickett, Apr. 11, 1943, CBLP.

35. ACB had met Geza Korvin in the summer of 1942, when he was performing in her mother's play *Love Is a Verb* in Abingdon, Virginia. Despite her hasty judgment of him, Geza, a graduate of the Sorbonne, was destined for starring roles opposite the likes of Merle Oberon as a contract player with Universal Studios.

36. ACB diary, Sept. 18, 1942, CBLP.

37. James Rea was a Phi Beta Kappa graduate of MIT and pilot employed by Pan Am. James Rea to CBL, Feb. 26, 1944, CBLP.

38. Wickett to SJM, Nov. 12, 1983, SJMP.

39. ACB to James Rea, July 1, 1943, CBLP.

40. ACB diary, Oct. 26, 1943, CBLP.

41. Walton Wickett to Norman Ross, another friend of Ann Brokaw, Nov. 4, 1987, WWP.

42. ACB to Wickett, Feb. 9, 1942, WWP.

43. Charles Willoughby to ACB, July 21, 1945, CBLP.

44. ACB to CBL, Aug. 2, 1943, CBLP.

45. While on reconnaissance thirty-five yards from the enemy lines at Bataan on Jan. 24, 1942, Willoughby had rescued a wounded officer. "Without a helmet and in disregard of his personal safety," the soldier afterward reported, "he made his way through the jungle to my position and assisted me to the rear through a concentration of hostile mortar fire." HQ report, Feb. 23, 1942, sent by Willoughby to CBL, CBLP.

46. DFB to CBL, July 28, 1943, CBLP.

47. Helen Lawrenson, *Stranger at the Party: A Memoir* (New York, 1972), 122. Quotations taken from Lawrenson's own summary of CBL's letter. Efforts to trace the original have been unsuccessful.

48. Ibid. Lawrenson was now married to Jack Lawrenson, a founder of the National Maritime Union.

49. Helen Lawrenson to CBL, July 27, 1943, CBLP.

50. CBL 1935 manuscript, CBLP.

51. *Bridgeport Herald*, Aug. 15, 1943.

52. CBL speech, Aug. 9, 1943, CBLP.

53. CBL to Sir Archibald Clarke Kerr, Dec. 18, 1942, CBLP. Indira Gandhi agreed. "My father," she said, "was the closest thing you could find to a saint in a normal man." But "he wasn't at all a politician. . . . He was sustained in his work only by a blind faith in India." Oriana Fallaci, *Interview with History* (New York, 1976), 173–74.

54. CBL admitted to having fallen "a bit in love" with the elegant Brahmin and immediately began to correspond with him on the subject closest to his heart: Indian independence. CBL to Colonel Frank Roberts, June 28, 1942, CBLP.

55. Nehru to CBL, May 5, 1942, CBLP; Morris, *Rage for Fame*, 457.

56. CBL to Nehru, June 4, 1942, CBLP.

57. Nehru to CBL, Oct. 7, 1958, CBLP.

58. Charles Willoughby to CBL, Dec. 29, 1943, CBLP.

6. LUMINOUS LADY

1. Washington's Stage Door Canteen opened on Oct. 4, 1942. It depended on donors for financing, and spent about $600 each night entertaining two thousand servicemen. Older women chaperoned the young hostesses, who wore red, white, and blue aprons and were forbidden to see the men when off duty. It closed on Jan. 23, 1946. General Eisenhower and his wife were the honored guests at the final party.

By then, six thousand volunteers had entertained more than two million service personnel. Sarah Booth Conroy, "Revisiting the Stage Door Canteen," *The Washington Post*, Jan. 31, 1991.

2. *Washington Times Herald*, Sept. 29, 1943.
3. CBL to HRL, "Sunday night," ca. Oct. 3, 1943, CBLP.
4. CBL to HRL, n.d., ca. Sept. 1943, SJMP.
5. Ibid.
6. CBL to Alice Basim, Oct. 27, 1943, ABP.
7. Ibid., Oct. 12, 1943, ABP.
8. CBL to ACB, "Wednesday," n.d. but possibly Oct. 20, 1943, CBLP.
9. John Billings diary, Dec. 20, 1943, JBP.
10. CBL to ACB, Oct. 29, 1943, CBLP.
11. Ibid. *Love Is a Verb*, a play about aphrodisiacs, was originally called *The Yohimbe Tree*. It was first performed under its new title at the Barter Theatre in Abingdon, Virginia, in Aug. 1942. To disguise her authorship, CBL mischievously adopted the pseudonym "Karl Weidenbach" for the Barter production. This was the name on Willoughby's German birth certificate. Morris, *Rage for Fame*, 463. The New York production did not take place.
12. Eventually, the Red Army would bring about some 75 percent of all German losses in manpower and matériel. John and Carol Garrard, in a letter to *The New York Times*, May 7, 2006.
13. Charles Willoughby to CBL, n.d., 1943, told her that her letters to him were never censored if they carried an appropriately coded address. CBLP.
14. Ibid.
15. Ibid.
16. Willoughby to CBL, Oct. 11, 1943, CBLP; *Time*, July 3, 1943.
17. Willoughby to CBL, Oct. 11, 1943, CBLP.
18. Ibid., Oct. 22, 1943, CBLP.
19. CBL to ACB, Nov. 7 [misdated Nov. 5], 1943, CBLP.
20. Ibid.
21. Morris, *Rage for Fame*, 442–45; CBL to HRL, Jan. 1, 1942, CBLP.
22. Jane Fletcher Geniesse, *Passionate Nomad: The Life of Freya Stark* (New York, 2001), 310–11; Caroline Moorehead, *Freya Stark* (New York, 1985), 86.
23. Ibid.
24. Faye Henle radio interview with Warren Bower, WNYC, Dec. 27, 1943, transcript in CBLP.
25. Harriman, "The Candor Kid."
26. Henle, *Au Clare de Luce*, 2.
27. Ibid., 20. Henle's biography was the first of an eventual eight biographies or book-length studies of CBL and her plays by 2014.
28. Faye Henle radio interview, CBLP.
29. John Billings diary, Aug. 28, 1943, JBP. When Billings first heard about the Henle book, he said he hoped it gave CBL "hell because she certainly has stuck her neck out and deserves it. Except I'm sorry for Harry. But then he chucked Lila and married Clare all of his own free will." John Billings diary, Aug. 12, 1943, JBP.
30. *Birmingham News*, Nov. 21, 1943; *Bridgeport Herald*, Dec. 5, 1943; *Chicago Sun*, Nov. 21, 1943, *Hartford Times*, Nov. 1, 1943.
31. *New York Post*, Nov. 22, 1943.
32. CBL to SJM verbally on many occasions.
33. CBL to ACB, ca. Dec. 1943, CBLP; CBL interview, Mar. 15, 1982. CBL accused HRL of being parsimonious over presents. Yet he often gave her a leather purse

with Time Inc. stock inside, along with extravagant "guilt" gifts of paintings and jewelry, usually when he was having an extramarital affair.

34. SJM notes on original tapestry, now privately owned. See also Joan Scobey and Lee Parr McGrath, *Celebrity Needlepoint* (New York, 1972), 75–77.

35. CBL to HRL, Nov. 23, 1943, CBLP.

36. CBL to SJM verbally on several occasions; CBL to ACB, Nov. 25, 1943, CBLP.

37. Burns, *Roosevelt*, 406–07.

38. Letters to CBL from Norman Stone of Maryland, Dec. 1, 1943; E. E. Evans of Kansas City, Dec. 4, 1943; and E. Willimon of Florida, Nov. 3, 1943, Congressional Correspondence for 1943, CBLP.

39. Julia McCarthy, "Capitol Pin-Up Girl," *New York Daily News*, Dec. 2, 1943.

40. *The New York Times*, Dec. 24, 1943.

41. *New York Daily News*, Dec. 4, 1943.

42. *Charleston Gazette* (W.Va.), Dec. 16, 1943.

43. *The New York Times*, quoting Noël Coward, Dec. 10, 1943.

44. Coward had been in Portugal en route from the United States, where he had stayed at the White House and interviewed Franklin Roosevelt. Barry Day, ed., *The Letters of Noël Coward* (New York, 2007), 398. Clare knew nothing of Noël's secret assignment in 1940, simply noting how pale and frightened he looked as he said that England would "never, never, surrender." She tried to cheer him up by quoting Shakespeare's "Once more unto the breach" soliloquy from *Henry V*. Morris, *Rage for Fame*, 86, 165, 386–87.

45. Graham Payne and Sheridan Morley, eds., *Noël Coward's Diaries* (Boston, 1982), 23.

46. On Dec. 14, 1943, CBL aired her views about America's postwar relations with China at the Wilson Auditorium in Cincinnati. On Dec. 15, she spoke in Fairmont, West Virginia, and derided FDR and the New Deal.

7. IMPACT

1. ACB to James Rea, Dec. 9, 1943, and July 1, 1943, CBLP.

2. ACB diary, Dec. 18 and Dec. 26, 1942, CBLP.

3. The Selznicks were occasional neighbors of the Luces at the Waldorf Towers. ACB considered the voluble and flamboyant producer of *Gone With the Wind* "revolting" and frowned on her parents' friendship with him. ACB diary, Dec. 21, 1942, CBLP; Morris, *Rage for Fame*, 438.

4. Irene Selznick interviews, Feb. 1988.

5. Ibid.

6. ACB diary, Aug. 19, 1942, CBLP.

7. Ibid., Dec. 3 and 13, 1942, CBLP.

8. Ibid., Jan. 25, 1943, CBLP.

9. Walton Wickett to CBL, Mar. 31, 1943, CBLP.

10. ACB to Wickett, Dec. 2, 1942, WWP.

11. Walton Wickett interview, Nov. 12, 1983, SJMP. Wickett later switched to Pan Am's engineering department. He was trained in rocketry, and in 1945 would move to the Manhattan Project and work on fitting atomic bombs into a modified B-29 as used at Hiroshima and Nagasaki.

12. Wickett to SJM, Nov. 6, 1983, SJMP.

13. In her diary on Dec. 28, 1942, ACB had written: "Well, here I am all but married to Mr. Wickett. I am so elated with the wonderful impression he has made on Mom and Pop and everyone . . . think I was a 'bad reporter' that he is quite handsome

even, that he is charming, poised and intelligent. Wheeeeeee! Now all I have to do is let my heart go ahead, and fall in love with him all it wants!" The next day she wrote: "Doubt has once more crept back into my mind." But later in the entry she said if, after graduating, she still liked "Walt and vice versa I will marry him." ACB diary, Dec. 29, 1942, CBLP.

14. Wickett to SJM, Nov. 6, 1983, SJMP.
15. ACB diary, Jan. 4, 1943, CBLP. ACB described Frances de Villers Fonda as "making a home for her slouch backed stupid acting husband, the pink eyed Henry Fonda." ACB diary, Jan. 4, 1943, and Nov. 22, 1941, CBLP. ACB's animus vis-à-vis Fonda might have been instigated by CBL. Fonda reportedly "couldn't stand Clare. He was not one for small talk, and she once said to him, 'Hank, don't you have anything to say for yourself?' He didn't care for her after that." Frances Brokaw Corrias interview, Feb. 24, 1988. After Henry Fonda asked his wife for a divorce, she committed suicide in Apr. 1950, on her forty-second birthday, by slashing her throat.
16. ACB to Mr. and Mrs. Thornburg, Jan. 3, 1944, CBLP.
17. Samuel Marx interview, Aug. 20, 1987.
18. *Spokane Spokesman*, Jan. 12, 1944.
19. CBL to Irene Selznick, Mar. 9, 1944, ISP.
20. ACB to Wickett, Dec. 2, 1942, Nov. 3, 1943, and Oct. 25, 1943, WWP. Wickett suspected that ABC and he were dating again only because she had broken up with James Rea. ACB to Wickett, Oct. 25, 1943, WWP; Wickett to ACB, Nov. 1, 1943, WWP; Wickett to SJM, Nov. 6, 1943, SJMP.
21. Sidney L. James, *Press Pass: The Journalist's Tale* (Walnut Creek, Calif., 1944), 171.
22. Report of Officer Ben Hickey, Jan. 12, 1944, CBLP.
23. Ibid. Dr. Anna F. Barnett declared Ann dead, and Dr. Blake C. Wilbur peformed the hospital examination.
24. *San Francisco Examiner*, Jan. 12, 1943.
25. List of contents of ACB's briefcase, CBLP.
26. CBL quoted in Isabel Hill to ACB, Nov. 22, 1943, CBLP.
27. Virginia L. Blood report on the events of the day, "Midnight, Jan. 11," CBLP.
28. CBL to SJM verbally on numerous occasions.
29. Rosalie Noland Gumbrill to SJM, Aug. 8, 1987, SJMP.
30. CBL to ACB, n.d., ca. 1943, CBLP.
31. Walton Wickett interview, Nov. 12, 1983. Ewell Sale told Wickett that she was asked "to knot Ann's hair, filament by filament, across the gash of the wound."
32. Colonel William Cobb to CBL, Jan. 11, 1944, CBLP.
33. Charles Hobbs to CBL, Nov. 21, 1942, CBLP; CBL to Hobbs, Nov. 29, 1942, CBLP.
34. Virginia Blood report, "Midnight, Jan. 11," 1944, CBLP.
35. James, *Press Pass*, 171; CBL to Irene Selznick, Mar. 9, 1944, ISP.
36. *The New York Times*, Jan. 12, 1944, reported HRL's arrival by train.
37. John Billings diary, Jan. 11, 1944, JBP.
38. Jean Dalrymple interview, Feb. 6, 1988. In Dalrymple's opinion, CBL had kept Ann in the background, because she herself looked young and "didn't want people to know she had a daughter that old." In fact, CBL never lied about her own age, and the more mature Ann became, the more she tried to include her in gatherings of her friends, eminent or not.
39. HRL wire to CBL, Jan. 11, 1944, CBLP.
40. Ibid.
41. John Billings diary, Jan. 11, 1944, JBP; HRL to CBL, Jan. 12, 1944, CBLP.

42. Virginia Blood report, "Midnight, Jan. 11," CBLP.
43. Ibid.
44. Walton Wickett interview, Nov. 13, 1983. It was clear, almost forty years later, that the wound of ACB's death was still raw for Wickett. As for the likelihood in 1944 of a rosy future with her, he remarked, "Happiness is determined by how well a man can deceive himself."
45. James, *Press Pass*, 171.
46. Norman Ross interview, Oct. 2, 1989.
47. Isabel Hill to DFB, Jan. 12, 1944, CBLP.
48. William B. Cobb to CBL, May 13, 1979, CBLP. Though Cobb's time with CBL was brief, he developed a tremendous respect for her, and in a letter to her thirty-five years later, he said that he never forgot her bravery and forbearance on the day of Ann's death. James, *Press Pass*, 173.
49. Kurt Bergel wire to CBL, 10:39 P.M., Sept. 11, 1944, CBLP.
50. Chief of Police H. A. Zinc of Palo Alto, reporting to HRL after "a careful investigation." Detailed notes written by Virginia Blood, "Thursday morning," Jan. 13, 1944, CBLP.
51. Report by Chief of Police H. A. Zink, on file at Palo Alto Police Department, as recorded by Virginia Blood, Sept. 13, 1944, CBLP. Also Officer Ben Hickey's reports dated Jan. 11 and 12, 1944, CBLP.
52. M. T. Moore memo to HRL, Feb. 3, 1944, CBLP. Lawyers advised HRL that none of Bergel's derelictions warranted civil or criminal action. Unless CBL elected to press charges, California authorities were unlikely to proceed, since proving negligence beyond a reasonable doubt would be next to impossible.
53. An undated draft of HRL's letter to Kurt Bergel, CBLP. Bergel was a married multilingual German-Jewish refugee who had tried unsuccessfully to enter the U.S Armed Forces. Memo to HRL from Henry G. Hayes, CBLP.
54. HRL to Charles Hobbs, Jan. 15, 1944, CBLP.
55. Walton Wickett interview, Nov. 12, 1983.
56. Ibid. The seals may have been those that appear on rocks near the Golden Gate Bridge.
57. Ibid.
58. Ibid. CBL pitied the young men who had loved her daughter. James Rea recalled a letter from her so warm and sympathetic that it brought tears to his eyes. James Rea to CBL, Feb. 6, 1944, CBLP.
59. Walton Wickett interview, Nov. 12, 1983.
60. Funeral arrangements and program, CBLP.
61. ACB thesis, CBLP.

8. AFTERMATH

1. Norman Ross interview, Oct. 2, 1989.
2. Al Morano interview, Oct. 6, 1981.
3. The Reverend Wallace Martin conducted Ann's service. CBLP has several pages of notes and memos on the funeral plans. The Luces and their guests spent Tuesday night at Yeamans Hall Club in Charleston. HRL was reimbursed $4,069.68 for ACB's funeral expenses by her estate.
4. John Billings diary, Feb. 26, 1944, JBP.
5. CBL cable to HRL, Jan. 27, 1944, CBLP.
6. John Billings diary, Jan. 28, 1943, JBP.
7. Ibid., Jan. 28 and 22, 1944, JBP.

8. Davis, "Clare Luce—What She Is and Why."

9. CBL to ER, Feb. 4, 1944, FDRL.

10. CBL to Laura Hobson, Feb. 1, 1944, LZHP.

11. JFK to CBL, Jan. 11, 1944, CBLP. CBL had recently given JFK an old gold coin that had belonged to her mother. He reciprocated by sending her a letter opener, the handle of which was made from a machine-gun shell, and the blade from a part of the PT boat that he was skippering in the Pacific when a Japanese destroyer cut it in two. He and his crew of ten survivors were missing for a week, and rescued after they sent an SOS on a coconut. The opener was inscribed, "PT-109 New Georgia, 8-2-43." Also see Morris, Rage for Fame, 436, 445.

12. DFB to CBL, Jan. 21, 1944, CBLP.

13. CBL's graying hair was mentioned in Davis, "Clare Luce—What She Is and Why."

14. The New York Times, Feb. 17, 1944.

15. Ibid., Apr. 16, 1943.

16. CBL to John Elson, June 13, 1968, TIA. CBL said that she "wanted to bow out" of her second campaign, but HRL "insisted she go forward."

17. Olive Clapper quoted by Alden Hatch in a series of interviews for his biography of CBL. Hereafter "Hatch interviews," AHP.

18. For new perspectives on the Italian campaign, see Matthew Parker, Monte Cassino: The Hardest-Fought Battle of World War II (New York, 1904), and Rick Atkinson, The Day of Battle: The War in Sicily and Italy, 1943–1944 (New York, 2007).

19. The New York Times, Mar. 22, 25, 1944.

20. Mark Clark, Calculated Risk (New York, 1950), 310; Shadegg, Clare Boothe Luce, 192. U.S. military strength had been on a par with Portugal in Dec. 1941.

21. Shadegg, Clare Boothe Luce, 192.

22. CBL to Gerald Heard, Nov. 20, 1959, copy in SJMP.

23. CBL to Irene Selznick, Mar. 9, 1944, ISP.

24. Ibid.

25. In a letter of Oct. 20, ca. 1943, CBL thanked her personal physician, Dr. Milton Rosenbluth, for his help over the last ten years. "It's not the pills, or the diet lists or the injections ... it's knowing always there's someone I can really talk to." CBLP.

26. Al Grover told Billings in 1948 that CBL "had been drunk for six months after her daughter's death." John Billings diary, Feb. 25, 1948, JBP. If true, this marked the resumption of CBL's tendency, dating back to Vanity Fair days, to use alcohol as a stimulant during late-night stints of writing and editing. At parties in the early 1930s, she had often drunk so much brandy that friends warned that she was becoming dependent on it. See Morris, Rage for Fame, 90, 132, 181, 199, 223, 254.

27. CBL to Alice Basim, Apr. 12, 1944, ABP.

9. CAMPAIGN '44

1. Geoffrey Perret, Old Soldiers Never Die: The Life of Douglas MacArthur (Holbrook, Mass., 1996), 386; D. Clayton James, The Years of MacArthur: 1941–1945, vol. 2 (Boston, 1975), 432, gives MacArthur fifteen delegates.

2. John Billings diary, Apr. 5, 1944, JBP.

3. J. Kenneth Bradley, Republican National Committee member from Connecticut, quoted in The New York Times, Apr. 16, 1944.

4. Erroneous impressions persist that CBL made the keynote speech at either the 1944 or 1948 Republican National Conventions.

5. Rafael Medoff, "Clare Boothe Luce and the Holocaust: A CT Congresswoman's

Fight for Justice," http://www.jewishledger.com/2012/04/clare-boothe-luce-and
-the-holocaust-a-ct-congresswomans-fight-for-justice/.

6. Ibid. Benzion Netanyahu was the father of the future Israeli Prime Minister Benjamin Netanyahu.

7. Ibid. On Oct. 5, 1945, CBL took up the Zionist cause again. Addressing a delegation of Zionists in Fairfield County, she lamented the large number of displaced Jews living in European camps, and cited the Balfour Declaration of 1917, which recognized the aspirations of Jews for a country of their own. She told the group that it was imperative the United States support the British government in its attempts to admit one hundred thousand immigrants from these temporary shelters into Palestine. If force was needed to overcome local Arab resistance, she recommended the use of American battleships and machine guns. It was cowardly, she said, for idealists to speak of the need for a Jewish homeland, while doing nothing to provide one. Some of the Zionists were astonished, saying that Mrs. Luce had gone beyond anything they had sought from her. *Bridgeport Telegram*, Oct. 6, 1945. For more on Anglo-American efforts to deal with the problem of displaced Jews, see Peter Clarke, *The Last Thousand Days of the British Empire: Churchill, Roosevelt and the Birth of the Pax Americana* (New York, 2008), 386–91, 460–63. Great Britain's Labor Party Zionist plank said there was no point in establishing a homeland for Jews unless they were allowed into it in sufficient numbers to be a majority. Clarke points out that the use of the word *holocaust* was not adopted almost exclusively to describe Nazi ill-treatment of Jews until July 1946. In fact, between 1942 and 1946 it had been used by *The New York Times* to emphasize other horrors, such as the siege of Stalingrad, the bombing of Berlin, and nuclear warfare. See Clarke, *The Last Thousand Days*, 387, 460–463, 456; *The New York Times*, Oct. 19, 1982.

8. ACB's estate was settled in Mar. 1945. One of the houses from which she had received rental income was the moated Brokaw mansion at Fifth Avenue and Seventy-ninth Street, where CBL had lived during her first marriage. The other was at Forty-fourth Street and Fifth Avenue, New York. CBL sued in Nov. 1945 to get ACB's trust funds and real estate assets. She lost the case and was advised by her lawyers not to appeal. A surrogate court had ruled some months before that the Brokaw trust fund set up for CBL by George Brokaw as part of her divorce settlement was exempt from taxes. Due to DFB's mishandling, its original worth of $425,000 was now reduced to $266,000. Details in CBLP.

9. Walton Wickett to SJM, Nov. 18, 1983, SJMP; James Rea to CBL, Feb. 26, 1944, CBLP; Norman Ross to SJM, July 1983, SJMP. Valuation certificate for Ann's violin, CBLP. The violin cost $1,700 in 1935. The piano was valued at $900. List in CBLP, dated Oct. 1944.

10. ACB's tempera watercolor portrait by Boris Chaliapin cost CBL $400 in 1945 and was appraised at $2,000 in 1967. An oil portrait of ACB by Paul Clemens, painted just before she died, cost $500. Memo, n.d., CBLP.

11. Walton Wickett to Stanford University, June 6, 1944, WWP. He gave the sum of $100 for five years.

12. List of speeches and articles in an office memo, June 4, 1944, CBLP; *PM*, June 4, 1944.

13. List of articles written between Apr. 28 and May 22, 1944, CBLP.

14. The sitting took place on May 16, 1944. Yousuf Karsh interview, Sept. 1989.

15. DFB to Isabel Hill, June 12, 1944, CBLP.

16. Charles Willoughby to CBL, May 4, and Jan. 13, 1944, CBLP.

17. Ibid.

18. DFB to CBL, Mar. 2, 1944, CBLP.

19. The GI Bill changed the lives of some 8 million veterans through advanced education. By 1947, half of all students on government grants were former servicemen or -women. Colleges turned out 360,000 teachers, 450,000 engineers, 240,000 accountants, 180,000 doctors or nurses, and 150,000 scientists. The United States was thus transformed from a nation of mostly blue-collar urban renters into one dominated by middle-class professionals, owning their own homes in fast-growing suburbs. *The New York Times*, June 22, 1994.

20. CBL to Herbert Hoover, n.d., June 1944, CBLP.

21. Hoover to CBL, June 19, 1944, HHP.

22. CBL to Hoover, June 20, 1944, CBLP.

23. Morris, *Rage for Fame*, 195–98.

24. *The New York Times*, June 28, 1944.

25. *PM*, Aug. 1, 1944.

26. CBL, "A Greater and Freer America: GI Joe's Future," delivered at the Republican National Convention June 27, 1944, and reprinted in *Vital Speeches of the Day* (New York, 1944).

27. Ibid.

28. Ibid. See also *Chicago Daily News*, June 28, 1944.

29. CBL said she was "almost prostrate" after leaving the Chicago Stadium podium. *McCall's*, July 1964.

30. Allene Talmey, "Clare Boothe . . . in a Velvet Glove," *Vogue*, Dec. 15, 1940; Morris, *Rage for Fame*, 329. *The New York Times* reported on June 28, 1944, that CBL's "ringing speech" was "undeniably the peak of the program" that night.

31. John Billings diary, June 27, 1944, JBP.

32. *National Review*, Apr. 30, 1982.

33. Russell Maloney, "Comment," *The New Yorker*, July 8, 1944, 13; *Time*, July 3, 1944, reported that CBL "gave the convention a new word for New Deal bureaucracy—bumbledom."

34. Photograph in the *Chicago Daily Tribune*, June 29, 1944.

35. *Sunday Worker*, Aug. 13, 1944; Max Spelke and J. Kenneth Bradley, Connecticut radio debate on CBL's voting record, Aug. 20, 1944, transcript in CBLP; *Philadelphia Record*, Sept. 1, 1944; *Reader's Scope*, Nov. 1945.

36. Obituary of Billings, *The New York Times*, Aug. 27, 1975. He was seventy-seven.

37. HRL office memo, Aug. 12, 1944, copy in JBP. Eric Hodgins, replying to HRL on behalf of *Time's* public relations committee, suggested that much of the current prejudice against CBL among the magazine's editors related to Republican campaign strategy. "So long as the wife of Publisher Luce is also Congresswoman Luce . . . the opposition will always have a handy weapon with which to make effective attack on CBL." Aug. 15, 1944, CBLP.

38. Neal, *Dark Horse*, 313–14.

39. James, *MacArthur*, 533; Burns, *Roosevelt*, 448–50.

40. Burns, *Roosevelt*, 424–25.

41. John Colville, *Winston Churchill and His Inner Circle* (New York, 1981), 126–27.

42. Carl M. Cannon, "Untruth and Consequences," *Atlantic*, Jan.–Feb. 2007. Truman's lunch with FDR was Aug. 18, 1944. *The New York Times*, July 14, 1998, said that FDR's blood pressure in 1944 rose from 180/90 to 240/130. Doctors told him to give up swimming, the only effective exercise for his wasted legs.

43. HRL office memo, Aug. 12, 1944, JBP.

44. Ibid., Aug. 9, 1944, JBP; *New York Herald Tribune*, Aug. 14, 1944; *The Boston Globe*, Aug. 9, 1944.

45. *The New Yorker*, Aug. 26, 1944.
46. John Billings diary, Aug. 25, 1944, JBP.
47. Beaverbrook displayed no feelings of guilt in having multiple affairs, a characteristic Harry envied. CBL to SJM verbally on numerous occasions.
48. CBL cable to HRL, ca. Sept. 7, 1944, CBLP.
49. Stephen Mellnik to CBL, Sept. 20, 1944, CBLP.
50. CBL to SJM, verbally, Jan. 16, 1982.
51. Shadegg, *Clare Boothe Luce*, 195.
52. Al Morano memo to CBL, 1944, CBLP. The phrase *political action committee*, now applicable to countless campaign organizations, related specifically to Hillman's group in 1944.
53. *New York Sun*, Nov. 8, 1944.
54. Chamberlain CBL profile, JBP.
55. Shadegg, *Clare Boothe Luce*, 195–97.
56. *Bridgeport World Telegram*, Nov. 3, 1944.
57. Ibid.
58. "Meet 'Big Bill' Brennan, an Honest Politician," *Bridgeport Sunday Post*, Aug. 18, 1946.
59. Al Morano interview, Oct. 6, 1981; CBL to John Elson, Oct. 9, 1967, TIA. CBL said that HRL sometimes helped with the content, if not the composition, of her speeches. CBL to John Elson, June 13, 1968, TIA.
60. *The Boston Globe*, Apr. 11, 1943.
61. *Time*, Nov. 20, 1944, analyzing CBL's victory.
62. *The New York Times*, Oct. 14, 1944.
63. Braden, *Women Politicians*, 44.
64. *The Christian Science Monitor*, Oct. 30, 1944.
65. CBL made more than one hundred speeches during the 1944 campaign. Twelve, on national or international issues, lasting thirty to forty-five minutes, were documented extensively and released to the press in advance of delivery. The rest were extemporaneous, "more or less reverberations or rewrites of the carefully prepared speeches to which I had added new facts and comments according to the news events of the day." David Hyatt, ed., "So You Have to Make a Speech by Heart," June 1961 scrapbook cutting, CBLP.
66. CBL to Charles Boothe, Oct. 19, 1944, CBLP.
67. CBL to HRL, Oct. 30, 1944, CBLP.
68. *Bridgeport Post*, Nov. 1, 1944; Margaret Case Harriman, "Or Would You Rather Be Clare Boothe?," *Reader's Scope*, 1945. Harriman wrote of CBL's record in Congress that in 1943, her first year, she had "been absent for 21 roll-call votes on legislation, out of a total of 71; in her first fifteen months she was listed as 'not voting' on four separate war appropriations bills . . . she also declined to vote on three labor bills—the President's veto of the Smith-Connally Bill, the Hobbs anti-racketeering bill, and a third bill granting overtime to 1.5 million federal workers." CBL had supported the GI Bill, but was on a speaking tour for the GOP at the time of its unanimous passage.
69. CBL to Bernard Baruch, Nov. 3, 1944, CBLP.
70. *New York Sun*, Nov. 8, 1944.
71. *New York Herald Tribune*, Nov. 9, 1944.
72. Connors spent $22,000 on her campaign and CBL $13,000, not counting Wes Bailey's salary, paid by Time Inc. HRL contributed $1,000 in cash to CBL's campaign and some $8,500 to various Republican groups, including $2,000 to the Fair-

field County Republican Association. He also gave about $9,600 to various Republican causes that year, including $3,000 to the National Republican Club and $1,000 to the CBL for Congress Committee. List in CBLP.

73. *New York Herald Tribune*, Nov. 9, 1944. See Geoffrey C. Ward, *Closest Companion: The Unknown Story of the Intimate Friendship Between Franklin Roosevelt and Marga- ret Suckley* (Boston, 1995), 340–41, for FDR remarks about CBL on Election Day 1944.

74. Shadegg, *Clare Boothe Luce*, 200, quoting *Bridgeport Post*.

75. Herbert Hoover to CBL, Nov. 7, 1944, HHP.

10. TO THE FRONT

1. John Billings diary, Nov. 8 and 11, 1944, JBP. The final count was FDR's 25.6 mil- lion to Dewey's 22 million.

2. *Time*, Nov. 20, 1944.

3. Time Inc. staffers reflected the split. Billings voted for Dewey, and reported that Harry was "hurt" that Al Grover, his personal aide, had voted for FDR. Others complained of their boss's "blind partisanship." John Billings diary, Nov. 7 and 8, 1944, JBP.

4. *Bridgeport Telegram*, Nov. 24, 1944.

5. U.S. forces numbered 231,306 and the British 253,859 in the final battle for Rome. Clark, along with Omar Bradley, would be given a fourth star in 1945, after victory in Europe. In his memoir, General Clark wrote that CBL's "special interest in our problems . . . gave all of us a real lift and helped to clarify the Italian war in the minds of the people back home." Clark, *Calculated Risk*, 423.

6. *Stars and Stripes*, Dec. 17, 1944.

7. Ibid.; Tere Pascone, "U.S. Doughboy Is 'Great Hero' of the War," *Bridgeport Post*, Jan. 2, 1945. Pascone made a scrapbook about CBL's European trip consisting of articles from the *Bridgeport Post* and *Bridgeport Herald*, Nov. 22 to Dec. 19, 1944, now in CBLP. When not otherwise indicated, documentary details in this chapter derive from this source.

8. Bernard Baruch to Lord Beaverbrook, July 26, 1935, CBL.

9. CBL to HRL, Nov. 28, 1944, CBLP.

10. For CBL's fact-finding tour of Western Europe at the onset of World War II, see Morris, *Rage for Fame*, 369–88.

11. CBL to HRL, Nov. 28, 1944, CBLP.

12. Morris, *Rage for Fame*, 106–09; CBL interview, May 3, 1982.

13. After returning to Washington, CBL heard from Simpson that he had been in London during her visit after all. He reported that as an army officer he had super- vised British police work in Palestine before the war. This suggests a career in military intelligence, and may explain his unavailability to her in the fall of 1944. He spoke vaguely of being personally dissatisfied, lonely, and having to live with his mother. Julian Simpson to CBL, Nov. 26, 1944, and Feb. 8, 1945, CBLP. For CBL's later, disillusioning reunion with her old lover, see chapter 21.

14. CBL to HRL, Nov. 28, 1944, CBLP.

15. Ibid.

16. *Bridgeport Post*, Nov. 27, 1944.

17. See Morris, *Rage for Fame*, 383–84.

18. *Bridgeport Post*, Dec. 2, 1944.

19. Burns, *Roosevelt*, 460. Unemployment plummeted, from 8 million to 670,000. Of huge social significance was the migration of large numbers of rural blacks to indus-

trial towns, where they were hired by armament factories to work alongside whites. A similar racial breakthrough, as CBL had tried to hasten in Congress, would eventually occur in the military, starting the United States on a fresh civil rights path.

20. CBL interviewed on CBS's 60 Minutes, Sept. 18, 1979, transcript in CBLP. Also see "Members of the Military Affairs Committee, including Clare Boothe Luce, visit various fronts," Dec. 29, 1944, http://www.youtube.com/watch?v=l3y_sk2t VYw, Human History Archive, published online Dec. 19, 2013.

21. Bridgeport Telegram, Dec. 7, 1944.

22. Stars and Stripes, Dec. 12, 1944.

23. Ibid.

24. Bill Mauldin, The Brass Ring (New York, 1971), 235; Mauldin obituary, The New York Times, Jan. 23, 2003. In 1945, Mauldin won a Pulitzer Prize for his war coverage.

25. Stars and Stripes, Dec. 16, 1944.

26. Ibid.

27. Ibid.

28. Ibid.; Bridgeport Post, Jan. 2, 1945.

29. CBL broadcast from Rome, Dec. 27, 1944, WNAB transcript in CBLP; Bridgeport Post, Jan. 2, 1945.

30. Bridgeport Post, Jan. 2, 1945. Years later, CBL would send a memo to her secretary: "It now becomes public policy for me to finish off Augusto's education. Will you send a cable with a check made out not to . . . his (drunken) father, but to the master of the Institute." CBL to Dorothy Farmer, n.d., 1953, CBLP. CBL also paid for Al Morano's son's schooling for several years.

31. Martin Blumenson, Mark Clark: The Last of the Great World War II Commanders (New York, 1984), 3.

32. Clark, Calculated Risk, 424–25. The Englishman whom Clark replaced, Field Marshal Sir Harold Alexander, became Supreme Allied Commander of the Mediterranean Theater.

33. Wilson A. Heefner, Dogface Soldier: The Life of General Lucian K. Truscott, Jr. (Columbia, Mo., 2010), 222–23; Chief of Military History, "North Apennines 1944–1945," U.S. Center for Military History website, http://www.history.army.mil/brochures/nap/72-34.htm/.

34. Generals Clark and Alexander had been at odds over separating American and British forces in order to capture Rome. Clark had wanted the glory of entering the capital, but Alexander preferred to keep the Allied armies together and have them encircle and destroy the German Tenth Army as they fled from the British Eighth Army. Clark won the argument, but German war memoirs confirm that by dividing their forces, the Allies had enabled them to flee, and hunker down to prolong the fight in the Apennines. Herbert Mitgang, "The Forgotten Front: For Soldiers Who Took Rome, Glory Was Fleeting," The New York Times, June 6, 1984.

35. CBL interview, Apr. 2, 1982; Arlington National Cemetery website on Lucian King Truscott, Jr. He had trained his Third Infantry Division to be the best in the Seventh Army. Battle-hardened from months of fighting in North Africa, Sicily, and Anzio, his troops had recently fought their way north to Bologna in record time. They accomplished this by marching, even through mountains, at four miles an hour instead of the usual two and a half, in what had become known as "the Truscott trot."

36. Mauldin, The Brass Ring, 241.

37. Life, Oct. 2, 1944.

38. Robert Geake, letter to *New York* magazine, Apr. 12, 1982.

39. Pascone, "U.S. Doughboy Is 'Great Hero' of the War."

40. *Stars and Stripes*, Dec. 18, 1944.

41. Ibid., Dec. 20, 1944.

42. *Time* staffer Tom Durrance cable to Filmore Calhoun, Dec. 30, 1944, TIA.

43. Mauldin, *The Brass Ring*, 234–39.

44. Ibid., 237–38.

45. CBL interview, April 2, 1982. CBL sent for the twenty-three-year-old Mauldin after their trip, and asked what he wanted to do after the war. Having already sold some drawings to Luce publications, he assumed she wanted to hire him. But face-to-face, he felt intimidated by the "most frightening person I'd ever met in my life." He said he had no long-term plans. Sensing that he might want to capitalize on his current fame, CBL advised him to get a college education first. "If you need any help," she said, "let us know." She seemed sincerely interested in his advancement, Mauldin thought, "in a power-wielding sort of way." But he was noncommittal. Later he found that lacking a degree did hold him back, and he regretted not having taken CBL's advice and offer. But he managed to win a second Pulitzer Prize and make the cover of *Time*. Mauldin, *The Brass Ring*, 234–39; see also Todd Depastino, *Bill Mauldin: A Life Up Front* (New York, 2008).

46. CBL interview, Apr. 2, 1982.

47. Ibid.; *Stars and Stripes*, Dec. 28, 1944.

48. Truscott to CBL, Apr. 10, 1945, CBLP.

49. Ibid., Mar. 18, 1945, CBLP.

50. John Billings diary, Dec. 22, 1944, JBP. Billings said that HRL was "demanding reservations by air to get back here Wednesday next"—i.e., Dec. 27.

51. *Stars and Stripes*, Dec. 26, 1944; CBL to Bernard Baruch, Mar. 2, 1945, CBLP.

52. Major James M. Wilson noted CBL's sincere desire to find out all she could "well in the forward area." *Louisville Courier-Journal*, CBL scrapbook, n.d.

53. CBL broadcast from Rome, Dec. 27, 1944, transcript in CBLP; *Stars and Stripes*, Dec. 26, 1944.

54. *Stars and Stripes*, Dec. 26, 1944; Pascone, "U.S. Doughboy Is 'Great Hero' of the War."

55. CBL broadcast from Rome, Dec. 27, 1944, transcript in CBLP.

56. Ibid; *Stars and Stripes*, Dec. 26, 1944.

57. Morris, *Rage for Fame*, 430–31, 441–42.

58. Ibid.

59. CBL interview, Apr. 2, 1982: "He had this death-grip on me."

60. Ibid.

61. CBL broadcast from Rome, Dec. 27, 1944, transcript in CBLP; *Bridgeport Post*, Jan. 2, 1945; photograph of *The Women* tent, *Life*, ca. Dec. 30, 1944.

62. CBL broadcast from Rome, Dec. 27, 1944, transcript in CBLP; *Bridgeport Post*, Jan. 2, 1945, CBLP.

63. *Stars and Stripes*, Dec. 26, 1944.

64. Ibid.

65. CBL, "Converts and the Blessed Sacrament," *Sentinel of the Blessed Sacrament*, Nov.–Dec. 1950.

66. Ibid.

67. *Stars and Stripes*, Dec. 26, 1944; CBL said that an American artillery officer broke the cease-fire to put a stop to "that irreverent nonsense," and "laid down quite a lot of thunder" on the revelers. CBL broadcast from Rome, Dec. 27, 1944, transcript in CBLP; *Bridgeport Post*, Jan. 2, 1945.

68. *Stars and Stripes*, Dec. 28, 1944.

69. Blumenson, *Mark Clark*, quoting Clark's diary, 239.

70. CBL wore the scarf often in Italy, and eventually gave it to the Arizona Costume Institute.

71. Michael Musmanno to CBL, Jan. 26, 1960, CBLP.

72. *Stars and Stripes*, Dec. 28, 1944. In response to CBL's suggestion that tired Fifth Army soldiers might benefit from being rotated home after a fixed period at the lines, Truscott pointed out that this would disrupt operations. "To rotate 10,000 men per month might require 72,000, unless the theater was to get along without the 10,000." Truscott to CBL, Jan. 7, 1945, CBLP.

73. CBL broadcast from Rome, Dec. 27, 1944, transcript in CBLP; *Stars and Stripes*, Dec. 29, 1944.

74. CBL to Truscott, ca. Jan. 1945, CBLP.

75. Truscott to CBL, Jan. 7, 1945, CBLP.

76. *The Washington Post*, Dec. 31, 1944.

77. *Bridgeport Post*, Jan. 2, 1945.

11. WANING DAYS OF WAR

1. *Passaic Herald News* (N.J.), Jan. 5, 1945; *D.C. News*, Jan. 4, 1945.

2. *Passaic Herald News* (N.J.), Jan. 5, 1945.

3. *Washington Times-Herald*, Jan. 3, 1945.

4. *Hollywood Citizen News*, Jan. 5, 1945. Gahagan Douglas was elected by a narrow margin, and the press immediately set her up as a rival to CBL. See chapter 3, "The 'Glamor Girls' of Congress," in Braden, *Women Politicians*.

5. General Dunlop to CBL, Jan. 10, 1945, CBLP.

6. Al Morano interview, Oct. 6, 1981; Army Report from HQ Thirty-second Division, Nov. 1, 1944, CBLP.

7. DFB to Isabel Hill, July 5, 1944, CBLP.

8. DFB to CBL, Aug. 17, 1944, CBLP; DFB to CBL, Mar. 10, 1944, CBLP.

9. *Bridgeport Post*, Jan. 15, 1945.

10. CBL to General Mark Clark, Jan. 24, 1945, enclosing a copy of her House speech. She ended the letter by saying she hoped to visit Clark's command again "in the not too distant future." CA.

11. *The New York Times*, Jan. 19, 1945.

12. *Stars and Stripes*, Jan. 18, 1945.

13. CBL repeated Truman's remark in a broadcast on WMAL Blue Nework on Feb. 9, 1945. Transcript in CA.

14. DFB to CBL, Jan. 25, 1945, CBLP. DFB left the hospital without a limp.

15. Ibid. Adding to CBL's black mood at this time was a legal dispute. Howard Crosby Brokaw, brother of George and the trustee of two funds set up by their father, had filed a claim in New York Surrogate Court to a part of Ann's legacy to which, as next of kin, Clare had assumed she was the sole heir. The plaintiff said that Isaac Brokaw's will was unclear regarding disposition of the money left to a grandchild who died during her minority. He therefore sought a share of cash from the two trust funds that in eight years had yielded Ann some $212,000. CBL was later declared the sole beneficiary of $14,655 left in her daughter's account at the time of her death. International News Service, Mar. 23, 1945, CBLP.

16. Heefner, *Dogface Soldier*, 222–23.

17. Clarke, *The Last Thousand Days*, 154–55.

18. CBL to Walter Winchell, May 17, 1945, CBLP.

19. Charles Willoughby to Senator Arthur Vandenberg, Feb. 4, 1945, CBLP.
20. Ibid.
21. Willoughby to CBL, Feb. 15, 1945, CBLP.
22. CAW to CBL, Feb. 15, 1945, CBLP.
23. CBL interview, Jan. 9, 1982.
24. Gerhard Peters and John T. Woolley, eds., *The American Presidency Project*, http://www.presidency.ucsb.edu/.
25. Burns, *Roosevelt*, 582.
26. *Naugatauk Daily News*, Mar. 3, 1945.

12. A GLORIOUS WOMAN

1. HRL to CBL, [Mar.] 3, 1945, CBLP.
2. CBL interview, Jan. 5, 1987.
3. Harold Alexander to CBL, ca. Mar. 8, 1945, CBLP. Also see CBL, "Outlines of Italian Trip," manuscript in CBLP.
4. Nevertheless, several of Alexander's tactical errors had been noticed. In Sicily, for example, he had allowed some sixty thousand Germans to flee with equipment across the Strait of Messina. Now, many months later, these escapees were still holding off half a million British and American troops in northern Italy.
5. The editor and artist Fleur Cowles said that CBL "slept with every general on the Western Front." Clementine Churchill was so incensed by rumors of CBL's vamping of Alexander that after the war she refused to sit at the same table with her at Hobcaw Barony. Fleur Cowles interview, Nov. 2, 1981; Elizabeth Navarro (Bernard Baruch's former nurse) interview, May 17, 1984.
6. CBL, "Outlines of Italian Trip," 1; U.S. Army Mediterranean Theater of Operations HQ, "Resume of Itinerary and Inspections for Mrs. Luce," transcript in CBLP, 1–2. Except where otherwise cited, all details of CBL's 1945 European itinerary come from these sources.
7. Arthur B. Dodge, Jr., interview, Aug. 28, 1988.
8. CBL interview, Feb. 5, 1983.
9. Bill Mauldin, *Up Front* (New York, 1945, 2000), 35–36.
10. Truscott to CBL, Apr. 10, 1945, CBLP.
11. CBL notes on 1945 Italian trip, CBLP; Blumenson, *Mark Clark*, 125.
12. CBL column, *Tucson Daily Citizen*, Apr. 2, 1945.
13. See also CBL, "The Forgotten Front," *Life*, May 14, 1945, and CBL in *Charleston Gazette* (W. Va.), Mar. 31, 1945.
14. CBL notes on 1945 Italian trip, CBLP. As early as 1934, in a syndicated article CBL celebrated the "beauty" of war machines.
15. Ibid.
16. Truscott to CBL, Mar. 18, 1945, CBLP.
17. Apr. 1, 1945, reprinted in PM, Apr. 3, 1945. The columnist Walter Winchell questioned CBL's motives for going abroad. "Insiders believe Congresswoman Luce visits Italy so often because in her campaign for the U.S. Senate [sic] she will fight for Italians. Her district (in Connecticut) has almost 40 percent Italian descent." *Burlington Daily Times News* (N.C.), Apr. 3, 1945.
18. CBL, "Miscellaneous Chit Chat: Items from here and there about this and that," transcript, ca. 1945, CBLP.
19. CBL miscellaneous undated notes on Italian trip, CBLP.
20. Ibid.
21. *Brazil Herald*, Mar. 3, 1959.

22. CBL and Vernon A. Walters, *History and the Nature of Man*, Vernon A. Walters Lectures in History, United States Naval Academy (Annapolis, Md., Jan. 10, 1979), 2.

23. Truscott to CBL, "Monday"—most likely Mar. 26, 1945, CBLP.

24. Ibid.

25. Harold Macmillan, *War Diaries: Politics and War in the Mediterranean 1943–1945* (New York, 1984), 724–25. Until otherwise convinced by HRL, CBL tended to side with Evelyn Waugh's axiom that punctuality was a virtue of the bored.

26. Ibid.

27. Arthur B. Dodge, Jr., interview, Mar. 18, 1989.

28. Ibid.; Dodge to SJM, May 2, 1989, SJMP.

29. Undated manuscript, CBLP.

30. *Coshocton Tribune* (Ohio), Apr. 8, 1945.

31. Colonel Ray J. Stecker to CBL, Jan. 31, 1945, CBLP.

32. Truscott to CBL, Apr. 10, 1945, CBLP. Berchtesgaden was Hitler's favorite getaway in the Bavarian Alps.

13. OPENING OF THE CAMPS

1. Burns, *Roosevelt*, 599–601.

2. CBL diary, Apr. 16, 1945, CBLP; *New York Herald Tribune*, Apr. 17, 1945.

3. Where not otherwise indicated, the following account of CBL's tour of the camps is based on her report to the House of Representatives, *Congressional Record*, May 3, 1945; CBL interview, June 9, 1981; *Bridgeport Telegram* and *Bridgeport Post*, Apr. 22 and 26, 1945.

4. "Liberation of Buchenwald Concentration Camp by 6th Armored Division of US Third Army," http://www.scrapbookpages.com/Buchenwald/Liberation0.html. When parts of the camp were dismantled after the war, some of the stone from the buildings was used to reconstruct Weimar. Mark Fisher, "Germans Rework Buchenwald's Dual History," *The Washington Post*, July 22, 1991.

5. Among the British delegates were Lords Stanhope and Addison, Sir Archibald Southby, Mavis Tate, and the rising Labour star Tom Driberg.

6. *Sunday Times Signal* (Lanesville, Ohio), Apr. 22, 1945.

7. *Congressional Record*, May 3, 1945.

8. Ibid.

9. Edward R. Murrow in "Broadcast from Buchenwald," Apr. 15, 1945, http://www.scrapbookpages.com/Buchenwald/Liberation3.html.

10. *Congressional Record*, May 3, 1945; *Port Arthur News* (Tex.), Apr. 21, 1945.

11. *Congressional Record*, May 3, 1945.

12. Ibid.

13. *Sheboygan Daily Press* (Wis.) and *Sunday Times-Signal* (Zanesville, Ohio), Apr. 21 and 22, 1945.

14. *Congressional Record*, May 3, 1945, British report.

15. Martin Gilbert, *The Day the War Ended* (New York, 1995), 49.

16. Richard J. Evans, *The Third Reich at War* (New York, 2009), 305. Also see Gilbert, *The Day the War Ended*, 148–49. Eichmann was caught in Argentina in 1960. He was tried by an Israeli court, found guilty of mass murder, and hanged in 1962.

17. Evans, *The Third Reich at War*, 696.

18. John Colville, *The Fringes of Power: 10 Downing Street Diaries 1939–1955* (New York, 1986), 591.

19. See http://www.jewishgen.org/ForgottenCamps/Camps/MainCampsEng.html.

20. *Congressional Record*, May 3, 1945. Martin Gilbert records that Americans had shipped four hundred tons of rocket equipment from Nordhausen to New Mexico by June 1, 1945, before the Russians arrived in what would be their zone of occupation. He also says that the rockets that killed three thousand were used between June and Dec. 1944. Gilbert, *The Day the War Ended*, 154, 387.
21. Evans, *The Third Reich at War*, 663–65.
22. CBL to John Chamberlain, n.d. [1946], JBP.
23. Richard Rhodes, *The Making of the Atomic Bomb* (New York, 1988), 624.
24. Anne Frank, *The Diary of a Young Girl: The Definitive Edition* (New York, 1995), 339.
25. CBL to *Bayonne Times* (N.J.), Mar. 2, 1945; CBL interview, June 9, 1981.

14. VICTORY IN EUROPE

1. *Dunkirk Evening Observer* (N.Y.), Apr. 26, 1945, reporting CBL broadcast from London.
2. CBL comments reported in *Bridgeport Telegraph* and *Bridgeport Post*, May 2, 1945.
3. CBL report to House of Representatives, *Congressional Record*, May 3, 1945.
4. Ibid.
5. Gilbert, *The Day the War Ended*, 70–71, quoting *Stars and Stripes*, May 5, 1945.
6. Almost fifty years later, on Sept. 1, 1994, the last occupying Russian troops would leave Germany by train from the Karlshorst railway station. See Gilbert, *The Day the War Ended*, 414.
7. Ibid., 1.
8. Brinkley, *Washington Goes to War*, 275; Gilbert, *The Day the War Ended*, 134–35.
9. Truman's broadcast was on May 7, a day before the official day of celebration.
10. Rhodes, *The Making of the Atomic Bomb*, 624.
11. Clark, *The Last Thousand Days*, 308. Spencer Warren, in "Churchill's Realism," *The National Interest* (Winter 1995–96), points out that the "Iron Curtain" phrase had been previously used by a Russian philosopher in 1918, by Joseph Goebbels in Feb. 1945, and twice by Winston Churchill, in a telegram to Truman in May 1945 (quoted in chapter 14) and in the House of Commons in Aug. 1945.
12. Speech transcript in CBLP.
13. CBL Blue Network broadcast of May 29, 1945, published in *Vital Speeches*, Aug. 15, 1945, 647–49.

15. FRAGMENTATION

1. Ray Stecker to CBL, n.d. [early summer 1945], CBLP.
2. Ibid., Jan. 22, 1946, CBLP.
3. Charles Willoughby to CBL, June 2, 1945, CBLP.
4. Ibid., May 9, 1945, CBLP.
5. Ibid., May 9 and June 2, 1945, CBLP.
6. Lucian Truscott to CBL, May 7, 1945, CBLP.
7. Ibid., June 11, 1945, CBLP.
8. Ibid. See also Heefner, *Dogface Soldier*, 247–48.
9. Truscott to CBL, May 31, 1945, CBLP.
10. Diary of Truscott's aide, June 24, 1945, quoted in Heefner, *Dogface Soldier*, 248.
11. Years later, Truscott's daughter, Mary, confirmed that her mother had been devastated by the general's obsession with CBL during World War II. Paul Hendrickson to SJM, Apr. 8, 1988, SJMP.

12. Truscott to CBL, May 13, 1945, CBLP. Truscott retired from the army in Sept. 1947, and had a desk job at the War Department determining which soldiers should be retained, promoted, or retired. In 1951 he joined the CIA as its covert senior representative in Germany. Allen Dulles promoted him in 1958 as deputy director for coordinating the agency's espionage network worldwide. He left the CIA in 1959, wrote his memoirs—omitting his years at the CIA—and died on Sept. 12, 1965, aged seventy.

13. Mrs. John Hill interview, Mar. 10, 1988.

14. John Billings diary, July 14, 1945, JBP.

15. Ibid.

16. George Waldo to CBL, n.d., ca. 1945 or 1946, CBLP.

17. Ibid., and July 16, 1945, CBLP.

18. This was the prototype atomic bomb known as "Fat Man," to be dropped if the Japanese continued to be defiant. When Truman shared his news with Stalin at Potsdam, the Soviet dictator showed no surprise. His spies had already penetrated Los Alamos. In fact, he knew about the bomb before Truman, who had not been told about it by FDR. Richard Lawrence Miller, *Truman: The Rise to Power* (New York, 1986), 387–88; Clarke, *Last Thousand Days*, 351.

19. John Billings diary, July 18, 1945, JBP. The ban applied only to *Time*. In *Life*, CBL's byline continued to appear on articles and photographs.

20. John Billings memo, July 21, 1945, JBP.

21. John Billings diary, July 23, 1945, JBP.

22. Chamberlain CBL profile, JBP.

23. CBL quoted in *Bridgeport Post*, July 24, 1945.

24. CBL once said *Saint Joan* was Shaw's greatest play, and the one she would most like to have written. Morris, *Rage for Fame*, 341.

25. George Bernard Shaw, *Complete Plays with Prefaces*, vol. 3 (New York, 1963), 213.

26. Ibid., passim.

27. Ibid., 227–29.

28. Ibid., 213.

29. Ibid., 265.

30. Tere Pascone, "Next Week in Person: CBL in *Candida*," *Bridgeport Post*, Aug. 2, 1945.

31. John Billings diary, Aug. 6, 1945, JBP. Subsequent official statistics put the bomb drop height at thirty thousand feet and the detonation height at one thousand nine hundred feet; http://atomicbombmuseum.org.

32. CBL to John Wilson, Aug. 18, 1945, CBLP.

33. *Bridgeport Telegram*, Aug. 7, 1945.

34. "Candida: The Audience Was Polite," *Newsweek*, Aug. 20, 1945. Apparently, the theater management prevented the distribution of the political literature.

35. *Bridgeport Telegram*, Aug. 7, 1945; CBL interview, Aug. 2, 1985.

36. Walcott Gibbs, "Candida Excursion," *The New Yorker*, Aug. 18, 1945. Gibbs made a point of telling his readers that he stayed only through the second act. Also see *New York Herald Tribune*, Aug. 7, 1945.

37. CBL interview, Aug. 2, 1985.

38. *Variety* front-page story, Aug. 15, 1945.

39. George Frazier, *The One with the Mustache Is Costello* (New York, 1947), 11–12.

40. Ibid.

41. "Summer Theater, *Candida*," *Life*, Aug. 20, 1945.

42. Ibid.; *Newsweek*, Aug. 20, 1945.

43. *Newsweek*, Jan. 24, 1955.

44. Guest lists for Aug. 6–11 entertaining at "The House," CBLP; CBL to John Wilson, Aug. 14, 1945, CBLP. Some of the bitterest comments on CBL's performance came from professional thespians who resented the intrusion of a politician onto their boards. Libby Holman gave her no quarter: "In the last ten minutes she warmed up to a cool icicle" (*Daily Variety*, Sept. 7, 1945). Humiliatingly for CBL, who had always made much of meeting George Bernard Shaw in 1939, the aging playwright failed to recall her when sent notices about the Stamford production. "I know nothing about the lady," he wrote, adding that he was "not surprised when I learnt that she had been so ill-advised as to attempt to act Katharine Cornell's leading part without the necessary four or five years training and stage practice." Shaw to Emarel Flesher, June 21, 1946, CBLP; also see Morris, *Rage for Fame*, 341–42.
45. John Billings diary, Aug. 7 and 12, 1945, JBP.
46. Ibid., Aug. 14, 1945, JBP.

16. BLACK HOUR

1. On Sept. 9, 1945, the National Institute for Human Relations announced that CBL and Madame Chiang Kai-shek had been named top female orators in the English language. Its speech consultant, Dr. James F. Bender, recommended CBL as "a model for business and professional women who must use their voices before large audiences without the benefit of public address or recording systems." *The New York Times Magazine*, Sept. 9, 1945, and *Bridgeport Post*, Sept. 15, 1945.
2. CBL, "The Real Reason," II, second part of a three-part series in *McCall's*, Feb., Mar., and Apr. 1947.
3. Ibid., III; John Kobler, *Luce: His Time, Life and Fortune* (New York, 1968), 131. Kobler interviewed CBL in the early 1960s.
4. CBL, "The Real Reason," I.
5. Ibid., II. CBL wrote: "Few people have ever found God in the analyst's office, but sometimes, years later, they may recall that was whom they were seeking." She concluded that analysis was one of the real reasons she became a Catholic. Anthony Storr, in *Solitude* (New York, 1988), 192, quotes Alfred Jung as saying that a problem for every one of his psychiatric patients over the age of thirty-five had been the inability to "find a religious outlook on life."
6. CBL, "The Real Reason," III. Also see Alden Hatch, *Ambassador Extraordinary: Clare Boothe Luce* (New York, 1955), 176–85. Waugh's novel had been published in England, but did not appear in the United States until Jan. 1946.
7. The article, "What One Woman Can Do," was about Madame Chiang Kai-shek's care of war orphans.
8. CBL, "The Real Reason," III.

17. CONVERSION

1. Ann Charnley interview, May 3, 1988; John Cooney, *The American Pope: The Life and Times of Francis Cardinal Spellman* (New York, 1984), 251. See also Fulton J. Sheen, *Treasure in Clay: The Autobiography of Fulton J. Sheen* (New York, 1980).
2. For Sheen's theatrical, almost hypnotic, screen presence, see, e.g., his TV broadcast *How to Improve Your Mind* (1956) on YouTube.
3. Sheen, *Treasure*, 337; Ann Charnley interview, Mar. 3, 1988.
4. Sheen quoted in Hatch interviews, Apr. 1955, AHP. Also see Hatch, *Ambassador*, 181–82.

5. Sheen quoted in Hatch interviews, Apr. 1955, AHP.

6. Hatch, *Ambassador*, 180.

7. CBL, "Converts and the Blessed Sacrament." The writer Katherine Anne Porter, also a convert, had a similar aesthetic response to the accoutrements of church architecture and the trappings of the Mass. Joan Givner, *Katherine Anne Porter: A Life* (New York, 1982), 101.

8. CBL, "Converts and the Blessed Sacrament."

9. Ibid.

10. Kobler, *Luce*, 131.

11. CBL interview, July 24, 1982. CBL frequently questioned why she clung to the relationship with HRL when it so often made her miserable.

12. CBL, "The Real Reason," I.

13. Maisie Ward, unpublished foreword to a proposed book edition of "The Real Reason," ca. 1956, CBLP.

14. CBL, "The Real Reason," III; Joan H. Fitzpatrick interview, Mar. 15, 1988.

15. Hatch, *Ambassador*, 183.

16. John Billings diary, Nov. 2, 1945, JBP. After HRL's return from China, Billings sensed he was less pro-Chiang than previously.

17. Al Morano interview, Oct. 6, 1981.

18. CBL, "The Real Reason," III.

19. CBL's House Resolution 101, proposing nuclear arms control, was presented concurrently on November 14, 1945, but no action was taken until 1946, when her principle emerged in the Atomic Energy Act.

20. *Congressional Record*, Nov. 14, 1945. CBL later remarked, apropos of the distinction between conventional and nuclear arms, "Conventional is simply a euphemism for obsolete." CBL, "Eisenhower Administration," Columbia University Oral History interview with John Luter, Jan. 11, 1968, Columbia University (New York, 1973), 76.

21. John K. Jessup, *The Ideas of Henry Luce* (New York, 1969), 355.

22. "I never had any shadow of a doubt that what my husband did was infinitely more important to the world than what I did." CBL quoted in *Family Circle*, Feb. 1954. She frequently expressed this opinion to SJM.

23. Bernard Baruch to CBL, Dec. 25, 1945, CBLP. Mary Bancroft, a confidante of HRL, believed that CBL should have married Baruch, since he was the one man who "would have made her happy, if any man could." Bancroft to W. A. Swanberg, May 1, 1971, MBP.

24. HRL to Billings, Nov. 28, 1945, JBP; Al Grover to Billings, Nov. 29, 1945, JBP.

25. Gladys Freeman interview, Feb. 20, 1982.

26. CBL, "The Real Reason," III.

27. Ibid. The last phrase is the title of a 1922 novel by H. G. Wells.

28. Fulton J. Sheen quoted in Hatch interviews, Apr. 1955, AHP. CBL's mood improved on Jan. 6, with a flattering contractual offer from Hollywood to spend six weeks filming in Hollywood as costar to George Raft, in a movie entitled *The Congresswoman*. Though the script was not specifically about her career, the action took place in the contemporary political arena. She was tempted by the $175,000 fee, but declined, saying she was far too busy being a Congresswoman to act one. The movie, retitled *Mr. Ace*, was released later that year with Sylvia Sidney taking a much reduced female lead. *The New York Times*, Jan. 8, 1946; CBL to Willi Schlamm, Jan. 7, 1946, CBLP; Mark Fearnow, *Clare Boothe Luce: A Research and Production Sourcebook* (Westport, Conn., 1995), 127.

29. Shadegg, *Clare Boothe Luce*, 209–11.

30. Sheen quoted in Hatch interviews, Apr. 1955, AHP.

31. Fulton J. Sheen, *The World's First Love: Mary Mother of God* (New York, 1952), 260; also see *Newsweek*, Jan. 24, 1955.

32. Sheen quoted in Hatch interviews, Apr. 1955, AHP.

33. CBL "The Real Reason," III.

34. Ibid.

35. Charles Willoughby to CBL, Nov. 2, 1945, CBLP. For extra biographical information on Willoughby, see Kenneth J. Campbell, "Charles A. Willoughby: A Mixed Performance," http://intellit.muskingum.edu/wwii_folder/wwiiepac_folder/wwiife pacwilloughby.html.

36. CBL to Willoughby, Jan. 5, 1946, CBLP.

37. Willoughby to CBL, Jan. 4, 1946, CBLP.

38. CBL, "The Real Reason," III.

39. CBL introduced HR 481 on Jan. 14, 1946. CBL, "On My Record in Congress— Bills Introduced. Remarks of Hon. Clare Boothe Luce of Connecticut in the House of Representatives, Wednesday, July 31, 1946," *Congressional Record*, July 31, 1946.

40. The house in Hobe Sound was owned by Sam Pryor of Pan Am.

41. CBL to Fulton J. Sheen, "Monday night, Jan. 21, Hobe Sound, Florida," CBLP. This handwritten four-page letter may not have been sent. CBL sometimes held back her epistolary effusions. See below, chapter 43, note 94.

42. Ray Stecker to CBL, Jan. 22, 1946, CBLP. Stecker divorced and remarried. He died of a heart attack in 1967 and was buried with full military honors at West Point.

43. Willoughby to CBL, Mar. 6, 1946, CBLP.

44. Ibid., Mar. 12, 1946, CBLP.

45. Ibid., ca. Mar. 7, 1946, CBLP.

46. *Emporia Gazette* (Kans.), Feb. 2, 1946.

47. Ibid.

48. *New York Sun*, Jan. 28, 1946. Since a senatorial candidacy by CBL would be the subject of much political jockeying in Connecticut over the next few years, the complicated history of this seat (junior to that of the Democratic Senator Brien McMahon) needs clarifying. Former Admiral Thomas C. Hart (R) was only a caretaker occupant, having been appointed to the seat after the death of Senator Francis T. Maloney (D). Hart served from Feb. 15, 1945, through Nov. 5, 1946, when Raymond E. Baldwin (R) was elected to fill out the remainder of Maloney's term, plus a full term in his own right. However, Baldwin resigned from the Senate on Dec. 16, 1949. His term was then completed by another appointee, William Benton (D), who subsequently lost the seat in the election of 1952. McMahon remained Connecticut's senior senator from 1945 until his death in 1952. For the wartime relations of CBL and Hart, see Morris, *Rage for Fame*, 426–28 and 440.

49. *Tucson Daily Citizen*, Feb. 8, 1946; *Santa Monica Outlook*, Feb. 21, 1946.

50. *PM*, Feb. 12, 1946.

51. Willoughby to CBL, dated only "In the night," CBLP.

52. CBL quoting G. K. Chesterton to the *Boston Pilot*, Nov. 24, 1951.

53. CBL, "Converts and the Blessed Sacrament."

54. Fulton J. Sheen quoted in Hatch interviews, Apr. 1955, AHP. Sheen told Hatch that most of his conversion courses took some fifty hours. "Clare's took hundreds." Even that of the probing questioner Evelyn Waugh had taken Father Martin D'Arcy only three months. Martin Stannard, *Evelyn Waugh: The Early Years 1903–1939* (London, 1986), 228.

55. Shadegg, *Clare Boothe Luce*, 211, quoting an interview with Sheen twenty-one years after CBL's conversion.

56. Sheen quoted in Hatch interviews, Apr. 1955, AHP.
57. Sheen told Gretta Palmer that he considered CBL "the most brilliant of his converts." Palmer, "The New Clare Boothe Luce"; Shadegg, *Clare Boothe Luce*, 209–10.

18. OTHER ARENAS

1. *The New York Times*, Feb. 17, 1946, and *Syracuse Post-Standard*, Feb. 17, 1946.
2. *New York Journal-American*, Feb. 19, 1946.
3. Tere Pascone to CBL, Feb. 17, 1945, CBLP.
4. Ibid.
5. Fulton J. Sheen to CBL, n.d., CBLP.
6. Leila Hadley Luce interview, May 1, 1997; Sir Isaiah Berlin interview, Nov. 20, 1988. Another visitor that fall noted that a statue of the Madonna and the figurines of the angels Cyprian and Felix had been added to CBL's bedroom decor. Constance O'Hara memo, ca. Oct. 1946, CBLP.
7. The Brockhurst portrait of Sheen hangs at American Catholic University in Washington, D.C.
8. CBL quoting Saint Augustine in "The Real Reason," II.
9. Jean Dalrymple interview, Feb. 5, 1988. Since mid-1945, Harry's aides had begun to speculate that the boss must have "a secret girl," because "he gets a haircut every few days, puts in a long private phone call every morning and disappears for hours from the office, with even Thrasher not knowing where he is." John Billings diary, Aug. 29, 1945, JBP.
10. Jean Dalrymple interviews, Feb. 5 and 6, 1988; CBL memo "To HRL's Psychiatrist," Mar. 10, 1960, CBLP. Dalrymple admitted to SJM, "I became a kind of fan of Clare. I admired her tremendously."
11. "I hear hair-raising stories about Harry and Clare—how they appear to be on the brink of divorce. Is Harry running around with other women? I'm sorry for Clare—because it must be hell-a-mile to be married to Harry." John Billings diary, June 22, 1943, JBP.
12. Jean Dalrymple interview, Feb. 6, 1988. Darlymple admitted to SJM that since a romantic disappointment in her teens, she had learned not to trust men, and HRL was no exception. Besides, he had never made "enough of an effort" to please her.
13. John Billings diary, Feb. 13, 1946, JBP.
14. Elizabeth Root Luce to CBL, Feb. 20, 1946, CBLP.
15. Constance O'Hara, *Heaven Was Not Enough* (New York, 1955), 288.
16. CBL to Wilfrid Sheed, June 15, 1982, CBLP.
17. Caroline Moorhead, ed., *Selected Letters of Martha Gellhorn* (New York, 2006), 179.
18. Quoted in Philip Dunne to Edmund Morris, April 15, 1987, SJMP.
19. Helen Lawrenson, "The Woman," *Esquire*, Aug. 1975. Sheen's pastoral attentions reportedly ceased when Jack lost his prominent position in the National Maritime Union. The tireless cleric had better luck with Buff Cobb Rogers, converting her despite her recent attempt to dissuade Clare from joining the Roman Church.
20. CBL, "The Real Reason," III.
21. Martin Gilbert, *Churchill: A Life* (New York, 1991), 865–67. *The Washington Post*, in a series entitled "The Century in the Post," excerpts from "the first rough drafts of history," Mar. 6, 1999.
22. John Billings diary, Mar. 14, 1946, JBP.
23. Morris, *Rage for Fame*, 238–39.
24. Warren, "Churchill's Realism." The following night, Under Secretary of State

Dean Acheson abruptly dropped out of an event at the Waldorf-Astoria where Churchill spoke.

25. John Billings diary, Mar. 14, 1946, JBP.

26. *Brooklyn Eagle*, Mar. 17, 1946.

27. CBL to Harry Truman, June 29 and Mar. 25, 1946, CBLP; *The New York Times*, Oct. 19, 1982; Clarke, *The Last Thousand Days*, 461. Between May 1946 and September 1947, America took in 5,718 Jews, an average of about 350 a month. Coupled with the 350 that Great Britain was allowing into Palestine meant it would take 143 years to disperse the 100,000 stateless Jews.

28. *Chicago Tribune*, Aug. 1, 1946, and Jan. 5, 1947.

29. "Why Clare Boothe Luce Went Home," scrapbook clipping, Jan. 5, 1947, CBLP.

30. *Chicago Tribune*, Aug. 1, 1946, and Jan. 5, 1947.

31. CBL to Harry Truman, June 29, 1946, CBLP. One sentence in her column read, "Senate nicknames for Harry (Pendergast Machine) Truman and Mrs. (Office Helper) Truman: 'Kickback Harry' and 'Overtime Bess.'" Robert Hannegan to CBL, Apr. 30, 1946, CBLP. The only East Room invitation CBL received that spring was to witness the President being presented with the first sheet of a new three-cent commemorative stamp.

32. *Philadelphia News*, Apr. 18, 1946.

33. "Are Communism and Democracy Mutually Antagonistic?" Radio debate transcript published by the Catholic Information Society, New York, May 21, 1946, CBLP.

34. DFB to CBL, Aug. 25, 1945, CBLP.

35. Ibid., Nov. 7, 1945, CBLP.

36. Ibid., Jan. 18, 1946, CBLP. DFB had just heard from CBL for the first time since Aug. 1945.

37. Charles Willoughby to CBL, Apr. 2, 1946, CBLP.

38. CBL to HRL, July 7, 1946, CBLP.

39. HRL to CBL, July 11, 1946, CBLP.

40. CBL interview, July 24, 1982. SJM: "He wanted you in the Congress to begin with." CBL: "Yes, but he didn't like it in the end. He tired of my not making it home at weekends."

41. CBL to HRL, July 11, 1946, CBLP.

42. *The New York Times*, July 18, 1946.

43. Palmer, "The New Clare Luce."

44. Unidentified scrapbook clipping, Mar. 27, 1946, CBLP.

45. Sterling Seagrave, *The Soong Dynasty* (New York, 1985), 431. In *The Washington Post Magazine*, Jan. 24, 1988, Walter Judd, a leader of the so-called China Lobby in the 1940s, said there was no such organization, merely a group of about fifty people "trying to save China in order to benefit the United States."

46. CBL's original bill, or the law it subsequently became, may have inspired a scene in William Wyler's 1946 movie, *The Best Years of Our Lives*.

47. CBL, "On My Record in Congress—Bills Introduced."

48. Stephen Shadegg, "It Was Never Nothing," unpublished autobiographical fragment, 326, CBLP.

19. IN LIMBO

1. John Billings diary, Aug. 15, 1946, JBP.

2. CBL to HRL, Aug. 15, 1952, CBLP.

3. Chamberlain CBL Profile, JBP.

4. CBL to SJM on several occasions.

5. *Greenwich Time*, Aug. 16, 1946. On Sept. 9, the *Bridgeport Post* reported that CBL had also been asked by the GOP to run for Governor of Connecticut. Her objections to being away from home in D.C. would not pertain, they said. CBL was reportedly "overwhelmed," but did not in the end agree to run.

6. Alice Longworth quoted in the *Bridgeport Post*, Sep. 22, 1946.

7. John Billings diary, Feb. 18, 1947, JBP.

8. Ibid., Sept. 3, 1946, JBP.

9. Ibid., Sept. 15 and 16, 1946, JBP.

10. DFB to CBL, "Duties of Captain Boothe," June 21, 1946, CBLP. According to Charles Willoughby to CBL, June 6, 1946, DFB seemed "happy and interested" in his job. CBLP.

11. Willoughby to CBL, Aug. 4, Sept. 6, ca. Oct. 8, and Nov. 4, 1946, CBLP.

12. DFB to CBL, Mar. 29, 1946, CBLP.

13. Ibid.; Mrs. John Hill interview, Mar. 10, 1988.

14. Mary Lois Purdy Vega interview, Aug. 12, 1988. CBL told Wilfrid Sheed that DFB had beaten up a Japanese in the street. Wilfrid Sheed, *Clare Boothe Luce* (New York, 1982), 49.

15. DFB to CBL, Dec. 29 and 30, 1946, CBLP.

16. Ibid., Dec. 31, 1945; CBL to DFB, Jan. 1, 1946, CBLP. DFB recalled his sister telling him to "sweat it out" in the army because he had no capabilities for business, and she could not back him "because I have no rich men that love me any more and besides when you got through with me there was nothing left." The last was a reference to DFB's sponging on her and HRL, as well as his mismanagement of her Brokaw alimony and other stocks. DFB to George Waldo, n.d., October 1947, CBLP.

17. Alexander Heymeyer of Cravath, Swaine & Moore to CBL, Mar. 4, 1946, and to Isabel Hill, May 23, 1946, CBLP.

18. The Washington group arrived in Tokyo on Aug. 24, 1946, minus CBL.

19. DFB to CBL, Aug. 26, 1946, CBLP. Willoughby's dalliance came to nothing. His only fantasies of a romantic nature remained those connected with CBL at Hobe Sound, of "curious flecks of gold, like a halo, around a beautiful head, with the classical purity of a marble profile."

20. Shadegg, *Clare Boothe Luce*, 214.

21. CBL to William Peterson of Guam Dredging Contractors, Nov. 30, 1946, CBLP.

22. DFB to George Waldo, Oct. 7, 1947, CBLP.

23. DFB to CBL, Nov. 11, 1946, CBLP.

24. Ibid.

25. Ibid., Dec. 29 and 30, 1946. CBL cabled DFB on Dec. 23, 1946, "It was a great joy to see you lots of love Sister."

26. Ibid., Jan. 15, 1945, CBLP.

27. Ibid., Dec. 29 and 30, 1946, CBLP. "Hate is so wicked, for it not only destroys your objective, but you yourself in the process."

28. CBL quoted in DFB to CBL, Jan. 5, 1947, and in DFB to George Waldo, ca. Oct. 1947, CBLP.

29. DFB to CBL, Jan. 5, 1947, CBLP.

30. Ibid.

31. Ibid., Jan. 20, 1947, CBLP. DFB's separation was effective June 1, 1947.

32. DFB to George Waldo, Oct. 15, 1947, CBLP. David sent a copy of this letter to CBL.

33. CBL quoted in DFB to CBL, Jan. 20, 1947; DFB to George Waldo, Oct. n.d., 1947, CBLP.

34. DFB to CBL, Jan. 20, 1947, CBLP.

35. Ibid.

36. See Hicks Stone, *Edward Durell Stone: A Son's Untold Story of a Legendary Architect* (New York, 2011).

37. CBL to John Billings, Mar. 3, 1947, CBLP. For the names of visitors to the plantation, see Mepkin guest book, CBLP.

38. CBL to Margaret Case, Feb. 27, 1947, CBLP.

39. DFB to CBL, Dec. 15, 1945, CBLP.

40. John Billings diary, Feb. 14, 18, and 20, 1947, JBP.

41. CBL interview, June 13, 1982.

42. Ibid., Dec. 12, 1981. Harry reappeared at the office with "all the spark and sparkle" gone out of him. John Billings diary, Feb. 20, 1947, JBP.

43. CBL to HRL, Mar. 20 and Apr. 8, 1947, responding to his issues, CBLP.

44. Ibid., Apr. 8, 1947, CBLP. CBL interview, Jan. 10, 1982.

45. CBL to HRL, Mar. 20, 1947, CBLP.

46. DFB to George Waldo, Oct. 15, 1947, CBLP. A copy of this letter went to CBL.

47. DFB to CBL, Jan. 5, 1947, CBLP. DFB conceded that he believed in God, and CBL told Sheen she saw that as progress. CBL to Fulton J. Sheen, Apr. 24, 1947, CBLP.

48. DFB to CBL, Jan. 20, 1947, CBLP.

49. Palmer, "The New Clare Luce."

50. Lawrenson, *Stranger,* 104.

51. Blanche Knopf to CBL, Apr. 23, 1947, CBLP.

52. The book version had been offered to Heinemann as well, annoying the London publisher Hamish Hamilton. He complained of CBL's defection, and she blamed her agent, George Bye. CBL to Hamish Hamilton, Apr. 2, 1947, CBLP.

53. The offer from Sheed to publish "The Real Reason" in book form came in 1953. CBL declined, feeling that republicizing her Catholicism would have a negative efffect on her image as Ambassador in the United States. Dorothy Farmer to Frank Sheed, Nov. 30, 1953.

54. Maisie Ward transcript, May 1953, CBLP. The editor of *McCall's* said he decided against having Clare respond to readers' letters in a Q&A column, because it might dissipate the effect of her work, "by making your Faith a matter of temporal controversy," and because "The Real Reason" had established her "as one of the leading lay spokesmen" of her church. Otis L. Wiese to CBL, May 6, 1947, CBLP.

55. CBL telegram to DFB, Apr. 24, 1947, CBLP.

56. Mrs. John Hill interview, Mar. 10, 1988. Mrs. Hill heard about DFB's stealing from her mother-in-law and CBL's secretary, Isabel Hill. The Hills met DFB at Mepkin, where they were on honeymoon from Apr. 19 to May 1, 1947.

20. A TERRIBLE MAELSTROM OF TROUBLE

1. *Vogue* featured Sugar Hill interiors in its March 1949 issue. The Luces left almost everything in the Greenwich house [NB: It was called "The House"] for its buyers. CBL had wanted to retrieve innumerable items before the sale, but Harry felt they would get a better price with a "completely furnished effect." He advised removing only irreplaceable antiques and items of sentiment.

2. DFB to CBL, May 7 and 8, 1947, CBLP. CBL hoped in vain that Sheen would be in Mobile at the same time as DFB and could complete his conversion. CBL to Fulton J. Sheen, Apr. 24, 1947, CBLP.

3. CBL, "A memo to Harry about Diminishments," ca. Aug. 1960, CBLP.

4. Ibid.

5. Ibid.; John Billings diary, June 17, 1947, JBP.

6. Ibid., June 18, 1947.

7. C. S. Lewis, *The Screwtape Letters* (London, 1942), 50, 48.

8. Ibid., 126–30.

9. Ibid., 94.

10. John Billings diary, July 14, 1947, JBP.

11. CBL, "To HRL's psychiatrist," Mar. 10, 1960, CBLP.

12. Ibid. Another reason HRL gave for his impotence was that he put CBL "on a pedestal." Morris, *Rage for Fame,* 308, 284–85, 357–60.

13. CBL to HRL, July 26, 1947, CBLP.

14. CBL, "To HRL's psychiatrist," Mar. 10, 1960, CBLP. HRL had potency problems even around the sexiest of women. Mary Bancroft quoted him as reporting that Pamela Churchill (later Harriman) once flagrantly tried to seduce him, but was "too businesslike" in ripping off her clothes, expecting his "automatic enthusiasm." When he failed to respond, she mocked him and broadcast the encounter to her friends. Bancroft to W. A. Swanberg, Apr. 19, 1971, MBP. For more on HRL's sexuality see Morris, *Rage for Fame,* 357–60.

15. CBL, "A memo to Harry about Diminishments," ca. Aug. 1960, CBLP.

16. CBL to HRL, July 26, 1947, CBLP; CBL interview, June 10, 1982.

17. CBL to HRL, Mar. 1, 1940, CBLP.

18. Ibid., July 26, 1947, CBLP. This last claim echoed one HRL had made some four years after their marriage. He said that from the start, "I loved you better than I loved myself . . . gladly would I have died for you—you know that—and if you had died I would have wished not to live." HRL to CBL, Mar. 18, 1940, CBLP.

19. John Billings diary, Aug. 4, 1947, JBP; Billings to Al Grover, Aug. 5, 1947, JBP.

20. John Billings diary, Aug. 5 and 6, 1947, JBP.

21. CBL memo to herself, imagining the affair from HRL's viewpoint, Sept. 8–10, 1959, CBLP; CBL interview, June 10, 1982.

22. CBL memo, Aug. 10, 1949, CBLP.

23. CBL, "To HRL's psychiatrist," Mar. 10, 1960, CBLP.

24. CBL quoted in DFB to George Waldo, Oct. 7, 1947, CBLP.

25. John Billings diary, Aug. 11, 1947, JBP.

26. Ibid.

27. Ibid.

28. CBL to HRL, n.d., Aug. 1947, CBLP.

29. CBL interviewed by Sally Quinn, *Chicago Sun Times,* Sunday, June 3, 1973.

30. DFB to CBL, "Friday," most likely Aug. 15, 1947, CBLP.

31. DFB to George Waldo, n.d., "Tuesday a.m.," Oct. 1947, CBLP. CBL sold the Boston house in May 1948.

32. John Billings diary, Aug. 19, 1947, JBP.

33. Ibid., Aug. 27, 1947, JBP.

34. Elizabeth Root Luce to HRL, July–Aug. 1948, SJMP.

35. Ibid.

36. John Billings diary, Aug. 25, 1947, JBP.

37. Jean Dalrymple interview, Feb. 5, 1988. Also see Alan Brinkley, *The Publisher: Henry Luce and His American Century* (New York, 2010), 321.

38. John Billings diary, Aug. 27, 1947, JBP.

39. Ibid.; Jean Dalrymple interview, Feb. 6, 1988. "Harry really loved me for twenty-four years. Our romance was not consummated. Never, actually, physically."

40. John Billings diary, Aug. 27, 1947, JBP.
41. CBL to HRL, n.d., CBLP.
42. HRL to CBL, "Monday," almost certainly Aug. 25, 1947, CBLP.
43. John Billings diary, Sept. 2, 1947, JBP. Mary Bancroft wrote HRL that Jackson liked to gossip about his boss outside the office, too. "I have not gathered that he hates the G.A. ["Guardian Angel," her nickname for CBL] as relentlessly as some—but apparently he regales people with the devastating effect on you. Probably all it means is that he'd like to be your G.A. himself and guide you along the paths *he* thinks you should follow." Mary Bancroft to HRL, Mar. 21, 1952, MBP.
44. John Billings diary, Sept. 2, 1947, JBP.
45. Ibid.
46. John Billings diary, Sept. 3, 1947, JBP; Al Grover to John Billings, Oct. 24, 1947, JBP.
47. John Billings diary, Sept. 17 and 18, 1947, JBP.
48. Ibid., Sept. 25, 1947, JBP.
49. DFB memo to CBL, July 30, 1947, CBLP; DFB quoting CBL to George Waldo, Oct. 7, 1947, CBLP.
50. DFB memo to CBL, July 30, 1947, CBLP.
51. DFB to George Waldo, Oct. 7, 1947, CBLP.
52. Ibid.
53. Ibid.
54. Ibid.

21. HOLLYWOOD

1. Payne and Morley, *The Noël Coward Diaries*, 93.
2. John Billings diary, Nov. 27, 1947, JBP. Janeway's dismissal was effective Jan. 1, 1948.
3. Robert E. Herzstein, "Five Years with Henry Luce: Second Thoughts," *Historian*, newsletter of the Department of History, University of South Carolina (Summer 1996).
4. C. S. Lewis to CBL, Oct. 26, 1947, CBLP.
5. CBL interview, June 20, 1982.
6. The Isenbrandt cost $20,000 and was meant to celebrate the Luces' decision to stay together, as well as Christmas.
7. List of Luce artworks, CBLP.
8. John Billings diary, Jan. 3, 1948, JBP.
9. Walter Graebner to John Billings, ca. Dec. 1947, JBP. HRL paid $750,000 for serial rights to Churchill's memoirs, sharing the privilege with *The New York Times*, which paid $400,000. The former Prime Minister thus earned an unprecedented rights total of $1.15 million. HRL had earlier paid Churchill $20,000 to reproduce his paintings in *Life*, and $50,000 to reprint some of his speeches. See Brinkley, *The Publisher*, 330–32.
10. CBL to Alice Austin, Dec. 26, 1947, CBLP. CBL admitted to her stepfather's wife that she had little to show for three weeks at the studio.
11. Ralph Ingersoll, *The Great Ones* (New York, 1948), 209–10.
12. CBL interview, June 10, 1982.
13. According to Philip Simpson, Julian's Australian cousin, Julian married Janet Knox, a member of New South Wales's first families. Philip Simpson, interviewed by Michael Teague, May 1990.
14. Julian Simpson to CBL, Feb. 2, 1948, CBLP.

15. In his later years, Julian Simpson was acknowledged to be homosexual. Philip Simpson, interviewed by Michael Teague, May 1990.
16. Booklet of CBL poems, CBLP.
17. CBL to Donald Ogden Stewart, Jan. 30, 1948, CBLP.
18. CBL to C. S. Lewis, Apr. 24, 1948, CBLP.
19. Ibid.
20. CBL to Donald Ogden Stewart, Jan. 30, 1948, CBLP.
21. Unidentified Connecticut scrapbook clipping, Oct. 5, 1946, CBLP. In her Waterbury speech, CBL recalled her own first sight of Monte Cassino during World War II, and drew parallels between the Christianity of St. Benedict's time, under siege in a "brutal, barbaric and pagan world," and contemporary Western democracy, similarly besieged by godless Communists. Ibid.
22. Darryl Zanuck to CBL, Jan. 30, 1948, CBLP. CBL's contract with Fox gave Gretta Palmer credit for research. She was paid $25,000 by Fox and gave most of it to the Reverend Mother Benedict at Regina Laudis, Bethlehem, Conn. Palmer to Kay Brown, Aug. 26, 1948, CBLP.
23. Meta Blackwell, in the *San Bernardino Sunday Telegraph*, Feb. 15, 1948; CBL to Darryl Zanuck, Mar. 2, 1948, CBLP.
24. Morton S. Biskind, MD, "DDT Poisoning and the Elusive 'Virus X': A New Cause for Gastroenteritis," *American Journal of Digestive Diseases* 16, no. 3 (1949).
25. John Billings diary, Feb. 25, 1948, JBP.

22. CROONERS OF CATASTROPHE

1. HRL to CBL and CBL to HRL, ca. Feb. 1948, notes exchanged on whether or not to part with Mepkin, CBLP. Before the war, CBL said it took forty gardeners at $1.00 each a day to keep up gardens and stables. After it, workers could make $5.00 a day in Charleston and no longer needed to work upriver, so improvements to the plantation ceased. CBL interview, June 14, 1982.
2. Sidney Lanier, *Hymns of the Marshes* (New York, 1907).
3. See Stone, *Edward Durell Stone*.
4. CBL to Sister Madeleva, Jan. 3, 1951, SJMP.
5. Morris, *Rage for Fame*, 285 and 296–302.
6. Irene Selznick interview, Feb. 4, 1988.
7. Elisabeth Luce Moore to HRL, Apr. 6, 1948, CBLP.
8. *Washington Times-Herald*, Jan. 10, 1950. The gossip columnist Hedda Hopper put out a rumor that Senator Vandenberg could not be nominated by the GOP because of an affair with CBL.
9. Mrs. John Hill interview, Mar. 1988.
10. CBL to Shirley Clurman, Mar. 18, 1973, CBLP.
11. Transcript in *Philadelphia Evening Bulletin*, June 22, 1948.
12. See http://www.ushistory.org/gop/convention_1948.htm.
13. Reuven Frank, "National Conventions," *The New York Times Magazine*, Apr. 17, 1988. *Life* publisher Andrew Heiskell arranged the deal for Time Inc. HRL never showed much interest in television.
14. Constance O'Hara to Brock Pemberton, Nov. 18, 1948, CBLP; O'Hara, *Heaven Was Not Enough*, 291–97. Most of the letters denigrating CBL's convention remarks were anonymous.
15. H. L. Mencken, "Decibels Hit Ceiling in Keynote-Night Din," *Baltimore Sun*, June 22, 1948. The author is indebted to Marion Elizabeth Rodgers, author of *Mencken: The American Iconoclast* (New York, 2005), for this item. Also see Joseph C. Goul-

den, ed., *Mencken's Last Campaign: H. L. Mencken on the 1948 Election* (Washington, D.C., 1976).

16. CBL in *McCall's*, June 1964, quoted a *World Telegram* newsman as reporting that "the blonde beauty from Connecticut looked like she'd been scalped."

17. CBL GOP convention speech, June 21, 1948, CBLP.

18. CBL in *McCall's*, June 1964. "Even though my speech . . . went on to praise Foster Dulles and Thomas Dewey, [GOP leaders] did not quite forgive me."

19. GOP convention speech, June 21, 1948, CBLP; CBL quoted in *Newsweek*, Jan. 24, 1955.

20. Unsigned letters, ca. June 1948, CBLP.

21. William F. Buckley, Jr., interview, Sept. 8, 1983; Beaverbrook to CBL, June, 27, 1948, CBLP.

22. John Billings diary, June 25, 1948, JBP.

23. *The New York Times*, July 2, 1948. Three days after announcing her plans, CBL attracted a record crowd in Fairfield.

24. *Newsweek*, July 12, 1948. Clare had long admired Mrs. Roosevelt, and had nothing but praise when on May 21, 1950, she spoke at a banquet honoring the former First Lady's work as chairman of the United Nations Commission on Human Rights. Stealing a line from the great Irish humorist Finley Peter Dunne, Clare said, "No woman has ever so comforted the distressed—or distressed the comfortable." A few narrow-minded Republicans frowned on this encomium, but Eleanor wrote to thank her. "You were more than kind in what you said at the Gold Medal Award, and I am deeply appreciative of your generous words and the fact that you attended the dinner." Eleanor Roosevelt to CBL, May 25, 1950, CBLP. Also see CBL quoted in David Remnick, "Memories of Eleanor," *The Washington Post*, Oct. 15, 1984.

25. Laura Z. Hobson, *Laura Z: A Life: Years of Fulfillment* (New York, 1986), 105–06.

26. HRL, probably at CBL's behest, made sure that *Time* "did not give too big a play to Helen G. Douglas" at the Democratic gathering. Its reports did not even mention the Congresswoman's name. John Billings diary, July 19, 1948, JBP.

27. Elizabeth Root Luce to HRL, "July–August, 1948," CBLP. Mrs. Luce died on November 7, 1948.

28. CBL thought HRL's "basically secretive nature" had caused much of the misunderstanding in the family. She learned late of Elizabeth Root Luce's liver cancer, and discovered Patricia Luce's pregnancy only by noticing her increasing size, although HRL had known about their coming grandchild for months. He was silent even about his own ailments. If Harry said he was "a little ill," she remarked, "it was time to send for an ambulance." CBL to Shirley Clurman, Oct. 5, 1972, CBLP.

29. Michael Mott, *The Seven Mountains of Thomas Merton* (Boston, 1984), 74–84, 120, 210–11.

30. Robert Giroux to CBL, July 30, 1948, CBLP; Mott, *Seven Mountains*, 243. By 1984, Merton's book had sold more than a million copies around the world.

31. *Time*, Dec. 31, 1984.

32. CBL to Thomas Merton, Aug. 12, 1948, CBLP.

33. CBL to Sister Madeleva, Sept. 11, 1948, CBLP.

34. CBL to Father Wilfrid J. Thibodeau, Mar. 13, 1949.

35. DFB to CBL, Aug. 31, 1948, CBLP.

36. *Oakland Tribune*, Sept. 8, 1948. Mary Lois Purdy Vega interview, Aug. 12, 1988. CBL told Ms. Vega, a former Time Inc. employee, that in a late-night phone call, DFB suggested she pray for him, "because I am going to kill myself." She appealed to a friend in California to find a good psychiatrist for him, saying that he wanted to commit suicide "so that he would not one day kill another."

23. OUTSIDE THE PALE

1. DFB to George Waldo, Oct. 7, 1947, CBLP.
2. Ibid.
3. George Waldo to DFB, Oct. 13, 1947, CBLP.
4. DFB to Waldo, Oct. 15, 1947, CBLP.
5. DFB to CBL, n.d., CBLP.
6. George Waldo to CBL, Jan. 28, 1948, CBLP.
7. Ibid., Nov. 23, 1947, CBLP.
8. Unidentified scrapbook clipping, Sept. 8, 1948, CBLP; *The New York Times*, Sept. 7, *New York World Telegram*, Sept. 8, and *New York Herald Tribune*, Sept. 9, 1948.
9. *New York Herald Tribune*, Sept. 9, 1948.

24. THE TWILIGHT OF GOD

1. CBL to Wilfrid J. Thibodeau, Feast of Saint Francis, Mar. 1949, SJMP; CBL interview, Dec. 12, 1981. CBL also said that DFB was a misanthrope, and could "never believe that the good and beautiful would triumph." CBL to Brigadier General S. M. Mellnik, n.d. 1969, CBLP. CBL admitted to SJM that there were many dark spots in her own life that she preferred not to go into. "Like you are afraid to go into a closet where you've heard a strange noise." CBL interview, June 13, 1982.
2. CBL to Thibodeau, Feast of Saint Francis, Mar. 1949, SJMP.
3. CBL recorded this frequent nightmare on June 7, 1949, CBLP. Unpersuaded by George Waldo that DFB might have crashed accidentally, she routinely referred to her brother's demise as "his suicide." George Waldo to CBL, Sept. 8, 1948; CBL, "To HRL's psychiatrist," Mar. 10, 1960, CBLP.
4. Dorothy Farmer to Allen Grover, Sept. 21, 1948, CBLP.
5. Article quoting Regina Foote in *San Antonio Light*, Sept. 12, 1948.
6. Dorothy Farmer to Allen Grover, Sept. 18, 1948, CBLP. DFB had sent CBL his Sept. premium notice for $20.90 after their last conversation. She paid it on Sept. 11, 1948, six days after his death, in an attempt to collect his death benefits.
7. Walter T. Stace, "Man Against Darkness," *Atlantic Monthly*, Sept. 1948.
8. Barnett's article appeared in the *Ladies' Home Journal*, Nov. 1948, McDonald's in the *American Ecclesiastical Review*, May 1948.
9. Clare Boothe Luce, *The Twilight of God* (Chicago, 1949).
10. Ibid., 34.
11. Ibid., 38.

25. COME TO THE STABLE

1. CBL interview, Apr. 16, 1982.
2. "The Great Upset of '49," PBS broadcast, Nov. 2, 1988; Fleur Cowles to CBL, Sept. 22, 1948, CBLP.
3. CBL interview, Apr. 16, 1982; CBL to Jane Abel, Dec. 30, 1948, CBLP. The biggest loser in the 1948 election was the Progressive candidate, Henry Wallace. But he did get a record number of 1,150,000 Communist Party votes. By the early 1980s, the United States would be "the only democratic industrialized nation in which not a single independent Socialist or Labor Party representative held elective office." Paul Johnson, *Modern Times* (New York, 1983), 213.
4. With Randolph Churchill's help. Churchill to CBL, Aug. 8, 1948, CBLP.
5. Mark Amory, ed., *The Letters of Evelyn Waugh* (New York, 1980), 287–89.

6. CBL interview, Jan. 8, 1982.

7. Unidentified scrapbook clipping, CBLP.

8. Ibid.

9. Ibid.

10. O'Hara, *Heaven Was Not Enough*, 296–97.

11. CBL to Wilfrid J. Thibodeau, Apr. 25, 1949, SJMP. In 1953, CBL was distressed to see in Merton's published journal impatient references to her. "I realized I had intruded on his contemplative life, which I ought never to have done." CBL to Father James of Mepkin Abbey, Jan. 25, 1953, CBLP.

12. Beaverbrook to Brendan Bracken, Jan. 17, 1949. It was the host's nurse who noticed HRL's familiarity with the Mass. The author is grateful to Sally Bedell Smith for this letter from the Beaverbrook archive in London.

13. CBL to Raimund von Hofmannsthal and Blanche Wise, Feb. 11, 1949, CBLP; CBL to George Bye, Feb. 2, 1949, CBLP.

14. CBL interview, June 20, 1982.

15. CBL to Darryl Zanuck, Mar. 2, 1948, CBLP. Her letter expressed disappointment at not being asked to do rewrites of *Bethlehem*.

16. Dorothy Farmer to CBL, n.d., Jan. 1949, CBLP.

17. Script of "Saint Anthony and the Gambler," CBLP; Samuel G. Engel to Kay Brown, Jan. 28, 1949, CBLP. CBL subsequently sent copies of "Saint Anthony" to Irene Dunne, Joseph P. Kennedy, Sam Goldwyn, Hedda Hopper, and Bob Hope. Only the last showed serious interest, saying he had forwarded the script to Paramount and asked if it could be rewritten to fit him. Nothing came of Hope's overture. Bob Hope to CBL's office, Dec. 19, 1949, CBLP; CBL cable to Bob Hope, Dec. 27, 1949, CBLP. As late as May 1, 1950, Hedda Hopper was suggesting in her column that Mary Martin and Bing Crosby should do CBL's "wonderful comedy" for Paramount. CBL was still writing revised versions as late as 1961. CBLP.

18. O'Hara, *Heaven Was Not Enough*, 321. CBL introduced O'Hara to Thibodeau that spring.

19. CBL to Thibodeau, Feb. 16, 1949, SJMP.

20. Ibid., Feb. 27, 1949, SJMP.

21. Ibid., Feb. 20, 1949, SJMP.

22. Ibid., Mar. 13, 1949, SJMP.

23. Ibid., Feb. 27, 1949, SJMP.

24. Curtis P. Freshel to CBL, Mar. 16 and Apr. 18, 1949, CBLP. Freshel said that he converted to Roman Catholicism because of his admiration for CBL. According to CBL, Freshel was a friend of George Bernard Shaw and an illegitimate son of Edward VII. She said that after his wife died in 1948, he gave her a diamond ring that the king had given to his mother. CBL interview, May 1, 1985.

25. O'Hara, *Heaven Was Not Enough*, 241. *Locusts* was part of Britain's 1938 Silver Jubilee Festival. It also played in Manchester. O'Hara anticipated a stellar career, but the onset of war foiled a revival of her play in London. A second script, *Honorable Estate*, based on the relationship of the English novelist George Eliot and her lover, George Lewes, was praised by the great actress Laurette Taylor, and a third, tinkered with by Brock Pemberton and Antoinette Perry, also failed to reach the stage. In despair by the fall of 1940, O'Hara attempted suicide. She recovered and persevered. But in 1946, *The Magnificent Heel*, produced by Pemberton, had opened and closed out of town.

26. O'Hara, *Heaven Was Not Enough*, 299

27. O'Hara to Dorothy Farmer, n.d. 1949, CBLP.

28. CBL to Dr. Karl Stern, Nov. 12, 1952, CBLP. Dr. Stern, a Catholic psychiatrist living in Montreal, Canada, contributed to CBL's book *Saints for Now*. She wrote him that she was concerned about the autobiography O'Hara was writing, and wanted to record her version of their friendship.

29. O'Hara, *Heaven Was Not Enough*, 300–03. At her mother's suggestion, O'Hara sent CBL a copy of *Years of the Locusts*. Georges Bernanos, author of *La Joie*, was a conservative French Catholic author who also wrote *Diary of a Country Priest* and the libretto for Poulenc's *Dialogues of the Carmelites*. He was anti-Vichy and spoke out against government intrusion into private life.

30. Ibid., 303. Brock Pemberton to CBL, Apr. 4, 1949, wrote, "Constance O'Hara tells me she is about to do some work for you. I hope she settles down enough to do it. I never saw anyone so excited." The producer seemed to hint at O'Hara's volatility. CBLP.

31. On June 7, 1949, CBL recorded various nightmares in which she was balding and losing teeth. CBLP.

32. O'Hara, *Heaven Was Not Enough*, 311.

33. Ibid., 310.

34. Ibid., 314–16.

35. Ibid., 316–22.

36. Ibid., 322–24.

37. CBL to Thibodeau, Apr. 17, 1949, CBLP.

38. CBL to Pope Pius XII, Easter day, Apr. 17, 1949, CBLP.

39. CBL to Thibodeau, Apr. 17, 1949, SJMP.

40. O'Hara, *Heaven Was Not Enough*, 330–31.

41. Elsa Maxwell, "Week-end Roundup," *New York Post*, May 1, 1949. In the week of May 1–7, the Posture Selection Committee of the International Chiropractors Association nominated CBL as "an outstanding example of good posture in the career woman classification." *Norwalk Hour* (Conn.), May 2, 1949.

42. Moss Hart to CBL, n.d. 1949, CBLP; Morris, *Rage for Fame*, 295.

43. *Walla Walla Union Bulletin*, Oct. 2, 1949, and *Reno Evening Gazette*, Oct. 20, 1949.

44. Connecticut's other senator, William Benton (D), in contrast, was sure only of the remaining two years of his appointive term. In 1952, he would be able to run for a full term in his own right. An Apr. 13, 1949, *Bridgeport Post* editorial described CBL as "one of the most gifted and far-sighted women ever to grace American public life."

45. CBL to Thibodeau, May 4, 1949, SJMP.

46. CBL to Beaverbrook, June 7, 1949, BP.

47. CBL, "The Mystery of Our China Policy," *Plain Talk*, July 1949.

48. The role of Sister Margaret was Loretta Young's ninetieth part. She had already won an Oscar for *The Farmer's Daughter*. Hugh Marlowe appeared in *Twelve O'Clock High* and costarred with Gene Tierney in *Night and the City*.

49. CBL to Darryl Zanuck, May 21, 1949, CBLP.

50. O'Hara, *Heaven Was Not Enough*, 334.

51. CBL to HRL, May 17, 1949, CBLP.

52. After the screening, Spellman said that he "enjoyed it immensely." Oren Root to CBL, May 20, 1949, CBLP.

53. CBL cable to Darryl Zanuck, May 21, 1949, CBLP.

54. Darryl Zanuck to CBL, June 1, 1949, CBLP.

55. Darryl Zanuck cable to CBL, quoting *Daily Variety* and *Hollywood Reporter* comments, June 22, 1949, CBLP.

56. *Variety*, June 22, 1949. *Life* helped to promote the movie by running a spread on Regina Laudis, the Connecticut nunnery on which CBL based her story. HRL told John Billings that CBL should be given full credit in the magazine for her input, because Hollywood would do the reverse. Memo, Apr. 8, 1949, CBLP; CBL to Beaverbrook, June 7, 1949, BP.

57. CBL to Thibodeau, June 6, 1949, SJMP.

58. CBL dream memo, June 13, 1949, CBLP.

59. CBL to Evelyn Waugh, June 9, 1949, CBLP.

60. O'Hara, *Heaven Was Not Enough*, 339.

61. The audiovisual Catechism was screened in Philadelphia later that year, with CBL cited as "Editorial Supervisor." The church hierarchy rejected it. O'Hara, *Heaven Was Not Enough*, 356–60.

62. Ibid., 355.

63. Ibid.

64. O'Hara, *Heaven Was Not Enough*, 366. O'Hara told Brock Pemberton that the "tragic termination" of her four-month intimacy with CBL had been due to "misunderstanding, my own temper, priestly indifference, lies and jealousy." O'Hara to Pemberton, n.d., CBLP.

65. O'Hara to CBL, ca. late 1949 or early 1950, CBLP. It is clear from O'Hara's other correspondence that by "church" she meant Monsignor Sheen. See O'Hara to Gretta Palmer, ca. Oct. 1949, CBLP; Palmer to O'Hara, Oct. 31, 1949, CBLP.

66. O'Hara to Palmer, n.d. 1949, CBLP. O'Hara also wrote to CBL, "Clare, it was obvious that I was very, very fond of you. . . . You never bored me dear." Undated letter, 1950, CBLP. O'Hara's autobiography, *Heaven Was Not Enough*, was published in 1955, to generally favorable reviews.

67. CBL to Thibodeau, Feb. 20, 1949, SJMP.

68. O'Hara had once told CBL that as a girl, she had described herself as the black sheep of her school. But CBL might also have been signaling that she considered the troubled Catholic a lost lamb who needed shepherding back into the Church. O'Hara, *Heaven Was Not Enough*, 363–64.

69. CBL to Dr. Karl Stern, Nov. 12, 1952, CBLP.

70. Sheed, *Clare Boothe Luce*, 5.

71. Morris, *Rage for Fame*, 26; Sheed, *Clare Boothe Luce*, 13.

72. The soubriquet "Little Flower" further distinguished her from the better-known Saint Teresa of Ávila.

73. Sheed, *Clare Boothe Luce*, 8.

74. CBL to Thibodeau, Aug. 11, 1949, SJMP.

75. Sheed, *Clare Boothe Luce*, 8–9.

76. Ibid., 17.

77. CBL to Thibodeau, Aug. 4, 1949, SJMP.

78. Sheed, *Clare Boothe Luce*, 7.

79. Ibid., 8.

80. CBL to Bernard Denenberg, May 20, 1969, CBLP. She bought the Chagall at an auction of Frank Crowninshield's artworks in 1943, and it would hang over her bed, wherever she had a house, for the next twenty-five years.

81. Sheed, *Clare Boothe Luce*, 8.

82. Ibid.; 21–22.

83. CBL to Thibodeau, Aug. 11, 1949, SJMP.

84. Sheed, *Clare Boothe Luce*, 35.

85. Ibid., 12.

86. Ibid., 8–10.

87. Ibid., 11.

88. *The New York Times,* July 28, 1949. When *Time's* critic gave the film short shift, calling it "a fluffy souffle" and its comedy "cute," HRL had the piece rewritten to be less negative.

89. CBL to Barbara Jenks, a Catholic admirer, May 17, 1949, CBLP.

90. *Come to the Stable* failed to win any Oscars.

26. PILGRIMAGES

1. Sheed, *Clare Boothe Luce,* 21. CBL told Sheed that "being a dramatist was the one thing she had *not* done just to prove she could do it." Paul Johnson, *Intellectuals* (New York, 1988), 313.

2. *Hartford Courant,* July 27, 1949; *New York Journal-American,* July 28, 1949.

3. *Hartford Times,* Sept. 24, 1949.

4. *New York Herald Tribune,* Sept. 22, 1949.

5. *Bridgeport Post,* Sept. 27 and June 5, 1949, quoting Thomas R. Harnett of the Mercantile Bank, Dallas.

6. CBL's speech slated for the Bridgeport Chamber of Commerce was entitled "Our American Way of Life and How We Can Best Defend Our System of Free Enterprise."

7. *Bridgeport Telegram,* Sept. 27, 1949, and *Williamsport Gazette and Bulletin* (Pa.), Sept. 29, 1949.

8. Robert J. Donovan, *Tumultuous Years: The Presidency of Harry S. Truman, 1949–1953* (New York, 1983), 101–03.

9. CBL, "Christianity and the Negro," *The New Leader,* Oct. 1, 1949; *Miami Daily News Record,* Oct. 10, 1949.

10. *Naugatuck News* (Conn.), Oct. 13, 1949.

11. *Charleston Gazette* (W. Va.), Nov. 22, 1949.

12. Wilfrid J. Thibodeau to CBL, Aug. 12, 1949, CBLP.

13. *Bridgeport Herald,* Nov. 27, 1949.

14. CBL to HRL, Oct. 31, 1949, CBLP. She added, "It would be swell wouldn't it. You could do such great good in that post, and yet never lose touch with your real metier, the interpretation of world events." Myron Taylor served as personal envoy from 1939 to 1950. Despite his strange title, he was extended ambassadorial status by the Vatican in 1940. The United States did not appoint an official Ambassador to the Holy See until 1984.

15. CBL in *Catholic Action of the South,* undated scrapbook clipping, CBLP.

16. CBL diary, Oct. 30, 1949, CBLP; CBL, "A Skull in the Catacombs," *The Pylon,* July 1950.

17. Elisabeth Cobb Rogers diary, Nov. 2, 1949, CBLP.

18. By mid-Nov., Chávez was in Paris at the same time as CBL, staying at the Hotel Georges V. They possibly dined together on Nov. 15, 1949.

19. Elisabeth Cobb Rogers diary, Nov. 3, 1949, CBLP.

20. Ibid., Nov. 14, 1949. On that day, the first contingent of monks moved from Kentucky to Mepkin.

21. The Hyde Park Hotel is where Waugh usually stayed when in town.

22. Amory, *The Letters of Evelyn Waugh,* 315.

23. CBL to HRL, Nov. 28, 1949, CBLP.

24. CBL to Thomas Merton, "Feast Day of St. Clare," Aug. 12, 1948; CBL to Abbot

M. James Fox, Dec. 2, 1948, CBLP. The Vatican approved the transfer to Mepkin in late November 1948. At the time of the move, 186 monks remained at Gethsemani.

25. CBL to Father Fox, Jan. 18, 1949, CBLP.
26. *Berkeley County Evening Post*, Nov. 15, 1949; AP clipping, Nov. 16, 1949, CBLP.

27. CARLOS AND CLARITA

1. HRL to Henry Luce III, Jan. 14, 1950, CBLP.
2. Ibid.
3. John Billings diary, Jan. 20, 1950, JBP; Robert Elson to Billings, May 22, 1970, JBP.
4. *The New York Times*, Feb. 1, 1950. Years afterward, CBL claimed that HRL commissioned a Connecticut poll that showed he could not win a Senate seat, whereas she could have beaten either Benton or McMahon. CBL interview, Jan. 10, 1982.
5. Al Morano to CBL, Jan. 11, 1950, CBLP; *Newport News*, Feb. 13, 1950, CBLP.
6. CBL to Carlos Chávez, Jan. 5, 1950, CCP.
7. CBL to Chávez, Feb. 6, 1950, CCP; Chávez to CBL, Feb. 7, 1950, CCP.
8. CBL, "Thoughts on Mexico," *Vogue*, Aug. 1950.
9. Carlos and Otilia Chávez had both been students of the eminent music teacher Luis Ogazon.
10. CBL eventually bequeathed *Between the Curtains* to the National Museum of Women in the Arts in Washington, D.C. In 1939, she commissioned Kahlo to paint a posthumous portrait of her friend, the suicidal actress Dorothy Hale. Kahlo, true to her own psychological makeup, depicted Hale jumping from a skyscraper, sequentially falling, and ending up splayed and bleeding on the sidewalk. Finding the painting too gruesome to live with, CBL left *The Suicide of Dorothy Hale* to the Phoenix Art Musem. For more on her relationship with Kahlo, see Morris, *Rage for Fame*, 326–32.
11. CBL, "Thoughts on Mexico."
12. Chávez once lent this house to Aaron Copland, who complained that he had difficulty composing there because of the "sensational" panorama. Copland to Chávez, Feb. 13, 1959, CCPN.
13. Robert L. Parker, *Carlos Chávez: Mexico's Modern-Day Orpheus* (Boston, 1983), 133–34.
14. CBL to Chávez, Apr. 1, 1950, CCP.
15. Ibid.
16. Ibid.
17. CBL quoting Chávez, Ash Wednesday, Feb. 22, 1950, CCP.
18. Fragment, CCP. While professing to follow CBL's thematic wishes, Chávez eventually wrote not a concerto but a four-movement symphony, his third.
19. CBL to Wilfrid J. Thibodeau, Mar. 1, 1950, SJMP.
20. Ibid.
21. Ibid.; CBL to Chávez, "Ash Wednesday," Feb. 22, 1950, CCP.
22. Ibid.
23. W. A. Swanberg, *Luce and His Empire* (New York, 1972), 290.
24. CBL to Thibodeau, Mar. 1, 1950, SJMP.
25. Joseph Mersand, *The American Drama Since 1930* (New York, 1949), quoted by Fearnow, *Luce*, 129–30.
26. CBL to Chávez, "Spring 1950," CCP. At CBL's prompting, Case sent a copy of the article to Chávez.

27. Schedule and guest list for Chávez's March visit, CBLP; *Alameda Times Star* (Calif.), Apr. 5, 1950.
28. CBL to Chávez, Mar. 29, 1950, CCP.
29. Ibid., Mar. 30, 1950, CCP.
30. Ibid., Apr. 1, 1950, CCP.
31. Ibid., n.d., ca. early Apr. 1950, CCP.
32. Ibid.
33. In a letter to Chávez, ca. May 1950, Margaret Case said she would tell him sometime "how I managed to get Clare on to the boards of the Stadium and Philharmonic in record-breaking time." CCP.
34. CBL to Chávez, "Spring 1950," CCP.
35. Ibid., May 3, 1950, CCP.
36. Ibid.
37. Ibid. Rieti avoided sentimentality and Germanic profundity in his scores, preferring the French neoclassical style adopted by Stravinsky in later life.
38. CBL to Chávez, May 3, 1950, CCP.
39. Ibid. Rufino Tamayo had shared a Greenwich Village apartment in New York with Chávez between 1926 and 1928. During those years, Chávez made friends with Aaron Copland, Edgard Varèse, and other North American composers.
40. CBL to Chávez, June 12, 1959, CCP.
41. Chávez to CBL, May 13, 1950, CCP.
42. CBL to Chávez, ca. Apr. 18, 1950, CCP.
43. CBL, "Saint Francis in Manhattan: A Synopsis for a Ballet," Apr. 18, 1950, CBLP.
44. Ibid.
45. CBL to Case, ca. early May, 1950, CBLP; Case to Chávez, ca. early May 1950, CCP.
46. CBL to Chávez, May 8, 1950, CCP.
47. Ibid.
48. Chávez to CBL, May 13, 1950, CCP.
49. Ibid., June 8, 1950, CCP. CBL to Chávez, June 12, 1950, CCP.
50. Chávez to CBL, June 8, 1950, CCP.
51. CBL to Chávez, July 7, 1950, CCP.

28. A RED VELVET TUFTED SOFA

1. Swanberg, *Luce*, 293.
2. Mary Bancroft quoted in Swanberg, *Luce*, 292.
3. CBL to HRL, Aug. 25, 1950, CBLP.
4. CBL's article appeared in *Flair* in Sept. 1950. This lavishly illustrated magazine was so expensive to produce that it ceased publication after only thirteen issues. Original copies have become collectors' items. A bound selection entitled *The Best of Flair*, edited by Fleur Cowles with a foreword by Dominick Dunne, was published in the United Kingdom in 1999. For CBL's essay, see 192–93.
5. Billy Baldwin, *Billy Baldwin Remembers* (New York, 1974) 163–67. The section describing his work with CBL is entitled "Paradise Lost."

29. PILATE'S WIFE

1. CBL to Father Fox of Gethsemani, Jan. 4, 1951.
2. Ibid.

3. CBL to Sister Madeleva, Jan. 3, 1951.

4. Lanier, *Hymns of the Marshes*.

5. CBL to Thomas Merton, Aug. 12, 1949; James Dodge interview, Mar. 18, 1989. A Trappist monk, James (later Father Linus), was the brother of Arthur Dodge, the young officer who had escorted CBL to her plane in Italy in 1945. He and Brother Emmanuel reinterred the two Anns in the spring of 1950.

6. CBL to HRL, Apr. 11, 1965, SJMP.

7. Carlos Chávez to CBL, Feb. 28, 1951, CCP.

8. *Daily Oklahoman*, Feb. 25, 1951.

9. After Vandenberg's interment, the officiating clergyman gave CBL a letter from the Senator that he had not had time to mail before dying. "They tell me, Clare, I am on my deathbed, but even if I am, if you decide to run for the Senate, I'll do something I never wanted to do again—I'll get up and campaign for you. We can win the next election with Eisenhower." Quoted in Shadegg, *Clare Boothe Luce*, 223.

10. CBL to Wilfrid J. Thibodeau, Apr. 17, 1951, SJMP.

11. Edwin Schallert, "Bible Movie to Fulfill Clare Luce Ambition," article clipping, ca. May 1951; CBL/RKO Pictures Agreement, Mar. 23, 1951; Kay Brown to CBL, Apr. 2, 1951, CBLP.

12. Undated RKO memo with *Pilate's Wife* material, CBLP.

13. CBL to Curt P. Freshel, June 22, 1951, CBLP.

14. Inez Wallace, "Clare Boothe Luce Chooses Screen to Explain Christianity," *Cleveland Plain Dealer*, Sept. 30, 1951.

15. CBL to Chávez, Aug. 24, 1951, CCP.

16. Quoted in *Chicago Tribune*, Nov. 18, 1951.

17. Script in CBLP.

18. Dorothy Farmer interview, July 29, 1982; CBL interview, Oct. 15, 1982.

19. *Bridgeport Post*, Oct. 26, 1951.

20. Ibid., Oct. 19, 1951.

21. *Box Office*, Oct. 27, 1951.

22. *Cleveland Plain Dealer*, Sunday, Sept. 30, 1951.

23. CBL to Mary Benson, Jan. 4, 1951, CBLP.

24. Chávez to CBL, Apr. 24, 1951, CCP.

25. Chávez's secretary, Josefina Napoles, to Dorothy Farmer, Oct. 1, 1951, CCP.

26. CBL's first thought at Ann's death in 1944 had been to have the university create a campus music room, which she would stock with audio equipment and records. But as time passed, her ambition for a more substantial monument grew, and she established the Ann Clare Brokaw Memorial Fund. The chapel site was the northwest corner of Cowper and Melville Streets, adjacent to the Newman House, a recreation center for Roman Catholic students. CBL estimated the cost of construction at $65,000, with an additional $5,000 for basic fixtures, and set aside approximately $20,000 in cash and *Time* stock from her currrent annual income of some $165,000. She continued this level of support for the next half decade or so. She also contributed $13,500 of the fee for her 1951 screenplay, *Pilate's Wife*. HRL's contribution was more than $55,000. Bernard Baruch gave $5,000, and George Waldo, $700. Ann's stepsister, Frances Brokaw, declined to subscribe, saying that her income from Brokaw trust funds "is just sufficient for my needs." Frances Brokaw to CBL, Jan. 1, 1951, CBLP. By Dec. 1954, the fund totaled $123,000. Chapel file, CBLP.

27. CBL to Kathleen Norris, Apr. 12, 1950, CBLP.

28. *San Francisco Chronicle*, Aug. 12, 1998.

29. Evelyn Waugh to CBL, Oct. 28, 1951, CBLP. CBL was about to publish an essay by Waugh in her compendium, *Saints for Now*.

30. Scrapbook clipping, n.d., CBLP; copies of *Child of the Morning* typescript in CBLP and New York Public Library Theatre Collection.

31. List in CBLP.

32. *Bridgeport Post*, Nov. 18, 1951.

33. *Springfield News*, Nov. 17, 1951.

34. *The Christian Science Monitor*, Nov. 19, *Boston Post*, Nov. 20, and *Boston Herald*, Nov. 20, 1951.

35. *Child of the Morning* was revived unsuccessfully off Broadway by the Blackfriars' Guild in Apr. 1958, and successfully for ten days at the Phoenix Little Theater in February 1959.

36. Charles Willoughby to CBL, Dec. 23, 1951, CBLP. Mrs. Pratt, a widow, was the former Marie Antoinette Becker. Willoughby's collaboration with John Chamberlain was a success, but MacArthur forbade direct quotes of his words, saying he wanted to save them for his memoirs. Nevertheless, *MacArthur 1941–1951* (New York, 1954) was reviewed favorably, *The New York Times* vaunting it as "the first comprehensive and authoritative account of MacArthur's decade of glory." Military historians, including D. Clayton James, MacArthur's most thorough biographer, found it a valuable, if overly worshipful, source. But Willoughby never got over his disillusionment at having to paraphrase MacArthur, blaming this lack for the loss of wide readership and sales. Willoughby reportedly used a serialization advance from *The Saturday Evening Post* to build a retirement house on Massachusetts Avenue in Washington, D.C. John Chamberlain, unpublished profile of CBL for *Time*, ca. 1946, CBLP. Willoughby published two other books about the Pacific war, *Reports of General MacArthur* (Washington, D.C., 1966) and *The Guerilla Resistance Movement in the Philippines* (New York, 1971).

37. *Film Bulletin*, Apr. 7, 1952, reported that RKO seemed to be "coasting on its backlog."

38. *Burlington News*, Apr. 13, 1952; Shadegg, *Clare Boothe Luce*, 227; *Chicago Sun Times*, Mar. 23, 1952; Philip Dunne to SJM, May 5, 1987, SJMP. CBL's appearance at the Oscars coincided with the death in Sidney, Australia, of her first great love, Julian Simpson.

39. CBL to Dorothy Farmer, Apr. 24, 1952.

40. CBL interview, Jan. 8, 1982. Also see Shadegg, *Clare Boothe Luce*, 227, and Jean Edward Smith, *Eisenhower in War and Peace* (New York, 2012), 525. Twelve days after his inauguration, Eisenhower joined his wife's church.

41. Chávez to CBL, Sunday, May 25, 1952, CCP.

30. BACK TO THE HUSTINGS

1. *New York Mirror*, June 10, 1952; John Billings diary, June 27, 1952, JBP. Edgar Albert Guest (1881–1959) wrote some eleven thousand sentimental poems that were syndicated in newspapers and collected in more than twenty books. Typical lines are "Home ain't a place that gold can buy or get up in a minute. / Afore it's home there's got t' be a heap o' living in it."

2. Mary Bancroft to "JGR," May 12, 1952, MBP; John Billings diary, June 4, 6, 19, and 23, 1952, JBP.

3. Swanberg, *Luce*, 326.

4. Perret, *Old Soldiers Never Die*, 575.

5. CBL interview, July 24, 1982.

6. Richard M. Nixon, *Leaders: Profiles and Reminiscences of Men Who Have Shaped the Modern World* (New York, 1982), 341. Nixon had no doubt that had Clare been selected, "she would have turned in a stellar performance."

7. Vega interview, Aug. 17, 1988. Also see Swanberg, *Luce*, 326–27.

8. T. S. Matthews, *Name and Address* (New York, 1960), 271–74.

9. CBL interview, July 24, 1982. "I'd kicked in five months among these fearful people, and it had got nowhere."

10. *New York World-Telegram and Sun*, July 29, 1952.

11. Hatch, *Ambassador*, 202.

12. *The New York Times*, Aug. 6, 1952.

13. CBL to John D. Lodge, Aug. 11, 1952, CBLP.

14. *Des Moines Register*, Aug. 19, 1952.

15. *Bridgeport Post*, Aug. 23, 1952, *The New York Times*, Aug. 26, 1952, *New York Herald Tribune*, Aug. 27, 1952.

16. *Hartford Courant*, Aug. 25, 1952.

17. *Stamford Advocate*, Aug. 29, 1952.

18. *Bridgeport Telegram*, Sept. 6, 1952.

19. *Bridgeport Post*, Sept. 6, 1952; *The New York Times*, Sept. 6, 1952; *Bridgeport Telegram*, Sept. 11, 1952. William Purtell had supported CBL to replace McMahon. A month after the convention, CBL wrote a friend that both Lodge and the GOP state chairman had told her she was "chiefly unacceptable" because she was a Catholic. But she continued to believe that the Governor had lured her into competing in the hope that in a deadlock he would be drafted. CBL to George Sokolsky, Oct. 8, 1952, CBLP.

20. *Bridgeport Telegram*, Sept. 6, 1952.

21. Beaverbrook to CBL, Sept. 20, 1952, CBLP; CBL to Beaverbrook, Oct. 8, 1952, BP. CBL's quip "No good deed goes unpunished" was penned by her in Oct. 1952. Google cites Letitia Baldrige's *Roman Candles* (Boston, 1956) as the first appearance in print of this now common saying. On p. 129 of this memoir, Baldrige wrote: "When I would entreat her to engage in resolving a specific case, she replied, 'No good deed goes unpunished, Tish, remember that?'" Other sources, citing no evidence, attribute the epigram to Billy Wilder, Oscar Wilde, and Andrew W. Mellon. A similar version appears in *Ego*, the autobiography of James Agate. "Pavia was in great form today: [Jan. 25, 1938]: 'Every good deed brings its own punishment.'" CBL remains the most frequently cited source, although Bartlett says its origin is unknown.

22. Carlos Chávez to CBL, Sept. 2, 1952, CCP.

23. Clare tried without success to recruit Ernest Hemingway, Grahame Greene, C. S. Lewis, T. S. Eliot, Dorothy Sayers, Vincent Sheean, Walter Lippmann, Christopher Isherwood, and Edna O'Brien as contributors. Perhaps the publisher's puny advance of $100 for four thousand to five thousand words (with a shared royalty of 15 percent on a print run of five thousand and over) had something to do with their refusal.

24. Clare Boothe Luce, ed., *Saints for Now* (New York, 1952).

25. *New York Herald Tribune*, Oct. 12, 1952; *The Voice of Saint Jude*, Dec. 1952.

26. George J. Marlin, *The American Catholic Voter* (South Bend, Ind., 2004), 231.

27. Ibid., 231–33; John Kenneth Galbraith, *Life in Our Times* (Boston, 1981), 297–98. Barnstorming for William Purtell against William Benton in Connecticut, Senator Joseph McCarthy made further inroads for the GOP among the state's 37 percent of Catholic voters.

28. Transcript, Sept. 28, 1952, CBLP.

29. John Billings diary, Sept. 24, 1952, JBP.

30. Smith, *Eisenhower*, 534.

31. Ibid., 538–42.; John Billings diary, Sept. 23, 1952, JBP.

32. Galbraith, *Life*, 298.

33. Dwight Eisenhower to CBL, Oct. 3, 1952, CBLP.

34. Chicago speech transcript, Oct. 24, 1952, SJMP. CBL's rhetoric, and that of other speakers from both parties, demonstrated why the 1952 campaign would be judged one of the most virulent of the century. Although on the trail the principals kept mostly above the fray, others on their teams made unproven insinuations, such as the existence of a Communist conspiracy in the Truman administration, and the possibility that the divorced, mild-mannered, and professorial Adlai Stevenson was homosexual.

35. *Longines Chronoscope*, Oct. 24, 1952, National Archives Identifier 95791. The program can be seen online. Truman was furious that Ike had not been specific about what he would do in Korea. If the GOP candidate had a plan to extricate us from the battleground, he said, he should reveal it immediately and "save a lot of lives." Smith, *Eisenhower*, 547.

36. CBL, "Eisenhower Administration," 15. In the waning days of the campaign, CBL would do two half-hour nationwide hookups that turned out to be so effective that Republican headquarters was flooded with compliments. "Everybody thought Ike was great and I was great," she recalled. See also *Time*, Feb. 1, 1953.

37. For accounts of the 1952 campaign, see Stephen Ambrose, *Eisenhower: Soldier and President* (New York, 1990), 268–87; Smith, *Eisenhower*, 544–49.

38. S. James to CBL, n.d. 1952, CBLP. Among a group of bettors, CBL was the only one to succeed in naming in advance six of the eight states lost by Eisenhower.

39. Marlin, *American Catholic Voter*, 234–37. Eisenhower also did well with ethnics (particularly German Americans), more than three million of whom switched their votes to him.

31. THE HEALING DRAUGHT

1. John Billings cable to HRL, Nov. 28, 1952, JBP.

2. CBL to HRL, Nov. 28, 1952, CBLP.

3. Steven F. White, "De Gasperi Through American Eyes: Media and Public Opinion, 1945–1953," *Review of the Conference Group on Italian Politics and Society*, no. 61 (Fall–Winter 2005). Many Americans were furious over this grant by the Truman administration, pointing out that Italy had been an enemy of the Allies in World War II. HRL, nevertheless, featured De Gasperi on the cover of *Time* on Apr. 19, 1948, just before the Prime Minister's historic reelection victory. The cover showed a red octopus trying to entwine itself around Italy, with the caption "Italian premier Alcide de Gasperi—can he cut the Red tentacles?"

4. In the hierarchy of diplomatic assignments in 1952, Rome was comparable in importance to London, Paris, Madrid, and Bonn, though probably not as crucial politically as Moscow. There had been other American female Ambassadors to less vital places such as Switzerland, Norway, Denmark, and Luxembourg, but CBL was the first to rate a top posting.

5. According to an Italian cabinet minister during CBL's tenure, the arch-Presbyterian Dulles did not initially approve Eisenhower's choice. "[He] practically solicited our government's 'nonagreement' to her appointment." Giulio Andreotti, *The U.S.A. Up Close: From the Atlantic Pact to Bush* (New York, 1992), 22–23.

6. CBL to HRL, Nov. 28, 1952, SJMP.

7. Margaret Case, "Maggie's Diary, June 3rd–September 15th, 1953," unpublished typescript in SJMP, 86.

8. Smith, *Eisenhower*, 557–60. The President-elect had been briefed on the Korean War by the Joint Chiefs. They advised going on indefinitely holding the current line, or committing more forces to achieve an outright military success. Ike rejected both scenarios, since he planned to spend three days on the battlefront assessing the situation for himself. Among those accompanying him were General Omar Bradley, Attorney General Herbert Brownell, Jr., Secretary of Defense Charles Wilson, and the now indispensable C. D. Jackson, who had transferred from HRL's staff as a senior White House aide. Admiral Arthur Radford was to join him en route, and at the front he hoped to see his son John, an army major.

9. John Billings to HRL in Jakarta, Dec. 10, 1952. Billings had discovered that HRL had not received a package of letters from CBL, which probably included her Nov. 28 one, detailing her meeting with Eisenhower. They were described as "three fat letters . . . carefully scotch-taped so I wouldn't steam 'em open." John Billings diary, Dec. 1, 1952.

10. Carlos Chávez to CBL, Dec. 17, 1952, CCP.

11. HRL was in a celebratory mood, having paid $500,000 to excerpt Harry Truman's memoirs in *Life*—half the price the President had hoped for.

12. CBL to Father James, Jan. 25, 1953, CBLP.

32. GAL FOR THE JOB

1. Howard Teichmann to CBL, Sept. 24, 1973, CBLP. Teichmann was working with Kaufman at the time of the intrusion.

2. John Billings diary, Jan. 21, 1953, JBP.

3. Ibid., Jan. 6, 1953, JBP.

4. *The New York Times*, Jan. 21, 1953.

5. *Women's Wear*, Jan. 21, 1953.

6. *Look* magazine, May 18, 1954.

7. Michael Stern interview, Feb. 2, 1988.

8. *The New York Times*, Jan. 30, 1953.

9. *New York News*, Feb. 24, 1953.

10. *McCall's*, "Without Portfolio," Mar. 1961. Dorothy Farmer and HRL moved to protect CBL from further misidentification, telling the head of Time-Life's Rome bureau to make sure reporters had the correct orthography of her name, and so avoid asking for the wrong articles and pictures from the morgues. Dorothy Farmer to Tom Dozier, Jan. 27, 1953; Dozier to Mrs. Farmer, Mar. 4, 1953, CBLP.

11. Mr. and Mrs. William Esty to Senator Herman Lehman, Feb. 15, 1953, and Rose A. Connor to Lehman, Mar. 29, 1953, HLP.

12. Luigi Criscuolo to Senator Alexander Wiley, Feb. 21, 1953, HLP. Al Grover discovered that CBL's appointment was unpopular in social circles in Madrid and London, to the extent that he felt compelled to slap "some mean sarcasm[s]" down. When CBL, apparently unaware of this, asked John Billings to help her answer "two thousand letters" of congratulation, he found the actual number to be nearer fifty. John Billings diary, Mar. 10 and Feb. 19, 1953, JBP.

13. Evelyn Waugh to CBL, Jan. 22, 1953, CBLP.

14. John Billings diary, Feb. 14, 1953, JBP.

15. *The New York Times*, Feb. 18, 1953.

16. CBL, "Eisenhower Administration," 75; Smith, *Eisenhower*, 552.

17. *New York Herald Tribune*, Mar. 4, 1953. "They never called me 'Ambassador,'"

CBL recalled in 1968, "because you know the difficulty, *ambasciatore* is masculine, *ambasciatrice* means the wife of an Ambassador, so they always called me . . . *Signora*." CBL, "Eisenhower Administration," 50. CBL misremembered. In fact, *ambasciatrice* is also used by Italians to denote a female ambassador.

18. Paul Ginsborg, *A History of Contemporary Italy: Society and Politics 1943–1988* (New York, 2003), 103, 143.

19. Gerald Miller to SJM, Nov. 18, 1983, SJMP. Miller's written account of his relationship with CBL was of immeasurable help in communicating the intricacies and nuances of Italian politics and American diplomacy in the 1950s.

20. On Mar. 11, 1948, the United States paid $151,000 for the Villa Taverna and $601,757 for the grounds, for a total of $732,757. Time Inc. memo, 1953, TIA.

21. Gretta Palmer, "The Lady and the Lion—in One," *Catholic Digest*, April 1953; *The New York Times*, Apr. 12, 1953; SJM notes taken during a visit to Rome with CBL in 1982, and interviews with embassy specialists Rex Hallman and Virginia Woofter, Apr. 18, 1985, SJMP. John Billings diary, Apr. 4, 1953, JBP.

22. *The New York Times*, Mar. 27, 1953.

23. CBL, "The Foreign Service as an Arm of U.S. Policy," transcript in *Department of State Bulletin*, May 11, 1953, 679–80.

24. *The New York Times*, Apr. 11, 1953.

25. Eleanor Roosevelt and Lorena A. Hickok, *Ladies of Courage* (New York, 1954), 230. Hickok also commented: "No appointment of a woman to a high government position was ever greeted with less enthusiasm by members of her own sex." Ibid., 231.

26. *Nevada State Journal*, Apr. 14, 1953.

27. Ibid., Apr. 11, 1953.

28. CBL to Wilfrid J. Thibodeau, Apr. 13, 1953, SJMP.

29. Thibodeau to SJM, June 19, 1983, SJMP.

33. LA LUCE

1. CBL interview, Oct. 30, 1983.

2. Elisabeth Moore interview, Nov. 22, 1983; CBL to Dorothy Farmer, Apr. 17, 1953, ACP.

3. In 1968, CBL listed her other fourteen missions as to (1) get Italy into the UN; (2) lessen American aid; (3) install a U.S. nuclear-capable division in Italy to defend the Ljubljana Gap; (4) get Italy to fulfill its minimal NATO commitment; (5) repatriate three American gangsters of dubious U.S. citizenship; (6) achieve an Italian ban on the production of heroin; (7) improve the lot of U.S. naval, air, and army forces stationed in Italy; (8) promote U.S.-Italian cultural relations; (9) increase Italian emigration to the United States while settling refugees from Iron Curtain countries in Italy; (10) perform full spectrum of consular functions; (11) assist U.S. congressional and other delegations; (12) improve relations with international agencies; (13) facilitate evacuations of U.S. nationals in emergencies; (14) make Italy an effective ally of U.S. in its "worldwide political, economic, and military struggle." CBL, "Eisenhower Administration," 32ff.

4. CBL to Wilfrid J. Thibodeau, Apr. 17, 1953, SJMP.

5. CBL to Dorothy Farmer, Apr. 17, 1953, ACP.

6. Carlos Chávez to CBL, Mar. 30, 1953, CCP.

7. CBL to Chávez, Apr. 20, 1953, CCP. CBL hinted that when Chávez had completed the score, she might arrange for a performance elsewhere in Italy, or in New York.

8. INCOM footage, Apr. 22, 1953, Archivio Storico Luce, http://www.archivioluce .com; *Time*, May 1, 1953.

9. Elbridge Durbrow interview, Dec. 12, 1983; AP and UPI dispatches, Apr. 22, 1953.

10. *The New York Times*, Apr. 23, 1953.

11. CBL to SJM in Rome, May 1985, SJMP; *The New York Times*, Apr. 23, 1953.

12. *Long Beach Independent*, Apr. 23, 1953.

13. "Villa La Pariola—Rome" [Villa Taverna], State Department booklet, U.S. State Department; Elisabeth Moore interview, Nov. 22, 1983.

14. CBL to SJM on joint tour of the Villa Taverna, May 25, 1985, SJMP.

15. Ibid. Durbrow told Alden Hatch that when CBL first saw the Villa Taverna, it was "as bare as a car barn." Hatch interviews, AHP.

16. Elisabeth Moore interview, Nov. 22, 1983. Soon CBL wore earplugs to cut out the animal noises. Baldrige, *A Lady*, 97.

17. Bernard Baruch to CBL, Jan. 24, 1953, CBLP.

18. Gerald Miller to SJM, Nov. 18, 1983, SJMP.

19. CBL to Joseph W. Martin, Jr., July 23, 1953, CBLP.

20. John Shea interview, Jan. 12, 1982.

21. Elbridge Durbrow interview, Dec. 12, 1983. Clare later heard from Ellsworth Bunker that Durbrow had expressed much the same sentiment to Foreign Service officials in the Palazzo Chigi. CBL, "Eisenhower Administration," 25. Bunker also told CBL "that at a certain point the conniving was so outrageous that he himself called together the whole staff and said, 'I do not wish anyone in this embassy to say anything that reflects on the capacities or the fitness of Mrs. Luce to be ambassador here. She is a friend of mine. . . . She is an able woman, and if I hear any more of it, I shall ask any officer indulging in it to be removed.'" Ibid.

22. AP and UPI dispatches, Apr. 23, 1953.

23. Ibid.

24. W. Stabler to Elbridge Durbrow, Apr. 20, 1953, CBLP-NA; UPI dispatch, Apr. 24, 1953; *Life*, "Ambassador Luce Takes Over," May 11, 1953.

25. Hatch, *Ambassador*, 211.

26. Luigi Barzini, "Ambassador Luce, As Italians See Her," *Harper's Magazine*, July 1955. CBL's translation of the motto was less cautionary than Talleyrand's original words, *Et surtout pas de zèle* ("And above all, no zeal").

27. Andreotti, *The U.S.A. Up Close*, 11.

28. Marco Rimanelli, "Italy's Diplomacy and the West: From Allied Occupation in World War II to Equality in NATO, 1940s–50s," http://fch.fiu.edu/FCH-1999/ Rimanelli-1999.htm; Morris, *Rage*, 370–71.

29. In March 1954, De Gasperi "almost wept" when he told a *New York Times* correspondent that CBL's efforts to encourage the Italian Right were misguided. "It is difficult to form a government with the Monarchists as your ambassador wants. . . . You cannot expect us democrats who fought fascism to join with fascism." C. L. Sulzberger, *A Long Row of Candles: Memoirs and Diaries, 1934–1954* (New York, 1969), 980.

30. CBL did not reveal that the State Department was doubtful Tagliotti could pull off such a reactionary coup.

31. Rimanelli, "Italy's Diplomacy"; Ginsborg, *History of Contemporary Italy*, 148, 200, 157.

32. Betty Carney Taussig, *A Warrior for Freedom* (Manhattan, Kans., 1955), 17.

33. Art Buchwald, "Europe's Lighter Side," *New York Herald Tribune*, May 17, 1953.

34. *New York Daily News*, May 5, 1953.

35. Ibid.

36. Hatch, *Ambassador*, 212.

37. *The New York Times*, May 5, 1953.

38. CBL to Joseph W. Martin, Jr., Apr. 30, 1953, CBLP-NA.

39. See, e.g., CBL to State Department, Feb. 23, 1956, CBLP-NA.

40. Gerald Miller to SJM, Nov. 18, 1983, SJMP.

41. Osvaldo Croci, "The Trieste Crisis," PhD thesis, McGill University (Montreal, 1991), 126.

42. Ibid., 151–152.

43. Ibid., 86–87.

44. Ibid., 206.

45. Ibid., 153.

46. Ibid.

47. Shadegg, *Clare Boothe Luce*, 240.

48. Ibid.

49. Hatch, *Ambassador*, 214; Elbridge Durbrow interview, Dec. 12, 1983.

50. *The New York Times*, May 13, 1953.

51. *Il Paese*, May 10, 1953.

52. *The Reporter*, May 26, 1953.

53. CBL to Joseph Martin, Jr., July 27, 1953, CBLP; CBL, "Eisenhower Administration," 30–31.

54. Milan address, May 28, 1953, CBL Speeches, CBLP.

55. *The New York Times*, May 30, 1953; Shadegg, *Clare Boothe Luce*, 243.

56. *The New York Times*, May 30, 1953; Hatch, *Ambassador*, 217.

57. Quoted in Hud Stoddard's Time Inc. memo, July 28, 1953, JBP.

58. CBL to John Foster Dulles, July 7, 1953, CBLP-NA.

59. Croci, "Trieste Crisis," 205.

60. John Billings diary, June 1, 1953.

61. Case, "Maggie's Diary," 85, SJMP.

62. Ginsborg, *History of Contemporary Italy*, 143.

63. CBL to State Department, June 26, 1953, CBLP-NA.

64. Case, "Maggie's Diary," 17, SJMP. CBL read Foot's remarks in the *Tribune* during a trip to Florence in mid-June.

65. *The New York Times*, June 15, 1953, and Jan. 30, 1954.

66. CBL to State Department, June 26, 1953, CBLP-NA. In a "melancholy" meeting with CBL on June 20, a weary-looking De Gasperi echoed this fear. "He said that if new elections were . . . precipitated in the present uncertain international situation, Italy might then go Communist." CBL, memorandum of conversation, June 20, 1953, CBLP-NA. The Prime Minister and CBL doubtless had in mind the riots of three days before in sixty East German cities, when tens of thousands of demonstrators calling for free elections were brutally suppressed by Soviet tanks. M. Steven Fish, "After Stalin's Death: The Anglo-American Debate over a New Cold War," *Diplomatic History* 10, no. 4 (Fall 1986), 339–40.

67. De Gasperi told CBL that "all sections of Italian opinion from Communist Left to Monarchist Right [had] advocated clemency" for the Rosenbergs. CBL memo, June 20, 1953, CBLP-NA; Case, "Maggie's Diary," 47, SJMP.

34. CRISIS AT SEA

1. Croci, "Trieste Crisis," 114–15. "She worked very diligently, but she never was fluent in Italian." Elbridge Durbrow interview, Dec. 12, 1983.

2. CBL to Wilfrid J. Thibodeau, May 3, 1956, SJMP; Cardinal Montini to CBL, March 11, 1953, CBLP.
3. Case, "Maggie's Diary," 32, SJMP.
4. Later, the number of personal letters dropped to an average of two hundred a week.
5. Hatch, *Ambassador*, 221.
6. Baldrige, *A Lady*, 87–88.
7. Italian for "excuse me" and "please"; Baldrige, *A Lady*, 95.
8. Ibid., 92.
9. *Time*, May 25, 1953, reported that Stokowski successfully conducted Menotti's opera in Florence.
10. Sir Victor Sassoon to CBL, Jan. 2, 1954, CBLP.
11. CBL to Chávez, May 29, 1953, CCP.
12. Case, "Maggie's Diary," 47–49, SJMP; *Minneapolis Star*, Aug. 18, 1953. Joking with the columnist Art Buchwald, CBL said, "The three things Americans who visit Rome want to see are the Holy Father, the Colosseum, and the American Ambassador." *New York Herald Tribune*, ca. Sept. 20, 1955, SJMP.
13. John Billings diary, June 9 and 17, 1953; Baldrige, *Roman Candles*, 34. Also see "Art File," CBLP.
14. John Billings diary, June 9 and 17, 1953; Baldrige, *A Lady*, 92.
15. John Billings diary, June 9 and 17, 1953. HRL added that he might consider buying the *Tribune*, but only if its owner, Mrs. Helen Reid, came to him with a proposition.
16. HRL to CBL, June 10, 1953, CBLP.
17. Croci, "Trieste Crisis," 189.
18. *Time*, Oct. 19, 1953.
19. Case, "Maggie's Diary," 70, SJMP.
20. Ibid., 67–68, SJMP.
21. The discussion concerned an urgent summons Durbrow had received to meet with Pella the following morning. Case, "Maggie's Diary," 74, SJMP.
22. Ibid., 73, SJMP.
23. Ibid., 74, SJMP; Croci, "Trieste Crisis," 195–96.
24. Case, "Maggie's Diary," 74, SJMP.
25. Durbrow to State Department, Aug. 29, 1953, NASD; Croci, "Trieste Crisis," 194.
26. Ibid., 196.
27. *The New York Times*, Aug. 30, 1953.
28. Case, "Maggie's Diary," 75, SJMP.
29. Ibid., 75–76, SJMP; Morris, *Rage for Fame*, 86. In his diary, Coward described the *Niki* as a "ghastly" Edwardian yacht. Fourteen years later, he wrote that women in power were a "menace. . . . Imagine the chaos that would ensue if our destinies were ruled, even temporarily, by Nancy Astor or Clare Booth [sic] Luce! Beatrice Lillie would be infinitely less perilous. Some day I must really settle down to writing a biography of that arch-idiot Joan of Arc." Payne and Morley, *Noël Coward Diaries*, 645–46.

35. PATIENCE AND COURAGE

1. Case, "Maggie's Diary," 77, SJMP; Croci, "Trieste Crisis," 198–99.
2. Alfred M. Gruenther to Eisenhower, Sept. 5, 1953, NASD.
3. CBL to State Department, Sept. 4, 1953, *Foreign Relations of the United States, 1952–1954*, vol. VIII (Washington, D.C., 1983), 248–50. Series title hereafter *FRUS*.
4. Ibid.; Case, "Maggie's Diary," 78, SJMP.

5. CBL memo to SD, Sept. 4, 1953, CBLP-NA.

6. Croci, "Trieste Crisis," 199.

7. Ibid., 202.

8. CBL to State Department, Sept. 4, 1953, *FRUS*, vol. VIII, 250–52.

9. Ibid., 252, 259.

10. CBL to C. D. Jackson, June 30 and Sept. 7, 1953, CBLP-NA. CBL had originally drafted the verse just after the Italian election in June, but refrained from sending it then because she felt Eisenhower had enough problems in Korea. Postscript to ibid.

11. Croci, "Trieste Crisis," 209.

12. Ibid., 205.

13. *The New York Times*, Sept. 6, 1953.

14. CBL to State Department, Sept. 4, 1953, *FRUS*, vol. VIII, 262–63.

15. Croce, "Trieste Crisis," 214, 216.

16. CBL to State Department, Sept. 5, 1953, CBLP-NA.

17. Croci, "Trieste Crisis," 200.

18. Case, "Maggie's Diary," 80, SJMP.

19. Unidentified British newspaper clipping, datelined Sept. 6, 1953, Trove Digitized Newspapers.

20. Sulzberger, *Candles*, 592.

21. Ibid., 851.

22. Ibid.; Croci, "Trieste Crisis," 203.

23. Hatch, *Ambassador*, 227.

24. Case, "Maggie's Diary," 81, SJMP.

25. Ibid. The State Department instructed CBL not to fly to Washington for consultations, as she was urgently needed to continue negotiating with Pella in Rome. *FRUS*, vol. VIII, 270–72.

26. CBL to State Department, Sept. 9, 1953.

27. Case, "Maggie's Diary," 82–83, SJMP.

28. Croci, "Trieste Crisis," 213.

29. Case, "Maggie's Diary," 82–84, SJMP.

30. Ibid., 84–85, SJMP. Not only was CBL "deeply comprehensive," Guareschi added, but she also had "a great heart. It isn't a compliment we pay her: it is a dutiful acknowledgment."

31. Case, "Maggie's Diary," 85, SJMP.

32. "Top Secret Security Information: Chief of Mission Meeting, Luxembourg, Sept. 18–19, 1953," CBLP-NA. Hereafter "Chief of Mission Meeting."

33. Sulzberger, *Candles*, 1018.

34. CBL, "Eisenhower Administration," 34.

35. Anthony Nutting, *Europe Will Not Wait* (London, 1960), 63.

36. Nelson Lankford, *The Last American Aristocrat: The Biography of Ambassador David K. E. Bruce, 1898–1977* (Boston, 1996), 256–57.

37. Ibid., 262–63.

38. CBL memo of a conversation with De Gasperi, June 20, 1953; CBL memo, "Subject of Pella at Conference in Luxembourg," Sept. 18, 1953, CBLP-NA.

39. Quoted by Case to CBL, Oct. 16, 1953, CBLP.

40. Sulzberger, *Candles*, 916. On Nov. 13, 1953, Sulzberger heard the story from Ambassador Chip Bohlen, who had been at the Sept. 18 dinner with CBL in Luxembourg.

41. "Chief of Mission Meeting," CBLP-NA.

42. Ambassador's Notes, and itinerary Sept. 17–22, 1953, CBLP-NA.

43. Croci, "Trieste Crisis," 221, 224, 227.
44. Ibid., 228.
45. Ibid.
46. Claire Sterling, "The Mess in Trieste," *The Reporter*, Nov. 10, 1953.
47. John Foster Dulles to CBL, 12:07 A.M., Oct. 10, 1953, CBLP-NA.
48. Case to CBL, quoting a CBS News broadcast, 8:00 A.M., Oct. 16, 1953, CBLP.
49. Croci, "Trieste Crisis," 272.
50. *The Reporter*, Nov. 10, 1953.
51. Croci, "Trieste Crisis," 278 and 281.
52. Ibid., 285.
53. Durbrow quoted in Hatch interviews, AHP.
54. Dorothy Farmer to Dorothea Philp, Oct. 19, 1953, CBLP.
55. Typed list of drug dosages, Oct. 23, 1953, CBLP.
56. CBL to John Foster Dulles, Oct 27, 1953; Dulles to CBL, Nov. 13, 1953, CBLP-NA.
57. Croci, "Trieste Crisis," 293–95.
58. CBL to Eisenhower and Dulles, Nov. 3, 1953, CBLP-NA. CBL confirmed sending this document in a letter to Walter Bedell Smith, Mar. 13, 1954, CBLP.
59. CBL to Eisenhower, Nov. 3, 1953, CBLP-NA.
60. Eisenhower to CBL, Nov. 7, 1953, CBLP-NA.
61. CBL to State Department, Nov. 6, 1953, NASD.
62. Gerald Miller to SJM, Nov. 18, 1983, SJMP; Hatch, *Ambassador*, 228–29. The protest incident took place on Nov. 6, 1953, not Oct. 10 as Hatch has it.
63. Michael Stern, *An American in Rome* (New York, 1964), 221–22.
64. Stan Swinton, Rome correspondent of the AP, remarked that in the 1950s "riots would stop at noon and start again at 2 p.m. for the mutual convenience of demonstrators and police." Stan Swinton interview, Apr. 12, 1982.
65. Eyewitness report of Michele Lanza, Nov. 7, 1953, copy in CBLP-NA.
66. U.S. Rome Embassy Despatch No. 1033, Nov. 10, 1953, CBLP-NA; Croci, "Trieste Crisis," 297, 340.
67. U.S. Rome Embassy Despatch No. 1033, Nov. 10, 1953, CBLP-NA; Croci, "Trieste Crisis," 299. Pella made his displeasure known to CBL, saying that Italian acceptance of the five-power conference was now impossible.
68. Ibid., 303.
69. Ibid., 307.
70. "Patience and courage." Hatch, *Ambassador*, 233.
71. Croci, "Trieste Crisis," 310–11.

36. EVIL EYE

1. According to Sulzberger, *Candles*, 973, Italian industrialists saw Fanfani as a "white Communist."
2. Croci, "Trieste Crisis," 356.
3. *The New York Times*, Jan. 3, 1954.
4. *New York Herald Tribune*, Jan., 24, 1954.
5. *U.S. News & World Report*, Feb. 19, 1954.
6. *New York Herald Tribune*, Mar. 28, 1954.
7. *Time* internal memo to Washington bureau, Mar. 28, 1954, transmitting a translation of an article in *L'Europeo*, same date.
8. AP report, Mar. 29, 1954.

9. Samuel Lubell to CBL, Jan. 9, 1954, CBLP.

10. John Billings diary, Jan. 7, 1954, JBP.

11. *The New York Times*, Jan. 12 and 13, 1954.

12. John Foster Dulles to CBL, Jan. 14, 1954, CBLP-NA.

13. CBL memo of conversation with Giuseppe Saragat, Jan. 16, 1954, CBLP-NA; Elbridge Durbrow interview, Dec. 12, 1983.

14. CBL memo of conversation with Giuseppe Saragat, Jan. 16, 1954, CBLP-NA.

15. CBL memo of conversation with Alfredo Covelli, Jan. 18, 1954, CBLP-NA.

16. CBL memo of conversation with Bruno Villabruna, Jan. 18, 1954, CBLP-NA.

17. CBL to Gerald Miller, Jan. 19, 1954, CBLP-NA.

18. CBL to Henry Luce III, Jan. 19, 1954, CBLP.

19. Croci, "Trieste Crisis," 359–61, 382.

20. *Time*, Feb. 8, 1954. The correspondent Dorothy Thompson, in a column defending CBL, cited two acquaintances who had to leave Italy after the superstition of the evil eye was attached to them. Like CBL, both had blue eyes, which to dark Italians seemed hypnotic. *Pittsburgh Post-Gazette*, Feb. 22, 1943.

21. *The New York Times*, Jan. 30, 1954.

22. *Time*, Feb. 8, 1954.

23. Ginsborg, *History of Contemporary Italy*, 130, 148.

24. HRL to C. D. Jackson, Feb. 18, 1954 (partially copied to Billings), JBP.

25. Swanberg, *Luce*, 361.

26. CBL to State Department, Feb. 24, 1954; ibid., Feb. 26, 1954, CBLP-NA.

27. Ginsborg, *History of Contemporary Italy*, 192. See also CBL memorandum of a conversation with Valletta on Oct. 6, 1954, CBLP-NA.

28. Sulzberger, *Candles*, 964. Sulzberger decided to make his tour on Feb. 10, the same day Scelba became Prime Minister.

29. Ibid., 980.

30. Ibid., 981.

31. Ibid., 965.

32. Ibid., 967.

33. Ibid., 974.

34. Ibid., 975.

35. Ibid., 976.

36. Ibid., 977.

37. Ibid., 974.

38. CBL to Walter Bedell Smith, Mar. 13, 1954, CBLP-NA.

39. Gerald Miller to SJM, Nov. 18, 1983, SJMP.

40. *The New Republic*, Feb. 15, 1954. Gorrell extensively quoted similar opinion from Britain's *Manchester Guardian*.

41. CBL to John Foster Dulles, Mar. 18, 1954, CBLP-NA.

42. *The New York Times*, Mar. 27, 1954.

43. Ibid.; *Congressional Record*, Senate, 5510, May 3, 1954.

44. CBL to HRL, Mar. 27, 1954, CBLP.

45. *Time* internal memo to Washington bureau, Mar. 28, 1954, transmitting a translation of an article in *L'Europeo*, same date.

46. CBL to HRL, Mar. 27, 1954, CBLP.

47. *The New York Times*, Apr. 1, 1954.

48. Homer S. Ferguson, in *Congressional Record*, Senate, 5510, May 3, 1954.

49. Baldrige, *Roman Candles*, 290.

50. CBL to Dulles, Apr. 5, 1954, CBLP-NA.

51. *The Jewels and Objects of Vertu of The Honorable Clare Boothe Luce*, Sotheby's Auction Catalogue, Apr. 19, 1988; Dorothy Farmer to HRL, Mar. 17, 1954, CBLP. Mrs. Farmer told HRL that CBL wanted the emeralds to be able to compete with the Roman aristocrats that he admired. After CBL's death, the necklace sold for $150,000 and a matching ring for $75,000.

52. Hatch, *Ambassador*, 235–36.

53. CBL to HRL, Apr. 10, 1954, CBLP. After discovering that HRL had paid $23,000 for *Madonna of the Roses*, CBL had it appraised by two New York experts. They informed her that the artist, Pier Francesco Fiorentino (1444–1497), was not of the first rank, and that the painting was worth between $3,500 and $12,000. "F.B." to CBL, Apr. 22, 1945, CBLP. In 1969, two years after HRL's death, CBL sold *Madonna of the Roses* for $40,000.

54. CBL's prescription drug file shows an order for two hundred of each of these pills, Apr. 16, 1954, CBLP.

55. Dr. M. Rosenbluth to CBL, June 14, 1954, CBLP.

56. CBL to Joseph W. Martin, Apr. 15, 1954, CBLP-NA.

57. Shadegg, *Clare Boothe Luce*, 249.

58. CBL to John Foster Dulles, May 5, 1954, CBLP-NA.

59. Elbridge Durbrow to CBL, Apr. 22, 1954, CBLP.

60. William Attwood, *Look*, "Mrs. Ambassador," May 18, 1954.

61. *Congressional Record*, Senate, 5510–12, May 3, 1954.

62. James B. Engle, memorandum of conversation between Dulles and Scelba, May 3, 1954, CBLP-NA. CBL attended the Geneva conference as an observer, and then accompanied Dulles to Milan. On May 1, the Italian Ambassador to Japan, Blasco Lanza d'Ajeta, privately told CBL that it was right for the United States to be "ruthlessly firm" until the Italian government, recovering from the "dope" of Marshall Plan aid, was scared into operating on its own Communist "cancer." CBL to State Department, May 4, 1954, CBLP-NA.

63. Roosevelt and Hickok, *Ladies of Courage*, 237–38.

64. Croci, "Trieste Crisis," 386–89.

65. Ibid., 389.

66. Ibid., 390. The Italian phase of the negotiations resumed on June 12.

67. Dorothy Farmer to Dorothea Philp, June 5, 1954, CBLP.

37. END OF THE DRAMA

1. CBL to HRL, June 11, 1954, CBLP.

2. CBL to Dorothy Farmer, June 10, 1954, CBLP.

3. *The New York Times*, July 10, 1954; Croci, "Trieste Crisis," 395.

4. *The New York Times*, July 12, 1954.

5. CBL to Remigio Grillo, June 17, 1954, CBLP-NA.

6. Dorothy Farmer to Dorothea Philp, Sept. 21, 1954, CBLP.

7. Robert H. Ferrell, ed., *The Diary of James C. Hagerty* (Bloomington, Ind., 1983), 114.

8. Barzini, "Ambassador Luce."

9. CBL to Eisenhower, Aug. 31, 1954, CBLP-NA. In his reply Eisenhower wrote, "Dear Clare: I have studied your secret letter of the 31st. The conclusions you present, as a result of your convictions and study, are not greatly different from my own instinctive feelings, based, however, on much flimsier foundations than are yours. I shall certainly do what I can." Eisenhower to CBL, Sept. 6, 1954, CBLP-NA.

10. CBL, "Eisenhower Administration," 39; Shadegg, *Clare Boothe Luce*, 250. CBL did

not reveal Low's identity to Shadegg, but did so in her Columbia University Oral History interview, which was to remain closed during her lifetime.

11. CBL, "Eisenhower Administration," 38–39.

12. Ibid., 39–40. CBL, interviewed in 1968, stated that the figure discussed was $18 million. Her memory was accurate as to the amount eventually paid Italy as part of the final settlement, but it is unlikely that in 1954 she was so specific.

13. "Arsenic for the Ambassador," *Time*, July 23, 1956.

14. Robert D. Murphy, *Diplomat Among Warriors* (New York, 1964), 422; CBL, "Eisenhower Administration," 40.

15. Ibid., 40–41.

16. Ibid., 40–41; Murphy, *Diplomat Among Warriors*, 422.

17. Ibid., 423.

18. Ibid., 422 ff.; *FRUS*, vol. VIII, 531–32.

19. Croci, "Trieste Crisis," 396–97.

20. Murphy, *Diplomat Among Warriors*, 424.

21. Ibid., 423. The main reason for Piccioni's resignation was the involvement of his son in a lurid Roman sex scandal known as "the Montesi case," the inspiration for Federico Fellini's 1960 movie, *La Dolce Vita*.

22. Croci, "Trieste Crisis," 398.

23. In late September, CBL received a disturbing letter from a security officer in the State Department. He said he had read a report, "which I know is accurate," that an Italian Ambassador to a Central American country had recently informed his U.S. counterpart that the Chigi Palace would "welcome Clare Luce's recall." The envoy stated further that other Italian missions "have similar instructions." Scott McLeod to CBL, Sept. 23, 1954, CBLP-NA. Although this alleged effort never came to anything, a likely explanation might be that Italian officials, worried by the concessions being forced on Ambassador Brosio in the Trieste negotiations, suspected that CBL favored a pro-Yugoslav settlement.

24. Copy of "Memorandum of Understanding Between the Governments [etc.]" in CBLP-NA; Croci, "Trieste Crisis," 399–400; Elbridge Durbrow to Letitia Baldrige, Nov. 9, 1967, CBLP.

25. Ibid.

26. CBL's arrival and the announcement in the Senate chamber can be seen on YouTube at http://www.youtube.com/watch?v=Vl1I_KUcWN4TK

27. Margaret Case to CBL, Oct. 6, 1954, SJMP.

28. Baldrige, *A Lady*, 110. An embassy staffer told Alden Hatch that during one weekend at the height of the Trieste crisis, forty-two "Top Secret" telegrams were decoded. Hatch interviews, AHP.

29. Hatch, *Ambassador*, 231–32.

30. Ibid.; *Newsweek*, Jan. 24, 1955. Still exulting over her Trieste triumph some eight months later, CBL invited the entire Sixth Fleet of the U.S. Navy to a Fourth of July party at the Villa Taverna, and made sure that they all knew they were there to celebrate Trieste. Baldrige, *A Lady*, 110.

31. Gianni Bartoli to Eisenhower, Oct. 21, 1953, NASD.

32. *Bridgeport Post*, Oct. 8, 1954.

33. *Time*, Oct. 28, 1954.

34. Dr. Milton Rosenbluth to CBL, Oct. 15, 1954, CBLP.

35. Dorothy Farmer to Rosenbluth, Oct. 27, 1954; Rosenbluth to CBL, Nov. 9, 1954, CBLP.

36. "Arsenic for the Ambassador," *Time*.

37. CBL to Joseph W. Martin, Nov. 20, 1954, CBLP.

38. Hatch, *Ambassador*, 240–41. Also see AP Rome dispatch, Dec. 26, 1954, quoted in *Congressional Record*, Jan. 6, 1955. This was the first of many similar Communist union losses in northern Italian factories in the winter of 1954–1955. CBL quoted by Elbridge Durbrow, Hatch interviews, AHP.
39. Carlos Chávez to CBL, Nov. 25, 1954, CCP.
40. Ibid., and Jan. 25, 1955, CCP; CBL to Robert Irving, Oct. 23, 1954, CBLP. The symphony had been completed on June 26, 1954. "I am extremely happy with this music," Chávez wrote CBL that day. Receipt of the score in Rome, while CBL was in the United States, had been acknowledged only by Letitia Baldrige, on Aug. 20, 1954, CCP.
41. Robert Irving to CBL, Oct. 25, 1954, CBLP.
42. Aaron Copland to Chávez, Dec. 9, 1954, CCPN; Parker, *Carlos Chávez*, 73.
43. Embassy Report to State Department, Dec. 17, 1954, CBLP-NA; Maura E. Hametz, *Making Trieste Italian: 1918–1954* (Rochester, N.Y., 2005), 160.
44. Embassy Report to State Department, Dec. 17, 1954, CBLP-NA; Jan Morris, *Destinations: Essays from Rolling Stone* (New York, 1980), 205–06.
45. Embassy Report to State Department, Dec. 17, 1954, CBLP-NA.
46. HRL to John Billings, Dec. 16, 1954, JBP.
47. CBL address, Dec. 17, 1954, transcript in UTA. "Thank you, dearest Rector, for having invited me to visit this great and youthful university, whose name is already celebrated in the story of Italian culture. . . . And for the honor that you desired to bestow upon me, for what it means to me personally and to the country I represent, allow me to offer my genuine gratitude. Now that Trieste is entering a new phase in its history, this university will have an even greater opportunity to enrich the life of its community and the Italian nation. . . . I wish to express the most heartfelt and sincere wishes of the American people for the glorious future of this eminent center of study and culture."

38. NO BED OF ROSES

1. *The New York Times*, Dec. 19, 1954. Divers attempted to retrieve bodies from Jamaica Bay, but were forced to stop when air pipes froze.
2. CBL to Livingston T. Merchant, Nov. 22, 1954, CBLP-NA. *Il Progresso Italo-Americano* contrasted CBL's largesse with "the proper expressions of regret" that other Ambassadors were content with. Hatch, *Ambassador*, 242.
3. CBS, *Longines Chronoscope*, Jan. 23, 1955, National Archives Identifier 95940. The program can be seen online.
4. *The New York Times*, Jan. 6, 1955; *Department of State Bulletin*, Jan. 24, 1955, 132–36.
5. *Newsweek*, Jan. 24, 1955. Virginia Kelly, researcher for the article, collected some negative material on CBL, but said later that her editor, Frank Gibney, suppressed it, because he hoped one day to work for HRL. Virginia Kelly to Michael Teague, assistant to SJM, ca. 1995, SJMP.
6. CBL to Malcolm Muir, president of *Newsweek*, thanking him profusely for an "excellent piece of research" and "tight writing," Jan. 22, 1955, CBLP; Dorothea Philp to Boris Chaliapin, Jan. 31, 1955, CBLP. CBL bought the latter's portrait of herself for $1,250. CBL interview, Jan. 4, 1982.
7. *Literaturnaya Gazeta*, Jan. 15, 1955, quoted in the *Bridgeport Telegram*, Jan. 16, 1955.
8. Elbridge Durbrow to CBL, Jan. 17, 1955, CBLP-NA; "Arsenic for the Ambassador," *Time*.
9. The only encouraging result from Bethesda was a screen test for lead-infused por-

phyrins that proved negative. Durbrow to CBL, Jan. 17, 1955, CBLP-NA; Durbrow interview, Dec. 12, 1983.

10. Durbrow to CBL, Jan. 17, 1955, CBLP-NA.

11. Gerald Miller to SJM, Nov. 18, 1983, SJMP; "Arsenic for the Ambassador," *Time*.

12. Durbrow interview, Dec. 12, 1983; CBL interview, Jan. 5, 1982; Gerald Miller to SJM, Nov. 18, 1983, SJMP; "Arsenic for the Ambassador," *Time*.

13. Ibid.; Durbrow interview, Dec. 12, 1983.

14. CBL to HRL, Feb. 2, 1955, CBLP. Letitia Baldrige, who also spent time working with CBL in that bedroom, wrote her on Aug. 6, 1956, "I had a bit more arsenic count in my system than you did. . . . But since I was a horse, exercised a lot (perspired a lot and got rid of it) I was never sickened." CBLP.

15. CBL to HRL, "Wednesday" [Mar. 9, 1955], CBLP.

16. Baldrige, *A Lady*, 116.

17. In 1967, CBL was asked why there had never been any official corroboration of the arsenic story, even after it broke in *Time* on July 23, 1956. She said there had never been an official denial, either. "CIA policy is known to be total anonymity. It never explains, discusses, or affirms, any of its activities, all of which are classified as secret. DOS [Department of State] refrains from any statements that would destroy this essential anonymity. As for the Italian government, my own story at the time indicates that it was not informed on the matter . . . for obvious 'reasons of state.'" CBL to Henry F. Graff, Aug. 10, 1967, SJMP.

18. Durbrow interview, Dec. 12, 1983. The breakfast tray tests appear to have been negative. Baldrige, *A Lady*, 117.

19. Letitia Baldrige to CBL, Mar. 28 and Apr. 6, 1955, CBLP.

20. Robert T. Elson, *The World of Time Inc: The Intimate History of a Publishing Enterprise, 1941–1960* (New York, 1973), 220.

21. *The New York Times*, Apr. 14, 1955.

22. Winston Churchill, *Painting as a Pastime* (New York, 1932, 1965), 7.

23. CBL to Eisenhower, May 2, 1955, CBLP. In his reply on May 10, Eisenhower wrote, "My 'painting' technique will never permit me, I am afraid, to have the audacity to attempt to give anyone a lesson." He offered to show CBL a portrait of Churchill that he had done from a print. CBLP.

24. CBL to Eisenhower, May 2, 1955, CBLP.

25. Churchill to CBL, Apr. 22, 1955, CBLP. CBL hung *Moroccan Landscape* by Churchill and a portrait of Lincoln by Eisenhower in the hall of the Villa Taverna. Hatch, *Ambassador*, 233.

26. Miss Pepper overpraised CBL's skills when talking to the same reporter. "She has a definite Matisse quality, yet her composition is original. Most surprising for an amateur, she draws very well." Undated newspaper clipping in CBL to Carlos Chávez, Sept. 1955, CCP.

27. Morris, *Rage for Fame*, 26.

28. Barzini, "Ambassador Luce." In April 1983, Barzini recalled that *Harper's* had wanted a derogatory piece on CBL. But he had seen no point in antagonizing the American Ambassador, at a time when Italy needed so much aid and support. Nan Talese interview, May 6, 1983.

29. *Newsweek*, Jan. 24, 1955. See also Ward Morehouse interview of CBL in the *New York World Telegram*, May 20, 1954.

30. CBL quoted by Cleveland Amory, *Pittsburgh Press*, Dec. 8, 1963.

31. Victor Sassoon to CBL, Jan. 2, 1954, CBLP; Barzini, "Ambassador Luce."

32. Letitia Baldrige interview, Apr. 4, 1988.

33. Baldrige, *Roman Candles*, 200, 202, 292.

34. Shadegg, *Clare Boothe Luce*, 257–58.

35. *Time*, May 9, 1955; Kobler, *Luce*, 246. The final total for Gronchi's election was 658 votes out of 883.

36. CBL memo of conversation with Count Vittorio Cini, May 25, 1955, CBLP-NA.

37. CBL secret memo to Durbrow and Miller, May 26, 1955, CBLP-NA.

38. CBL to Dorothy Farmer, June 20, 1955, CBLP.

39. Drew Pearson, "This Time She Intends to Start Early," *Mobile Register* (Ala.), June 17, 1955.

40. Elbridge Durbrow interview, Dec. 12, 1983.

41. See Ilka Chase, *Past Imperfect* (New York, 1942),78, for further information about Maine Chance.

42. Eleanor Nangle to SJM, Dec. 22, 1981; UPI news report, *Bridgeport Post*, June 15, 1955.

43. Eleanor Nangle to SJM, Dec. 22, 1981, SJMP.

44. Ibid.

45. Ibid.

46. Ibid.

47. *FRUS, 1955–1957*, vol. XVIII (Washington, D.C., 1989), 276.

48. Fish, "After Stalin's Death." Before going to Geneva, Eisenhower had considerately written to assure the out-of-power Churchill that he and Dulles were continuing his quest for peace. Emmet John Hughes, *The Ordeal of Power: A Political Memoir of the Eisenhower Years* (New York, 1963), 168.

49. CBL to HRL, July 20, 1955, CBLP.

50. Stassen to CBL, Aug. 1, 1955, CBLP.

51. Smith, *Eisenhower*, 670.

52. CBL to Eisenhower (fragment), Aug. 22, 1955. SJMP.

53. CBL told Art Buchwald in late Sept. 1955 that "in the last two months we've had 416 members of Congressional parties and sixty-nine official visitors, plus hundreds of unofficial visitors such as clubwomen, labor leaders, delegates of conferences, tourists and friends." *New York Herald Tribune*, ca. Sept. 22, 1955.

54. *Cleveland Plain Dealer*, Aug. 28, 1955.

55. Ibid. On Aug. 25, 1955, CBL went to the Venice Film Festival, where she caused a stir by declining to attend a showing of *Blackboard Jungle*, an MGM movie about hooliganism in an American school. When the movie was withdrawn from exhibition, she was accused of censorship. The State Department issued a denial, saying that Ambassador Luce "did not believe she should give official endorsement to *Blackboard Jungle* by her presence at the Festival when she believed that the film would create a seriously distorted impression of American youth and American public schools and, thus, abet the anti-U.S. propaganda of the Communists in Italy." *Department of State Bulletin*, Oct. 3, 1955.

56. Baldrige, *A Lady*, 96. In the early 1950s, CBL was spending $20,000 a year on clothes, but in 1952, she—or HRL—cut her budget to $18,000. She gave discards to thrift shops, friends, and institutions such as the Chicago Historical Society. John Billings diary, Oct. 17, 1952, JBP. Also see *McCall's*, Apr. 1961. Bill Blass remarked in *Vogue* in Aug. 1997 that CBL "had no sense of clothes at all."

57. CBL to Richard Nixon, n.d., ca. Sept. 26, 1955, CBLP. In a telephone conversation on Nov. 26, 1957, Richard Nixon referred to this longhand letter and told CBL, "I'll never forget it." CBL transcript of their talk in CBLP.

58. CBL memo to herself, ca. mid-Oct. 1955, CBLP.

59. Letitia Baldrige to Dorothy Farmer, Oct. 11, 1955, CBLP.

60. CBL to HRL, Oct. 16, 1955, CBLP. See also HRL to CBL, Oct. 21 and 23, 1955, CBLP.
61. Baldrige, *Roman Candles*, 251; HRL to CBL, Oct. 23 and 27, 1955, CBLP.
62. CBL to HRL, Nov. 10, 1955, CBLP; Wharton Hubbard to Dorothy Farmer, Nov. 7, 1955, CBLP; Gretel Steinfadt to Dorothy Farmer, Nov. 8, 1955, CBLP.
63. Michael Davy, ed., *The Diaries of Evelyn Waugh* (Boston, 1976), 746.
64. CBL memo, n.d., ca. Dec. 1955, CBLP.
65. *Brownsville Herald*, Jan. 12, 1956.
66. *Middlesboro Daily News* (Ky.), Jan. 16, 1956; *New York Post*, Jan. 16, 1956.
67. *The New York Times*, Jan 14, 1956.
68. Ibid., Jan. 21, 1956. The event was expected to raise $1 million.
69. Letitia Baldrige interview, Apr. 4, 1988. "Alden was in love with Clare. . . . She knew the biography would be a puff piece."
70. *National Catholic Weekly Review*, Mar. 10, 1956; Marya Mannes, "The Remarkable Mrs. Luce," *The Reporter*, Feb. 9, 1956; *The Spectator*, Oct. 26, 1956.
71. CBL, "Eisenhower Administration," 59; *New York Herald Tribune*, Jan. 27, 1956; CBL to Gerald Miller, Feb. 28, 1956, CBLP.
72. *New York Herald Tribune*, Jan. 27, 1956; CBL, "Eisenhower Administration," 59. On Jan. 22, Walter Winchell broadcast a report on WOR: "The resignation of Ambassador Clare Boothe Luce is now on the desk of Mr. Secretary of State Dulles, to be effective before the Italian spring election."
73. CBL to Henry Graff, Aug. 10, 1967, SJMP.
74. *New York Mirror*, Jan. 26, 1956.
75. Guest list, CBLP.
76. *The New York Times*, Jan. 27, 1956.
77. In July 1955, CBL listened to a tape recording of the symphony, performed at the Festival of the Society of Contemporary Music in Baden-Baden on June 17, 1955. "I've heard the Symphony for Ann," she wrote Chávez on Aug. 12, 1955. "Not as I would have liked to have heard it—with you conducting. But in a pleasant enough way . . . in my own salon here at the Villa, surrounded by friends. . . . Carlos it is very very fine. I liked it much better than I dared hope." CCP.
78. Analysis based on the London Symphony Orchestra recording of Chávez's Symphony No. 3, conducted by Eduardo Mata in 1981.
79. *The New York Times*, Jan. 27, 1956; *Time*, Feb. 6, 1956. Aaron Copland, writing in *Tempo* (Spring 1955), described the symphony as "very personal and uncompromising. Its four brief and connected movements have an almost sadistic force that compels attention. The symphony is powerful but not music that can be easily loved." Quoted in Parker, *Chávez*, 76.
80. *The New York Times*, Feb. 3, 1956; CBL to Dorothy Farmer, Apr. 16, 1956, CBLP.
81. CBL to HRL, and Wharton Hubbard to Dorothy Farmer, Feb. 20, 1956, CBLP; CBL to Gerald Miller, Feb. 20, 1956, SJMP.
82. Eisenhower praised Gronchi as one of few foreign leaders "who came with a sense of determination and sacrifice rather than as a supplicant." General J. H. Michaelis to CBL, Apr. 13, 1956, CBLP.
83. *San Francisco Chronicle*, Mar. 9, 1956.
84. CBL to Gerald Miller, Feb. 28, 1956, CBLP.
85. Shirley Potash press release, Mar. 10, 1956, CBLP.
86. Edmund Stevens, Moscow correspondent of *Look*, published his interview with Gronchi in *The Christian Science Monitor*, Feb. 3, 1956.
87. John Lewis Gaddis, *The Cold War: A New History* (New York, 2005), 108. Khrush-

chev's speech had been delivered on Feb. 22, 1956, but was not released to the West until March 18.

88. Thomas A. Bailey, *A Diplomatic History of the American People* (New York, 1968), 837.

89. Mary Nix cable to Dorothy Farmer, Apr. 5, 1956, asking for more penicillin.

90. CBL secret memo to State Department, Apr. 12, 1956, CBLP-NA. Around this time, CBL declined an invitation to the wedding of Grace Kelly and Prince Rainier on Apr. 19, citing pressure of diplomatic engagements.

91. Drew Pearson syndicated column, May 21, 1956, scrapbook clipping in CBLP.

92. CBL to Gerald Miller, May 15, 1956, CBLP.

93. CBL to Wilfrid J. Thibodeau, May 3, 1956, SJMP. On Aug. 23, 1965, the priest and CBL had a brief reunion in New York.

94. CBL to Dorothy Farmer, May 4, 1956, CBLP.

95. *The New York Times*, May 11, 1956; *New York Daily News*, May 11, 1956.

96. CBL to Gerald Miller, May 15, 1956, CBLP.

97. CBL, "A memo to Harry about Diminishments," ca. Aug. 1960, CBLP.

98. *The New York Times*, May 18, 1956; CBL to Gerald Miller, May 15, 1956, CBLP. In a famous British case of Nov. 1921, a Mrs. Annie Black appeared to have died of gastroenteritis. But when a postmortem revealed arsenic in her tissues, her husband was convicted of murder.

99. CBL to Ruth and Wiley Buchanan, May 31, 1956, CBLP.

100. CBL to Joseph P. Kennedy, June 1, 1956, CBLP. *The New York Times* noted that Communists particularly lost ground in the South, where the government programs CBL had encouraged, particularly agrarian reform and public works, were cooling workers' enthusiasm for extreme left politicians. June 1, 1956.

101. "Luce Vindicates Ike and State Department," Spadea Syndicate release, May 23, 1956. In addition, Drew Pearson touted CBL for Secretary of State; Ruth Montgomery cited "three good reasons" why she should be Secretary of Health, Education and Welfare; George E. Sokolsky praised her success in a "man-sized job." *New York Mirror*, May 25, 1956; *New York Daily News*, May 26, 1956; *New York Journal-American*, May 28, 1956.

102. James Bell to CBL, May n.d., 1956; Raymond von Hofmannsthal to CBL, May n.d., 1956, CBLP.

103. *Washington Evening Star*, June 27, 1956; Dorothy Farmer to "Joan," July 3, 1956, CBLP.

104. CBL suspected that Eisenhower might have been the innocent originator of the leak, by sharing her confidential arsenic story with his press secretary, James Hagerty, or someone else who "mentioned it in the press dining room." CBL, "Eisenhower Administration," 60.

105. "Arsenic for the Ambassador," *Time*. On successive days, *The New York Times* headlined CLARE BOOTHE LUCE'S ILLNESS IS TRACED TO ARSENIC DUST FROM CEILING OF VILLA and STORY OF MRS. LUCE'S POISONING IN ROME VILLA AMAZES ITALIANS.

106. "Arsenic for the Ambassador," *Time*.

39. THIS FRAGILE BLONDE

1. Translation marked "New York, July" of undated *Il Ore* article, SJMP.

2. Mary Bancroft to W. S. Swanberg, May 1, 1971, MBP.

3. *New York Daily News*, July 18, 1956.

4. *Washington Evening Star*, July 19, 1956. Increasing the confusion of the debate that followed the *Time* article and was to last the rest of CBL's life, the acting head of

the Naval Medical School in Bethesda stated that it was "impossible" for his laboratory to have determined in early 1955 that "Mrs. Luce was suffering from arsenic poisoning." *The New York Times*, July 22, 1956.

5. CBL to Dorothy Farmer, undated postcard from the *Creole*, July 1956, CBLP.

6. CBL to HRL, July 24 and 26, 1956, CBLP.

7. CBL to Stavros and Eugenie Niarchos, Aug. 8, 1956, CBLP.

8. David Sulzberger to SJM in an unrecorded conversation.

9. CBL to HRL, July 24, 1956, and HRL to CBL, July 28, 1956, CBLP. HRL was amenable, but when CBL realized that the work of owning a yacht would devolve on her, she gave up on the idea.

10. CBL to HRL, July 31, 1956, CBLP. The ship collided with a Swedish liner, and forty-six from the *Andrea Doria* died.

11. CBL to HRL, July 31, 1956, CBLP.

12. CBL interview, Jan. 9, 1982; CBL to Dorothy Farmer, Aug. 10, 1956, CBLP.

13. Ibid.

14. S. N. Behrman, *People in a Diary: A Memoir* (Boston, 1972), 289.

15. CBL to Dorothy Farmer, Aug. 10, 1956, CBLP. Her stomach was "consistently out of wack," she wrote.

16. Somerset Maugham to CBL, Apr. 6, 1957, CBLP. Ruth Buchanan, who also saw CBL at this time, remembered that she "could barely get out of her chair she was so weak and thin." Ruth Buchanan interview, Jan. 24, 1984.

17. David Nasaw, *The Patriarch: The Remarkable Life and Turbulent Times of Joseph P. Kennedy* (New York, 2012), 703. JFK came second to Senator Estes Kefauver of Tennessee in a "free vote" for the number two spot on a ticket headed by Adlai E. Stevenson. Joseph Kennedy was not displeased, because he was sure Eisenhower would be reelected, and preferred his son to run for President in 1960.

18. Durbrow was soon to become Ambassador to South Vietnam. By now he had lost his early misgivings about CBL. "As an old careerist, I could ask for no better boss," he told Alden Hatch. "One gets so used to laughing and smiling when one works for her." Hatch interviews.

19. CBL to HRL, Sept. 16, 1956, CBLP.

20. Ibid.

21. Sept. 28, 1956, CBLP-NA.

22. Tim Weiner, *Legacy of Ashes: The History of the CIA* (New York, 2008), 150; Charles Gati in Council on Foreign Relations, "Hungary-Suez Crisis: Fifty Years On: Session 2," transcript, Oct. 24, 2006; Timothy Foote, "But If Enough of Us Get Killed Something May Happen . . ." *Smithsonian* 17, no. 8 (Nov. 1986).

23. John Prados, *Lost Crusader: the Secret Wars of CIA Director William Colby* (New York, 2003), 61; "Little Outside Information," http://www2.gwu.edu/~nsarchiv/NSAEBB/NSAEBB206/.

24. Gerald Miller to CBL, Dec. 14, 1969, CBLP. Shadegg, *Clare Boothe Luce*, 270; Weiner, *Legacy of Ashes*, 153.

25. Many years later, declassified documents revealed that there was collusion among Israel, Great Britain, and France in timing the two invasions. At a secret meeting in Sèvres, France, on Oct. 22–24, 1956, representatives of the three powers approved a scheme of Prime Minister Anthony Eden that Israel should strike first, in order to give the others an excuse to intervene and "prevent" a war between nations. This would enable retaking the Suez Canal. The Sèvres Protocol was later destroyed on Eden's orders. Bodleian Timeline, http://www.bodleian.ox.ac.uk/dept/scwmss/projects/suez/suez/html.

26. CBL, "Eisenhower Administration," 84–85; *Time*, Dec. 3, 1956. The evacuation

beginning on Oct. 30 was successfully completed by Nov. 5. *The New York Times,* Nov. 6, 1956.

27. Smith, *Eisenhower,* 694–95.
28. Ibid., 698–99; Bailey, *Diplomatic History,* 843.
29. CBL to Eisenhower, Nov. 4, 1956, CBLP-NA.
30. Attila J. Ürményházi, *The Hungarian Revolution-Uprising, Budapest 1956* (Hobart, Tasmania, Feb. 2006), 15, http://www.americanhungarianfederation.org/docs/Urmenyhazi_HungarianRevolution_1956.pdf.
31. Gati, in Council on Foreign Relations, "Hungary-Suez Crisis."
32. CBL to HRL, dated Nov. 5, 1956, but actually written at 2:00 A.M. on Nov. 6.
33. Bulganin to Eisenhower, Nov. 5, 1956, *FRUS, July 26–Dec. 31, 1956,* vol. XVI, *Suez Crisis* (Washington, D.C., 1990), document 505. The cable was received in Washington at 3:03 P.M.
34. Smith, *Eisenhower,* 702; *The New York Times,* Nov. 6, 1956.
35. Smith, *Eisenhower,* 703. France and Israel followed suit. In the aftermath of the Suez debacle, Anthony Eden resigned, his health and spirit broken. Harold Macmillan succeeded him on Jan. 10, 1957.
36. *The Washington Post,* Nov. 20, 1956.
37. *New York Journal-American,* Apr. 7, 1957.
38. CBL to Gerald Miller, Nov. 20, 1956, SJMP.
39. Ibid.
40. Shadegg, *Clare Boothe Luce,* 271; CBL speech file, Dec. 20, 1956, CBLP-NA; *Il Tempo,* Dec. 21, 1956.
41. *Il Tempo,* Dec. 21, 1956, translation in CBLP.
42. UPI dispatch, *Tulsa Tribune,* Dec. 27, 1956.
43. UPI dispatch, *Indianapolis Star,* Dec. 28, 1956.
44. Between 1952 and 1956, the MDAP had helped Italy increase its number of infantry and armored divisions from 9 to 13, its combat support units from 13 to 136, and its air force squadrons from 7 nonoperational to 18 combat-ready. Charles E. Rogers memo to CBL, n.d., 1956, CBLP.
45. Christopher Isherwood, *Diaries, 1939–1960* (New York, 1997), Nov. 14, 1955; *Time,* Dec. 3, 1956. For two critical articles on CBL's years in Rome, see Alessandro Brogi, "Ambassador Clare Boothe Luce and the Evolution of Psychological Warfare in Italy," *Cold War History* 12, no. 2 (May 2012), and Mario del Pero, "American Pressures and Their Containment in Italy During the Ambassadorship of Clare Boothe Luce, 1953–1956," *Diplomatic History* 28, no. 3 (June 2004).

40. LIQUID PARADISE

1. *The New York Times,* Dec. 21, 1956–Jan. 1, 1957.
2. CBL to Martin Luther King, Jr., Jan. 2, 1957, CBLP.
3. Taylor Branch, *Parting the Waters: America in the King Years, 1954–63* (New York, 1988), 203. Morrow (1906–1994) was administrative officer for special projects.
4. CBL to Gerald Miller, Dec. 31, 1956, CBLP.
5. Ibid., and Jan. 3, 1957, SJMP. Miller had written to Allen Dulles on Dec. 13, 1956, suggesting CBL as Chief of Mission in Paris. Copy in SJMP.
6. CBL to Shadegg, Feb. 10, 1969, CBLP; CBL to Kay Brown, Mar. 29, 1957, CBLP (Brown was to become CBL's new agent); *The New York Times,* Mar. 12, 1957; Elsa Maxwell in *New York Journal-American,* Apr. 6, 1957.
7. *New York Journal-American,* Apr. 7, 1957.
8. CBL to Guy Hannaford, Mar. 18, 1957, CBLP.

9. Ibid.
10. Shadegg, *Clare Boothe Luce*, 274; SJM notes on visit to Phoenix site, June 26, 1987, SJMP.
11. *The New York Times*, Apr. 9, 1957.
12. Ibid., and *New York Herald Tribune*, Apr. 9, 1957.
13. *The New York Times*, Apr. 9, 1957, *New York Journal-American*, Apr. 10, 1957.
14. CBL to Luigi Barzini, July 28, 1957, CBLP.
15. CBL to Dorothy Farmer, May 24, 1957. "Please note what I have become! Any surprise?"
16. CBL to John Foster Dulles, June 3, 1957, CBLP.
17. *The New York Times*, June 17, 18, 1957; CBL memo of conversation with Sherman Adams, June 18, 1957, CBLP.
18. Ibid.
19. CBL's disillusionment with the Eisenhower administration became public on Sept. 8, when the *Stamford Sunday Herald* published a report that she was "seriously considering" running in 1958 as an independent for the Connecticut seat of Senator William Purtell (R). The paper said that she particularly disapproved of the way Ike's "palace guard" was influencing foreign policy and slowing the pace of Southern integration.
20. CBL to André Girard, June 22, 1957, CBLP.
21. Richard Park Breck to SJM, Mar. 14, 1988, SJMP.
22. "Notes from Park Breck," ca. Feb. 10, 1988, SJMP.
23. CBL, "God's Little Underwater Acre," part 1, *Sports Illustrated*, Sept. 9, 1957.
24. Ibid.
25. Ibid.
26. Ibid.
27. "Notes from Park Breck," ca. Feb. 10, 1988, SJMP.
28. CBL, "God's Little Underwater Acre," part 1.
29. Ibid.
30. When CBL admitted to taking Miltown, a drug whose popularity would reach epidemic proportions in the early 1960s, Jeanne Breck told her that she and Park used them to cut down on smoking. "Notes from Jeanne Breck," ca. Feb. 10, 1988, SJMP.
31. CBL, "God's Little Underwater Acre," part 1.
32. Ibid.; CBL, "God's Little Underwater Acre," part 2, *Sports Illustrated*, Sept. 16, 1957.
33. Ibid.
34. "Notes from Park Breck," ca. Feb. 10, 1988, SJMP.
35. *Philadelphia Evening Bulletin*, July 17, 1957; unidentified Italian newspaper clippings, SJMP.
36. CBL to Luigi Barzini, July 28, 1957, CBLP; CBL to Gaetano Martino, July 28, 1957, CBLP.
37. CBL to Ernest Hocking, July 25, 1957, CBLP; Thomas Traherne, *Centuries of Meditations*, "The First Century" (London, 1908), section 29.
38. CBL to Mortimer J. Adler, July 26, 1957, CBLP.
39. Somerset Maugham to CBL, Aug. 15, 1957, CBLP.
40. CBL to Luigi Barzini, July 28, 1957, CBLP.
41. Simon Michael Bessie interview, Nov. 21, 1983; Mina Shaughnessy to CBL, Sept. 18, 1957, CBLP.
42. CBL to Luigi Barzini, July 28, 1957, CBLP; CBL to Clarita de Forceville, July 27, 1957, CBLP.

43. *New York Journal-American*, Aug. 30, 1957.

44. Walter Guzzardi to CBL, Apr. 29, 1957, CBLP; Count Dino Grandi to CBL, Aug. 8, 1957, CBLP.

45. CBL to Nellie Lante, ca. early Sept. 1957, CBLP; CBL to HRL, Sept. 12, 1957, CBLP.

46. Morris, *Rage for Fame*, 103–05; Heinz Dielke, "She Is an 'Old' Berliner," *Berliner Zeitung*, Sept. 20, 1957, translation in CBLP.

47. CBL Berlin speech, Sept. 19, 1957, copy in SJMP. Secretary Dulles's sister Eleanor was the inspiration behind the building of Congress Hall, now known as Haus der Kulturen der Velt ("House of the Cultures of the World"). See http://www.galinsky .com/buildings/congress/.

48. *New York Post*, Oct. 9, 1957; CBL in *McCall's*, July 1961.

49. CBL interview, Apr. 3, 1982.

50. CBL to Henry Graff, Aug. 10, 1967, SJMP.

51. CBL, "Little Rock and the Muscovite Moon," speech transcript, Oct. 17, 1957, SJMP.

52. Irving R. Kaufmann to CBL, and to Spellman, Oct. 18, 1957, CBLP.

41. NO ONE STARED

1. Hobson, *Laura Z*, 180.

2. CBL to HRL, Oct. 28, 1957, CBLP.

3. Book contract for diving book, Oct. 14, 1957, copy in CBLP. The book, to have an introduction by Park Breck, was not written.

4. Sister Madeleva to CBL, Oct. 22, 1957, CBLP.

5. Shadegg, *Clare Boothe Luce*, 276. "Arthur" or "Art" Little's real name was Artemis.

6. CBL to Peter Grimm, Nov. 23, 1957, CBLP.

7. The Soviets launched a second *Sputnik* on Nov. 3, 1957, this time with a dog inside. Twelve days later, Khrushchev tauntingly challenged the United States to a "rocket-range shooting match." On Dec. 6, the United States was further humiliated when its first satellite rocket rose only four feet before toppling and exploding at Cape Canaveral, Florida. On Dec. 17, however, the United States successfully launched an *Atlas* ICBM.

8. George H. Dunne, *King's Pawn: The Memoirs of George H. Dunne* (Los Angeles, 1990), 189.

9. Ibid. CBL's secretary typed a memo of her conversation with Nixon, which apparently had been taped. He wanted to bolster his prestige by going to the Paris mid-December NATO meeting of heads of state in the ailing Eisenhower's stead. He asked CBL four times to press Dulles in favor of this plan. She was as evasive as he was persistent. In the end Ike made the trip, and it was a great personal success. CBL, memorandum of conversation, Nov. 26, 1957, and follow-up memo, Nov. 27, 1957, CBLP.

10. "Notes from Park Breck," ca. Feb. 10, 1988, SJMP; CBL to Lillian Gish, Nov. 20, 1957, CBLP.

11. CBL, outline of an autobiography (fragment, ca. 1957), CBLP.

12. CBL to [illegible], Jan. 17, 1958, CBLP.

13. CBL to Nelson A. Rockefeller, Jan. 9, 1958, NRP.

14. Dunne, *King's Pawn*, 192–93. Probably unbeknown to both CBL and Dunne, Frank Brophy's wife, Anna, was Jewish. See Brophy obituary in *Jewish News of Greater Phoenix*, Sept. 10, 2004.

15. Hobson, *Laura Z*, 180–82.

16. Elson, *The World of Time Inc.*, 428. Elson's and Hobson's accounts of HRL's medical crisis of Feb. 1–5, 1958, are somewhat confused as to chronology. This account is based on the records of the attending physician, Dr. Hayes Caldwell, as cited in an interview with the author on June 26, 1987, SJMP.
17. Hobson, *Laura Z*, 183.
18. Ibid., 183.
19. Hayes Caldwell interview, June 26, 1987.
20. Ibid.
21. Hobson, *Laura Z*, 183–84.
22. Ibid., 184.
23. *Tucson Daily Citizen*, Feb. 14, 1958.
24. *Arizona Republic*, Feb. 23 and Mar. 21, 1958.
25. Ibid., Mar. 21, 1958.
26. CBL to Ernest Hocking, Jan. 17, 1957, SJMP. On Apr. 13, CBL was a guest of honor at a Screen Producers Guild dinner for Spyros Skouras in Hollywood. Nunnally Johnson was no more impressed with her than he had been at the 1952 Academy Awards. "Somebody once told Clare that she looked like a pale goddess and clearly she has never got over this. . . . She is the phoniest snob I have ever come up against." Unidentified scrapbook clipping, ca. Apr. 14, 1958, CBLP; Dorris Johnson and Ellen Leventhal, *The Letters of Nunnally Johnson* (New York, 1981), 166. Johnson had been seated next to CBL at a dinner the night before, and said, "As nearly as I could get it, she was doing her best to be gracious among colored folks." Ibid., 165–67. Later Skouras asked CBL to write the story line and dialogue for a 20th Century-Fox Bible epic even more ambitious than *Pilate's Wife*. It was to be called *The Greatest Story Ever Told*. She turned down the offer. CBL to Gerald Miller, May 18, 1958, SJMP; CBL to Ned Brown, May 27, 1960, CBLP. The four-hour-twenty-minute movie, released seven years later, was a critical and box office disaster.
27. CBL to Gerald Miller, May 18, 1958, SJMP.
28. *Miami Herald*, June 8, 1958; *New York Mirror*, Aug. 8, 1958; CBL, "The Heaven Below," *Sports Illustrated*, Aug. 11 and 18, 1958.
29. CBL to Somerset Maugham, July 28, 1957, CBLP.
30. William F. Buckley, Jr., interview, Sept. 8, 1983.
31. CBL told Worth, "I have been relying on others to feed me all my life." Helen Worth interview, May 9, 1988; Helen Worth to SJM, May 11, 1988; CBL in *Catholic Transcript*, Sept. 18, 1958; Mae Talley interview, Apr. 15, 1988.
32. CBL to Chávez, ca. mid-Dec. 1958, CCP.
33. Joseph. A. Owens, "Renewing Self in Simple Ways, Says Mrs. Clare Boothe Luce," *Catholic Transcript*, Sept. 18, 1958.
34. CBL became so enthusiastic about bridge that she persuaded Harry to employ Charles Goren as a regular columnist in *Sports Illustrated*. Goren quoted in *Chicago Tribune Magazine*, Aug. 1, 1965.
35. Owens, "Renewing Self."
36. CBL to Gerald Heard, Nov. 20, 1959, copy in SJMP; CBL, "The Double-Bind," 73, CBLP.
37. CBL to Gerald Heard, Nov. 20, 1959, copy in SJMP.
38. Ibid.
39. Ibid.; *Arizona Republic*, Nov. 24, 1958.
40. "Schedule for Secretary's Visit to Rome, October 18–19, 1958," CBLP.
41. Maggie Savoy, "L'Ambasciatrice at Home Here," *Arizona Republic*, Nov. 24, 1958.
42. Ibid.
43. Ibid.; *Phoenix Gazette*, Dec. 8, 1958.

42. SERPENT'S TONGUE

1. CBL, "Eisenhower Administration," 60ff.; Shadegg, *Luce*, 278–79. On Jan. 12, 1959, HRL called John Foster Dulles to tell him that CBL "would be inclined to take on Cuba." Senior State Department officials ruled that "she is not the one for Cuba," whereupon Dulles offered her Brazil. *FRUS, 1958–1960*, vol. VI, *Cuba* (Washington, D.C., 1991), document 223.

2. CBL to Henry Graff, Aug. 10, 1967, SJMP.

3. CBL to Guy Hannaford, Mar. 24, 1959, CBLP; Dr. Hayes Caldwell interview, June 26, 1987; CBL interview, July 24, 1982.

4. Ibid.; CBL to Guy Hannaford, Mar. 24, 1959, CBLP.

5. CBL to Stan Swinton, Feb. 28, 1959, CBLP; *The New York Times*, Jan. 27, 1959; Shadegg, *Luce*, 279.

6. *The New York Times*, Feb. 27, 1959.

7. Ibid. Stan Swinton of the Associated Press wrote CBL on Mar. 5, 1959, "There was hell to pay at the *Times* over their profile on you. I gather from someone who was there that [Arthur Ochs] Sulzberger thought that use of the old saw about trying to convert the Pope was in poor taste and that heads fell as a result." CBLP.

8. Eric Sevareid, "Radio News Analysis," transcript, Feb. 26, 1959, SJMP.

9. HRL to CBL, Feb. 26, 1959, CBLP.

10. Other senators on the Foreign Relations Committee were Theodore F. Green (D-RI), John Sparkman (D-AL), Russell B. Long (D-LA), Albert Gore, Sr. (D-TN), Frank Church (D-ID), Alexander Wiley (R-WI), Bourke B. Hickenlooper (R-IA), Homer E. Capehart (R-IN), and Frank Carlson (R-KS).

11. Eighty-sixth Congress, First Session, 1959, *Executive Sessions of the Senate Foreign Relations Committee*, Historical Series, vol. XI (Washington, D.C., 1982), 186–87. Hereafter *Executive Sessions*.

12. Ibid., 201.

13. Ibid., 202–06.

14. Ibid., 241.

15. Beverly Smith, Jr., "Things They Wish They Hadn't Said," *The Saturday Evening Post*, Sept. 19, 1959; Ellis O. Briggs, *Farewell to Foggy Bottom: The Recollections of a Career Diplomat* (New York, 1968), 145.

16. AP report, Mar. 4, 1959.

17. *The Washington Post*, Mar. 6, 1959.

18. *Cincinnati Post*, Mar. 5, 1959. CBL called Acting Secretary of State Christian Herter and offered to withdraw her nomination, if it became an embarrassment to the administration. He declined her offer. *New York Herald Tribune*, Apr. 29, 1929.

19. *Arizona Republic*, Mar. 3, 1959; CBL to Elisabeth Cobb Rogers, Mar. 3, 1959, CBLP; CBL to Nelson A. Rockefeller, Mar. 14, 1959, NRP; Briggs, *Farewell to Foggy Bottom*, 125.

20. CBL to Louisa Jenkins, Mar. 19, 1959, CBLP.

21. "Nomination of Clare Boothe Luce. Hearing Before the Committee on Foreign Relations, United States Senate, Eighty-sixth Congress, First Session, April 15, 1959" (Washington, D.C., 1959), 2. Hereafter "Nomination of CBL."

22. Ibid., 2–8.

23. *National Review*, June 2, 1962.

24. "Nomination of CBL," 8. The rest of Morse's interrogation is from ibid., 8–17.

25. Willis, "The Persuasion of Clare Boothe Luce," 142, points out that in 1944 Thomas E. Dewey was privy to information leaked from the White House that the Roosevelt administration had suppressed Japanese code breaks presaging an attack

on Pearl Harbor. "Given [CBL's] involvement in the Dewey campaign, he may have told Luce what he discovered."

26. "Nomination of CBL," 11.

27. Ibid., 11–17.

28. Jack H. Pollack, "JFK Considered a Woman Veep," *Washington Weekly*, Sept. 10, 1984. Pollack reported that in early Apr. 1959, JFK said that when "someday" a woman ran for the presidency, she would need "the political sagacity of Clare Boothe Luce."

29. "Nomination of CBL," 17.

30. Mrs. John Hill interview, Mar. 1988.

31. "Nomination of CBL," 18. Senator Lausche said he had been reading a book called *The Ugly American* and wondered how much American envoys were able to mix with ordinary people. CBL said it was not easy, given the frequency of meetings with officials, but "one tries to do as well as one can."

32. "Nomination of CBL," 18–26.

33. Ibid., 247.

34. *Executive Sessions*, 247–54; *Foreign Affairs*, Oct. 1957.

35. *The New York Times*, Apr. 16 and 17, 1959; *Bridgeport Post*, Apr. 21, 1959.

36. *Washington Evening Star*, Apr. 10, 1959; unidentified scrapbook clipping, CBLP.

37. James P. Philbin, "Charles Austin Beard: Liberal Foe of American Internationalism," *Humanitas* 8, no. 2 (2000); Robert E. Sherwood, *Roosevelt and Hopkins: An Intimate History* (New York, 1948), 274, 299. It should be noted that Sherwood approvingly quoted Beard on the subject of "binding agreements," as well as the latter's opinion that FDR deserved to be impeached for his dealings with Great Britain and the Soviet Union. Beard's revisionist book was savagely attacked by the academic establishment, and his reputation plummeted. In recent years, a new revisionism has substantially confirmed his charges against FDR, in particular his warnings that the postwar United States was committed to "perpetual war for perpetual peace." See, for example, John Toland, *Infamy: Pearl Harbor and Its Aftermath* (New York, 1982), and Robert B. Stinnett, *Day of Deceit: The Truth About FDR and Pearl Harbor* (New York, 2000).

38. UPI report, Apr. 27, 1959; *New York Herald Tribune*, Apr. 28, 1959; *The New York Times*, Apr. 28, 1959.

39. *Time*, May 11, 1959.

40. "Got up early and dictated a speech for Wayne Morse on Clare Luce." Tyler Abell, ed., *Drew Pearson: Diaries 1949–1959* (New York, 1974), 517, 519. On the floor of the Senate, Fulbright voted in favor of CBL's nomination.

41. Ibid., 520.

42. Shirley Clurman memo, n.d., CBLP; Stan Swinton interview, Apr. 12, 1982; CBL interview, July 24, 1982.

43. Undated memo to CBL, CBLP; Mary Lois Purdy Vega interview, Aug. 17, 1988.

44. Stan Swinton interview, Apr. 12, 1982; Shirley Clurman memo, n.d., CBLP.

45. AP release, *Milwaukee Journal*, Apr. 28, 1959.

46. *New York Herald Tribune*, Apr. 29, 1959; *Time*, May 11, 1959.

47. *New York Herald Tribune*, Apr. 29, 1959.

48. Ibid.; *The New York Times*, Apr. 30, 1959.

49. CBL to Gerald Heard, Nov. 20, 1959, copy in SJMP; CBL interview, July 24, 1982. Years later a perceptive friend of CBL's remarked, "I don't think Harry was ever totally sure of what she'd do. That's one of the holds she had on him. She was so unpredictable." Simon Michael Bessie interview, Nov. 21, 1983.

50. *New York Herald Tribune*, Apr. 29, 1959.

51. Ibid., Apr. 30, 1957.

52. *Última Hora*, May 4, 1959; *Tribuna do Ceará*, Apr. 24, 1959.

53. *The New York Times*, Apr. 30, 1959; William Watson, *New Poems* (Cambridge, Mass., 1909), 32–33.

54. Transcript in SJMP.

55. CBL to Gerald Heard, Nov. 20, 1959; CBL interview notes for Carole Hyatt and Linda Gottlieb's *When Smart People Fail: Rebuilding Yourself for Success* (New York, 1987), 5, CBLP.

56. *New York Journal-American*, May 1, 1959.

43. AN UNSHARED LIFE

1. Quoted in *Time*, May 11, 1959, and Elson, *The World of Time Inc.*, 450.

2. CBL to Jack Shea, Aug. 22, 1960, CBLP; *Sharon Herald* (Pa.), May 9, 1959.

3. *New York Herald Tribune*, Apr. 30, 1959.

4. *The New York Times*, Apr. 30, 1959.

5. *Washington Evening Star*, May 6, 1959. CBL's successor in Brazil was John Moors Cabot.

6. Ibid.; Lawrenson, *Stranger*, 128; CBL to Claire Luce, July 22, 1959, CBLP; Ruth Montgomery, "Clare Finds Change of Mind a Costly Deal," *San Francisco Examiner*, May 8, 1959.

7. Edna Ferber to CBL, May 11, 1959, CBLP.

8. CBL to Allen Dulles, July 22, 1959, CBLP.

9. Notes taken of CBL's LSD session by J. Michael Barrie, May 16, 1959, CBLP.

10. Ibid.

11. CBL interview, Feb. 10, 1987.

12. Heard may be watched in conversational action at http://www.youtube.com/watch?v=1pI5XZxpQaI.

13. Ibid. See also Gerald Heard, *The Five Ages of Man* (New York, 1963), 332. For a recent reassessment of Heard, see Alison Falby, *Between the Pigeonholes: Gerald Heard, 1889–1971* (Newcastle, UK, 2008).

14. Sidney Cohen, "Complications Associated with Lysergic Acid Diethylamide (LSD-25)," *Journal of the American Medical Association* 181, no. 2 (July 14, 1962).

15. Gerald Heard to CBL, Dec. 15, 1959, CBLP.

16. Notes taken of CBL's LSD session by J. Michael Barrie, Mar. 11, 1959, SJMP. During her second session at the Fairmont Hotel in San Francisco, CBL said she never saw the architectural and geometric figures that Aldous Huxley saw on his trips, but did experience a heightened sensitivity to the smell of violets, and perceived that everything at the center of a camellia "composes." She rambled about keeping a parakeet, but not in captivity because "I'm in a cage." Ibid., Apr. 4, 1959, SJMP.

17. CBL to Dr. Cohen, n.d., ca. 1963, CBLP. CBL thanked LSD for the serenity she professedly felt during her Senate hearings, and for "the burst of creative vitality which took me, a month later, to Caneel Bay, to write my first book after ten non-creative years." But the book, a detective novel, was never completed.

18. "CBL Literary Notes," CBLP. In the early 1960s, CBL tried to recast her memoir as a roman à clef entitled "The Double-Bind." She offered it to Simon Michael Bessie in 1963, but abandoned it after one hundred pages. The manuscript survives in CBLP, and is remarkable for its descriptions of adult suicide attempts and childhood sexual traumas. See Simon Michael Bessie to CBL, Mar. 29, 1963, CBLP; Morris, *Rage for Fame*, chapters 1 and 2.

19. CBL to Gerald Heard, Nov. 20, 1959, CBLP; CBL to Dorothy Farmer, June 26, 1959, CBLP.

20. Dr. Hayes Caldwell of Phoenix reported in the spring of 1959 that despite an earlier finding of residuals in HRL's bladder, he saw "none of the usual symptoms of prostatism." HRL, however, complained of "some loss of *potentia* and libido." Caldwell suspected that his current urethral obstruction might be "on a neurogenic basis and that possibility should be eliminated before surgical interference is considered." Caldwell, "To Whom It May Concern" memo, Apr. 1, 1959, SJMP.

21. CBL to Gerald Miller, July 18, 1959, CBLP; Mina Shaughnessy to CBL, June 17, 1959, CBLP; CBL to Shaughnessy, July 20, 1959, CBLP.

22. CBL to HRL, July 21, 1959, CBLP.

23. Ibid.

24. John Courtney Murray to CBL, July 31, 1959, SJMP.

25. CBL interview, Mar. 31, 1982.

26. Murray to CBL, July 31, 1959, CBLP.

27. CBL, "Caneel Bay Notebook," Aug. 6, 1959, CBLP.

28. CBL to HRL, ca. mid-Aug. 1959, CBLP; CBL to HRL, Feb. 29, 1960, CBLP.

29. Murray to CBL, Aug. 15, [1959], CBLP.

30. Ibid., Aug. 26, 1959, CBLP.

31. CBL to HRL, Apr. 27, 1960, CBLP.

32. CBL undated memo, ca. late summer 1959, CBLP. This document was forwarded by HRL to his sister and adviser, Elisabeth Moore.

33. CBL memo, "Frequent Dream—1959 summer," CBLP.

34. CBL to HRL, Oct. 9, 1959, CBLP.

35. Ralph G. Martin, *Harry and Clare: An Intimate Portrait of the Luces* (New York, 1991), 337.

36. Jeanne Campbell interview, Apr. 6, 1988.

37. Serrell Hillman (a former Time Incer) to SJM, Mar. 18, 1988, SJMP.

38. Martin, *Harry and Clare*, 341. Jeanne Campbell had kept hundreds of letters from HRL in a safety deposit box at the Plaza Hotel. All but three or four were lost in a burglary there in the early 1970s. Jeanne Campbell interview, Apr. 12, 1988.

39. Ibid.

40. Ibid., Apr. 18, 1988.

41. Ibid.; Jeanne Campbell interview, Apr. 6, 1988.

42. Jeanne Campbell interview, Apr. 17, 1988.

43. CBL to Gerald Heard, Nov. 20, 1959, copy in SJMP.

44. Ibid.

45. CBL to HRL, Feb. 29, 1960, CBLP.

46. Clare Boothe, *The Women* (New York, 1937), 97.

47. CBL to HRL, Oct. 10, 1959, CBLP.

48. CBL to HRL, Mar. 1, 1960, CBLP. CBL admitted to shouting, crying, and cursing in HRL's presence, and he told his former wife, Lila, about her gutter vocabulary at this time. See Martin, *Henry and Clare*, 370.

49. CBL to HRL, ca. Oct. 9, 1959, CBLP.

50. Ibid., Feb. 29, 1960, CBLP.

51. Ibid., ca. Oct. 9, 1959, CBLP.

52. Ibid., Feb. 29, 1960, CBLP.

53. Ibid. and Oct. 10, 1959, CBLP.

54. Ibid., Feb. 29, 1960, CBLP.

55. Ibid. and Mar. 1, 1960, CBLP.

56. Murray to HRL, Sept. 23, 1959, SJMP.

57. Boothe, *The Women*, 56.

58. Shirley Clurman interview, Apr. 8, 1988. An undated memo in CBLP, "Overseas Press Mentions," lists fifty-seven international newspapers that reported the Luce divorce rumor, thirty-four of them in Italy.

59. Jeanne Campbell interview, Apr. 19, 1988. Tex Moore was a colleague of Gilpatric's at Cravath, Swaine & Moore. According to Mary Bancroft, some of HRL's close associates at Time Inc. thought that his sister Elisabeth "would have been 'the right wife' for him," making him "more Presbyterian, more ruthless." Bancroft to W. A. Swanberg, Apr. 19, 1971, MBP.

60. Murray to HRL, Oct. 2, 1959, CBLP.

61. CBL interview, Mar. 31, 1982.

62. Ibid. and June 16, 1982; Murray to CBL, Aug. 1, [1962], CBLP.

63. Dorothy Farmer interview, Sept. 8, 1981.

64. *Time*, Dec. 12, 1960. HRL even signed over his Buick automobile for the priest's use in Maryland. Dorothea Philp to Murray, Apr. 26 and May 2, 1951, JCMP.

65. CBL to Dr. Cohen, "Sunday," n.d., ca. 1963, CBLP.

66. CBL to Murray, Apr. 5, 1960, CBLP.

67. Murray to HRL, n.d., ca. Oct. 5, 1959, CBLP.

68. CBL to HRL, Oct. 10, 1959, CBLP.

69. CBL to HRL, "Oct. 1959 en route to S.F.," CBLP.

70. CBL to Jeanne Campbell, ca. mid-October 1959 [unfinished and unsent], CBLP.

71. CBL memo ca. early spring 1960, a list of reasons for the failure of her marriage, and whether she and HRL should separate or divorce, CBLP. Gilpatric later became JFK's Deputy Secretary of Defense.

72. Jeanne Campbell interview, Apr. 18, 1988; Leila Luce interview, Apr. 8, 1996.

73. Nancy Randolph, "Chit-Chat," *New York Daily News*, Oct. 21, 1959.

74. Jeanne Campbell interview, Apr. 18, 1988; Randolph, "Chit-Chat."

75. Joseph X. Dever, "Society Today," *The Wall Street Journal*, Oct. 22, 1959.

76. CBL to HRL, Oct. 19, 1959. "Dear—there's everything ready so you won't be interrupted. I am down in 38H. . . . You can get me there when you want me. Always WIFE." CBLP.

77. Jeanne Campbell interview, Apr. 18, 1988.

78. Ibid.

79. Ibid.

80. Ruth Buchanan interview, Jan. 24, 1984 ("She took her place and never lowered her head. She was there as proud as you please and she was Mrs. Henry Luce"); Earl Wilson syndicated column, Oct. 28, 1959.

81. CBL to Gerald Miller, Nov. 5, CBLP.

82. Morris, *Rage for Fame*, 307.

83. CBL diary, Aug. 24, 1960, SJMP.

84. CBL to Gerald Heard, Nov. 20, 1959, SJMP.

85. Jeanne Campbell interview, Apr. 18, 1988.

86. *McCall's*, Feb. 1960.

87. Gerald Heard to CBL, Feb. 13, 1960, CBLP; CBL interview, Feb. 10, 1985; Kobler, *Luce*, 102.

88. Dr. Cohen to CBL, Dec. 14, 1960, CBLP.

89. Sidney Cohen, "Lysergic Acid Diethylamide: Side Effects and Complications," *Journal of Nervous and Mental Disease* 130 (Jan. 1960).

90. CBL to Dr. Cohen, ca. Sept. 1963, CBLP.

91. Ibid.

92. Dr. Cohen to CBL, Feb. 10, 1960, CBLP.

93. CBL to HRL, Mar. 1, 1960, CBLP.

94. Ibid.; CBL to Murray, Apr. 5, 1960, CBLP. The former letter was the first of several lengthy documents, amounting to some one hundred thousand words, that CBL wrote for therapeutic reasons over the next few days.

95. HRL got this phrase from Mary Bancroft. Bancroft, "Reflections," May 23, 1958, MBP. A man asked her if she had some Irish whiskey, and she told HRL, "Evidently the map of Ireland is still very evident on my face!"

96. CBL to Murray, ca. Mar. 3, 1960, CBLP.

97. Ibid., Apr. 5, 1960, CBLP. HRL's "dying Gaul" reference was to a Hellenistic statue in Rome's Capitoline Museums.

98. CBL to Louisa Jenkins, Mar. 7, 1960; CBL to Murray, ca. Mar. 3, 1960, CBLP.

99. Gerald Heard to CBL, Mar. 12, 1960, CBLP.

100. CBL, untitled description of HRL, ca. Mar. 1960, CBLP; CBL interview, Feb. 10, 1985.

101. CBL untitled description of HRL, ca. Mar. 1960, CBLP.

102. *The New York Times* and *The Washington Post*, Apr. 22, 1960, *Austin American* (Tex.), Apr. 26, 1960; Marya Mannes, *Out of My Time* (New York, 1971), 153–54.

103. CBL to HRL, Apr. 27 and May 16, 1960, CBLP.

104. Jeanne Campbell interview, Apr. 18, 1988.

105. Clipping of Cholly Knickerbocker column, ca. late Apr. 1960, found in HRL's wallet after his death and shown by CBL to SJM on June 18, 1982.

106. HRL cable to CBL, May 10, 1960, CBLP.

107. CBL to HRL, May 10, 1960, CBLP.

108. CBL cable copy, 12:47 A.M., June 1, 1960, CBLP; CBL interview, June 20, 1982.

109. "Conference Between CBL and HRL—Waldorf Apartment—June 1, 1960," SJMP.

110. Jeanne Campbell interview, Apr. 6, 1988.

111. HRL to CBL, July 20, 1960, CBLP. CBL's sudden interest in divorce may have been prompted by Bernard Baruch's counsel, "Don't you budge for less than seventeen million." Lawrenson, "The Woman."

112. Jeanne Campbell interviews, June 18 and Apr. 6, 1988; Martin, *Harry and Clare*, 369.

113. Jeanne Campbell interview, Apr. 6, 1988.

114. Quoted in CBL to Murray, July 16, 1962, CBLP.

115. HRL to CBL, July 20, 1960, CBLP; Murray to CBL, Dec. 29, 1961, CBLP; HRL to CBL, June 19, 1969, CBLP. CBL already had joint ownership of the Phoenix house. Acquiring similar rights to Sugar Hill would give her prohibitive tax liabilities.

116. CBL to HRL, June 2, 1960, CBLP.

117. Jeanne Campbell interview, Apr. 6, 1988.

118. CBL to Letitia Baldrige, May 20, 1963, CBLP. CBL quoted Joseph Kennedy as saying, "Harry, he couldn't have made it without the breaks you gave him." See also Swanberg, *Luce*, 410; Nasaw, *The Patriarch*, 739–40.

119. *New York Herald Tribune*, July 22, 1960. CBL met Tunney in the late 1920s when he was world heavyweight champion. Harry Evans, "Broadway Diary," *Family Circle*, Apr. 21, 1939.

120. CBL interview, Apr. 2, 1982.

121. CBL, "The Double-Bind," 8, CBLP.

122. CBL to Dr. Cohen, n.d., ca. 1962, CBLP. CBL was referring to Cohen, on whom

she had a crush, and whom she described as "an extraordinarily compassionate man." She believed he loved her and was the only one who really knew her.

123. AP report, July 23, 1960; *The New York Times*, July 24 and 25, 1960.

124. Randolph Churchill to CBL, Aug. 4, 1960, CBLP; Jeanne Campbell interview, Apr. 13, 1988; Dr. Michael Rosenbluth interview, May 7, 1984.

125. Louisa Jenkins to CBL, July 25, 1960, CBLP.

126. Randolph Churchill to CBL, Aug. 4, 1960, CBLP. CBL never saw Randolph again, but he wrote her on Jan. 6, 1963: "My personal feelings for you are unchanged from when we met at Chartwell and the Ritz Hotel, Paris, and before you had the misfortune to meet Robinson." CBLP.

127. CBL to Murray, Aug. 1, 1960, CBLP; CBL's LSD notes, Aug. 8, 1960, CBLP; Gerald Heard to CBL, Aug 1, 1960, CBLP; CBL to Dr. Cohen, n.d., ca. 1963, CBLP; Jeanne Campbell interview, Apr. 18, 1988.

128. *New York World-Telegram and Sun*, Aug. 30, 1960; CBL vacation diary, Aug. 19–25, 1960, SJMP.

129. Kobler, *Luce*, 4.

130. Ibid.; CBL told SJM that HRL had speculated that his sexual "deficiency" with women might be due to latent homosexuality. Mary Bancroft wrote to HRL's biographer, W. A. Swanberg, for his private "enlightenment" about the possibility, and he replied saying he had decided not to publish whatever suspicions or evidence he had because he felt the subject could not be mentioned "until the biographer of 2001 comes along." Swanberg to Mary Bancroft, Jan. 23, 1971, MBP.

44. A NEW ERA

1. Jeanne Campbell interview, Apr. 18, 1988.

2. Erich Maria Remarque to CBL, Sept. 2 and n.d., 1960, SJMP; Hedda Hopper in *Houston Post*, Sept. 30, 1960; CBL to HRL, Sept. 17, 23, 26, and 29, 1960, CBLP; HRL to CBL, "Thursday" [Sept. 29,] 1960 ("I am delighted to have the pleasure of taking care of the Balenciaga raid!"), CBLP; Ferdinando Gazzoni to CBL, Sept. 19 and Nov. 11, 1960 ("AM IN POSSESSION OF RENOWNED DRUG. PLEASE CABLE WHICH USE INTENDED FOR OTHERWISE SHIPPING IMPOSSIBLE"), CBLP. CBL continued to try other potential sources for LSD, including a Greek professor in Athens and the Buddhist scholar Alan Watts. In the last case, she appears to have been successful. N. C. Louros to CBL, Oct. 18, 1960, and Alan Watts to CBL, Oct. 13, 1960, CBLP.

3. CBL to HRL, Sept. 23, 1960, CBLP.

4. Nancy A. Walker, *Shaping Our Mothers' World: American Women's Magazines* (Jackson, Miss., 2000), 13.

5. CBL to Wilfrid Sheed, May 30, 1973, CBLP.

6. Richard Nixon to CBL, Sept. 9, 1960, CBLP.

7. CBL to Letitia Baldrige, May 20, 1963, CBLP.

8. Swanberg, *Luce*, 410–13; Elson, *The World of Time Inc.*, 474–75; Brinkley, *The Publisher*, 425.

9. Randolph Churchill to HRL, Aug. 13, 1960 [CBL copy], SJMP. Randolph chided CBL for avoiding his phone calls. "I expect better treatment than I have had from you. Pray God to make you a better girl." Aug. 13, 1960, SJMP.

10. John Courtney Murray to Dr. Cohen, Nov. 20, 1960, SCP.

11. Ibid.; Cohen to Murray, Nov. 22, 1960, SCP.

12. CBL to Cohen, Dec. 6, 1960, JCMP. In a letter to Murray dated Dec. 11, 1960, Cohen said he had seen CBL exactly two weeks before.

13. Cohen to CBL, Dec. 14, 1960, SCP.

14. CBL to Cohen, n.d., but probably early Jan. 1961, SCP.
15. Ibid., Apr. 2, 1962, SCP.
16. Cohen to CBL, Apr. 18, 1961, SCP.
17. CBL to Cohen, n.d., and perhaps unsent. CBLP.
18. Ibid.
19. Ibid.
20. Ibid. CBL asked Cohen to advise her—for a fee—on the character of a psychiatrist in her play *Love Is a Verb*. He agreed and was sent a copy. Dorothy Farmer to Dr. Cohen, Apr. 9, 1962, SCP. The play never made it to Broadway.
21. Copy of Cohen's book in CBLP.
22. Although CBL complained about her loss of creative writing ability, in early 1961 she published two substantial articles: "Italy After One Hundred Years," *Foreign Affairs* (Jan. 1961), and "America's Image Abroad," *Modern Age* 5, no. 1 (Winter 1960–1961).
23. CBL interview, Jan. 6, 1982. CBL to Letitia Baldrige, May 20, 1963, quotes Johnson saying to her and HRL, "hand on heart" before the 1960 convention, "I wouldn't be on his team if he got down on his knees." At JFK's Inaugural Ball, the Luces sat in a box with Joseph and Rose Kennedy.
24. CBL to "Dr. Thompkins," Mar. 17, 1961, CBLP; CBL to Murray, Dec. 26, 1961, CBLP.
25. CBL to Thompkins, Mar. 17, 1961, CBLP; Cohen to CBL, Apr. 18, 1961, SCP; Jeanne Campbell interview, Apr. 18, 1988.
26. CBL to Thompkins, Mar. 17, 1961, CBLP.
27. Dr. Michael Rosenbluth interview, May 7, 1984; CBL to Dr. Thompkins, Mar. 17, 1961, CBLP.
28. Jeanne Campbell had the impression that HRL had her under surveillance, because after telephoning her some five times a day previously, he now stopped altogether. Jeanne Campbell interview, Apr. 18, 1988.
29. CBL to Cohen, Apr. 25, 1961, SCP.
30. CBL to Stan Swinton, Jan. 27, 1961, CBLP.
31. CBL to HRL, ca. mid-Dec. 1961, CBLP; CBL to Murray, Dec. 26, 1961, CBLP.
32. Ibid.; Henry Luce III interview, Sept. 6, 1983; Dorothy Farmer to CBL, July 27, 1983, CBLP; Shirley Clurman in *Vanity Fair*, Oct. 28, 1987. In 1961, Dorothy Farmer overheard HRL asking CBL what she wanted for Christmas. She replied, "Why don't you put the things you've already given me in my name?" Ann Charnley interview, Feb. 13, 1990. Friends variously recalled the cost of the pearl necklace as being between $150,000 and $300,000.
33. *Arizona Republic*, Jan. 30, 1962.
34. *New York Herald Tribune*, Jan. 23, 1962.
35. JFK to CBL, Mar. 28, 1962; CBL to JFK, Apr. 10, 1962, CBLP. The cultural center opened after the President's death and was named after him.
36. Dorothy Farmer to Rosemary Wood, Apr. 2, 1962, CBLP. *Six Crises* became a bestseller, earning Nixon $250,000 and burnishing his credentials for another presidential run.
37. Chávez to CBL, May 12, 1962, CCP; Murray to CBL, July 8, 1962, CBLP.
38. Ibid.; Chávez to CBL, Oct. 30, 1957, CCP.
39. CBL to Murray, July 16, 1962, CBLP; Murray to CBL, July 8 and Aug. 1, 1962, CBLP.
40. Murray to CBL, July 8 and Aug. 1, 1962, CBLP.
41. William Harlan Hale, *Hannibal Hooker* (New York, 1939), 104ff.
42. William Harlan Hale to CBL, Dec. 3, 1962, CBLP. Morris, *Rage for Fame*, 200–02.

43. Hale to CBL, June 24, 1962, CBLP. His visit to Ridgefield appears to have been on June 14, 1962.
44. CBL, "A Balearic Breakfast," *New York Post-Gazette,* Nov. 21, 1934.
45. CBL to Ilse and Sidney Cohen, July 21, 1962, SCP.
46. CBL to Murray, July 16, 1962, CBLP.
47. Ibid.; CBL Majorca calendar, July–Sept. 1962, CBLP.
48. CBL 1962 scrapbook, CBLP; CBL, "Christmas in August," *McCall's,* Dec. 1962.
49. Letitia Baldrige interview, Apr. 4, 1988. Her friend reportedly "ended up later in a bad way in North Africa somewhere."
50. Hale to CBL, Oct. 2, 1963, and Oct. 29, 1962, CBLP. He told his wife he was going to Majorca, then wrote CBL, "This lifts the burden of subterfuge that I haven't liked." Aug. 7, 1962, CBLP.
51. Gerald Heard to Dr. Cohen, Aug. 16, 1962, SCP.
52. *Journal of the American Medical Association* 181 (July 14, 1962).
53. CBL, "Eisenhower Administration," 87. For annoyance in the Kennedy White House at *Time's* perceived bias, see, e.g., Theodore Sorenson memo to JFK, Aug. 3, 1961, HRL to JFK, Sept. 21, 1962, and JFK to HRL, Oct.1, 1962, Special Correspondence Series, JFKP.
54. The main source for this account of CBL's meeting with JFK is CBL, memorandum of conversation, Sept. 26, 1962, CBLP. Years later, she recalled JFK as being "sexy as a goat," with "his hand on the charm spigot." CBL to Wilfrid Sheed, May 30, 1973, and June 15, 1982, CBLP. To SJM she remarked, "Jack couldn't keep his hands off women, and once made a pass at me." CBL interview, June 12, 1982.
55. Hugh Sidey interview, Feb, 15, 1983.
56. CBL to JFK, Oct. 4, 1962, draft copy in CBLP.
57. CBL draft article on JFK, and letter of rejection from John N. Wheeler of the North American Newspaper Alliance to CBL, Oct. 16, 1962, SJMP.
58. At a reunion of crisis participants on March 5, 1987, Robert McNamara admitted that the White House never had hard evidence of the presence of nuclear warheads in Cuba, "but it was prudent for us to act as if they were."
59. "Nuclear Files: Key Issues . . . Cuban Missile Crisis: Timeline," http://www.nuclear files.org.
60. CBL to Betty Beale, *The Washington Post,* Nov. 16, 1975, CBLP. Allen Dulles had been succeeded at this time as Director of the CIA by John McCone, but remained clandestinely active in agency affairs. According to Gaeton Fonzi in "The Last Investigation," Cuban Information Archives, http://www.cuban-exile.com, CBL gave anti-Castro Cubans $600.
61. Ibid.; *The Washington Post,* Nov. 16, 1975.
62. See, e.g., CBL's Cuba-related articles in the *New York Herald Tribune,* Sept. 30, 1962, *Life,* Oct. 5, 1962, and a series for the *Chicago American* published in the fall of 1962; also *Washington Star,* Feb. 3, 1963, *Buffalo News,* Feb. 12, 1963, and *Los Angeles Times,* Feb. 17, 1963.
63. Speech typescript, Jan. 1963, CBLP.
64. *The New York Times,* Jan. 2, 1963; CBL, "De Gaulle Upheld on Nuclear Stand," *Washington Star,* Feb. 3, 1963.
65. *Congressional Record,* Feb. 4, 1963.
66. CBL to JFK, Feb. 5, 1963, CBLP.
67. Bundy to CBL, Feb. 12, 1963, CBLP; *The New York Times,* Feb. 15, 1963.
68. JFK to CBL, Feb. 19, 1963, CBLP. Emphasis in original.
69. Ibid.
70. Ted Widmer, ed., *Listening In: The Secret White House Recordings of John F. Kennedy*

(New York, 2012), 80–81. Widmer labels this conversation as "date unknown," but it clearly took place in the late winter of 1963, because JFK declined HRL's invitation to the *Time* party on Mar. 12, 1963.

71. JFK to HRL, Mar. 12, 1963, JFKP.

72. Curtis Prendergast with Geoffrey Colvin, *The World of Time Inc.: The Intimate History of a Changing Enterprise*, vol. 3, *1960–1980* (New York, 1986), 115.

73. Coverage in CBL scrapbook, CBLP; Swanberg, *Luce*, 432–33. By May 1963, there had been a total of two thousand *Time* cover subjects.

74. CBL, "The Inner Space Proposition," July 4, 1963, copy in JFKP. See *Arizona Republic*, July 5, 1963. On Aug. 18, 1963, CBL wrote to Senator Barry Goldwater, asking him to vocally support JFK's "worthy" oceanographic research program, in order to start a Republican congressional movement in its favor, which would coax the administration to relinquish Project Apollo in favor of a "Project Neptune," her own suggested name for the enterprise. CBLP. The name appealed to JFK but was not officially adopted.

75. JFK to CBL, Aug. 23, 1963, JFKP.

76. CBL quoted in *Chicago Tribune*, Nov. 27, 1963; Morris, *Rage for Fame*, 445; CBL articles for the North American Newspaper Alliance, Sept. 29 and 30, Oct. 1 and 2, 1963; *New York Sunday Herald*, Sept. 8, 1963. CBL made a further calculation that by the twenty-second century, JPK's progeny would total 20,267,777.

77. Typescript, Nov. 24, 1963, CBLP. CBL's essay does not appear to have been published.

> Lee Harvey Oswald was charged with the assassination of President Kennedy, and two days later was shot dead by Jack Ruby in the basement of the Dallas police headquarters. Back in Phoenix on the morning of Wednesday, Nov. 27, CBL received a telephone call from Justin McCarthy, public relations coordinator for the anti-Castro DRE (Directorio Revolucionario Estudiantil), whose young members had run the "Flying Tigers" Cuba surveillance operation before the CIA discontinued it. It had been he, a devout Catholic, and Bill Pawley who originally involved CBL in supporting a motorboat run by three particularly idealistic youths. McCarthy, calling from Washington, was highly excited and said he was in a state of "despair." According to notes that CBL took at the time, he gave her astonishing news. " 'My boys— the 3 young men who are the moving spirits of the DRE—know all about Mr. Oswald.' He said that Oswald returned from Moscow and tried to infiltrate (in New Orleans? or Miami?) the DRE. They were right away suspicious of him. They said he was not a fanatic at all. He was highly intelligent and full of zeal. What they were suspicious of was that he spoke no Spanish. They could not understand why he would then want to join the DRE. They . . . did not take him . . . but they were so suspicious that they followed his movements." The next thing they discovered was that Oswald, inexplicably, had started a chapter in New Orleans of the pro-Castro "Fair Play for Cuba Committee," a national group providing grassroots support for the Cuban Revolution. Apparently he had boasted to chapter recruits that he had gone to Russia with the hope of becoming a Soviet citizen, and "after having spent a week with Mikoyan's group in the south," he had been told that he "could do *more* for Russia by going back to the United States." He claimed that for a year he had trained in techniques of subversion and assassination. McCarthy said that he believed this story, since the authorities had subsequently allowed Oswald to leave with a Russian wife. The most dramatic information that the DRE boys had gathered during their counter-

infiltration of his chapter consisted of tape recordings of an ideological debate in which Oswald had participated, and photographs of him passing out pro-Castro handbills on the streets of New Orleans. "They have the tapes and the handbills," CBL noted. "After Oswald's move to Texas, members of the Dallas DRE had warned the FBI about him. When the President was assassinated, [the DRE] began to track Oswald's movements down, and [found] that he was in communication with Rubenstein [the birth name of Jack Ruby] and that undoubtedly he was silenced by Rubenstein. He was seen by the DRE boys in Rubenstein's night club two nights before the assassination. McCarthy said that the GOP approached the DRE boys, asking them for their tapes and that then the FBI called on them last night to tell them that if they talked they would all be jailed, and that they musn't tell what they know. He said that the FBI demanded the tapes, demanded the photostatic copies of the handbills, (which they had saved) and said that if they (the DRE) contacted anyone they would be put in jail. The DRE boys said that there was 'a piece of paper'—a letter or document which showed that Oswald and Rubenstein had been in touch and that the police of Dallas has been told to pass this over to the FBI and to shut up about it!" CBL, "Memorandum of a telephone conversation with Justin McCarthy and Clare Boothe Luce—[Tuesday,] November 26, 1963," CBLP.

45. TOGETHER AT THE END

1. *The Washington Post*, Feb. 5, 1964.
2. *New York Herald Tribune*, Feb. 23, 1964.
3. Ibid., Apr. 12, 1964.
4. CBL to her lawyer Sol Rosenblatt, Apr. 13, 1964, CBLP.
5. CBL in *The New York Times*, Aug. 18, 1979, and to SJM on numerous occasions.
6. CBL to Sol Rosenblatt, Apr. 13, 1964, CBLP; CBL, "Psychology of Artists," draft manuscript for *McCall's*, 1966, copy in SJMP.
7. CBL to Simon Michael Bessie, Feb. 28, 1964, CBLP.
8. Had John Billings not retired, he would probably have succeeded HRL.
9. Swanberg, *Luce*, 444.
10. William J. Miller, "The Unforgettable Henry Luce," *Reader's Digest*, Nov. 1972.
11. CBL to Simon Michael Bessie, ca. Oct. 1963, CBLP.
12. Eileen Lindgren, CBL's Phoenix secretary, to Carlos Chávez, Mar. 30, 1964, CCP.
13. CBL attended the world premiere in Los Angeles on Oct. 11, 1965.
14. The article was published in the Aug. 7, 1964, issue, marking the second anniversary of Monroe's death.
15. Transcript, June 14, 1964, SJMP; Swanberg, *Luce*, 450; Willis, "The Persuasion of CBL," 178.
16. Walter Lippmann to CBL, June 26, 1964, CBLP.
17. CBL, "Tears for the Grand Old Party," *National Review*, June 30, 1964.
18. Barry Goldwater to CBL, July 5, 1964, CBLP.
19. Jeanne Campbell interview, Apr. 18, 1988. Lord Beaverbrook died at age eighty-five, expecting Jeanne's mother to pass on her inheritance to her daughter, but this did not happen. In the days after meeting Jeanne, HRL phoned her frequently, but thought better of trying to see her.
20. See http://www.millercenter.org/president/nixon.
21. In Chicago on Dec. 10, 1964, CBL said that although she was personally opposed to the admission of Red China to the UN, she would accept it as inevitable, pro-

viding Taiwan's security was never compromised. Later, appearing with HRL on a Californian television panel on China, she insisted, "We must soon find ways of living at peace with half the human race." HRL made his standard praise of Taiwan, but was then challenged aggressively by another panelist, the British sinologist Felix Greene, for Time Inc.'s distortion of the truth about China. CBL defended her husband, but the audience loudly applauded Greene. Willis, "The Persuasion of CBL," 15; Swanberg, *Luce,* 453.

22. Henry Luce III interview, Aug. 9, 1984.

23. Irene Selznick to SJM, Feb. 4, 1988, SJMP. Shirley Clurman also remarked that CBL had cosmetic surgery—performed by Dr. Thomas Rees.

24. CBL to Dorothy Farmer, Aug. 8, 1965, CBLP.

25. CBL to Louisa Jenkins, Aug. 24, 1965, CBLP; Phyllis Battelle in unidentified newspaper, dateline Honolulu, Aug. 18, 1965, SJMP.

26. Gerald Heard to CBL, ca. spring 1965, CBLP; Luce real estate memo, ca. Aug. 1965, CBLP. Heard appears to have seen the property before the Luces, writing to tell them he felt sure they would "replace these haphazard housings with a structure that will fulfill Sir Henry Wotton's three basic requirements of Architecture: 'Commodity, Firmness and Delight.'"

27. *Honolulu Advertiser,* July 29, 1965.

28. John B. Judis, *William F. Buckley, Jr.: Patron Saint of the Conservatives* (New York, 1988), 235–55; Marvin Liebman, *Coming Out Conservative: An Autobiography* (San Francisco, 1992), 200–02.

29. William F. Buckley, Jr., interview, Sept. 8, 1983; CBL in *National Review,* Nov. 5, 1963.

30. CBL to William F. Buckley, Jr., Sept. 17, 1969, CBLP.

31. William F. Buckley, Jr., interview, Sept. 8, 1983; Liebman, *Coming Out Conservative,* 200–02.

32. CBL at Woodrow Wilson International Center for Scholars, SJM notes, Mar. 2, 1983, SJMP. Around this time, CBL gave Reagan one of her paintings of a big cat, writing on the back, "The Democrats had better not awaken this sleeping tiger." *Gold Coast Skyliner* (Honolulu), June 1983.

33. Walter Lippmann, *The Good Society* (Boston, 1937); *National Review,* Nov. 30, 1965.

34. See Stephen Siff, "Henry Luce's Strange Trip: Coverage of LSD in *Time* and *Life,* 1954–68," *Journalism History* 34, no. 3 (Fall 2008).

35. CBL to Dr. Cohen, Dec. 2, 1965, SJMP.

36. Dr. Cohen to CBL, Dec. 12, 1965, SJMP. Todd Gitlin, in *The Sixties: Years of Hope, Days of Rage* (New York, 1987, 1993), 202, expresses the escapist point of view of the drug-taking, baby boom counterculture of 1965. "On these luminous occasions, the tension of a political life dissolved; you could take refuge from the Vietnam war, from your own hope, terror, anguish. . . . Drugs planted utopia in your own mind. . . . Did anybody ever do this before? The straights talk about martinis, but they're so uptight, they don't know how to wonder, they don't know what they're missing." In Mar. 1966, CBL's article "The Answer to Youthful Drug Addiction" was published in *McCall's.* She warned against legal barbiturates and amphetamines as well as illegal hallucinogens, neglecting to say how often she had taken them herself.

37. CBL to Walton Wickett, Jan. 21, 1976, SJMP.

38. Shadegg, "It Was Never Nothing," 322; Shadegg to SJM, Aug. 30, 1989, SJMP. If the proceeds of the book exceeded $25,000, Shadegg was required to begin reimbursing CBL for the research expense advance. Copy of contract, SJMP.

39. CBL, "Interview with President Johnson," June 2, 1966, CBLP. Horace Busby, an aide to LBJ, claimed that LBJ had an affair with CBL when they were in the House together. Michael Beschloss to SJM, July 29, 1997, SJMP.

40. Brinkley, *The Publisher*, 450.

41. Swanberg, *Luce*, 478. CBL gave her 168 handmade Christmas ornaments to the Henri Bendel store in New York, to be sold at $10 each for charity.

42. Boothe, *The Women*, 57–58; CBL to HRL, Oct. 3, 1965, CBLP.

43. William F. Buckley, Jr., in *World Journal Tribune*, Mar. 12, 1967. *Firing Line* began broadcasting on Apr. 30, 1966, and CBL made the first of many appearances on the show on July 6, 1966.

44. CBL to John Courtney Murray, ca. July 1962, CBLP; CBL interview, May 3, 1982; CBL to Dorothy Farmer, May 20, 1981, CBLP. Sheen was as enamored as ever of CBL, and after returning home wrote, "Years collapsed, months telescoped and time lost its horizon on the occasion of my visit. The same brilliance! The same charm! The same Clare! Dear Lord in heaven: I see many people but I come back to putting you at the head of the list." Fulton J. Sheen to CBL, Jan. n.d., 1966, CBLP.

45. The box was designed by William Comyns, London, 1897.

46. Kobler, *Luce*, 283.

47. Swanberg, *Luce*, 480; Jean Dalrymple interview, Feb. 6, 1988.

48. Frank Sheed to CBL, Mar. 12, 1967, CBLP.

49. CBL speech reprinted in *The Commonwealth*, Feb. 1967, 63–65; Swanberg, *Luce*, 481.

50. Kobler, *Luce*, 286–87.

51. Ibid., 288–89.

52. Ibid., 289.

53. Ibid., 289–90; Hayes Caldwell interview, July 26, 1987.

54. Kobler, *Luce*, 290.

55. Hayes Caldwell interview, July 26, 1987; Kobler, *Luce*, 290–91.

46. A DELUXE LONELINESS

1. CBL interview, January 8, 1962. HRL to CBL, Mar. 3, 1945, CBLP.

2. Elisabeth Moore interview, Nov. 22, 1983.

3. CBL interview, Jan. 8, 1982.

4. John Jessup to Dan Longwell, Mar. 15, 1967, JBP.

5. *The New York Times*, Mar. 4, 1967; Reverend David Read, Memorial Address transcript in SJMP.

6. "Story of Our Lady of Mepkin," vol. 2, 1965–1967, 10–11, CBLP.

7. John Jessup to Dan Longwell, Mar. 15, 1967, JBP; Mary Longwell to John Billings, Mar. 30, 1967, JBP.

8. HRL to CBL, Dec. 8, 1938, CBLP.

9. Henry Luce III interview, Sept. 6, 1983; CBL to Laura Z. Hobson, Apr. 1967, LZHP; CBL to Dorothy Farmer, July 20, 1967, CBLP.

10. Frank Sheed to CBL, Mar. 12, 1967, CBLP.

11. "Estate of Henry R. Luce," Mar. 6, 1967, CBLP.

12. David Alevy, CPA, to Sol Rosenblatt, Jan. 19, 1968, CBLP.

13. Alevy to Dorothy Farmer, Aug. 7, 1967, and CBL statement of net worth, Nov. 1, 1965, CBLP; Shadegg, *Clare Boothe Luce*, 297; "Estate of Henry R. Luce," Mar. 6, 1967, CBL to Alevy, May 20, 1967, and Alevy to CBL, June 27, 1969, CBLP.

14. Louisa Jenkins to CBL, Feb. 28, 1967, CBLP; Lawrenson, "The Woman"; CBL to

Chávez, Mar. 30, 1967, CCP. From 1974 to 1978, Chávez lived opposite Lincoln Center in New York. Poor health and finances had compelled him to sell his house in Lomas de Chapultepec. He saw CBL for the last time in May 1978 while in Washington, D.C., to conduct his Concerto for Trombone at the Kennedy Center. It turned out to be his final performance. That August, he died during a visit to Mexico to see his daughter, Juanita. Bard College in New York State planned a summer festival of his music for 2015.

15. CBL to Richard L. Russell, May 10, 1967, CBLP.

16. Dorothy Farmer to Ann Charnley, July 4, 1967, ACP.

17. Ibid.

18. William Benton to CBL, May 17, 1967, CBLP.

19. CBL to Dorothy Farmer, July 20, 1967, CBLP.

20. Dorothy Farmer to Ann Charnley, Sept. 26, 1967, ACP.

21. Ossipoff was not amused by CBL's wisecrack. While conceding her brilliance, he said she was a difficult client. "To hear her tell it later, the layout was all her doing. She never gave anybody credit." David W. Eyre, *Clare: The Honolulu Years* (Honolulu, 2007), 35, 38, 42.

22. CBL, "Eisenhower Administration," 98–99.

23. Dorothy Farmer to Ann Charnley, Nov. 19, 1967, ACP.

24. Henry Kissinger, *White House Years* (Boston, 1979), 9; Kissinger interview, Oct. 19, 2013; CBL interview with Martha Weinman Lear, *The New York Times Magazine*, Apr. 22, 1973.

25. CBL to Louisa Jenkins, Dec. 18, 1967; CBL to Helen Wrigley, Dec. 24, 1967, CBLP.

26. Barry Goldwater to CBL, Apr. 4, 1968, CBLP.

27. CBL to Al Morano, Jan. 29, 1968; CBL to Richard Nixon, n.d., CBLP. In July, CBL joined an action committee called "Ambassadors for Nixon." Nixon to CBL, thanking her for the check, July 31, 1968, CBLP.

28. CBL, "Eisenhower Administration," 107–08.

29. Nixon to CBL, Aug. 21, 1968, CBLP.

30. CBL to Gerry Miller, Aug. 27, 1968, CBLP.

31. Dorothy Farmer to Ann Charnley, Nov. 3, 1968, ACP; CBL to Helen Lawrenson, Sept. 11, 1968, CBLP.

32. James H. R. Cromwell to CBL, Sept. 18, 1968, CBLP. "To me, you are the most desirable woman in the world. . . . I truly believe I could love you more than any other girl in my life." CBL to "Mr. Purdy," Shadegg's editor, Dec. 16, 1968, CBLP.

33. CBL to Chávez, ca. Dec. 31, 1968, CCP.

34. CBL to Sheldon Severinghaus, Jan. 16, 1969, CBLP.

35. CBL to Norman Chandler, Jan. 27, 1969, CBLP.

36. For a detailed description of the architectural and design work that went into Halenai'a, see Eyre, *Clare*, chapters 4 and 5. Eyre quotes Jane Ashley, one of CBL's decorators: "I felt sheer frustration because the architect had given her such a beautiful home . . . but it was principally a messy assemblage of things." Ibid., 51.

37. In 1987, Halenai'a was gutted by the Japanese financier who bought it from CBL. Only the footprint of Ossipoff's design survived.

38. CBL on *Firing Line*, Jan. 7, 1972. Recalling the same incident a year later, CBL quoted Nixon as saying, "We have to make progress there, but the time hasn't come." *The New York Times Magazine*, Apr. 22, 1973.

39. Eyre, *Clare*, 71.

40. John Richardson interview, December 6, 1991.

41. The following anecdote comes from William Herbert Kennedy to SJM, June 10, 1997, SJMP.

42. Some of CBL's art had been sold a year earlier, in 1968. Those works included two Pissarros, two Giorgio Morandi still lifes, a Matisse, two Redons, a De Segonzac, an Alfred Sisley, a Fantin-Latour, and a Mary Cassatt. Paintings not sold by Kennedy were consigned to the dealer Danenberg/Beilin for a 1969 total of thirty-four. Among those were works by Chagall, Corot, Dufy, Goya, Renoir, Roualt, Utrillo, and Vuillard, as well as the Fragonard that Richardson admired, and Fiorentino's *Madonna of the Roses*, CBL's 51st birthday gift from Harry. Revenue from the three sales amounted to $1,342,000 before commissions, netting about triple the Luces' original investment. Art sale memos, Feb. 23, 1968, and June 10, 1969, CBLP. CBL sold other items later, including HRL's chinoiserie to his son Hank for $250,000. Artworks she still owned at her death included a number of portraits of herself: two caricatures by Covarrubias, a 1930s watercolor by Cecil Beaton, a marble bust by Noguchi, the aborted 1954 Boris Chaliapin *Time* cover, and a full-length oil rendering of her as Ambassador by René Bouché. There were also a Chaliapin portrait of Ann Brokaw and works by Frida Kahlo, Chagall, and Magritte.

43. Eyre, *Clare*, 71.

44. "Suzy Says," *Daily News*, Mar. 24, 1971; master list of Halenai'a guests, 1967–1981, CBPL.

45. Dorothy Farmer to Ann Charnley, Nov. 3, 1968, ACP; CBL to William P. Rogers, Aug. 19, 1969, CBLP; *Washington Star*, Sept. 17, 1969.

46. In 1969, CBL's furs and jewelry were assessed at $914,926, and her insurance premium was $21,092. Notes on CBL finances, CBLP.

47. Eyre, *Clare*, 25–34. Eyre's copiously illustrated book features fine reproductions of CBL's paintings, as well as the other art and furnishings in Halenai'a.

48. Ibid., 34.

49. CBL to Count Dino Grandi, Mar. 23, 1970, CBLP.

50. *New York Daily News*, Mar. 26 and June 16, 1970; CBL to Dorothy Farmer, ca. June 1970; CBL to Gerry Miller, July 13, 1970; Ann Pierce (Honolulu secretary) to CBL, Nov. 20, 1970, CBLP. In spite of endless socializing, CBL complained to Dorothy Farmer, "I know a lot of nobodies." She was disappointed that friends like Bill Buckley, whom she adored, failed to invite her for more weekends at their country or seaside houses. One reason was that she neglected to ingratiate herself sufficiently with wives. Dorothy Farmer to SJM verbally, 1982.

51. Clare Boothe Luce, *Slam the Door Softly* (New York, 1971). Also see Fearnow, *Luce*, 56–58.

52. *Life*'s publication of the play elicited much favorable comment. One reader sympathetic to Thaw wrote a second act in which Nora returns. There was talk of presenting the play onstage in Los Angeles and Honolulu. It was translated into Norwegian and Swedish, and CBL collected $500 in royalties from university productions in Oslo and elsewhere. She advised Peter C. Gillette, director of the Media Division at the University of Kentucky, to follow a production of her play with panel discussions (including men) about the women's liberation movement. CBL to Gillette, June 13, 1973.

53. CBL to Stephen Shadegg, Feb. 4 and 10, 1969, CBLP; Shadegg, "It Was Never Nothing," 328–29; Shadegg to SJM, Aug. 30, 1989, SJMP.

54. *The New York Times Book Review*, Apr. 11, 1971.

55. CBLP.

56. Margaret Case to CBL, Oct. 6, 1968. Case had been let go in early August, and killed herself at 8:00 A.M. on Wednesday, August 25, 1971. *The New York Times*, Aug. 26, 1971; Hugo Vickers, *Cecil Beaton: A Biography* (Boston, 1985), 550–51.

By no means hard up, as she led others to believe, Case left her maid $50,000 and her great-niece her cooperative apartment, retirement benefits, and some $500,000. *The New York Times*, Sept. 2, 1971.

57. *New York* magazine, Sept. 27, 1971, *Los Angeles Times*, Oct. 18, 1971, *Chicago Tribune*, Oct. 24, 1971, and *Lakeland Ledger*, Oct. 31, 1971. A television version of *The Women* appeared in 1955. A second movie adaptation starring June Allyson came out in 1956 under the title *The Opposite Sex*, and a third, with Meg Ryan, Annette Bening, and Candice Bergen, in 2008. CBL told SJM that for 50 years she never earned less than $7,000 annually in royalties from *The Women*.

58. Unidentified scrapbook clipping, CBLP.

59. CBL to William Benton, Aug. 17, 1972, CBLP.

60. *The New York Times Magazine*, Sept. 3, 1972.

61. *Honolulu Advertiser* and *Honolulu Star-Bulletin*, Aug. 31, 1972.

62. CBL to Dorothy Farmer, Apr. 6, 1972, CBLP.

63. Lawrenson, "The Woman"; CBL to Dorothy Farmer, Apr. 6, 1972, ACP; Estrellita Karsh interview, Sept. 6, 1989.

64. Eyre, *Clare*, 141–44; CBL to Dorothy Farmer, Apr. [1972]. CBL was capable of waking Louise at 3:00 A.M. to ask for a cup of tea. Eyre, *Clare*, 88.

65. Nesta Obermer to CBL, Apr. 17, [1972], CBLP.

66. *National Review*, Sept. 1972.

67. See, e.g., *The Washington Post*, Nov. 20, 1981.

68. The festivities extended to Washington, D.C., where CBL's former Rome Embassy staff gave a party on Apr. 9 at Rive Gauche, and on April 19 the Italian Ambassador held a reception for eight hundred.

69. "Suzy Says," *New York Daily News*, Apr. 20, 1973, and *Time*, Apr. 23, 1973.

70. *Newsweek*, Apr. 23, 1973.

71. CBL to Gerald Clarke, quoted in *Time*, Apr. 30, 1973; see also Morris, *Rage for Fame*, prologue and 277–79 for more about *Abide with Me*.

72. *Time*, Apr. 30, 1973.

73. *Village Voice*, May 3, and *New York* magazine, May 14, 1973.

74. CBL, "Woman: A Technological Castaway," *Encyclopaedia Britannica Yearbook 1973*.

75. CBL to James P. McFadden, Dec. 19, 1973, CBLP.

76. CBL to Henry Luce III, June 4, 1973, Henry Luce III private collection.

77. Henry A. Kissinger, White House memorandum of conversation, Apr. 14, 1973, GFL.

78. Kenneth M. Absher, Michael C. Desch, and Roman Popadiuk, *Privileged and Confidential: The Secret History of the President's Intelligence Advisory Board* (Lexington, Ky., 2012), 156.

79. Kissinger, memorandum of conversation, Aug. 3, 1973, GFL.

80. Ann Pearce to CBL, quoting Edward J. Koczak, Jr., of the National Security Agency, Aug. 10, 1973, CBLP.

81. Shana Alexander, *Newsweek*, Nov. 26, 1973.

82. On November 12, 1973, *Time* had published an editorial, the first in its fifty-year history, calling for Nixon's resignation even before Ford had been approved as the new Vice President. CBL wrote an angry letter to the magazine, but the editor, Henry Grunwald, persuaded her to withdraw it, saying that printing it would "unquestionably lead to widely and gleefully publicized stories about a feud between you and the editors of *Time*." By April 1974, however, she was no longer able to suppress her anger at *Time*'s "below the belt" coverage of Nixon. "Whatever Nixon

is or not," she wrote, "he is one hell of a gutsy fighter." The magazine published these remarks. CBL to Henry Grunwald, Nov. 19, 1973, CBLP; Prendergast, *The World of Time Inc.*, 362; *The New York Times*, Apr. 2, 1974.

83. *The New York Times*, Jan. 11, 1974; CBL to Barry Goldwater, Feb. 6, 1974, CBLP.

84. CBL interview, Apr. 15. Nixon confirmed that CBL's note had cheered him up. Richard Nixon, *In the Arena* (New York, 1990), 25.

85. Serrell Hillman to SJM, Apr. 1, 1988, SJMP; CBL to Barry Goldwater, Aug. 12, 1974, CBLP.

86. CBL to Shirley Clurman, July 19, 1974, CBLP; Lawrenson to CBL, May 20, 1973, CBLP; CBL to Lawrenson, June 1, 1973, SJMP; CBL to Al Morano, Aug. n.d., 1974, AMP. CBL had offered to have Joanna Lawrenson stay with her in Hawaii, but when she heard about her brother's acute psychological problems, she wrote to tell her to give the airfare money to her mother to pay medical bills. CBL to Helen Lawrenson, June 1, 1973, CBLP.

87. Absher, Desch, and Popadiuk, *Privileged and Confidential*, 234.

88. The following account of the PFIAB meetings of Oct. 3–4, 1974, is taken from Absher, Desch, and Popadiuk, *Privileged and Confidential*, 201–02.

89. CBL to SJM on numerous occasions.

90. Jimmy Carter to CBL, May 4, 1977, CBLP; Absher, Desch, and Popadiuk, *Privileged and Confidential*, 225. Carter belatedly realized the need for an independent advisory body in intelligence. In 1980, Leo Cherne was invited to reconstitute the board, but declined until Ronald Reagan renewed the request in 1981. See Absher, Desch, and Popadiuk, *Privileged and Confidential*, 228–29.

91. Gladys Freeman decorated CBL's bedrooms in both places.

92. CBL to Al Morano, Oct. 17, 1976, AMP; CBL to Henry Luce III, July 22, 1976, CBLP.

93. Quoted in Edwin M. Adams to CBL, Apr. 24, 1979, CBLP.

94. Arthur Little to Dorothy Farmer, Aug. 11, 1975, and CBL to Dorothy Farmer, ca. July 1975, ACP. Little had worked for CBL for twenty-four years, and left without a long-promised pension. See also Eyre, *Clare*, 140.

95. CBL interview, June 10, 1982.

96. "I've known 18 of the 21 past winners," CBL told a reporter, "and I think it's a case of fame by association." *Honolulu Star Bulletin*, Oct. 11, 1979.

97. At the time of *The New York Times* interview, Reagan was running ahead of Carter in the polls.

98. Ronald Reagan to CBL, Sept. 14 and Oct. 3, 1979, CBLP.

99. *60 Minutes* transcript in SJMP.

100. *West Point Assembly* 38, no. 3 (Dec. 1979).

101. Ann Pearce to Paul Czarnowski of Alevy and Kantor, Apr. 1, 1980, CBLP.

102. CBL interviewed by Stephen R. Conn, *Town and Country*, Jan. 1981.

103. June 11, 1980, CBLP. In the same letter, CBL called Carter "the worst President of this century."

104. CBL to John L. Harmer, June 17, 1980, CBLP.

105. CBL, "The Ghost at Westminster," John Findley Green Foundation Lecture, transcript in CBLP.

106. The electoral college results were Reagan 489 and Carter 49. On the day the new President was sworn in, the American hostages were released, and Carter, at Reagan's request, flew to Frankfurt to welcome them.

107. Parts of these two paragraphs, and the Epilogue that follows, appeared in an article entitled "In Search of Clare Boothe Luce" by Sylvia Jukes Morris, *The New York Times Magazine*, Jan. 31, 1988.

INDEX

ABOUT THE AUTHOR

SYLVIA JUKES MORRIS was born and educated in England, where she taught history and English literature before immigrating to America. She is the author of *Edith Kermit Roosevelt: Portrait of a First Lady* and *Rage for Fame: The Ascent of Clare Boothe Luce*. With her husband and fellow biographer, Edmund Morris, she lives in New York City and Kent, Connecticut.